A CANADIAN PERSPECTIVE

EDITED BY PETER R.E. CROCKER

SPORT PSYCHOLOGY

PEARSON

Prentice
Hall

Toronto

Library and Archives Canada Cataloguing in Publication

Sport psychology: a Canadian perspective / Peter R. E. Crocker, editor.

Includes bibliographical references and index.
ISBN 0-13-196572-7

1. Sports—Psychological aspects—Textbooks. I. Crocker, Peter R. E. (Peter Ronald Earl)

GV706.4.S66 2006   796.01   C2006-901825-1

ISBN 0-13-196572-7

Vice-President, Editorial Director: Michael J. Young
Editor-in-Chief: Gary Bennett
Acquisitions Editor: Michelle Sartor
Marketing Manager: Janet Piper
Developmental Editor: Maurice Esses and Kimberley Hermans
Production Editor: Cheryl Jackson
Copy Editor: Judy Hernandez
Proofreader: Dawn Hunter
Production Coordinator: Andrea Falkenberg
Page Layout: Debbie Kumpf
Permissions Manager: Susan Wallace-Cox
Permissions Researcher: Lynn McIntyre
Photo Researcher: Christina Beamish
Art Director: Julia Hall
Cover and Interior Design: Jennifer Stimson
Cover Image: David Roth/Getty Images

3 4 5   11 10 09 08

Printed and bound in United States of America

I would like to dedicate this book to my life partner, Linda; to my mother, Dorothy; and to the memory of my father, Ellard.

About the Editor

Peter R.E. Crocker

Dr. Peter R. E. Crocker is a professor in the School of Human Kinetics and an associate faculty member of the Department of Psychology at the University of British Columbia. He was the director of the school from 1999 to 2004. His research focuses on stress and adaptation, with a particular interest in understanding health-related behaviour. His ongoing research includes physical self-perceptions and health in adolescent girls, coping with social physique anxiety in adolescence, and identifying key psychological determinants of physical activity in children and youth. The *World Sport Psychology Sourcebook* (2001) identified Dr. Crocker as one of the top three sport psychology researchers in Canada.

Dr. Crocker is a two-time president of the Canadian Society for Psychomotor Learning and Sport Psychology (SCAPPS). In 2004, he was recognized as a Fellow of the Association of Applied Sport Psychology. He is also active in the North American Society for the Psychology of Sport and Physical Activity. He is a former editor of *The Sport Psychologist* (1996–1999) and is actively involved as a reviewer for several scholarly journals and granting agencies. He is also an editorial board member of the *Journal of Applied Sport Psychology* and the *Journal of Sport & Exercise Psychology*. Dr. Crocker has also served as a consultant for athletes in gymnastics, volleyball, and baseball. He has been a soccer coach for several university and provincial-select soccer teams.

Dr. Crocker completed an undergraduate degree in psychology and a Masters degree in Kinesiology at Simon Fraser University. His PhD studies, under the supervision of Dr. Rikk Alderman at the University of Alberta, focused on sport psychology and skill learning. He has taught at Lakehead University (1986–1990) and the University of Saskatchewan (1990–1999). In his leisure time he coaches recreational youth soccer and struggles with golf. He lives in Vancouver with his wife Linda and two teenage children, Julisa and Douglas.

About the Contributors

Dr. Joseph Baker is an assistant professor in the School of Kinesiology and Health Science at York University. His research examines the development and maintenance of expert performance and the psychosocial factors influencing involvement in physical activity across the lifespan.

Dr. Enrique Garcia Bengoechea is an Assistant Professor in the Department of Kinesiology and Physical Education at McGill University. His major research interests are in the pedagogical and psychosocial dimensions of children's and adolescents' involvement in physical education, sport, and physical activity. In his leisure time, Enrique particularly enjoys a game of tennis, and playing his guitar.

Dr. Gordon A. Bloom is an Associate Professor in the Department of Kinesiology & Physical Education at McGill University. He teaches courses in sport psychology, coaching psychology, and pedagogy. His research interests lie in coaching, team building, hockey aggression, and concussions.

Dr. Jean Côté is an associate professor in the School of Physical and Health Education at Queen's University. His research interests are in the areas of children in sport, positive youth development, and coaching. Dr. Côté is on the editorial boards of the *Journal of Applied Sport Psychology*, *The Sport Psychologist*, *Revue International des Sciences du Sport et de l'Education Physique*, and *Physical Education and Sport Pedagogy*. He is a section editor for the *International Journal of Sport and Exercise Psychology* and the *Asian Journal of Exercise and Sport Science*.

Dr. Kim D. Dorsch is an associate professor in the Faculty of Kinesiology and Health Studies at the University of Regina. Her current research interests include examining the influence of body checking upon many psychosocial concepts (including perceptions of aggression and motivation) in minor hockey. She is also intrigued by collective efficacy expectations and their relationship to other group factors like cohesion, performance, and performance outcome. Another line of research that she pursues is that of investigating sources of stress and practical applications of coping among officials.

Ms. Jessica Fraser-Thomas is a doctoral candidate in the School of Physical and Health Education at Queen's University. Her doctoral research focuses on dropout and prolonged engagement in youth sport, with a focus on healthy psychosocial development through sport. Prior to pursuing graduate studies, Jessica was a junior high physical education teacher. She is a certified NCCP Level 2 coach in swimming, track and field, and triathlon, and has competed internationally in triathlon. She enjoys organizing the annual Kids of Steel triathlon in her community, and training with her husband.

Dr. Craig Hall is a professor in the School of Kinesiology at The University of Western Ontario. He has been conducting research in sport and exercise psychology for over 25 years. His research has focused on imagery use in sport, exercise, and athletic injury rehabilitation, but he has also investigated other topics including self-efficacy, self-talk, deliberate practice, and observational learning. He has also conducted mental training programs with athletes at all competitive levels.

Dr. Sharleen D. Hoar is an assistant professor in the Department of Kinesiology and Physical Education at the University of Lethbridge. A former competitive figure skater, her research focuses on stress and coping, and positive emotional development of children and adolescents through participation in sport and physical activity.

Dr. Kimberley L. Gammage is an Assistant Professor at Brock University. Her research includes investigation on self-presentational influences on exercise and health behaviour, body image, and exercise imagery. She is also currently involved in research examining osteoporosis knowledge and beliefs in young adults.

Dr. Kent C. Kowalski is an Associate Professor of Kinesiology at the University of Saskatchewan. His general area of interest includes coping with stress and emotion in sport and physical activity. He is also currently an assistant coach with the University of Saskatchewan Huskies Men's soccer program and a Level 3 course conductor in the National Coaching Certification Program.

Dr. Todd M. Loughead is currently an assistant professor in the Kinesiology Department at the University of Windsor. His current research interests include group dynamics in sport and exercise, and aggression in hockey. Specifically, his interests are investigating cohesion in sport teams and exercise groups and how cohesion affects athlete satisfaction, leadership, exercise adherence, motivation, and future participation. Dr. Loughead is also investigating the psychosocial variables that influence aggression in hockey and its effect on enjoyment and participation.

Ms. Meghan H. McDonough is a Ph.D. student in the School of Human Kinetics at the University of British Columbia. Her research focuses mainly on social relationships and motivation in sport and physical activity. Her dissertation examines the role of social relationships in self-determined motivation among adult dragon boat participants. She has conducted a number of studies examining the role of friendships in coping with stress and motivation for sport among adolescents.

Dr. Krista Munroe-Chandler is an associate professor in the Kinesiology Department at the University of Windsor. Her research interests include imagery use in sport and exercise as well as youth sport development. She works with athletes of all ages, levels, and sports, helping them achieve their personal performance goals.

Dr. David M. Paskevich is an assistant professor in the Faculty of Kinesiology at the University of Calgary. His research examines collective efficacy in sport; disordered eating in sport and exercise; obesity, Type II diabetes, and physical activity; cardiac rehab and social psychological variables; and volunteer activity in sport and culture.

Dr. David Scott is an associate professor of Sport Psychology in the Faculty of Kinesiology at the University of New Brunswick in Fredericton. He teaches and does research in the area of sport and exercise psychology, focusing primarily on performance enhancement and physical activity and mental health. He has been a psychological consultant with a number of national teams in addition to working with teams in the National Hockey League.

Dr. Whitney A. Sedgwick is a registered psychologist at the University of British Columbia's Counselling Services. She has taught undergraduate and graduate sport psychology courses at three Canadian universities and recently co-authored a mental training book for triathletes. Whitney has also been consulting with athletes at all levels for the past 10 years, including a year in Paris, France, where she worked with national team and Olympic athletes.

Dr. Kevin S. Spink is a professor in the College of Kinesiology at the University of Saskatchewan, specializing in group dynamics, specifically cohesion. He teaches courses involving the application of social psychology to exercise and sport behaviour. His research interests focus on cohesiveness in the exercise and sport setting.

Dr. Diane E. Stevens is an associate professor in the Department of Physical Education and Kinesiology at Brock University. Research interests include cognitive and behavioural manifestations of self-presentation on health behaviours. Her interest has extended to knowledge specific to physical activity and dietary intake in young adults and bone health. In her down time she can be found with her family, both two- and four-legged versions.

Ms. Lindsay Waddell is currently a second-year MA student in the Applied Health Sciences program at Brock University, with a specialization in sport and exercise psychology. In her spare time she enjoys competing in various sporting activities, such as volleyball, basketball, and softball.

Dr. Philip M. Wilson is an assistant professor of Physical Education and Kinesiology in the Faculty of Applied Health Sciences at Brock University. His research interests focus on the interplay between measurement and theory for understanding motivational processes responsible for health behaviours. In his spare time, Phil can be found enjoying active living with Diane and Wembley, and following his two favourite football teams (Liverpool F.C. and England).

Brief Contents

Contents

Preface

Sport psychology has come to play an increasingly prominent role in sport and exercise sciences. Although most people associate sport psychology with elite athletics, sport psychology research and practice cover all competitive levels and age groups to increase athletes' success and satisfaction. Today, many Canadian scholars are recognized as world leaders in this research and practice. Their important work has influenced the lives of the many Canadians involved in sporting activity. This book celebrates their contributions.

In this book we cover key concepts that are supported in the sport psychology literature, and we provide Canadian examples of them. Three unique features characterize this book. First, the chapters are written by Canadian scholars who are actively teaching undergraduate courses in sport psychology. Second, the book provides many Canadian examples to illustrate important concepts. Third, the book highlights research by Canadian scholars while recognizing the contribution of other scholars around the world.

This book is written specifically for a Canadian introductory undergraduate course in sport psychology. We use the term *sport psychology* in a broad sense to encompass many areas of physical activity, including exercise. Although the book emphasizes sport, many authors have included examples from exercise and recreational physical activity. The book presents an overview of sport psychology and provides a solid foundation in core concepts required for upper-level undergraduate courses.

Organization

The 13 chapters of this book present most of the key topics covered in a typical introductory course. The chapters may be viewed in three large groups. In Chapters 1–5, we introduce the basic domains of sport psychology. Here, we provide an overview of the field and discuss research perspectives, personality, motivation, and anxiety and arousal. In Chapters 6–9, we proceed to the more general themes of stress and coping, aggression, psychological interventions, and group cohesion. Then in Chapters 10–13, we interface the basic domains and general themes with the more global topics of coaching psychology, youth sport, older athletes, and female athletes and gender issues.

Chapter 1 provides an overview of the field. Topics include the diverse nature of sport psychology, differences in career orientations and educational training opportunities, a brief history of sport psychology in Canada and the world, ethics in sport psychology, and predicted trends. The contributions of Canadians and Canadian organizations are highlighted.

Chapter 2 focuses on research perspectives in sport psychology. This chapter covers a number of basic research concepts, such as applied versus theoretical research, the role of theories and models in sport psychology, qualitative versus quantitative methods, different types of research designs used in sport psychology, psychological testing, and the ethics of using test scores. We believe this chapter is crucial for many students because it helps them understand the strengths and limitations of sport psychology research.

Chapter 3 deals with personality perspectives in sport. It covers personality measurement, ethics related to measuring personality, recent findings in sport psychology personality research, and the limitations of personality in explaining athletic behaviour and performance.

Chapter 4 focuses on cognitive-evaluative approaches to motivation in sport. It includes various theories and models of motivation applied to sport, such as attribution theory, competence theory, self-efficacy theory, achievement goal theory, self-determination theory, and sport commitment.

Chapter 5 deals with anxiety, arousal, and sport performance. It defines anxiety and arousal, provides the basic models of anxiety and arousal (including multidimensional anxiety theory, zones of optimal functioning, and catastrophe theory), discusses how anxiety and arousal impact underlying mechanisms related to performance, and describes the facilitative and debilitative aspects of anxiety.

Chapter 6 focuses on stress and coping. We cover this area in more detail than most undergraduate textbooks because it is a key component of sport psychology. Students are very interested in stress. The chapter emphasizes types of cognitive evaluations, types of coping, and the relationship between appraisal, stress, and diverse emotions, such as anger, happiness, anxiety, and fear. This chapter also integrates information from the previous chapters on motivation and on anxiety and arousal.

Chapter 7 focuses on aggression in sport. The chapter differentiates between aggression, assertion, and violence. It discusses key theories useful for understanding why athletes (and spectators) behave aggressively. It also explores how personal, situational, and group factors influence aggressive behaviour and examines ways to reduce aggressive behaviour in sport.

Chapter 8, on sport psychology interventions, integrates knowledge and concepts from the previous chapters. It addresses specific intervention techniques for arousal control, discusses emotion management, and describes psychological and coping skills training. Specific topics include relaxation procedures, psyching strategies, attention-control, self-talk, imagery, and goal setting. The chapter features many applied examples and exercises.

Chapter 9 provides a comprehensive review of group cohesion in sport. Students will learn about group dynamics, group cohesion and its measurement, how and why cohesion affects behaviour in both sport and exercise settings, a conceptual model of cohesion, team-building concepts, and important correlates of cohesion. The chapter also covers social loafing, self-handicapping, role clarity and acceptance, and leader behaviour.

Chapter 10 describes the complexity of coaching psychology. It discusses the structure and process of coaching education in Canada, the steps to becoming an elite coach, and the common characteristics and coaching principles of youth-sport coaches. The chapter also explains a coaching model, discusses effective coaching, and considers the psychological factors involved in coaching.

Chapter 11 focuses on the health and developmental benefits of youth-sport participation. The chapter describes the outcomes that can result from youth-sport participation, principles of positive youth development, how youth sport programs lead to positive sport experiences, and the role of parents and coaches in this process. It also reviews key models of youth-sport motivation and sport development.

Chapter 12 covers the psychological factors related to sport and physical activity in the older athlete. This chapter is unique to sport psychology undergraduate textbooks. One of the main reasons we have included this chapter is to acknowledge that many "older" Canadians are, and should be, involved in physical activity. The chapter covers a wide range of issues, including the factors influencing sport and physical activity involvement in this group, the impact of societal perceptions of aging on physical and cognitive performance, and strategies for increasing sport and physical activity involvement in older adult populations.

Chapter 13 explores gender issues related to sport psychology. The chapter differentiates between various theoretical approaches to gender research. It discusses gender differences in cognition and social experiences and their relative influence on sporting behaviour and beliefs. In the context of gender, the chapter also discusses sex and gender stereotypes, gender and self-identity, the role of media and socialization, eating disorders, the drive for muscularity, and stress.

Instructors may wish to vary the sequence in which the chapters are studied. The first five chapters serve as the foundation for the following chapters. These foundation chapters should be covered in the order presented, although the research perspective chapter may be redundant for students who have already completed a research methods course. Some instructors may wish to cover psychological interventions before aggression. Chapters 10, 11, 12, and 13 can be sequenced according to instructors' preferences.

Pedagogical Features

We have made a special effort with this book to facilitate learning and enhance understanding by incorporating the following pedagogical features.

- **Chapter Objectives.** A set of four to eight learning objectives at the beginning of each chapter provides a road map to help students read the material more effectively. The learning objectives also form the basis of the review questions found near the end of the chapter.
- **Vignette.** Each chapter begins with a scenario, many of which are real, that raises issues and topics to be addressed in the chapter.
- **Common Myths.** Each chapter includes three to five common myths about the subject of the chapter. We clarify and dispel each myth by presenting clear evidence to the contrary. Then we address the issue raised in the myths.
- **Key Terms.** Key terms are boldfaced where they are introduced in the text, and they are listed at the end of each chapter.
- **Case Studies.** Case studies are included in some chapters to clarify key ideas and concepts.
- **Reflections Boxes.** Each chapter contains several reflection boxes that require students to integrate key concepts and ideas into their personal knowledge and experiences.
- **Canadian Examples.** Numerous Canadian examples are used to help clarify and highlight concepts.
- **Figures and Tables.** Diagrams, graphs, and tables are provided in the chapters to illustrate and clarify important points.
- **Photos.** Numerous photos throughout the book serve to emphasize Canadian athletes and participants in physical activity.
- **Weblinks.** References to useful websites are interspersed in the chapters where appropriate. They include links to sport psychology sites, advanced papers, scholarly organizations, and scholarly journals.
- **Chapter Summary.** A summary of the main points is provided near the end of each chapter.

- **Review Questions.** A set of review questions requiring short answers will help instructors and students determine whether the learning objectives have been mastered.
- **Suggested Reading.** Each chapter closes with a list of several selected advanced readings for the interested student.
- **References.** All references cited in the text are listed at the end of each chapter.
- **Glossary.** All the key terms are collated with their definitions in a glossary at the back of the book.

Supplements

To aid instructors in presenting lectures, fostering class discussion, and administering examinations, we have carefully prepared an Instructor's Resource CD-ROM that contains the following three items:

- **Instructor's Manual.** The Instructor's Manual is designed to enhance the organization and presentation of course materials. Each chapter includes:
  - Chapter Overview
  - Learning Objectives
  - Key Terms
  - Lecture Outline
  - Projects and Assignments
  - Answers to Review Questions
  - Discussion Questions
  - Additional Teaching Resources
- **PowerPoint® Slides.** PowerPoint slides are available for each chapter that can be used in electronic form to present materials in class or in printed form to guide the preparation of new lecture notes. Over 250 slides are available in total.
- **Pearson TestGen.** The Pearson Education Canada TestGen is a special computerized version of the Test Item File that enables instructors to view and edit the existing questions, add questions, generate tests, and print the tests in several formats. Powerful search and sort functions make it easy to locate questions and arrange them in any order. TestGen also enables instructors to administer tests on a local area network, have the tests graded electronically, and have the results prepared in electronic or printed reports. Issued on a CD-ROM, the TestGen is compatible with Windows or Macintosh operating systems. The TestGen includes over 650 questions in total, including multiple choice and short answer questions. For each question, the following information is provided:
  - The correct answer
  - The question's difficulty level (easy, moderate, or challenging)
  - The question's skill type (recall or applied)
  - The relevant page reference from the text

Acknowledgments

I would like to acknowledge all the contributors to this textbook. These individuals represent the future of sport psychology in Canada, and they have all made a special contribution. I also want to thank several doctoral students—Meghan McDonough, Cathi Sabiston, and Valerie Hadd—whose suggestions and work kept this book on track.

We would also like to recognize those instructors who provided us with formal reviews of parts of the manuscript. Their observations, ideas, and comments greatly improved the quality of all chapters.

- L. J. Bilek (St. Francis Xavier University)
- Kimberley Ann Dawson (Wilfrid Laurier University)
- Michelle M. Dionne (Ryerson University)
- Joey Farrell (Lakehead University)
- Deborah Flynn (Nipissing University)
- Bruce Howe (University of Victoria)
- Steve Kamps (College of the Rockies)
- Basil Kavanagh (Memorial University of Newfoundland)
- Larry Leith (University of Toronto)
- Lynda Mainwaring (University of Toronto)
- Tom Patrick (University of Winnipeg)
- Janet Starkes (McMaster University)
- Gary L. Worrell (University of New Brunswick)

Finally, I greatly appreciate all the staff at Pearson Education Canada: Michelle Sartor (Acquisitions Editor); Maurice Esses (Developmental Editor); Kimberley Hermans (Assistant Editor); Cheryl Jackson (Production Editor); Andrea Falkenberg (Production Coordinator); Jennifer Stimson (Designer); Debbie Kumpf (Senior Composition Specialist); Christina Beamish (Photo Researcher); and Lynn McIntyre (Permissions Researcher). Their talent, support, and patience were so critical in completing this book.

CHAPTER 1

Peter R. E. Crocker
David Scott

Introducing Sport Psychology

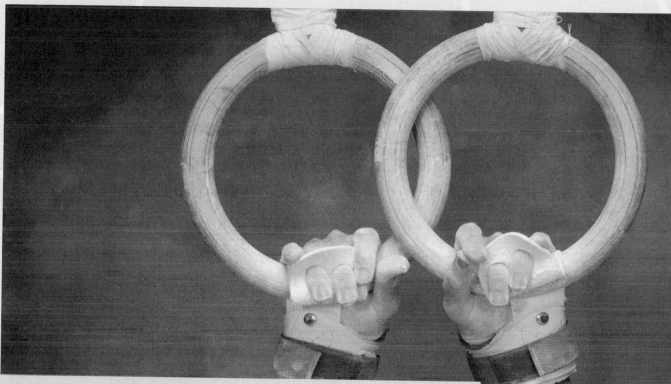

Chapter Objectives

After reading this chapter, you should be able to do the following:

1. Explain what sport psychology is and what sport psychology specialists do.
2. Explain the differences between educational and counselling/clinical orientations in sport psychology.
3. List the diverse educational training opportunities in sport psychology.
4. Outline the basic standards of conduct and service in sport psychology.
5. Relate the history of sport psychology in Canada.
6. Outline developments in sport psychology around the world.
7. List key sport psychology journals and scholarly organizations.
8. Describe future trends in sport psychology.

Courtney is a 15-year-old soccer player. She has been playing soccer for eight years and has had her share of successes and failures. At soccer practice she works hard and is always enthusiastic and positive. She is keen to learn and completes drills and other practice activities with great confidence and expertise.

Although she loves soccer, she recently has found that she is not enjoying the intensely competitive games. She reports that prior to competitive games she feels anxious, does not look forward to playing, gets extremely nervous, and sometimes feels physically ill. As the anxiety about upcoming performances starts to mount, her confidence decreases. This is compounded by her belief that she is letting down herself, her teammates, her coaches, her family, and her friends. As a consequence, Courtney's on-field performance is often at a level far below expectations. Not surprisingly, she reports that she is enjoying soccer less and less. The situation has become so bad that she is thinking of giving up soccer.

After a series of meetings, Courtney, her parents, and her coaches decide that she could benefit from professional help. Through the Canadian Mental Training Registry, Courtney's parents are able to contact Dr. Holowalchuk, who is a professor of sport psychology at the local university. Dr. Holowalchuk is well known for her research on stress and coping in youth athletes. What can Dr. Holowalchuk do to help?

The above vignette illustrates a common situation that involves the services of a qualified sport psychology consultant. To help Courtney, a sport psychology consultant must have expertise in a number of areas. These areas include theoretical knowledge of how psychological factors may influence performance; sport knowledge of the technical, physical, and psychological demands of soccer; assessment knowledge to determine the psychological skills of the athlete and the source of the problem; and intervention skills to design and implement an effective intervention. For example, a consultant may suspect that anxiety is the "villain of the piece." The consultant will be familiar with various theories of the link between anxiety and performance and will have knowledge of the relationship between different types of anxiety and self-confidence. A proper assessment protocol would be necessary. If anxiety is a central problem, it is important that the consultant have an understanding of various strategies for managing feelings of anxiety and promoting self-confidence. Once the sport psychology consultant has identified the source of the problem, devised strategies for dealing with it, and explained them to Courtney, there then follows a period of application. During this stage, the consultant has moved from a theorist position to one of practitioner. The consultant must now have the ability to teach Courtney mental skills that will help her enjoy and perform better in competitive games.

Is performance enhancement the only role of sport psychology specialists in Canada? How does one become a sport psychology specialist? In this chapter, we will discuss the various roles and training in sport psychology. As students will discover, sport psychology specialists work in a variety of settings, have a multiplicity of educational training opportunities, and possess varying competencies. There are also ethical issues that govern the application of sport psychology principles. Many of the practices and controversies in sport psychology, especially in applied sport psychology, were shaped by its history, a history unlike those of other fields in psychology. In this chapter, we will address many of these issues related to sport psychology, but before we go any further, it is important to address some common myths about sport psychology.

Some Common Myths about Sport Psychology

MYTH: *Only athletes with serious mental problems need a sport psychologist.*

Any athlete can benefit from the services of a qualified sport psychology specialist. Specialists design the majority of interventions to prepare athletes to manage the demands of training and competition and to enhance their well-being. Athletes can learn to develop and apply effective psychological skills to manage stress, focus attention, and augment motivation. In addition, specialists can teach coaches how to develop more effective training environments. These psychological interventions and skills are discussed in more detail throughout this book.

MYTH: *Sport psychologists are shrinks.*

Shrink is a slang term for a psychiatrist, a medically trained professional who specializes in the study, prevention, and treatment of mental disorders. Some psychiatrists do work in sport settings, and there is a small scholarly society called the International Society for Sport Psychiatry (www.theissp.com). However, the vast majority of sport psychology specialists are not trained in psychiatry. They have an array of educational training experiences that might include sport sciences, research methodology and statistics, counselling psychology, and clinical psychology.

MYTH: *All sport psychology specialists work with elite athletes to enhance their performance.*

This is a restrictive view of sport psychology. In Canada, the majority of sport psychology specialists work in universities and colleges, primarily as teachers and researchers. Others may work as independent consultants, in schools, in government, or in private clinical and counselling settings. Many of these professionals do provide services to athletes to facilitate performance and promote psychological growth and development. The athletes (and coaches) range from young to old, and the athletes perform from developmental to elite competitive levels. Furthermore, sport psychology specialists are increasingly working with people in other areas of physical activity, including physical fitness and rehabilitation.

Introduction

Sport and exercise are important elements of Canadian life. Sporting experiences might involve running a 10K race along the seawall in Vancouver; playing hockey on an outdoor rink in the Prairies; canoeing the waterways of the Yukon, Quebec, or Ontario; or competing in a golf tournament on the Highlands Links on Cape Breton Island.

Sport is complex and involves many subdisciplines in the sport sciences, including sport psychology. Reflect on your own experiences of participating in and watching sports. How do we make sense of athletes who are unable to concentrate or control anxiety in crucial situations, of acts of aggression by athletes and fans, of athletes' feelings of joy or shame after events, and of individual differences in the interpretation and reactions to sporting situations? What are the characteristics and behaviours of effective coaches? How do we answer even the seemingly simple question of why people choose to participate and continue in a physical activity? It is little wonder that people are interested in sport psychology.

Sport psychology has made major advances throughout the world as a legitimate scientific and applied discipline (Lidor, Morris, Bardaxoglou, & Becker, 2001) and is an important component of the sport sciences in Canada. National accreditation standards identify sport psychology as a core discipline in undergraduate kinesiology and physical education programs (www.ccupeka.ca). Yet there remain many misconceptions and limitations in understanding what sport psychology is all about. We will provide students with a clearer understanding about sport psychology, especially in Canada.

The Nature of Sport Psychology

The term *sport psychology* means different things to a variety of people in an array of situations. If you entered "definition of sport psychology" into an internet search engine, the webpages would reveal an array of definitions. Some definitions would emphasize sport science, some would emphasize performance enhancement, and still others would address psychological principles applied to sport settings. The only consistency among the many definitions is some reference to psychology and sport/exercise/physical activity (see Feltz & Kontos, 2002).

As we will see in a later section, sport psychology in Canada and the United States has its parentage primarily in the sport sciences. In Canada, students can take sport psychology courses in most sport science programs (kinesiology, physical education, human kinetics). Most university professors in sport psychology also work in sport science programs. Thus, Gill (2000, p. 7) suggested, "sport psychology is the branch of sport science that involves the scientific study of human behavior in sport and in the practical application of that knowledge in sport."

However, some professionals may see sport psychology more as a subdiscipline of psychology, much like health psychology or abnormal psychology. In this sense, sport psychology is "a science in which the principles of psychology are applied in a sport or exercise setting" (Cox, 1998, p. 4). Sport psychology is also recognized within the American Psychological Association (Division 47). Further, an increasing number of psychology programs are offering sport psychology courses at the undergraduate level. Although there are outstanding Canadian researchers and practitioners in psychology programs, such as Dr. Robert Vallerand (Université du Québec à Montréal) and Dr. David Cox (Simon Fraser University), the Canadian Psychological Association (CPA) does not identify sport and exercise psychology as unique subdisciplines of psychology (www.cpa.ca).

Does it matter whether one views sport psychology as a subdiscipline of either sport sciences or psychology? We believe that such perspectives are limiting and will hamper the scientific growth of the field. Sport psychology is an interdisciplinary scientific and applied field that embraces the integration of sport science and psychological knowledge. As the following sections reveal, sport psychology is dynamic and constantly evolving.

Careers in Sport Psychology

Specialists in sport psychology are involved in a number of career options that typically require graduate-level degrees. These options can be classified into three major areas: teaching, research, and consulting. We will briefly discuss each of these roles below.

Teaching

Most sport psychology specialists are employed in universities and colleges and have a primary responsibility for teaching undergraduate and graduate courses. Courses may

<Teaching is an important role for many sport psychology specialists.
Photograph by John MacLeod, University of British Columbia.

range from introductory sport psychology to more specialized courses, such as applied sport psychology, mental training, developmental and lifespan sport psychology, counselling in sport, and behavioural medicine. Some sport psychologists also provide educational services to community and sport organizations (Anshel, 2003). These teaching situations may involve increasing the awareness of sport psychology, teaching basic principles of sport psychology, and helping athletes to develop and use psychological skills to enhance performance (Cox, 1998).

Research

A primary responsibility of sport psychology specialists working in universities is to advance knowledge. Through specialized training, scholars are able to design, conduct, and evaluate research. There are many areas of research that will be described in this textbook, including personality, motivation, anxiety, stress and coping, psychological skills training, aggression, group cohesion, leadership and coaching, youth sport, and lifespan and gender issues. Researchers in these areas seek to describe, predict, explain, and sometimes change cognition, emotion, and behaviour in physical activity settings. Their research can range from basic to applied. For example, they would conduct basic research to study the underlying mechanisms or principles (e.g., cognitive, motivational, or neurological) of how or why imagery works in basketball. In applied research they would try to determine what type of imagery program will increase shooting performance in basketball. Sport psychology researchers not only conduct research under strict ethical guidelines but also present their findings at scholarly conferences and in refereed journals and books (see Tables 1.1 and 1.2 on page 6 for a listing of scholarly organizations and journals). These presentations and publications allow scholars to engage in discussions and debates about the strengths and limitations of various theories, methods, and paradigms. The research process is described in greater detail in Chapter 2.

Table 1.1   Selected Sport Psychology Professional Organizations

Canadian Society for Psychomotor Learning and Sport Psychology/Société Canadienne D'Apprentissage Psychomoteur et de Psychologie du Sport (SCAPPS) *www.scapps.org*

International Society of Sport Psychology (ISSP) *www.issponline.org*

European Federation of Sport Psychology/Fédération Européenne de Psychologie des Sports et des Activités Corporelles (FEPSAC) *www.fepsac.org*

Association for the Advancement of Applied Sport Psychology (AAASP) *www.aaasponline.org*

American Psychological Association Division 47: Exercise and Sport Psychology *www.apa47.org*

North American Society for the Psychology of Sport and Physical Activity (NASPSPA) *www.naspspa.org*

Australian Psychological Society: College of Sport Psychologists *www.psychology.org.au/units/colleges/sport*

Table 1.2   Representative Sport Psychology Journals

Journal of Sport & Exercise Psychology—www.humankinetics.com/JSEP/journalAbout.cfm

Journal of Applied Sport Psychology—www.tandf.co.uk/journals/tf/10413200.html

The Sport Psychologist—www.humankinetics.com/TSP/journalAbout.cfm

International Journal of Sport and Exercise Psychology—www.meyer-meyer-sports.com/verlag_english/start.cfm

Psychology of Sport and Exercise—www.sciencedirect.com/science/journal/14690292

Athletic Insight (online journal)—www.athleticinsight.com

Consulting

A third major role of the sport psychology specialist is to help individuals and teams improve performance, manage sport and life demands, and enhance personal well-being. These specialists providing consulting services might be licensed sport psychologists. Other specialists providing services might be individuals who have strong educational and psychological skills knowledge but are not formally licensed. The issues concerning who can provide sport psychology services and who can call themselves sport psychologists are discussed later in this chapter.

In Canada, many professional sport teams and national sport organizations employ sport psychology consultants. In the United States, many major universities have full-time consultants (Weinberg & Gould, 2003), but this is not the case in Canada. However, an increasing number of Canadian universities do use sport psychology

An increasing role of sport psychology specialists is consultant to athletes. Dr. Whitney Sedgwick and University of British Columbia basketball player Pasha Bains discuss psychological strategies to enhance performance.

Photograph by John MacLeod, University of British Columbia.

consultants on a limited basis. There are also consultants working in the fitness industry, in rehabilitation settings, and progressively more in the business community (Anshel, 2003). In Canada, there are very few individuals who make their living as full-time sport psychology consultants. Most sport psychology specialists combine sport consulting with university or college careers or psychological consulting in other areas.

Sport psychology consultants tend to work in three general roles. Educational consultants typically teach athletes psychological skills to facilitate performance. Counselling consultants help athletes with developmental concerns, adjustment, and challenges (Petitpas, 1996). Clinical psychology consultants can assist athletes in educational and counselling areas, but they also have special training in psychopathology. We will discuss the specialized training required in the next section.

Training to Be a Sport Psychology Specialist

Since sport psychology is an interdisciplinary field, there are multiple career pathways. Training to be a sport psychology specialist, however, is contentious and is a source of constant debate. Silva (2002) noted there was little controversy in the 1960s and 1970s since most sport psychology specialists were academically oriented. Now an increasing number of students and academics are interested in applied sport psychology. However, working in applied settings requires a different set of competencies from those required in academic settings.

So what kind of training is required? Unfortunately there is no easy answer! To a large extent, educational training depends on what career path a person chooses. There are multiple career tracks that combine teaching, research, performance enhancement, and the provision of clinical/counselling services. The American Psychological Association provides some guidance on graduate training and career possibilities in exercise and sport psychology (www.psyc.unt.edu/apadiv47/gradtrain. htm). For simplicity we will briefly describe two general training orientations: sport science education and clinical/counselling sport psychology.

Sport Science Education

In Canada most sport psychology specialists work in university and college settings and thus require strong teaching and research skills. Typically they are extensively trained in the sport sciences and research methods and take additional courses in psychology and/or counselling (see Table 1.3). Nevertheless, there are trends toward more interdisciplinary training that combines the sport sciences and psychology. Currently a wide range of academic programs that provide varied learning experiences are available to students. The interested student can find important information in a directory of graduate programs in Canada, the United States, Australia, and Great Britain published for the Association for the Advancement of Applied Sport Psychology (www.aaasponline.org).

Clinical and Counselling Sport Psychology

Clinical psychology and counselling psychology are closely associated fields. Clinical psychology training typically focuses on the assessment and rehabilitation of serious psychological dysfunctions. Counselling training tends to focus more on helping people with adjustment or development problems. However, there is significant overlap in the training of clinical and counselling psychologists (see Petitpas, 1996).

The training of clinical and counselling psychologists is well grounded in psychological theory, assessment, intervention, research methods, and ethics and often requires a supervised internship (see Table 1.3). Clinical and counselling psychologists who work as sport psychologists usually have completed graduate courses or supplementary training in the sport sciences. The specific training for clinical psychologists is linked to the registration (licensing) standards of individual provincial and territorial regulatory bodies. Students interested in the specific requirements and accredited academic programs can visit the Canadian Psychological Association website for appropriate weblinks (www.cpa.ca).

Table 1.3   Examples of Graduate Courses in Sport Psychology

Sport Science Orientation	Clinical/Counselling Orientation
Sport Psychology	Psychological Assessment
Exercise Psychology	Psychotherapy
Skill Acquisition	Psychopathology
Motor Development	Cognitive Behavioural Therapy
Adapted Physical Activity	Counselling Theory
Psychological Intervention in Sport	Health Psychology
Research Methods	Social Psychology
Advanced Statistics	Professional Ethics
Professional Ethics	Research Methods
Sport Psychology Internship	Advanced Statistics
Behavioural Medicine	Internship

Courses and Programs for Undergraduate Students

Entry into either a sport science or a psychology graduate program often requires very different undergraduate coursework. So what should a student do to prepare for a career in sport psychology? Ideally, a student should take a double major in sport sciences and psychology. This background would allow the greatest flexibility in pursuing graduate work. If this is not possible, then a student should combine a major and a minor in an undergraduate degree. However, the exact program and courses will be determined by (a) the career path and (b) the entrance requirements of various sport science or psychology (clinical and counselling) programs. It is hoped that, in the near future, more universities will create more opportunities that will allow students greater flexibility to pursue academic programs in both the sport sciences and psychology.

Licensing of Sport Psychologists

Many individuals providing performance enhancement services to athletes are called sport psychologists by the media. However, is this appropriate? In Canada, provincial and territorial laws regulate use of the term *psychologist*. These laws were enacted to protect people from being exploited, possibly by untrained individuals. In most cases, psychologists must complete specific types of educational training and pass examinations set by psychological licensing boards. The specific rules for the use of the title *psychologist* vary across provinces and territories, and there are exemptions in some jurisdictions for people working in hospitals, government, education, and universities (www.cpa.ca/licensing.html).

There are a number of professionals who are well trained in the sport sciences, psychology, and performance enhancement techniques, but they are not licensed sport psychologists. Unless they met the exemption criteria, they should not call themselves sport psychologists. Within universities and colleges, such titles as instructor or professor of sport psychology might be appropriate if it describes the individual's teaching or research responsibilities. In applied settings, people have used such designations as mental trainer, sport psychology consultant, and sport science consultant. Regardless of the title that practitioners adopt, they are responsible for meeting standards of conduct when providing sport psychology services. The Canadian Mental Training Registry (see Table 1.4) and AAASP have been proactive in identifying the necessary standards and competencies required for providing sport psychology services to athletes. The next section discusses these standards and competencies.

Table 1.4   Membership Criteria for the Canadian Mental Training Registry

The Canadian Mental Training Registry (www.coach.ca/e/mental_training) lists mental training consultants who fulfill the following basic criteria:

- educational experience in mental training for performer and performance enhancement

- background understanding of the sport sciences

- first-hand experience in sport

- mental training consulting experience

- favourable client evaluation

Standards of Conduct and Practitioner Competencies in Sport Psychology

An increasing role for sport psychology specialists is that of consultant for athletes, teams, and coaches. However, who should provide specific types of sport psychology services? How do consultants deal with conflicts of interest, demands from coaches for athletes' private information, challenges that exceed their professional competencies, or potential romantic interests in clients? The style in which each individual consultant works with an athlete or a team will probably differ considerably from one consultant to another. Nevertheless, a number of basic standards of conduct and service always apply when a sport psychology consultant interacts with clients.

Ethics is concerned with matters of right and wrong as they relate to human behaviour. With regard to the duties and responsibilities of a sport psychology consultant, ethics also refers to the nature, terms, and parameters of the relationship between the consultant and the client. Consultants provide a service, but they must be mindful that this service can be both beneficial and harmful to clients. Consultants have an ethical responsibility (at best) to assist athletes and (at worst) to do no harm. However, consultants often find themselves faced with situations in which the right course of action is far from clear (Moore, 2003). This is where ethical codes become invaluable because they provide guidelines for what to do, when to do it, and how to do it (see Case Study 1.1).

A number of professional organizations have drawn up codes of ethics or guidelines that govern the relationship between a practitioner and a client. Two of these codes of ethics are particularly relevant to the sport psychology consultant working in Canada: one was developed by the Canadian Psychological Association (www.cpa.ca/ethics2000.html), and the other was formulated by the Association for

Case Study 1.1
Sport Psychology Competencies and Referral

Professor Kim has been working with the university volleyball team as a sport psychology consultant. Dr. Kim is a full professor with academic responsibilities in sport and exercise psychology. She is a certified consultant (AAASP), a member of the Canadian Mental Training Registry, and a member of the Canadian Psychological Association. However, she is not a registered (licensed) psychologist. Dr. Kim's role with the team falls clearly within the educational orientation, and she provides psychological skills training. At the beginning of each year, Dr. Kim clearly defines her role with the team, her areas of competence, and the boundaries of her services. She also distinctly outlines a referral process for dealing with issues outside her role and competencies (i.e., that she will help the athlete(s) to get the appropriate assistance).

This year the implementation of the psychological skills training program seemed to be going smoothly. Athletes were well motivated and participating fully. Dr. Kim had developed a strong rapport with most players, and all seemed satisfied. One day an athlete asked to talk to Dr. Kim in private. The athlete disclosed his substance-abuse problem and asked for Dr. Kim's help to deal with this issue. Although Dr. Kim has taken graduate courses in counselling psychology, it was clear that this request required careful consideration of the standards of conduct as outlined by the CPA and AAASP codes of ethics. She does not have the professional competencies to deal with substance abuse. Furthermore, this area was clearly outside her prescribed roles of service with the volleyball team. Dr. Kim was able to refer the athlete to university counselling services. This referral process went smoothly because of (1) the athlete's early knowledge of Dr. Kim's roles and competencies, (2) a clear outline of the referral process, and (3) an established referral mechanism with University Counselling Services.

the Advancement of Applied Sport Psychology (www.aaasponline.org/governance/committees/ethics/standards.php). Professional ethics are normally covered in more detail in advanced sport and exercise psychology courses. We provide a brief overview of the AAASP guidelines in Table 1.5. However, students should be aware that ethical standards are complex and are constantly being modified and refined (see Moore, 2003; Whelan, Meyers, & Elkin, 2002).

Table 1.5   Association for the Advancement of Applied Sport Psychology: Code of Ethics

The code is made up of six general principles, which are summarized below:

Principle A: Competence

This principle reinforces the importance of providing only those services that one is qualified to provide, remaining knowledgeable about those services, and recognizing the limitations of one's expertise.

Principle B: Integrity

This principle reminds sport psychology consultants of the need to accurately portray both themselves and their services and to avoid the development of inappropriate relationships with clients.

Principle C: Professional and Scientific Responsibility

This principle addresses the responsibility of the sport psychology consultant to uphold acceptable professional standards and to encourage colleagues to comply with such standards.

Principle D: Respect for People's Rights and Dignity

This principle emphasizes the importance of respecting all athletes' rights to privacy, confidentiality, and autonomy. In addition, consultants must avoid all unfair discriminatory practices. Consultants should also be conscious of individual differences, including those due to age, gender, ethnicity, culture, religion, sexual orientation, disability, language, and socioeconomic status.

Principle E: Concern for Others' Welfare

This principle states that sport psychology consultants have professional relationships with athletes and that consultants must be sensitive to differences in power that may exist between the two parties. Furthermore, consultants must not seek to take advantage of such a situation. It is critical that consultants do not take advantage of or mislead clients during or after professional relationships.

Principle F: Social Responsibility

This principle reminds sport psychology consultants that they have a duty to participate in the advancement of the discipline through the dissemination of knowledge that may serve to promote athlete and public welfare.

Reflections 1.1
A practitioner in Ontario is providing sport psychology services to athletes of various competitive levels. The specialist is teaching performance enhancement strategies through psychological skills training. There were, however, some questions about the specialist's knowledge and practices. Although the person is a former elite athlete, there was no indication that the specialist had formal training in the theory and use of performance enhancement strategies in sport. What principles might the specialist have violated, based on the AAASP standards of conduct?

Sport Psychology in Canada and the United States

The previous sections have highlighted how sport psychology is a multidisciplinary field that involves both psychology and the sport sciences, but how did it evolve into its present condition in Canada and the United States? The development of sport psychology in both countries has been closely intertwined. A brief history will allow the student to more clearly understand the present day issues, challenges, and status of sport psychology in Canada.

In the early 20th century, Canadian universities were few and enrolment was low. In sport psychology, there was little evidence of systematic research or teaching. However, south of the border, Dr. Coleman Griffith developed a sport psychology laboratory at the University of Illinois in 1925. His research focused on understanding psychological and social factors that influenced skill performance (Gould & Pick, 1995), and he was a consultant for the Chicago Cubs baseball team. Griffith penned two of the first sport psychology texts: *The Psychology of Coaching* (1926) and *Psychology and Athletics* (1928). Despite Griffith's early work, sport psychology witnessed little development during the 1930s and 1940s.

The post–World War II expansion of universities in the United States had an important impact on sport psychology. Several universities established laboratories in motor learning and behaviour, seeking to determine how people learned motor skills and how practice and feedback influenced learning. Dr. Franklin Henry, a faculty member at the University of California, Berkeley also became a strong advocate of a scholarly and scientific approach to physical education studies. Notably, two graduates of Dr. Henry's laboratory became prominent pioneering sport psychology researchers in Canada: Dr. Rikk Alderman and Dr. Albert Carron. In North America, many sport psychology instructors were trained in motor behaviour in physical education departments.

Nurtured primarily by academics in the movement and sport sciences, sport psychology began to grow in both Canada and the United States during the 1960s and 1970s (Gould & Pick, 1995). This growth corresponded with the establishment of many new universities and junior colleges. The teaching of sport psychology courses became widespread and graduate training programs began to appear in the major universities, such as the University of Illinois, the University of Florida, and the University of Alberta. Psychology departments also became more interested in teaching sport psychology, although there seemed to be an overemphasis on abnormal or problem behaviour. For example, in 1966, clinical psychologists Bruce Ogilvie and Thomas Tutko published the influential textbook *Problem Athletes and How to Handle Them*. (See Table 1.6 on page 15 for a list of some important sport psychology textbooks by Canadians.)

In Canada, Dr. Rikk Alderman at the University of Alberta developed the first PhD program. Along with Dr. Albert Carron, Alderman could be considered one of the modern parents of sport psychology in Canada. Under the guidance of Dr. Alderman and Dr. Robert Wilberg (a motor behaviour specialist), the University of Alberta program produced several influential Canadian sport psychology researchers and practitioners in the 1970s. They include John Salmela (Université de Montréal, University of Ottawa), Terry Orlick (University of Ottawa), Cal Botterill (University of Winnipeg), Len Wankel (University of Alberta), and Peter Klavora (University of Toronto).

Two major scholarly professional organizations were established in the United States and Canada. The North American Society for the Psychology of Sport and Physical Activity (NASPSPA) was formed in 1967. It reflected the close ties between the training of specialists in motor learning and in sport psychology in the 1960s. NASPSPA focused on improving the quality of research and teaching in the psychology of sport, motor development, and motor learning and control. The Canadian Society for Psychomotor Learning and Sport Psychology (Société Canadienne D'Apprentissage Psychomoteur et de Psychologie du Sport (SCAPPS)) had its beginnings in Edmonton in 1969 but was founded as a society in Banff, Alberta, in 1977. Its main objectives were similar to NASPSPA's, with a primary focus on research. Dr. Robert Wilberg was its first unofficial president in 1969, followed by Dr. Jack Leavitt of the University of Windsor. Many sport psychology specialists have served as president, including Brent Rushall (Lakehead University), John Salmela (Université de Montréal), Peter Klavora (University of Toronto), John Albinson (Queen's University), Wendy Rodgers (University of Alberta), and Peter Crocker (University of British Columbia). A unique feature of SCAPPS is its recognition of scholarly research by student members through the Franklin Henry Young Scientist Awards. SCAPPS continues to have a strong influence on the professional and academic development of sport psychology in Canada.

The late 1970s and 1980s were periods of consolidation in sport psychology as it separated from its motor learning parentage. Many universities had specialists in sport psychology, more graduate programs were established, and quality research flourished. The practice of sport psychology also became more widespread. In the United States, the Olympic Committee developed a sport psychology advisory board around 1980, organized a sport psychology registry, and hired a full-time sport psychologist in 1985 (Weinberg & Gould, 2003). Sport psychology services were increasingly sought by professional and Olympic sport organizations. The American Psychological Association developed a special division—Division 47: Exercise and Sport Psychology—to bring together psychologists interested in this area. In Canada, sport psychology practices were included in the National Coaching Certification Program (NCCP). Three prominent sport psychology journals were established: *The Journal of Sport Psychology* (1979), *The Sport Psychologist* (1986), and the *Journal of Applied Sport Psychology* (1989).

A key event was the formation of the Association for the Advancement of Applied Sport Psychology (AAASP) in 1986. Many Canadian sport psychology scholars became active members, with Dr. Larry Brawley (University of Waterloo, University of Saskatchewan) as one of its earliest presidents. AAASP is now the largest organization devoted to the promotion of applied sport (and exercise) psychology. AAASP conferences highlight research and professional issues in sport, exercise, and health psychology, as well as provide continuing education workshops.

Dr. Albert Carron: A Canadian Profile.

Photograph courtesy of Dr. A. Carron.

Dr. Albert (Bert) Carron is recognized as one of the modern founders of sport and exercise psychology in Canada. Born in Edmonton, Alberta, he completed his undergraduate physical education degree at the University of Alberta (1963), where he also starred as a football player. In 1967 he completed his EdD degree at the University of California, Berkeley and became a faculty member at the University of Saskatchewan.

He has been at the University of Western Ontario in the School of Kinesiology since 1974, where he established one of the top sport and exercise psychology research programs in the world. Dr. Carron is widely acknowledged as the world expert on group cohesion and group dynamics in sport and exercise. Dr. Carron collaborated with Dr. Larry Brawley and Dr. Neil Widmeyer to produce the Group Environment Questionnaire, at present the best research instrument to assess group cohesion in sport teams (see Chapter 9). This work has been cited in more than 100 research studies. He has published 10 books and more than 120 research publications.

His colleagues have recognized his contributions by awarding him Fellow status in three professional organizations: the American Academy of Kinesiology and Physical Education, the Association for the Advancement of Applied Sport Psychology, and the Canadian Society for Psychomotor Learning and Sport Psychology (SCAPPS). A Fellow designation is reserved for top scholars who have demonstrated high standards of scholarly practice and made significant contributions to scientific knowledge. SCAPPS has also named its senior scholar presentation in sport and exercise psychology after Dr. Carron.

He has consulted with the Spanish and British Olympic Committees, the London Knights of the Ontario Hockey League, and the University of Western Ontario's men's and women's ice hockey teams. His remarkable career and contributions establish the standard for all sport and exercise scholars.

Since the 1990s there has been tremendous growth in sport psychology in North America. There are now numerous opportunities for research, teaching, and practice in this expanded field. Within universities, the growth of sport psychology has been propelled and shaped by societal concerns about health and health costs. Many programs currently place an emphasis on health and health promotion through physical activity. One impact of this health movement has been the diversification and expansion of exercise and health psychology. Research topics now increasingly focus on body image, self-esteem, well-being, behavioural change, self-presentation, exercise adherence, eating disorders, and other health behaviours affected by physical activity. Many university programs presently offer undergraduate courses in sport psychology, exercise psychology, exercise and health psychology, behavioural medicine, applied sport and exercise psychology, and the like. Major granting agencies in Canada and the United States are directing significant research funding to sport and exercise psychology researchers, especially if the work is linked to health.

Practitioners are also working with major organizations to provide sport organizations and athletes with better access to certified mental or psychological skills consultants. To this end, the Canadian Mental Training Registry was established in the early 1990s, and AAASP developed a process to certify qualified consultants (www. aaasponline.org/cc/index.php).

Table 1.6   Representative Academic and Professional Sport Psychology Textbooks by Canadians

1974	*Psychological behaviour in sport.*	R. Alderman
1975	*Every kid can win.*	T. Orlick & C. Botterill
1976	*Psychology of sport: The behavior, motivation, personality and performance of athletes.*	S. Butt
1980	*Social psychology of sport.*	A. Carron
1980	*In pursuit of excellence.*	T. Orlick
1983	*Behavior modification and coaching: Principles, procedures, and research.*	G. L. Martin & D. Hrycaiko
1986	*Psyching for sport: Mental training for athletes.*	T. Orlick
1988	*The mental game plan: A training program for all sports.*	J. Albinson & S. Bull
1998	*Exercising your way to better mental health.*	L. M. Leith
1998	*Group dynamics in sport.*	A. Carron & H. Hausenblas
2003	*The psychology of physical activity.*	A. Carron, H. Hausenblas, & P. Estabrooks
2003	*The psychology of coaching team sports: A self-help guide.*	L. M. Leith
2003	*Sport psychology: Practical guidelines from behavior analysis.*	G. L. Martin

Sport Psychology around the World

The discipline and profession of sport psychology has witnessed tremendous growth in many parts of the world over the last 25 years. Lidor et al. (2001) estimated there were several thousand sport and exercise psychologists working in numerous countries. Socio-cultural, economic, and political forces have shaped the evolution of sport psychology in various regions. Not surprisingly, sport psychology is best developed in the wealthiest economic regions, such as North America, Europe, the United Kingdom, Australia, and Japan. Reviewing the worldwide developments in sport psychology is beyond the scope of this chapter. We will, however, provide a snapshot of prominent organizations and events. Those students interested in more details are encouraged to read the third edition of *The World Sport Psychology Sourcebook* by Lidor et al.

The former Soviet Union boasted one of the first sport psychology programs. Around 1919 the Institute for the Study of Sport and Physical Culture was established in Petrograd (later Leningrad, now St. Petersburg). The Institute developed a systematic approach to the application of sport sciences. Psychologists worked with other sport scientists to develop and apply training and competition principles to maximize performance. This system was adopted by more than 130 sport institutes throughout the former Soviet Union and later in the Soviet-controlled eastern European bloc (Silva, 2002). With the collapse of the Soviet Union beginning in the 1980s, there were insufficient resources and political power to maintain the high level of training and practice of sport psychology.

In the rest of Europe, with the possible exception of Germany, there was little significant support for and development of sport psychology before 1960. However, two major events occurred in the 1960s that played significant roles in the establishment of sport psychology. First, under the persuasive leadership of Ferruccio Antonelli of Italy, the first World Congress of Sport Psychology was held in Rome in 1965. This lead to the formation of the International Society of Sport Psychology (ISSP), with more than 25 countries represented. ISSP also sponsored the first scholarly sport psychology journal, the *International Journal of Sport Psychology*. The second event was the founding of the European Federation of Sport Psychology/Fédération Européenne de Psychologie des Sports et des Activités Corporelles (FEPSAC). In 2005, FEPSAC had representation from more than 24 European sport and exercise psychology organizations. Both ISSP and FEPSAC have had a major impact on the advancement of sport psychology in Europe and throughout the world.

By 2005, there were many strong academic programs and professional organizations throughout the world. In Britain, sport and exercise psychology courses are widespread in the university system. Coaches can learn about sport psychology applications through sports coach UK (formerly the National Coaching Foundation), and the British Association of Sport and Exercise Sciences (BASES) offers individual accreditation in sport psychology. In Australia, psychology departments co-operate with sport science programs to offer graduate training. Sport psychology is well accepted by the Australian sporting community and is fully integrated into the Australian Institute of Sport (www.ais.org.au/psychology). In Asia, the leading countries are Japan, China, and Korea. Recent or impending major sporting events (Olympics, Asian Games) have fuelled the practice of applied sport psychology and other sport sciences. Unfortunately, academic and professional development have been slow in many poorer areas of the world, such as Africa and Central America. Sport psychology organizations are working with dedicated professionals in these areas to improve educational and professional opportunities in sport psychology.

∧

Canadian Dr. John Salmela served on the executive of the International Society of Sport Psychology for 16 years.

Photograph courtesy of John Salmela.

Key Historical World Events in Sport Psychology

- Institute for the Study of Sport and Physical Culture established in Soviet Union (1919)
- First World Congress of Sport Psychology held in Rome (1965)
- International Society of Sport Psychology (ISSP) founded (1965)
- European Federation of Sport Psychology/Fédération Européenne de Psychologie des Sports et des Activités Corporelles (FEPSAC) established (1969)
- First issue of the *International Journal of Sport Psychology* (1970)
- Japanese Society of Sport Psychology founded (1973)
- World Congress of Sport Psychology held in Ottawa, Canada (1981)
- British Association for Sport Sciences (now Sport & Exercise Sciences) formed—establish a distinct Sport Psychology section (1985)
- Australian Applied Sport Psychology Association founded (1986)
- German Association for Sport Psychology formed in 1969, but first meeting after unification held in Cologne (1991)
- First Congress of Asian and South Pacific Association for Sport Psychology (1991)
- First issue of *Psychology of Sport and Exercise* (a FEPSAC journal) (2000)
- ISSP sponsors *International Journal of Sport and Exercise Psychology* (2004)

Predicted Trends and Issues in Canada

Sport psychology is an interdisciplinary field involving researchers, educators, and practitioners from both the sport sciences and psychology. Many social, economic, and political forces have shaped the present state of sport psychology in Canada. It has faced many challenges and growing pains but has made very impressive gains in the last two decades. So what does the future hold? We believe there are a number of trends and issues that will dominate the advancement of sport psychology over the next 20 years.

Increased Specialization and Diversification

Federal and provincial or territorial health initiatives and policies, combined with knowledge development, will drive increased specialization and diversification. Much of the growth in the field will be in exercise and health primarily because physical activity is an effective, and relatively inexpensive, way to maintain or improve health. Hot topics are likely to be exercise adherence, obesity, aging, and youth development. There will be continued expansion of sport and exercise psychology principles in clinical settings in the study and treatment of cancer, stroke, spinal cord injuries, and Parkinson's disease.

Increased Research and Teaching Opportunities

Most Canadian universities and colleges offer sport and exercise psychology courses. Because of continued specialization and diversification, the number and types of courses will continue to grow at both undergraduate and graduate levels. Research opportunities will increase as major funding agencies—Social Sciences and Humanities Research Council of Canada (SSHRC), Canadian Institutes of Health

Research (CIHR), and the Heart and Stroke Foundation of Canada—recognize the quality and applicability of sport and exercise psychology research. Although funding for sport-related research has improved in the last few years, the major focus for increased funding will be on health-related research.

Limited Opportunities in Applied Sport Psychology

Opportunities will continue to be limited in applied sport psychology, primarily because of the lack of large-scale investment by professional sport organizations. Unlike its U.S. counterparts, Canadian university athletic programs do not have the resources to pay for continuous applied sport psychology services. Similar constraints exist for many national and provincial sport organizations. However, in 2005, the Canadian Olympic Committee announced a plan (Own the Podium 2010) that called for increased funding for sport sciences services, including sport psychology.

Increased Demands for Training in Counselling Psychology and Clinical Psychology

Working in diverse sport and exercise settings will require a range of sport science and psychological competencies. Students will demand and require counselling training and possibly clinical psychology training. Unfortunately, Canadian (and U.S.) universities have been slow to respond to this demand. Kinesiology and exercise science programs largely focus on research and teaching, and few psychology departments offer sport psychology programs. This leaves students with two choices. First, students in kinesiology programs can supplement their training by taking appropriate counselling courses in psychology or educational psychology programs. However, there seldom is the opportunity for supervised internships in applied sport psychology. Second, students can do a graduate degree in counselling or clinical psychology. An advantage to this route is generalized training that is applicable to many domains. Unfortunately, most counselling and clinical programs lack a critical mass of faculty trained in applied sport psychology.

Interdepartmental Collaboration in Teaching, Research, and Practice

As sport and exercise psychology expands, there will be a need for faculty to collaborate across departments of sport science, psychology, education, public health, and rehabilitation sciences. There is a need to break down traditional and artificial academic barriers and to create joint or multidepartmental programs. A major challenge, however, is determining the necessary requisite courses and experiences for specific careers at undergraduate and graduate levels.

Ethics and Competencies

There will be increased pressure on practitioners to adhere to the professional standards of conduct when working with clients. Regulatory bodies are likely to become more vigilant in monitoring the use of the title *sport psychologist* as well as the practices of sport psychology consultants. Consultants from both sport science educational and clinical and counselling psychology backgrounds will need to acquire and demonstrate competencies to work with specific populations in sport and exercise.

Tension between Academic and Applied Sport Psychology

In Canada, the majority of sport psychology professionals are employed in academic programs in universities and colleges. There are, however, many highly qualified applied practitioners. Some practitioners may feel ignored by universities and professional organizations like SCAPPS, which emphasize research generation and dissemination. Academic sport psychologists are typically not overly concerned with professional practice issues, certification, advocacy, or professional lobbying. This situation is not much different in the United States. Although Silva, Conroy, and Zizzi (1999) have argued for the need for better training and supervision in the application of sport psychology principles with clients, Hale and Danish (1999) note that applied sport psychology remains a minor area in North America.

Knowledge Translation

There is a critical need to bridge the gap between research evidence and professional practice in sport psychology. Knowledge must be accessible, understandable, and useful for practitioners, such as applied sport psychologists, physical educators, coaches, rehabilitation specialists, and fitness specialists. Traditional knowledge translation methods have been primarily of a top-down nature. These methods have included university courses, textbooks, coaching manuals, and workshops taught by specialists. However, these traditional methods are not always effective. Partnerships among researchers, educators, and practitioners are required—partnerships that produce an exchange and ethically based application of sport psychology knowledge.

Reflections 1.2
What is the future of sport psychology in Canada? Will there be an increased need for sport psychologists in educational, research, and consulting areas? Where do you see the biggest potential for growth?

Chapter Summary

Sport psychology is an interdisciplinary field that is recognized in Canada as a core discipline within kinesiology and physical education programs. Sport psychology specialists are involved in teaching, research, and service roles, although most specialists in Canada are employed in universities and colleges. Various educational pathways involve training in the sport sciences, clinical psychology, or counselling psychology. Specific training is often dependent on career objectives, whether as an academic (in either sport sciences or psychology) or as a practitioner. Some scholarly organizations, such as AAASP, do provide a certification process for consultants. There is also a mental training registry in Canada. However, provincial and territorial bodies regulate the use of the term *psychologist* as well as the specific training and examinations required to become a registered psychologist. All sport psychology consultants are guided by standards of conduct set out by organizations such as the Canadian Psychological Association and AAASP. Although the term *psychologist* has a specific legal meaning, throughout this book we will use the term *sport psychologists* to refer to specialists in the three areas of teaching, research, and consulting.

The state of sport psychology in Canada, including its strengths and controversies, has been shaped by its parentage. In North America, sport psychology has been nurtured primarily in the sport sciences. The major Canadian scholarly professional organization is the Canadian Society for Psychomotor Learning and Sport Psychology (SCAPPS), although many academics and practitioners also affiliate with the North American Society for the Psychology of Sport and Physical Activity (NASPSPA) and AAASP. At present, sport psychology is taught in most universities, and research is flourishing. There has also been increased diversification into exercise, health, and clinical populations. Sport psychology also continues to flourish around the world, with major scholarly organizations in Europe, Australia, New Zealand, the United Kingdom, and Asia.

The next twenty years should witness several major trends including increased specialization, diversification, research, and teaching opportunities. There will be pressure to improve educational opportunities and training of specific competencies for applied sport psychology services. It is hoped that faculty in programs in psychology, educational psychology, and sport science will collaborate to enhance the future development of sport psychology, instead of engaging in futile turf wars. Lastly, there is a critical need to bridge the gap between research evidence and professional practice in sport psychology. This process will require effective partnerships among practitioners, educators, and researchers so that sport and exercise principles can be effectively applied across multiple settings of physical activity to enhance performance, increase participation, and enhance well-being.

Review Questions

1. What are the three major roles of a sport psychology specialist? Are different types of training needed for the three roles?
2. What are the differences between a sport psychology specialist trained in sport sciences and one trained in clinical or counselling psychology?
3. Is a counselling psychologist able to work with athletes to provide performance enhancement strategies? What standards of conduct guide such decisions?
4. How would the principles of Integrity and of Respect for People's Rights and Dignity help guide your decision to reveal information about an athlete's psychological state to a coach who demands it?
5. What are three major sport psychology organizations around the world? What is the major Canadian organization that promotes sport psychology research?
6. What is knowledge translation, and why is it important for the advancement of sport psychology?

Suggested Reading

Feltz, D. L., & Kontos, A. P. (2002). The nature of sport psychology. In T. Horn (Ed.), *Advances in sport psychology* (2nd ed., pp. 3–19.). Champaign, IL: Human Kinetics.

Lidor, R., Morris, T., Bardaxoglou, N., & Becker, B. (2001). *The world sport psychology sourcebook* (3rd ed.). Morgantown, WV: Fitness Information Technology.

Moore, Z. E. (2003). Ethical dilemmas in sport psychology: Discussion and recommendations for practice. *Professional Psychology: Research & Practice, 34*, 601–610.

References

Albinson, J. G., & Bull, S. J. (1988). *The mental game plan: A training program for all sports*. London, ON: Spodym.

Alderman, R. (1974). *Psychological behaviour in sport*. Toronto: W. B. Saunders.

Anshel, M. H. (2003). *Sport psychology: From theory to practice* (4th ed.). San Francisco: Benjamin Cummings.

Butt, D. S. (1976). *Psychology of sport: The behavior, motivation, personality and performance of athletes*. New York: Van Nostrand Reinhold.

Carron, A. V. (1980). *Social psychology of sport*. Ithaca, NY: Mouvement.

Carron, A. V., & Hausenblas, H. A. (1998). *Group dynamics in sport*. Morgantown, WV: Fitness Information Technology.

Carron, A. V., Hausenblas, H. A., & Estabrooks, P. A. (2003). *The psychology of physical activity*. St Louis, MO: McGraw-Hill.

Cox, R. H. (1998). *Sport psychology: Concepts and applications* (4th ed.). Boston: McGraw-Hill.

Feltz, D. L., & Kontos, A. P. (2002). The nature of sport psychology. In T. Horn (Ed.), *Advances in sport psychology* (2nd ed., pp. 3–19.). Champaign, IL: Human Kinetics.

Gill, D. (2000). *Psychological dynamics of sport and exercise* (2nd ed.). Champaign, IL: Human Kinetics.

Gould, D., & Pick, S. (1995). Sport psychology: The Griffith era, 1920–1940. *The Sport Psychologist, 9*, 391–405.

Griffith, C. R. (1926). The *psychology of coaching*. New York: Scribner's.

Griffith, C. R. (1928). *Psychology and athletics*. New York: Scribner's.

Hale, B. D., & Danish, S. J. (1999). Putting the accreditation cart before the AAASP horse! A reply to Silva, Conroy, & Zizzi. *Journal of Applied Sport Psychology, 11*, 298–320.

Leith, L. M. (1998). *Exercising your way to better mental health: Combat stress, fight depression and improve your overall mood and self-concept with these simple exercises*. Morgantown, WV: Fitness Information Technology.

Leith, L. M. (2003). *The psychology of coaching team sports: A self-help guide*. Toronto: Sport Book.

Lidor, R., Morris, T., Bardaxoglou, N., & Becker, B. (2001). *The world sport psychology sourcebook* (3rd ed.). Morgantown, WV: Fitness Information Technology.

Martin, G. L. (2003). *Sport psychology: Practical guidelines from behavior analysis*. Winnipeg, MB: Sport Science Press.

Martin, G. L., & Hrycaiko, D. (1983). *Behavior modification and coaching: Principles, procedures, and research*. Springfield, IL: C. C. Thomas.

Moore, Z. E. (2003). Ethical dilemmas in sport psychology: Discussion and recommendations for practice. *Professional Psychology: Research & Practice, 34*, 601–610.

Ogilvie, B. C., & Tutko, T. A. (1966). *Problem athletes and how to handle them*. London: Palham Books.

Orlick, T. (1980). *In pursuit of excellence*. Champaign, IL: Human Kinetics.

Orlick, T. (1986). *Psyching for sport: Mental training for athletes*. Champaign, IL: Leisure Press.

Orlick, T., & Botterill, C. (1975). *Every kid can win*. Chicago: Nelson-Hall.

Petitpas, A. J. (1996). Counseling interventions in applied sport psychology. In J. L. Van Raalte & B.W. Brewer (Eds.), *Exploring sport and exercise psychology* (pp. 189–204). Washington, DC: American Psychological Association.

Silva, J. M. (2002). The evolution of sport psychology. In J. M. Silva & D. E. Stevens (Eds.), *Psychological foundation of sport*. Toronto: Allyn and Bacon.

Silva, J. M., Conroy, D. E., & Zizzi, S. J. (1999). Critical issues confronting the advancement of applied sport psychology. *Journal of Applied Sport Psychology, 11*, 298–320.

Weinberg, R., & Gould, D. (2003). *Foundations of sport and exercise psychology* (3rd ed.). Champaign, IL: Human Kinetics.

Whelan, J. P., Meyers, A. W., & Elkin, T. D. (2002). Ethics in sport and exercise psychology. In J. L. Van Raalte (Ed.), *Exploring sport and exercise psychology* (2nd ed., pp. 503–523). Washington, DC: American Psychological Association.

Philip M. Wilson
Enrique Garcia Bengoechea

CHAPTER 2

Research Perspectives in Sport Psychology

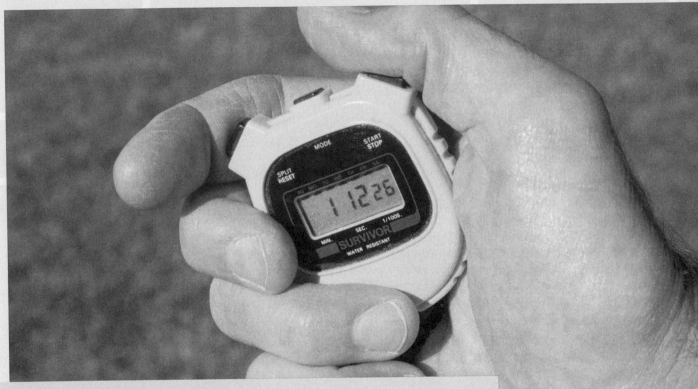

Chapter Objectives

After reading this chapter, you should be able to do the following:

1. Differentiate scientific research from other sources of knowledge.
2. Define the basic terminology of research methods.
3. Discuss the importance of research ethics.
4. Explain the role of measurement in the research process.
5. Explain the importance of sampling and design in sport psychology research.
6. Discuss the utility of qualitative inquiry in sport psychology research.

* We would like to acknowledge the mentorship of Dr. W. Todd Rogers (Professor and Director of the Centre for Applied Measurement and Evaluation, University of Alberta) and Dr. Marcel Bouffard (Professor, Faculty of Physical Education & Recreation, University of Alberta). Together, they shaped our own interests in research during our sojourns in Edmonton. Both of them bring personal meaning for us to Sir Isaac Newton's 1676 dictum, "if I have seen a little further it is because I stand on the shoulders of giants." We would also like to thank Dr. Sandy O'Brien Cousins (University of Alberta) for her helpful comments on a previous draft of this chapter.

Coach Powell is the director of St. Catharines United, a high-performance soccer team that provides a forum for young players in the Niagara region to develop their soccer abilities. In his role of overseeing soccer development in the Niagara region, Coach Powell has covered all aspects of player development from the grassroots to the professional levels. During his time in charge, Coach Powell has watched some of the finest soccer players emerge from the region and go on to participate in both the Olympic Games and the Under-18 World Cup finals. Despite his enthusiasm for player development, Coach Powell is frustrated by the poor training habits exhibited by some of his most talented players.

Considering his current team roster, Coach Powell ponders why some players give maximum effort during every training session while others seem to be nothing more than practice players. Although Coach Powell is not a man of science, he has attempted to answer some of his questions by monitoring his players' habits during practice (using daily performance diaries) and by completing interviews with his players following game-tape analyses of previous matches.

Coach Powell and his staff frequently review each player's evidence and use it in an attempt to motivate more consistently high training performances throughout the team during their season and tournament plays. Based on his personal playing experiences, Powell is often convinced that the difference between players is motivational in nature and that some players just "want it" more than others, which drives them to excel in all aspects of preparation. Several of his staff coaches, however, believe that motivation can be affected by coaching and training methods.

The aforementioned scenario might sound familiar to any youth-sport coach or the parent of a gifted young athlete. It is common for coaches to have questions regarding the performance of their players and to seek different (sometimes creative and inventive) ways of collecting evidence that allows the coaching staff to answer those questions. Such answers will often lead to changes in player preparation, training regimens, coach-athlete interactions, or in some instances, team selection. In other words, the process of acquiring information (data) that answers relevant questions often serves as the springboard that initiates coaching decisions and roster changes. Sometimes the changes produce the desired effects, but at other times the changes have undesired consequences on player performances. Based on Coach Powell's experiences, this process of seeking answers to important questions will invariably lead to more research regarding player preparation for the coaching staff to undertake.

The Coach Powell scenario depicts the acquisition of knowledge through a sequence of events that is known as the research process. The process of conducting research is considered by many to be the cornerstone of scientific inquiry. This chapter will highlight factors about sport psychology research that are worth considering. The scenario depicted by Coach Powell's predicament raises a number of interesting questions. For example, how will the coach measure training performance? What would be the best way to test Coach Powell's hunch that motivation is the major influence on training performance? Could other factors (such as illness, family problems, team chemistry, and weather) influence the player's daily training performances? Can the findings derived from Coach Powell's observations of his own players be applied to other soccer teams or other sports with players of similar age and gender? In this chapter, we will provide you with some guidelines to address these and other questions that contribute to the research process. To gain a greater appreciation for scientific research, we will attempt to distinguish scientific research from other forms of knowledge acquisition after examining some pervasive myths about scientific research in sport psychology.

Some Common Myths about Research in Sport Psychology

MYTH: *Research is defined by subject matter and uses a single method.*
Many people believe that scientific research is confined to certain disciplines (such as biomechanics and exercise physiology) and can be completed only by using a single method or approach. Assuming you accept the idea that research is simply a knowledge-collecting process that is fraught with pitfalls and imperfections (Okasha, 2002), it seems reasonable to contend that it can be performed in a number of disciplines using multiple methods.

MYTH: *Validity is another name for reliability.*
Many people think that *reliability* and *validity*, which represent components of applied measurement, are abstract terms for the same concept. In fact, reliability is concerned with the precision of test scores whereas validity is concerned with the appropriateness of the decisions made by the test user based on the observed test scores. We will address this issue later in the chapter.

MYTH: *Qualitative research is not a rigorous research method.*
When thinking about qualitative research, some people still think of it as a less rigorous form of inquiry than its quantitative counterpart. However, qualitative research is a demanding, systematic, and time-consuming process that requires careful planning and decision making. Sport psychologists using qualitative methods are guided by a set of standards or criteria to judge the quality of their work, much like their quantitatively inclined colleagues.

Introduction

Recent international competitions have reinforced the dominant role of science in high-performance sport. Consider a selection of events from recent Olympic Games. Swimmers competed against one another wearing aerodynamically efficient bodysuits. Cyclists hurtled around an oval-shaped track wearing drag-reducing helmets. Hockey players used sticks made from various high-tech materials to gain power on their shots. In addition to using these legitimate products of scientific knowledge, some athletes adopt a less scrupulous approach and use banned substances, such as erythropoietin, anabolic steroids, and caffeine, for performance enhancement. These examples imply that sport and science have become inextricably joined at higher levels of competition. In conjunction with this emphasis on the use of science in high-performance sport, an emerging body of information suggests that science is active in other contexts, such as in physical education. For example, a recent publication by the Canadian Fitness and Lifestyle Research Institute (Craig & Cameron, 2004) suggests that the majority of Canadian children and youth fail to accumulate sufficient amounts of daily physical activity necessary for health promotion. These examples underscore the role that science plays in the realm of competitive sport and physical activity in our society.

The application of scientific principles to the study of sport performance is hardly novel in sport psychology. However, the recent emphasis on promoting healthy levels of physical activity in all Canadians has brought into the spotlight other aspects of scientific inquiry, such as enhanced quality of life and sustained involvement in the right type and amount of physical activity for health enhancement. Although some might argue that science and research have no place in sport psychology, others contend that the current emphasis on evidence-based practice makes scientific research an important component of contemporary sport psychology (Gill, 1997).

Science and Scientific Research

The notion of science is often confused with the stereotypical media image of a scientist as a middle-aged, unfit, spectacled person who is running around a large laboratory (full of test tubes emitting green gases) and screaming, "Eureka!" ("I've found it!") It is prudent to highlight the fact that the notions of science and scientific inquiry are matters of contemporary debate (Bouffard, 1997); however, **science** has been defined as a dynamic yet imperfect process of knowledge accumulation through the process of research (Kerlinger, 1979). In a perfect world, such research endeavours would fall nicely into one of two distinct categories that are often used to classify research in sport psychology (Baumgartner, Strong, & Hensley, 2002).

The first category is labelled **basic research** and deals with testing fundamental mechanisms that produce conditions or events, without undue concern for the practical utility of such mechanisms. Conversely, **applied research** focuses on generating solutions to immediate problems irrespective of mechanism details that form the focus of basic research. Although some researchers have found it useful to dichotomize research into these two camps, we suspect that the majority of sport psychology research falls somewhere between these two extremes. Perhaps an example of basic research will help illustrate this point. Consider a sport psychologist who is interested in determining the utility of a psychological skills training intervention (PSTI) with a university hockey team. The sport psychologist could set up a variety of motor performance tasks in a controlled laboratory setting, provide half the athletes with the PSTI and the other half with a placebo (no known effect on the motor performance tasks), and then observe the athletes' performance differences on the motor tests. Though it would be illuminating to find that the intervention group outperformed the placebo group on the tasks, the finding may be useless unless those differences translated into on-ice performance differences. Although the study is a useful (albeit hypothetical) example of basic research, it seems likely that the majority of sport psychology research requires practical endpoints. Therefore, we believe it is useful to think about basic and applied research as two ends of a continuum, with most research falling between these points.

Most sport psychology research falls between the extreme categories of basic and applied research.

Photograph by Richard Lam, courtesy of University of British Columbia Athletics.

Scientific methods of knowledge acquisition differ from other sources of information that athletes and coaches could easily resort to in the pursuit of optimal performance. These other knowledge sources include intuition, tradition, authorities, and logic (Pelham & Blanton, 2003). **Intuition** refers to the development of an implicit understanding of the phenomena of interest in the absence of formal training. **Tradition** refers to knowledge that is historically rooted, with no emphasis on current information. **Authorities** are experts whose opinions are considered the final word in knowledge acquisition, or in other words, "What the expert says, goes!" Finally, **logic** refers to knowledge generated through the application of formal rules of reasoning to the problem in question. For instance, logic could be inductively derived (moving from a specific observation to a general principle) or deductively derived (moving from a general principle to a specific observation) depending on the rules applied to the problem.

Reflections 2.1

Scotty Bowman's professional record in the National Hockey League would make him (in most people's estimation) an expert coach. What sources of knowledge do you think he relied on most when making (a) team selection decisions and (b) tactical changes? Can you provide two examples for intuition, tradition, authority, and logic that Bowman may have used when making selection or tactical decisions during his coaching career?

In contrast to these approaches, most sport psychology researchers interested in evidence-based knowledge advocate the use of the **scientific method**. The scientific method is a series of steps that are executed sequentially to generate knowledge (Baumgartner et al., 2002); however, experts (often disguised as university professors) disagree on the level of objectivity and number of steps involved in the scientific method. Nevertheless, it is generally accepted that this approach is an attempt to find the best solutions to answerable questions (unlike such questions as "What is the meaning of life?" or "Are humans inherently good or evil?"). Despite a lack of consensus about the components of this approach, it is important to recognize that the scientific method is guided by the sequential nature of research unfolding over time, rather than governed by dogmatic adherence to a formalized set of prescriptive (often prohibitive) steps. Common steps in the scientific method include identification of a problem, generation of a hypothesis, analysis of collected data, and integration of conclusions with directions for additional study (Okasha, 2002).

The majority of researchers in sport psychology attempt to describe, predict, or explain phenomena of interest. **Descriptive research** provides in-depth portrayals of a phenomenon of interest, either in general or for specific participant groups. A useful example of descriptive research in sport psychology is a study that describes athletes' use of imagery in sport (Munroe, Giacobbi, Hall, & Weinberg, 2000). In contrast to descriptive research, **predictive research** is concerned with establishing directional relationships among phenomena of interest. For example, Green-Demers, Pelletier, Stewart, and Gushue (1998) examined the relationship between enhancement strategies and interest toward tasks that varied in their degree of attraction to recreational and competitive-level figure skaters. The results suggested that challenges, task variety, and task relevance predicted greater interest in both stimulating tasks and boring tasks in sport.

Although descriptive and predictive studies are useful, the overall goal of most scientific research is explanation. Research to explain phenomena moves beyond mere description and prediction and includes arguments for why observations occurred. Typically, researchers couch their research within a *theory*. In scientific inquiry, a **theory** is an interconnected set of concepts that explain how and why phenomena work together (Okasha, 2002). For example, a study by Pelletier, Fortier, Vallerand, and Brière (2001) provides a good example of sport psychology research that embraces theory testing in an attempt to explain participation in swimming. In this study, the researchers tested propositions from self-determination theory (SDT; Deci & Ryan, 1985) with data collected from age-group swimmers to explain persistence and dropout behaviours. Consistent with propositions in SDT, they noted that swimming behaviour was explained by more self-determined motives for participation, irrespective of their intrinsic or extrinsic nature.

Basic Research Terminology

Consider for a moment the following conversation between two old friends:

Fred: "Yeah. Since my injury I prefer to adopt a less arduous training regimen and usually complete 3 sets of 10–13 reps at 40–55% of my 1RM."

Mary: "Really? I prefer to work through a series of ballistic exercises stressing antagonistic muscle groups using a high-sets (4–6) low-reps (2–4) approach at 80% of my 1RM."

We suspect that such terms as *reps, sets, antagonistic, 1RM,* and *ballistic exercises* may seem foreign to some students, depending on their familiarity with resistance training. Consistent with other occupations and cultures, research boasts a vocabulary that forms a common language, allowing scholars to converse (Trochim, 2001). Some research methods terminology require our attention before we proceed to more advanced topics in the research process.

The first word commonly used by members of the research fraternity is *variable*. A **variable** is any attribute or characteristic that can change or vary, thereby taking on more than one value. In sport psychology research, variables can take on different values, such as motivation, confidence, arousal, anxiety, and performance. In the context of research methods, variables can be identified as one of two types, depending on the status afforded those variables in a particular study. The first is the **independent variable** (IV), which is the manipulated variable explaining (or causing) the study outcomes. In contrast, the **dependent variable** (DV) in a particular study is the phenomenon of interest that you expect to change because of manipulating the independent variable.

Perhaps an example from a recent study by Elston and Martin-Ginis (2004) will clarify the distinction between IVs and DVs. The researchers compared the effects of self-set versus assigned goals (IV) on participants' self-efficacy to perform a strength exercise (DV). They noted that the experimental group (those receiving the IV) reported higher levels of self-efficacy post-intervention than the comparison group (those not receiving the IV). However, is it possible that any other variables could influence self-efficacy to perform strength-related tasks? The answer is "Yes." Researchers refer to such factors as **extraneous variables** (EVs). An EV is any variable other than the IV that could influence the DV in a research study.

> ## Reflections 2.2
> Consider for a moment your own physical activity experiences. What extraneous variables do you think could influence your confidence to perform a strength-related task other than goal setting?

Another word found in the research methods lexicon is **nomothetic**, which concerns attempts to isolate rules or observations that pertain to most cases on most occasions or in most contexts (Bouffard, 1997). For example, a recent study attempted to understand the independent influences of physical activity and obesity on health complaints, with the intent of discovering a general pattern of relationships that could be applied on most occasions to the majority of Canadian youth (Janssen, Katzmarzyk, Boyce, & Pickett, 2004). By contrast, the term **idiographic** is used when research concerns a special or unique case that does not apply to most people on the majority of occasions. Sport psychologists have become interested in studying career termination as it pertains to movement out of elite sport. For example, a study by Lotysz and Short (2004), using an autobiographical account, examines the experiences of a former professional athlete who had his career terminated prematurely because of complications associated with a knee injury. The insights into this athlete's experiences would be individual in nature and represent information derived from a single person about one incident in his career.

The third entry in the research methods vocabulary is **hypothesis**. A hypothesis is an educated guess regarding the outcome of a research study (Trochim, 2001). Although variation exists in the use of the word *hypothesis*, the most common extensions pertain to the use of hypothesis testing in statistics. In a study, the **null hypothesis** indicates that there is no relationship between the variables under study or that there is no difference between the groups receiving or not receiving the independent variable. In contrast, the **alternative hypothesis** is the researcher's educated guess regarding what the researcher expects to find when conducting the study. A recent study by Martin, Sinden, and Fleming (2000) may help clarify the difference between these hypotheses. In this study, the authors were interested in determining if an individual's exercise habits influenced the impressions others formed of him or her; the impressions were measured using personality dimensions. The null hypothesis stated that an individual's exercise habits had no effect on people's impressions of that individual whereas the alternative hypothesis contended that exercise habits would positively or negatively influence the impressions people formed of an individual's personality.

A fourth word (and one of the most contentious issues in contemporary science) permeating the research methods literature is **causal**. This word refers to the process of identifying agents that when manipulated will bring about the desired changes in the dependent variables of interest (Trochim, 2001). Generally, three conditions are necessary before researchers can make a causal inference in scientific research. First, the proposed cause (independent variable) must be correlated with the observed effect (dependent variable). This condition is sometimes called *systematic covariation*. Second, the proposed cause must precede the effect, or there must be evidence of what methodologists refer to as *temporal precedence*. Finally, all other possible causes (extraneous variables) must be systematically ruled out as the causal mechanism.

An effective coaching style can enhance athletes' enjoyment of sport.
Photo courtesy of Photo Disc/Getty Images.

Here is a case example in determining causation. Suppose Dr. Etheridge, a well-known sport psychologist in the Niagara region, is interested in helping Coach Powell improve his squad's performances in major tournaments. Considering her options carefully, Dr. Etheridge implements a goal-setting program designed specifically to enhance team performance, which will be measured by the team's win-loss record during regular season competitive play. This seems like a credible idea given the large volume of sport psychology literature that suggests goal setting can have a positive effect on sport performance (Burton, Naylor & Holliday, 2000). At the end of the competitive season, Dr. Etheridge compares the performances of Coach Powell's team with those of another soccer team that did not get the intervention but is of similar age and gender and playing in the same league. Coach Powell's team outperformed the comparison group on all dependent variables examined in Dr. Etheridge's study. Confidently, she concludes that the goal-setting intervention caused the observed differences in the teams' performances. But, wait just a minute! Did Dr. Etheridge satisfy all of the conditions needed to make a causal inference? Let us take a closer look at what happened in her study.

The first condition of causation is that a correlational relationship exist between the proposed cause and the desired effect. This is perhaps the easiest of the conditions to satisfy, and some literature does suggest that goal setting can influence sport performance (Burton et al., 2000). Understanding this aspect of the cause-effect debate, Dr. Etheridge collected data that confirmed through a manipulation check that the intervention group (Coach Powell's team) set goals that had a positive relationship with team performance, as indexed by the ratio of games won to lost over the season.

The second condition is that the presumed cause (independent variable) precede the observation of the effect (dependent variable). Given that Dr. Etheridge introduced the goal-setting intervention during the team's pre-season training camp and then monitored their performances across the entire season, it does seem reasonable to claim that the proposed cause did precede the effect. It seems reasonable to suggest that the first two conditions of causation have been satisfied.

Is the third condition of causation satisfied? This condition requires that all other possible causal factors be systematically ruled out. Although the goal-setting sport-performance hypothesis seems tenable at first glance, extraneous variables, including psychological characteristics (e.g., personality, confidence, motivation, cohesion) and contextual considerations (e.g., friendship networks, luck, weather, and league schedule), may have contributed to the changes in the team's performance. Given that we cannot typically rule out the influence of extraneous variables in a single study, it would seem wise to be hesitant about accepting the causal inferences derived from Dr. Etheridge's study prior to the study's replication and extension in future research.

Approval for Sport Psychology Research

In addition to understanding the language of research and their area of study, most researchers require administrative approval prior to initiating data collection (this applies equally to research with animals). In Canada, the relevant administrative body is a **Research Ethics Board (REB)**, which oversees the policies and procedures of the Interagency Advisory Panel on Research Ethics. The REB ensures that research is conducted in a manner that protects the integrity and safety of the participants and the researchers. However, does all research require REB approval? The answer is that it depends on whether the activity undertaken meets the criteria for exemption outlined by the Interagency Advisory Panel's *Tri-Council Policy Statement: Ethical Conduct for Research Involving Humans*. Table 2.1 contains a summary of research that either does or does not require REB approval.

Assuming that the lion's share of sport psychology research involves collecting data directly from sport participants, it seems reasonable to suggest that most sport psychologists will need to familiarize themselves with REB requirements for ethical review, prior to undertaking their research. The *Tri-Council Policy Statement* highlights all aspects of the research process that a sport psychologist should attend to, and it

Table 2.1   Type of Research and Ethical Review Requirements

Research Requiring Ethical Review	Sport Psychology Example
All research involving human participants	Experimental studies examining the impact of mental skills training on athletic performance
	Non-experimental studies examining the association between coping skills and athletic performance
All research involving biophysical specimens or the use of human remains	Longitudinal studies examining mood disturbances in athletes using performance-enhancing substances
Research Not Requiring Ethical Review	**Sport Psychology Example**
Research based exclusively on publicly accessible information	Non-experimental studies examining the home-venue advantage (using various archival data)

amalgamates information from key ethical documents that guide decision making in scientific research (www.pre.ethics.gc.ca/english/policystatement/policystatement.cfm). Three broad issues emanating from this report are central to good ethical conduct in scientific research and warrant careful consideration for sport psychology research.

The first issue is that of **respecting participants** and concerns the anonymity and confidentiality of participant data through a process known as *informed consent*. **Anonymity** refers to the inability to identify a participant involved in the research project, whereas **confidentiality** refers to the retention of all participant data in confidence so that an individual's data is not identifiable by others. It is appropriate in scientific research to make participants aware of the degree to which their anonymity will be compromised as a function of participating in the research project. As a result, participants are fully informed of their rights and responsibilities during the research project. This process is often referred to as **informed consent**, and it indicates that the research participants have been informed of what their participation will entail and how the data provided will be treated during the research project. Students interested in finding out more information about key features of the informed consent process could consult the Office of Research Services at Brock University for guidance (www.brocku. ca/researchservices/ethics/humanethics/humanethics_informed_checklist.php).

Does the process of respecting participants raise concerns for sport psychology research? Consider for a moment a hypothetical publication, titled "Wrestling with the psychology of elite female performance: An Olympian's perspective," in which a sport psychologist describes the results of an interview with a female athlete who won Canada's first Olympic wrestling medal. Though the name of the athlete is not disclosed, sufficient information is provided that allows the reader to identify the athlete and thereby breach confidentiality, assuming the interviewee was assured of confidentiality in the informed consent process. Respecting the rights and privileges of all participants is the responsibility of the researcher and is the hallmark of good ethical practice in sport psychology research. The second major ethical issue is **beneficence**, which concerns the degree to which the proposed research will maximize the potential benefits while minimizing the possible harm to the research participants. Toward this end, this principle does not guarantee that participants face no risk, given that even non-invasive research carries risks, such as disclosure of personal information or heightened emotional sensitization. This principle does contend that it is the researcher's responsibility to ensure that the benefits of the study (either to the participant directly or to the scientific community at large) come with the assumption of justifiable risk and thereby outweigh the costs of research.

The third key ethical issue associated with scientific research is concerned with the notion of justice that pertains directly to the selection of participants for the purposes of research. Central to this idea of **justice** is the notion that participants in research should be the ones who derive the benefits from the results of the study. For example, consider a scenario in which a sport psychologist is interested in understanding the effects of Canada's coaching education program on moral development in youth sport participants. Imagine that the sport psychologist is housed in a West Coast university but is able (though former connections in his/her home province) to collect all of the data from Wolfville, Nova Scotia. If all of the participants were active in youth-sport programs in Wolfville but the applications of the research were to be promoted only on the West Coast, then the principle of justice is likely violated, given that the participants providing the data will never reap the benefits of changes made to the coaching education programs.

Reflections 2.3

Think back to a research study that you have read about in the media. What information do you think the research team would have needed to provide to people prior to enrolling participants in the study? What benefits and risks do you think would be associated with participation in the study? In what way will the results of this study benefit other people beyond the sample under study?

Measurement in the Research Process

The practice of measurement in sport psychology is considered particularly difficult given that most of the variables are invisible to the naked eye. What do we mean by this? Well, consider the major variables discussed in other chapters composing this text. Variables, such as arousal, anxiety, confidence, motivation, personality, and stress, are all important psychological concepts that are not observed directly. To illustrate this fact, consider the concept of gravity for a moment. Many of you may be wondering what does gravity have to do with the variables of interest to a sport psychologist? Well, can you actually see gravity? Moreover, could you show your friends gravity if we asked you to? Our guess is that you might throw a pen into the air and say, "Look! Gravity!" But if you stop and think about it, you are not seeing gravity but merely observing what we believe to be gravity's effects on the pen when it is pulled back to the Earth. The key point to keep in mind here is quite simple: Most of the things we are interested in measuring in sport psychology are not much different from other variables, in the sense that they cannot be observed with our senses. Nevertheless, this does not mean that we cannot measure them; it only means that we have to take some leaps of faith (scientists often call these *assumptions*) when doing measurements in research.

Levels of Measurement

Irrespective of the nature of the research question, measurement issues will arise during any research project that attempts to quantify variables. In the classic sense, **measurement** refers to the process of assigning numbers to variables according to specific rules (Stevens, 1946). **Levels of measurement** represent different ways of assigning numbers to variables. The most rudimentary level of measurement is referred to as **nominal**. When numbers are assigned to variables in a nominal fashion, they represent measurement only as labels. In other words, the number 15 assigned to Kara Lang (Canadian Women's Soccer Team) does not mean that she is 3 times better than number 5, Andrea Neil. The numbers simply represent a unique label used to identify a soccer player.

The next level of measurement is termed **ordinal** and reflects the assignment of numbers in such a fashion that the variable can be ranked. An example is the assignment of medals representing first, second, and third places on the Olympic medal podium. The distance between the gold and silver medal winners does not have to be equivalent to the distance between the silver and bronze medal winners. The numbers simply reflect the order in which the athletes finished.

The third level of measurement is called **interval** and reflects the assignment of numbers to variables so that the distances between consecutive numbers are equal. For example, daily temperature records throughout events, such as the Olympic Games, represent interval measurement.

The final and most useful level of measurement is labelled **ratio** and concerns the assignment of numbers in such a manner that a true zero exists representing a complete absence of the variable under study. One example of ratio level measurement in sport psychology is the number of rehabilitation sessions attended by an injured athlete as a measure of adherence. If the athlete attends none of the prescribed sessions, then he or she has a complete absence of the variable measuring adherence.

Reflections 2.4

Keeping in mind the levels of measurement outlined in the previous section, consider some of the variables involved in sports or physical activities (e.g., speed, strength, goals, points, motivation, confidence, arousal, anxiety). How is each variable typically measured? What level of measurement is represented by each variable, based on the rules used to assign numbers to those variables?

Basic Measurement Concepts

The subject of measurement is vast and covers a broad spectrum of issues within several fields, most notably the field of **psychometrics**, which is concerned with the measurement of psychological variables. There are two concepts associated with variable measurement that require consideration: reliability and validity. These concepts form the cornerstone of sound measurement practice in research. Although they will be presented separately in the following sections, these concepts are inextricably linked in sport psychology research. Our discussion of these concepts will be succinct, so the interested reader is directed to Bill Trochim's website for further insights (www.social researchmethods.net/).

RELIABILITY   **Reliability** concerns the consistency or stability of scores derived from single or multiple tests or measurement procedures (Vogt, 1993). Along these lines, reliability is concerned with the degree of precision inherent in a particular score or set of scores. But what does it really mean for a score on a test to be considered reliable? Perhaps an example of the model that scientists have traditionally used to estimate reliability will help address this question.

The classic approach to estimating reliability is known as the true score model since reliability is concerned with knowing how precisely we can measure a person's true score on a variable of interest (see Figure 2.1). According to the true score model, every recorded score is composed of components that provide a numerical index of test-score reliability. The **observed score** is the actual numerical value derived from the test. The observed score is composed of a person's **true score** on the variable of interest plus some **error of measurement** (or Observed Score = True Score + Measurement Error).

Figure 2.1   Classical true score model of reliability

Observed Score = True Score + Measurement Error

Let us consider an example that might enhance your understanding of the classical true score model. Imagine a coach is interested in monitoring athletes' responses to training and he decides to use blood pressure as a key variable. After each training session, the coach measures the athletes' blood pressure to determine the consistency of each athlete's responses to the demands of training. The team has 20 athletes who all complete 10 training sessions, resulting in a total of 200 blood pressure recordings. These are the observed scores. Think about the factors that could influence the accuracy of each blood pressure measurement. Scores are likely to be influenced by the auditory ability and experience of the technician taking the blood pressure readings and by environmental noise. Participant non-compliance, improper use of the sphygmomanometer, and physiological nuances of the athlete might also influence the precision with which the technician can account for each athlete's blood pressure. This means that each blood pressure value is an observed score that is composed of the athlete's *true* blood pressure value plus some *measurement error*.

What sources of evidence can the sport psychologist use to estimate score reliability in research? According to measurement experts (Crocker & Algina, 1986), three sources of evidence can be used to demonstrate the reliability of scores. The first source, the coefficient of stability, concerns the assessment of the same participants at two or more different time points and is sometimes referred to as test-retest reliability. The second source of evidence, the coefficient of equivalence, involves an examination of the consistency between scores from two different versions of a test designed to measure the same variable. One obvious limitation of both these approaches is that they require the administration of two tests, either at different points in time or at a single point in time using two different test formats. To counteract this problem, sport psychologists can use the third source of evidence, the coefficient of internal consistency, to measure the reliability of a participant's scores across multiple test items administered on a single occasion.

VALIDITY The second concept that forms the cornerstone of sound measurement practice is validity. Whereas reliability is concerned with the accuracy or precision inherent in scores used to measure a variable, **validity** is concerned with meaningfulness of the inferences that can be drawn from the numbers once they have been generated (Messick, 1995). Put slightly differently, validity refers to the extent to which test scores, when interpreted, serve their intended function. Consider the simple example of height (measured in metres) and weight (measured in kilograms). The instrument used to measure body weight (a scale) could produce reliable scores. Would those scores be useful in determining how tall a person is at the time of data collection? They would not be useful that way because measures of weight were never intended to be interpreted as an index of a person's height! Although this may seem straightforward, validity is one of the most controversial topics in applied measurement and evaluation research today (Downing, 2003; Messick 1995). Let us look at some sources of validity information used in sport psychology research.

Evidence of validity has traditionally been collected from multiple sources in the sport psychology literature (see Figure 2.2). One source is called *content validity*, which assesses the degree to which test items (e.g., questionnaire items) adequately represent the variable of interest and is usually assessed by expert review (Dunn, Bouffard, & Rogers, 1999). Another source of validity evidence is known as *criterion validity*, which assesses the degree to which test scores (e.g., Sport Competition Anxiety Test scores) are empirically associated with a criterion of interest (e.g., indices of sport performance). This can be accomplished by using an approach in which scores on the test in question

Figure 2.2   Sources of data contributing to construct validity evidence

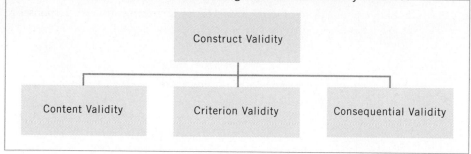

are collected before the measurement of the criterion. For example, a test measuring aggressiveness (the test) is administered to hockey players and then aggressive actions (the criterion) are recorded for the next 10 weeks. In another approach, the sport psychologist collects data on the test and criterion variables at about the same time (Pedhazur & Schmelkin, 1991). Yet another source of validity evidence is *consequential validity*, which involves the actual and potential consequences stemming from test score use, and although these sources of evidence can be examined individually, a contemporary view of validation contends that the combined sources of evidence reflect the construct validity of test scores (Messick, 1995).

Sampling in Sport Psychology Research

Sampling refers to the process of selecting observations for the purposes of your research study (Babbie, 1995). We suspect that many of you are very familiar with the concept of sampling and engage in sampling procedures regularly. The media (including the internet) are constantly polling people about their opinions. These polls include such topics as whether hockey fights should be banned, whether funding should be increased for women's sports, or who are the greatest Canadian female and male athletes of the last century. Clearly, the intent of such informal opinion polls is to represent the opinions of the public. However, do the opinions of the sample represent the opinions of all people? This underscores the basic idea behind sampling, which involves studying a small part of a group to ascertain answers to your research questions about the whole group. However, sampling is critical! Research conclusions and policy decisions affecting many people are made according to findings generated from specific samples. Let us look at some of the terminology associated with sampling and then examine some of the common approaches to sampling employed in sport psychology.

The literature on sampling is permeated by a highly specialized vocabulary that makes it difficult to comprehend without formal exposure or training. A **sample** is a selection of observations that you are going to study in your research project (Babbie, 1995). However, what is the researcher selecting the observations from during sampling? The answer is a **population** that can be a **theoretical population** (all of the possible elements) or a **study population** (all of the accessible elements). An obvious question at this stage is why sample from a population. Well, the advantages of sampling—namely, cost reduction, feasibility, or accuracy—allow sport psychologists to study a selection of elements from which he or she can make inferences about the study population. How then does the sport psychologist collect a sample to study in a research project? Figure 2.3 provides a schematic overview of the sampling process, and

Figure 2.3   Overview of the sampling process

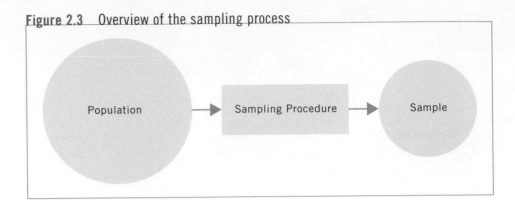

Trochim (2001) suggests two general procedures employed to collect samples for the purposes of research.

Sampling Procedures

The first class of sampling procedures are labelled **probability-based sampling**. In these approaches, researchers make use of the mathematical laws from probability theory so that they can ensure that at a study's outset every element of the target population has an equal chance of being randomly selected into the study sample. This can be accomplished by taking a simple random sample from the entire population of elements, or dividing the entire population of elements into groups and then sampling from each group to ensure representation in the final sample. An alternative class of procedures known as **non-probability-based sampling** (Trochim, 2001) relies on non-mathematical criteria for sampling observations. Non-probability-based procedures are problematic because they do not require the researcher to define the target population before collecting the data, which makes generalizing the study results beyond the confines of the study difficult, if not impossible. The use of non-probability approaches, however, is not without merit and can provide useful data about complex psychological phenomena that the restrictions associated with probability-based procedures struggle to accomplish. Typical non-probability approaches to sampling in the sport psychology research include collecting data from samples that are readily accessible to the researcher (known as **convenience sampling**) or from samples that have a defining set of unique characteristics that are of interest to the sport psychologist (known as **purposive sampling**).

Reflections 2.5

You want to identify the greatest university coach in Canada in the last 25 years. What sampling process would you use to collect the data? Could you provide a rationale for choosing your sampling method and give the strengths and weaknesses associated with this approach?

Photo © tomas del amo/Alamy.

Research Design: A Blueprint for Action

Design is an integral portion of the research process in sport psychology. A **research design** is a plan the sport psychologist will follow to execute the study (Vogt, 1993). Perhaps a simple analogy will help solidify the importance of the research design. Imagine trying to assemble a piece of furniture (such as IKEA's) without the instructions that provide you with an idea of which piece goes where, how they fit together, and what the finished product should look like. Well, the research design is similar to assembly instructions in the sense that it provides a blueprint for action that will guide the proposed study to completion.

Why is research design so important? The answer to this query lies at the heart of what the sport psychologist is interested in concluding once the study has been completed. Most sport psychology research is interested in understanding what causes events or behaviours to happen. Such questions as "Why did he choke under pressure?" or "Why does she excel when we go a goal behind in tight games?" are examples of questions that researchers seek to answer about the underlying cause of an athlete's behaviour. In the language of research design, **internal validity** concerns the extent to which the results of a study can be attributed to a treatment or intervention rather than to a design flaw (Vogt, 1993). If we stop for a moment to consider the types of questions most sport psychology researchers seek to answer, we suspect that the vast majority of those questions are causal in nature. As such, the choice of research design is critically important because some designs provide better evidence for causation than others (Trochim, 2001).

Some designs are more prone to threats than others by virtue of their composition. An **internal validity threat** represents another plausible explanation for the study findings, irrespective of the treatment or independent variable manipulated in the study. In the language of research methods, internal validity threats are extraneous variables that represent plausible alternative explanations for changes in the dependent variable. Table 2.2 (next page) contains a summary of common threats to internal validity and suggests their implications for causal inference in the research process. Let us take a closer look at the three major categories of research design proposed in the research methods literature along with some sport psychology examples.

True Experimental Designs

The first set of research designs that offer the strongest evidence for causality are known as **true experimental designs**. True experimental designs have two hallmark characteristics that distinguish them from other designs (Trochim, 2001). The first characteristic is that they randomly assign study participants to different conditions (sometimes referred to as different levels of the independent variable). The second hallmark characteristic is the manipulation of the independent variable(s). Recall from our earlier discussion that the independent variable is the proposed causal agent inherent in your research project. Within the category of true experimental designs, a variety of approaches could be taken, depending on resources, time, and available expertise.

What does a true experimental design look like in practice? A recent study conducted by Blanchard, Rodgers, Wilson, and Bell (2004) serves as a useful example of how such true experimental designs can be tailored to examine sport psychology issues. Blanchard et al. examined the influence of two different training conditions on partic-

Table 2.2   Common Internal Validity Threats in Sport Psychology Research

Name of Threat	Nature of Internal Validity Threat
Maturation	Change in participants as a function of biological growth or development or of fatigue
History	Influence of an unusual yet powerful external event
Selection	Non-random placement of participants into the groups for an intervention research study
Mortality	Departure of participants from studies that use repeated assessments of the dependent variables
Testing	Influence of earlier test scores on later scores when a test is administered on multiple occasions
Instrumentation	Alterations in the nature or reliability of the test used to measure the dependent variable
Regression to the Mean	Natural tendency of extreme scores to "regress" closer to the typical population value during subsequent testing
Diffusion of Treatment	Adoption of intervention-type responses by participants in the control group when they learn of the treatment provided to the intervention group
Resentful Demoralization	Resentment by participants in the control group when they learn of the treatment administered to the intervention group but not to them

ipants' feeling states while equating the total volume of work between conditions. Participants were community residents who were randomly assigned to either a High Intensity Short Duration (HISD) or a Low Intensity Long Duration (LILD) supervised exercise program for 12 weeks. In essence, this study manipulated exercise training across multiple levels (intensity and duration). The study indicated that positive changes in feeling states were reported from pre- to post-test in both experimental groups, after equating for total volume of work completed within each condition.

Quasi-experimental Designs

The second class of approaches to designing research studies are known collectively as **quasi-experimental designs**. These designs attempt to unearth the cause of change in the dependent variables without randomly assigning participants to different conditions within the study (Trochim, 2001). Why does this happen? Well, in some instances, random assignment is not possible, practical, or even desirable. For example, if a sport psychologist were interested in comparing the influence of a coaching development program on soccer coaches residing in British Columbia and Ontario, it is neither possible nor desirable to assign participants to either province.

Stevens and Bloom (2003) provide a useful example of a study using a quasi-experimental design. They examined the effectiveness of a sport psychology intervention program designed to enhance team effectiveness in collegiate softball players. One team was exposed to a multifaceted intervention designed to enhance team effectiveness; the other team served as a comparison group and did not receive the intervention.

Examination of post-intervention differences in scores from the Group Integration subscales of the Group Environment Questionnaire (GEQ; Carron, Widmeyer, & Brawley, 1985) indicated higher levels of task and social group integration (indicative of greater team effectiveness) reported by the team in the intervention condition compared with the team in the comparison condition.

Reflections 2.6
Considering the study conducted by Stevens and Bloom (2003), what threats to internal validity do you believe could influence the interpretation of their data?

Non-experimental Designs

The final design category, which is more common in sport psychology research than the previous two approaches, is known as **non-experimental designs** (Trochim, 2001). These designs establish patterns of relationships between the variables of interest in the absence of group assignment or variable manipulation. In non-experimental designs, researchers place emphasis on testing theoretical arguments or predicting criterion variables of interest to the sport psychologist, rather than on establishing causality. Often in the sport psychology literature, these designs are labelled as passive observational or correlational designs, given that the intent of collecting data in this manner is to establish relationships between variables of interest rather than to identify the causal mechanisms that influence a given dependent variable.

One example of a non-experimental design is a study examining predictors of social physique anxiety (SPA) in adolescent females competing in provincial- or national-level sport (Crocker, Snyder, Kowalski, & Hoar, 2000). In this study, perceptions of body fatness and coordination were associated with elevated SPA while the nature of the sport (objectively vs. aesthetically evaluated) had no relationship with SPA. These data suggest that perceptions of one's physical and athletic selves appear to be the critical factors predicting physique-related anxiety, as opposed to the manner in which success within the sport is accomplished. Does this study satisfy the conditions required to claim with confidence that self-perceptions cause SPA? Let us examine the evidence in relation to the criteria required for causality presented earlier in this chapter. First, the data support the presence of a relationship between self-perceptions and SPA. Second, all of the data were collected at the same point in time, making it difficult to satisfy the assumption of temporal precedence. Finally, all possible factors contributing to SPA were not included or controlled for in this study; therefore, it is possible that variables other than self-perceptions influenced SPA in these athletes. Considering these points carefully in relation to the criteria for causality, we cannot say with confidence that self-perceptions cause SPA in adolescent female athletes. The key point to keep in mind here is that causation requires more than the demonstration of an association between two or more variables, or as some might argue, "Correlation does not equal causation!"

Qualitative Research in Sport Psychology

Much of the aforementioned discussion on measurement, sampling, and design is consistent with what some have labelled quantitative research. **Quantitative inquiry** concerns an approach to knowledge acquisition that focuses on quantification or counting the amount of a particular variable or set of variables (Vogt, 1993). In recent years, there has been growing advocacy for the use of **qualitative inquiry** in sport psychology research. Qualitative inquiry encompasses a set of practices through which researchers seek to understand the world from the perspectives of those being studied or, as Merriam (1998) points out, to understand the phenomenon of interest from the participants' point of view (e.g., Coach Powell and his players). This participant-centred approach is sometimes referred to as attempting to capture the emic, or insider's perspective, as opposed to the etic or outsider's view. Part of the appeal of qualitative inquiry is that such methods provide a wealth of detailed information and depth of understanding not typically found in traditional quantitative methods (Gould, 1996). Consequently, during the last decade, there has been an increase in the number of studies using qualitative methodologies published in sport psychology journals.

Characteristics of Qualitative Inquiry

Qualitative inquiry has traditionally been associated with various disciplines, such as anthropology, sociology, and clinical psychology (Merriam, 1998). More recently, however, there has been a proliferation of approaches emerging from such areas as cultural and feminist studies that have been embraced by scholars interested in qualitative research (Denzin & Lincoln, 2003). Although the notions of what constitutes qualitative inquiry are divergent, given the multidisciplinary roots of this approach to research, experts in this area of inquiry have reached some consensus on the hallmarks of qualitative inquiry.

Let us look at a core group of characteristics that provide a common thread between different approaches to qualitative inquiry found in sport psychology research. Core characteristics of qualitative research are that it occurs in naturalistic contexts and that it uses multiple methods of inquiry to interpret phenomena of interest (Denzin & Lincoln, 2003). This means that researchers are interested in people's experiences and their associated meanings in the real, natural settings of everyday life—the home, the school, the workplace, or the gym. Moreover, qualitative inquiry (unlike its numerical counterpart) is not method bound. It draws from a variety of data collection practices, such as formal and informal interviews, field observations, and document gathering, to access the data illuminating the issues under study (Patton, 2002).

Another important characteristic common to most forms of qualitative inquiry is that participants are sampled because of their potential to offer informative and illustrative manifestations of the phenomenon of interest. Sampling, then, is purposeful (Patton, 2002) or theoretical (e.g., Merriam, 1998), rather than random using probability-based procedures. Thus, qualitative research often involves an in-depth study of a small number of participants.

A comparative summary of the characteristics defining qualitative and quantitative approaches to research has been provided in Table 2.3.

Common Approaches to Doing Qualitative Research

Qualitative research is characterized by a remarkable variety of approaches and dynamism, which is considered one of its strengths. Irrespective of this diversity, a number of central approaches appear to be gaining prominence in the sport psychology literature as academics embrace qualitative methods as a legitimate approach to

Table 2.3   Qualitative vs. Quantitative Approaches to Research

Research Component	Qualitative Approach	Quantitative Approach
Major Assumptions	Accepting the important subjective role of a researcher's background and perspective; providing descriptions of behaviour or building theories inductively	Striving for scientific theories that are objective and confirmable; collating data that corroborates pre-existing theoretical arguments
Sampling	Non-probability-based, typically purposive sampling; generalization to a larger population not important	Non-probability- and probability-based; generalization to a larger population in most instances
Context	The environment in which behaviour naturally occurs because behaviour is context bound	Laboratories in which behaviour is best studied by being isolated from contextual interferences
Data	Text derived from interviews, documents, or personal observations that are trustworthy	Numbers derived from standardized instruments that meet acceptable standards of psychometric rigour
Design	Non-experimental design that is flexible and open to any necessary changes during data collection	True, quasi-, and non-experimental designs, most of which are fixed prior to data collection
Data Analysis	Focus on description and inductive interpretation	Focus on hypothesis testing and statistical properties

research. The following section examines some of the common approaches to qualitative research found in the sport psychology literature.

BASIC INTERPRETIVE QUALITATIVE STUDIES   Basic interpretive qualitative studies are used by researchers who seek to understand a particular phenomenon or process, the perspectives and perceptions of the participants, or a combination of these (Merriam, 2002). Typically, the researcher collects data through interviews, observations, or document examination and analyzes the data to identify patterns and themes. The researcher then presents a descriptive account of the findings and discusses it in reference to the literature that initially framed the study. For example, Jean Côté's (1999) study of family influences on the development of talent in sport is situated in the talent-development literature. Retrospective interviews with athletes, parents, and siblings allowed Côté to identify three distinct periods or stages of sport development from early childhood to late adolescence. Each of these stages is characterized by specific patterns in the dynamics of family involvement in the children's sport as well as patterns in processes of social influence.

PHENOMENOLOGY APPROACH   Phenomenology is a philosophical tradition that concerns the structure or essence of a lived experience (phenomenon) for an individual or group of people (Merriam, 2002). In this approach, the researcher has to bracket (temporarily put aside) his or her preconceptions and beliefs about the phenomenon or experience being studied. In a study by Fitzpatrick and Watkinson (2003), data from retrospective interviews with adults elaborated on what it meant to be physically awkward as a child (i.e., the lived experience). The data generated from this phenomenological approach provides useful data, encouraging teachers, coaches, and others to be aware of the emotional and social consequences stemming from physical awkwardness.

Reflections 2.7

Consider for a moment what the phrase "hitting the wall" means to a competitive marathon runner. An exercise physiologist would describe this phenomenon as resulting from glycogen depletion that reduces the energy available to the body to meet activity demands. How do you think a phenomenologist would describe the experience of "hitting the wall"?

GROUNDED THEORY APPROACH   The term **grounded theory** refers to a specific approach to qualitative inquiry in which the researcher develops a theory that is inductively derived from (or "grounded" in) the participants' data. Grounded theory developed from the seminal work of sociologists Glaser and Strauss (1967). The development of grounded theory is assisted by analytic procedures, such as different forms of coding the data, and the constant comparison method, which involves comparing one participant's experiences with another participant's experiences, using an iterative process. The type of theory developed is usually substantive in nature, as opposed to an omnibus theory that attempts to explain a broad array of phenomena. **Substantive theory** is "localized, dealing with particular real-world situations" (Merriam 2002, p. 7). For example, Holt and Dunn (2004) used grounded theory to identify four major psychosocial competencies (Discipline, Commitment, Social Support, and Resilience) that promote success in elite youth soccer.

CASE STUDY APPROACH   **Case studies** refer to "intensive descriptions and analyses of a single unit or bounded system such as an individual, program, event, group, intervention, or community" (Merriam, 1998, p. 19). Case studies can and do often incorporate a variety of disciplinary and methodological perspectives. Krane, Greenleaf, and Snow's (1997) examination of the experiences of a former elite gymnast provide an illustrative example of a case study using qualitative inquiry. Grounded in a feminist view of sport and research, the findings showed how an ego-involved motivational environment was developed and reinforced by the gymnast's coaches and parents. The results also revealed that this athlete developed an ego-involved motivational orientation that had negative consequences for her sport participation and experience.

ETHNOGRAPHY APPROACH   **Ethnography** is concerned with the study of the culture operating within or around a group or a team. The term *ethnography* was initially used in anthropology to refer to a set of techniques used to collect data and to the final written product of using ethnographic methods. Ethnography can be distinguished from methods commonly found in ethnographic research (such as participant observation) when the data are interpreted and presented within a sociocultural framework (Merriam, 2002). This point is nicely illustrated in a classic study by Fine (1987) who spent three years studying boys' moral development in Little League baseball. After extensive fieldwork, he concluded that the moral messages conveyed to the boys by the coaches and parents were heard and interpreted in terms of the boys' socio-cultural context. As 11-year-old males, they were concerned primarily with being accepted by peers and with learning what it means to be a man in U.S. culture.

NARRATIVE ANALYSIS APPROACH   **Narrative analysis** is an approach to qualitative inquiry that collects data for the purposes of presenting a story, and more specifically, a story told in first person, which distinguishes this method from other presentations of scientific writing. Other terms used to refer to this type of qualitative research are *biography*, *autobiography*, *life story*, *autoethnography*, and *life narratives* (Merriam, 2002). Tsang (2000) has provided an example of use of the narrative as a way of writing about experiences of sport, specifically her own experiences of identity development within high-performance sport as a member of the Canadian National Rowing Team.

Judging the Merit of Qualitative Research

For many years, qualitative researchers have sought to develop criteria to evaluate and judge their work—criteria that are consistent with the fundamental assumptions of the qualitative paradigm or worldview (Denzin & Lincoln, 2003). For example, qualitative researchers often assume that there is no single reality "out there" for us to apprehend, but, rather, multiple subjective realities. Thus, in qualitative research, such criteria as credibility, rigour, and usefulness of the study (Rossman & Rallis, 2003) typically substitute for validity and reliability claims made with quantitative approaches to research. Some strategies that qualitative researchers employ to ensure credibility of the findings and of the methodological rigour include triangulation (use of multiple data sources or perspectives), prolonged fieldwork, member checking (participant confirmation of a researcher's data interpretation), and use of a "peer debriefer" to check assumptions and conclusions as the study proceeds.

Chapter Summary

At the outset of this chapter on research perspectives in sport psychology, we introduced Coach Powell and the "practice player" problem. Now, it might be prudent to return to this scenario and provide an answer to the perplexed coach regarding how to improve the training habits of his soccer players. Although such an answer might be feasible considering the content of other chapters in this text, a single answer to Coach Powell's question may be inappropriate, given the variety of approaches that could generate information for the coach's quandary.

A naive methodologist may be inclined to be more forthright in giving advice to Coach Powell. Those indoctrinated within the quantitative tradition might suggest that Coach Powell randomly assign soccer players to separate conditions and administer a psychological skills training intervention to one group of players in an attempt to establish the scientific credence of such techniques. Alternatively, others who have heeded Martens' (1987) call for methodological diversity might advocate a phenomenological approach to the problem whereby athletes exemplifying both good and poor practice habits will be interviewed to help Coach Powell understand his players' viewpoints. In her article examining the "state of the union" in sport and exercise psychology research, Gill (1997) lamented the proliferation of authoritative advice treated as dogmatic gospel with this statement, "Give us a hammer, and everything looks like a nail" (p. 50). Methodological advances, including the diversification of approaches to science, offer the sport psychologist numerous options (and difficult decisions) in addressing questions with inherent practical appeal, such as those faced by Coach Powell. Rather than stamping any single approach (or combination of approaches) as the "gateway to acceptability" (Gill, p. 50), we recommend that neophytes consider what question(s) they seek to answer and select the most useful approach available, perhaps even combining some of the methods presented in this chapter.

Our brief journey through the methodological literature has described and illustrated various issues and components of the research process that have bearing on Coach Powell's predicament. To turn to an inquisitive person (such as the student reading these pages) and simply provide a single answer to Coach Powell's situation would seem trite and would trivialize what we have tried to convey about the nature of research. Perhaps a famous quote from British Prime Minister Winston Churchill puts it best when he claimed, "This is not the end. It is not even the beginning of the end. But it is, perhaps, the end of the beginning." Churchill's words encapsulate quite nicely the food for thought we would like you to consider after reading this chapter—namely, that any journey (or research in sport psychology) starts with an interesting question but in essence does not require a final destination, merely a path to traverse and a direction to follow!

Review Questions

1. Discuss and contrast the different sources of knowledge that could be used in the process of knowledge production in science.
2. Can you classify and provide examples of the types of variables used in research?
3. Define and discuss the major principles associated with measurement in sport psychology research. Can you provide examples that illustrate your understanding of the key components involved in the measurement process?
4. Define and discuss some of the major ethical principles guiding research in sport psychology. Please describe two situations that give examples of activities that require ethical approval for a sport psychologist.
5. What types of research design could an applied sport psychologist use to determine the effectiveness of mental skills training programs?
6. What different approaches to qualitative research were presented in this chapter? Can you identify differences and similarities among the approaches?

Suggested Reading

Berg, B. L. (2004). *Qualitative research methods for the social sciences* (5th ed.). Toronto: Allyn & Bacon.

Shadish, W. R., Cook, T. D., & Campbell, D. T. (2002). *Experimental and quasi-experimental designs for generalized causal inference*. New York: Houghton Mifflin.

Trochim, W. (2001). *The research methods knowledge base* (2nd ed.). Cincinnati, OH: Atomic Dog.

References

Babbie, E. (1995). *The practice of social research* (7th ed.). Toronto: Wadsworth.

Baumgartner, T. A., Strong, C. H., & Hensley, L. D. (2002). *Conducting and reading research in health and human performance* (3rd ed.). Montreal: McGraw-Hill.

Blanchard, C. M., Rodgers, W. M., Wilson, P. M., & Bell, G. J. (2004). Does equating total volume of work between two different exercise conditions matter when examining exercise-induced feeling states? *Research Quarterly for Exercise & Sport, 75*, 209–215.

Bouffard, M. (1997). Using old research ideas to study contemporary problems in adapted physical activity. *Adapted Physical Activity Quarterly, 1*, 71–87.

Burton, D., Naylor, S., & Holliday, B. (2000). Goal setting in sport: Investigating the goal effectiveness paradox. In R. N. Singer, H. A. Hausenblas, & C. M. Janelle (Eds.), *Handbook of sport psychology* (2nd ed., pp. 497–528). New York: Wiley.

Carron, A. V., Widmeyer, W. N., & Brawley, L. R. (1985). The development of an instrument to assess cohesion in sport teams: The group environment questionnaire. *Journal of Sport Psychology, 7*, 244–266.

Côté, J. (1999). The influence of the family in the development of talent in sport. *The Sport Psychologist, 13*, 395–417.

Craig, C. L., & Cameron, C. (2004). *Increasing physical activity: Assessing trends from 1998–2003.* Ottawa: Canadian Fitness and Lifestyle Research Institute.

Crocker, L., & Algina, L. (1986). *Introduction to classical and modern test theory.* New York: Holt, Rinehart and Winston.

Crocker, P. R. E., Snyder, J., Kowalski, K. C., & Hoar, S. (2000). Don't let me be fat or physically incompetent! The relationship between physical self-concept and social physique anxiety in Canadian high-performance female adolescent athletes. *Avante, 6*, 16–23.

Deci, E. L., & Ryan, R. M. (1985). *Intrinsic motivation and self-determination in human behavior.* New York: Plenum.

Denzin, N. K., & Lincoln, Y. (2003). The discipline and practice of qualitative research. In N. K. Denzin & Y. Lincoln (Eds.), *Strategies of qualitative inquiry* (2nd ed., pp. 1–45). Thousand Oaks, CA: Sage.

Downing, S. M. (2003). Validity: On the meaningful interpretation of assessment data. *Medical Education, 37*, 830–837.

Dunn, J. G. H., Bouffard, M., & Rogers, W. T. (1999). Assessing item content-relevance in sport psychology scale-construction research: Issues and recommendations. *Measurement in Physical Education and Exercise Science, 3*, 15–36.

Elston, T. L., & Martin-Ginis, K. A. (2004). The effects of self-set versus assigned goals on exercisers' self-efficacy for an unfamiliar task. *Journal of Sport & Exercise Psychology, 26*, 500–504.

Fine, G. A. (1987). *With the boys: Little League baseball and preadolescent culture.* Chicago: University of Chicago Press.

Fitzpatrick, D. A., & Watkinson, E. J. (2003). The lived experience of physical awkwardness: Adults' retrospective views. *Adapted Physical Activity Quarterly, 20*, 279–297.

Gill, D. L. (1997). Measurement, statistics, and research design issues in sport and exercise psychology. *Measurement in Physical Education & Exercise Science, 1*, 39–53.

Glaser, B., & Strauss, A. L. (1967). *The discovery of grounded theory: Strategies for qualitative research.* Chicago, IL: Aldine.

Gould, D. (1996). Sport psychology: Future directions in youth sport research. In F. L. Smoll & R. E. Smith (Eds.), *Children and youth in sport: A biopsychosocial perspective* (pp. 405–422). Dubuque, IA: Brown & Benchmark.

Green-Demers, I., Pelletier, L. G., Stewart, D. G., & Gushue, N. R. (1998). Coping with less interesting aspects of training: Toward a model of interest and motivation enhancement in individual sports. *Basic and Applied Social Psychology, 20*, 251–261.

Holt, N. L., & Dunn, J. G. H. (2004). Toward a grounded theory of the psychosocial competencies and environmental conditions associated with soccer success. *Journal of Applied Sport Psychology, 16*, 199–219.

Janssen, I., Katzmarzyk, P. T., Boyce, W. T., & Pickett, W. (2004). The independent influence of physical inactivity and obesity on health complaints in 6th to 10th grade Canadian youth. *Journal of Physical Activity and Health, 1*, 331–343.

Kerlinger, F. N. (1979). *Behavioral research: A conceptual approach.* Toronto: Holt, Rinehart and Winston.

Krane, V., Greenleaf, C. A., & Snow, J. (1997). Reaching for gold and the price of glory: A motivational case study of an elite gymnast. *The Sport Psychologist, 11*, 53–71.

Lotysz, G., & Short, S. (2004, December). "What ever happened to . . .": The effects of career termination from the National Football League. *Athletic Insight, 6.* Retrieved June 8, 2005, from http://www.athleticinsight.com/Vol6Iss3/WhatEverHappened.htm

Martens, R. (1987). Science, knowledge, and sport psychology. *The Sport Psychologist, 1*, 29–55.

Martin, K. A., Sinden, A. R., & Fleming, J. C. (2000). Inactivity may be hazardous to your image: The effects of exercise participation on impression formation. *Journal of Sport & Exercise Psychology, 22*, 309–317.

Merriam, S. B. (1998). *Qualitative research and case study applications in education.* San Francisco: Jossey-Bass.

Merriam, S. B. (2002). *Qualitative research in practice: Examples for discussion and analysis.* San Francisco: Jossey-Bass.

Messick, S. (1995). Validity of psychological assessment: Validation of inferences from persons' responses and performances as scientific inquiry into score meaning. *American Psychologist, 50*, 741–749.

Munroe, K. J., Giacobbi, P. R., Hall, C. R., & Weinberg, R. S. (2000). The four w's of imagery use: Where, when, why, and what? *The Sport Psychologist, 14*, 119–137.

Okasha, S. (2002). *Philosophy of science: A very short introduction.* Oxford: Oxford University Press.

Patton, M. Q. (2002). *Qualitative research evaluation and methods* (3rd ed.). Thousand Oaks, CA: Sage.

Pedhazur, E. J., & Schmelkin, L. P. (1991). *Measurement, design & analysis: An integrated approach.* Mahwah, NJ: Lawrence Erlbaum.

Pelham, B. W., & Blanton, H. (2003). *Conducting research in psychology: Measuring the weight of smoke* (2nd ed.). Pacific Grove, CA: International Thompson.

Pelletier, L. G., Fortier, M. S., Vallerand, R. J., & Brière, N. M. (2001). Associations among perceived autonomy support, forms of self-regulation, and persistence: A prospective study. *Motivation & Emotion, 25*, 279–306.

Rossman, G. B., & Rallis, S. F. (2003). *Learning in the field: An introduction to qualitative research* (2nd ed.). Thousand Oaks, CA: Sage.

Stevens, D. E., & Bloom, G. A. (2003). The effect of team building on cohesion. *Avante, 9*, 43–54.

Stevens, S. S. (1946). On the theory of scales of measurement. *Science, 103*, 677–680.

Trochim, W. (2001). *The research methods knowledge base* (2nd ed.). Cincinnati, OH: Atomic Dog.

Tsang, T. (2000). Let me tell you a story: A narrative exploration of identity in high-performance sport. *Sociology of Sport Journal, 17*, 44–59.

Vogt, W. P. (1993). *Dictionary of statistics and methodology: A nontechnical guide for the social sciences.* Thousand Oaks, CA: Sage.

CHAPTER 3

Whitney A. Sedgwick
Peter R. E. Crocker

Personality in Sport

Chapter Objectives

After reading this chapter, you should be able to do the following:

1. Define personality and differentiate it from other concepts, such as traits and disposition.

2. Describe Hollander's (1976) components of personality.

3. Discuss key personality perspectives, including trait, humanist, learning/behaviourism, social learning, and interactionist.

4. Briefly explain personality measurement tools, including both objective and projective tests and sport-specific measures.

5. Discuss the potential dangers or hazards and ethics related to measuring personality.

6. Explain recent findings in sport psychology personality research. This includes risk taking/sensation seeking, competitiveness, perfectionism, and mental toughness.

7. Discuss the limitations of personality in explaining athletic behaviour and performance.

Subha and Bob play Rep Bantam Hockey for the New Westminster Bobcats. They are a contrast in personalities. Off the ice, Subha is well mannered but considered somewhat reserved and quiet. She excels in school and volunteers at the food bank. On the ice, Subha seems to be transformed when playing hockey. A highly skilled and swift forward, she is a tenacious checker and is third on the team in penalties.

Her coach, even opposing coaches, loves her playing style. Subha exclaims, "Hockey just brings out the fire in me! I love the speed and contact. Maybe it is from all those nights of watching *Hockey Night in Canada* and listening to Don Cherry. The boys seem surprised that a girl can be so good. Every night I try to play my best and improve. I can be a little hard on myself when I am not playing well. I hope to play for Canada's Olympic team one day. You have to set high standards for yourself."

Bob is a physical presence at more than 6'2", with a happy-go-lucky, friendly disposition both on and off the ice. He has many friends and is a good student. Bob is the biggest, fastest, and most skilled Bobcat player, but his coach sees him as an underachiever. He seldom challenges opposing players who constantly rough him up. Bob often jokes with opposing players, and all of his teammates like hanging around with him.

Bob states, "I like hockey and hanging with my friends, but it is not the only thing in the world. Coaches and some of the parents are always pressuring me to play tougher. I hate the rough stuff and all the pressure. Who needs that crap? Why are adults always trying to change you? All they talk about is the need to get drafted by a junior team, scholarships, and the NHL. I wish they would all back off and just let me enjoy hockey."

Coach Hartley has strong opinions about both Bob and Subha. "Bob has such great physical potential but doesn't have the right personality for hockey," he says. "Subha, on the other hand, has the right stuff. She is aggressive, confident, never gives up—a real fighter. She will go a long way." Manager Campbell says, "I think Subha's aggressiveness is genetic. Her father was a tough nut back in his hockey days. Bob is soft, no mental toughness." Bob's dad feels his son is doing all right. "Bob is a good kid. Because he is so big, the coaches expect too much. They always compare him to Subha. They are different kids. I think the coaches can develop Bob's on-ice personality. They just don't know how."

In the above scenario a number of different descriptors are used to describe the behaviours of Subha and Bob. We often describe others in terms of specific traits with words like *shy*, *aggressive*, *impulsive*, *happy-go-lucky*, and *social*. These terms imply that we expect people to behave or display these characteristics across time. In the scenario, coaches and parents attempt to understand and explain the two athletes' sport performance and motivation by referring to the construct of personality. The coach goes even further by suggesting that there is a right type of personality for hockey.

The above scenario raises a number of questions when we consider personality in sport. Is the uniqueness of a person consistent across situations, or can a person be different in different contexts, like sport and school? Can personality predict sport performance? Is there a distinct sport personality? Does personality interact with the environment to influence sporting performance? For that matter, what is personality? In this chapter we will address these and several other questions related to personality in sport. To gain a better understanding of personality in sport, let us begin by dispelling some common myths.

Some Common Myths about Personality in Sport

MYTH: *A distinct elite athlete personality profile exists.*

The reality is that despite multiple research studies, finding specific characteristics common to elite athletes remains elusive (Vealey, 2002). There are many individual differences among elite athletes both within and across sports and genders. Some people believe that competitiveness and self-confidence are necessary qualities for elite athletes to rise to the highest levels of sport. This seemingly logical belief has only been partially supported in the literature (Gould, Dieffenbach, & Moffett, 2002). This means that some world champions and Olympic gold medallists do not rank themselves high on self-confidence or competitiveness scales. Furthermore, some relatively unsuccessful athletes rate themselves high in self-confidence and competitiveness.

MYTH: *Team athletes are more extroverted than individual-sport athletes, who are considered to be more introverted.*

The reality is that it is not accurate to generalize that all, or even most, team athletes share the same traits. So, it would be an incorrect generalization to say that members of a boys' football team are more extroverted than boys of the same age who are distance runners. There are athletes who are reserved and contribute in many ways in team sports, and there are outgoing athletes who compete and perform well in individual sports.

MYTH: *Contact-sport athletes consistently score high on aggression measures.*

If you've played in a contact team sport, take a moment to consider your teammates. It is likely that they varied in aggressiveness. The reality is that not all football and rugby players are aggressive on and off the playing field. Some contact-sport athletes may play more aggressively or accrue more fouls or penalties, but this does not necessarily mean they possess high aggression as a trait.

Introduction

Personality is a complex, integral part of human individuality. Although researchers find personality challenging to define, the average person freely uses descriptors to describe others' (and their own) personalities. In Canadian sport, spectators and the media might use *cheerful* to describe golfer Lori Kane and *aggressive* to describe hockey player Tie Domi. Not surprisingly, sport researchers have been interested in personality for many decades. Students should realize that there are many complex questions regarding personality in sport, and there are many disagreements among sport researchers and consultants about the importance of personality in sport (for more detailed discussions see Vanden Auweele, De Cuyper, Van Mele, & Rzewnicki, 1993; Vanden Auweele, Nys, Rzewnicki, & Van Mele, 2001; Vealey, 2002). In the 1970s and 1980s, there was a heated debate, termed the credulous-skeptical argument, about the ability to use personality to predict sport behaviour. Those on the **credulous side** believed that personality was an important factor in sport and that personality traits could predict success. Those on the **skeptical side** argued that there was no consistent scientific evidence that personality could provide a meaningful prediction of success in sport, and some writers went so far as to say that personality research in sport should be abandoned. As with most arguments, extreme positions do not really capture the relevance of personality in sport research in the 21st century. Sport-personality research dropped off in the 1980s and 1990s because of perceived difficulties in

Sport researchers have long been interested in studying the personalities of sport performers.

Photograph by Richard Lam, courtesy of University of British Columbia Athletics.

measuring personality and disagreements about the importance of personality in sport. Yet many psychological factors investigated in sport psychology today are related to personality. These include, among many others, trait confidence, trait anxiety, identity, attentional style, mental toughness, hardiness, competitiveness, ego and mastery goal orientation, perfectionism, temperament, conscientiousness, and extroversion (sometimes called *extraversion*). You will see many of these psychological terms throughout this book.

Introduction to Personality

Personality involves the distinct characteristics that make an individual unique. It has been defined as "a dynamic organization, inside the person, of psychophysical systems that create a person's characteristic patterns of behavior, thoughts, and feelings" (Carver & Scheier, 2000, p. 5). The term *dynamic* suggests that people are continually adapting to situations. As well, these authors suggest that physical components are part of our personality composition (i.e., levels of the stress hormone cortisol). Finally, a person's thoughts, feelings, and behaviours are experienced in individual ways and expressed in distinct manners. Personality is relatively stable over time and the combination of personality characteristics contributes to the uniqueness of individuals.

Another term often used in sport-personality research is **disposition**, defined as "broad, pervasive, encompassing ways of relating to particular types of people . . . or situations" (Lazarus & Folkman, 1984, p. 120). For example, to say a teammate has a cheerful disposition would mean this person is typically upbeat, regardless of whom she is talking with or the environment. In sport research, the term *disposition* is often applied to constructs that are relatively stable, such as competitiveness, optimism, and motivational orientation.

Most students have probably heard of personality traits. A **trait** is a relatively stable characteristic or quality that is a portion of one's personality. For example, extroversion refers to being concerned with, or being responsive to, things outside the self. Extroverts are typically sociable, outgoing, friendly, confident, and impulsive. As you will see, traits and trait theory have had a major impact on personality research in sport.

Reflections 3.1

Carefully consider Carver and Scheier's definition of personality. Think about Canadian golfer Mike Weir when he made a crucial 2-metre putt on the 18th hole to get into the playoff in the 2003 Masters. On observing his behaviour throughout 18 holes, *Globe and Mail* columnist Lorne Rubenstein stated, "All day he had been a study in tenacity." Can you make inferences about an athlete's personality simply by watching him or her in specific situations? What types of information would you need to determine an athlete's personality?

Components of Personality and Behaviour

Psychologists have found that some behavioural aspects of personality seem to be moderately stable in many individuals but that other aspects of specific behaviour are constantly in flux. There are many different ways to conceptualize the various facets of personality. One helpful framework is a three-level model provided by Hollander (1976). The three levels are arranged in concentric circles with a psychological core at the centre, typical responses in the middle circle, and role-related behaviour in the outer circle (see Figure 3.1). The **psychological core** represents the most basic foundation of an individual's personality. The core contains the values, motives, attitudes, memories, and expectations that make each person unique. The core also includes one's self-perceptions and is the hardest element of personality to change. For example, you might consider yourself to be a determined, hard-working, and thoughtful person. This means that, regardless of the situation, you will present yourself in this manner. Whether in sport, in school, or at work, the majority of your thoughts, feelings, and behaviours would be a reflection of your core self-perceptions.

Typical responses, in the middle circle, are the ways in which an individual would react to events. If you describe yourself as aggressive with a competitive nature, this

Figure 3.1 Diagram of Hollander's (1976) personality model

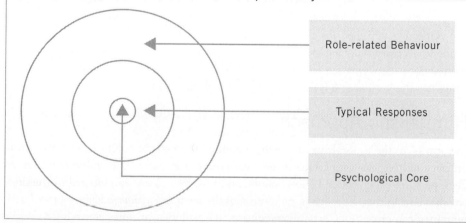

might be demonstrated on the playing field. These middle elements could also be similar to values in the underlying core, but it is important to note that this is not always the case. It is not advised to infer someone's core characteristics based simply on behaviour alone. Someone might behave in an aggressive manner but could actually be quite shy in character. A contextual factor (e.g., playing against a long-term rival) could be a primary reason for this athlete's presentation. Therefore, various contexts or situations, as well as temporal factors, need to be considered when determining a person's typical responses.

Role-related behaviour is the easiest component of personality to change. The immediate situation and expectations of how one *should* behave compose this outer component of the personality model. A person may have multiple life roles: sibling, team captain, student, and boyfriend or girlfriend. Each role may be markedly different from the others. However, one would expect that the role-related behaviours would not be radically inconsistent with core elements.

Approaches to Studying Personality

The study of personality has been shaped by various viewpoints, ranging from biological to socio-cultural. The conceptual approaches to studying personality have emphasized different theories: psychodynamic, humanist, trait, learning (behaviourism), social learning, and interactionist. The following sections are overviews of these psychological approaches that will aid in illustrating the development of personality research.

Psychodynamic Approach

The **psychodynamic approach** to personality grew out of the psychoanalytic movement founded and practiced by Sigmund Freud. The psychodynamic approach suggests that all behaviour is interconnected and driven by unconscious forces. As well, Freud's work contained an underlying theme that thoughts and feelings motivate our behaviours—a premise that is widely held to this day. Freud devised a structure of personality that includes the id, the ego, and the superego. The **id** is considered the instinctual and driving force of personality, the pleasure principle centre. The **ego** mediates the individual's relationship with the environment, the reality principle. Finally, the **superego** is the voice of the conscience and morality, the should/should not principle. The ego is considered a mediator, or the reality-tester, between the id and **superego**. Freud proposed that all behaviour stems from conflict and compromise, among the wants of the id, the defences of the ego, and the morality of the superego.

Although the theories of Freud and those who followed him contributed major elements to the advancement of the study of personality, there is little application to current sport performance enhancement. Psychodynamic work has been criticized as being too theoretical and is an incredibly difficult area to test.

Humanistic Approach

In contrast to the inner drives of psychodynamics, humanistic psychology focuses more on personal responsibility, human growth, personal striving, and individual dignity. Each person's experiences, beliefs, values, and perceptions are emphasized in the present moment in this approach. One often sees the term *self-actualization* associated with humanistic approaches. Certainly in competitive athletics, athletes are trying to be the best they can be, to reach their potential; this is a quick way to summarize self-actualization. Dr. Terry Orlick of the University of Ottawa has been a strong proponent of humanistic approaches to sport psychology consulting. He emphasizes that it is important to understand the needs and desires of athletes, to respect their perceptions and ideas, and to view their athletic participation in the bigger picture of personal growth (Orlick, 1989).

Carl Rogers (1959) was a humanist psychologist who contributed greatly to the field of personality study. Rogers believed that when there is a discrepancy between a person's self-perceptions and what is being experienced, this person might deny what is actually happening. Abraham Maslow (1943) was another of the founding humanist psychologists. He published a hierarchy of needs in a five-tiered triangular model (see Figure 3.2), which suggests that as our basic human needs (lower tiers of the pyramid) are met, we strive to meet higher needs. The base of the triangle represents physiological needs, such as food, water, sleep, and shelter. The second tier up represents safety needs, provided in personal and social settings. If physiological and safety needs are met, then the individual moves to the third tier to satisfy social needs: feelings of belonging, connections to others, the acts of giving and receiving love. The fourth tier of the triangle is for esteem needs, which can be internal (i.e., self-respect and achievement) or external (i.e., recognition and status). **Self-actualization**, at the top of the pyramid, refers to the constant striving to make the most of one's special abilities. Olympic champions or individuals who have succeeded in spite of physical or mental disabilities (such as Terry Fox and Rick Hansen) could be considered self-actualized.

Trait Approach

The trait approach to personality proposes that certain traits exist, that all people have varying levels of these traits, and that these traits influence specific behaviours. As previously stated, the definition for traits is similar to that of personality—stable qualities used to explain an individual's behaviour across time and situations. Hans Eysenck, a

Figure 3.2   Maslow's hierarchy of needs pyramid

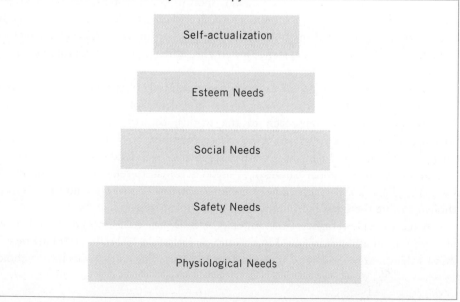

behavioural psychologist with a strong biological orientation, began studying temperament in the 1940s. From a list of personality traits, he devised two main personality-assessment scales: Extraversion-Introversion and Neuroticism-Stability. He also devised two popular instruments to assess personality, the Eysenck Personality Inventory (Eysenck & Eysenck, 1964) and the Eysenck Personality Questionnaire (Eysenck & Eysenck, 1975).

Contrary to traits, **states**, refer to momentary feelings and thoughts that change depending on the situation and time. Take the following example. In a 2004 NHL hockey game, the Vancouver Canucks' Todd Bertuzzi hit the Colorado Avalanche's Steve Moore from behind and drove him headfirst into the ice. The hit fractured Moore's neck and Bertuzzi was later charged with assault causing bodily harm. Were Bertuzzi's actions representative of the trait of aggression, or were they the result of a temporary atypical state? This is a very difficult question. Your opinions may differ, but the example highlights questions regarding athletic personality (not to mention the influence of game situations, societal influences or expectations, and the nature of the sport).

A common assumption in many trait models of personality is that traits have a normal distribution throughout the population. This means most people have moderate levels of a specific trait, with only a small percentage having extremely low or extremely high levels of the trait. These traits are thought to direct behaviour. For example, athletes high in aggression are believed to be more likely to exhibit aggressive behaviours and thoughts across a variety of situations compared with their teammates who are moderate or low in aggression. What makes the prediction of behaviour difficult, however, is that personality is composed of several different traits that combine to influence specific behaviours.

Various trait models have been developed over time, with many having been applied in sport psychology research. Two example models are Cattell's (1946, 1995) trait personality model and Costa and McCrae's (1992) five-factor model. Cattell's model proposes there are 16 personality factors, called source traits, that capture personality. These factors are warmth, reasoning, dominance, liveliness, social boldness, rule consciousness, sensitivity, vigilance, abstractedness, privateness, apprehension, openness to change, self-reliance, perfectionism, tension, and emotional stability. Cattell's work was a primary source for many sport psychology studies in the 1960s and the 1970s. Some sport psychologists argued that successful athletes shared specific traits, like dominance and emotional stability, but over time researchers have realized that there is little consistent evidence for an elite athletic personality profile (Vanden Auweele et al., 2001).

Costa and McCrae's (1992) five-factor model (FFM) of personality suggests that all people can be described in terms of the prevalence of five factors: *extroversion* (assertiveness, energetic approach to the world), *conscientiousness* (achievement-striving, self-discipline), *openness to experience* (opposite of closed-mindedness, curious), *agreeableness* (compliance, positive approach toward others), and *neuroticism* (feelings of tension and nervousness). A useful acronym to remember these factors is OCEAN. This model has become a pre-eminent theory in personality psychology, though to date there has been limited sport psychology research using it.

A recent study (Hughes, Case, Stuempfle, & Evans, 2003) looked at the personality profiles of athletes involved in an ultra-marathon, a 100-mile (160 km) race in Alaska that must be completed in fewer than 48 hours. The participants have a choice of competing on foot, snowshoes, cross-country skis, or bicycle. In addition they have to carry their own survival gear. The researchers found that participants' scores were higher on the extroversion and openness dimensions compared with data from a general adult sample. Further research in exercise psychology by Rhodes, Courneya, and Hayduk (2002) suggests that personality variables may moderate motivational variables in the prediction of exercise behaviour. For example, individuals higher in extroversion and conscientiousness are more likely to meet their intentions to exercise. These two studies suggest that examining the potential role of these five personality variables may shed light on specific dimensions of sport and exercise behaviour.

Reflections 3.2

Look closely at the factors associated with the five-factor model of personality. How might these characteristics affect training and competitive behaviours of athletes? How would you rate yourself on these characteristics? Are they consistent across various aspects of your life?

Behaviourism, Learning, and Social Learning Theory

Early learning theories suggested that behaviour was not determined by inner drives but by interactions (involving reward and punishment) with the environment. The learning perspective suggests that all behaviour is learned through experience, and it discards notions of disposition, drives, or instincts proposed by other personality theories. B. F. Skinner (1999) argued that behaviour that is followed by a reward would increase in probability of reoccurrence, whereas behaviour that is followed by punishment would decrease in probability of reoccurrence. The extreme behaviourists rejected the importance of internal causes of behaviour, including such factors as goals, intentions, traits, and expectancies. Over time other psychologists argued that learning was very complex and involved such aspects as beliefs, expectancies, and goals.

Other learning theorists have taken a less absolute, rigid approach to the influence of the environment on personality. Such views as social learning theory and social cognitive theory have influenced contemporary personality research. Rotter (1954) determined that three factors would influence behaviour: situational expectancies, generalized expectancies, and reinforcement value. More simply, Rotter believed that people are motivated to seek out positive stimulation and to avoid negative interactions or stimulation. Rotter suggested that behaviour and personality are changeable; furthermore, if you change a situation or the way a person thinks, you would subsequently change that person's behaviour and personality.

Albert Bandura (1977, 1997) emphasized the importance of observational learning and modelling. He determined that individuals can learn simply by being exposed to, or by observing, the behaviours of others. For example, watching the behaviours of an athlete can influence a person's future behaviour. Bandura's work demonstrated that people can and do learn from multiple sources, such as television, magazines, and social interactions. We know that individuals are more likely to adopt a behaviour if it results in valued outcomes. If a baseball player behaves in a co-operative manner and that behaviour results in his team winning an important game, then an observer is more likely to imitate that behaviour in a similar sport setting.

Learning theories focus on how situations and individuals reciprocally influence each other. If a situation has an influence on an individual (or vice versa), this influence could subsequently have a lasting effect on his or her personality. Simply put, the strict learning behaviourists suggest that personality is the sum of all that you do, not of what you think or feel. However, social learning theorists believe that people are active agents in shaping their behaviour, with many factors determining a person's actions. It should not be surprising then, that there are multiple applications of social learning theory in sport.

Reflections 3.3

Bandura argues that through observing role models, people learn that aggression in sport is often acceptable. When spectators and teammates cheer on combatants, young players learn that this type of behaviour is expected and valued. Do you think that athletes can adopt sport personalities by this process of modelling and imitation? Think of your own behaviour. Who are your role models, and are your behaviours similar to those of your role models?

Interactionist Approach: Combining Personality and the Environment

The interactionist perspective came into vogue in the 1970s in response to perceived limitations of the personality-versus-environment approaches. According to Endler and Magnusson's interactionist approach, it is the situational interplay between the person and the environment that determines the specific behaviours of an individual (1976). Their interactionist work differentiates mechanistic from dynamic interactions. **Mechanistic interactions** refers to the structure of the interaction between the person and the situation, versus the process; **dynamic interactions** refers to the simultaneous reciprocal effect of the person and the situation.

Most current research of personality in sport emphasizes an interactionist approach (Vanden Auweele et al., 2001). This acknowledges that each athlete brings specific dispositions, experiences, and genetic variables to a sporting situation. Neither the individual's personality nor the situation exclusively dictates behaviour. In 1935, Kurt Lewin suggested that the individual's personality (P), the social environment (E), and behaviour (B) were dynamic and constantly changing. A simple equation, $B = f(P, E)$ represents both Lewin's ideas and the interactionist approach that behaviour is a function of the interaction between personality and the social environment. However, because there is a vast number of personal, situational, and environmental factors in situations, this simple equation can become quite complex when applied to real life.

Instead of searching for stability of behaviour across all situations, interactionist researchers are trying to understand how various traits or dispositions affect behaviour, depending on the sport context. In this view, we can consider the interplay among the stable characteristics of the person, goals and motivations of the person, and

Athletes can demonstrate different behaviours depending on their personality and the competitive context.

Photographs by Richard Lam, courtesy of University of British Columbia Athletics.

opportunities and appropriateness of specific behaviours in the sport context. In addition, the athlete's perceptions of the situation cannot be underestimated. For example, Ann is a talented player on her university varsity volleyball team. She is known by her own teammates as being very calm, sometimes to her own detriment. Coming into the last game, her play seems overly relaxed and the team is losing the match. During the last portion of the final game, Ann's game becomes quick, determined, and driven, and she perceives herself to be competent and up to the challenge. She works hard on the offense and repeatedly hits winning shots to tie the score at 25–25. This is a hypothetical example of how it is important to consider the person's typical pattern of behaviour (Ann's calm, non-assertive tendencies) with the goals or expectancies that become activated during game contexts (importance of team success), along with the types of behaviours that are deemed appropriate in this context and the athlete's perceptions.

The Measurement of Personality

Many inventories have been developed to measure personality. The reliability and validity of most of these measures have been tested, and the measures have been used across and within genders, populations, and cultures worldwide. Because many varied tests are available, it follows that the applicability and relevance of these tests to athletes will vary. You should be aware, however, that many sport psychology researchers have been critical of how some psychologists and sporting teams have used personality tests in sport (Vealey, 2002). Before we discuss the ethics of testing, it will be useful to discuss the various types of measures used in personality research and then talk about some sport-specific measures.

Measures of personality can be divided into projective and objective categories. **Projective tests** contain open-ended questions, which provides a subjective perspective. The test taker is not provided with possible answers to the test questions. Researchers believe that the questions will reveal an individual's hidden feelings and thoughts. These tests are not typically used in sport personality research. **Objective tests**, on the other hand, are highly standardized tests that do not require the tester to interpret the meaning of the participant's responses. These tests typically present the individual with choices, as in true/false questions or a choice of responses in a scale. For example, a statement used to assess extroversion might be, "I see myself as someone who is talkative." A person would indicate on a five-point scale how much she or he agrees or disagrees with this statement. Examples of objectives tests are Cattell's 16 Personality Factors (16PF; Cattell, 1946), the Minnesota Multiphasic Personality Inventory-2 (MMPI-2; Hathaway & McKinley, 1943; Hathaway, McKinley, & Butcher, 1989), and the Neuroticism Extroversion Openness Five Factor Inventory (NEO-FFI; Costa & McCrae, 1994).

Two important issues to consider in the measurement of personality is whether the test is appropriate for athletic settings and whether the research questions are specific to sporting populations. For example, the MMPI-2 includes 10 clinical scales, which measure different facets of personality, including depression, paranoia, hypomania, and social introversion. The original MMPI was designed for use with in-patients in psychiatric hospital units. The MMPI-2 is one of the most widely used tests, but it is a still a test of adult psychopathology. The test is used to assist in the diagnosis and treatment of mental disorders and therefore is not appropriate for use with athletes in sport settings. Yet a search of the database SIRC SportDiscus reveals several studies that have used the MMPI-2 in an attempt to answer many non-clinical research questions.

Not surprisingly, trait measures of personality have been very popular in sport research. The 16PF combines both the state and the trait approach to personality study and assesses different personality trait dichotomies. The database SIRC SportDiscus indicates over 140 references to the 16PF. The majority of research studies using the 16PF in sport occurred between 1960 and 1980, and there was still research in the 1990s using this measure to attempt to differentiate between different levels of sport performers. The majority of personality research in sport today, however, uses measures that have been developed specifically for sport.

Sport-specific Measures

There are numerous sport-specific measures that are used to measure either global or specific aspects of athletes' personalities. Many of these measures relate to motivation, anxiety, stress, physical self-perceptions, self-esteem, and aggression and will be discussed in later chapters. Clearly we cannot discuss all of these measures, many of which are documented in detail in Ostrow's (1996) *Directory of Psychological Tests in the Sport & Exercise Sciences*. We will address three representative measures that attempt to assess various aspects of personality in sport: the Athletic Motivation Inventory (Tutko, Lyon, & Ogilvie, 1969), the Sport Competition Anxiety Test (Martens, 1977), and the Profile of Mood States (McNair, Lorr, & Droppleman, 1971, 1992).

ATHLETIC MOTIVATION INVENTORY   The Athletic Motivation Inventory (AMI) was designed to measure the personality and motivation of athletes participating in competitive sports. It was the first sport-specific psychological test to be developed, and it has been widely used in schools and by private and professional athletic organizations. Specifically, the AMI measures personality such areas as ability to cope with emotional stress, dedication to the coach and sport, and traits predictive of athletic success. The inventory was correlated with the variables on the 16PF, including emotional control, aggression, leadership, conscientiousness, tough-mindedness, trust, self-confidence, and guilt-proneness. The AMI measures personality traits within a specific sport.

Research using the AMI provides equivocal results in terms of its validity. For example, researchers Thomas and Sinclair (1978) examined Canadian women intercollegiate basketball players using both the AMI and the 16PF. The results indicated that, when compared with controls, athletes were slightly above average in mental toughness and self-confidence. However, the AMI was later critiqued by Hap Davis (1991), a Canadian sport psychologist based in Calgary. He examined the validity of the instrument by having hockey scouts rate the NHL draft players' psychological strengths by observing their on-ice play. Davis found that only a small number of the hockey players' on-ice behaviours representing psychological strength were related to what the AMI measured. This type of research then has implications for draft screening procedures and for determining whether the use of instruments, such as the AMI, is optimal in assessing athletes' psychological strengths.

SPORT COMPETITION ANXIETY TEST   The Sport Competition Anxiety Test (SCAT), developed by Martens (1977), is a sport-specific measure designed to capture competitive trait anxiety. **Trait anxiety** was heavily investigated in psychology and refers to a general disposition to respond to a variety of situations with feelings of concern or worry, along with having heightened physiological arousal. According to Martens, athletes who have high competitive trait anxiety would be more likely to experience high trait anxiety across many competitive situations, regardless of situational variables. Ten anxiety statements measured sport competitive trait anxiety. An example is, "Before I compete I get a queasy feeling in my stomach." Each SCAT item is scored on a three-point scale: (1) *hardly ever*, (2) *sometimes*, (3) *often*. The SCAT has been used in many studies to investigate numerous research questions related to trait anxiety in sport. Trait anxiety and the use of the SCAT are discussed in more detail in Chapter 5, the chapter on anxiety and arousal.

PROFILE OF MOOD STATES   A predominant instrument used in sport personality and mood research is the Profile of Moods States (POMS; McNair et al., 1971, 1992). Interestingly, the POMS is not really a stable personality type test since it was designed to assess state affect in psychiatric populations. Yet, it became popular in sport psychology based on the work of Morgan and colleagues (Morgan, 1980; Morgan & Pollock, 1977) The POMS assesses six discrete affective states: *tension-anxiety* (TEN), *depression-dejection* (DEP), *anger-hostility* (ANG), *vigor* (VIG), *fatigue* (FAT), *and confusion-bewilderment* (CON). A Total Mood Score can be calculated by subtracting the score for Vigor from the sum of the other five scores. Participants in the initial sport study of the POMS (Morgan & Pollock, 1977) included rowers, distance runners, and wrestlers. The research findings suggested that elite athletes with positive affect reported what has been termed an *iceberg profile*, scoring low on tension, depression, anger, fatigue, and confusion but high on vigour (Figure 3.3 on the next page). This makes sense because it would be more challenging to perform well—and even harder to aim for a personal best—if one were feeling down, frustrated, tired, or uncertain. If your energy levels are high, you would likely rate your vigour as high, which can aid in creating a positive mood and ultimately positively influence performance.

Morgan and Pollock's work (1977) generated great interest in the link between scores on POMS and sport performance and resulted in more than 200 references to the POMS on SIRC SportDiscus. However, subsequent research on the iceberg profile has reached mixed conclusions, with many studies failing to support the profile. Rowley, Landers, Kyllo, and Etnier (1995) conducted a meta-analysis (a research technique in which the results of many studies are combined) on studies that had used the

Figure 3.3   Example of an iceberg profile for successful and unsuccessful athletes

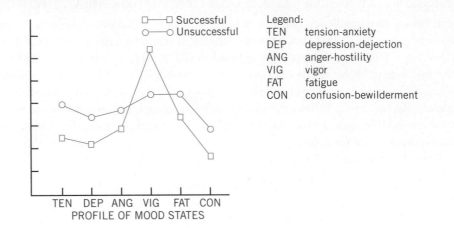

□——□ Successful
○——○ Unsuccessful

Legend:
TEN   tension-anxiety
DEP   depression-dejection
ANG   anger-hostility
VIG   vigor
FAT   fatigue
CON   confusion-bewilderment

TEN DEP ANG VIG FAT CON
PROFILE OF MOOD STATES

Note: Wann, Daniel L., Sport Psychology, First Edition, © 1997, p.65. Reprinted by permission of Pearson Education, Inc., Upper Saddle River, NJ.

POMS. They determined that there was weak support for Morgan and Pollock's findings of the iceberg profile (i.e., that across studies, successful athletes did report more positive affect); the difference between successful and unsuccessful athletes was very small. The meta-analysis results indicated that mood accounted for less than 1% of the athletes' performances! Nevertheless, there still appears to be much interest in the POMS and sport performance, with the *Journal of Applied Sport Psychology* devoting an entire volume in 2000 to research on the POMS.

Potential Hazards of Personality Measurement

We have seen that multiple tools exist to measure personality characteristics of athletes. However, under what conditions should a personality test be used? Should these tests be utilized to screen or select athletes? Whether the test is objective, projective, sport-specific, or general, there are a number of factors that we need to consider. First, what is the research evidence that supports the use of test scores for a specific purpose? Tests have been developed and validated for specific populations and contexts. To use a clinical tool, like the MMPI-2, to screen athletes for a team would be inappropriate. The MMPI was not developed for such a purpose, nor is there any evidence that it can discriminate successful from unsuccessful athletes. Second, only qualified people should administer and assess scores from a measurement tool. You wouldn't want a layperson to give you a medical exam and diagnosis, so the same standard should hold for the use of psychological assessments. This second consideration leads us into the ethics of personality testing and assessment.

Ethical principles are typically devised by a specific organization and used by members of this same organization to shape professional judgment and behaviour (see the website for the Association for the Advancement of Applied Sport Psychology: www.aaasponline.org/governance/committees/ethics/standards.php). Integrity and the responsibility to protect the public's well-being are examples of ethical issues. With respect to psychological testing, athletes need to be informed of the nature of tests, how the results will be used, and who will have access to the results. Using tests or

Sport research indicates there does not appear to be a distinct elite sport personality.

Photographs by Richard Lam, courtesy of University of British Columbia Athletics.

inventories for team selection is frowned upon since there is little evidence to support the validity of such use. Some professional teams have used psychological tests in team selection or to explore an athlete's personality. However, many professional organizations, like the NFL Players Association, have forbidden the use of such tests with its members. Breaches in confidentiality and the potential financial cost of testing athletes are also considerations when using psychological tests with athletic populations. As well, the person administering the test must be qualified. This person must be competent, meaning that he or she has a broad range of experience administering, scoring, and interpreting the particular test. Licensed psychologists or individuals with specialized training in test administration are usually the best resources for psychological testing and interpretation. For students wanting more information, Etzel, Yura, and Perna (1998) provide an excellent discussion of ethics in assessment and testing in sport and exercise psychology.

Reflections 3.4

You are an undergraduate student working with a high-school soccer team. The team is struggling, and the coach is searching for solutions to improve their performance. The coach believes that specific personalities are needed for his sport. He asks you to administer a personality test to determine the personality profile of each player. What would you do? What are the ethical issues involved?

Personality Research in Sport

In the following section we will provide some examples of sport research studies that have emphasized a personality approach. We have selected representative research from four areas that give students an idea of how specific personality factors might affect sport behaviour. These research areas are risk taking/sensation seeking, competitiveness, perfectionism, and mental toughness.

Risk-taking and Sensation-seeking Behaviours

When you consider Canadian Olympic divers Emilie Heymans and Blythe Hartley, 10M platform silver medalists at the Olympic Games in Athens, they epitomize sensation-seeking athletes. To stand on a tower 10 metres high, the equivalent of a three-storey building, and then execute a complicated routine with somersaults and twists and enter the water flawlessly is a challenging feat. Or consider Lori-Ann Muenzer, Athens Olympic gold medalist in cycling, who, in that particular race, averaged 56 km/h on a bicycle with no brakes and her feet attached to the pedals. These athletes became experts in sports where the thrill of heights and speed is inherent.

The terms *risk taking* and *sensation seeking* (or *stimulus seeking*) have been used interchangeably in sport psychology literature. **Risk taking** involves narrowing the margin of safety, both physically and psychologically (Anshel, 2003). The elements of danger, possibility of bodily harm, injury, and physical loss are inherent in some sports, such as skydiving, race-car driving, and downhill skiing. Do the athletes who participate in these sports have different personalities from those who remain rooted to the ground, participating in what might be considered safer sports? **Sensation (stimulus) seeking** has been defined as "the seeking of varied, novel, complex and intense sensations and experiences, and the willingness to take physical, social, legal and financial risks for the sake of such experiences" (Zuckerman, 1994, p. 27). Malone (1985) characterized stimulus seeking as a motivational factor for athletes to not only participate in sport but also to engage in risk-taking behaviours. There is research that suggests that stimulus seekers have higher physiological activation levels or chronic levels of high excitation, which is rewarded when they take risks in sport.

Malone (1985) conducted a review of the literature on risk taking in sport and concluded that the perception of danger creates excitement in athletes. They also have a desire to conquer the situation. This is seen in the previously cited study of the personalities of Iditasport (Alaskan ultra-marathon) athletes (Hughes et al., 2003). The athletes completed personality inventories and results indicated they were higher than average on extroversion, openness, and experience-seeking scales from two different instruments. The authors suggest that the athletes' curiosity and optimism contribute to their ability to complete this demanding race.

Other researchers have been interested in particular aspects of sensation seeking, such as thrill and adventure seeking, experience seeking, boredom susceptibility, and disinhibition. Zarevski, Marusic, Zolotic, Bunjevac, and Vukosav (1998) were able to discriminate between Croatian males involved in high-risk sport (parachuting, scuba diving, gliding, and climbing) and those in low-risk sport (athletics, rowing, bowling, and table tennis). Thrill and adventure seeking and experience seeking were the two most important factors. Their data demonstrated, however, that there were large individual differences within each of the two groups of athletes.

With respect to gender and age, it would appear that sensation seeking declines with age and that males are more drawn to high-risk sports than are females. In a recent

Although males generally score higher in sensation seeking, there are many females who compete in high-risk sport.

Photo courtesy of PhotoDisc/Getty Images.

study that examined sensation-seeking levels in both parents and children (Butkovic & Bratko, 2003), the children expressed higher levels of sensation seeking than their parents. As well, males scored higher than female participants on total sensation seeking, thrill and adventure seeking, disinhibition, and boredom susceptibility. These findings support other research that has been conducted in England, the United States, Australia, and Canada. Nevertheless, many women excel in high-risk sport; examples are Canadian mountain bikers Marie-Helene Premont and Alison Sydor.

Competitiveness

We all know athletes who seem to possess that "killer instinct," those athletes who attack competition and even regular training workouts with high levels of intensity. These athletes want to succeed and are determined to do everything within their power to achieve this goal. Canadian athletes, such as Sue Holloway, have demonstrated such competitiveness and positive determination. Holloway was the first Canadian woman ever to compete in both the 1976 Winter (cross-country skiing) and 1984 Summer (kayaking) Olympic Games.

Competitiveness is conceptualized as a desire to engage in and strive for success in sport achievement situations (Gill & Deeter, 1988). Gill and Deeter devised the Sport Orientation Questionnaire to measure athletes' desire to win, along three specific dimensions. These dimensions are competitiveness, win orientation, and goal orientation. These researchers compared non-athletes and athletes and found that athletes scored higher on all three dimensions and that males scored higher than females. Interestingly, Gill & Dzewaltowski (1988) found that high-level athletes enjoy performing successfully and place more emphasis on performance, or personal best goals, than on outcome, or winning goals.

As well, Gould et al. (2002) have studied competitiveness as a psychological characteristic of Olympic champions. They found competitiveness, adaptive perfectionism, mental toughness, and mental resiliency to be present in Olympic medal winners.

Durand-Bush and Salmela (2002), sport researchers from the University of Ottawa, conducted interviews with Canadian World or Olympic medalists. Their research indicated that competitiveness was an important characteristic of these elite athletes. Houston, Carter, and Smithers (1997) examined competitiveness in professional and amateur tennis players and concluded that the professional players reported higher levels of competitiveness. Contrary to other findings, this study found that the female tennis professionals reported more competitiveness than the male players. Not surprisingly, the research results across studies are varied with respect to gender differences and competitiveness. In another study, Acevedo, Gill, and Dzewaltowski (1987) found that ultra-marathoners (a 100-mile or 160 km race) had competitiveness scores only slightly higher than university-age runners. The ultra-marathoners' scores for competitiveness were actually lower than those of a comparison group of intercollegiate athletes.

Simply put, competitiveness involves how motivated one is toward achievement. Gender, sport level, and cultural differences have been studied in relation to competitiveness, with varying results. Again, individual differences should not be discounted because people can interpret the notion of competitiveness differently. As you will see in the following chapter on motivation, there are various ways to describe the dispositions related to achieving goals and success in sport.

Perfectionism

Catriona LeMay Doan, Olympic speed skating champion, and Helen Simard, Paralympic gold medallist in wheelchair tennis, are two outstanding Canadian athletes who trained for numerous years to achieve sporting excellence. Success at this elite level would seem to require that athletes need to (a) set high personal standards for performance, (b) monitor progress toward these standards, (c) be highly organized, and (d) manage the pressure and expectations of significant others, such as parents, coaches, teammates, and partners. But what about athletes who incur psychological or physical costs while engaging in the drive for success? The danger is that setting unrealistic, high standards could lead to stress and anxiety, and could subsequently result in maladaptive behaviours, such as hostility, disordered eating, steroid use, training when injured, and dropping out of sport.

Perfectionism is a relatively stable personality construct that involves unrealistic, high standards; inappropriate levels of expectations; and high self-criticism (Flett & Hewitt, 2002; Frost, Marten, Lahart, & Rosenblate, 1990). Psychology researchers have recognized that perfectionism has multiple dimensions that involve both the self and significant others. Frost et al. (1990) state that self-perfectionism involves high personal standards, doubts about actions, high concern over mistakes, and organization. High parental expectations and parental criticism are two factors of the interpersonal aspects of perfectionism. Given that many of these behaviours are present in competitive sport, it is not surprising that sport psychologists have become increasingly interested in the study of perfectionism. Other dimensions and frameworks for perfectionism have been proposed (Flett & Hewitt, 2002), but sport researchers have primarily used the conceptualization of Frost et al.

It sounds as if perfectionism might lead to destructive behaviour patterns in athletes. Some sport researchers, however, believe that there are both healthy and unhealthy aspects of perfectionism (Anshel & Eom, 2003; Dunn, Causgrove, Dunn, & Syrotuik, 2002). **Maladaptive or unhealthy perfectionism** would involve excessive, unrealistic standards of performance, high doubt, high self-criticism, fear of failure, and high distress. **Healthy or adaptive perfectionism** consists of realistic goal setting, judging success through personal improvement and effort (task orientation), self-discipline, and achievement striving. Indeed, many of the behaviours associated with healthy perfectionism are the same as for conscientiousness.

Sport research has generally found that extreme perfectionism will lead to negative emotions, dropping out, poor or maladaptive coping, and perceptions of low competence (Anshel & Eom, 2003). Frost and Henderson (1991) found that athletes who scored high on a scale designed to measure concern over mistakes also had higher competitive anxiety and reacted more negatively to mistakes in competition. Hall, Kerr, and Matthews (1998) found that anxiety was associated with perfectionism in high-school male and female cross-country runners. Gould, Tuffey, Udry, and Loehr (1997) identified elements of perfectionism in association with burnout of youth high-performance tennis players. Krane, Greenleaf, and Snow (1997) reported a case study of a gymnast who internalized the pressure to be perfect (cited in Flett & Hewitt, 2002). This athlete manifested numerous maladaptive behaviours, including high anxiety, engaging in unhealthy behaviour, and practising while seriously injured.

Dr. John Dunn of the University of Alberta has recently been investigating healthy and unhealthy perfectionism in sport. Dunn et al. (2002) studied the link between perfectionism, ego motivation, and task achievement motivation in high-school football players. Ego motivation involves judging success in terms of being better than others. Task achievement motivation involves judging success in terms of personal improvement and effort (these concepts will be more thoroughly described in Chapter 4). Dunn et al. defined unhealthy, or maladaptive, perfectionism as having high personal standards, high concerns with mistakes, and high concern with coach and parent pressure. Healthy, or adaptive, perfectionism was reflected by moderate

< Perfectionism in sport can be both healthy and unhealthy.

Photograph by Richard Lam, courtesy of University of British Columbia Athletics.

standards and low concern with mistakes and low pressure from coaches and parents. They found that unhealthy perfectionism was positively related to an ego orientation whereas healthy perfectionism was associated with a task orientation. Dunn, Gotwals, Causgrove-Dunn, and Syrotuik (2004) also found that football players with unhealthy perfectionism had a greater likelihood of experiencing anger when playing poorly. Vallance and Dunn (2002) replicated this finding with male youth competitive hockey players. Lastly, in a study of competitive figure skaters, Dunham, Dunn, and Hogg (2002) found that negative attitudes toward body image were associated with maladaptive perfectionism whereas adaptive perfectionists had more positive attitudes. Overall, the existing research evidence indicates that perfectionism can have both beneficial and destructive aspects for athletes.

Mental Toughness

In 1992, Canadian rower Silken Laumann looked as if she had the world in her hands. She was the reigning World Cup champion and was highly favoured for gold in the Barcelona Olympics. Shockingly, 10 weeks before the Olympics she suffered serious leg injuries as a result of a boat collision during a race warm-up. Her Olympic dreams, and possibly her rowing career, seemed shattered. Nevertheless, with the assistance of a special brace to stabilize her leg, Silken endured incredible pain to finish third in the 1992 Olympics (see www.silkenlaumann.com). Sport commentators spoke glowingly about her courage and mental toughness.

Mental toughness has been identified as one of the most critical psychological characteristics for achieving excellence in elite sport (Jones, Hanton, & Connaughton, 2002; Loehr, 1995). For example, in a special issue of the *Journal of Applied Sport Psychology* on athletic excellence, three separate articles identified mental toughness as a personal characteristic of elite performers (Durand-Bush & Salmela, 2002; Gould et al., 2002; Jones et al., 2002). What is mental toughness? Is it a personality variable or a motivational factor? Jones et al. argued that coaches, athletes, and sport psychologists often use the term *mental toughness* though it is poorly understood. Jones et al. found that it has been described as a personality trait (Kroll, 1967), an outward expression of an inner commitment (Goldberg, 1998), and as a collection of psychological attributes and skills (Loehr, 1995). Psychological characteristics associated with mental toughness have included control, competitiveness, concentration, confidence, commitment, determination, desire, focus, persistence, and optimism (see Goldberg, 1998; Gould, Hodge, Peterson, & Petlichkoff, 1987; Jones et al., 2002; Loehr, 1995).

In an attempt to better understand athletes' perspectives on mental toughness, Jones et al. (2002) had 10 international athletes (7 men and 3 women) identify the qualities and characteristics of mental toughness. Using qualitative research methods for focus groups, they found many similarities with the results of previous research. Mental toughness was a skill that allowed athletes to cope with competition demands better than their opponents did. Some athletes thought this skill was innate whereas others believed mental toughness could be developed over time with the right competitive experiences. Ten key characteristics in three broad categories were identified: (1) very strong self-confidence and motivation, (2) ability to manage the stress of competition and training, and (3) ability to maintain or regain focus in the face of distraction.

The key characteristics identified by Jones et al. (2002) are consistent with findings on athletic excellence in Canadian athletes. Orlick and Partington's (1988)

 High-level performance requires athletes to be mentally tough.

Photograph by Richard Lam, courtesy of University of British Columbia Athletics.

research with Olympians found that high levels of commitment and the ability to focus and refocus when confronted with distractions were two elements that distinguish more successful athletes from less successful athletes. Durand-Bush and Salmela's (2002) interviews with 10 World or Olympic champions revealed that competitiveness, self-confidence, and motivation were important personal characteristics of excellence. They also found that athletes reported the use of psychological skills that help manage stress and allow a strong competition and training focus.

In summary, the research indicates that **mental toughness** involves a number of personal characteristics and psychological skills that allow athletes to cope with stress and anxiety while remaining focused on competition demands. Some of these personal characteristics may be dispositional, such as competitiveness; others may be motivational, such as self-confidence. The latter characteristics can be developed or enhanced through psychological training and experience. The chapters on motivation, stress and coping, anxiety and arousal, and psychological skills interventions will discuss many of these psychological topics in more detail.

Chapter Summary

You were introduced to many ideas in this chapter. From these ideas and concepts, what is known about personality in sport? Most researchers would probably accept the following key points about personality in sport today.

Personality is a very complex subject, and numerous theories represent various conceptual approaches. There has been a shift from grand, or global, theories toward more specific key aspects of personality. Investigations and viewpoints are influenced by the particular conceptualizations of personality. These conceptualizations range from psychodynamic, to humanistic, to social learning, to trait theories. Furthermore, researchers are investigating how specific personality factors interact with other psychological factors, like motivation, in specific athletic contexts.

Measurement of personality requires careful ethical considerations. There are various means to assess an athlete's personality, including the use of projective and objectives tests. Sport researchers have utilized both general objective personality tests and sport-specific tests. Personality tests should be administered and interpreted only by individuals with appropriate qualifications. Personality tests should not be used to select athletes for teams or positions within teams.

There is no distinct athletic personality. Athletes have varied personality profiles. There is little evidence that a specific personality profile describes successful athletes. Personality, however, will interact with the competition environment to influence behaviour, cognitions, and emotions.

There is no consistent personality trait profile that separates one group of athletes from another group: team from individual sport, contact from non-contact, successful from unsuccessful. Furthermore, no consistent personality trait separates athletes from non-athletes. Studies that find statistically significant group differences in a particular trait or a cluster of personality traits tend to find that the differences are small (practically meaningless). In many cases the findings of these studies cannot be replicated. However, large individual differences in personality traits are commonly found.

Some aspects of personality can be shaped by experience. This implies that sport can change personality. However, research indicates that sport has little impact on core personality traits. This research finding may be due to two reasons. First, to determine the long-term impact of sport on personality would require extensive longitudinal research covering many years. Such research does not exist. Second, many youths enter intensive competitive sport in later adolescence. They bring many years of socialization that have already had a major influence on their personality development. Coaches are likely to have more success shaping the specific role behaviours of athletes.

Personality can influence the behaviours of individual athletes in various contexts. Predicting the strength of personality influence on specific behaviours across athletes or even within a specific athlete across multiple events is often difficult, because of contextual and unstable personal factors. Contextual factors include sociocultural norms, the culture and structure of a given sport, and the specific dynamics within a particular sporting event. Unstable personal factors might be physiological states, emotional states, psychological strategies, and motivation. These latter factors will be covered in the following chapters.

Review Questions

1. How does the definition of *personality* differ from that of *disposition*?
2. Explain the three components of personality according to Hollander (1976).
3. Compare and contrast the humanistic perspective with the trait perspective of personality. Why do you think the trait perspective has had a greater impact on research in sport psychology?
4. What is the interactionist approach to personality in sport?
5. What are the differences between projective tests and objectives tests of personality?

6. What are the advantages of sport-specific tests of personality?
7. List the ethical considerations for using personality tests in sport settings.
8. Can a personality test tell you which athletes are going to be successful in a specific sport? Why or why not?
9. What are the differences between competitiveness and sensation seeking?
10. What are the differences between maladaptive and adaptive perfectionism?
11. List the attributes of mental toughness. Try to identify an athlete who has demonstrated all or most of these attributes.

Suggested Reading

Vanden Auweele, Y., Nys, K., Rzewnicki, R., & Van Mele, V. (2001). Personality and the athlete. In R. N. Singer, H. A. Hausenblas, & C. M. Janelle (Eds.), *Handbook of sport psychology* (2nd ed., pp. 239–268). New York: Wiley.

Vealey, R. S. (2002). Personality and sport behavior. In T. Horn (Ed.), *Advances in sport psychology* (2nd ed., pp. 43–82). Champaign, IL: Human Kinetics.

References

Acevedo, E. O., Gill, D., & Dzewaltowski, D. A. (1987, September). *Sport-specific psychological characteristics of ultramarathoners*. Paper presented at the annual conference of the Association for the Advancement of Applied Sport Psychology, Newport Beach, CA.

Anshel, M. H. (2003). *Sport psychology: From theory to practice*. (4th ed.). San Francisco: Benjamin Cummings.

Anshel, M. H., & Eom, H. J. (2003). Exploring the dimensions of perfectionism in sport. *International Journal of Sport Psychology, 34*, 255–271.

Bandura, A. (1977). *Social learning theory*. New York: General Learning Press.

Bandura, A. (1997). *Self-efficacy: The exercise of control*. New York: W. H. Freeman.

Butkovic, A., & Bratko, D. (2003). Generation and sex differences in sensation seeking: results of the family study. *Perceptual and Motor Skills, 97*, 965–970.

Carver, C. S., & Scheier, M. F. (2000). *Perspectives on personality* (4th ed). Boston: Allyn & Bacon.

Cattell, R. B. (1946). *Description and measurement of personality*. New York: Harcourt, Brace & World.

Cattell, R. B. (1995). Personality structure and the new fifth edition of the 16PF. *Educational & Psychological Measurement, 55*, 926–937.

Costa, P. T., Jr., & McCrae, R. R. (1992). The five-factor model of personality and its relevance to personality disorders. *Journal of Personality Disorders, 6*, 343–359.

Costa, P. T., Jr., & McCrae, R. R. (1994). *Neuroticism Extroversion Openness (NEO) Five Factor Inventory*. Lutz, FL: Psychological Assessment Resources.

Davis, H. (1991). Criterion validity of the Athletic Motivation Inventory: Issues in professional sport. *Journal of Applied Sport Psychology, 3*, 176–182.

Dunham, J. M., Dunn, J. G. H., & Hogg, J. M. (2002, October). *Perfectionism and attitudinal body image in competitive female figure skaters*. Paper presented at the annual conference of the Association for the Advancement of Applied Sport Psychology, Tucson, AZ.

Dunn, J. G. H., Causgrove, J., Dunn, J., & Syrotuik, D. G. (2002). Relationship between multidimensional perfectionism and goal orientations in sport. *Journal of Sport & Exercise Psychology, 24*, 376–395.

Dunn, J. G. H., Gotwals, J. K., Causgrove-Dunn, J., & Syrotuik, D. G. (2004). *Examining the relationship between perfectionism and trait anger in competitive sport*. Manuscript submitted for publication.

Durand-Bush, N., & Salmela, J. H. (2002). The development and maintenance of expert athletic performance: Perceptions of World & Olympic Champions. *Journal of Applied Sport Psychology, 14*, 154–171.

Endler, N. S., & Magnusson, D. (1976). Toward an interactional psychology of personality. *Psychological Bulletin, 83,* 956–974.

Etzel, E., Yura, M. T., & Perna, F. (1998). Ethics in assessment and testing in sport and exercise psychology. In J. L. Duda (Ed.), *Advances in sport and exercise psychology measurement* (pp. 423–432). Morgantown, WV: Fitness Information Technology.

Eysenck, H. J., & Eysenck, S. B. J. (1964). *Manual of the Eysenck Personality Inventory.* London: University of London Press.

Eysenck, H. J., & Eysenck, S. B. J. (1975). *Manual for the Eysenck Personality Questionnaire.* San Diego, CA: EdITS.

Flett, G. L., & Hewitt, P. L. (2002). Perfectionism and maladjustment: An overview of theoretical delinational, and treatment issues. In G. L. Flett & P. L. Hewitt (Eds.). *Perfectionism: Theory, research, and treatment* (pp. 5–31). Washington, DC: American Psychological Association.

Frost, R. O., & Henderson, K. J. (1991). Perfectionism and reactions to athletic competition. *Journal of Sport & Exercise Psychology, 13,* 323–335.

Frost, R. O., Marten, P., Lahart, C., & Rosenblate, R. (1990). The dimensions of perfectionism. *Cognitive Therapy and Research, 14,* 449–468.

Gill, D. L., & Deeter, T. E. (1988). Development of the sport orientation questionnaire. *Research Quarterly for Exercise and Sport, 59,* 191–202.

Gill, D. L., & Dzewaltowski, D.A. (1988). Competitive orientations among intercollegiate athletes: Is winning the only thing? *The Sport Psychologist, 2,* 212–221.

Goldberg, A. S. (1998). *Sports slump busting: 10 steps to mental toughness and peak performance.* Champaign, IL: Human Kinetics.

Gould, D., Dieffenbach, K., & Moffett, A. (2002). Personal characteristics and their development in Olympic Champions. *Journal of Applied Sport Psychology, 14,* 172–204.

Gould, D., Hodge, K., Peterson, K., & Petlichkoff, L. (1987). Psychological foundations of coaching: Similarities and differences among intercollegiate wrestling coaches. *The Sport Psychologist, 1,* 293–308.

Gould, D., Tuffey, S., Udry, E., & Loehr, J. (1997). Burnout in competitive junior tennis players: III. Individual differences in the burnout experience. *The Sport Psychologist, 11,* 257–276.

Hall, H. K., Kerr, A. W., & Matthews, J. (1998). Pre-competitive anxiety in sport: The contribution of achievement goals and perfectionism. *Journal of Sport & Exercise Psychology, 20,* 194–217.

Hathaway, S. R., & McKinley, J. C. (1943). *Manual for the Minnesota Multiphasic Personality Inventory.* New York: Psychological Corporation.

Hathaway, S. R., McKinley, J.C., & Butcher, J. N. (1989). *MMPI-2, Minnesota Multiphasic Personality Inventory-2: User's guide.* Minneapolis, MN: National Computer Systems.

Hollander, E. P. (1976). *Principles and methods of social psychology.* New York: Oxford University Press.

Houston, J. M., Carter, D., & Smithers, R. D. (1997). Competitiveness in elite professional athletes. *Perceptual and Motor Skills, 84,* 1447–1454.

Hughes, S. L., Case, H. S., Stuempfle, K. J., & Evans, D. S. (2003). Personality profiles of Iditasport ultra-marathon participants. *Journal of Applied Sport Psychology, 15,* 256–261.

Jones, G., Hanton, S., & Connaughton, D. (2002). What is this thing called mental toughness? An investigation of elite sports performers. *Journal of Applied Sport Psychology, 14,* 205–218.

Krane, V., Greenleaf, C. A., & Snow, J. (1997). Reaching for gold and the price of glory: A motivational case study of an elite gymnast. *Journal of Sport & Exercise Psychology, 19,* 53–71.

Kroll, W. (1967). Sixteen personality factor profiles of collegiate wrestlers. *Research Quarterly, 38,* 49–57.

Lazarus, R. S., & Folkman, S. (1984). *Stress, appraisal and coping.* New York: Springer.

Lewin, K. (1935). *A dynamic theory of personality.* New York: McGraw-Hill.

Loehr, J. E. (1995). *The new toughness training for sports.* New York: Plume.

Malone, C. (1985). Risk-taking in sport. In L. K. Bunker, R. J. Rotella, & A. S. Reilly (Eds.), *Sport psychology: Psychological considerations in maximizing sport performance* (pp. 264–281). Ithaca, NY: Mouvement.

Martens, R. (1976). Competition: In need of a theory. In D. M. Landers (Ed.), *Social problems in athletics* (pp. 9–17). Urbana, IL: University of Illinois Press.

Martens, R. (1977). *Sport competition anxiety test.* Champaign, IL: Human Kinetics.

Maslow, A. H. (1943). A theory of human motivation. *Psychological Review, 50,* 370–396.

McNair, D. M., Lorr, M., & Droppleman, L. F. (1971). *Profile of Mood States.* San Diego, CA: Educational and Industrial Testing Service.

McNair, D. M., Lorr, M., & Droppleman, L. F. (1992). *Revised manual for the Profile of Mood States.* San Diego, CA: Educational and Industrial Testing Service.

Morgan, W.P. (1980). Personality dynamics and sport. In R. Suinn (Ed.), *Psychology in sport—methods and application* (pp. 145–155). Minneapolis, MN: Burgess.

Morgan, W. P., & Pollock, M. L. (1977). Psychological characterization of the elite distance runner. *Annals of the New York Academy of Science, 301,* 382–403.

Orlick, T. (1989). Reflections on sport psych consulting with individual and team sport athletes at Summer and Winter Olympic Games. *The Sport Psychologist, 3,* 358–365.

Orlick, T., & Partington, J. (1988). Mental links to excellence. *The Sport Psychologist, 2,* 105–130.

Ostrow, A. C. (1996). *Directory of psychological tests in the sport & exercise sciences.* Morgantown, WV: Fitness Information Technology.

Rhodes, R. E., Courneya, K. E., & Hayduk, L. A. (2002). Does personality moderate the theory of planned behavior in the exercise domain? *Journal of Sport & Exercise Psychology, 24,* 120–132.

Rogers, C. R. (1959). A theory of therapy, personality and interpersonal relationships as developed in the client-centered framework. In S. Koch (Ed.). *Psychology: A study of a science: Vol. III. Formulations of the person and the social context* (pp. 184–256). New York: McGraw-Hill.

Rotter, J. B. (1954). *Social learning and clinical psychology.* New York: Prentice Hall.

Rowley, A. J., Landers, D. M., Kyllo, L. B., & Etnier, J. L. (1995). Does the iceberg profile discriminate between successful and less successful athletes? A meta-analysis. *Journal of Sport & Exercise Psychology, 17,* 185–199.

Skinner, B. F. (1999). *The behavior of organisms: An experimental analysis.* New York: D. Appleton Century. (Original work published 1938).

Thomas, G. C., & Sinclair, G. D. (1978). Relationship between personality and performance of Canadian women intercollegiate basketball players. In *Human performance and behaviour.* Banff, AB: University of Calgary. Retrieved from the SIRC SportDiscus database.

Tutko, T. A., Lyon, L. P., & Ogilvie, B. C. (1969). *Athletic Motivation Inventory.* San Jose, CA: Institute for the Study of Athletic Motivation.

Vallance, J. K. H., & Dunn, J. G. H. (2002, October). *Multidimensional sport-perfectionism and trait anger in competitive youth ice hockey.* Paper presented at the annual conference of the Association for the Advancement of Applied Sport Psychology, Tucson, AZ.

Vanden Auweele, Y., De Cuyper, B., Van Mele, V., & Rzewnicki, R. (1993). Elite performance and personality: From description and prediction to diagnosis and intervention. In R. N. Singer, M. Murphey, & L. K. Tenant (Eds.), *Handbook of research in sport psychology* (pp. 257–289). New York: Macmillan.

Vanden Auweele, Y., Nys, K., Rzewnicki, R., & Van Mele, V. (2001). Personality and the athlete. In R. N. Singer, H. A. Hausenblas, & C. M. Janelle (Eds.), *Handbook of sport psychology* (2nd ed., pp. 239–268). New York: Wiley.

Vealey, R. S. (2002). Personality and sport behaviour. In T. Horn (Ed.), *Advances in sport psychology* (2nd ed., pp. 43–82). Champaign, IL: Human Kinetics.

Wann, D.L. (1997). *Sport psychology.* Upper Saddle River, NJ: Prentice Hall.

Zarevski, P., Marusic, I., Zolotic, S., Bunjevac, T., & Vukosav, Z. (1998). Contribution of Arnett's inventory of sensation seeking and Zuckerman's sensation seeking scale to the differentiation of athletes engaged in high and low risk sports. *Personality and Individual Differences, 25,* 763–768.

Zuckerman, M. (1994). *Behavioral expressions and biosocial bases of sensation seeking.* New York: Cambridge University Press.

David M. Paskevich
Kim D. Dorsch
Meghan H. McDonough
Peter R. E. Crocker

CHAPTER 4

Motivation in Sport

Chapter Objectives

After reading this chapter, you should be able to do the following:

1. Define motivation and its components of direction, intensity, and persistence.

2. Explain the difference between intrinsic and extrinsic motivation.

3. Describe the three general motivation views: trait-centred, situation-centred, and interaction-centred.

4. Discuss key theories and models of motivation, including attribution theory, competence motivation, achievement goal theory, self-efficacy, self-determination theory, and the sport commitment model.

5. Summarize the key guidelines for sport motivation.

Ben and Julie are both 14 years old and play elite-level hockey for the Woodbine Rockets Hockey Club. At school, Ben is an excellent student and often asks the teacher for additional work, all for the satisfaction of learning as much as he can about a particular subject. Ben likes playing hockey, and the most exciting part of the game for him is scoring goals. His parents, particularly his father, have told him since he started playing hockey eight years ago that the only players who get any recognition are the goal scorers. Thus, to increase Ben's goal-scoring production, his father has told Ben that for every goal he scores he will receive five dollars. Ben states, "Hockey is okay, but it's most fun when I score a lot of goals. If I ever want to make it to the next level, I need to be the leading scorer on my team. It has to be my focus."

Julie is an excellent student and is motivated in her studies to get top grades. Julie continually compares herself with her peers and is competitive when doing assignments and in-class work. She is passionate about hockey. After watching Canada win the 2002 Olympic gold medal, Julie set her sights on trying to make the national team. She works extremely hard in practice and is truly committed to developing the skills needed to become an elite hockey player. Julie states, "I love the game of hockey and want to be the best I can be. I realize that it's going to take a lot of hard work and practice. My parents are very supportive of my goals, and my coaches always try to motivate me; however, I know that if I am to realize my dream that it's up to me. I have to be the one who takes responsibility and does the work in order to realize MY dream."

Ben, whose focus is on scoring goals and winning games, seems to be losing interest halfway through the hockey season. His goal-scoring production is down, and his team has been losing more than winning. When Ben is at the rink, he seems down, and unless he scores a goal early in the game, his effort is greatly reduced. He has become more critical of his teammates recently for not "getting him the puck." When Ben's team does win, he is not excited for his teammates unless he has scored at least one goal, and in many instances he resents the fact that others on the team have had greater success.

Julie, whose focus has been on the development and refinement of her hockey skills, is really enjoying her season. Though her team has had only moderate success, Julie has identified weaknesses in her game and has striven in both practices and games to increase her abilities. Her goal is to become the best player she can be. By pushing herself and her teammates, she sees progress at both the individual and team level, and she takes great pride in seeing these positive changes.

The above vignette shows that both Ben's and Julie's efforts and interests seem to be related to the activities they are engaged in. You should also notice that both Ben and Julie are motivated by shared and unique motives. Some people use the term *motivated* as a descriptor, as in saying that Ben is a highly motivated student. Others may refer to motivation as coming from an external source: for example, Ben has to receive five dollars to get him interested in scoring goals. Yet a third reference to motivation would be as an explanation of an individual's behaviour; for example, Julie is a consistently hard worker in order to reach her dream of playing hockey for Canada.

The above scenario raises a number of questions when we consider motivation in sport. Is the motivation of an athlete consistent across situations, or can athletes be differentially motivated in various contexts, like sport and school? Can an athlete's level of motivation predict sport performance? What are the factors that affect motivated behaviour? Is there a distinct motivational style that will allow an athlete to be successful in sport? Does internal motivation interact with external motivators to influence sporting behaviour? For that matter, what is motivation? In this chapter, we will address these and several other questions related to motivation in sport.

Some Common Myths about Motivation in Sport

MYTH: *Money is the ideal way to motivate an individual.*
Money can be, and has definitely been, used as a motivator (have you ever done something only because you were paid for it?). However, it is only one form of motivator and in some instances will not be successful, regardless of the amount. Many elite athletes have retired, despite being offered millions of dollars to continue their career. Furthermore, many amateur athletes train long hours in obscurity with few financial incentives.

MYTH: *A focus on winning provides the greatest motivation.*
In sport, particularly Olympic and professional sport, winning is a primary objective. Many athletes aspire to be on the podium or to win a championship. That being said, having a singular focus on winning can have a negative impact. Staying focused only on winning during the Olympics (or any other competition) may drain an athlete physically and emotionally. As you will see later in the chapter, there are multiple ways to define success, and multiple internal and external factors motivate athletes.

MYTH: *Either you have it (motivation) or you don't.*
Some coaches seem to think that motivation in sport is something an athlete is born with or that motivation is very difficult to change. As the story goes, basketball great Michael Jordan was cut from his high-school basketball team. Did he not "have it"? Athletes do have personal characteristics that will influence motivated behaviour. Some of these characteristics are more changeable than others. Furthermore, research indicates that coaches can create learning and competitive environments that enhance motivation and performance over time.

Introduction

The subject of motivation in sport raises many important questions. Why do people participate, and why do some people stop? What factors influence effort and persistence in sport? For many coaches, if they could ask a sport psychologist one question, it would be "How do I motivate my athletes?" Exercise instructors and fitness club owners ask "How do we motivate people to keep exercising?" Physiotherapists often ask "How do we motivate our clients to complete their rehabilitation program?" Motivation is one of the most fundamental topics in sport and exercise psychology.

Understanding motivation is a key factor in maximizing human performance and positive emotions in sport. If you think back on your own sporting experiences, you may have come across many talented teammates or opponents who never seemed to maximize their potential. Were they uncaring and lazy? Perhaps there was another reason. Likewise, you may have known (or perhaps even been) the athlete who had only marginal talent yet was able to perform at a level superior to more talented others. Thus, understanding the construct of motivation and having the ability to motivate yourself and others (e.g., as a teammate, coach, or parent) may make the difference between being good and being great.

To facilitate understanding the concept of motivation, we must first define it and its behavioural indices; then we will examine several major theories and models that explore the relationship between motivation and sport participation and performance. Unlike other chapters, we will not review measurement in motivation because, as you will see, there are numerous motivational variables and associated concepts. For the

Understanding motivation in sport is critical to maximizing performance and enjoyment.
Photo courtesy of Zoran Milich/Masterfile.

interested student, several books cover the measurement of motivation in sport and exercise (see Duda, 1998; Roberts, 2001).

Defining Motivation

In the sport psychology literature, there are various ways to define **motivation**. Under the umbrella term *motivation*, several specific forms—including achievement motivation, competence motivation, intrinsic motivation, and extrinsic motivation—have been identified. From a literal perspective, the word *motivation* is derived from the Latin root *movere*, which means "to move." Vallerand and Thill (1993) have defined motivation as "the hypothetical construct used to describe the internal and/or external forces that produce the initiation, direction, and persistence of behaviour" (p. 18, translated from French). This definition directs our attention to the three important components of motivation: direction, intensity, and persistence.

Direction, Intensity, and Persistence of Motivation

Before one attempts interventions designed to facilitate motivation, it is important to have a theoretical understanding of the construct, and we will start with a focus on direction, intensity, and persistence. The **direction of effort** in relation to motivation refers to those situations that an athlete seeks out, approaches, or is attracted to. For example, athletes can make decisions about which of many types of activities to engage in. What makes some activities more attractive, and what would cause an athlete to disengage from sport?

The amount of effort one is willing to put forth in a particular situation or event is termed **intensity of effort**. An athlete may play for the varsity soccer team (direction of effort); however, in practices and games she does not put forth much effort.

Conversely, a hockey player who finds himself in the seventh game of a playoff series may direct too much intensity of effort and try to do too much. You, as a student, are likely to choose to take certain classes, yet you might have tremendous variation in the intensity of effort with which you participate in different classes and study for exams.

Persistence refers to maintaining intensity of effort over a continuous period. High-level success requires persistent effort over multiple occasions. Persistence is also critical when an athlete encounters obstacles. Opponents might utilize specific tactics to counteract an athlete's skills. The athlete might lose focus or emotional control, or conversely, might search for solutions to maximize individual or team performance. During a season, an athlete may encounter many obstacles, including injuries and illness, poor weather, coaching decisions, questionable referee decisions, and difficult opponents. Understanding why some athletes persist in intensity and direction is a key aspect of understanding motivation.

Intrinsic and Extrinsic Motivation

Intrinsic motivation applies to behaviours that we engage in because of interest and enjoyment. For example, if you belong to a rowing club and row because you enjoy the experience of just rowing, you find it is interesting, and you derive a tremendous sense of pleasure from it, you would be rowing for intrinsic reasons. You want to learn how to row to the best of your ability, have fun, and take pride in the gains that you make. Intrinsic motivation is a powerful force since the athlete does not need to be enticed by external motivators.

In contrast, **extrinsic motivation** applies to behaviours that we engage in to attain rewards or outcomes that lie outside the activity itself. If the main reason you row is to win the club rowing regatta at year's end, you would be extrinsically motivated. The use of extrinsic rewards is extensive in the world of sport. Ribbons, medals, trophies, and money are all examples of extrinsic rewards.

Reflections 4.1
Extrinsic rewards, such as medals, are a central feature of competitive sport; however, athletes still compete for intrinsic reasons. Think of your own experiences in sport. Did you start playing sport for intrinsic reasons? Did the reasons change as you continued to play? If you have remained in sport, what motivates you now?

Photo courtesy of CP/Frank Gunn.

Sources of Motivation

Why does one athlete seem more motivated than a teammate, and what might contribute to this motivated state? Why is one coach more successful than his or her peers when motivating athletes? More fundamentally, where does motivation come from?

You will recall from Chapter 3 on personality in sport that there are various views in the study of sport behaviour. Likewise, there are various views about the sources of motivation. Some researchers have focused on what the athlete brings to the situation. This is often referred to as the **trait-centred view**. Other researchers have argued that environmental factors are critical; this is the **situation-centred view** of sport motivation. The third view recognizes that sport motivation is best explained by an interaction between personal and environmental factors; it is termed the **interaction-centred view** (Anshel, 2003; Duda, 1993; Roberts, 1993).

In the trait-centred view (also called the participant-centred view) the primary sources of motivation are thought to be personal dispositions or individual characteristics of the athlete. Personal attributes, such as levels of perceived ability, achievement goal orientation, competitiveness, perfectionism, self-confidence, and optimism, can explain individual differences in intensity, direction, and persistence in sport. There is no doubt that these personal factors are an important component of motivation, but most sport psychologists would be reluctant to endorse solely personal factors.

The situation-centred view proposes that motivation levels are primarily determined by key features in the environment. This view holds that external conditions produce motivation and play a more important role in determining motivation than do personality traits or personal factors. For example, in the opening vignette, Ben was highly motivated to perform well in school; however, when he wasn't scoring goals while playing hockey, his level of motivation in hockey decreased. This suggests differences in the environment are important. There are a number of potential situational variables that can affect an athlete's motivational level, including coach and parent feedback, training conditions, playing at home versus playing on the road, weather conditions, type of activity, friends, extrinsic rewards, and difficulty of skills and opponents. By manipulating the athletic training and competitive environment, coaches should be able to facilitate (or debilitate) any athlete's direction, intensity, and persistence of effort. However, it seems naive to believe that an athlete's personal characteristics play no role in sport motivation. Most sport psychologists would not endorse solely environmental factors.

Most sport psychologists would state that the best way to understand motivation is by examining the interaction of personal characteristics with the situation, rather than by examining either factor alone. This participant-by-situation view is referred to as the interaction-centred view. Knowing only an athlete's personal characteristics and not acknowledging the importance of the situation (or vice-versa) could seriously limit our ability to describe, explain, or predict sport motivation.

An example of the interaction-centred view can be found in Anshel's (1995) work with elite and non-elite male swimmers. In the elite group, he found a combination of high achievement needs, intrinsic motivation, and extreme commitment (participant-centred) along with situation factors, such as strong parental support, positive and trustworthy feedback from the coach, and the use of coaching feedback. Thus, if we truly want to understand motivated behaviour in sport, we must examine the interaction of personal factors and situational factors (see Figure 4.1 on next page.)

Reflections 4.2
Think of a recent situation in which you demonstrated high intensity of effort. Why were you so motivated? What personal and situational variables were at play?

Figure 4.1   Example of an interactional view of motivation

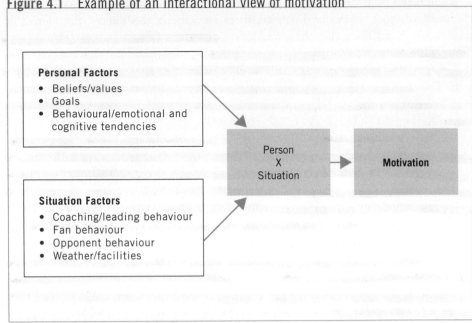

Theories and Models of Motivation

A number of theories and approaches have evolved over the years to help describe, explain, and predict what motivates athletes to behave the way they do. There are more than 30 different theories that have been applied to sport motivation (Roberts, 2001). Descriptions of all these theories would overwhelm even the most motivated undergraduate student. We have selected several theories and models that emphasize a cognitive-evaluative perspective. These theories have been very popular in sport research and practice over the last 25 years. We will cover only the basic principles of the theories, so students should appreciate that the theories are far more complex than presented here.

Attribution Theory

In the 2004 Canadian Golf Open, Mike Weir failed to hold a multiple-stroke lead over Vijay Singh and lost in a playoff. In the 2002 Olympics, the Canadian men's and women's hockey teams both won gold. What do you think caused these outcomes: luck, ability, effort, mental skills, opponent's ability and effort, weather, crowd support or noise, or officials? How do you think the athletes felt, and, maybe more importantly, how would the events affect their future motivation? **Attribution theory focuses on how individuals explain success and failure.** The type of attribution with which athletes explain their successes and failures directly affects motivation and emotion. Two researchers, Heider (1958) and Weiner (1985, 1986), have contended that literally thousands of possible explanations (or *attributions*) for success and failure can be classified into a few categories. Attribution research in sport has been dominated by Weiner's model of achievement attributions.

DIMENSIONS OF ATTRIBUTION   Early work by Weiner, Frieze, Kukla, Reed, Rest, & Rosenbaum (1971) suggested that the causes of success and failure fall into four categories: ability, task difficulty, effort, and luck. These achievement attributions could be classified along two attribution dimensions: stability and locus of causality. The **stability** dimension refers to the extent to which the attributed quality is relatively enduring or stable over time. For example, factors that would be considered relatively stable include personal ability and task difficulty. When compared with more variable or unstable factors, such as one's effort or luck, it can be seen that an athlete's ability will not change dramatically over a short span of time nor would the difficulty of a task change dramatically in a short time period. **Locus of causality** refers to whether the attributed quality is internal or external to the athlete. Factors, such as one's ability and effort, are internal to the athlete while external attributes would include task difficulty and luck.

In 1979, Weiner added the controllability dimension. The dimension of **controllability** differentiated between factors that are under one's control, such as one's effort, and those factors that are not under one's control, such as illness. Thus, current attribution theory is set into three dimensions: stability, locus of causality, and controllability (see Figure 4.2).

The importance of attributions is that they may affect an athlete's motivation and performance outcome. Weiner (1986) argued that the stability of attributions should affect the athlete's expectations regarding future success. Stable attributions lead to an increased certainty that future outcomes will be positive (versus unstable attributions that lead to greater uncertainty). Let's go back to the Mike Weir example. If he believed the outcome was due to stable factors (his ability or Vijay Singh's ability), he might expect similar results in the future. However, if the outcome was attributed to more unstable factors (a bear hug from a fan on an earlier hole or some poor shot decisions), then he might expect different results in the future. Obviously, athletes can attribute a particular success or failure to several factors that can vary in stability, controllability, and locus of causality. These will all combine to affect future motivated behaviour.

SPORT RESEARCH EVIDENCE ABOUT ATTRIBUTION THEORY   Research on attribution theory has found that sport participants tend to attribute winning to internal causes (e.g., ability and effort) but attribute losing to external causes (e.g., luck and task difficulty; Bukowski & Moore, 1980). However, *perceptions* of success or failure are

Figure 4.2   Three causal dimensions and representative attributions based on Weiner's model of attribution

		LOCUS OF CAUSALITY			
		INTERNAL		EXTERNAL	
	STABILITY	Stable	Unstable	Stable	Unstable
CONTROLLABILITY	Controllable	Individual's Stable Effort	Individual's Unstable Effort	Others' Stable Effort	Others' Unstable Effort
	Uncontrollable	Ability	Illness	Task Difficulty	Luck

better predictors of attributions than are winning or losing (Spink & Roberts, 1980). In other words, perceived outcomes are more important predictors of attributions than objective outcomes. A number of studies have linked attributions to emotional outcomes, but the findings of these studies have not fully supported attribution theory. Attributions are weak predictors of emotions, and particular attributions are not linked with specific emotions (Graham, Kowalski, & Crocker, 2002; McAuley & Duncan, 1989; Vlachopoulos, Biddle, & Fox, 1996). One of the most consistent findings about attributions has been support for the **self-serving bias**. This bias suggests that athletes will tend to attribute outcomes more to internal causes when they are successful and more to external causes when they are unsuccessful. The self-serving bias hypothesis has been generally supported; however, it is more of a difference of degree than of attributional pattern. All athletes tend to use internal, controllable attributions in general, but in conditions of success they tend to score higher on the internal and controllable dimensions than in conditions of failure (Mullen & Riordan, 1988).

Theory of Competence Motivation

Children seem to have an inherent need to master their surroundings. White (1959) argued that behaviour is directed, selective, and owing to "an intrinsic need to deal (effectively) with the environment" (p. 318); he called this concept **effectance motivation**. Susan Harter (1978, 1982) concluded that individuals are innately motivated to be competent in all areas of human achievement, with sport being one such area. Her theory of effectance, or theory of competence motivation, provides a framework for examining children's and adolescents' motivation. Basically, this theory holds that perceptions of one's competence and control in a particular activity that is perceived as valuable or important will produce motivation to continue participating in that activity. Harter's theory has had a major impact on sport research on children and adolescents (see Weiss & Williams, 2004).

A key aspect of Harter's (1982) ideas on competence motivation was that self-concept was multidimensional; that is, people have a number of domains that compose their sense of self. In children, these include social, athletic, physical appearance, behavioural conduct, and academic domains (see Figure 4.3). As people mature cognitively, the number of domains increase and become more differentiated to include such areas as romantic appeal, close friendships, and job competence. Perceptions of

Figure 4.3   The self-perception model for children

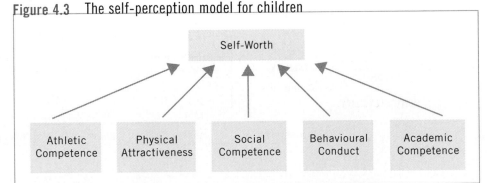

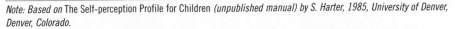

Note: Based on The Self-perception Profile for Children *(unpublished manual) by S. Harter, 1985, University of Denver, Denver, Colorado.*

competence and value in these domains contribute to feelings of self-worth or self-esteem and to motivation to continue pursuing activities in that domain.

Another feature to Harter's theory (1978, 1982) is that perceptions of competence in a particular domain will enhance self-worth and subsequent motivation if the individual values competence in that domain. For example, if an adolescent sees herself as having exceptional athletic skills and values competence in sports, she will have high perceptions of self-worth. If she perceives her athletic competence as low and values sport, her self-worth will be low.

COMPONENTS OF THE COMPETENCE MOTIVATION MODEL   The basic components of Harter's theory (1978, 1982) are shown in Figure 4.4. A young athlete's perceptions of athletic competence and control will lead to emotional states, which combine to facilitate motivation to engage in specific sporting behaviour. If the athlete experiences success in his or her endeavours, then these sporting experiences lead to positive emotional states (e.g., pride, happiness, enjoyment). The sporting experiences will also affect feedback received from significant others (e.g., coaches, parents, teammates) as well as self-evaluation. The result is that, in a cyclical fashion, these feelings and feedback will lead to a recurrent incentive to participate in the sport environment. Equally, those individuals who receive negative evaluations about their personal competence or mastery will have heightened levels of anxiety and other mood disturbances, which would have the impact of reducing motivated behaviour.

The central principle to Harter's theory is that individuals in sport who hold high perceptions of competence and self-control will exert greater effort, persist longer in the face of failure, and experience more positive affect than individuals who hold lower levels of perceived competence. For example, if a young speed skater is training hard and receiving positive feedback in terms of successful attempts and in feelings of competence, this behaviour will result in an increase in pride and happiness. With increased self-confidence, it is likely that this speed skater will continue to participate with increased vigour and motivation.

Harter (1987) modified her basic theory of competence motivation and suggested that perceptions of competence and importance in each domain and social support or positive regard contribute to perceptions of self-worth, which, in turn, lead to affect

Figure 4.4   Basic components of Harter's competence motivation model (1978, 1982)

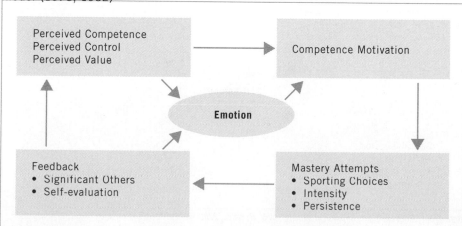

and motivation. Weiss (2000) and Weiss and Ebbeck (1996) adapted Harter's (1987) mediational model of self-worth to explain motivated behaviour in the physical domain. Their model suggests that perceptions of physical competence and social support predict self-esteem, which in turn predicts both sport enjoyment and physical activity behaviour (see Figure 4.5).

SPORT RESEARCH EVIDENCE ABOUT COMPETENCE MOTIVATION   There is a substantial body of research evidence supporting various aspects of the competence motivation theory in sport. There is strong evidence that positive feedback increases

Figure 4.5   Mediational model of global self-esteem customized for the physical domain

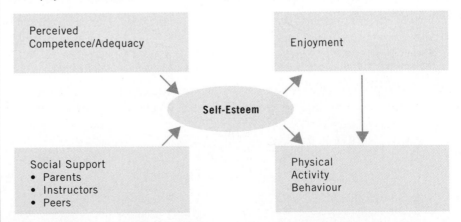

Note: From "Motivating kids in physical activity," by M. R. Weiss, 2000, The President's Council on Physical Fitness and Sports Research Digest, *3, p. 1. Reprinted with permission.*

perceived physical competence and that motivated sport and physical activity behaviour is related to perceptions of athletic and physical competence (see Horn, 2004; Weiss & Williams, 2004). Physical competence and enjoyment are related, and both affect motivated behaviour (Weiss, 1993). Indeed, enjoyment has consistently been found to be a strong predictor of motivated behaviour in children (Crocker, Hoar, McDonough, Kowalski, & Neifer, 2004; Scanlan & Simons, 1992; Scanlan, Carpenter, Schmidt, Simons, & Keeler, 1993; Wankel & Sefton, 1989). Enjoyment is not only related to physical competence but also to personal control, mastery-focused teaching environments, team friendships, pleasing significant others, and being involved in challenging activities (see Crocker et al., 2004; Weiss & Stuntz, 2004). Brustad (1993, 1996) found that parent's behaviour could also influence motivated behaviour. Greater levels of parental encouragement and enjoyment were related to higher perceptions of competence and attraction to physical activity in children.

Unfortunately, Harter's mediational model (1987) is not entirely consistent with the sport research. In a study on middle-school students (12–15 years old), Smith (1999) tested a model based on Harter's mediational model but used measures of physical self-worth and of affect related to physical activity as mediators, rather than global self-esteem and affect. He found that perceptions of social acceptance and having close friends were related to physical self-worth and physical activity-related affect, which predicted 80% of the variance in cognitive motivation (Smith, 1999). McDonough and Crocker (2005) found that sport commitment in female adolescent recreational sports participants was weakly related to global self-worth but was better predicted directly by aspects of sport friendship and physical competence.

Reflections 4.3

If you were coaching a community baseball team, what type of feedback and reinforcement would you provide to your athletes to maximize their perceived competence and sense of control? If one of your athletes were unhappy, could you use the framework of competence motivation theory to help explain the behaviour and plan a course of action that could positively affect the athlete's happiness and enjoyment?

Achievement Goal Theory

Many motivation theories have recognized that success and failure, along with demonstrating ability, are vital features in achievement. Duda (2001) noted there are two central antecedents to achievement motivation: how people evaluate their competence and how people define success and failure. Achievement goal theory tries to account for how individual differences in dealing with these two antecedents influence motivated behaviour (Nicholls, 1989; Roberts, 2001). A central principle in this theory is that a person's achievement behaviour is dependent upon the personal meaning one assigns to perceived success and failure (Maehr & Braskamp, 1986; Maehr and Nicholls, 1980). Although in sport we often think about success and failure as an objective state (determined by score and rankings), achievement goal theory holds that success and failure are *subjective psychological states* (Roberts, 2001). Take the example of Brittany Reimer, 2005 World Aquatics 1500-metre bronze medalist, who stated, "I've worked my butt off for this. I had a bad year last year, [so] I'm just happy I could get up there and go for it this year" ("Reimer swims," 2005, ¶4). How an athlete interprets her or his achievement behaviours in terms of desirable qualities, such as effort and ability, determines the perception of success and subsequent motivated processes (Roberts, 2001).

KEY CONCEPTS OF ACHIEVEMENT GOAL THEORY   There are several key concepts in achievement goal theory. These include conceptions of ability, psychological achievement goal state, dispositional achievement goals, and motivational climate. We will briefly review each of these concepts.

The first key concept of achievement goal theory is that people are motivated to demonstrate ability (competence) and to avoid demonstrating inability (incompetence) (Weiss & Williams, 2004). But what is ability? Nicholls (1980) stated that there are two conceptions of ability. The first is an **undifferentiated concept of ability**, which refers to an inability to, or a choice not to, differentiate between ability and effort. In this sense, working hard is equated with ability. The second type is a **differentiated concept of ability**, which refers to an ability to, or a choice to, differentiate between ability and effort.

There are important developmental aspects to consider in conceptions of ability. The skill to differentiate between ability and effort requires cognitive maturity. Younger children are unable to differentiate among various aspects of achieving a task, for example, among luck, task difficulty, and effort (Fry, 2001; Weiss & Williams, 2004). With cognitive maturity, children by the age of 12 to 13 years are able to differentiate among luck, effort, and task difficulty. This mature understanding of ability allows youth to understand that (a) no amount of effort can change success or failure on luck tasks, (b) ability will limit the impact of effort on performance, and (c) better performance with less effort reflects more ability (Weiss & Williams, 2004).

Concepts of ability reflect the theory's second key concept, the psychological achievement goal state of an athlete. Nicholls (1989) identified state achievement goal behaviour that utilizes the undifferentiated concept of ability as **task involvement**. Athletes in a state of task involvement focus on learning, mastery, and improvement. For example, in the opening vignette, although Julie liked to compete and win hockey games, her focus was on developing her skills to the best of her ability. In this instance, Julie was task involved and getting better each time she was on the ice. In contrast, using a differentiated concept of ability for achievement is called **ego involvement**. Athletes who are ego involved need to demonstrate ability relative to others. Looking for favourable judgments, having superior performance to others (especially with less effort), and focusing on winning an event all reflect ego involvement (Duda, 2001; Roberts, 2001).

The third key concept of the theory relates to dispositional achievement goals. These are goal orientations that are more stable cognitive schemas, and they influence how athletes evaluate situations (Roberts, 2001; Duda, 2001). **Task goal orientation** (sometimes called mastery orientation) reflects a tendency to engage in mastery and skill improvement behaviour. **Ego goal orientation** (sometimes called outcome orientation) reflects the tendency to focus on outcome and being better than others. Goal orientations bias the likelihood that an athlete will become either task or ego involved in a specific situation.

Perceived **motivational climate**, the final key concept of the theory, refers to athletes' perceptions of achievement goals promoted by coaches (and significant others, such as parents). Coaches and instructors can structure the teaching setting to emphasize various achievement goals (Ames, 1992). Environments that stress interpersonal competition, winning, and social comparison tend to evoke ego involvement. On the other hand, an emphasis on mastery learning, effort, individual improvement, and cooperation tends to evoke task involvement (Roberts, 2001; Treasure & Roberts, 1995). Motivational climate combines with developmental factors and goal orientation to produce either an ego or a task involvement (see Figure 4.6).

SPORT RESEARCH EVIDENCE ABOUT ACHIEVEMENT GOAL THEORY   Achievement goal theory has become a prominent motivation theory in sport and exercise (Roberts, 2001). There is a substantial evidence base that says that athletes vary in dispositional task and ego goal orientation and that these orientations affect motivated behaviour (see Duda, 2001; Duda & Hall, 2001). For example, task goal orientation is associated with greater enjoyment and intrinsic motivation (Duda, Chi, Newton, Walliling, & Catley, 1995; Duda, Fox, Biddle, & Armstrong, 1992). There is also evidence that goal orientations predict fair play. For example, in a study of British soccer players, Carpenter & Yates (1997) found that a strong task goal orientation and a low ego goal orientation were negatively associated with willingness to do whatever necessary to win, such as breaking the rules. There is evidence that task goal orientation is characterized by greater effort and higher perceived competence whereas ego goal orientation is associated with lower effort (Duda & Hall, 2001). Although research suggests that coaches should foster task involvement, some research indicates that elite athletes with high competence and high ego goal orientation may not be satisfied with a mastery (task) oriented environment (Hardy, 1997). Overall, the research evidence shows that achievement goal theory provides a good understanding of motivated behaviour in sport.

Figure 4.6   Key factors influencing motivated behaviour in achievement goal theory

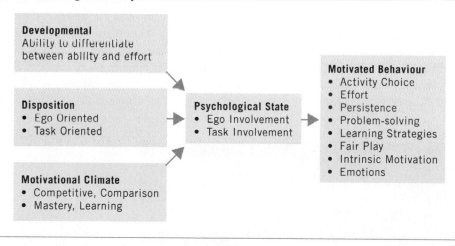

Reflections 4.4
You are the keynote speaker at a coaching conference, and the organization would like you to speak about structuring the coaching environment for youth sport. According to achievement goal theory, what are the important differences between task and ego involvement? Which might be more appropriate for youth settings? How should the coaches you are talking to structure their training programs to develop the type of involvement you have chosen?

Self-efficacy Theory

Many athletes and coaches believe that confidence is a critical factor for successful sport performance. Self-confidence is one of the most frequently cited psychological factors thought to affect athletic performance (Feltz, 1992; Hardy, Jones, & Gould, 1996; Manzo, 2002). As Canadian golfer Lorie Kane commented about the mental attitude of fellow golfers Annika Sorenstam and Karrie Webb, "Maybe they won't win every week, but having that attitude and feeling the confidence that that attitude brings definitely raises your play and just makes everything a little easier" ("Lori Kane chosen," n.d., ¶8). Therefore, it is hardly surprising that sport researchers are highly interested in the motivational aspects of self-confidence.

A prominent theory in sport and exercise self-confidence research is Bandura's (1986, 1997) self-efficacy theory. In sport and exercise settings, self-confidence can be conceptualized in varying ways, ranging from trait sport confidence (Vealey, 1986), through perceived ability in specific domains like sport (Harter, 1987), to confidence in specific sporting situations (Bandura, 1997; Feltz & Chase, 1998). However, Bandura suggests that **self-efficacy**, or situational self-confidence, is the best predictor of motivated behaviour. Athletes with high self-efficacy would work harder, show greater persistence when facing adversity, and be more likely to participate and have better performance (Feltz & Lirgg, 2001; Standage & Duda, 2004).

Self-efficacy refers to "beliefs in one's capabilities to organize and execute the courses of action required to produce given attainments" (Bandura, 1997, p. 3). Self-efficacy is not about the skills a person possesses but about a person's beliefs that he or she will be able to produce a specific outcome with those skills. For example, a high jumper may have very good technical and physical skills and is able to perform very well in practice settings. Nevertheless, what is the strength of the athlete's self-efficacy belief when faced with clearing a 2.0-metre bar in front of 5000 fans to win a gold medal in a provincial championship? Self-efficacy can also indirectly influence performance (and other self-regulated actions) through its positive effects on setting personal goals and developing performance strategies (Dawson, Gyurcsik, Culos-Reed, and Brawley, 2001; Kane, Marks, Zaccaro, & Blair, 1996; Poag & McAuley, 1992)

Efficacy beliefs should not be confused with **outcome expectations**, which are related to expected consequences associated with specific behaviour. In the high jump

> An athlete's self-efficacy beliefs can have a major impact on successful performance.

Photograph by Richard Lam, courtesy of University of British Columbia Athletics.

scenario, the athlete's successful completion of the jump might be associated with outcome expectations of social recognition, self-satisfaction, a gold medal, and an invitation to the national team. Both efficacy beliefs and outcome expectations combine to affect motivated behaviour.

INFLUENCES ON SELF-EFFICACY   An attractive feature of Bandura's theory is that self-efficacy beliefs can be changed. An athlete's self-efficacy is determined from a complex evaluation of personal and environmental factors. There are four sources of information that will influence the perception of self-efficacy: enactive mastery experience, vicarious experiences, verbal persuasion, and physiological and affective states (see Figure 4.7). **Enactive mastery experience** refers to previous performances that could influence one's belief in his or her capability to repeat such actions in a similar setting. Success in similar situations will enhance self-efficacy and, not surprisingly, is the most influential source of self-efficacy information. **Vicarious experiences** occur when athletes compare themselves with others who have similar skills and attributes. **Verbal persuasion** include self-talk and encouragement from coaches and significant others. Finally, **physiological and affective states** refer to the physical and emotional cues associated with different performances.

SPORT RESEARCH EVIDENCE ABOUT SELF-EFFICACY THEORY   The sport research has generally supported Bandura's self-efficacy theory in a variety of settings (e.g., Earley & Lituchy, 1991; Feltz, 1988; Kane et al., 1996; Lirgg & Feltz, 1991; Theodorakis, 1995; Treasure, Monson, & Lox, 1996) although most research has examined relationships between performance and self-efficacy. A meta-analysis based on 45 studies reported a moderate relationship between self-efficacy and performance (Moritz,

Figure 4.7   Relationship among sources of efficacy information, efficacy beliefs, and consequences

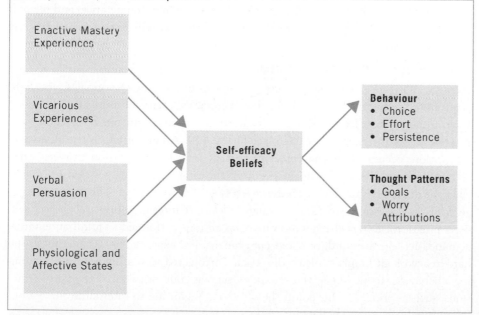

Feltz, Fahrbach, & Mack, 2000). Furthermore, self-efficacy theory has been applied in many physical activity settings, including in exercise and rehabilitation across the life-span (see McAuley & Blissmer, 2002; Standage & Duda, 2004). Research also indicates that there is a reciprocal relationship between self-efficacy and sport and exercise behaviour (Feltz & Lirgg, 2001; McAuley & Katula, 1998). That is, self-efficacy can enhance motivated behaviour, which in turn can enhance self-efficacy. Unfortunately, the same reciprocal relationship can also undermine self-efficacy beliefs.

In closing, self-efficacy theory has identified important factors in understanding motivation in sport, such as performance accomplishments and vicarious experiences. It suggests that self-confidence can be enhanced, but it will take time and systematic intervention.

Reflections 4.5

A coach asks you for advice to enhance his swimmer's self-confidence. Use Bandura's self-efficacy theory to develop some basic guidelines. Do you think that you can change the swimmer's confidence in a short period?

Self-determination Theory

The theories reviewed thus far indicate that perceptions of ability, task demands, inter-personal factors, and feedback can affect motivated behaviour in sport and exercise. Another influential theory, self-determination theory (Deci & Ryan, 1985, 1991; Ryan & Deci, 2002), ties many of these factors together with psychological needs. The theory has two main concepts that work together to explain motivated behaviour: (1) that motivation is a multidimensional construct and (2) that the type of motivation an athlete experiences in a sporting situation will be determined by how well the situation meets that person's basic psychological needs for autonomy, competence, and related-ness (Deci & Ryan, 1991). Since the theory is complex, we will first discuss each of the above two concepts.

THE MOTIVATIONAL CONTINUUM Throughout this chapter, intrinsic and extrinsic motivation have been portrayed as two discrete motivational states. Self-determination theory, however, holds that there are six types of motivation, lying on a continuum from least self-determined, or externally controlled, to most self-determined, or internally controlled (see Figure 4.8). **Amotivation**, or the absence of motivation, occurs when one perceives that there is no connection between one's actions and outcomes. This might occur when an athlete perceives that no matter what she does, it has no impact on the coach's decision to play her. The next four types are forms of extrinsic motivation but range in levels of internalization and choice (self-determination). **External regulation** involves actions performed to fulfill an external demand, achieve a reward, or avoid punishment. For example, an athlete might run hard in a workout simply to please the coach. **Introjected regulation** involves perform-ing a behaviour to avoid negative emotions, such as guilt, or to enhance positive emo-tions, such as pride. At this point, the athlete is beginning to internalize the reasons for personal behaviour (Vallerand, 2001).

Identified regulation occurs when sporting behaviour is linked to personal impor-tance and value. Now the athlete runs hard in practice because she or he has made a

Figure 4.8 The motivational continuum

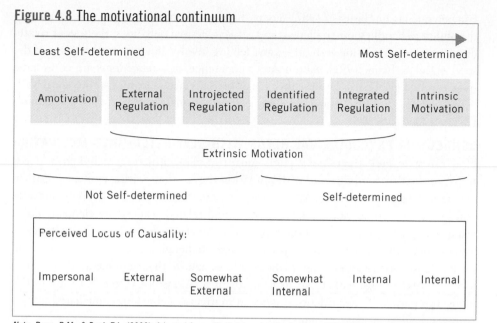

Note: Ryan, R.M., & Deci, E.L. (2000). Adapted from: "Self-determination theory and the facilitation of intrinsic motivation, social development, and well-being." American Psychologist, 55, 68–78. Copyright © 2000 by the American Psychological Association. Adapted with permission.

choice and believes that running hard has personal importance beyond external factors. **Integrated regulation** involves making choices about behaviours that are part of the whole self. For example, an athlete might decide not to drink and dance at a social outing because she perceives herself to be an athlete and wants to be at her best for the upcoming competition.

Intrinsic motivation is involved when an athlete performs a behaviour because it is inherently satisfying, interesting, or enjoyable. Work out of the University of Ottawa (Pelletier, Fortier, Vallerand, Tuson, Brière, & Blais, 1995) has further subdivided intrinsic motivation into three types. These are **intrinsic motivation to know**, performing a behaviour for the sake of learning, exploring, or understanding something new; **intrinsic motivation to accomplish**, participating for the satisfaction of striving to improve upon one's personal best performances and achieve new personal objectives; and **intrinsic motivation to experience stimulation**, engaging in an activity to experience sensations such as sensory pleasure, aesthetic experience, fun, excitement, and so on.

Reflections 4.6
Consider your involvement in sport or exercise. Were there aspects of your behaviour that involved the various types of motivation? Did these change over time or across situations?

THE THREE PSYCHOLOGICAL NEEDS   Self-determination theory proposes there are three basic psychological needs: autonomy, competence, and relatedness (Deci & Ryan, 1985). The need for **autonomy** is met when athletes feel they have choices and are in control of their own behaviour. The need for autonomy is considered the most important for self-determination. Athletes must feel that they have some power and choice in sport in order to feel their behaviour is internally controlled. Feelings of

competence, as in Harter's (1987) model, happen when athletes perceive they have the ability to handle sport challenges and achieve desired outcomes. Feelings of **relatedness** involve connecting with others and feeling involved in the social context of the sport (Deci & Ryan, 1991). Autonomy, competence, and relatedness are considered basic psychological needs because they are universally necessary for psychological well-being and for the growth and development of personality and cognitive structures (Ryan & Deci, 2002).

CONNECTING PSYCHOLOGICAL NEEDS WITH SELF-DETERMINED MOTIVATION

How can sport best structure the environment to allow athletes' psychological needs to be satisfied? According to self-determination theory, the sporting context is critical (Frederick-Recasicino, 2002). When specific elements are present in sport, athletes will be able to feel autonomous, competent, and related. Autonomy elements allow athletes to make choices about training and competitive behaviour. Competence is enhanced by the achievement of personal and challenging goals and informational feedback. Relatedness is enhanced when athletes believe that significant others in the sport context engage with them in meaningful relationships (Deci & Ryan, 1991). Thus, the impact of the athletic context on motivated behaviour is mediated in part by psychological needs (see Figure 4.9).

The satisfaction of psychological needs is more likely to be associated with self-determined forms of motivation. For example, if athletes feel they have a choice over competitive behaviours, demonstrate competence, and feel socially accepted by teammates and coaches, then they will more likely have a self-determined type of motivation to engage in sporting behaviour. However, athletes can still feel competent (and related to others) without necessarily being self-determined. In an attempt to maximize team success, many coaches control athletes' behaviour in training and competition. Although this might increase success and increase the coach's sense of self-determination (since he or she is making all the choices), it might undermine the athlete's autonomy and self-determined motivation, reduce cognitive involvement, and produce negative emotions.

EFFECTS OF FEEDBACK ON SELF-DETERMINATION
A key feature of sport is that there is constant feedback on performance and other behaviour. This feedback includes external rewards (trophies), event outcomes (win/loss, rankings, performance times), verbal and nonverbal feedback from coaches and significant others, and information available from social comparisons with peers. Typically, one would think that positive feedback would enhance self-determined behaviour whereas negative feedback would have the opposite effect. As Deci and colleagues (Deci & Ryan, 1985;

Figure 4.9 The motivational sequence proposed by self-determination theory

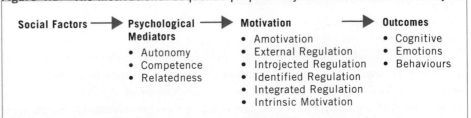

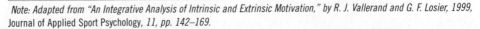

Note: Adapted from "An Integrative Analysis of Intrinsic and Extrinsic Motivation," by R. J. Vallerand and G. F. Losier, 1999, Journal of Applied Sport Psychology, *11,* pp. 142–169.

Frederick & Ryan, 1995) have shown, the impact of feedback depends on how athletes perceive it. Deci and colleagues argued that two external reward features could influence intrinsic motivation: an **informational factor** and a **controlling factor**. Rewards perceived as informational should increase intrinsic motivation whereas rewards viewed as controlling should decrease intrinsic motivation.

The informational factor could affect intrinsic motivation by affecting how competent one feels. If feelings of competence are increased because of the information that an athlete receives (e.g., wins the most valuable player award), this should result in an increase in intrinsic motivation. If a coach provides an athlete with negative information about his or her competence, the impact could result in a decrease in perceived self-worth and level of intrinsic motivation. Finally, if an athlete is focused primarily on the outcome of a competition or reward in relation to an event (e.g., win or lose, win most valuable player) and has not been able to accomplish what she or he set out to do, feelings of competence may be negatively affected with a resulting decrease in intrinsic motivation.

Every reward has the potential to be either informational or controlling. Thus, the functional significance of the reward, or how the reward is interpreted, ultimately dictates its impact on intrinsic motivation (Deci & Ryan, 1985). For example, a coach may make the same comment to two of her or his athletes. One athlete may interpret the comment as (informational) praise, a reflection of his or her competence and hard work. The second athlete may view the remark as controlling (the coach is just trying to make sure I work harder at practice tomorrow).

SPORT RESEARCH EVIDENCE ABOUT SELF-DETERMINATION THEORY   Research in sport and exercise has provided support for various components related to self-determination theory. There is empirical support for the link between competence and motivated behaviour in physical activity settings (e.g., Gagne, Ryan, & Bargmann, 2003; Kowal & Fortier, 1999, 2000; Sarrazin, Vallerand, Guillet, Pelletier, & Cury, 2002; Wilson & Rodgers, 2002). Controlling environments reduce self-determined behaviour and intrinsic motivation (Vallerand & Reid, 1984; Wilson, Rodgers, & Fraser, 2002). Although there is limited research on relatedness, Kowal and Fortier (2000) did find that relatedness was a good predictor of self-determined behaviour in masters-level swimmers.

There is also strong evidence that self-determined motivation is associated with many positive aspects in sport and exercise. More self-determined forms of motivation are associated with higher levels of effort, intentions to participate, persistence, positive affect, fair play, exercise behaviour, optimism, and perceived behavioural control, and with lower levels of distraction, boredom, and dropping out (e.g., Farrell, Crocker, McDonough, & Sedgwick, 2004; Kowal & Fortier, 1999, 2000; Lutz, Lochbaum, & Turnbow, 2003; Ntoumanis, 2001; Pelletier et al., 1995; Sarrazin et al., 2002; Standage, Duda, & Ntoumanis, 2003; Vallerand & Losier, 1999; Vlachopoulos, Karageorghis, & Terry, 2000; Wilson, Rodgers, & Fraser, 2002). Overall, this research evidence supports the utility of self-determination theory in sport and exercise.

Sport Commitment Model

To be successful in sport, athletes need to spend many hours in training, have to overcome a variety of challenging obstacles, and are often required to make many sacrifices (socially and financially). Clearly, success in sport requires commitment. Scanlan,

Carpenter and colleagues. sought to understand commitment as it relates to sport and physical activity, with **sport commitment** identified as "the psychological state representing the desire or resolve to continue sport participation" (1993, p. 6). Commitment accounts for situations in which individuals either want to continue their involvement in an activity for satisfaction and self-identification or have to continue their involvement, because of social pressure (Carpenter & Coleman, 1998).

PRIMARY DETERMINANTS OF THE SPORT COMMITMENT MODEL The **sport** commitment model (see Figure 4.10) consists of six primary determinants (Carpenter & Coleman, 1998; Scanlan, Simons, Carpenter, Schmidt, & Keeler, 1993). These determinants were identified from previous psychological work in various fields. **Sport enjoyment**, much as in Harter's model, refers to positive feelings related to the sport experience. **Involvement alternatives** refer to the degree to which athletes feel alternative activities are more or less desirable in relation to participating in their current sport program. **Involvement opportunities** are opportunities that arise through playing in the sport. These opportunities might include developing skill and fitness, being with sport friends, going on trips, getting social recognition, and the like. **Personal investment** refers to the personal resources devoted to the sport. Typical personal resources include time, effort, and money. **Social constraints** are social expectations or norms that make a person feel obligated to remain in the sport and involve social pressures to continue participating. **Social support** refers to the perceived help and encouragement received from significant others while participating in the sport. Involvement alternatives have a negative effect on sport commitment.

SPORT RESEARCH EVIDENCE ABOUT THE SPORT COMMITMENT MODEL The research has generally supported the model in various youth-sport activities, such as tennis, cricket, soccer, football, and volleyball (Carpenter & Coleman, 1998; Carpenter, Scanlan, Simons, & Lobel, 1993; Carpenter & Scanlan, 1998; Scanlan, Simons, et al., 1993; Scanlan, Carpenter, et al., 1993; Weiss, Kimmel, & Smith, 2001). However, not all determinants have been significant predictors across all studies. For

Figure 4.10 Sport commitment model

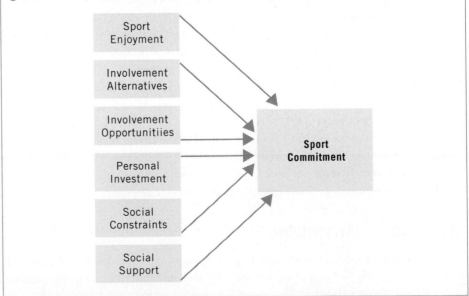

example, Carpenter and Scanlan (1998) demonstrated that longitudinal changes in only selected constructs—involvement opportunities and sport enjoyment—predicted associated changes in sport commitment among youth high-school soccer players.

The sport commitment model has also been investigated in adult athletes of varying ability. Using qualitative methods, Scanlan, Russell, Beals, and Scanlan (2003) found that all determinants, except social constraints, were important in understanding commitment in 15 New Zealand All Black rugby players. Recent work from the University of British Columbia has found gender differences in predicting commitment determinants in age-group adult triathletes (Augaitis & Crocker, 2005). For males, the determinants of sport enjoyment, involvement opportunities, involvement alternatives, and personal investment predicted sport commitment. For females, only involvement opportunities, involvement alternatives, and personal investment were significant predictors. However, there were no significant gender differences in levels of sport commitment on any of the six determinants.

In summary, the sport commitment model has provided insight into the factors related to why athletes continue to participate in sport at both the youth and the adult levels. However, there is little information about the effectiveness of the model to predict specific aspects of motivated behaviour (such as intensity and persistence) in specific sporting situations.

Reflections 4.7
Several key determinants shape an athlete's commitment to sport. Think of your own experiences in sport. Using the sport commitment model, identify the key determinants of your sport commitment. What was the most important and why?

Photograph by Richard Lam, courtesy of University of British Columbia Athletics.

Using Theory for Practice

Based on what you have covered in this chapter, it is now time to put this theoretical knowledge to work in the field. The application of the knowledge gained is, after all, the goal when working with individuals involved in sport. Recognizing that each individual and situation is unique, we can follow certain guidelines that aid us in our decision-making process. In addition to these guidelines, goal setting can be used to enhance motivation in sport and exercise settings. Goal-setting strategies are covered in Chapter 8: "Sport Psychology Interventions."

Guideline 1: Use the interactional model of motivation. It should be clear that the interaction of the individual and the situation influences behaviour. Be aware that participant-centred factors will bias how an athlete perceives and reacts to the sporting environment. Athletes are not blank slates that are easily manipulated by the environment. There are large individual differences in perceived ability, self-efficacy, goals, psychological needs, achievement goal orientations, and developmental maturity. Additionally, you will want to consider the impact that situational factors, such as the motivational climate, are having on the athlete's behaviour. This participant-by-situation view will allow for the fullest understanding of an athlete's motivation. Once we have a full appreciation of the factors influencing behaviour, we are better able to make informed choices in our attempts to influence individual behaviour.

Guideline 2: Emphasize perceptions of competence and self-control. It is important in the sport environment that we build in successful endeavours and mastery experiences, particularly at the youth level. If we want individuals to continue to participate and have a positive sport experience, then we should try to ensure that participants are focusing on the pride, happiness, enjoyment, and self-confidence they are gaining from these experiences. To enhance intrinsic motivation, it is important that we help athletes develop high perceptions of competence, value, and control. If this guideline is properly followed, athletes will exert greater effort, persist longer in the face of failure, and continue to experience greater positive affect.

Guideline 3: Develop confidence (self-efficacy) through challenging tasks and positive feedback. The development of competence and self-efficacy arise primarily through mastery experiences. Although such sources as encouragement, vicarious experience, and physiological states can have some influence, previous success in similar situations is the primary determinant of self-efficacy. Thus, it will take time to change self-efficacy through careful structuring of the training situations to ensure success in personally challenging tasks.

Guideline 4: Develop a mastery motivational climate to encourage task involvement. If the personal meaning one assigns to perceived success and failure is related to achievement behaviour, would it not seem important for parents, coaches, and the athletes themselves to understand the consequences of such beliefs? If athlete development—the continuous improvement of performance in competitive environments—is an important goal, then it is important to have athletes become more task involved. This can be facilitated by creating a mastery motivational climate in which there is an emphasis on learning challenging goals and getting positive feedback. Furthermore, athletes can learn to adopt task goals, rather than outcome goals. Task goals (also called mastery goals) have the athlete focus on improving in relation to his or her best past performances. Athletes can set goals that are moderately difficult, choose opponents or tasks that present a challenge, persist longer in the face of failure, and feel good about themselves, regardless of having won or lost.

Ego involvement (focusing on outcome and being better than others) is particularly harmful to those athletes who also have low perceived competence. Because failure (i.e., losing) is bound to occur often, these individuals reduce their efforts, stop trying, or make excuses, all to protect their self-worth. They often select tasks that are either extremely easy or difficult and perform poorly in evaluative situations. Thus, if the sport environment can be constructed to promote task goal involvement, then there is a greater likelihood of adaptive motivation patterns.

Guideline 5: Ensure rewards are perceived as informational. We have already stated that if we want to increase the intrinsic motivation of athletes, then we should try to increase feelings of competence, self-worth, and self-determination. Thus, the feedback we provide to athletes should be perceived by them as informational. If the information or feedback given to the athletes is perceived as controlling, a resultant decrease in intrinsic motivation may occur.

Guideline 6: Understand the importance of causal attributions in performance. The attributional statements that athletes make to themselves may have tremendous impact on their motivation and performance. Since these statements are often reflected in self-talk, it is imperative that athletes become conscious of the statements they make regarding success and failure. The feedback that they receive from their peers, coaches, and parents is also going to affect the attributions that they make regarding their performance.

Ultimately, we would like athletes to ascribe their performance to factors that are under their control (e.g., ability and effort) rather than to factors outside their control, such as luck and task difficulty. When an athlete experiences success, attributional statements made about stable, internal causes and factors under her or his control result in increased expectation of success, increased pride, and increased motivation. If athletes constantly have maladaptive attibutional statements, they may benefit from undergoing some form of attribution retraining.

Guideline 7: Ensure that autonomy and relatedness needs are met. Competitive sport tends to emphasize winning, with limited athlete autonomy and high coaching control. All these factors can undermine self-determination and intrinsic motivation. Structure your sporting environment to allow athletes to make more choices. Although this might result in more errors, the trade-off will be an increase in athletes' self-determination and intrinsic motivation for the activity. Furthermore, athletes have a need for relatedness. Allow opportunities within your sport for athletes to foster meaningful social relationships with other athletes. Activities, such as team parties, social time before and after practice, and breaks within practices, can facilitate friendships. Prevent demeaning coaching situations or other activities (such as degrading initiations) that may cause athletes to feel humiliated in front of their peers.

Chapter Summary

Motivation involves three central components of direction, intensity, and persistence of effort. Athletes (and coaches) can choose various sports and choose to expend effort in specific sports skills or activities. The intensity of effort relates to how much effort an individual is willing to put forth in a particular situation or event. Persistence refers to the continuation of effort over time, especially in the face of obstacles.

Motivation typically ranges on a continuum from extrinsic to intrinsic. Intrinsic motivation is behind the behaviours athletes engage in for interest or enjoyment sake. These activities provide fun and a sense of pleasure, and athletes do not expect any external rewards. Extrinsic motivation entails behaviours athletes engage in to attain rewards or outcomes that lie outside the activity itself. Sport behaviour is influenced by both intrinsic and extrinsic motivation, although intrinsic motivation is considered more powerful over the long term.

There are three general views of motivation. Recognizing that there are countless theories of motivation, research on motivation can fit within one of three general views. In the trait-centred view, the primary sources of motivation are linked to the individual characteristics of the athlete. The situation-centred view proposes that motivation levels are determined primarily by the situation. The interactional view, which has the strongest support from sport psychology researchers, proposes that the best way to understand motivation is by examining the interaction of personal characteristics with the situation, rather than from personal or situational characteristics alone.

This chapter has described several key theories and models applied in sport motivation research and practice. These theories and models attempt to describe, explain, and predict what motivates athletes to behave the way they do. Attribution theory focuses on how individuals explain success and failure. The numerous possible explanations for success and failure have been classified into three dimensions: stability, locus of causality, and controllability. The importance of causal attributions is that they may provide insight into an athlete's expectancies, motivation, and performance.

Competence motivation theory holds that athletes have an inherent need to master their surroundings. High perceptions of competence and self-control will lead to greater effort, persistence in the face of failure, and higher levels of enjoyment. Feedback from significant others (and oneself) can influence perceptions of competence, self-control, self-worth, and positive emotions.

Achievement goal theory states that an athlete's achievement behaviour is dependent upon the personal meaning she or he assigns to perceived success and failure. Athletes can adopt two types of psychological involvement related to achievement: task and ego. In a task goal involvement, the focus of the performer is on learning and improving relative to his or her own past performances. In contrast, an ego goal involvement centres on social comparison and being better than others. Psychological goal involvement is influenced by developmental factors, dispositional goal orientation, and motivational climate.

Self-efficacy theory postulates that the belief that one can produce the necessary actions to achieve a performance goal is the best predictor of direction, intensity, and persistence of effort. These self-efficacy beliefs combine with the athlete's expectations of outcome consequences (intrinsic and extrinsic rewards) to explain behaviour. Self-efficacy beliefs are primarily influenced by previous performances in similar settings, although vicarious experience, verbal persuasions, and physiological and affective states can also enhance beliefs.

Self-determination theory holds that people have psychological needs for competence, autonomy, and relatedness. Sporting environments that satisfy these three psychological needs will facilitate more self-determined forms of motivation, such as integrated regulation and intrinsic motivation. Feedback from significant others (coaches, teammates, and parents) can be perceived as either informational or controlling. Informational feedback following success can enhance feelings of competence and, thus, intrinsic motivation. Controlling feedback, which is often associated with lack of autonomy, can reduce intrinsic motivation.

The sport commitment model attempts to explain why athletes want to continue in sport. There are six primary determinants, four positive and two negative. Athletes are more likely to show sport commitment when there are high levels of personal investment, involvement opportunities, social support, and sport enjoyment. Sport commitment is undermined by social constraints and involvement alternatives.

Motivation has been, and will continue to be, one of the key psychological constructs that receives attention from sport researchers. Because of the complexity of human behaviour, we may never be able to predict with absolute certainty the *why* and *what* of sporting actions. This chapter has provided an overview of several key ideas and theories about sport motivation. Throughout the rest of this sport psychology book, you will see repeated references to these theories and ideas. Using the knowledge you have gained, you should have a better understanding of athletes' (and coaches', fans', and parents') behaviours. It is hoped that the guidelines provided will improve your ability to enhance athletes' experiences in sport.

Review Questions

1. What are the three components of motivation? Give specific examples from sport.
2. What are the limitations of exclusively applying either a trait-centred or a situation-centred approach to sport motivation?
3. What is the difference between intrinsic and extrinsic motivation? Can extrinsic motivation range along a continuum? If so, what are some key differences in types of extrinsic motivation?
4. Identify the theories of motivation that emphasize perceived competence.
5. What theories of motivation emphasize internal or innate drives or needs? Identify one theory that did not emphasize internal drives or needs.
6. How would you enhance self-efficacy in young athletes who have limited experience in a specific sport?
7. What are the key components of sport commitment? Do you think the relative importance of these components might be different between youth and adult sport? Explain.

Suggested Reading

Roberts, G. C. (Ed.). (2001). *Advances in motivation in sport and exercise*. Champaign, IL: Human Kinetics.

Standage, M., & Duda, J. L. (2004). Motivation processes among older adults in sport and exercise settings. In M. R. Weiss (Ed.), *Developmental sport and exercise psychology: A lifespan perspective* (pp. 357–381). Morgantown, WV: Fitness Information Technology.

Weiss, M. R., & Williams, L. (2004). The why of youth sport involvement: A developmental perspective on motivational processes. In M. R. Weiss (Ed.), *Developmental sport and exercise psychology: A lifespan perspective* (pp. 223–268). Morgantown, WV: Fitness Information Technology.

References

Augaitis, L., & Crocker, P. R. E. (2005, November). The sport commitment model: Commitment and outcome behaviours of age-group triathletes. Paper presented at the annual conference of the Canadian Society for Psychomotor Learning and Sport Psychology (SCAPPS).

Ames, C. (1992). Achievement goals, motivational climate, and motivational processes. In G. C. Roberts (Ed.), *Motivation in sport and exercise* (pp. 161–176). Champaign, IL: Human Kinetics.

Anshel, M. H. (1995). An examination of self-regulatory cognitive-behavioural strategies of Australian elite and non-elite competitive male swimmers. *Australian Psychologist, 30,* 78–83.

Anshel, M. H. (2003). *Sport psychology: From theory to practice* (4th ed.). New York: Benjamin Cummings.

Bandura, A. (1986). *Social foundations of thought and actions: A social cognitive theory*. Englewood Cliffs, NJ: Prentice Hall.

Bandura, A. (1997). *Self-efficacy: The exercise of control*. New York: W. H. Freeman.

Brustad, R. J. (1993). Who will go out and play? Parental and psychological influences on children's attraction to physical activity. *Pediatric Exercise Science, 5,* 210–223.

Brustad, R. J. (1996). Parental and peer influences on children's psychological development through sport. In F. L. Smoll & R. E. Smith (Eds.), *Children and youth in sport: A biopsychosocial perspective* (pp. 112–124). Toronto: Brown & Benchmark.

Bukowski, W. M., & Moore, D. (1980). Winners' and losers' attributions for success and failure in a series of athletic events. *Journal of Sport Psychology, 2,* 195–210.

Carpenter, P. J., & Coleman, R. (1998). A longitudinal study of elite youth cricketers' commitment. *International Journal of Sport Psychology, 29,* 195–210.

Carpenter, P. J., & Scanlan, T. K. (1998). Changes over time in the determinants of sport commitment. *Pediatric Exercise Science, 10,* 356–365.

Carpenter, P. J., Scanlan, T. K., Simons, J. P., & Lobel, M. (1993). A test of the sport commitment model using structural equation modeling. *Journal of Sport & Exercise Psychology, 15,* 119–133.

Carpenter, P. J., & Yates, B. (1997). Relationship between achievement goals and the perceived purposes of soccer for semiprofessional and amateur players. *Journal of Sport & Exercise Psychology, 19,* 302–311.

Crocker, P. R. E., Hoar, S. D., McDonough, M. H., Kowalski, K. C., & Niefer, C. B. (2004). Emotional experience in youth sport. In M. R. Weiss (Ed.), *Developmental sport and exercise psychology: A lifespan perspective* (pp.197–222). Morgantown, WV: Fitness Information Technology.

Dawson, K. A., Gyurcsik, N. C., Culos-Reed, S. N., & Brawley, L. R. (2001). Perceived control: A construct that bridges theories of motivated behaviour. In G. C. Roberts (Ed.), *Advances in motivation in sport and exercise* (pp. 321–356). Champaign, IL: Human Kinetics.

Deci, E. L., & Ryan, R. M. (1985). *Intrinsic motivation and self-determination in human behavior.* New York: Plenum Press.

Deci, E. L., & Ryan, R. M. (1991). A motivational approach to self: Integration in personality. In R. Dienstbier (Ed.), *Nebraska Symposium on Motivation: Vol. 38. Perspectives on motivation* (pp. 237–288). Lincoln: University of Nebraska Press.

Duda, J. L. (1993). Goals: A social-cognitive approach to the study of achievement motivation in sport. In R. N. Singer, M. Murphey, & L. K. Tennant (Eds.), *Handbook of research on sport psychology* (pp. 421–436). New York: Macmillan.

Duda, J. L. (1998). *Advances in sport and exercise psychology measurement.* Morgantown, WV: Fitness Information Technology.

Duda, J. L. (2001). Achievement goal research in sport: Pushing the boundaries and clarifying some misunderstanding. In G. C. Roberts (Ed.), *Advances in motivation in sport and exercise* (pp. 129–182). Champaign, IL: Human Kinetics.

Duda, J. L., Chi, L., Newton, M. L., Walliling, M. D., & Catley, D. (1995). Task and ego orientation and intrinsic motivation in sport. *International Journal of Sport Psychology, 26,* 40–63.

Duda, J. L., Fox, K. R., Biddle, S. J. H., & Armstrong, N. (1992). Children's achievement goals and beliefs about success in sport. *British Journal of Educational Psychology, 62,* 313–323.

Duda, J. L., & Hall, H. (2001). Achievement goal theory in sport: Recent extensions and future directions. In R. N. Singer, H. A. Hausenblas, & C. M. Janelle (Eds.), *Handbook of sport psychology* (2nd ed., pp. 417–443). New York: Wiley.

Earley, P. S., & Lituchy, T. R. (1991). Delineating goal and efficacy effects: A test of three models. *Journal of Applied Psychology, 76,* 81–98.

Farrell, R. J., Crocker, P. R. E., McDonough, M. H., & Sedgwick, W. A. (2004). The driving force: Motivation in Special Olympians. *Adapted Physical Activity Quarterly, 21,* 153–166.

Feltz, D. L. (1988). Gender differences in the causal elements of self-efficacy on a high avoidance motor task. *Journal of Sport & Exercise Psychology, 10,* 151–166.

Feltz, D. L. (1992). Understanding motivation in sport: A self-efficacy perspective. In G. C. Roberts (Ed.), *Motivation in sport and exercise* (pp. 107–128). Champaign, IL: Human Kinetics.

Feltz, D. L., & Chase, M. A. (1998). The measurement of self-efficacy and confidence in sport. In J. L. Duda (Ed.), *Advances in sport and exercise psychology measurement* (pp. 65–80). Morgantown, WV: Fitness Information Technology.

Feltz, D. L., & Lirgg, C. D. (2001). Self-efficacy beliefs of athletes, teams, and coaches. In R. N. Singer, H. A. Hausenblas, & C. M. Janelle (Eds.), *Handbook of sport psychology* (2nd ed., pp. 340–361). New York: Wiley.

Frederick, C. M., & Ryan, R. M. (1995). Self-determination in sport: A review using cognitive evaluation theory. *International Journal of Sport Psychology, 26,* 5–23.

Frederick-Recasicino, C. M. (2002). Self-determination theory and participation motivation research in the sport and exercise domain. In E. L. Deci & R. M. Ryan (Eds.), *Handbook of self-determination research* (pp. 277–294). Rochester, NY: University of Rochester Press.

Fry, M. D. (2001). The development of motivation in children. In G. C. Roberts (Ed.), *Advances in motivation in sport and exercise* (pp. 51–78). Champaign, IL: Human Kinetics.

Gagne, M., Ryan, R. M., & Bargmann, K. (2003). Autonomy support and need satisfaction in the motivation and well-being of gymnasts. *Journal of Applied Sport Psychology, 15*, 372–390.

Graham, T. R., Kowalski, K. C., & Crocker, P. R. E. (2002). The contributions of goal characteristics and causal attributions to emotional experience in youth sport participants. *Psychology of Sport and Exercise, 3*, 273–291.

Hardy, L. (1997). The Coleman Roberts Griffin Address: Three myths about applied consultancy work. *Journal of Applied Sport Psychology, 9*, 277–294.

Hardy, L., Jones, G., & Gould, D. (1996). *Understanding psychological preparation for sport: Theory and practice of elite performers.* New York: Wiley.

Harter, S. (1978). Effectance motivation reconsidered: Toward a developmental model. *Human Development, 21*, 34–64.

Harter, S. (1982). The perceived competence scale for children. *Child Development, 53*, 87–97.

Harter, S. (1985). *The self-perception profile for children.* Unpublished manual, University of Denver, Denver, CO.

Harter, S. (1987). The determinants and mediational role of self-esteem in children. In N. Eisenberg (Ed.), *Contemporary topics in developmental psychology* (pp. 219–242). New York: Wiley.

Heider, F. (1958). *The psychology of interpersonal relations.* New York: Wiley.

Horn, T. S. (2004). Developmental perspectives on self-perceptions in children and adolescents. In M. R. Weiss (Ed.), *Developmental sport and exercise psychology. A lifespan perspective* (pp. 101–144). Morgantown, WV: Fitness Information Technology.

Kane, T. D., Marks, M. A., Zaccaro, S. J., & Blair, V. (1996). Self-efficacy, personal goals, and wrestlers' self-regulation. *Journal of Sport & Exercise Psychology, 18*, 36–48.

Kowal, J., & Fortier, M. S. (1999). Motivational determinants of flow: Contributions from self-determination theory. *The Journal of Social Psychology, 139*, 355–368.

Kowal, J., & Fortier, M. S. (2000). Testing relationships from the hierarchical model of intrinsic and extrinsic motivation using flow as a motivational consequence. *Research Quarterly for Exercise and Sport, 71*, 171–181.

Lori Kane chosen for the Bobbie Rosenfeld award. (n.d.). Retrieved from www.caaws.ca/girlsatplay/stuff/awards/lori_kane.htm

Lirgg, C. D. & Feltz, D. L. (1991). Teacher versus peer models revisited: Effects on motor performance and self-efficacy. *Research Quarterly for Exercise and Sport, 62*, 217–224.

Lutz, R., Lochbaum, M., & Turnbow, K. (2003). The role of relative autonomy in post-exercise affect responding. *Journal of Sport Behavior, 26*, 137–154.

Maehr, M. L., & Braskamp, L. A. (1986). *The motivation factor: A theory of personal investment.* Lexington, MA: Lexington Books/D. C. Heath.

Maehr, M., & Nicholls, J. (1980). Culture and achievement motivation: A second look. In N. Warren (Ed.), *Studies in cross-cultural psychology* (Vol. 2, pp. 53–75). New York: Academic Press.

Manzo, L. (2002). Enhancing sport performance: The role of confidence and concentration. In J. M. Silva III & D. E. Stevens (Eds.), *Psychological foundations of sport* (pp. 247–271). Boston: Allyn & Bacon.

McAuley, E., & Blissmer, B. (2002). Self-efficacy and attributional processes in physical activity. In T. S. Horn (Ed.), *Advances in sport psychology* (pp. 185–205). Champaign, IL: Human Kinetics.

McAuley, E., & Duncan, T. (1989). Cognitive attributions and affective reactions to disconfirming outcomes in motor performance. *Journal of Sport & Exercise Psychology, 11*, 187–200.

McAuley, E., & Katula, J. (1998). Physical activity intervention in the elderly: Influence on physical health and psychological function. *Annual Review of Gerontology and Geriatrics, 18*, 115–154.

McDonough, M. H., & Crocker, P. R. E. (2005). Sport participation motivation in young adolescent girls: The role of friendship quality and self-concept. *Research Quarterly for Exercise and Sport, 76*, 456–467.

Moritz, S. E., Feltz, D. L., Fahrbach, K. R., & Mack, D. E. (2000). The relation of self-efficacy measures to sport performance: A meta-analytic review. *Research Quarterly for Exercise and Sport, 71*, 280–300.

Mullen, B., & Riordan, C. A. (1988). Self-serving attributions for performance in naturalistic settings: A meta-analytic review. *Journal of Applied Social Psychology, 18*, 3–22.

Nicholls, J. G. (1980). The development of the concept of difficulty. *Merrill-Palmer Quarterly, 26,* 271–281.

Nicholls, J. G. (1989). *The competitive ethos and democratic education.* Cambridge, MA: Harvard University Press.

Ntoumanis, N. (2001). A self-determination approach to the understanding of motivation in physical education. *British Journal of Educational Psychology, 71,* 225–242.

Pelletier, L. G., Fortier, M. S., Vallerand, R. J., Tuson, K. M., Brière, N. M., & Blais, M. R. (1995). Toward a new measure of intrinsic motivation, extrinsic motivation, and amotivation in sports: The sport motivation scale (SMS). *Journal of Sport & Exercise Psychology, 17,* 35–53.

Poag, K. A., & McAuley, E. (1992). Goal setting, self-efficacy and exercise behaviour. *Journal of Sport & Exercise Psychology, 14,* 352–360.

Reimer swims to bronze medal at aquatic worlds. (2005, July 27). CBC News. Retrieved from http://montreal.cbc.ca/regional/servlet/View?filename=qc-reimer20050727

Roberts, G. C. (1993). Motivation in sport: Understanding and enhancing the motivation and achievement of children. In R. N. Singer, M. Murphey, & L. K. Tennant (Eds.), *Handbook of research on sport psychology* (pp. 405–420). New York: Macmillan.

Roberts, G. C. (2001). Understanding the dynamics of motivation in physical activity: The influence of achievement goals on motivational processes. In G. C. Roberts (Ed.), *Advances in motivation in sport and exercise* (pp. 1–50). Champaign, IL: Human Kinetics.

Ryan, R. M., & Deci, E. L. (2000). Self-determination theory and the facilitation of intrinsic motivation, social development, and well-being. *American Psychologist, 55,* 68–78.

Ryan, R. M., & Deci, E. L. (2002). Overview of self-determination theory: An organismic dialectical perspective. In E. L. Deci & R. M. Ryan (Eds.), *Handbook of self-determination research* (pp. 3–33). Rochester, NY: University of Rochester Press.

Sarrazin, P., Vallerand, R. J., Guillet, E., Pelletier, L. G., & Cury, F. (2002). Motivation and dropout in female handballers: A 21-month prospective study. *European Journal of Social Psychology, 32,* 395–418.

Scanlan, T. K., Carpenter, P. J., Schmidt, G. W., Simons, J. P., & Keeler, B. (1993). An introduction to the sport commitment model. *Journal of Sport & Exercise Psychology, 15,* 1–15.

Scanlan, T. K., Russell, D. G., Beals, K. P., & Scanlan, L. A. (2003). Project on elite athlete commitment (PEAK): II. A direct test and expansion of the sport commitment model with elite amateur sportsmen. *Journal of Sport & Exercise Psychology, 25,* 377–401.

Scanlan, T. K., & Simons, J. P. (1992). The construct of sport enjoyment. In G. C. Roberts (Ed.), *Motivation in sport and exercise* (pp. 199–215). Champaign, IL: Human Kinetics.

Scanlan, T. K., Simons, J. P., Carpenter, P. J., Schmidt, G. W., & Keeler, B. (1993). The sport commitment model: Measurement development for the youth-sport domain. *Journal of Sport & Exercise Psychology, 15,* 16–38.

Smith, A. L. (1999). Perceptions of peer relationships and physical activity participation in early adolescence. *Journal of Sport & Exercise Psychology, 21,* 329–350.

Spink, K. S., & Roberts, G. C. (1980). Ambiguity of outcome and causal attributions. *Journal of Sport Psychology, 2,* 237–244.

Standage, M., & Duda, J. L. (2004). Motivation processes among older adults in sport and exercise settings. In M. R. Weiss (Ed.), *Developmental sport and exercise psychology: A lifespan perspective* (pp. 357–381). Morgantown, WV: Fitness Information Technology.

Standage, M., Duda, J. L., & Ntoumanis, N. (2003). A model of contextual motivation in physical education: Using constructs from self-determination and achievement goal theories to predict physical activity intentions. *Journal of Educational Psychology, 95,* 97–110.

Theodorakis, Y. (1995). Effects of self-efficacy, satisfaction, and personal goals on swimming performance. *The Sport Psychologist, 9,* 245–253.

Treasure, D. C., Monson, J., & Lox, C. L. (1996). Relationship between self-efficacy, wrestling performance, and affect prior to competition. *The Sport Psychologist, 10,* 73–83.

Treasure, D. C., & Roberts, G. C. (1995). Application of achievement goal theory to physical education: Implications for enhancing motivation. *Quest, 47,* 475–489.

Vallerand, R. J. (2001). A hierarchical model of intrinsic and extrinsic motivation in sport and exercise. In G. C. Roberts (Ed.), *Advances in motivation in sport and exercise* (pp. 263–320). Champaign, IL: Human Kinetics.

Vallerand, R. J., & Losier, G. F. (1999). An integrative analysis of intrinsic and extrinsic motivation. *Journal of Applied Sport Psychology, 11*, 142–169.

Vallerand, R. J., & Reid, G. (1984). On the causal effects of perceived competence on intrinsic motivation: A test of cognitive evaluation theory. *Journal of Sport Psychology, 6*, 94–102.

Vallerand, R. J., & Thill, E. E. (1993). Introduction au concept de motivation [Introduction to the concept of motivation]. In R. J. Vallerand & E. E. Thill (Eds.), *Introduction à la psychologie de la motivation* (pp. 3–39). Laval, QC: Éditions Études Vivantes.

Vealey, R. S. (1986). Conceptualization of sport-confidence and competitive orientation: Preliminary investigation and instrument development. *Journal of Sport Psychology, 8*, 221–246.

Vlachopoulos, S., Biddle, S. J. H., & Fox, K. R. (1996). A social-cognitive investigation into the mechanisms of affect generation in children's physical activity. *Journal of Sport & Exercise Psychology, 18*, 174–193.

Vlachopoulos, S. P., Karageorghis, C. I., & Terry, P. C. (2000). Motivation profiles in sport: A self-determination theory perspective. *Research Quarterly for Exercise and Sport, 71*, 387–397.

Wankel, L. M., & Sefton, J. M. (1989). A season long investigation of fun in youth sports. *Journal of Sport & Exercise Psychology, 11*, 355–366.

Weiner, B. (1979). A theory of motivation for some classroom experiences. *Journal of Educational Psychology, 71*, 3–25.

Weiner, B. (1985). An attributional theory of achievement motivation and emotion. *Psychological Review, 92*, 548–573.

Weiner, B. (1986). Attribution, emotion, and action. In R. M. Sorrentino & E. T. Higgins (Eds.), *Handbook of motivation and cognition: Foundations of social behavior* (pp. 281–312). New York: Guilford Press.

Weiner, B., Frieze, I., Kukla, A., Reed, L., Rest, S., & Rosenbaum, R. M. (1971). *Perceiving the causes of success and failure.* Morristown, NJ: General Learning Press.

Weiss, M. R. (1993). Children's participation in physical activity: Are we having fun yet? *Pediatric Exercise Science, 5*, 205–209.

Weiss, M. R. (2000). Motivating kids in physical activity. *The President's Council on Physical Fitness and Sports Research Digest, 3*, 1–6, 8.

Weiss, M. R., & Ebbeck, V. (1996). Self-esteem and perceptions of competence in youth sports: Theory, research and enhancement strategies. In O. Bar-Or (Ed.), *The encyclopedia of sports medicine* (Vol. VI, pp. 364–382). Oxford, England: Blackwell Science.

Weiss, M. R., Kimmel, L. A., & Smith, A. L. (2001). Determinants of sport commitment among junior tennis players: Enjoyment as a mediating variable. *Pediatric Exercise Science, 13*, 131 144.

Weiss, M. R., & Stuntz, C. P. (2004). A little friendly competition: Peer relationships and psychosocial development in youth sport and physical activity contexts. In M. R. Weiss (Ed.), *Developmental sport and exercise psychology: A lifespan perspective* (pp. 165–196). Morgantown, WV: Fitness Information Technology.

Weiss, M. R., & Williams, L. (2004). The why of youth sport involvement: A developmental perspective on motivational processes. In M. R. Weiss (Ed.), *Developmental sport and exercise psychology: A lifespan perspective* (pp. 223–268). Morgantown, WV: Fitness Information Technology.

White, R. W. (1959). Motivation reconsidered: The concept of competence. *Psychological Review, 66*, 297–333.

Wilson, P. M., & Rodgers, W. M. (2002). The relationship between exercise motives and physical self-esteem in female exercise participants: An application of self-determination theory. *Journal of Applied Biobehavioral Research, 7*, 30–43.

Wilson, P. M., Rodgers, W. M., & Fraser, S. N. (2002). Examining the psychometric properties of the behavioral regulation in exercise questionnaire. *Measurement in Physical Education and Exercise Science, 6*, 1–21.

Sharleen D. Hoar

CHAPTER 5

Arousal, Anxiety, and Sport Performance

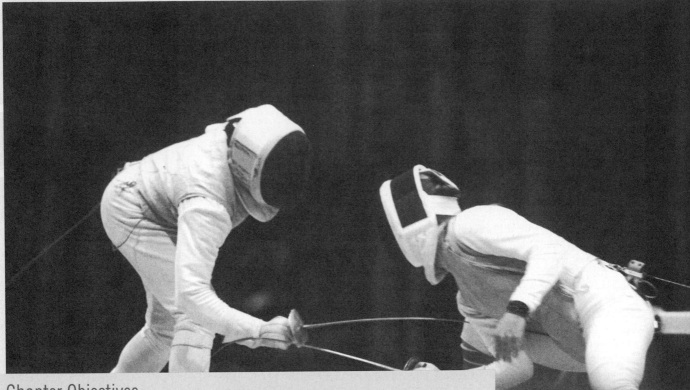

Chapter Objectives

After reading this chapter, you should be able to do the following:

1. Define and differentiate among different anxiety-related terms, such as *trait anxiety*, *state anxiety*, *competitive anxiety*, *cognitive anxiety*, *somatic anxiety*, and *arousal*.

2. Briefly describe measurement tools that have been primarily used to study anxiety-related emotions in sport settings, including strengths and weaknesses inherent to the tests.

3. List and describe personal and situational sources of competitive anxiety.

4. Explain how arousal and anxiety-related emotions affect sport performance according to four different proposed models.

5. Describe two mechanisms that explain why arousal and anxiety-related emotions affect sport performance.

* I would like to acknowledge Ms. Jayme Battershill for all her contributions to this chapter.

Naomi, a starting collegiate volleyball player, started her morning thinking, "Today is game day." She had her ritual game-day breakfast and proceeded to get ready for her morning classes. She was able to arrange her school schedule so that she had Friday classes only in the morning. For home games she needed the afternoons to rest and prepare for the Friday matches.

Thinking about the match, Naomi knew that a win that night was important. They were playing a rival school team, and both teams were even in points in the standings. That meant that this was going to be a challenging match, and as a starting player for the team, she told herself that it was her responsibility to be on her game in order to lead the team to a win. Her teammates depended on her. Also, her parents were travelling three hours to watch her play that night. She didn't want to disappoint her teammates or her parents.

Naomi tried to concentrate in class, but her thoughts kept drifting off to critical game points. She visualized herself making a series of perfect serves. In her mind she saw herself making important blocks and defensive digs. She imagined the feelings of excitement as her team gained momentum going into the final set. After classes were over, Naomi performed her ritual pre-game routine as she waited for the 6:30 p.m. start. She took a nap and then had a pre-game meal around 3:00 p.m. She then just tried to relax by watching TV and talking to her roommates.

Arriving at the team room at the gym at 5:30 p.m., Naomi began to feel the physical and mental sensations of nervousness. Her thoughts were racing, and she couldn't focus on the game plan. Her stomach was feeling queasy, her hands were slightly sweaty, and her heart was beating faster than normal. "This doesn't feel too good," she thought to herself. "I hope that things go all right for me on the court tonight, but if I keep feeling this way I'm not too sure it will!"

The effects of psychological pressure and eagerness is no doubt a part of competitive sport. It is often described by athletes, coaches, sports writers, and sport psychology researchers in different ways. For example, Mike Weir explains that what he felt in the final round of the 2003 Masters Tournament was "gut wrenching" (Jarrett, 2003, p. 40). Other terms that are commonly used to refer to this psychological state include *nervous wreck*, *emotional basketcase*, *stressed*, *pumped*, *psyched*, and *competitive anxiety*. Competitive anxiety can result from hundreds of different events that occur prior to, during, and after competitive contests. In the opening vignette, Naomi felt pressure because of the perceived importance of the match, teammate and parent expectations, and the need to play perfectly. Many athletes fall victim to competitive anxiety. There are, however, a few athletes who thrive on the pressure of competition and produce personal-best performances, such as Canadian gymnast Kyle Shewfelt, a 2004 Olympic gold medalist. In this chapter, the following questions will be addressed: What is competitive anxiety? What causes competitive anxiety? What effect does competitive anxiety have on the athletic performance of Canadian athletes? To obtain a better understanding of competitive anxiety, let's first begin by dispelling three common myths.

Some Common Myths about Arousal, Anxiety, and Sport Performance

MYTH: *Pre-competitive anxiety symptoms are generally the same for all athletes.*

The reality is that an anxiety response to a competitive event is specific to the individual athlete. Sport psychology researchers state that pre-competitive anxiety symptoms can differ with respect to the kind of symptom (e.g., gut-wrenching or concerns about past failed performance), intensity of felt anxiety (e.g., high or low), frequency in occurrence of symptom, and in duration of the felt anxiety (Jones, 1995). The individual anxiety response displayed by athletes is important to understanding how competitive anxiety affects athletic performance.

MYTH: *Competitive anxiety is produced by the high demands of sport.*

The reality is that athletes at all competitive levels can experience anxiety. Anxiety is not only produced by real high demands but also by athletes' *perceptions* that the specific competitive demands are high (whether it is objectively high or not). Thus, competitive anxiety is shaped by factors that are within the person (i.e., personality, beliefs, gender) as well as by the competitive environment.

MYTH: *Pre-competitive anxiety always negatively affects sport performance.*

Traditional research efforts assumed that elevated levels of pre-competitive anxiety were always detrimental to athletic performance. However, for many athletes this assumption is false! There are many examples where Canadian athletes have excelled in elite competition despite their feelings of pre-competitive nervousness. At the 2004 Olympic Games, gymnast Kyle Shewfelt performed personal-best routines on both the vault and floor individual apparatus competitions. Similarly, 2004 Olympic kayaker Adam van Koeverden finished first and third in his 500M and 1000M events, respectively, at his first Olympic Games. If you reflect on your own competitive sport performances, it is likely that you can recall a time when you also enjoyed the benefits of competitive anxiety. Today most sport psychology researchers agree that pre-competitive anxiety can have both positive (e.g., facilitative) and negative (e.g., debilitative) consequences for sport performance.

Introduction

Sport competitive anxiety has been of great interest to athletes, coaches, and sport psychology researchers for many years (Smith, Smoll, & Wiechman, 1998). Often, the difference between successful sport performances (e.g., a personal best or a winning performance) and those that are failures lies in athletes' ability to manage their nervousness or competitive anxiety. Because it was assumed that elevated levels of competitive anxiety are debilitating for sport performance, sport psychology scientists have sought to better understand the causes and consequences of this psychological state in athletes.

Reflections 5.1

Sport researchers have long been interested in the causes and consequences of competitive anxiety. Think about your own sport performance when you felt nervous or under pressure prior to an important competitive event. What caused you to feel nervous? How did the anxiety affect your performance?

Photograph by Richard Lam, courtesy of University of British Columbia Athletics.

Definitions and Basic Concepts

In this section, the terms relating to competitive anxiety are defined. To understand the ways in which competitive anxiety affects athletes' sport performance, it is important to have a working definition of what competitive anxiety is. Traditional research used the terms *arousal* and *anxiety* interchangeably. This resulted in a body of research with contradictory results, thereby limiting the understanding of the competitive anxiety construct. Today, sport psychology researchers emphasize the importance of distinguishing between arousal and anxiety, to enhance our knowledge about their influences on sport performance. Specifically, key anxiety terms, such *as arousal, anxiety, state anxiety, trait anxiety, cognitive anxiety, and somatic anxiety*, will be defined.

Arousal and Anxiety Defined

Arousal is a blend of physiological and psychological activation within a person and varies in intensity on a continuum ranging from deep sleep to peak activation or frenzy (Gould, Greenleaf, & Krane, 2002). At the high end of the arousal continuum, high-arousal athletes commonly exhibit both physiological and psychological symptoms: a racing heart, shallow breathing, sweaty palms, tunnel vision, and possibly confusion. Arousal is thought to be neither a pleasant nor an unpleasant experience. Increases in arousal states can occur from positive and exciting events as well as from negative and potentially threatening events.

Anxiety is a negative emotional state and is made up of multiple components (Smith et al., 1998). How sport researchers define anxiety has undergone considerable refinement over the years, but in general, anxiety is characterized by worrying, apprehension, and high arousal or physiological activation of the body (Smith et al., 1998; Speilberger, 1966). Specifically, three sets of distinctions are important for understanding how competitive anxiety is related to athletic performance. Sport researchers discriminate among (a) trait and state anxiety, (b) global and situation-specific anxiety, and (c) cognitive and somatic anxiety.

Trait Anxiety and State Anxiety

Anxiety is both a part of our personality and a (state-dependent) response that fluctuates from situation to situation. **State anxiety** is the type of anxiety that is associated with worries and apprehension that change from moment to moment. For example, a basketball player may experience mild symptoms of anxiety when entering the team dressing room, with symptoms increasing in intensity in the moments prior to warming up on the court. During the warm up, the anxiety symptoms may subside and the player feels ready to play. More formally, state anxiety is understood to be "anxiety states [that are] characterized by subjective, consciously perceived feelings of apprehension and tension, accompanied by or associated with activation of the autonomic nervous system" (Speilberger, 1966, p. 17).

Trait anxiety is a stable part of an individual's personality and predisposes the individual to perceive situations as physically or psychologically threatening. Because of the tendency to evaluate situations as threatening, high trait-anxiety individuals are more likely to experience state anxiety in more situations compared with those individuals with low trait anxiety. Furthermore, high trait-anxious sport performers are likely to have state anxiety responses of greater intensity and duration than low trait-

> Trait anxiety will affect an athlete's state anxiety in specific competitive situation.

Photo courtesy of AP Photo/Jack Dempsey.

anxious individuals (Smith et al., 1998). For example, consider two female intercollegiate hockey players, having equal skill, being placed in the identical situation (e.g., to score against the goalie in a shootout to determine the winner of a tied game). Because of different personality dispositions toward anxiety, both players have very different state anxiety responses in the shootout situation. Stephanie, a low trait-anxious athlete, responds to the shootout with a moderate level of state anxiety. Tammy, a high trait-anxious athlete, views the potential of missing her shot and causing her team to lose as extremely threatening. She responds with a disproportionately high amount of state anxiety.

Reflections 5.2

Carefully consider the definitions of state and trait anxiety. In this critical moment in the basketball game, at what intensity would this player's state anxiety be if he had low trait anxiety? At what intensity would his state anxiety be if he had high trait anxiety?

Global Trait Anxiety and Situation-Specific Trait Anxiety

Although state anxiety by definition is always situation-specific, sport researchers consider trait anxiety to be either a global personality trait or a situation-specific personality trait (Smith et al., 1998). As a global trait, individuals with high trait anxiety evaluate *all* situations (e.g., sport competition, public speaking, social situations, and academic exams) as having some degree of potential danger and threat. Researchers, however, have had limited success in predicting levels of state anxiety in sport-specific situations (e.g., competition) with global trait-anxiety. This result makes sense when one considers the fact that different situations have different associated threat sources.

Sport psychology researchers are better able to evaluate state anxiety experienced in sport-specific situations with a situation-specific trait-anxiety measure. Martens (1977) coined the term **competitive trait anxiety** to describe the specific trait anxiety associated with sport competition. It is formally defined as "a tendency to perceive competitive situations as threatening and to respond to these situations with feelings of apprehension or tension" (p. 23). It is assumed that athletes high in competitive trait anxiety are more likely to experience stronger intensity of state anxiety in competitive situations than athletes low in competitive trait anxiety.

Recently, Canadian sport psychology researchers (e.g., Hausenblas & Mack, 2001; Martin & Mack, 1996; Wilson & Eklund, 1998) and others have turned their attention to another situation-specific anxiety experienced in sport and exercise settings. **Social physique anxiety** is the tendency to experience anxiety as a result of the perception an individual holds about others' evaluation of his or her physique in social settings (Martin & Mack, 1996). In sport, there are many opportunities for public evaluation of athletes' bodies. For example, 2005 World Aquatics diving champion Blythe Hartley may be judged for both her physique and her physical abilities. In aesthetic sports like figure skating, gymnastics, and diving, competitive scores are based not only on athletic skill abilities but also on how pleasing the physical figure is to the judge's eye. Athletes who are high in social physique anxiety have great concerns about making favourable impressions with their bodies.

Cognitive Anxiety and Somatic Anxiety

Anxiety is multidimensional in nature and is experienced by athletes in different ways. Some athletes report feeling nauseated or having heavy legs while others report images of disaster. Canadian Olympic diver Blythe Hartley joked about how viewers at home would be able to identify her: "I'm pretty much a nervous wreck the whole competition. . . . I don't look happy, but that's what works for me" (Gatehouse, 2004, p. 28). Competitive anxiety is composed of two components, a mental and a physical component. The mental component is called **cognitive anxiety**, and it reflects the athlete's concerns or worries and the reduced ability to focus or concentrate (Krane, 1994). The other component, called **somatic anxiety**, is defined as "the physiological and affective elements of the anxiety experience that develop directly from autonomic arousal" (Martens, Vealey, & Burton, 1990, p. 6). Somatic anxiety is distinct from arousal in that somatic anxiety is not merely a reflection of the level of physiological arousal that is experienced. Rather, somatic anxiety is the *perception* of the symptom manifestations of arousal (Cohen, Pargman, & Tenenbaum, 2003). Thus, somatic anxiety is only experienced to the degree that the athlete becomes aware of arousal symptoms, such as clammy hands and a racing heartbeat. Although cognitive and somatic anxiety are conceptualized to be independent and distinct, studies reveal that cognitive and somatic anxiety responses are moderately interrelated and that levels of *both* anxiety responses are experienced in most competitive events (e.g., Burton, 1988; Gould, Petlichkoff, & Weinberg, 1984; Krane & Williams, 1994).

There is empirical evidence that cognitive and somatic anxiety are associated with different antecedent factors. Cognitive anxiety results in situations where an athlete has negative expectations about success or negative self-evaluations (Craft, Magyar, Becker, & Feltz, 2003; Martens, Vealey et al., 1990). Somatic anxiety is proposed to be a conditioned response to the competitive environment, such as when an athlete first enters a stadium prior to the beginning of a contest or when an athlete hears the cheers of the audience (Krane, 1994). Additionally, there are differences in the ways that cognitive and somatic anxiety relate to sport performance. Cognitive anxiety is almost always related to sport performance whereas some athletes do not report experiencing somatic anxiety prior to or during competition (e.g., Burton, 1988, 1998; Krane, 1994).

There is also empirical evidence that cognitive and somatic anxiety have different temporal patterns prior to, during, and after competition (e.g., Burton, 1998; Gould et al., 1984; Jones, Swain, & Cale, 1990; Martens, Vealey et al., 1990). Martens, Vealey et al. proposed that somatic anxiety remains at a low intensity until several hours prior to competition, after which there is a sharp rise until the onset of performance. During and after competition, the intensity level of somatic anxiety is hypothesized to decrease. Cognitive anxiety, on the other hand, is proposed to demonstrate a different pattern. Unless there is a change in athletes' evaluation about the potential for success prior to competition, no changes in the intensity level of cognitive anxiety are expected to occur prior to competition. After the onset of competition, there is a steady decline in the felt intensity of cognitive anxiety. Figure 5.1 displays the hypothesized temporal pattern of somatic anxiety and cognitive anxiety in relation to the time before and after the athletic competition.

Figure 5.1   Hypothesized temporal patterning of cognitive anxiety and somatic anxiety before and after a sport performance

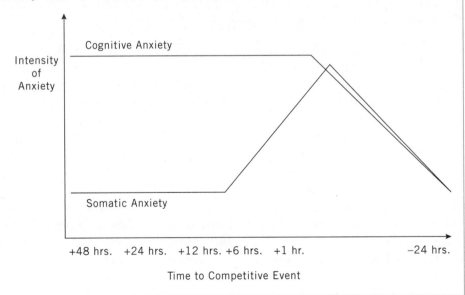

Note: Parfitt, G., Jones, J.G., & Hardy, Lew (1990). "Multidimensional anxiety and performance." In J.G. Jones & L. Hardy (eds.), Stress and Performance in Sport. *John Wiley & Sons Limited. Reproduced with permission.*

Reflections 5.3
Reflect on a time when you watched an important sporting competition. Were the players jittery and fidgeting? Did they appear to be distracted, concentrating on something other than the national anthem? Considering the multidimensional nature of anxiety, what mental and physical symptoms of anxiety were present? What was likely causing the elevation in competitive anxiety as the players anticipated the beginning of the contest? Do you think the intensity of somatic and cognitive anxiety changed during the contest?

Measurement of Arousal and Anxiety

The last 40 years of research investigating competitive anxiety have resulted in the development and use of a wide variety of measurement tools. In fact, the latest edition of the *Directory of Psychological Tests in the Sport and Exercise Sciences* cites approximately 30 different questionnaires to assess arousal and anxiety of sport performers (Ostrow, 1996). The measurement of arousal and anxiety is important for both scientific and practical reasons. Scientifically, evaluating athletes' competitive anxiety and arousal levels permits better understanding about their relationship to sport performance and other important outcomes, such as emotional well-being, sport injury, and burnout. From a practical perspective, measurement of arousal and anxiety allows athletes and sport professionals to monitor athletes' competitive anxiety levels prior to and during sport performance. In this section only those measurement tools that are the best and most commonly used are briefly reviewed.

Measurement of Arousal

Athletes' arousal levels are typically assessed through three different methods. Physiologically based assessments measure changes in heart rate, blood pressure, respiration rate, electrocortical activity, electromyography, and galvinic skin response. Biochemical assessments involve drawing blood or taking urine samples to assess changes in levels of circulating hormones associated with arousal responses, such as epinephrine, norepinephrine, and cortisol. Physiologically based and biochemical assessments are objective types of arousal measurement and are not commonly used by sport psychology researchers. Conversely, sport researchers are more apt to assess athletes' arousal levels through self-report questionnaires, such as the Activation-Deactivation Adjective Checklist (AD-ACL; Thayer, 1967) and the Somatic Perception Questionnaire (SPQ; Landy & Stern, 1971). The reader is referred to Landers and Arent (2001) for further information on the arousal measures used by sport researchers.

Measurements of Competitive Trait Anxiety

Two self-report questionnaires have been used predominantly by sport researchers to assess athletes' tendency to experience somatic and cognitive anxiety in competitive sport situations: the Sport Competition Anxiety Test (SCAT, Martens, 1977) and the Sport Anxiety Scale (SAS, Smith, Smoll, & Schutz, 1990). Using rigorous scientific methods Martens developed the SCAT to assess competitive trait anxiety. The SCAT contains 15 items, with 10 statements asking about trait anxiety symptoms (the other 5 items do not relate to competitive trait anxiety). Two versions of the scale are available, the SCAT-A for athletes who are 15 years or older and the SCAT-C for children between the ages of 10 and 14. An example of an item of the SCAT reads, "Before I compete I get a queasy feeling in my stomach."

   In the process of developing the SCAT, Martens (1977) conducted a series of carefully planned laboratory and field-based studies to assess the instrument's measurement properties. Findings from these studies and additional studies by other sport researchers have demonstrated that the SCAT has impressive reliability and validity (Smith et al., 1998). The SCAT was also better able to predict competitive state anxiety compared with general trait anxiety measures. The wide application of the SCAT in sport anxiety research attests to the strength of the measure. A weakness of the SCAT, however, is its inability to differentiate between cognitive and somatic anxiety. (If you want to complete the SCAT online, the questionnaire can be found at www.brianmac.demon. co.uk/scat.htm.)

Smith et al. (1990) developed the SAS to fill the need for a multidimensional competitive trait anxiety measure. The SAS is made up of 22 items, divided into three subscales. Two of the subscales, *concentration disruption* and *worry*, operationalize cognitive anxiety, while the third is a description of *somatic anxiety*. The following are example items from each of the three subscales of the SAS:

- I have lapses in concentration during competition because of nervousness. (concentration disruption)
- I'm concerned about performing poorly. (worry)
- My body feels tense. (somatic anxiety)

Research has found the SAS to be a reliable and valid instrument for assessing athletes' tendency to experience cognitive and somatic anxiety during competitive situations. Smith et al. (1990) reveal that (a) the subscales of the SAS achieve moderately strong relationship with the SCAT and that (b) the SAS is able to predict negative mood states, competitive state anxiety, and performance. Taken together, this is solid evidence that the SAS is a valid instrument to measure competitive trait anxiety.

Measurements of Competitive State Anxiety

Two self-report questionnaires have commonly been used to assess competitive state anxiety. The Competitive Sport Anxiety Inventory-2 (CSAI-2, Martens, Burton, Vealey, Bump, & Smith, 1990) is the most widely used sport-specific anxiety measure used by sport psychology scientists in the past 15 years of laboratory and field-based research (Craft et al., 2003). The Mental Readiness Form (MRF, Krane, 1994; Murphy, Greenspan, Jowdy, & Tammen, 1989), a measure based on the CSAI-2, has been primarily used in field-based studies for the assessment of competitive state anxiety immediately prior to or during competition.

The CSAI-2 was systematically developed and tested based on theoretical propositions about multiple components of state anxiety (Martens, Vealey et al., 1990). The CSAI-2 has 27 items and three subscales: *cognitive anxiety, somatic anxiety,* and *self-confidence*. The following are example items from each scale.

- I'm concerned about performing poorly. (cognitive anxiety)
- I feel nervous. (somatic anxiety)
- I feel self-confident. (self-confidence)

The 16 studies used in the development of the CSAI-2 and the 49 independent investigations that followed together provide empirical evidence of reliability and validity (Naylor, Burton, & Crocker, 2002). However, recent investigations with the CSAI-2 have led sport psychology researchers to note a number of measurement shortcomings associated with the instrument (e.g., Cox, Martens, & Russell, 2003; Craft et al., 2003; Jones, 1995; Woodman & Hardy, 2003). First, a number of studies demonstrate that the items written to represent the same type of anxiety (e.g., cognitive anxiety subscale items) do not always relate to each other. Second, Lane, Sewell, Terry, Bartman, and Nesti (1999) argue that the terms used in the questions to describe anxiety may be inappropriate. That is, terms such as *concern* may represent an acknowledgement of an important competition, rather than cognitive anxiety. Third, the length of the CSAI-2 has been criticized as burdensome for athletes to complete in the final minutes prior to competition (Krane, 1994; Murphey et al., 1989). Nevertheless, the CSAI-2 continues to be influential in sport research, as evidenced by its continued use by sport researchers and its use as a prototype for other measurement scales, such as the Collegiate Hockey and Football Worry scales developed by Canadian researcher John Dunn and his colleagues (Dunn, 1999; Dunn & Dunn, 2001; Dunn & Syrotuik, 2003) at the University of Alberta.

In light of the criticisms of the CSAI-2, the MRF was developed to facilitate field research of athletes' immediate subjective experiences of cognitive and somatic anxiety (Krane, 1994; Murphey et al., 1989). The MRF is a three-item version of the CSAI-2 (see Figure 5.2). Krane modified the original version to improve the measurement properties. Krane changed the anchor descriptors to *not worried-worried, not tense-tense, not confident-confident* and used an 11-point Likert scale to assess how athletes feel in the immediate competitive situation. Results from testing of the modified MRF with two different intercollegiate samples of athletes led Krane to conclude that it had adequate reliability and validity and was a superior test of cognitive and somatic anxiety than the original version (Krane, 1994; Krane, Joyce, & Rafeld, 1994).

Figure 5.2   Mental Readiness Form Modified Version 3

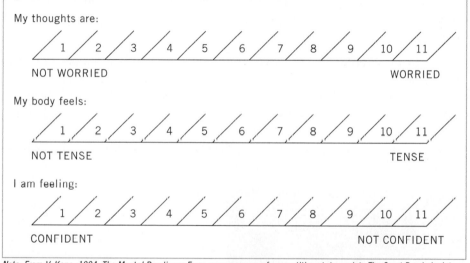

Note: From V. Kane, 1994, The Mental Readiness Form as a measure of competitive state anxiety, The Sport Psychologist 8(2): 192, figure 2. © 1994 by Human Kinetics Publishers, Inc. Reprinted with permission from Human Kinetics (Champaign, IL).

Reflections 5.4

Different measurement tools have been developed to assess anxiety-related emotions of athletes. Considering the common assessment tools that sport psychology scientists use to evaluate anxiety-related emotions, how would you solve the following problem? As a coach of a female volleyball team, you are concerned about the state anxiety levels of your athletes, particularly during important matches. What instrument would you select to monitor your athletes' state anxiety levels? Why would that instrument be the most appropriate? How could you find out which athletes may be most susceptible to increases in competitive state anxiety? Based on ethical issues discussed in Chapter 1, what dangers are there with such testing?

Sources of Arousal and Anxiety

Athletes experience increases in felt levels of arousal and competitive anxiety for a number of specific reasons. For example, anxiety may be elevated during sport competition by events relevant to the contest itself, such as its importance, critical situations occurring during the competition, as well as the location of the competition (i.e., home vs. away games). Anxiety can also be provoked by (a) personality predispositions to worry and experience anxiety in competitive or evaluative situations, (b) inexperience with competition or with a specific opponent, (c) worries about performing up to personal and others' expectations about ability, and (d) beliefs held about competitive success and personal ability to control arousal or anxiety symptoms. These specific sources of arousal and anxiety can be classified into categories determined by the situation or the person.

Situation-based Sources of Arousal and Anxiety

SPORT TYPE   There is evidence that the type of sport that an athlete participates in affects trait and state anxiety responses (e.g., Dunn & Nielsen, 1993; Hammermeister & Burton, 2001; Wong, Lox, & Clark, 1993). Athletes competing in individual sports experience higher levels of both trait and state anxiety compared with athletes competing in team sports. There is also evidence that youth athletes in individual contact sports, like wrestling, report higher state anxiety than youth athletes in individual non-contact sports like swimming (Simons & Martens, 1979).

LOCATION OF COMPETITION   Canadian researcher Steven Bray and his colleagues (Bray, Jones, & Owen, 2002; Bray & Martin, 2003; Bray, Martin, & Widmeyer, 2000) have investigated the influence of the home-team advantage on various psychological factors related to sport performance. The **home-team advantage hypothesis** states that athletes should perform better and be more successful in front of a supportive home-team crowd than before a less supportive and antagonistic opposition crowd (Courneya & Carron, 1992). Research results demonstrate that Canadian athletes report lower

> The ability to control anxiety and arousal is critical for competitive success.

Photograph by Richard Lam, courtesy of University of British Columbia Athletics.

levels of state anxiety while performing in front of a home-team crowd than while playing away. Similar empirical findings have been reported with non-Canadian athletes (Thuot, Kavouras, & Kenefick, 1998).

IMPORTANCE AND CRITICALITY OF COMPETITION   Research with youth and collegiate-level athletes reports that the more important the game and the more critical the situation during the contest, the higher the state anxiety response (e.g., Krane et al., 1994). Thus, athletes are prone to experience higher levels of state anxiety during playoff games than during the regular season. Similarly, athletes experience elevated state anxiety responses during critical moments in a competition. Examples of such situations might be while shooting free throws near the end of a tied basketball game, taking a penalty shot in soccer, and serving for or against match point in volleyball. How an individual athlete manages these situations can vary over time. Although golfer Mike Weir managed his nervousness in the 2003 Masters, he was not as successful in the 2004 Canadian Open, when he lost his lead over the last nine holes with some uncharacteristically poor shots. Playing in front of a huge and boisterous crowd and under intense media scrutiny, he commented later that he felt the weight of the country's golfing hopes on his shoulders.

TYPE OF ROLE HELD ON THE TEAM   Empirical evidence reveals that specific roles held on a team are more anxiety provoking than other roles. Sewell and Edmondson (1996) surveyed 121 university soccer and field hockey players and found that players in different role positions experienced anxiety symptoms differently. Goalkeepers had the highest levels compared with players in all other positions. Midfielders and forwards were reported to have higher levels of somatic anxiety compared with athletes who held defensive roles. Additionally, Beauchamp, Bray, Eys, and Carron (2003) suggest that athletes experience anxiety when they do not fully understand their team roles. Their work suggests that when team roles are unclear, athletes experience elevated levels of cognitive and somatic state anxiety.

Reflections 5.5
Consider this moment for golfer Mike Weir at the 2003 Masters Cup.

It was a moment of exquisite pressure. Having reached the green in two, lying 45 feet away and needing two putts to tie Mattiace, Weir followed the line laid out for him by the putt of his playing partner, Jeff Maggert. Once Maggart putted out {and} walked off the green, Weir, alone in a sea of people and cameras and the psychic weight of millions, leaned over his ball. He struck it short and took the longest walk of his career, then leaned over it again. The crowd began screaming the moment the ball moved. When it dropped, Weir looked like he hadn't slept in a week. "It was a gut wrenching day, [with] a lot of comeback putts that I needed to make and was able to make," Weir said afterward. (Jarrett, 2003, p. 40).

Which situational factors are most influential in Weir's anxiety response: situation criticality, playing in front of a supportive crowd, or playing an individual sport? Would he have a different anxiety response in a different competitive situation?

Person-related Sources of Arousal and Anxiety

Not all athletes have the same anxiety-related emotional responses to predisposing situational factors. For example, two teammates of a volleyball team may have different opinions about the importance of the match. One teammate may view the match to be critical for the team's ranking for a playoff position, whereas the other teammate believes that the match is not very important because the team is guaranteed a playoff position. Why would athletes have such different beliefs and what are the ramifications for anxiety and arousal? Sport psychology researchers have exerted considerable attention to identifying important personal sources of competitive arousal and anxiety. Specifically, there are six categories of personal sources of anxiety that have been studied, including (a) personality, (b) beliefs and attitudes related to success in competition, (c) goals and expectancies, (d) age, experience, and skill level of athletes, (e) gender, and (f) use of coping skills for managing anxiety symptoms.

PERSONALITY   Athletes who are higher in the personality traits of external locus of control, perfectionism, pessimism, trait anxiety, or self-handicapping have a tendency to experience elevations in anxiety prior to competitive events; those athletes higher in self-esteem and optimism generally experience relatively lower levels of competitive state anxiety (Gould et al., 1984; Hanton, Evans, & Neil, 2003; Wilson, Raglin, & Pritchard, 2002). Of the personality traits that have been investigated, competitive trait anxiety has received the most attention by sport psychology researchers. Athletes who are higher in trait anxiety have a greater propensity to judge competitive situations as potentially threatening and anxiety provoking.

Self-esteem and self-handicapping have also been found to relate to anxiety responses of athletes. Athletes with low self-esteem are more likely to experience higher levels of state anxiety during competition compared with their high-esteem counterparts (e.g., Martin & Gill, 1991). This finding makes sense in that athletes who are low in self-esteem generally perceive evaluative events (e.g., sport competition) to be potentially threatening to their ability to display athletic competence. Additionally, athletes with low self-esteem are inclined to engage in **self-handicapping behaviours**, such as diminishing their efforts during training, exaggerating the pain associated with an injury, or complaining illegitimately about the fairness of the referee, in order to obscure whether performance failure is due to athletic ability or due to external problems that the athlete had to manage (Prapavessis, Grove, Maddison, & Zillmann, 2003). Generally, athletes who have a higher tendency to handicap themselves also experience higher levels of cognitive state anxiety.

PERSONAL BELIEFS AND ATTITUDES ABOUT COMPETITIVE SUCCESS   The athlete's personal beliefs about her or his potential for success are a critical source of anxiety. In general, research reveals that positive beliefs about competence (i.e., self-confidence), readiness for competition, ability to exert control in the competition, and ability to perform better than one's opponent are related to *lower* levels of state anxiety (Bray et al., 2000; Hammermeister & Burton, 2001; Hanton & Jones, 1997; Jones, Swain, & Cale, 1990; Jones, Swain, & Hardy, 1993; Lane, Terry, & Karageorghis, 1995; White & Zellner, 1996). Canadian researchers have also identified that beliefs relating to the competitive success of the group or team are also influential for athletes' pre-competitive anxiety responses. Specifically, athletes who hold positive beliefs about their group's ability to work together to achieve success report having less pre-competitive state anxiety compared with those whose beliefs are negative (Eys, Hardy, Carron, & Beauchamp, 2003; Prapavessis & Carron, 1996).

GOALS AND EXPECTANCIES   Personal beliefs about success in sport are tied to the goals and expectancies that athletes hold. Therefore, different types of achievement goals also influence athletes' emotional responses, such as competitive anxiety. These different types of goals were discussed in the motivation chapter. In general, results from studies demonstrate that athletes who hold *outcome goals* (focusing on competitive result) experience higher elevated levels of pre-competitive anxiety compared with athletes who hold *performance* or *process goals* (focusing on actions to achieve performance objectives) (Burton, 1988; Jones et al., 1990; Krane, Williams, & Feltz, 1992; Lane et al., 1995; White, 1998). These types of goals are further discussed in Chapter 8.

EXPERIENCE, SKILL LEVEL, AND AGE   Early research from Walter Fenz and his associates from the University of Waterloo demonstrated that novice parachute jumpers differed from expert jumpers in their arousal responses to jumping from an airplane (Fenz & Epstein, 1967; Fenz & Jones, 1972). Specifically, their work demonstrated that the arousal symptoms of expert jumpers were elevated upon their entering the plane and continued to increase in intensity as the plane neared the jump zone. On reaching the drop zone, the intensity in arousal symptoms decreased until the time of the jump. In contrast, novice parachute jumpers displayed relatively lower arousal symptoms on entering the plane, after which intensity levels of arousal continued to increase up to the time of the actual jump. This early work has been replicated in a number of more recent studies investigating cognitive and somatic state anxiety responses (Hanton & Jones, 1997; Hanton, Thomas, & Maynard, 2004; Williams & Elliott, 1999). In general, results have demonstrated that (a) more experienced sport performers report lower levels of state anxiety; (b) collegiate athletes report lower levels of worry and somatic anxiety symptoms compared with high-school athletes; and (c) expert athletes view anxiety symptoms to be more *facilitative* toward their competitive performance. The facilitative and debilitative influences of competitive anxiety for athletic performance will be discussed in the final section of this chapter.

GENDER   The research on gender differences has been inconsistent over the years. Early research has provided some evidence that female athletes report higher intensities of state anxiety symptoms prior to competition in comparison with male athletes (e.g., Clingman & Hilliard, 1994; Jones & Cale, 1989; Krane & Williams, 1994). Krane and Williams suggested that differences in competitive anxiety responses could be attributed to the adoption of traditional feminine and masculine gender roles. A traditional masculine gender role, whether the person is a female or a male, is characterized by independence, dominance, and a willingness to take risks (Krane & Williams, 1994). These are all characteristics that could be advantageous for sport. In contrast, a traditional feminine gender role is characterized by being relationship-oriented, emotional, gentle, and tender. The competitive and achievement-oriented nature of sport typically does not favour the traditional feminine gender role. According to this explanation, competitive sport is more threatening and anxiety-provoking for athletes who take up the traditional feminine gender role. More recent research, however, has failed to find differences in male and female competitive anxiety responses (e.g., Hammermeister & Burton, 2004). This finding may be related to changes in cultural values and beliefs related to gender roles. Gender issues in sport psychology are covered in more detail in Chapter 13.

COPING SKILLS   Canadian researchers have been instrumental in studying the influence of specific coping skills that athletes use to manage their pre-competitive anxiety symptoms (e.g., Crocker, Alderman, & Smith, 1988; Haney, 2004; Kerr & Leith, 1993; Savoy, 1993; Savoy & Beitel, 1997; Terry, Mayer, & Howe, 1998). Some coping skills are specific behaviours or actions that an athlete can use to adjust physiological arousal and degree of worry or concern that is experienced prior to competition (Hardy, Jones, & Gould, 1996). Common coping skills used by athletes are relaxation skills, self-talk and cognitive restructuring, and imagery. Research with Canadian Olympic athletes revealed that the most important factor distinguishing medal winners from non-medal-winners was the ability to use coping skills to manage anxiety responses prior to and during competitive performances (Orlick & Partington, 1988). Recent work by Haney (2004) involved a six-month coping skills intervention with 47 Canadian female adult athletes. She found that sport performers in the relaxation training and cognitive restructuring groups reduced their somatic and cognitive anxiety pre-competitive responses. Coping skills, stress, and emotion are covered in detail in Chapter 6.

Reflections 5.6

In this section, six personal factors were identified as important determinants of athletes' anxiety responses. As a coach of a waterpolo team, how can you account for the differences in the anxiety experienced by two of your players, Jeoun and Pervaiz? What personal factors account for the differences described below?

Jeoun is a 20-year-old student who is very serious about performing well in her swimming. She sets high standards for herself and feels successful when she has outscored her teammates. Jeoun doesn't believe that she needs imagery or other "hokey" mental skills in order to perform well. It is her physical skill and determination that causes her to be successful. Before games, Jeoun becomes extremely tense and difficult to talk to.

In comparison with Jeoun, Pervaiz is easy-going. He is a 22-year-old student and plays on the team as an outlet for stress. He feels successful when he has put in a good performance and played his personal best. He is a very talented swimmer and is fairly optimistic in his ability to score goals. Before games, Pervaiz is excited to play and uses self-talk skills to focus his mind on the game plan.

Consequences of Competitive Anxiety: Anxiety-Performance Relationships

What effect does competitive anxiety have on sport performers? One obvious consequence of competitive anxiety is its potential effect on sport performance. Athletes who consistently experience high levels of worry and apprehension prior to

---

Reflections 5.7

Think about your own competitive sport performance. How do you respond to high-pressure situations? Is your performance enhanced or diminished by competitive anxiety?

Photo courtesy of PhotoDisc/Getty Images.

sport competition also tend to have lowered levels of enjoyment with sport, increased susceptibility to athletic injury, enhanced feelings of burnout, and increased dropout rates (Brustad, 1993; Smith et al., 1998). Although these outcomes are important to understand, most of the scientific studies of competitive anxiety consequences have focused on athletic performance. Thus, we will focus on the research investigating the relationship between competitive anxiety and sport performance.

Anxiety-Performance Relationship Models

INVERTED-U THEORY   For nearly 25 years beginning in the early 1970s, the inverted-U theory was the dominant model to explain the relationship between sport performance and anxiety (Gould & Tuffey, 1996). Its theoretical tenets, however, are not based on changes in anxiety, but rather on changes in arousal. The theory proposes that increases in arousal are associated with corresponding increases in sport perform-ance *up to a certain point*, at which time further increases in arousal (i.e., over-the-top) produces a decrease in performance (Yerkes & Dodson, 1908). This theory predicts that moderate levels of arousal should produce optimal sport performance (see Figure 5.3).

Let's take a look at how the inverted-U theory may be used to explain an athlete's performance under various intensities of arousal. Tina is a starting point guard for her basketball team. According to the inverted-U theory, we could expect that when Tina is relaxed or overly aroused (e.g., sweaty palms, a racing heartbeat, and "jelly" legs) that her performance will be less than optimal. In this state she is likely to miss passes more frequently, make poor decisions that may lead to turnovers, and sustain a low free-throw percentage. However, when Tina is moderately aroused, the inverted-U theory predicts that she will be on her game and performing optimally: making good passes, using appropriate judgement in her decision making, and completing most of her free throws.

Sport scientists have determined that the moderate level of arousal required for optimal sport performance differs according to the complexity of the sport skills and

Figure 5.3   Inverted-U model predicting the relationship between arousal and performance for the individual

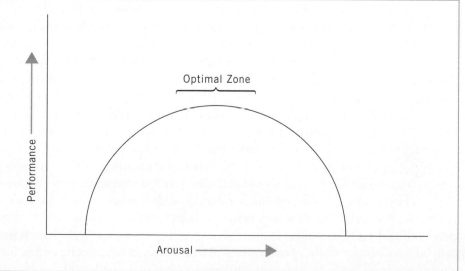

the kind of sport that an athlete participates in (Jones, 1990; Oxendine, 1984). Sport skills that involve strength, speed, and endurance and that are generally low in complexity are believed to require high arousal levels for optimum performance. On the other hand, low levels of arousal are required for optimal performance of sport skills that are complex in nature, involving fine muscle movements, co-ordination, steadiness, and general concentration (Hardy et al., 1996; Jones, 1990). Thus, power weightlifters and sprinters are likely to require high levels of arousal for optimal competitive performance while golfers and archers may achieve optimal performance levels with low levels of arousal.

Although there is no doubt that the matching of different types of sport performance with arousal requirements is intuitively appealing, sport researchers are highly critical of this approach. The inverted-U hypothesis has failed to accurately predict performance levels, to consider the multidimensional nature of anxiety and arousal, and to explain *why* arousal influences sport performance (Gould & Tuffey, 1996). Moreover, this approach does not explain why some athletes achieve peak athletic performances under instances of either high arousal or low arousal. Hence, sport psychology researchers have abandoned the inverted-U as a viable model explaining the relationship between competitive anxiety and athletic performance. However, students should be aware of this hypothesis as it still surfaces in popular sporting magazines and other media sources.

ZONES OF OPTIMAL FUNCTIONING THEORY   In his work with Russian athletes, Yuri Hanin (1980) noted that athletes demonstrated considerable variability in the level of pre-competitive state anxiety that was associated with optimal athletic performance. Some athletes performed best with high levels of state anxiety, while others achieved superior performances with moderate or low levels of state anxiety. These observations led Hanin to contend, like the inverted-U hypothesis, that best performances are more likely to occur with optimal levels of state anxiety. Unlike the inverted-U hypothesis, however, Hanin asserted that optimal state anxiety is a *bandwidth or zone of state anxiety intensity scores* (not a specific value) that is specific to the individual athlete and is dependent neither on motor skill requirements of the sport nor on the athlete's skill level (Raglin & Hanin, 2000).

Practically speaking, this theory suggests that the optimal intensity zone of competitive state anxiety required for optimal performance from members of a men's hockey team (or any other sport team) is likely to differ among the players. Some hockey players may play their best in wide zones of competitive state anxiety whereas others may play best in narrow zones of competitive state anxiety. Moreover, some of the team members may require a low to moderate intensity band of competitive state anxiety, while others display personal best performances when experiencing moderate to high levels of competitive anxiety. The point is that each hockey player's optimal intensity band of competitive state anxiety is individual and is dependent on the player, not the type of sport or sport skills that the athlete is to perform.

Thus, the central tenet of the Zones of Optimal Functioning (ZOF) hypothesis is that an athlete who is within his identified competitive state anxiety zone will be more likely to have a best athletic performance than an athlete who is outside his zone of optimal state anxiety. The ZOF hypothesis has been tested in a number of investigations with athletes from a wide variety of countries. The research reveals that, in general, athletes who are within personally identified optimal zones of competitive state anxiety are more likely to have best performances compared with athletes who are outside the determined optimal zone (see Gould & Tuffey, 1996). This result, unfortunately, does not occur for every athlete (e.g., Annesi, 1997; Imlay, Carda, Stanbrough, Dreiling, & O'Connor, 1995). Despite the intuitive appeal of the ZOF, there are important limitations of the theory. The most serious limitations are that the ZOF hypothesis makes no attempt to identify (a) why one athlete is different from another in the levels of competitive state anxiety that are optimal for achieving best performances and (b) how zones of optimal zones of functioning affect performance.

CATASTROPHE THEORY   The **cusp catastrophe theory** attempts to describe the combined influences of cognitive state anxiety and physiological arousal on athletic performance (Fazey & Hardy, 1988; Hardy, 1990). Few sport psychology researchers have applied this model to understanding the relationship between arousal/anxiety and sport performance, and it has been criticized for being overly complex (e.g., Gill, 1994). But why would one expect anxiety and performance relationships to be simple? Canadian downhill ski racer Steve Podborski describes how his competitive anxiety affected his athletic performance:

> I discovered that after a certain point of nervousness, I would start to deteriorate pretty rapidly. There was a real drop-off point in my ability to perform if I got too nervous . . . so it was just being able to find that little narrow comfort zone. (cited in Orlick & Partington, 1986, p. 162)

The advantage to using the cusp catastrophe theory to describe relationships between anxiety and athletic performance is that the theory recognizes that athletic performance is a complex behaviour (see Case Study 5.1) and that the variables that affect it, such as anxiety, do not do so in simplistic, uniform ways (Cohen et al., 2003; Hardy, 1996). Essentially this model makes five predictions (see Figure 5.4; Hardy, 1996).

1. When cognitive state anxiety is low, the relationship between physiological arousal and performance is uniform or in an inverted-U shape (as shown by the back face of Figure 5.4).
2. When physiological arousal is low, elevations in cognitive state anxiety are associated with enhanced performance relative to baseline (as shown by the left-hand side of Figure 5.4).
3. When physiological arousal is high, elevations in cognitive state anxiety are associated with declines in performance (as shown by the right-hand side of Figure 5.4).
4. When cognitive state anxiety is high (as shown by the front face of Figure 5.4), the effects of elevations in physiological arousal can be positive or negative for performance (relative to baseline performance). It is proposed that the combined effect of high cognitive state anxiety and moderately low levels of physiological arousal should produce more successful performances (compared with those produced under conditions of low cognitive arousal). This proposition implies that a high level of cognitive anxiety is not always detrimental to sport performance. For athletes who are able to sustain moderately low levels of physiological arousal, an increase in worry and concern can function to enhance athletic performance (Hardy, 1990).
5. When physiological arousal is moderately high (i.e., over-the-top physiological arousal) and cognitive state anxiety is high, it is predicted that a dramatic performance drop (similar to that described by Steve Podborski), called a *catastrophe*, will occur. To improve performance after the catastrophe, a decrease in physiological arousal is required. A performance catastrophe is not proposed to occur when cognitive state anxiety is low.

Figure 5.4   Catastrophe theory describing the interactions of cognitive state anxiety, physiological arousal, and sport performance

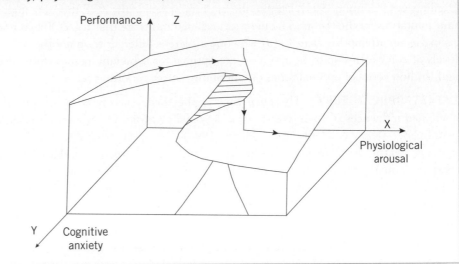

Note: From "A Catastrophe Model of Performance in Sport," by L. Hardy, 1990. In G. Jones & L. Hardy (Eds.), Stress and Performance in Sport (p. 88). New York: Wiley. Copyright 1990 by Wiley. Reproduced with permission.

Case Study 5.1:

Carefully consider the tenets of the different competitive-anxiety performance models. Can we explain Perdita Felicien's performance in her final race at the 2004 Olympic Games? She was ranked No. 1 in the world in the 110M hurdles. At the Olympic Games, she performed well in her heats and easily qualified for the finals. However, what happened in the final race was what she described as "my worst nightmare come true" ("This is,"

2004, ¶2). A few metres into the race she missed a hurdle, hitting the barrier instead. Losing her balance, she fell into another competitor and fell to the ground. She could not complete her race and was disqualified.

How might each of the models presented in this chapter describe Perdita's competitive anxiety in relation to her performance?

Underlying Mechanisms of the Anxiety-Performance Relationship

Despite important advancements in documenting anxiety and performance relationships, sport psychology researchers still do not completely know why this relationship forms at all. That is, the question "Why does competitive anxiety affect athletic performance?" still remains unanswered. Two primary mechanisms have been hypothesized to explain the effect of anxiety on athletic performance: cognitive information processing and neuromuscular control systems (Gould et al., 2002; Gould & Tuffey, 1996; Jones, 1995; Naylor et al., 2002). Optimal performance of any motor skill requires at least the following: (a) the cognitive processing of relevant amounts and types of information from the environment and (b) the appropriate levels and coordination of muscle activation. Consider Lori Kane attempting a putt. It looks like an easy task, but she must focus her attention on numerous external stimuli, such as the speed and slope of the green, distance from the hole, her stance and grip on the club, and wind conditions. She must then generate an action plan and translate this plan into a movement program to produce the appropriate putting stroke. If there are problems in either the action plan or the movement program, the putt will not be effective (i.e., go into the cup). Sport researchers believe that competitive anxiety and arousal processes affect sport performance through interfering either with the cognitive processing of external and internal stimuli or with the neuromuscular control systems, or both.

There is sufficient empirical evidence to support the hypothesis that changes in cognitive processing are associated with heightened state anxiety, which in turn, influence motor performance (Parfitt & Hardy, 1993; Parfitt, Hardy, & Pates, 1995). Specifically, sport psychology scientists have tested this hypothesis with two lines of research: (a) attentional focus and selectivity and (b) hyperdistraction. The **attentional focus and selectivity hypothesis** holds that an elevation in state anxiety reduces the ability to attend to and process information (Easterbrook, 1959). An increase in competitive state anxiety is associated with the narrowing of attentional focus, likened to travelling down a tunnel (Gould & Tuffey, 1996; Naylor et al., 2002). This narrowing is believed to be beneficial only for motor skills that need few sources of input stimuli for optimal execution. These may include well-learned (automatic) skills; skills that require quick decision making; and simple gross motor activities (Hardy et al., 1996). With a narrow attentional focus, there is an increased possibility that the athlete attends to *only* task-relevant sources of information, so some anxiety or arousal may be beneficial. However, too narrow an attentional focus will result in missed task-relevant information, producing a diminished performance.

The second line of research examining cognitive changes in processing demonstrates that highly anxious athletes experience hyperdistraction (Eysenck, 1982). **Hyperdistraction** is a state in which an athlete's attentional focus shifts rapidly among different sources of stimuli. In this state, a highly anxious golfer would rapidly shift her attentional focus among the crowd's cheering, the feel of the golf club in her hand, the caddy's instructional cues, the previous shot performed by her opponent, the worries or concerns related to the upcoming drive, and the like.

The relationship between competitive anxiety and athletic performance can also be explained through anxiety-related changes to the functional patterns of muscles (Landers & Arent, 2001; Parfitt, Jones, & Hardy, 1990). Increased physiological arousal disrupts the performance of motor skills that require manual dexterity and fine motor control (Parfitt et al., 1990). Further, under a heightened cognitive anxiety state, some athletes invest more psychic energy and cognitive resources into thinking about how to do well-learned tasks. Increased conscious control of the motor skill, especially skills that must be performed rapidly, will disrupt the automatic flow of movement.

Reflections 5.8

Think about your own competitive performance errors. When were the errors primarily a result of missed cues within the situation? When were the errors primarily a result of over-activation of your muscles?

Photo courtesy of PhotoDisc/Getty Images.

Facilitative vs. Debilitative Effects of Anxiety

Traditional sport psychology research, particularly in Canada and the United States, has assumed that competitive anxiety negatively affects athletic performance. That is, when Canadian athletes, such as Larry Walker or Perdita Felicien, experience increases in felt arousal or anxiety symptoms prior to competition, it is assumed that these feelings will almost always result in a poor performance. This assumption is a myth. Competitive anxiety does not necessarily lead to diminished athletic performance.

Graham Jones and his associates introduced the idea that anxiety symptoms have a direction dimension (i.e., debilitative/facilitative) in addition to the well-studied intensity dimension (Jones, 1991; Jones, Swain, & Hardy, 1993; Jones & Swain, 1995; Jones & Hanton, 1996). The **directional interpretation of competitive anxiety** refers to how sport performers label, or perceive, their cognitive and physiological competitive anxiety symptoms on a debilitative–facilitative continuum. Think about how two elite Canadian athletes described the implications of their anxiety symptoms for future athletic performances. Blythe Hartley (Olympic diver) stated that the feelings of being a "nervous wreck" are positively interpreted as being in a state of readiness for competition. Alternatively, Steve Podborski (Olympic ski racer) referred to a specific intensity of nervousness that, if reached, will result in poor performance. These reports by Canadian athletes anecdotally support the idea that athletes interpret and give meaning to competitive anxiety symptoms in terms of potential optimal performance. Jones (1995) proposed that athletes' perceptions of anxiety as debilitative or facilitative for athletic performance is likely to be a function of their beliefs about their personal ability to exert control over the competition environment and themselves (i.e., athletic skill), as well as beliefs about their ability to manage their anxiety.

Considerable empirical support is mounting to allow researchers to conclude that intensity and direction are two distinct qualities or dimensions of state and trait competitive anxiety (Butt, Weinberg, & Horn, 2003; Jones & Hanton, 1996; Jones & Swain, 1995; Jones et al., 1993; Ntoumanis & Jones, 1998). In summary, the results of the studies with elite and non-elite athletes from a variety of sports reveal the following:

- Athletes who report high intensity of cognitive and somatic anxiety typically view their symptoms to be more negative.
- The reported direction of state anxiety symptoms predicts more successful and less successful sport performance to a greater extent than state anxiety intensity.
- Highly successful athletes view anxiety symptoms as facilitating for performance to a greater extent than less successful athletes.
- Elite athletes have a tendency to view anxiety symptoms as facilitative, compared with non-elite athletes.
- Fluctuations in the intensity of felt cognitive anxiety across stages of a competition is associated with changes in directional interpretation.

Chapter Summary

Competitive sport can create anxiety-related emotions in athletes, coaches, and spectators. What does more than 40 years of research reveal to us about anxiety-related emotions in sport? The following key points are conclusions that are generally accepted by sport psychology researchers about the effects of competitive anxiety in sport.

Competitive anxiety is a complex multidimensional psychological construct. A number of conceptual terms have been identified and delineated to describe competitive anxiety. Anxiety-related terms include trait anxiety, somatic anxiety, cognitive anxiety, and arousal. It is important to distinguish among these different components of competitive anxiety in order to understand (a) what causes competitive anxiety to occur and (b) what effects competitive anxiety has on athletic performance and other important outcomes.

Competitive anxiety is caused by a number of personal and situational factors within sport. Competitive anxiety is not solely the result of factors within the person, nor is it shaped only by the competitive sport environment. Rather, it is the interaction between personal and situational factors that gives rise to competitive anxiety. In this chapter, six personal variables and four competitive situational variables were discussed.

High levels of competitive anxiety may lead to a host of negative outcomes for sport performers, including poor athletic performance. The most widely studied outcome of excessively high levels of competitive anxiety is poor sport performance. Generally, most athletes with extremely high competitive anxiety perform more poorly than athletes with relatively lower levels of competitive anxiety. Recently, researchers have demonstrated that in some situations high competitive anxiety can function to facilitate rather than debilitate sport performance. Sport psychology scientists are continuing to investigate the validity of findings that demonstrate a negative relationship between high competitive anxiety and competitive sport performance.

Competitive anxiety has a complex relationship with sport performance that is individual for each athlete. Early views asserted that an inverted-U shape described the relationship between athletic performance and competitive anxiety. More recent advances in sport psychology researchers' understanding about this relationship reveal that an inverted-U is too simplistic to accurately describe this relationship. Alternatively, the zones of optimal functioning theory and catastrophe theory are deemed more appropriate in explaining how competitive anxiety influences sport performance. Competitive anxiety is not necessarily debilitating for all athletes.

Changes to cognitive processes and neuromuscular control systems explain why competitive anxiety affects athletic performance. Competitive anxiety affects how athletes process the information they receive from internal and external environments. Research also demonstrates that anxiety-related emotion affects the tension production and coordination of muscle action. Both mechanisms are directly related to sport performance.

Review Questions

1. Distinguish among competitive anxiety, trait anxiety, state anxiety, cognitive anxiety, somatic anxiety, and arousal. What are some major signs and symptoms that can lead a coach to believe that an athlete has elevated levels of competitive anxiety?
2. How can you measure arousal?
3. List two self-report measures that have been used by sport psychology researchers to assess competitive trait anxiety. List two self-report measures that have been used to assess competitive state anxiety. What is a strength and limitation of each instrument?

4. Identify four situational sources of competitive anxiety.
5. Describe six personal sources of competitive anxiety.
6. Discuss the major differences in how the following theories explain how competitive anxiety affects sport performance:
   - inverted-U hypothesis
   - zones of optimal functioning
   - catastrophe theory
7. Describe two mechanisms that are likely responsible for the relationship between competitive anxiety and sport performance.
8. What argument could you present that competitive anxiety is not always negative for sport performance?

Suggested Reading

Jones, G. (1990). A cognitive perspective on the processes underlying the relationship between stress and performance in sport. In G. Jones & L. Hardy (Eds.), *Stress and performance in sport* (pp. 17–42). New York: Wiley.

Landers, D. M., & Arent, S. M. (2001). Arousal-performance relationships. In J. Williams (Ed.), *Applied sport psychology* (4th ed., pp. 164–184). Palo Alto, CA: Mayfield.

Parfitt, G., Jones, J. G., & Hardy, L. (1990). Multidimensional anxiety and performance. In G. Jones & L. Hardy (Eds.), *Stress and performance in sport* (pp. 43–80). New York: Wiley.

References

Annesi, J. J. (1997). Three-dimensional state anxiety recall: Implications for Individual Zone of Optimal Functioning research and application. *The Sport Psychologist, 11*, 43–52.

Beauchamp, M. R., Bray, S. R., Eys, M. A., & Carron, A. V. (2003). The effect of role ambiguity on competitive state anxiety. *Journal of Sport & Exercise Psychology, 25*, 77–92.

Bray, S. R., Jones, M. V., & Owen, S. (2002). The influence of competition location on athletes' psychological states. *Journal of Sport Behavior, 25*, 231–242.

Bray, S. R., & Martin, K. A. (2003). The effect of competitive location on individual athlete performance and psychological states. *Psychology of Sport and Exercise, 4*, 117–123.

Bray, S. R., Martin, K. A., & Widmeyer, W. N. (2000). The relationship between evaluative concerns and sport competition state anxiety among youth skiers. *Journal of Sport Sciences, 18*, 353–361.

Brustad, R. J. (1993). Youth in sport: Psychological considerations. In R. N. Singer, M. Murphey, & L. K. Tennant (Eds.), *Handbook of research on sport psychology* (pp. 695–717). New York: Macmillan.

Burton, D. (1988). Do anxious swimmers swim slower? Reexamining the elusive anxiety-performance relationship. *Journal of Sport & Exercise Psychology, 10*, 45–61.

Burton, D. (1998). Measuring competitive state anxiety. In J. Duda (Ed.), *Advances in sport and exercise psychology measurement* (pp. 129–148). Morgantown, WV: Fitness Information Technology.

Butt, J., Weinberg, R., & Horn, T. (2003). The intensity and directional interpretation of anxiety: Fluctuations throughout competition and relationship to performance. *The Sport Psychologist, 17*, 35–54.

Clingman, J. M., & Hilliard, D. V. (1994). Anxiety reduction in competitive running as a function of success. *Journal of Sport Behavior, 17*, 121–129.

Cohen, A., Pargman, D., & Tenenbaum, G. (2003). Critical elaboration and empirical investigation of the Cusp Catastrophe Model: A lesson for practitioners. *Journal of Applied Sport Psychology, 15*, 144–159.

Courneya, K. S., & Carron, A. V. (1992). The home advantage in sport competition: A literature review. *Journal of Sport & Exercise Psychology, 14*, 13–27.

Cox, R. H., Martens, M. P., & Russell, W. D. (2003). Measuring anxiety in athletics: The revised competitive state anxiety inventory-2. *Journal of Sport & Exercise Psychology, 25*, 519–533.

Craft, L. L., Magyar, T. M., Becker, B. J., & Feltz, D. L. (2003). The relationship between the competitive state anxiety inventory-2 and sport performance: A meta-analysis. *Journal of Sport & Exercise Psychology, 25*, 44–65.

Crocker, P. R. E., Alderman, R. B., & Smith, F. M. R. (1988). Cognitive-affective stress management training with high performance youth volleyball players: Effects on affect, cognition, and performance. *Journal of Sport & Exercise Psychology, 10*, 448–460.

Dunn, J. G. H. (1999). A theoretical framework for structuring the content of competitive worry in ice hockey. *Journal of Sport & Exercise Psychology, 21*, 259–279.

Dunn, J. G. H., & Dunn, J. C. (2001). Relationships among the sport competition anxiety test, the sport anxiety scale, and the collegiate hockey worry scale. *Journal of Applied Sport Psychology, 13*, 411–429.

Dunn, J. G. H., & Nielsen, A. B. (1993). A between-sport comparison of situational threat perceptions in ice hockey and soccer. *Journal of Sport & Exercise Psychology, 15*, 449–465.

Dunn, J. G. H., & Syrotuik, D. G. (2003). An investigation of multidimensional worry dispositions in a high contact sport. *Psychology of Sport and Exercise, 4*, 265–282.

Easterbrook, J. A. (1959). The effect of emotion on cue utilization and the organization of behavior. *Psychological Review, 66*, 183–201.

Eys, M. A., Hardy, J., Carron, A. V., & Beauchamp, M. R. (2003). The relationship between task cohesion and competitive state anxiety. *Journal of Sport & Exercise Psychology, 25*, 66–76.

Eysenck, M. W. (1982). *Attention and arousal: Cognition and performance*. Berlin: Springer-Verlag.

Fazey, J. A., & Hardy, L. (1988). The inverted-U hypothesis: A catastrophe for sport psychology. *British Association of Sports Sciences Monograph, 1*.

Fenz, W. D., & Epstein, S. (1967). Gradients of physiological arousal in parachutists as a function of an approaching jump. *Psychosomatic Medicine, 29*, 33–51.

Fenz, W. D., & Jones, G. B. (1972). Individual differences in physiologic arousal and performance in sport parachutists. *Psychosomatic Medicine, 34*, 1–8.

Gatehouse, J. (2004, August 16). Athens '04. *Maclean's, 117*, 26–35.

Gould, D., Greenleaf, C., & Krane, V. (2002). Arousal-anxiety and sport behavior. In T. Horn (Ed.), *Advances in sport psychology* (2nd ed., pp. 207–241). Champaign, IL: Human Kinetics.

Gould, D., Petlichkoff, L., & Weinberg, R. S. (1984). Antecedents of, temporal changes in, and relationships between CSAI-2 subcomponents. *Journal of Sport Psychology, 6*, 289–304.

Gould, D., & Tuffey, S. (1996). Zones of optimal functioning research: A review and critique. *Anxiety, Stress, and Coping, 9*, 53–68.

Gill, D. L. (1994). A sport and exercise psychology perspective on stress. *Quest, 46*, 20–27.

Hammermeister, J., & Burton, D. (2001). Stress, appraisal, and coping revisited: Examining the antecedents of competitive state anxiety with endurance athletes. *The Sport Psychologist, 15*, 66–90.

Hammermeister, J., & Burton, D. (2004). Gender differences in coping with endurance sport stress: Are men from Mars and women from Venus? *Journal of Sport Behavior, 27*, 148–164.

Haney, C. J. (2004). Stress-management interventions for female athletes: Relaxation and cognitive restructuring. *International Journal of Sport Psychology, 35*, 109–118.

Hanin, Y. (1980). A study of anxiety in sports. In W. F. Straub (Ed.), *Sport psychology: An analysis of athlete behaviour* (pp. 236–249). Ithaca, NY: Mouvement.

Hanton, S., Evans, L., & Neil, R. (2003). Hardiness and the competitive trait anxiety response. *Anxiety, Stress, and Coping, 16*, 167–184.

Hanton, S., & Jones, G. (1997). Antecedents of intensity and direction dimensions of competitive anxiety as a function of skill. *Psychological Reports, 81*, 1139–1147.

Hanton, S., Thomas, O., & Maynard, I. (2004). Competitive anxiety responses in the week leading up to competition: The role of intensity, direction, and frequency dimensions. *Psychology of Sport and Exercise, 5*, 169–181.

Hardy, L. (1990). A catastrophe model of performance in sport. In G. Jones & L. Hardy (Eds.), *Stress and performance in sport* (pp. 81–106). New York: Wiley.

Hardy, L. (1996). Testing the predictions of the cusp catastrophe model of anxiety and performance. *The Sport Psychologist, 10,* 140–156.

Hardy, L., Jones, J. G., & Gould, D. (1996). *The psychological preparation of elite sports performers.* Chichester, UK: Wiley.

Hausenblas, H. A., & Mack, D. E. (2001). Social physique anxiety and eating disorder correlates among female athletic and nonathletic populations. *Journal of Sport Behavior, 22,* 502–513.

Imlay, G. J., Carda, R. D., Stanbrough, M. E., Dreiling, A. M., & O'Connor, P. J. (1995). Anxiety and athletic performance: A test of zone of optimal function theory. *International Journal of Sport Psychology, 26,* 295–306.

Jarrett, R. (2003, April 21). New man of the moment. *Sports Illustrated, 98,* 38–44.

Jones, G. (1990). A cognitive perspective on the processes underlying the relationship between stress and performance in sport. In G. Jones & L. Hardy (Eds.), *Stress and performance in sport* (pp. 17–42). New York: Wiley.

Jones, G. (1991). Recent developments and current issues in competitive state anxiety research. *The Sport Psychologist, 4,* 152–155.

Jones, G. (1995). More than just a game: Research developments and issues in competitive anxiety in sport. *British Journal of Psychology, 86,* 449–478.

Jones, G., & Cale, A. (1989). Precompetition temporal patterning of anxiety self-confidence in males and females. *Journal of Sport Behavior, 12,* 183–195.

Jones, G., & Hanton, S. (1996). Interpretation of competitive anxiety symptoms and goal attainment expectancies. *Journal of Sport & Exercise Psychology, 18,* 144–157.

Jones, G., & Swain, A. (1995). Predispositions to experience debilitative and facilitative anxiety in elite and nonelite performers. *The Sport Psychologist, 9,* 201–211.

Jones, G., Swain, A., & Cale, A. (1990). Antecedents of multidimensional competitive state anxiety and self-confidence in elite intercollegiate middle-distance runners. *The Sport Psychologist, 4,* 107–118.

Jones, G., Swain, A., & Hardy, L. (1993). Intensity and direction dimensions of competitive state anxiety and relationships with performance. *Journal of Sports Sciences, 11,* 525–532.

Kerr, G., & Leith, L. (1993). Stress management and athletic performance. *The Sport Psychologist, 7,* 221–231.

Krane, V. (1994). The mental readiness form as a measure of competitive state anxiety. *The Sport Psychologist, 8,* 189–202.

Krane, V., Joyce, D., & Rafeld, J. (1994). Competitive anxiety, situation criticality, and softball performance. *The Sport Psychologist, 8,* 58–72.

Krane, V., & Williams, J. M. (1994). Cognitive anxiety, somatic anxiety, and confidence in track and field athletes: The impact of gender, competitive level, and task characteristics. *International Journal of Sport Psychology, 25,* 203–217.

Krane, V., Williams, J. M., & Feltz, D. (1992). Path analysis examining relationships among cognitive anxiety, somatic anxiety, state confidence, performance expectations, and golf performance. *Journal of Sport Performance, 15,* 279–295.

Landers, D. M., & Arent, S. M. (2001). Arousal-performance relationships. In J. Williams (Ed.), *Applied sport psychology* (4th ed., pp. 164–184). Palo Alto, CA: Mayfield.

Landy, F. J., & Stern, R. M. (1971). Factor analysis of a somatic perception questionnaire. *Journal of Psychosomatic Research, 15,* 179–181.

Lane, A. M., Sewell, D. F., Terry, P. C., Bartman, D., & Nesti, M. S. (1999). Confirmatory factor analysis of the competitive state anxiety inventory-2. *Journal of Sports Sciences, 17,* 505–512.

Lane, A., Terry, P., & Karageorghis, C. (1995). Antecedents of multidimensional competitive state anxiety and self-confidence in duathletes. *Perceptual and Motor Skills, 80,* 911–919.

Martens, R. (1977). *Sport Competition Anxiety Test.* Champaign, IL: Human Kinetics.

Martens, R., Burton, D., Vealey, R. S., Bump, L., & Smith, D. E. (1990). A multidimensional theory of competitive state anxiety. In R. Martens, R. S. Vealey, & D. Burton (Eds.) *Competitive anxiety in sport* (pp. 119–126). Champaign, IL: Human Kinetics.

Martens, R., Vealey, R. S., & Burton, D. (Eds.). (1990). *Competitive anxiety in sport.* Champaign, IL: Human Kinetics.

Martin, J. J., & Gill, D. L. (1991). The relationships among competitive orientation, sport-confidence, self-efficacy, anxiety, and performance. *Journal of Sport & Exercise Psychology, 13,* 149–159.

Martin, K. A., & Mack, D. (1996). Relationships between physical self-presentation and sport competition trait anxiety: A preliminary study. *Journal of Sport & Exercise Psychology, 18,* 75–82.

Murphy, S., Greenspan, M., Jowdy, D., & Tammen, V. (1989, October). *Development of a brief rating instrument of competitive anxiety: Comparison with the CSAI-2.* Paper presented at the national conference of the American Alliance for Health, Physical Education, Recreation and Dance, Atlanta, GA.

Naylor, S., Burton, D., & Crocker, P. R. E. (2002). Competitive anxiety and sport performance. In J. M. Silva III & D. E. Stevens (Eds.), *Psychological foundations of sport* (pp. 132–154). Boston: Allyn & Bacon.

Ntoumanis, N., & Jones, G. (1998). Interpretation of competitive trait anxiety symptoms as a function of locus of control beliefs. *International Journal of Sports Psychology, 29,* 99–114.

Orlick, T., & Partington, J. (1986). *Inner views of winning: Psyched.* Ottawa: Coaching Association of Canada.

Orlick, T., & Partington, J. (1988). Mental links to excellence. *The Sport Psychologist, 2,* 105–130.

Ostrow, A. C. (1996). *Directory of psychological tests in the sport and exercise sciences* (2nd ed.). Morgantown, WV: Fitness Information Technology.

Oxendine, J. B. (1984). *Psychology of motor learning.* Englewood Cliffs, NJ: Prentice Hall.

Parfitt, G., & Hardy, L. (1993). The effects of competitive anxiety on memory span and rebounding shooting tasks in basketball players. *Journal of Sports Sciences, 11,* 517–524.

Parfitt, G., Hardy, L., & Pates, J. (1995). Somatic anxiety and physiological arousal: Their effects upon a high anaerobic, low memory demand task. *International Journal of Sport Psychology, 26,* 196–213.

Parfitt, G., Jones, J. G., & Hardy, L. (1990). Multidimensional anxiety and performance. In G. Jones & L. Hardy (Eds.), *Stress and performance in sport* (pp. 43–80). New York: Wiley.

Prapavessis, H., & Carron, A. V. (1996). The effect of group cohesion on competitive state anxiety. *Journal of Sport & Exercise Psychology, 18,* 64–74.

Prapavessis, H., Grove, J. R., Maddison, R., & Zillmann, N. (2003). Self-handicapping tendencies, coping, and anxiety responses among athletes. *Psychology of Sport and Exercise, 4,* 357–375.

Raglin, J. S., & Hanin, Y. L. (2000). Competitive anxiety. In Y. Hanin (Ed.), *Emotions in sport* (pp. 93–112). Champaign, IL: Human Kinetics.

Savoy, C. (1993). A yearly mental training program for a college basketball player. *The Sport Psychologist, 7,* 173–190.

Savoy, C., & Beitel, P. (1997). The relative effect of a group and group/individualized program on state anxiety and state self-confidence. *Journal of Sport Performance, 20,* 364–376.

Sewell, D. F., & Edmondson, A. M. (1996). Relationships between field position and pre-match competitive state anxiety in soccer and field hockey. *International Journal of Sport Psychology, 27,* 159–172.

Simons, J., & Martens, R. (1979). Children's anxiety in sport and nonsport evaluative activities. *Journal of Sport Psychology, 1,* 160–169.

Smith, R. E., Smoll, F. L., & Schutz, R. W. (1990). Measurement and correlates of sport-specific cognitive and somatic trait anxiety: The sport anxiety scale. *Anxiety Research, 2,* 263–280.

Smith, R. E., Smoll, F. L., & Wiechman, S. A. (1998). Measurement of trait anxiety in sport. In J. Duda (Ed.), *Advancement in sport and exercise psychology measurement* (pp. 105–127). Morgantown, WV: Fitness Information Technology.

Speilberger, C. D. (1966). Theory and research on anxiety. In C. D. Speilberger (Ed.), *Anxiety and behaviour* (pp. 3–22). New York: Academic.

Terry, P. C., Mayer, J. L., & Howe, B. L. (1998). Effectiveness of a mental training program for novice scuba divers. *Journal of Applied Sport Psychology, 10,* 251–267.

Thayer, R. E. (1967). Measurement of activation through self-report. *Psychological Reports, 20,* 663–679.

"This is my worst nightmare come true": Felicien. (2004, August 25). *CBC Sports Online.* Retrieved January 31, 2005, from http://www.cbc.ca/story/olympics/national/2004/08/24/Sports/ perdita040824 .html

Thuot, S. M., Kavouras, S. A., & Kenefick, R. W. (1998). Effect of perceived ability, game location, and state anxiety on basketball performance. *Journal of Sport Behavior, 21,* 311–321.

White, S. A. (1998). Adolescent goal profiles, perceptions of parent-initiated motivational climate, and competitive trait anxiety. *The Sport Psychologist, 12,* 16–28.

White, S. A., & Zellner, S. R. (1996). The relationship between goal orientation, beliefs about the causes of sport success, and trait anxiety among high school, intercollegiate, and recreational sport participants. *The Sport Psychologist, 10,* 58–72.

Williams, A. M., & Elliott, D. (1999). Anxiety, expertise, and visual search strategy in karate. *Journal of Sport & Exercise Psychology, 21,* 362–375.

Wilson, G. S., Raglin, J. S., & Pritchard, M. E. (2002). Optimism, pessimism, and precompetition anxiety in college athletes. *Personality and Individual Differences, 32,* 893–902.

Wilson, P., & Eklund, R. C. (1998). The relationship between competitive anxiety and self-presentational concerns. *Journal of Sport & Exercise Psychology, 20,* 81–97.

Woodman, T., & Hardy, L. (2003). The relative impact of cognitive anxiety and self-confidence upon sport performance: A meta-analysis. *Journal of Sports Sciences, 21,* 443–457.

Wong, E. H., Lox, C., & Clark, S. E. (1993). Relation between sports context, competitive trait anxiety, perceived ability, and self-presentation confidence. *Perceptual and Motor Skills, 76,* 847–850.

Yerkes, R. M., & Dodson, J. D. (1908). The relation of strength of stimulus to rapidity of habit formation. *Journal of Comparative Neurology and Psychology, 18,* 459–482.

Kent C. Kowalski

CHAPTER 6

Stress and Coping in Sport

Chapter Objectives

After reading this chapter, you should be able to do the following:

1. Define the concepts of stress and coping.
2. Describe the relationship between stress and the emotions.
3. Explain the role of cognitive appraisal and coping in the stress process.
4. Distinguish between coping and coping outcomes.
5. Identify predictors of coping in sport.

* I would like to thank Cory Niefer, Ivan Tam, and Huskie Athletics (University of Saskatchewan). I would like to say a special thanks to Sarah Junkin, whose undergraduate thesis research helped to shape the fictional vignette presented in the chapter. Last, but not least, I would like to thank Cathy Magnus and the rest of the SPAACE SQUAD for their artwork and feedback on this chapter.

Many of the truths we cling to depend greatly on our point of view. —Obi-Wan Kenobi, *Star Wars*

"Sport has always fascinated me. On the one hand, it seems like it's a never-ending source of stress for me, but on the other hand, I can't imagine my life without it," said 20-year-old Natalie, an elite Canadian track-and-field sprinter. "Don't get me wrong; I would never want to give up sprinting, but I really wish that I could deal with the stress better. After all, the main reason I came to this university was so that I could compete in track. It just seems like there are so many things that worry me. I do my best to cope with my feelings, and that sometimes helps, but often I don't even know what to do."

Natalie reflected upon her feelings further and said, "I'm probably most stressed right before a race. From the time I finish my warm-up until the time the gun goes, I get really, really nervous. I've always been really afraid of failure, so even the possibility that I might come last really bothers me right before the race. I'm always wondering about things like what my coach and my boyfriend are going to think of me if I don't win. But it's not only that; it's also that darn bodysuit that I have to wear. I know I need to wear it to go faster, but couldn't they just add maybe a little more fabric to it? I feel like I'm naked out there and wonder what might be hanging out here and there, if you know what I mean. I do my best just to focus on the race through deep breathing and things like that, but my mind can never really get off those other things. Once the race starts, I'm fine. My mind goes totally on the race, and nothing else seems to matter. I think that's why I do well despite getting so nervous beforehand."

"Another thing that really stresses me out about sport is that we never seem to get enough money to train properly. I always have to take part-time jobs here and there just so that I can go to nationals or get new spikes for competition. That's time that I really should be using for proper training. Plus, my coach gets mad at me for being so tired at practice 'cause I had to be up until 1 a.m. carrying boxes the night before. I feel like I'm letting the team down, but I really don't have any other options other than to be poor and starve."

A unique source of stress was her conflicting feelings about her "sport" body. She continued, "Being all muscular and strong really helps me go fast, but it's not so cool when I'm trying on these, like, size 8 pants, and I can't even get my legs in the leg holes because my legs are too big from running and weight training. I fit in pretty good when I'm at the track, but I think that when I'm in public, people are looking at me and thinking 'what kind of steroids is she taking?' I just pretend I don't see them or just laugh it off when they say something. It actually doesn't even bother me all that much anyways because I'm proud that I'm a strong, fit, athletic woman. If they don't like it, they can just suck it up (laughs)."

The use of the term *stress* is commonplace in modern Canadian society. Although it certainly isn't an experience limited to sport, athletes' ability to manage stress is often thought to be critical to elite performance. What does it mean when an athlete says that he or she is stressed? And what role does coping play in the experience of stress? Natalie's story provides us with some insight into the complexity of stress and the coping process. Athletes don't just find themselves in a stressful situation, resolve it, and then move on to the next situation. Instead, there are many facets to an athlete's life, often competing with one another and making the management of stress extremely challenging. Such is the case with Natalie and her conflicted feelings about having a strong, muscular body. In addition, seldom are situations easily resolved. Often they play out over a long period of time and significantly strain athletes' personal resources as they attempt to cope.

Canadians have played a prominent role in sport stress and coping research in recent years (Figure 6.1). The work of Peter Crocker in the late 1980s really acted as a catalyst for coping research in Canada over the past two decades (e.g., Crocker, 1989a; Crocker,

1989b; Crocker, Alderman, & Smith, 1988). Since then, contributions to the field have been made by many scholars. In this chapter, the concepts of stress and coping in sport will be explored, with special emphasis on Canadian perspectives and examples. Although definitions of stress and coping have changed over time, one constant theme is that these two concepts are intimately linked.

Figure 6.1   Over the past two decades, stress and coping have been a focus of research in Canada to help *us* help *athletes* deal more effectively with the many demands of sport

Illustration by Kent Kowalski.

Some Common Myths about Stress and Coping in Sport

MYTH: *Elite sport is inherently stressful.*
How athletes interpret specific situations is the key factor that will determine whether or not they experience stress (and what level of stress). Even situations that one might think should be stressful might not cause stress, depending on a particular athlete's goals and interpretation of what is happening. For example, an apparently stressful event, such as breaking an ankle, might be interpreted by an athlete as an opportunity to avoid the performance demands of sport. Thus, to understand stress, we need to know athletes' goals and what they are thinking.

MYTH: *We can determine how athletes are coping by observing their behaviour.*
Observable coping behaviour, such as yelling at a referee or trying a new swimming stroke technique, is only one type of coping. Athletes' non-observable efforts, such as re-interpreting the reason a coach is yelling at them or wishing they were somewhere else, are also potential ways to cope with stress. Watching athletes respond to stress will give us only part of the coping picture.

MYTH: *Dropping out of sport is an ineffective coping strategy.*

Although in many cases dropping out of sport may not be the best or preferable option to manage stress, in some cases this action might well be the most effective coping strategy. Coping strategies are not inherently good or bad. Effective coping depends on the match between the situation, the athlete's goals and values, and the strategy that is used.

Introduction

Any starting point of a conversation about stress and coping in sport needs to begin by addressing the basic question: What is stress? Is stress involved in your going to the Olympics? Is stress involved when you choose the wrong ski wax before sending yourself sailing down a large mountain? Is stress involved in facing an opponent whom you have never beaten but must face again? The answer to these questions is a resounding "maybe." As we will discuss, situations are not inherently stressful. Instead, athletes play an active role in how they interpret the situations they face, and often it is very difficult to predict when stress will occur. For example, Canadian baseball pitcher Eric Gagne ("Expos 7, Dodgers 3," 2004) reported, "I was a little bit nervous about not throwing strikes." What's most interesting is that he reported this following a spring training game in 2004, the year after he won the National League Cy Young Award as a member of the Los Angeles Dodgers! If Eric Gagne can experience stress in a spring training game as a Cy Young Award winner, which we might not expect, then defining stress is clearly not a simple matter.

The Concept of Stress

Carpenter (1992) described how the concept of stress most often has one of two meanings. First, stress can represent what is often referred to as the *stress response*, which consists of physiological, cognitive, affective, and behavioural reactions when we are faced with heavy demands. For example, if a hitter in baseball sees a fastball coming straight toward his head, he experiences increased blood pressure, heart rate, and perspiration, as well as the fight or flight reaction (e.g., duck out of the way) because of sympathetic nervous system arousal. This response serves a very adaptive function for human beings, and athletes are more able to get pumped up or get the adrenaline flowing to achieve peak performance when there is sympathetic nervous system arousal (Aldwin, 2000; see Buckworth & Dishman, 2002, for an overview of the physiological mechanisms of the stress response).

A second approach to defining stress is to consider it as a *process* that links situational demands to an athlete's reactions to the outcomes of that experience. This second definition is consistent with cognitive-based models of stress that emphasize the dynamic interrelationships among the environment, people, and their reactions to the environment. A limitation in defining stress as simply a reaction to an external event is that it ignores the role of a person's perception, or cognitive appraisal, in the experience of stress. What is stressful for someone might not be stressful for someone else or even for that same person at another time (Aldwin, 2000). Hence, **stress** can be defined as an experience that is produced through a person-situation relationship that is perceived as taxing or exceeding the athlete's resources.

Stressors, on the other hand, are the external events, forces, or situations that have the potential to be interpreted as stressful. Examples of potential stressors include playing in a championship match, getting injured, being yelled at by a coach, and losing national team funding. The implication is that each athlete might interpret situations and stressors in unique ways. For example, although playing a televised game on *Hockey Night in Canada* might be extremely stressful for one player because of a concern over making a mistake with so many people watching, another player might interpret it as no big deal.

As we can see from the definition of stress, **cognitive appraisal**, or someone's interpretation of a situation, is a key concept. Richard Lazarus (1991, 2000a, 2000b) distinguished between primary and secondary cognitive appraisal. **Primary appraisal** is an evaluation of what is at stake for an athlete in a situation. Whether or not something is at stake depends on whether what is happening is relevant to the athlete's goals and whether the situation is interpreted as having the potential to be beneficial or harmful to her or him. Alternatively, **secondary appraisal** is an evaluation of what can be done in the situation, which will depend on an athlete's available resources, level of perceived control, and expectations regarding what is likely to occur in the future.

The cognitive appraisal process can result in various kinds of stress, including harm/loss, threat, and challenge (Lazarus, 1993a, 1993b). **Harm/loss** refers to an appraisal of a situation in which psychological damage has already been done and the loss is irrevocable. For example, a university athlete might experience stress over not being able to play Canadian interuniversity sport as a result of using up her five years of eligibility. Her personal identity might be strongly tied to being a member of the university team, and once that identity is taken away she could really struggle in her search for a new identity. A **threat** appraisal refers to the anticipation of harm that might occur or is likely to occur. An example would be a young gymnast who is fearful of falling off the balance beam at an upcoming competition because falling might jeopardize her chances of winning and be a source of embarrassment. **Challenge**, on the other hand, stems from the interpretation of potential benefits from succeeding in a situation that presents difficult demands. For example, a rugby player might relish the opportunity to prove herself in a championship game even though she realizes that the opponent is much stronger than she.

When different types of stress are considered, it seems clear that not all stress is negative and to be avoided. The potential for stress to be both beneficial and harmful has long been recognized (see Selye, 1993, for an overview of the history of the stress concept). Hans Selye was one of the pioneers of the stress concept in the 20th century and was a professor at McGill University and the Université de Montréal. He distinguished between **eustress** (good stress) and **distress** (bad stress). He suggested that stress can be useful for performance and well-being (eustress) but that at a certain point it becomes too high (distress) and results in various mental, emotional, and physiological limitations (Buckworth & Dishman, 2002). Thus, we really need to consider the type of stress that people are experiencing because this knowledge informs us of how situations are being interpreted and the potential consequences of the stressful experience. It is also important to note that we will experience stress only if the situation is meaningful or important to us. If an athlete doesn't really care about what happens, then the situation won't be perceived as stressful. An example would be a young goalkeeper who gets scored on in a game of soccer but is indifferent to letting in a goal or losing the competition. However, if the game were important to him, then letting in a goal, especially if he felt blamed for it, would indeed likely be a source of stress.

Reflections 6.1

What makes a situation stressful for an athlete? Are there certain types of situations that are more likely to be interpreted as stressful?

Illustration by Kent Kowalski.

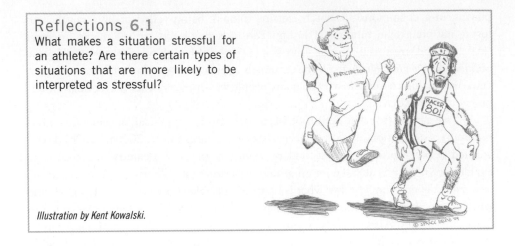

Stress and Emotion

Before we discuss specific sources of stress in sport, it is important to point out that the concept of stress is closely tied to the concept of emotion (Lazarus, 1999). Richard Lazarus provided the framework for the way in which many researchers study and interpret stress and coping. He suggested that the concepts of stress and emotion are similar; however, he also said that we can learn more about what someone is experiencing, what a situation means to an individual, and how she or he is likely to respond to it by looking at the specific emotion that is experienced, rather than by looking at the more general concept of stress. He stated:

> Despite these subdivisions of stress types (harm/loss, threat, and challenge), the typical idea of stress is much simpler than that of the emotions. Either as a single dimension, or with only a few functional categories, stress tells us relatively little about the details of a person's struggle to adapt. Emotion, conversely, includes at least 15 different varieties, greatly increasing the richness of what can be said about a person's adaptational struggle. (Lazarus, 1999, p. 33)

The 15 emotions Lazarus identified, including both positive and negative emotions, are shown in Table 6.1. Each of these emotions is important because there is a core relational theme for each emotion that describes the nature of the relationship between an athlete and her or his environment. For example, the core relational theme of anxiety is that the person is *facing an uncertain, existential threat*, suggesting that when an athlete is experiencing anxiety, he or she is not sure of what will happen, when it will happen, or even what can be done about it (Lazarus, 2000a). If we look at competitive anxiety in sport, much of the stress that is experienced is simply the result of not knowing what the outcome will be (e.g., "Will I perform well today?"). We can see an example of this in Eric Gagne's report that he was nervous in a pre-season baseball game because he did not know whether he would be able to throw strikes in the game. Ultimately, in that game he pitched a perfect inning and reported that he felt great, most likely reflecting, in part, the positive experience of being able to throw strikes. Clearly, knowing about a specific emotion does tell us more about what is going on with an athlete than just knowing that he or she is stressed. However, despite Lazarus' recommendation to focus more on specific emotions, as opposed to general stress relationships, there is an abundance of sport research on general aspects of stress. A major focus of research has been on identifying sources of stress.

Table 6.1   The Core Relational Theme for Each Emotion with Sport Examples

Emotion	Theme	Sport Examples
Anger	A demeaning offence against me and mine.	A bad call by a basketball official causes an athlete to foul out of an important game.
Anxiety	Facing uncertain, existential threat.	A football player does not know how she will perform in the championship game.
Fright	An immediate, concrete, and overwhelming physical danger.	A gymnast loses his grip on the parallel bars.
Guilt	Having transgressed a moral imperative.	A soccer player lies to her coach about why she missed practice.
Shame	Failing to live up to an ego-ideal.	A discus thrower comes last in a competition that she expected to win.
Sadness	Having experienced an irrevocable loss.	An athlete loses her world championship wrestling title.
Envy	Wanting what someone else has and feeling deprived of it but justified in having it.	A rookie NHL player wants the same ice time or money as other team members because he feels he deserves it.
Jealousy	Resenting a third party for loss or threat to another's affection or favor.	A speed skater's coach decides not to continue to coach him because a better athlete who needs coaching has come along.
Happiness	Making reasonable progress toward the realization of a goal.	A bobsledder wins an Olympic gold medal, which was her ultimate goal.
Pride	Enhancement of one's ego-identity by taking credit for a valued object or achievement, either one's own or that of someone or group with whom one identifies.	A volleyball player believes the team won because of his blocking ability.
Relief	A distressing goal-incongruent condition that has changed for the better or gone away.	A race-car driver escapes a crash without injury when injury was seen as likely.
Hope	Fearing the worst but yearning for better, and believing the improvement is possible.	A fencer believes she has no chance of winning the world championship but hopes for victory.
Love	Desiring or participating in affection, usually but not necessarily reciprocated.	A swimmer desires a teammate's affection.
Gratitude	Appreciation for an altruistic gift that provides personal benefit.	A young goalkeeper is helped by a veteran goalkeeper to develop his skills even though the veteran might lose his starting position to the younger goalkeeper.
Compassion	Moved by another's suffering and wanting to help.	A boxer sees another boxer injured and wants to help.

Note: "Table 3.4" modified from Emotion and Adaptation by Richard S. Lazarus, copyright © 1991 by Oxford University Press, Inc. Used by permission of Oxford University Press, Inc.

Sources of Stress in Sport

General Dimensions

Think about the complexity inherent in the numerous types and competitive levels of sport. To help understand the various sources of stress, researchers have proposed the use of general dimensions or concerns. In their research with American national champion figure skaters and national teams for alpine and freestyle skiers, Daniel Gould and his colleagues found that general sources of stress identified by athletes included (1) psychological concerns, such as competitive stress, self-doubt, losing, fear of injury, and mental readiness to perform, (2) physical concerns, such as injury, body weight, pain, and physical inactivity, (3) social concerns, such as negative relationships with others, lack of attention, coaching changes, and others' expectations, (4) environmental concerns, such as financial stress and media demands, and (5) career and life direction concerns (Gould, Finch, & Jackson, 1993; Gould, Udry, Bridges, & Beck, 1997).

Similar general sources of stress have been found in research with Canadian adolescents involved in sport (Kowalski, 1999; Kowalski & Crocker, 2001). Examples of physical sources of stress included injury and illness. More specifically, one young athlete reported that a source of stress was having to "watch the team play when I was out with an injury." Psychological sources of stress included pressure to perform and important upcoming competitions. An example of a psychological source of stress can be seen in the following quote, "Tryout for city team in guys' singles badminton against the number one player in the school. He was one grade older than me." Examples of specific sources of environmental stress included time management and financial concerns. One young athlete wrote, "Playing on an AAA hockey team, which is an hour away from practice every day. There is no time for anything after school. I eat and then I'm off to practice." Finally, social concerns and relationships that caused stress were those with coaches, parents, and other athletes. One young woman stated, "A girl on my basketball team believed she was 'the boss.' Nothing was ever her fault. Somebody else was always in the wrong even if it was her fault." Overall, sport participants reported a wide range of stress sources and males and females reported similar dimensions of sources. Although there was little evidence of life direction concerns, this dimension of stress likely becomes more important as athletes get older.

Another group of Canadian researchers looked at sources of stress for members of a women's national soccer team during preparations for the 1999 women's soccer World Cup finals (Holt & Hogg, 2002). They wanted to know about sources of stress in a team sport during a six-week preparation camp leading up to the World Cup event, in part because most of the previous research had been with individual sports. They found four main categories of stressors: coaches' communication, demands of international soccer, competitive stressors, and distractions. Examples of coaches' communication stressors included a negative, punitive coach-player interaction during training and negative, excessive feedback during the games. Demands of international soccer that they identified revolved primarily around the need to adjust to the technical and tactical demands of a fast-paced international game. A number of competitive stressors were identified by the players, including having pre-game anxiety, having high expectations of going to the Olympics, making mistakes, coming off the bench, fearing being cut from the team, and getting evaluations of individual player's performance. The two primary distractions that the athletes mentioned were the fatigue from practising twice a day during camp and opponent aggression. As Holt and Hogg identified, one of the unique aspects of their study was finding that many of the stressors were related to the social interactions that are part of a team environment.

Subtypes of Stressors

An alternative approach when looking at stress in sport is to be more specific in identifying subtypes of stressors that athletes face. Three distinctions made in the literature are acute vs. chronic stressors, expected vs. unexpected stressors, and competitive vs. non-competitive stressors. **Chronic stress** occurs over a long period of time, such as in the case of ongoing harassment, relationship issues, and chronic pain (Anshel, Kim, Kim, Chang, & Eom, 2001); **acute stress** occurs over a shorter period of time and its onset is much more sudden (Anshel, Gregory, & Kaczmarek, 1990). Mark Anshel and his colleagues have identified a number of acute stressors that athletes might face, such as making a physical or mental error, being criticized or reprimanded by a coach, observing an opponent cheating, sustaining pain or injury, receiving a bad call by an official, seeing an opponent play really well, performing poorly because of bad weather or substandard playing conditions, and being distracted by a crowd (Anshel, 2001; Anshel, Jamieson, & Raviv, 2001). If acute stressors are not managed effectively, they can lead to long-term chronic stress and burnout (Anshel, Kim, et al., 2001). For example, we have probably all seen situations in which a coach makes a negative comment to an athlete during a practice or competition, but nothing is done to resolve the conflict; then, later on many other relationship issues develop between the coach and the athlete.

A second distinction that has been made is between expected and unexpected stressors (Dugdale, Eklund, & Gordon, 2002). An **expected stressor** is one that an athlete plans or prepares for whereas an **unexpected stressor** is one that is not anticipated. Dugdale et al. asked 91 athletes representing New Zealand at the 1998 Commonwealth Games (ages 14 to 46) to identify the most stressful experience they had prior to or during the Games. The experiences were then rated as expected or unexpected. They found that more than two-thirds of athletes who reported stress said that the source of stress was unexpected. Examples given by the athletes included things like transportation delays, poor food, and bad refereeing decisions. One of the study's most interesting findings was that the athletes perceived the unexpected stressors to be more threatening than the expected ones, suggesting that athletes might experience more or less stress, depending on the type of stress source they face. Surely the extreme distress that Canadian track-and-field hurdler Perdita Felicien (and the nation) experienced after her fall in the 2004 Olympic final 100-metre hurdles was a result of not only the importance of the race but also of the unexpectedness of her fall, based on her previous performances.

A third distinction that has been made is between competitive and non-competitive stressors (Dugdale et al., 2002; Gould, Eklund, & Jackson, 1993; Noblet & Gifford, 2002). **Competitive stressors** would be those that are experienced prior to, during, or immediately following competition; they include injury, poor officiating, and expectations from others. **Non-competitive stressors** would be those that are related to sport but are not directly part of an actual competition performance; they include having to deal with the media, travel, rehabilitation, and team meetings. For example, Noblet and Gifford interviewed professional Australian Football League players. The players reported competitive stressors like poor technique, constant pressure to perform, and high performance expectations, as well as a wide variety of non-competitive stressors, including job insecurity, long training sessions, lack of feedback, constant public scrutiny, and difficulty balancing sport with other commitments. The vignette of Natalie presented at the beginning of this chapter provides an additional example of how athletes can experience both competitive (e.g., fear of not winning) and non-competitive (e.g., having a muscular body in social settings) stressors in sport.

It is important to recognize that specific sports might have unique sources of stress that athletes within those sports are more likely to face than are other athletes. For example, the professional Australian Football League players in the Noblet and Gifford (2002) study had to deal with stressors associated with being in a professional, high-profile league—job insecurity and constant public scrutiny—that other athletes might not have to face. Another example of sport-specific stressors is provided by Campbell and Jones (2002) who looked at stress experienced by male wheelchair basketball players. They interviewed 10 members of Great Britain's men's wheelchair basketball team and found a variety of common sources of stress, including pre-event concerns, negative match preparation, on-court concerns, post-match performance concerns, negative aspects of a major event, poor group interaction and communication, negative coaching style or behaviour, and relationship issues. However, they also found stressors that many athletes in other sports don't have to contend with, such as the demands or costs of wheelchair basketball and people's lack of disability awareness. These two examples show that there are a number of stressors that are common to many athletes but that there are also often unique demands that athletes face, depending on the nature of their sport.

Reflections 6.2
Think back to your own experiences in sport. What different types of acute/ chronic, expected/unexpected, and competitive/non-competitive sources of stress have you witnessed as an athlete, a spectator, or a coach?

The Concept of Coping

When athletes are faced with stress and emotion, how they attempt to manage their experiences can take many forms. For example, Paralympian Chantal Petitclerc's response to being co-winner of Canada's top track-and-field athlete of the year award was to decline her award. Petitclerc won five gold medals and set three world records at the 2004 Paralympics Games in Athens, but she declined to share the award with Perdita Felicien, who fell in the Olympic 100-metre hurdles final. As Christie (2004) reports online in *The Globe and Mail*, Petitclerc said:

> It's always a little shocking to see what Paralympics medals and world records are worth, to really see it. After Athens, you feel you've come a certain way and had a certain achievement and your sport has grown and been recognized, that you're finally there. And this is shocking.

Hence, she declined the award as a way to protest the perceived value of Paralympics performances in comparison with those of able-bodied Olympic counterparts. Was declining the award the only way she could have reacted to the stress of feeling her achievements were not valued? There were probably many other coping options, including seeking social support from coaches, friends, and teammates; suppressing her feelings; or reappraising the meaning of the award. Most likely her attempts to cope were not all-or-none approaches; she likely attempted to deal with the situation in multiple ways. However, her most newsworthy strategy was the one that was publicized in the media. Ultimately, how athletes cope with stress in sport is a very complex process.

Clearly the concept of coping is closely linked to stress. First, if athletes believe that they can effectively manage a situation, they will be less likely to experience stress. Second, the ways in which athletes attempt to cope with stress can affect both the level and the type of stress that they experience. For example, if athletes cope effectively with a situation, it should reduce their stress level. Also, the type of stress might change from one of perceived threat to one of challenge. If stress is experienced when a situation taxes athletes' perceived resources (i.e., an important goal is harmed/lost, threatened, or challenged), then coping is the way in which they attempt to deal with that psychological stress (Lazarus, 1999).

An important question is "what is coping?" A formal definition of coping was provided by Lazarus (1991), who described **coping** as " . . . cognitive and behavioural efforts to manage specific external or internal demands (and conflicts between them) that are appraised as taxing or exceeding the resources of the person" (p. 112). Consequently, although coping does include actual physical actions, it is not limited to them. For example, if Natalie from the opening vignette tries to convince herself that nobody is looking at her in her bodysuit, she is coping as much as if she had changed her competition outfit to one that is less revealing. However, within Lazarus' definition it is important to also point out that coping has to be an effortful process to manage stress. If athletes engage in behaviours that are routine but that still help them to avoid problems, such as going to practice every day, that is not coping per se. Instead, routine behaviours are **management skills** that help prevent stress from happening in the first place; these behaviours themselves might have developed initially from learning to cope (Aldwin, 2000). For example, a soccer player might have initially begun wearing shin pads as a way to cope with being kicked; however, once that behaviour (wearing shin pads) becomes relatively automatic, it is better considered a management skill rather than actual coping. Most importantly, what Lazarus' definition of coping suggests is that efforts to manage stress are constantly changing and are extremely complex. Athletes' coping will depend, in part, on both available coping resources and expectations. Their coping efforts then must shift as the effectiveness of particular strategies becomes evident and as the situation itself changes over time.

Micro- and Macro-analytic Levels of Coping

There are different models of coping, but one common notion across models is that there are different levels of coping. A **micro-analytic** approach to coping involves the specific coping strategies or families of coping strategies that athletes engage in to cope with stress. An example of a micro-analytic approach to coping is provided by Crocker and Graham (1995). They assessed the coping strategies of 377 competitive athletes who had used the strategies in a recent athletic situation—either a practice or a game—in which there was a performance difficulty or pressure to perform. The strategies Crocker and Graham assessed were active coping, seeking social support for instrumental or emotional reasons, planning, denial, humour, behavioural disengagement, venting of emotion, and suppression of competing activities.

At a practical level, each of these coping dimensions is made up of various instances of coping, or specific coping efforts. For example, while one athlete might yell at a coach as a way to vent emotions, another might cry. In another example, two wrestlers might cope with competition stress by using social support for instrumental reasons (coping dimension); however, one athlete might speak to a fellow wrestler to find out the schedule of events for the day (coping instance 1) while another might speak to the coach to find out an opponent's strengths and weaknesses (coping instance 2). Finally, two coaches might cope with the stress of dealing with a non-cohesive group of athletes by using active coping (coping dimension); however, one coach might bring in a conflict management specialist to improve the team's communication skills (coping instance 1) whereas another might make the practices harder in an effort to help the team bond together in the face of adversity (coping instance 2).

A major challenge in the coping in sport literature is that there is no consistent set of micro-level coping strategies across studies. However, this lack of consistency not only reflects the difficulty in understanding the coping process, but it also seems that a variety of strategies is necessary in order to understand coping in different sports or situations. For example, a coping strategy, such as on-field task communication, might be entirely appropriate for international level soccer, but it might be entirely inappropriate for singles figure skating or gymnastics, in which communication with teammates during the actual performance is absent and irrelevant. Thus, researchers are always trying to find the delicate balance between including coping strategies that are appropriate for their population and sport, but still allowing for comparison between athletes and sports. A balanced approach better allows researchers to examine situations that have relevance across sports, such as relationships between coping and variables like burnout or injury. Another limitation with the micro-level approach is that knowing the specific coping strategies being used tells us little about why athletes are using those particular strategies or what goals they are trying to accomplish via coping efforts.

Thus, at the **macro-level** it is the goals, or functions, of the strategies that are often assessed. An important macro-level distinction that is often made in the literature is between problem-focused coping and emotion-focused coping. **Problem-focused coping** refers to efforts that help athletes change the actual situation in some way. For example, a few years ago many Canadian speed skaters began using the clap skate (with a spring-loaded hinge under the heel) in order to more effectively deal with the stress of increasing performance demands in world-class speed skating. **Emotion-focused coping**, on the other hand, is an attempt to change the way a situation is attended to or interpreted. For example, an athlete might be comforted by a parent who tells her that the coach is only trying to get the best out of her athletes with her punitive behaviour. Another distinct type of coping often included in the literature is **avoidance coping**, in which athletes attempt to remove themselves from the stressful situation (e.g., Amirkhan, 1990; Endler & Parker, 1994; Kowalski & Crocker, 2001). A common example of avoidance coping in sport would be an athlete's quitting a team.

Some researchers have attempted to merge micro- and macro-analytic approaches. Gaudreau and Blondin (2002, 2004) developed a framework for coping to assess both micro- and macro-level coping in competitive sport settings. Their model consists of 10 micro-level coping strategies that fall under three macro-level dimensions of coping. The macro-level dimensions are task-oriented coping, distraction-oriented coping, and disengagement coping (see Figure 6.2).

Figure 6.2 Micro- and macro-level coping in competitive sport

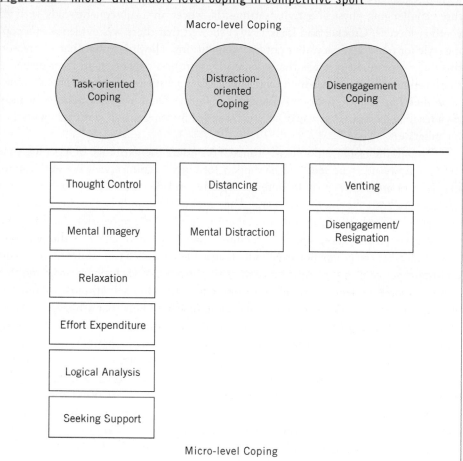

Note: Adapted from "Development of a Questionnaire for the Assessment of Coping Strategies Employed by Athletes in Competitive Sport Settings," by P. Gaudreau and J. P. Blondin, 2002, Psychology of Sport and Exercise, 3, pp. 1–34; and from "Different Athletes Cope Differently: A Cluster Analysis of Coping," by P. Gaudreau and J. P. Blondin, 2004, Personality and Individual Differences, 36, pp. 1865–1877.

Coping Style

Despite the dynamic nature of coping, one notion is that people attempt to cope in similar ways across different situations and over time. In other words, athletes have preferred **coping styles** that make them consistent in the ways they attempt to manage stress. For example, if an athlete's coping style is to use humour, then regardless of whether the stress is a conflict with a coach, an upcoming important competition, or a bad call by an official, that athlete will have a tendency to use humour as a coping strategy. Coping style is contrasted with a state-like, or situational, approach that emphasizes coping changes, depending on the situation. A state-like view of coping would predict coping to be much more variable, as athletes would attempt to match their coping strategy to the specific stressor, rather than having a tendency to rely on a consistent coping style.

There is a growing body of literature on coping styles in the sport domain. In support of a state-like view of coping, Bouffard and Crocker (1992) found that individuals with physical disabilities did not consistently use the same coping strategies across three challenging physical activity settings. However, in a subsequent study with 25 youth swimmers, Crocker and Isaak (1997) showed that there was evidence of a coping style for training sessions but not for competitions. They suggested that one reason this difference might occur is that competitions are less consistent in their demands than workouts in practice, which tend to be fairly repetitive. Competitions often differ in their importance, in other swimmers in the race, and in who is watching the race. As a result, a more diverse way of coping is needed in competition compared with during practice.

Overall, the results are somewhat mixed regarding the existence of a coping style in sport; however, there seems to be support for both a coping style view and a state-like view of coping in sport. Gaudreau, Lapierre, and Blondin (2001) showed direct evidence for both approaches to coping. They studied the stability of coping across pre-competitive, competitive, and post-competitive phases of competition for 33 junior competitive golfers. There was considerable variability in coping across the phases of competition for the group; however, individual athletes tended to maintain a relatively consistent position in the group on each coping strategy at each phase, meaning that there was some evidence of stability in coping for the individual athletes, despite the changes in coping across phases of competition. It seems likely that athletes have preferred ways of coping with stress, but that the choice of strategies is flexible depending on the type of stress that is being faced. This is consistent with Lazarus' (1991) view of coping as a process; that is, athletes' coping is constantly changing in an attempt to meet the demands of a situation. Thus, while an athlete might prefer to problem-solve as a way of coping, problem-solving is only likely to be used in situations in which problem-solving is perceived to be beneficial, or it may be attempted and then abandoned once perceived as ineffective. Understanding the role of coping styles versus a state-like approach might best be summed up by Crocker, Kowalski, and Graham (1998) who stated, "Overemphasizing either person or environmental characteristics may lead to distorted understanding of the role of coping in the stress process" (p. 150).

> Athletes appear to have preferred ways of coping with stress; however, coping requires flexibility to select strategies that best match the situation.

Photo courtesy of PhotoDisc/Getty Images.

Both the person and environment are important factors in athletes' coping, as Lazarus originally suggested. What takes on more importance is likely determined by who is doing the coping and what they are coping with.

Coping and Outcomes of Coping

An important distinction to be made when trying to understand coping in sport is the distinction between the concept of coping and outcomes of the coping process. Coping is an effort to deal with stress. An **outcome of coping** is the result (good or bad) of those coping efforts. One of the most interesting aspects of sport is that sport itself can be either a coping strategy or an outcome of coping. For example, children who stay involved in sport are not necessarily coping with stress by staying in the sport. They might be using a variety of other coping efforts, such as social support from peers, that allows their continued participation in sport. However, some children might actually be using involvement in sport as a coping strategy to deal with other stressors in their lives, such as academic or family stress. Thus, although it is often difficult to distinguish between coping and coping outcomes, it is an important distinction to make. It is also critical to remember that because the experience of stress is a process, the outcomes of coping influence subsequent coping efforts. For example, if a field hockey player has an unsuccessful performance in a competition as a result of coping with stress by eating fast food as a form of emotional comfort, the outcome of that performance will likely prompt the search for alternative coping strategies. Likewise, successful performance reinforces coping efforts.

A group of Canadian researchers recently completed a review of the coping in sport literature and showed that coping was related to a number of functional, emotional, and psychosomatic outcomes (Hoar, Kowalski, Gaudreau, & Crocker, in press). Functional outcomes of coping include things like sport performance and goal attainment, as well as the desire to continue in sport. Surprisingly, there is little evidence in sport to suggest that coping is strongly related to high performance. As an example of this, Haney and Long (1995) found only weak relationships between coping and performance in basketball free throws and soccer or field hockey penalty shots. However, there is evidence to suggest that coping might play a more important role in whether or not athletes perceive that they are able to attain their goals, and problem-focused strategies tended to be related to higher perceived goal attainment (Gaudreau & Blondin, 2002). For example, athletes who use planning as a coping strategy to deal with the demands of sport would be more likely to think that they could attain their sport goals, compared with athletes who do not use planning. A recent study with Korean and American athletes found that problem-focused coping was related to the desire to continue in sport whereas avoidance coping was predictive of a lower intention to continue (Kim & Duda, 2003).

The most common emotional outcomes in sport coping research are emotional states. Although competitive anxiety has been related to higher use of disengagement strategies (e.g., Gaudreau & Blondin, 2002; Ntoumanis & Biddle, 2000), it is difficult to know whether the coping or the anxiety comes first. Does the use of disengagement-type strategies, such as avoidance of a coach, lead to increased anxiety in competition? Or is disengagement coping more likely to occur when stress and anxiety get to a point where the athlete becomes overwhelmed, leaving him or her with little option but to avoid the situation as a way to control the stress level? Most likely it acts like a spiral, whereby avoidance of the coach would lead to increased anxiety, which in turn would make more avoidance even more likely; however, these dynamic interplays between outcomes and coping have been rarely studied in sport.

It is also difficult to draw conclusions about the relationship between coping and general affective (emotional) states. Generally, problem-focused coping strategies, like active coping and planning, are positively related to positive affect. Emotion-focused strategies, like seeking social support for emotional reasons and avoidance strategies, are more related to negative affect (e.g., Crocker & Graham, 1995; Gaudreau & Blondin, 2002; Kim & Duda, 2003). However, the reasons for these relationships are not clear. Problem-focused strategies might help people get closer to their goals, thereby increasing positive affect (Gaudreau, Blondin, & Lapierre, 2002).

The psychosomatic outcomes of coping that have been studied in sport include rehabilitation from athletic injury and burnout. Coping has been recognized as an important factor by sport trainers and athletic therapists for effective injury rehabilitation (Ford & Gordon, 1998), and there is some evidence to suggest that coping can contribute to a more rapid return to competition and a lower chance of repeat injuries (Udry, 1997). Knowing what specific strategies lead to a more effective recovery from injury is a more difficult question to answer. Cornelius (2002) suggested it is likely that both problem-focused and emotion-focused coping strategies are important for athletes to use.

As for burnout, the second psychosomatic outcome, it results from the inability to effectively manage excessive demands in training and competition (Smith, 1986). It is not uncommon to hear athletes, especially elite athletes, speak about being burned out. However, as Gould, Udry, Tuffey, and Loehr (1996) pointed out, sport does not exist in isolation. Athletes often have to deal with a variety of demands, all of which can contribute to burnout. We can see the potential for burnout in Natalie, who described in the vignette the fatigue she was experiencing that resulted from the need to both work and train. However, it is not only athletes who experience burnout in sport. Coaches and athletic directors are also at risk because of the many demands of sport (Kelley, Eklund, & Ritter, 1999; Martin, Kelley, & Eklund, 1999).

Reflections 6.3
It is important to distinguish between *coping* and *outcomes of coping*. Reflecting on your own experiences, has your involvement in sport been more of a stress release, or has it just been another source of stress in your life?

Coping Effectiveness

A question we often face in sport is "Are some coping strategies better for athletes to use than others?" In other words, are some coping strategies more *effective* than others? Few of us would suggest that a bench-clearing brawl in youth soccer would be an effective way to deal with a dirty tackle by the opposing team. What then do we make of the reactions to a brawl during a game between the Edmonton Oilers and the Atlanta Thrashers of the National Hockey League in which even the goalies got into a scuffle? Thrashers' goalie Pasi Numinen was quoted by CBS Sportsline.com after the game as saying, "It's always fun. Just give a couple of punches, take a couple punches, still alive"; even Oilers' coach Craig MacTavish said, "A brawl like that always brings a team together" ("Goalies join," 2004). It would be hard to conclude from these reactions that fighting is inherently an ineffective coping strategy. As with many other aspects of coping, the effectiveness of any coping strategy depends on the situation. Depending on the athlete and the situation, even such strategies as dropping out from sport can be effective as a way to prevent excessive long-term stress and burnout.

Susan Folkman (1992) presented a **goodness-of-fit model of coping** in which the effectiveness of coping depends on two fits: (1) the fit between reality and appraisal, which reflects the match between what is actually going on in the situation and how that situation is appraised by someone, and (2) the fit between appraisal and coping, which reflects the match between one's *perceived* controllability of a situation and the *actual* control someone has. If we look back at the vignette, we can't necessarily conclude that because of Natalie's acceptance of wearing the bodysuit and her high level of performance in track that she is effectively coping with her body issues, especially over the long term. Alternatively, she might have overestimated how much others are actually looking at her body, possibly resulting in her choosing less revealing clothing that could potentially impede even better race times. As well, her high stress right before her performance might have resulted from feelings of lack of control over the situation and perceived inability to do anything about it when, in fact, she might have been able to implement a number of mental skills training techniques to manage her stress (see Chapter 8 for examples).

Just knowing the coping strategies that are used by athletes tells us little about the effectiveness of those coping attempts. Coping strategies assist us in coordinating our actions, our social resources, and our preferences and available options in a given situation. Thus, all coping is aimed at helping athletes adapt to stress. Having said that, Skinner, Edge, Altman, and Sherwood (2003) did say that if we take a slightly different look at the concept of coping, a distinction can be made between good news and bad news coping. **Good news coping** attempts would be organized, flexible, and constructive whereas **bad news coping** would be rigid, disorganized, and destructive responses to unmanageable levels of stress. Athletes who use such ways of coping as helplessness, constant opposition to others, and social withdrawal might be at risk for long-term consequences, such as low self-confidence or depression.

Reflections 6.4

From your own experiences in sport, what would you consider to be athletes' good news and bad news ways of coping with sport stress?

Kim and Duda (2003) suggested that if we want to understand the effectiveness of athletes' coping, we need to consider both the short- and long-term results of their coping efforts. Some strategies that athletes use might be effective in the short term but result in negative consequences in the long term. In a study with 318 U.S. athletes and 404 Korean athletes who reported coping with psychological difficulties during important competitions, Kim and Duda found that both problem-focused coping and avoidance coping strategies were related to perceived short-term effectiveness. Alternatively, only problem-focused coping was considered to be effective over the long term. In addition, situations that were perceived as more controllable resulted in higher use of problem-focused coping; this is consistent with Folkman's goodness-of-fit model.

The difficulty in trying to determine the effectiveness of athletes' coping efforts is that in most cases any strategy will have a combination of positive and negative consequences, depending on how we look at it. For example, although Natalie's decision to continue to race in the bodysuit likely has positive performance results, it might compound her body issues. Coping is part of a dynamic stress process that involves the many, often competing, demands that athletes face; thus, identifying what strategies athletes should use is going to continue to be a challenge.

Predictors of Coping

Although we might not necessarily know how athletes should be coping, the work that has been discussed suggests that we at least have some idea of how athletes might effectively cope with stress. We have often seen athletes do things that have not worked, such as telling a coach to take a hike in less than a politically correct way. In addition, we have seen different athletes react to similar stressors in very different ways. For example, one athlete might embrace an upcoming World Cup event; another might be terrified. Thus, at a very practical level as coaches and athletes, we often still want to know what predicts how someone will cope with stress. A number of variables that have been shown to be predictive of coping in sport have been identified (Hoar et al., in press). Some of the strongest predictors of athletes' coping include gender, culture, cognitive appraisal, and personal resources.

Gender

Studies that look at differences in coping between males and females have been of great interest to sport researchers, especially over the last 10 years. This literature has demonstrated one of the most consistent findings in the sport coping literature: males and females do appear to cope differently in sport! Overall, females tend to use more social support, help-seeking, increased effort, and emotion-focused coping than males, to manage sport stress (e.g., Crocker & Graham, 1995; Goyen & Anshel, 1998; Kowalski & Crocker, 2001; Maniar, Curry, Sommers-Flanagan, & Walsh, 2001). In general, the combined sport and general psychology literature has shown that females tend to cope more than males (Tamres, Janicki, & Helgeson, 2002). However, these differences might be due to differences in the type of stressors males and females face. **Role constraint theory** states that differences in stress are primarily the result of the different roles men and women play in society, as opposed to any inherent gender differences (see Tamres et al., 2002). Even in the vignette, we see Natalie dealing with the stress of having to wear a revealing bodysuit to compete in. If males on her team wear less revealing bodysuits to compete in, then the bodysuit would present a potential source of stress that is accentuated for the female competitors. Hence, Natalie will have to develop coping strategies that the males on her team will not have to, simply because of the expectations of what they are required to compete in. However, gender differences might not emerge simply because of different sources of stress. The **gender socialization hypothesis** predicts that males and females learn to use different coping strategies to manage the same types of situations (Crocker et al., 1998; Hoar et al., in press). Through sex-role stereotyping and role expectations, females are generally encouraged to express their emotions and turn to others for emotional support more than males. All in all, although the finding of gender differences is one of the most consistent results in sport coping research, why males and females differ is less clear.

Reflections 6.5

Although there is growing body of evidence to suggest that males and females cope with stress in sport differently, we don't really know why they are coping differently. Two possible explanations are (1) males and females experience different sources of stress and (2) there are socially defined expectations as to what are acceptable ways of coping for males and females. Are there particular aspects of Canadian culture that strengthen or weaken gender differences in coping?

Culture

There is a growing body of evidence demonstrating cultural differences in coping with stress in sport. Culture has relevance to coping because once a cultural group is established, it tends to persist and present more or less stable rules of conduct for members of the group (Lazarus, 1991). Thus, culture can play an important role in the way athletes attempt to deal with stress. For example, a number of studies have shown the particular importance of prayer as a coping strategy for Korean athletes (Kim & Duda, 2003; Park, 2000; Yoo, 2000, 2001). Similarly, Anshel, Jamieson, and Raviv (2001) have found that Israeli athletes use a high number of avoidance coping strategies to manage difficult coping situations. They suggested this behaviour was a result of cultural beliefs that focusing away from a task is an effective coping strategy when there is low control. In most studies, athletes from other countries are compared with U.S. athletes to determine whether or not there are cultural differences. Anshel, Williams, and Williams (2000) demonstrated more use of approach-emotion coping among Australian athletes than among U.S. athletes; in this coping strategy, athletes stay engaged in the situation and use emotion-focused strategies.

There have been surprisingly few studies to see if Canadians have a particular way of coping with stress in sport. Holt and Hogg (2002) showed that coaches were not used as sources of social support for, what is presumed to be, the Canadian national soccer team; this result differed from previous reports of players from other countries, including Germany, Norway, Sweden, and the United States. However, as Holt and Hogg noted, in their sample the coaches were a source of stress; therefore, it is not surprising they were not used as part of the coping efforts to manage other stressors. Although this might be considered to reflect a particularly Canadian source of stress and way of coping, it more likely simply reflects the dynamics of that particular team rather than a cultural difference in coping.

Overall, although there is some evidence of cultural differences in the coping literature, it remains an extremely complex area of study because cultures are not easily defined (Crocker, Kowalski, Hoar, & McDonough, 2004). Furthermore, there has been little study of coping with athletic stress even within more well-defined cultures in Canada, such as Inuit and urban European Canadians. There are many different sporting subcultures within Canada that likely differ in their sources of stress and ways of coping. The acceptance of fighting as a coping strategy in organized junior hockey but not in youth soccer is just one example of why it would be so difficult to establish a particularly Canadian way of coping with stress in sport. The same judgment requires us to be cautious about the findings demonstrating particular ways of coping among other cultures outside Canada.

Cognitive Appraisal

Throughout this chapter, the importance of cognitive appraisal in the experience of stress and subsequent coping efforts has been emphasized, and research supports the importance of appraisal in the prediction of coping. Particularly important appear to be the level of threat that is perceived at various stages of competition and perceptions of control (Hoar et al., in press). Gaudreau et al. (2001) showed that a number of coping strategies, such as active coping, increased effort, suppression of competing activities, seeking social support, positive reappraisal, and wishful thinking, were used less during a golf tournament compared with the days leading up to it. This finding is consistent with Lazarus' (1991) notion that it becomes more difficult to effectively apply coping strategies as appraisals of threat reach high levels. We often see this with athletes who seem to lose control over their behaviour when they experience high levels of stress. How often have we heard of major league baseball pitchers breaking a hand or thumb by punching a water cooler or wall after a particularly poor performance? Similarly, perceptions of control have been shown to be related to coping efforts in sport and non-sport literature, typically showing perceived control related to an increased use of problem-focused coping strategies (Carver, Scheier, & Weintraub, 1989; Kim & Duda, 2003). The relationship between perceived control and emotion-focused coping is less clear. Compas, Banez, Malcarne, and Worsham (1991) suggested that emotion-focused coping should be more related to overall level of stress than perceptions of control, since more efforts have to be directed toward emotional regulation.

Personal Resources

It should be no surprise that **personal resources** are expected to influence coping. An important coping resource for athletes can be psychological skills, which include coping with adversity, peaking under pressure, goal setting and mental preparation, ability to concentrate, freedom from worry, confidence and achievement motivation, and coachability (Smith, Schutz, Smoll, & Ptacek, 1995). These psychological skills can act as coping resources that athletes can use when facing stressful situations in sport (Crocker et al., 1998). When athletes are not coping effectively with stress in sport, it might simply be a reflection that they do not have the appropriate resources to cope; thus, the development of coping resources is a key component of stress and coping interventions.

Reflections 6.6

Psychological skills act as coping resources that athletes draw upon to use as strategies to cope with stress in sport. What psychological skills do you possess that help you cope with stress? What skills do you need to develop or enhance in order to improve your ability to cope with stress in sport?

Photo courtesy of Jon Feingersh/Masterfile.

Coping Interventions

Although the complexity of coping is likely evident in this chapter, despite all the unknowns, we still often want or need to know how to help athletes cope with stress in sport. Interventions in sport psychology are covered in more detail in Chapter 8. Many of them are ultimately designed to help athletes maintain or regain emotional control; thus, they will be touched upon only briefly here. However, it is important to point out that there have been interventions designed to specifically target stress and emotion management in sport. Three prominent coping interventions that have been used in sport are stress inoculation training, stress management training, and COPE training.

The development of an athlete's coping resources combined with an application of those skills in practice and competition is a key component of all of these programs. It is really the manner of the application that makes them distinct from one another. In Meichenbaum's (1993) stress inoculation training, athletes learn to develop and rehearse a wide range of coping skills or learn to better use the coping skills that they already have. It is called stress *inoculation* training because when athletes practise their coping skills, they start with small manageable doses of stress and gradually progress to more stress-inducing situations (see www.apa.org/divisions/div12/rev_est/sit_stress. html for more information and references regarding stress inoculation training).

In Smith's (1980) stress management training, athletes develop an "integrated coping response," which can be used across a wide variety of stressful situations in sport and generally consists of muscular relaxation and self-talk statements. In stress management training, contrary to stress inoculation training, athletes do not practise coping with gradually increasing stress. Instead, the training uses a procedure called *induced affect* in which athletes learn to turn off a high level of stress via the implementation of their integrated coping response (see Case Study 6.1).

Finally, Anshel's (1990) COPE training is similar to the other two interventions in that athletes learn coping strategies in a planned sequence while recognizing that different strategies are going to be more or less effective, depending on the specific situation. However, a specific emphasis of COPE training is on the management of acute stress, as opposed to chronic stress.

Research has generally confirmed the effectiveness of these programs in helping athletes cope with stress in sport (see Crocker, Kowalski, & Graham, 2002; Hoar et al.,

Reflections 6.7

Stress and coping interventions help athletes develop coping skills, and these interventions provide athletes with an opportunity to learn how to use their coping skills in practice and competition. How can coaches set up practices to allow athletes an opportunity to practise their coping skills?

Illustration courtesy of Cathy Magnus.

in press). In addition, although not specifically termed coping materials, Canadian sporting bodies have resource materials that help facilitate a positive emotional environment for parents, coaches, and athletes. Examples include Sask Sport's Children in Sport Skill Development Program (see www.sasksport.sk.ca/cis/cis.html) and Softball Canada's Learn to Play Program (see www.softball.ca/LearnToPlay). These programs aim to make the sporting environment a positive experience for all involved in youth sport, and they challenge our current sport models, which often make sport a stressful experience for young athletes.

Case Study 6.1: Coping Intervention

One of the challenges in developing a coping intervention in sport is determining how to develop a program for a specific group of athletes or team. As an example of how a coping intervention can be tailored to a specific sport and team, Crocker et al. (1988) implemented a stress management training (SMT) program with 31 volleyball players (16 males, 15 females) on the 1987 Alberta Canada Games Team (under 19 yrs). Their SMT program consisted of eight one-hour sessions that were offered to the athletes over eight weeks.

Week 1: A discussion with the players was conducted regarding the concept of stress, emphasizing the role of cognitive appraisal in coping. In addition, a progressive muscle relaxation technique was taught; in this technique muscle groups are tensed and relaxed.

Week 2: Athletes identified key thoughts and feelings that triggered stress.

Week 3: The role of irrational beliefs (e.g., "everyone will hate me if I don't win") in the stress process was discussed, and athletes developed substitute statements to replace irrational thoughts and self-talk.

Week 4: Induced-affect procedures, in which athletes attain high levels of emotional arousal, were introduced to the athletes. They were required to turn off the resulting stress by using relaxation.

Week 5: Players were shown how self-talk could help them cope with stress, specifically before serving or waiting for service reception. A former Canadian national volleyball team member was brought in to model the use of self-talk.

Week 6: Using the same induced-affect procedures as in week 4, the volleyball players used self-talk to turn off the stress they experienced.

Week 7: Players learned how to develop and implement an integrated coping response, which combined relaxation and self-talk. In their integrated coping response, self-talk statements were used during the inspiration cycle of deep breathing, while the relaxation response was used during the expiration cycle. They were encouraged to practise their integrated coping response in practice and competition.

Week 8: The players learned meditation as a form of relaxation.

Chapter Summary

If we reflect on the opening vignette of the chapter, we can see the complexity of stress and coping in sport. Sport is obviously important to Natalie, and, as a result, she is dealing with a number of stress sources ranging from time management and financial concerns to concerns about wearing a bodysuit in competition. In addition, these stress sources range from actual competition stressors, such as the fear of losing, to more general self-presentation issues, such as having a highly muscular physique in non-sport settings. Her ways of coping are numerous, with efforts ranging from using humour ("I just laugh it off when they say something") to the use of deep-breathing techniques. She even acknowledged that often she doesn't even know what to do to cope with her feelings. Clearly, an understanding of stress and coping in sport helps us understand why she is experiencing stress, how she attempts to deal with that stress, and how we can help her to effectively cope with stress in sport. The following represent some of the conclusions that are generally accepted by most sport psychology researchers today.

Cognitive appraisal is a key component of the stress experience. How athletes interpret the situations they face in sport is now generally considered as important as the situations themselves. Athletes are not passive agents who must succumb to the demands placed upon them. Instead, they interpret situations in relation to their goals and their perceived coping options. This cognitive appraisal process is critical to the experience of stress in sport. General sources of stress that athletes often report as threatening, challenging, or as a harm/loss include various psychological, physical, social, environmental, and career demands. These general sources include acute and chronic stressors, expected and unexpected stressors, and competitive and non-competitive stressors.

Coping is a dynamic process. It is a response to stress that includes a wide variety of cognitive and behavioural efforts. These efforts can range from accepting the situation to making a plan of action to leaving the situation altogether. Often, multiple coping efforts are made in any given situation as an athlete tries to figure out the most effective way to manage the demands she or he faces. These coping efforts themselves then re-shape the situation and possibly the athlete's cognitive appraisal of the situation, making new coping attempts necessary (if stress remains). The distinction between micro- and macro-analytic approaches to coping is useful to understanding the dynamic process of coping, because not only will specific coping strategies change but so too might the goals of the strategies.

Coping seems to reflect both coping styles and characteristics of the situation. There is growing evidence that athletes might have preferences for coping in particular ways but that despite these preferences, coping can still be quite variable across different situations. Whether or not a particular coping style can be used across different situations likely depends on how similar those situations are to one another and whether the coping style is appropriate for the situations. One of the limitations in many situations is that there are constraints on what can be done to cope; thus, athletes must often seek out alternative ways to manage the demands placed upon them.

Coping strategies are neither inherently effective nor ineffective. Whether or not a coping strategy is effective depends on the fit between the coping efforts and the stress that is experienced. Although there is some evidence to suggest that, in general, problem-focused coping efforts are most effective in the long term, ultimately the effectiveness of coping needs to be considered in relation to an athlete's goals and well-being, which themselves sometimes contradict each other.

Much more work is needed in establishing predictors of coping in sport. Although we discussed important predictors—gender, culture, cognitive appraisal, and personal resources—even within these categories relatively little is known. The challenge is that all situations seem to be relatively unique at some level because not only do the characteristics of situations change but so too do individual athlete's appraisals of those situations. Researchers have only begun to look at consistencies across situations that might help establish whether strong predictors of coping in sport can be established.

Despite the many unknowns regarding stress and coping in sport, coping intervention programs seem to be effective in helping athletes manage stress. Coping interventions, such as stress inoculation training, stress management training, and COPE training, all seem to have much potential for helping athletes develop a set of resources that allow them to more effectively meet the demands of sport. Ultimately, however, an interest in stress and coping in sport stems from a desire to not only help athletes meet the demands of sport in a healthy way but also to promote a lifetime of enjoyable sport involvement.

Review Questions

1. What does it mean to describe stress as a "process"?
2. What roles do cognitive appraisal and coping play in the experience of stress?
3. How are the concepts of stress and emotion related?
4. Discuss why it is important to distinguish between *coping* and *outcomes of coping*.
5. Compare and contrast micro-level and macro-level dimensions of coping.
6. What four predictors of coping in sport were discussed in the chapter? What relationship do they have to coping?
7. Discuss challenges to understanding stress and coping in sport and in developing effective intervention programs for athletes.

Suggested Reading

Crocker, P. R. E., Kowalski, K. C., & Graham, T. R. (1998). Measurement of coping strategies in sport. In J. L. Duda (Ed.), *Advances in sport and exercise psychology measurement* (pp. 149–161). Morgantown, WV: Fitness Information Technology.

Crocker, P. R. E., Kowalski, K. C., & Graham, T.R. (2002). Emotional control and intervention. In J. M. Silva III & D. E. Stevens (Eds.), *Psychological foundations of sport* (pp. 155–176). Boston: Allyn & Bacon.

Hoar, S. D., Kowalski, K. C., Gaudreau, P., & Crocker, P. R. E. (in press). A review of coping in sport. In S. Hanton & S. Mellalieu (Eds.), *Literature reviews in sport psychology*. Hauppauge, NY: Nova Science.

Lazarus, R. S. (2000b). How emotions influence performance in competitive sports. *The Sport Psychologist, 14,* 229–252.

References

Aldwin, C. M. (2000). *Stress, coping, and development: An integrative perspective*. New York: Guildford.

Amirkhan, J. H. (1990). A factor analytically derived measure of coping: The coping strategy Indicator. *Journal of Personality and Social Psychology, 59,* 1066–1074.

Anshel, M. H. (1990). Toward validation of a model for coping with acute stress in sport. *International Journal of Sport Psychology, 21,* 58–83.

Anshel, M. H. (2001). Qualitative validation of a model for coping with acute stress in sport. *Journal of Sport Behavior, 24,* 223–245.

Anshel, M. H., Gregory, W. L., & Kaczmarek, M. (1990). The effectiveness of a stress training program in coping with criticism in sport: A test of the COPE model. *Journal of Sport Behavior, 13,* 194–217.

Anshel, M. H., Jamieson, J., & Raviv, S. (2001). Coping with acute stress among male and female Israeli athletes. *International Journal of Sport Psychology, 32,* 271–289.

Anshel, M. H., Kim, K., Kim, B., Chang, K., & Eom, H. (2001). A model for coping with stressful events in sport: Theory, application, and future directions. *International Journal of Sport Psychology, 32,* 43–75.

Anshel, M. H., Williams, L. R. T., & Williams, S. M. (2000). Coping style following acute stress in competitive sport. *Journal of Social Psychology, 140,* 751–773.

Bouffard, M., & Crocker, P. R. E. (1992). Coping by individuals with physical disabilities with perceived challenge in physical activity: Are people consistent? *Research Quarterly for Exercise and Sport, 63,* 410–417.

Buckworth, J., & Dishman, R. K. (2002). *Exercise psychology*. Champaign, IL: Human Kinetics.

Campbell, E., & Jones, G. (2002). Cognitive appraisal of sources of stress experienced by elite male wheelchair basketball players. *Adapted Physical Activity Quarterly, 19,* 100–108.

Carpenter, B. N. (1992). Issues and advances in coping research. In B. N. Carpenter (Ed.), *Personal coping: Theory, research, and application* (pp. 1–13). Westport, CT: Praeger.

Carver, C. S., Scheier, M. F., & Weintraub, J. K. (1989). Assessing coping strategies: A theoretically based approach. *Journal of Personality and Social Psychology, 56,* 267–283.

Christie, J. (2004, December 3). Who's the top track star? *The Globe and Mail.* Retrieved December 20, 2004, from http://theglobeandmail.ca.

Compas, B. E., Banez, G. A., Malcarne, V., & Worsham, N. (1991). Perceived control and coping with stress: A developmental perspective. *Journal of Social Issues, 47,* 23–34.

Cornelius, A. (2002). Psychological interventions for the injured athlete. In J. M. Silva III & D. E. Stevens (Eds.), *Psychological foundations of sport* (pp. 224–246). Boston: Allyn & Bacon.

Crocker, P. R. E. (1989a). A follow-up of cognitive-affective stress management training. *Journal of Sport & Exercise Psychology, 11,* 236–242.

Crocker, P. R. E. (1989b). Evaluating stress management training under competition conditions. *International Journal of Sport Psychology, 20,* 191–204.

Crocker, P. R. E., Alderman, R. B., & Smith, F. M. (1988). Cognitive-affective stress management training with high performance youth volleyball players: Effects on affect, cognition, and performance. *Journal of Sport & Exercise Psychology, 10,* 448–460.

Crocker, P. R. E., & Graham, T. R. (1995). Coping by competitive athletes with performance stress: Gender differences and relationships with affect. *The Sport Psychologist, 9,* 325–338.

Crocker, P. R. E., & Isaak, K. (1997). Coping during competitions and training sessions: Are youth swimmers consistent? *International Journal of Sport Psychology, 28,* 355–369.

Crocker, P. R. E., Kowalski, K. C., & Graham, T. R. (1998). Measurement of coping strategies in sport. In J. L. Duda (Ed.), *Advances in sport and exercise psychology measurement* (pp. 149–161). Morgantown, WV: Fitness Information Technology.

Crocker, P. R. E., Kowalski, K. C., & Graham, T. R. (2002). Emotional control and intervention. In J. M. Silva III & D. E. Stevens (Eds.), *Psychological foundations of sport* (pp. 155–176). Boston: Allyn & Bacon.

Crocker, P. R. E., Kowalski, K. C., Hoar, S. D., & McDonough, M. H. (2004). Emotion in sport across adulthood. In M. R. Weiss (Ed.), *Developmental sport and exercise psychology: A lifespan perspective* (pp. 333–355). Morgantown, WV: Fitness Information Technology.

Dugdale, J. R., Eklund, R. C., & Gordon, S. (2002). Expected and unexpected stressors in major international competition: Appraisal, coping, and performance. *The Sport Psychologist, 16,* 20–33.

Expos 7, Dodgers 3. (2004, March 9). *CBS SportsLine.com* Wire Reports. Retrieved December 12, 2004, from http://cbs.sportsline.com

Endler, N. S., & Parker, J. D. (1994). Assessment of multidimensional coping: Task, emotion, and avoidance strategies. *Psychological Assessment, 6,* 50–60.

Folkman, S. (1992). Making the case for coping. In B. N. Carpenter (Ed.), *Personal coping: Theory, research, and application* (pp. 31–46). Westport, CT: Praeger.

Ford, I. W., & Gordon, S. (1998). Perspective of sport trainers and athletic therapists on the psychological content of their practice and training. *Journal of Sport Rehabilitation, 7,* 79–94.

Gaudreau, P., & Blondin, J. P. (2002). Development of a questionnaire for the assessment of coping strategies employed by athletes in competitive sport settings. *Psychology of Sport and Exercise, 3,* 1–34.

Gaudreau, P., & Blondin, J. P. (2004). Different athletes cope differently: A cluster analysis of coping. *Personality and Individual Differences, 36,* 1865–1877.

Gaudreau, P., Blondin, J. P., & Lapierre, A. M. (2002). Athletes' coping during a competition: Relationship of coping strategies with positive affect, negative affect, and performance-goal discrepancy. *Psychology of Sport and Exercise, 3,* 125–150.

Gaudreau, P., Lapierre, A. M., & Blondin, J. P. (2001). Coping at three phases of a competition: Comparison between pre-competitive, competitive, and post-competitive utilization of the same strategy. *International Journal of Sport Psychology, 32,* 369–385.

Goalies join wild brawl at end of Oilers-Thrashers game. (2004, February 12). *CBS SportsLine.com* Wire Reports. Retrieved February 18, 2004, from http://cbs.sportsline.com

Gould, D., Eklund, R. C., & Jackson, S. A. (1993). Coping strategies used by U.S. Olympic wrestlers. *Research Quarterly for Exercise and Sport, 64,* 83–93.

Gould, D., Finch, L. M., & Jackson, S. A. (1993). Coping strategies used by national champion figure skaters. *Research Quarterly for Exercise and Sport, 64,* 453–468.

Gould, D., Udry, E., Bridges, D., & Beck, L. (1997). Stress sources encountered when rehabilitating from season-ending ski injuries. *The Sport Psychologist, 11,* 361–378.

Gould, D., Udry, E., Tuffey, S., & Loehr, J. (1996). Burnout in competitive junior tennis players: I. A quantitative psychological assessment. *The Sport Psychologist, 10,* 322–340.

Goyen, M. J., & Anshel, M. H. (1998). Sources of acute competitive stress and use of coping strategies as a function of age and gender. *Journal of Applied Developmental Psychology, 19,* 469–486.

Haney, C. J., & Long, B. C. (1995). Coping effectiveness: A path analysis of self-efficacy, control, coping, and performance in sport competitions. *Journal of Applied Social Psychology, 25*, 1726–1746.

Hoar, S. D., Kowalski, K. C., Gaudreau, P., & Crocker, P. R. E. (in press). A review of coping in sport. In S. Hanton & S. Mellalieu (Eds.), *Literature reviews in sport psychology*. Hauppauge, NY: Nova Science.

Holt, N. L., & Hogg, J. M. (2002). Perceptions of stress and coping during preparations for the 1999 women's soccer World Cup finals. *The Sport Psychologist, 16*, 251–271.

Kelley, B. C., Eklund, R. C., & Ritter, T. M. (1999). Stress and burnout among collegiate tennis coaches. *Journal of Sport & Exercise Psychology, 21*, 113–130.

Kim, M. S., & Duda, J. L. (2003). The coping process: Cognitive appraisals of stress, coping strategies, and coping effectiveness. *The Sport Psychologist, 17*, 406–425.

Kowalski, K. C. (1999, October). *Sources of stress experienced by adolescents in sport*. Paper presented at the meeting of the Canadian Society for Psychomotor Learning and Sport Psychology, Edmonton, AB.

Kowalski, K. C., & Crocker, P. R. E. (2001). Development and validation of the coping function questionnaire for adolescents in sport. *Journal of Sport & Exercise Psychology, 23*, 136–155.

Lazarus, R. S. (1991). *Emotion and adaptation*. New York: Oxford University Press.

Lazarus, R. S. (1993a). From psychological stress to the emotions: A history of changing outlooks. *Annual Reviews of Psychology, 44*, 1–21.

Lazarus, R. S. (1993b). Why we should think of stress as a subset of emotion. In L. Goldberger & S. Brenznitz (Eds.), *Handbook of stress: Theoretical and clinical aspects* (2nd ed., pp. 21–39). New York: The Free Press.

Lazarus, R. S. (1999). *Stress and emotion: A new synthesis*. New York: Springer.

Lazarus, R. S. (2000a). Cognitive-motivational-relational theory of emotion. In Y. L. Hanin (Ed.), *Emotions in sport* (pp. 39–63). Champaign, IL: Human Kinetics.

Lazarus, R. S. (2000b). How emotions influence performance in competitive sports. *The Sport Psychologist, 14*, 229–252.

Maniar, S. D., Curry, L. A., Sommers-Flanagan, J., & Walsh, J. A. (2001). Student-athlete preferences in seeking help when confronted with sport performance problems. *The Sport Psychologist, 15*, 205–223.

Martin, J. J., Kelley, B., & Eklund, R. C. (1999). A model of stress and burnout in male high school athletic directors. *Journal of Sport & Exercise Psychology, 21*, 280–294.

Meichenbaum, D. (1993). Stress inoculation training: A 20-year update. In P. M. Lehrer & R. L. Woolfolk (Eds.), *Principles and practices of stress management* (2nd ed., pp. 373–406). New York: Guildford.

Noblet, A. J., & Gifford, S. M. (2002). The sources of stress experienced by professional Australian footballers. *Journal of Applied Sport Psychology, 14*, 1–13.

Ntoumanis, N., & Biddle, S. J. H. (2000). Relationship of intensity and direction of competitive anxiety with coping strategies. *The Sport Psychologist, 14*, 360–371.

Park, J. K. (2000). Coping strategies used by Korean national athletes. *The Sport Psychologist, 14*, 63–80.

Selye, H. (1993). History of the stress concept. In L. Goldberger & S. Brenznitz (Eds.), *Handbook of stress: Theoretical and clinical aspects* (2nd ed., pp. 7–17). New York: The Free Press.

Skinner, E. A., Edge, K., Altman, J., & Sherwood, H. (2003). Searching for the structure of coping: A review and critique of category systems for classifying ways of coping. *Psychological Bulletin, 129*, 216–269.

Smith, R. E. (1980). A cognitive-affective approach to stress management training for athletes. In C. Nadeau, W. Halliwell, K. Newell, & G. Roberts (Eds.), *Psychology of motor behavior and sport—1979* (pp. 54–73). Champaign, IL: Human Kinetics.

Smith, R. E. (1986). Toward a cognitive-affective model of athletic burnout. *Journal of Sport Psychology, 8*, 36–50.

Smith, R. E., Schutz, R. W., Smoll, F. L., & Ptacek, J. T. (1995). Development and validation of a multidimensional measure of sport-specific psychological skills: The athletic coping skills inventory-28. *Journal of Sport & Exercise Psychology, 17*, 379–398.

Tamres, L. K., Janicki, D., & Helgeson, V. S. (2002). Sex differences in coping behavior: A meta-analytic review and an examination of relative coping. *Personality and Social Psychology Review, 6*, 2–30.

Udry, E. (1997). Coping and social support among injured athletes following surgery. *Journal of Sport & Exercise Psychology, 19*, 71–90.

Yoo, J. (2000). Factorial validity of the coping scale for Korean athletes. *International Journal of Sport Psychology, 31*, 391–404.

Yoo, J. (2001). Coping profile of Korean competitive athletes. *International Journal of Sport Psychology, 32*, 290–303.

CHAPTER 7

Kim D. Dorsch
David M. Paskevich
Todd M. Loughead

Aggression in Sport

Chapter Objectives

After reading this chapter, you should be able to do the following:

1. Define aggression and differentiate it from other terms, such as *assertion* and *violence*.

2. Explain the complexities involved in measuring aggressive behaviour.

3. Discuss key theories useful for understanding why people behave aggressively.

4. Describe how some personal, situational, and group factors influence aggressive behaviour.

5. List the consequences of aggressive behaviour to athletes and spectators.

6. Discuss ways to reduce aggressive behaviour in sport.

On February 21, 2000, the Boston Bruins of the National Hockey League (NHL) played the Vancouver Canucks. Approximately three minutes into the game, the designated enforcers for the teams, Marty McSorley of Boston and Donald Brashear of Vancouver, engaged in a fight. As the game progressed, the Canucks took the lead, and McSorley made attempts to re-engage Brashear in another altercation. Brashear did not oblige. Finally, with fewer than three seconds left in the third period and the Bruins down by three goals, McSorley raised his stick and struck Brashear on the head, causing Brashear to fall backwards. Brashear banged the back of his head on the ice, lost consciousness for a few moments, and sustained a concussion. After several weeks of recovery and many post-concussion symptoms, Brashear recovered fully and returned to play. Marty McSorley, on the other hand, received a penalty for deliberate injury of an opponent, was suspended by the NHL for the remainder of the season, and was charged in criminal court for assault with a weapon.

During the trial, McSorley informed the court that he was trying to strike Brashear around his shoulder, with the goal of goading him into a fight. He stated, "I was trying to strike Donald on the number above the sleeve. It happened so fast" ("Meant no harm," 2000, ¶6). He continued to say that he had no idea that he had hit him in the head. When asked if he had intended to injure Brashear, McSorley replied, "No" ("Meant no harm," 2000, ¶4). "My intention was not to hurt him with the stick. My intention was to force a confrontation and it went badly, and he got hurt because of it. And (for) that, I feel very badly, very, very badly" (Tuchman, 2000, ¶11). Marty McSorley was given a conditional discharge of assault with a weapon; the charges would be dropped from his record as long as he completed 18 months of probation and did not play against Donald Brashear during that time.

The vignette above describes incidents that can occur in ice hockey. In fact, the late comedian Rodney Dangerfield once said, "I went to the fights the other night and a hockey game broke out." Nevertheless, acts of aggression tarnish sports other than hockey. In baseball, we often see bench-clearing brawls, brush-back pitches, or deliberate "beanings" of hitters. In basketball, elbows are thrown and players assault their coaches. For example, Latrell Sprewell of the Golden State Warriors in the National Basketball Association allegedly choked his coach, P. J. Carlesimo. Basketball players also get into altercations with fans; Ron Artest of the Indiana Pacers was banned for the 2004/05 season for attacking a fan who reportedly threw a beverage on him during a game. Aggressive behaviours occur so often in sport that Russell (1993) suggested that "outside of wartime, sports is perhaps the only setting in which acts of interpersonal aggression are not only tolerated but enthusiastically applauded by large segments of society" (p. 191).

There are also aggressive behaviours in individual sports, such as tennis. An extremely aggressive act in tennis occurred in April 1993 when a fan stabbed Monica Seles, who was then ranked number one in women's play. The fan did it because he wanted Steffi Graf to regain her number one ranking. Then, approximately eight months later an assailant struck figure skater Nancy Kerrigan, a 1992 Olympic bronze medalist, on the knee just before the 1994 Winter Olympic Games. Also, consider the incident that occurred during the men's marathon in the 2004 Summer Olympic Games held in Athens, Greece. Five kilometres from the finish line, a spectator grabbed the leader of the race, Vanderlei de Lima of Brazil, and pulled him into the crowd. Even though other spectators rescued de Lima, he lost valuable time, was slightly injured, but still managed to win the bronze medal.

It is because we hear and see such incidents as those described above that we need to become aware of what aggressive behaviour is, why it occurs, what factors cause it, and, perhaps most importantly, what we can do to try to change these behaviours. In this chapter, we will address these issues with respect to aggression in sport.

Some Common Myths about Aggression in Sport

MYTH: *Aggression in sport is a good characteristic, something to be encouraged in players.*
Most coaches, when asked what kind of player they want on their team, would include *aggressive* in their description of the ideal player. However, from a sport psychology perspective, aggression is not a good thing. An aggressive act is one in which the player intentionally tries to hurt his or her opponent. The behaviours that coaches and parents should try to encourage in their athletes and children are correctly labelled *assertive* behaviours.

MYTH: *Aggression is only a physical behaviour.*
A classic scene in the movie *Slapshot* refutes this myth. An opponent was trying to get the Chiefs' goalie off his game, so he skated by the goalie and said something insulting about a member of the goalie's family. The Chiefs' goalie then skated after the opposing player, trying to slash him with his stick. A verbal insult, like this type of trash talk, can be considered an aggressive act, as it is an intentional attempt to psychologically hurt (and distract or intimidate) a person.

MYTH: *An aggressive act has to be one that succeeds in physically or psychologically injuring the opponent.*
The key point in defining an act as aggressive is not whether or not the player succeeds in injuring an opponent but whether or not the player *intends* to injure an opponent. If you have ever watched the cartoon show of Wile E. Coyote and Road Runner, you will know that Wile E. Coyote's very existence revolves around attempting to injure Road Runner. Try as he may, though, his intentionally harmful aggressive actions never succeed.

MYTH: *Participating in physical sports will decrease the desire to behave aggressively.*
It is widely believed that people can get rid of their aggressive urges by participating in a sport or activity that has a lot of physical contact (e.g., football, hockey, dodge ball) and that by this participation we will be able to reduce aggressive behaviour. This notion of catharsis has not found any support in the literature and will be discussed in detail later in the chapter.

MYTH: *Aggressive behaviours are always against the rules.*
Most sports have written rules that disallow the intentional injury of players. However, there are often examples of aggressive behaviours that can occur within the rules. For example, in boxing, the ultimate goal is to knock an opponent unconscious, a legal yet aggressive act. Similarly, the rugby flanker often tackles the fly-half with as much force as possible in order to make the fly-half think twice about carrying the ball.

Introduction

Storr (1968) stated, "When a word becomes so diffusely applied that it is used both of the competitive striving of the footballer and the bloody violence of a murderer, it ought to be dropped or more closely defined" (p. *x*). What he meant by this quote is that we often hear the word *aggression* used in everyday society in a variety of ways. In sport settings in particular, we often hear about a baseball player aggressively running the bases or the volleyball player aggressively digging the ball. From a sport psychology perspective, however, this is not the correct use of the term. In an attempt to try to define the term more closely, Silva (1980) suggested that **aggression** is any overt verbal or physical act that is intended to psychologically or physically injure another living organism. **Violent behaviours** are extreme acts of physical aggression that bear "no direct relationship to the competitive goals of sport, and relates to incidents of uncontrolled aggression outside the rules of sport" (Terry & Jackson, 1985, p. 27). Keep in mind that because the aggressive action is directed at another living organism, there is always an aggressor and a victim in an aggressive or violent act.

Using Silva's (1980) definition, the term aggression is not appropriate for the description of the baseball and volleyball players' behaviours mentioned earlier. Sport psychologists prefer to describe those behaviours as **assertive**. The difference between an aggressive and an assertive action is that the latter behaviour does not include the intent to harm another living being. Assertive behaviours are those actions that are forceful, vigorous, and legitimate, but the individual performing this behaviour does not intend to injure an opponent (e.g., most body checks in hockey). Therefore, when a coach or a parent tells an athlete or child to play more aggressively, in most situations what they are encouraging is behaviour that is assertive.

Consequently, defining aggressive behaviour involves four key points:

- It is a behaviour (i.e., an act), not an emotion or a feeling.
- It can be verbal or physical.
- It is intended to physically or psychologically harm.
- It is directed toward another living organism.

Let's go back to the image of aggression in sport that was presented at the beginning of this chapter. Marty McSorley took his stick and hit Donald Brashear, knocking him unconscious. However, when asked if he intended to hurt Brashear, McSorley stated that he never intended to hurt Donald but simply wanted to get his attention and start another fight. Based on the definition of aggression provided above, this behaviour would not be considered aggression because the intent to harm was not involved.

Aggressive and violent behaviours in sport are not accidental; they are done with the intent to injure either physically or psychologically. However, sport psychologists go further in defining acts of aggression by looking at the reason for the behaviour, at what the individual wanted to accomplish. Consider the following example: In the dying seconds of a November 2004 Canadian Football League semi-final game between the Saskatchewan Roughriders and the BC Lions, Roughrider kicker Paul McCallum missed a field goal that would have sent his team to the Grey Cup. After McCallum returned home to Regina, an irate fan made a phone call to McCallum's residence and uttered threats against McCallum and his family. In the strictest sense of the definition, this was an overt verbal act that was intended to frighten (i.e., psychologically harm) McCallum and his family. Contained within this act of aggression, the perpetrator's ultimate goal was the injury of the 'Rider kicker. This type of aggressive behaviour is known as **reactive or hostile aggression**.

In other scenarios in sport, the ultimate goal of the athlete is not the injury of the person but some other tangible reward, like praise or victory. Sport examples would also include the vigorous tackling of a receiver so that he would fumble the ball or become intimidated; then next time he would "hear footsteps" behind him and become distracted from his play. It is important to keep in mind that even though the aggressor wanted something else to result from the act (i.e., a fumble or distraction), the intent to injure the opponent was still a key factor in the behaviour. This type of aggression is known as **instrumental aggression**. The stabbing of tennis star Monica Seles (described in the introductory paragraphs) is another example of an instrumentally aggressive act. The fan did it because he wanted Steffi Graf to regain her number one ranking. In order to achieve this goal, he stabbed the current number one ranked individual. The aggressive behaviour was a means to an end.

Reflections 7.1

The following are scenarios that could occur in sport. Using the definitional criteria of aggressive behaviour, decide whether the behaviours are aggressive or not.

1. After striking out, a baseball player throws her bat into the dugout and it hits the coach.
2. Samantha, a left-winger in soccer, purposely kicks an opposing player in the shins in retaliation for the same being done to her.
3. In order to win a game of dodge ball, Luke deliberately aims for Jake's face and throws the ball as hard as he can, but Jake ducks out of the way, so the ball misses.
4. With 3.2 seconds left in the championship game and the opposing team down by one, at the free throw line, Coach Jones calls a time out in order to make the shooter worry and think about missing the shot.
5. After missing the tournament-winning putt, Steve wraps his putter around the light pole.

Answers:

1. Not aggressive: The act was not intended to injure anyone; it was an accident.
2. Aggressive: Samantha's goal was to hurt another player; it is an act of reactive/ hostile aggression.
3. Aggressive: Despite the fact that the ball did not hit Jake, Luke wanted to injure him in order to win the game; therefore, it is a case of instrumental aggression.
4. Aggressive: The intent of Coach Jones was to instill anxiety in the opposing team's shooter (i.e., a form of psychological harm); therefore, it was an act of instrumental aggression.
5. Not aggressive: Although he was probably angry, Steve did not intend to harm another living being.

Although the act definitely has to contain the aggressor's intent to injure, some researchers suggest that the behaviour also has to go against the prevailing norms within the sport-specific culture (Mummendey, Bornewasser, Löschper, & Linneweber, 1982; Mummendey, Linneweber, & Löschper, 1984a). Each sport has its own written and unwritten rules. It is through socialization and experience gained through participation in the sport that the participants become knowledgeable regarding the normative standards (i.e., unwritten rules) of that sport. Therefore, acts that may be aggressive in one sport are not necessarily considered aggressive in another sport. Fighting in ice hockey is a prime example of this. Many people involved in the subculture of ice hockey (i.e., players and coaches) do not believe that fights are aggressive actions (Colburn, 1986). These individuals believe that fighting is not an attempt to injure but an attempt to control some of the more potentially harmful behaviours, like stick work, kicking, or kneeing. Players like Marty McSorley have stated that "fighting is not only accepted but an important part of NHL hockey. The job of a tough guy is to inspire team-mates and to ensure the team's skilled players are not intimidated" ("Meant no harm," 2000, ¶13). Should this same act occur in another sport, like volleyball or basketball, where the unwritten rules do not sanction fighting, the perception of the act as non-aggressive would definitely change.

Reflections 7.2

Think about the role of fighting in different types of sports. Some coaches talk about "controlled" aggression. Do you think there is a place for aggression in sport?

Another factor that influences the perception of aggression is the viewpoint from which one is involved in the behaviour. The actor (alleged aggressor) will usually view his or her action as appropriate and not aggressive, whereas the actor's opponent (alleged victim) will usually perceive the behaviour as inappropriate or aggressive (Mummendey, Linneweber, & Löschper, 1984b). For example, a wrestler may subtly "work against the joint," intentionally inflicting pain on an opponent in order to pin him or her on the mat. The actor may think he or she is just doing what it takes to win; however, the opponent more than likely believes it was a deliberate attempt to injure and may subsequently question the "attacker's" sportsmanship. In most cases of allegedly aggressive behaviour, in addition to the actor and the opponent, there is usually an observer. The psychological closeness of this observer to the actor influences the observer's perception of whether or not the act was aggressive. In a classic study, Hastorf and Cantril (1954) demonstrated this relationship between the affiliation of the viewers and their perception of the behaviour of a sports team. They examined the perceptions of fans regarding the amount of aggression exhibited by one of two football teams in an exceptionally physical football game played between teams from Dartmouth and Princeton universities. Fans of Dartmouth perceived Princeton players to have committed many more intentionally harmful acts than the Dartmouth players, and fans of Princeton believed Dartmouth was the more aggressive of the two teams.

Another factor that tends to influence a person's perception of whether or not an act is aggressive is the outcome of the act (i.e., did someone get hurt?). However, if you refer to the definition of aggression, the key point is the intent to harm another living being. This description does not mean that an aggressor has to succeed in harming an

---

Reflections 7.3

If you were in charge of handing out suspensions for a sport governing body, on what evidence would you base the length of time of the suspension? A good link that discusses the law and aggression in sport is http://www.sport law.ca/articles/other/article9.html or http://www.lawconnection.ca/modules/ php?name=News&file=article&sid=35

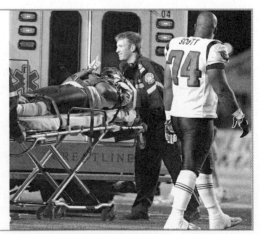

Photo courtesy of CP/Marianne Helm.

opponent, but only that he or she intends to harm the other individual. If an act is committed with the intent of psychologically intimidating an opponent but does not succeed, it is still aggressive behaviour. Let us revisit the action of Luke described in the Reflections 7.1 box. He tried to physically injure Jake by throwing the ball at his face. Just because Jake dodged the ball, rendering Luke's attempt futile, this does not negate the fact that Luke's actions were aggressive. The intent to do harm was still there.

Theories of Aggression

What are the reasons that some athletes lose control and act aggressively? Are people born to be aggressive, or are they products of their environment? In order to explain what causes athletes to be aggressive, scientists have advanced several theories and explanations. These theories and explanations can be classified into five groups: instinct, frustration-aggression, physiological, moral reasoning, and social learning.

Instinct Theory

Based on the writings of Sigmund Freud, instinct theory offered the earliest explanation of why humans engage in aggressive behaviour. This theory holds that humans are born with certain behavioural tendencies that will cause them to act in certain ways. For example, Freud (1925) believed that aggressive behaviour is an innate, natural response that evolved primarily through a struggle for survival. Aggression builds up naturally and must be released. Freud believed that numerous socially approved methods existed for releasing this pent-up aggression. Sport is one such socially acceptable activity that could curtail the negative results of aggression. This releasing process was termed **catharsis**, a word derived from the Greek term *katharsis*, which means to purge or cleanse the body. According to this theory, hitting an opponent in sport serves as a catharsis, or release, of built up aggression.

The instinct theory has far more detractors than supporters. Albert Bandura (1973) noted that a large body of research, involving either direct or vicarious aggressive experiences, has demonstrated that aggression will actually be maintained, rather than reduced. Further, the probability of subsequent aggression will increase rather than diminish! These findings are also apparent in a sport setting, where research has found no draining of aggressive tendencies through participation in physical activities. In fact, many sport researchers have argued that exposure to violence in sport serves as a reinforcer, not as a catharsis. Many scientists have rejected the instinct theory; they suggest that sport provides a better framework for the learning, rather than the venting, of aggression. Therefore, it is fair to conclude that instinct theory has little support today and certainly is of limited use in understanding aggression in sport.

Frustration-Aggression Theory

Rejecting Freud's notion of an aggressive instinct, Dollard, Doob, Miller, Mowrer, and Sears first proposed the frustration-aggression theory in 1939. This theory viewed aggression as a natural response to frustration. Originally, it was hypothesized that all aggression was due to frustration and that frustration always leads to aggression. For instance, a rugby player who has been tackled high and hard might become frustrated and punch his opponent in retaliation. Although, this theory has intuitive appeal because it seems reasonable that most aggression occurs when individuals are frustrated, the frustration-aggression theory has some definite shortcomings. For example, individuals are able to deal with their frustrations in non-aggressive ways. Consequently, Berkowitz (1989) proposed a **revised frustration-aggression theory**, recognizing that aggression can have causes other than frustration and that frustration can lead to behaviours other than aggression, such as withdrawal from sport. Berkowitz suggested that when an individual is frustrated, an emotional reaction of anger is produced that does not automatically lead to aggression but rather to a readiness to be aggressive. Although, Berkowitz's revisions made the theory more palatable, some scientists have been reluctant to accept this theory since it implies an instinctual mechanism that accounts for the frustration-anger link.

Reflections 7.4
What are some of the ways in which a person could deal with her or his frustration?

Physiological Explanations

Proponents who believe that aggression is physiological in nature use two supportive mechanisms: brain pathology and blood chemistry. Insofar as brain pathology is concerned, research has shown that aggressive behaviour is often characteristic of people with brain tumours. In these people, aggressive behaviours can be elicited by stimulating various parts of the brain. As for blood chemistry, aggression has been linked primarily to the hormone testosterone. Although researchers have found a link between testosterone and aggressive behaviour in animal species, the relationship is less consistent in humans. That is, testosterone may cause individuals to be aggressive, but it is difficult to explain why people who possess high levels of this hormone are aggressive in some situations and not in others. As well, it is difficult to explain why people, such as females, who possess little or low amounts of testosterone can act aggressively.

Although physiological explanations have been used to explain aggression in animal species, rarely has this explanation been forwarded as a cause of aggression in sport. One exception concerns the use of steroids, most notably by athletes in power and strength sports like weightlifting, football, baseball, and track and field. The links between steroid use and feelings of aggressiveness, and between steroid use and aggressive behaviour, have been frequently documented among athletes (e.g., Yates, Perry, & Murray, 1992). For instance, studies have shown that athletes who take steroids have higher levels of aggression toward objects, of verbal aggression, and of aggressiveness while training. It should be pointed out that when the athletes stopped using steroids, these characteristics disappeared (Parrott, Choi, & Davies, 1994).

Moral Reasoning Theory

Brenda Bredemeier and her colleagues (e.g., Bredemeier & Shields, 1984; Bredemeier, 1994; Shields, Bredemeier, Gardner, & Bostrom, 1995) have been strong proponents of the relationship between moral reasoning and athletic aggression. These researchers view aggression as unethical and argue that a relationship should exist between a person's level of moral maturity and their acts of athletic aggression. In other words, individuals are aggressive because they have not matured enough to realize that what they are doing is wrong. Despite their promising findings, the study of morality in a sport context is in its infancy.

Social Learning Theory

The most supported explanation of why aggression occurs is social learning theory. The leading advocate for this theory, relative to aggression, is Albert Bandura. According to social learning theory, a person is neither driven by inner forces nor controlled solely by environmental influences. Instead, Bandura (1973) believes people are aggressive because they have learned that aggression pays. In other words, the use of aggressive behaviours can lead to success.

Bandura (1973) theorized that two forms of social interaction lead to the development of aggressive behaviours. The first form of interaction involves modelling. In its simplest form, modelling suggests that people can acquire aggressive behaviours from observing aggressive models and can retain these aggressive tendencies over time. For instance, Michael Smith (1983) has suggested that youth hockey players learn to be aggressive by watching their role models from professional leagues, like the NHL.

The other form of interaction involves learning or acquiring new responses because of reinforcement. When an action is performed and then positively reinforced (i.e., rewarded), the behaviour is strengthened. The behaviour will be discontinued if it is not rewarded or is punished. For example, research has suggested that parents, teammates, and coaches are the most influential providers of social reinforcement, especially for young athletes (Smith, 1979). In 1974, Smith surveyed minor league hockey players and found that those who engaged in fighting believed that their parents, teammates, and coaches approved of this behaviour. Specifically, Smith found that 31% of players said their fathers would approve of fighting, and 21% said their mothers would approve. Similarly, hockey players said that 64% of their teammates and 26% of their coaches approved of fighting.

Approval is not the only possible reinforcer of aggression. The belief that aggression is related to success also can influence aggressive behaviours. Luxbacher (1986)

< The social learning theory suggests that since aggressive behaviour is learned, it can be unlearned.
Photo courtesy of CP/John Ulano.

investigated the influence of the coach's attitude toward winning on aggression in youth soccer. The findings showed players who perceived their coach to have a win-at-all-cost attitude expressed higher levels of aggression and were more willing to use illegal, aggressive tactics to win.

In short, social learning theory is a strong force in contemporary research, linking aggression to the environment and the individual. It is a model that contains provisions for direct learning and for vicarious learning. Furthermore, Bandura's (1973) theory contains a cognitive dimension that had been previously missing from other theories regarding aggression. Finally, since aggression allegedly does not originate internally and its environmental determinants are alterable, social learning theory holds a more optimistic view of reducing aggression in humans.

Summary of Theories of Aggression

Five major theoretical frameworks have been utilized in the study of aggressive behaviour. These theoretical frameworks attempt to explain or predict an individual's aggressive behaviour. We often hear people trying to explain aggression by saying such things as "boys will be boys" or "they are just blowing off steam." The belief in the basic tenets of instinct theory and the frustration-aggression theory has had an impact upon the sporting sphere. People will often justify aggression as natural and necessary. These justifications occur although research indicates that these theories are not effective means of explaining aggressive behaviour. Although Bredemeier's and her colleagues' attempts to explain aggression from a moral reasoning viewpoint is still in its infancy, this perspective gives us another useful avenue to use in our quest for understanding. Up to this point, however, the social learning theory provides the most plausible and empirically supported foundation for describing, understanding, predicting, and ultimately controlling aggressive behaviour in sport (see Table 7.1).

Table 7.1   Theories Regarding Aggressive Behaviour

Theory	Major Tenet
Instinct Theory	Humans are born with the instinct for aggression.
Frustration-aggression Theory	A blocked goal causes the individual to become frustrated, and frustration produces aggression.
Revised Frustration-aggression Theory	A blocked goal causes emotional reactions (e.g., anger), which lead to a readiness to behave aggressively; appropriate environmental cues cause this readiness to develop into aggression.
Physiological Theories	Aggressive behaviour occurs because individuals have either a brain pathology or excess testosterone.
Moral Reasoning Theory	Aggressive behaviour is perpetrated by individuals who do not know it is wrong.
Social Learning Theory	Individuals are aggressive because they have learned that aggression pays.

> **Reflections 7.5**
> Think back to a time when you behaved aggressively, you saw someone behaving aggressively, or you were a victim of another's aggressive action. Using the theories just discussed, try to explain why you or this other individual behaved in this manner.

Measurement of Aggression

The only way that we can try to get a picture of aggression in sport is to start with the conceptual definition. Therefore, any measure of aggression has to include the intent to physically or psychologically harm another living being. Typically, in sport research, we find two perspectives utilized, an external and an internal perspective (Widmeyer, Dorsch, Bray, & McGuire, 2002). The **external perspective** focuses on behaviours in the sport that are generally thought to be performed with the intent to harm. The drawback of using this perspective is that no consideration is given to the actor's actual intent. Consequently, we see other research using an **internal perspective**. From this standpoint, individuals are asked to describe their desire to behave aggressively or their perceptions of what is aggressive behaviour. The methodologies used in each perspective are briefly described below. For a more in-depth examination of various ways of measuring aggression, the reader is referred to Widmeyer, Dorsch et al. (2002) or Stephens (1998).

External Perspectives in Measurement

Methods that fall under the external perspective category usually involve examining behaviours that are typically thought to involve the intent to injure. Game sheets that record penalties are a common source for this type of information. A limitation of this method is that it is not possible to know the true intent of the actor. Researchers have attempted to overcome the limitation that exists with using these statistics by trying to find out which penalties typically involve the intent to injure. For example, Widmeyer and colleagues (Widmeyer & Birch, 1984; Widmeyer & McGuire, 1997), in a study of aggression in ice hockey, asked professional hockey players to indicate the percentage of time they typically used the penalized behaviour to injure their opponent physically or psychologically. This approach yielded a list of 14 penalties that are performed usually with the intent to injure: charging, boarding, kneeing, elbowing, roughing, fighting, high sticking, slashing, cross checking, butt ending, spearing, instigating, checking from behind, and head butting. Other behaviours, such as tripping and hooking, were not included on this list and are usually not used when trying to measure aggressive behaviour in ice hockey since the intent is not to harm the opponent. Widmeyer (1997) performed a similar study in football, resulting in a list of five aggressive actions: unnecessary roughness, late hit, roughing the passer, roughing the kicker, and unsportsmanlike conduct.

One of the problems that we encounter with this method is that officials do not see all of the infractions; consequently, some intentionally harmful behaviour goes unpenalized. Consider this fact in light of what was said earlier regarding the social learning theory. The intentionally harmful behaviours that are not penalized usually lead to a successful outcome in the immediate future. Consequently, these behaviours could be seen as being successful and being subsequently reinforced by the lack of a penalty (Sheldon & Aimar, 2001).

Now let's think about using penalties as an indicator of aggression from a different angle. In other words, not all penalties assessed by an official may be acts of aggression;

some legitimate behaviours in sport may be aggressive in nature. For example, think about the football athlete playing the safety position who viciously tackles the receiver in the middle of the field to make sure the opposing team thinks twice about passing up the middle. Or consider the defenceman in hockey who delivers an open-ice body check to the forward, who is racing up the centre of the ice with his head down, in order to make him "see stars" and lose the puck. If the intention of both these players is to psychologically intimidate their opponents, then these behaviours can be considered acts of instrumental aggression.

Another external methodology that has been used by some researchers involves the use of video technology. For example, Kirker, Tenenbaum, & Mattson (2000) examined aggression in hockey and basketball using this method. Because the context in which the act occurs helps the observer determine the actor's intent (Dorsch & Widmeyer, 1996), this method of measurement could be particularly useful if it is coupled with ratings of aggressive behaviour from individuals who are members of the subculture under examination.

Internal Perspectives in Measurement

Methods that fall under the internal perspective category usually involve asking individuals, via surveys or interviews, about their desire to behave aggressively or about their actual aggressive behaviour. Using a survey approach, individuals identify how often during a contest they want to both physically injure and psychologically injure or intimidate an opponent (Brice, 1990; Dorsch & Widmeyer, 1993; Sanszole, 1995; Widmeyer, Dorsch, & Sanszole, 1995). Although one could argue that wanting to behave aggressively does not necessarily lead to an actual aggressive incident, Dorsch and Widmeyer (1993) found a relationship between an athlete's desire to behave aggressively and the number of aggressive penalties the athlete actually received. Therefore, this method provides some value in measuring aggressive intent particularly when there is no opportunity to utilize more than one method.

A group of Canadian researchers from McGill University has also used a qualitative approach. Todd Loughead, Gordon Bloom, and their colleagues (cited in later sections) have involved athletes in focus groups and one-on-one interviews to discuss actual behaviours in ice hockey. This paradigm allows the researchers to get an understanding of athletes' views of sport and their behaviours within it, particularly whether or not they ever actually want to or attempt to injure opposing players.

Summary of Measurement of Aggression

Measuring aggression is a complex undertaking. Many different ways have been used to try to get a better understanding of how often aggression occurs in sport and to ultimately try to understand why this behaviour continues to occur. Typically, researchers use one of two perspectives to measure this behaviour. External methodologies rely upon the observation of the researchers or other individuals and carry the risk of mistakenly inferring the intent of the actor. Internal methodologies, while doing a better job of looking at intent, are often not linked to specific acts of aggression within the sport. Shapcott, Bloom, and Loughead (2005) have linked the two perspectives by videotaping athletic contests and subsequently interviewing the players involved about their intentions surrounding their behaviour. This is perhaps the most promising way to help us understand why people behave in this fashion.

Factors Causing Aggression

Being frustrated or wanting reinforcement may partially explain why athletes behave aggressively. There are, however, other personal, situational, and group factors that help us to understand when aggression is more likely to occur. Within this section, we will briefly discuss some of these factors. The findings for many of these factors will be equivocal, considering the lack of research done in the sport setting and the many ways in which researchers have measured aggression.

Personal Factors Influencing Aggression

FEMALE ATHLETES AND AGGRESSION   Historically, the majority of research examining aggression in sport has primarily examined male athletes. Consequently, the majority of the information presented so far in this chapter has been discovered while studying males. Recently, there has been more interest shown in sport behaviours exhibited by women, particularly in aggressive behaviours. In ice hockey, where women's participation has increased more than 600% in the last decade, female athletes have shown a tendency to engage in aggressive behaviours, similar to their male counterparts. For instance, a 15-year-old female hockey player was charged with assault after she repeatedly punched an opponent in the head, causing her opponent to suffer whiplash and neck bruises (McGregor, 2002).

Given that female athletes appear to be displaying similar aggressive behaviours to their male counterparts, Canadian researchers Bloom and Vanier (2004) and Vanier, Bloom, and Loughead (2004) have conducted a series of studies specifically examining aggression in women's hockey. They discovered that the majority of aggressive behaviour in women's hockey occurs to (a) protect the goalie, (b) gain a competitive advantage, and (c) get the opponent to retaliate and draw a penalty. They also found that these women tended to rely more on psychological aggression in the form of verbally taunting and provoking their opponents into taking retaliatory penalties.

Reflections 7.6
Would boxing be considered aggressive behaviour? When and why do women behave aggressively in sport?

Photo courtesy of CP/Andrew Vaughan.

Taking into consideration the limitations discussed earlier regarding measuring aggression, Shapcott et al. (2005) videotaped and then individually queried female university hockey players from one team about their aggressive intentions during game play. Using videotaped game footage, the researchers selected clips that included any aggressive acts committed by the participant. The interview began by showing the aggressive video clips, and then the researchers asked the player to explain the intent influencing her aggressive behaviours. The results of these interviews revealed that female players used aggression for five reasons. The most frequent reason was to obtain the puck from their opponents even if it meant using aggression to do it. The second reason was related to strategy; the players indicated that their coach taught them various aggressive behaviours as a method of impeding their opponents' progress. Another strategy used by the players was to utilize aggression as a way of preventing the opposition from scoring and as a way to draw penalties. A third reason for using aggression was to protect themselves or their teammates from being hit by the opposition. A fourth reason was to intimidate their opponents; this included using verbal and physical aggression. The fifth reason was for no other purpose than simply to hit their opponents. Interestingly, all the players indicated that they never intended to physically injure anyone.

AGE AND AGGRESSION   No conclusive statement can be made regarding the relationship between age and aggressive behaviour, considering the fact that not a lot of studies have looked at age as the specific variable of interest. One study by Kirker et al. (2000) examined the aggressive behaviours of elite ice hockey and basketball athletes and discovered that athletes believed they became more aggressive with age. The athletes suggested their increased aggressive behaviour occurred in conjunction with their increased confidence (including being better and bigger) and because they believed the

Figure 7.1   At different levels of competition, the desire of male ice hockey players to physically and psychologically injure an opponent at least once per period

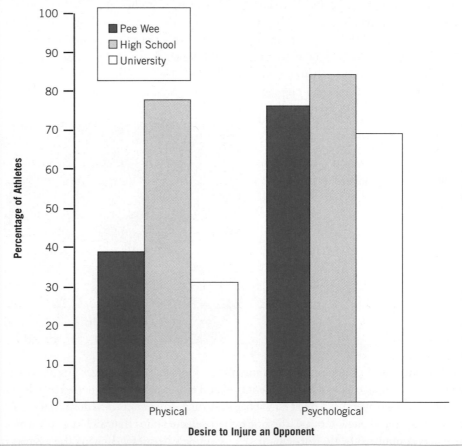

games were more serious and that aggressive behaviours were needed to keep themselves on the team. Silva (1983) also found that players' perceptions of the acceptability of aggression increased as a function of the number of years the athlete played the sport.

There are contrary findings to the argument that there is a positive relationship between age and aggressive behaviour. Several studies have examined statements regarding the desire to behave aggressively among male Pee Wee–level (ages 12–13) ice hockey players (Dorsch, 1992), high-school ice hockey players (Sanszole, 1995), and university ice hockey players (Brice, 1990). As can be seen in Figure 7.1, desires to physically and psychologically injure opposing players peak during the middle years. Consequently, we cannot definitively state the direction of the relationship between age and aggressive behaviour until more research examines this variable in particular.

PHYSICAL SIZE AND AGGRESSION   One might think that bigger players are more likely to use their size to their advantage; however, one could also imagine that larger athletes may be aware of their size and not want to engage in activities that may injure an opponent. In one study, looking at Pee Wee hockey players (ages 12–13), Dorsch (1992) found that both height and weight positively correlated with the number of aggressive penalties. This size-aggression relationship was supported by Lemieux, McKelvie, and Stout (2002) who compared the aggressive behaviour of athletes involved in contact sports (e.g., football and rugby), athletes involved in non-contact sports (e.g., track, baseball, golf, and volleyball), and individuals not involved in any sports. They found that regardless of whether an individual was an athlete or not, the bigger the person, the more likely he reported being involved in a fight in a non-sport setting.

RETALIATION MOTIVES AND AGGRESSION   Brice's (1990) study of university ice hockey players and Sanszole's (1995) study involving a variety of male and female athletes found that many athletes expressed wanting to physically harm an opponent because the opponent had attempted to injure them or a teammate. Although these researchers did not directly examine the link between these retaliation motives and the athletes' aggressive behaviour, Harrell (1980) did find the strongest predictor of high-school basketball players' aggressive behaviour was the aggression of their opponents. In another study of basketball and ice hockey players, Kirker et al. (2000) found that the most severe aggressive acts were preceded by aggressive acts, often committed by the opponent. These retaliatory acts often led to further acts of aggression.

ANNOYANCES AND AGGRESSION   Widmeyer, Bray, Dorsch, and McGuire (2002) suggested that some athletes might become aggressive because they are annoyed. Annoyances in sport could take the form of inconsistent calls by an official, mannerisms of opponents, or taunting by opposing players, coaches, or fans. For example, imagine how the opposition felt when Terrell Owens, then of the San Francisco 49ers (National Football League), scored a touchdown and pulled a Sharpie marker out of his sock to sign the football—while still in the end zone!

Brice (1990) found that officiating inconsistencies were one of the most annoying and most prevalent sources of anger for ice hockey athletes. Although Brice did not examine whether these feelings of anger resulted in subsequent acts of aggression, Kirker et al. (2000) found that verbal abuse of officials was the most frequent aggressive act occurring in ice hockey and basketball games (30% and 26% of aggressive acts, respectively). Officials in many other sports have reported being the victims of verbal abuse. For example, in soccer, 24.3% of referees stated that players had physically threatened them, and 63.6% said players had verbally abused them (Folkesson, Nyberg,

Archer, & Norlander, 2002). Even in squash, officials state that verbal abuse occurs on average once every five to ten matches (Dorsch, McAuliffe, & Paskevich, 2000).

Although officials are usually the victims of verbal aggressive actions, sometimes the aggression becomes physical. In soccer, Folkesson et al. (2002) found that 12.1% of referees had suffered from some form of physical aggression from players. In baseball and softball, Rainey (1994) discovered that 11% of umpires reported some form of assault, usually pushing, shoving, grabbing, hitting, or punching.

It is not so much the angry feelings themselves that cause an individual to behave aggressively; it might be the rumination on these feelings that leads to aggression. The **cognitive neoassociation theory** (Berkowitz, 1990) suggests that paying attention to and focusing on angry feelings primes more angry feelings, thereby increasing the possibility of further aggressive behaviour. Indeed, Bushman (2002) found that the long-held therapeutic value of imagining the face of one's attacker while hitting a punching bag, worked, in fact, in the opposite direction. Not only were the people in this study not relieved of their aggressive intent, but their feelings of anger were intensified.

SELF-PRESENTATION AND AGGRESSION   Sport psychologists often refer to **self-presentation** as the way individuals present themselves (i.e., behave, dress) in social situations. Some sport psychologists believe that some athletes may behave aggressively in order to convey or maintain an image of toughness to opponents and observers, particularly within contact sports, such as football, basketball, or ice hockey (Widmeyer, Bray, et al., 2002). In support of this notion, Wann (1997) found that intercollegiate ice hockey and football players whose names were printed on the backs of their jerseys were more aggressive. He surmised that because the players were now identifiable to others, they needed to portray a certain image. Similarly, McGuire (1990) found that professional ice hockey players who did not wear facemasks were more aggressive than those who did. A possible explanation for this finding is that because the players' identities are more apparent without the facial protection, the need to present themselves in a manner consistent with the norms of the game becomes more prevalent.

The contrasting viewpoint would suggest that aggressive impulses are increased when the individual feels less identifiable. This process, known as **deindividuation**, is particularly apparent from war stories. Soldiers have often said that it is much easier to pull the trigger when the target is 150 feet (45 metres) away versus shooting an enemy who is close enough to see their eyes. In a sport context, Rehm, Steinleitner, and Lilli (1987) found that handball teams whose members wore the same jersey and consequently appeared similar to each other (i.e., high anonymity) committed more aggressive acts than the team in which each individual wore his own shirt. This finding supports the assumption that higher levels of anonymity contribute to actions that are more aggressive.

Reflections 7.7
Consider the findings on self-presentation. Most of these studies use correlational research methods. Thinking back to what you read in the research perspectives chapter (Chapter 2), what are the limitations of this research in drawing conclusive causal statements about identifiability and aggression?

ACHIEVEMENT MOTIVATION AND AGGRESSION   As you learned in the chapter on motivation, individuals with a high ego-orientation base their perceptions of their ability on their comparisons with the abilities of others. High task-oriented individuals, on the other hand, base their perceptions of their ability on their past performances and improvement of their skills. Although there has been no research examining the link between these achievement orientations and actual aggressive behaviour, past research has shown that athletes with a high ego-orientation are more inclined to approve of aggressive behaviour (Dunn & Dunn, 1999) or to perceive aggressive behaviours as more legitimate (Duda, Olsen, & Templin, 1991).

Situational Factors Influencing Aggression

COMPETITIVE SITUATIONS AND AGGRESSION   A classic study, by Sherif and Sherif in 1953, demonstrated that friendships were destroyed, hostilities were created, and aggressive behaviour escalated when competition was introduced into a summer camp setting. Hoping to replicate these findings in a laboratory setting, Leith (1977) found that people who were placed in a competitive physical activity situation exhibited more aggressive behaviour than those who were in a co-operative physical activity setting, or the control situation. These studies would suggest that competitive situations have an impact on displayed aggression.

Some researchers have taken this finding a step further and believe that a competitive situation coupled with an environment in which physical contact is allowed increases aggressive behaviour even further. In support of this assumption, Zillman, Johnson, and Day (1974) found that contact-sport athletes behaved more aggressively than non-contact-sport athletes. Lemieux et al. (2002) also found that athletes involved in contact sports reported more acts of hostile aggression than those who were involved in non-contact sports. Taken together, these studies would suggest that more aggression takes place in competitive situations where physical contact is integral.

To complicate this straightforward finding, Lemieux et al. (2002) found that there were no differences with respect to the number of hostile aggressive acts the individuals reported engaging in when the contact athletes were size-matched to a group of non-athletes. This suggests that it was perhaps the size differential between the contact athletes and non-athletes that was leading to the differences in aggressive behaviour. Another study that calls into question the positive relationship between competition and aggression is one of the few natural experimental studies of aggressive behaviour. Dorsch et al. (2004) found that the inclusion of body checking did not increase the desire to behave aggressively in Atom ice hockey (ages 9 and 10). More specifically, those athletes who played in a league that allowed body checking did not express more frequent attempts to be aggressive than those athletes who played in a league where no body checking was allowed. Although body contact was still allowed in both leagues, the increased physicality of a body-checking environment did not seem to have an impact on these athletes' stated attempts to injure opponents either physically or psychologically.

FREQUENCY OF COMPETITION AND AGGRESSION   As there appears to be some evidence for a relationship between competition and aggression, it is not a stretch to think then that the number of times competitors meet may have an impact on the amount of aggressive behaviour demonstrated in these matches. Indeed, Widmeyer and McGuire (1997) did find that aggressive behaviours occurred more often in intra-divisional professional ice hockey games (i.e., seven to eight games in a season) than in interdivisional games (i.e., three games in a season).

HOME-FIELD ADVANTAGE AND AGGRESSION A study by McGuire, Courneya, Widmeyer, and Carron (1992) examined whether home teams exhibited more aggressive behaviours than visiting teams and whether or not this type of behaviour had an impact upon the outcome of the game. They found that there was indeed a home-field advantage with the home teams winning 58.5% of decided games. Furthermore, home teams received more aggressive penalties in games they won while visiting teams incurred more aggressive penalties in games they lost.

POINT DIFFERENTIALS AND AGGRESSION Losing is often thought to be a frustrating situation. If this assumption is true, then according to the frustration-aggression hypothesis, individuals should behave in an aggressive manner when they are losing. When researchers examined the influence of losing situations in general and took into account the score when an aggressive act occurred, these situations in team sports, such as ice hockey (McGuire, 1990) and soccer (Lefebvre & Passer, 1974), were not related to aggressive behaviours. There was, however, a relationship between losing and aggressive actions in the individual sport of wrestling (Martin, 1976). In this sport, it seems that when an individual is behind in points, there is an increase in the tendency to behave in an aggressive manner.

Despite the fact that there does not seem to be a relationship between aggressive behaviour and losing situations in general, there does seem to be some support for the occurrence of aggressive behaviours in various specific losing situations. For example, several studies in ice hockey (e.g., Kirker et al., 2000; Wankel, 1973) have found that teams *losing late in the game* tend to be more aggressive. Other researchers have found that teams *losing* by a large margin, particularly three or more goals, tend to display more aggressive actions (Harrell, 1980; McGuire, 1990; Wankel, 1973). Taking this finding even further, Cullen and Cullen (1975) found that winning teams committed more total penalties when only one or two, or more than five, goals separated the two teams. Losing teams, on the other hand, committed more penalties when the score differential was three or four goals.

GAME-TIME TEMPERATURE AND AGGRESSION There is limited research examining the influence of temperature on aggressive behaviours in sport. For example, Riefman, Larrick, and Fein (1991) examined the relationship between aggressive behaviour and temperature in major league baseball. Using the number of times that pitchers hit batters as their measure of aggressive behaviour, they found a significant positive relationship between temperature at game time and the number of batters hit. At lower temperatures (e.g., 70° to 79° F or 21° to 26°C), relatively few batters were hit, but as the temperature started to climb into the 80s (above 26° C) and higher, more batters were hit by pitchers.

Group Factors Influencing Aggression

As discussed previously in this chapter, the psychological closeness of an observer to an aggressor will influence the observer's perception of the aggressor's intent. Similarly, belonging to a group will have an impact on an individual's willingness to behave aggressively. Within a group, such factors as the role the individual plays, group norms, group cohesion, and the group's collective efficacy for aggression will impact the individual's and consequently the team's aggressive behaviour.

INDIVIDUAL'S ROLE AND AGGRESSION Individuals who occupy a specific role on a team are generally expected to behave in a manner consistent with the behaviours that are expected of their roles. Within sports like ice hockey, we often see players designated as the "enforcer" or "policeman." The players who fill these roles are expected, and may even be recruited, to behave in an aggressive manner. As Marty McSorley, former Boston Bruin enforcer, stated during his trial, "The job of a tough guy is to inspire team-mates and to ensure the team's skilled players are not intimidated" ("Meant no harm," 2000, ¶13).

GROUP NORMS AND AGGRESSION   **Group norms** are the "standards for the behaviour that is expected of members of the group" (Carron & Hausenblas, 1998, p. 134). Typically referred to as the unwritten rules of the game, norms provide the team player with the information necessary to know what is or is not acceptable behaviour. Stephens (2000) found that the best predictor of girls' likelihood to engage in aggressive behaviours in a soccer game was their belief that their teammates would play unfairly. It is this expectation of unfair play as being the team norm that subsequently guided the athletes' behaviours.

COLLECTIVE EFFICACY FOR AGGRESSION   As teams develop an acceptance of aggressive behaviour and a subsequent expectation that it is needed for success, they develop a perception of their ability to use aggressive behaviour as a tactic or strategy within the game. This perception of their ability to use aggression as a strategy (i.e., **collective efficacy for aggression)** is similar to the sense of collective competence they feel for their offensive or defensive skills. A study of Canadian university and junior ice hockey teams by Dorsch (1997) found that collective efficacy for strategic aggression did predict future team aggressive behaviours. Furthermore, these perceptions were more similar among team members than between teams, which suggests that it is a group perception.

GROUP COHESION AND AGGRESSION   Dorsch, Widmeyer, Paskevich, and Brawley (1996) examined perceptions of team cohesion and aggressive behaviour among Canadian junior ice hockey teams. They found that as the teams became more united, or cohesive, in pursuit of their goals and objectives (Carron, 1988), they exhibited more aggressive behaviours. In a study of baseball and softball players, Shields et al. (1995) found further support to suggest that task cohesion predicted team norms regarding cheating and aggressive behaviour. Together these studies lead to the suggestion that group cohesion may in fact be a group factor that influences aggressive behaviour.

Reflections 7.8
As a sport psychology consultant, you have been asked by a youth hockey league to help reduce aggression levels. Which factors—personal, situational, or both—would you target and why?

Consequences of Aggressive Behaviour

All aggressive acts have both an aggressor and a victim. Furthermore, most of these acts in a sport setting also have at least one observer. Consequently, within an aggressive interaction, there can be consequences to the aggressor, the victim, and the observer. The most obvious of these consequences is injury. Although many studies have examined the incidence of injury in sports, few have related the cause of the injury to aggressive behaviour. In an attempt to address this limitation, Katorji and Cahoon (1992) reported that trainers and players in Canadian Junior B hockey said that approximately 59% of injuries occurred because of an opponent's aggressive act. Katorji and Cahoon also found that of the injuries that occurred to the aggressor, approximately 27% occurred when the aggressor was attempting to harm his opponent.

Falling back upon the definition of an aggressive behaviour, intimidation or psychological harm is another possible consequence of an aggressive altercation. Even though it is very difficult to measure the amount of psychological harm that occurs within a sporting event, we can sometimes infer from a player's behaviour that the aggressor's intent has succeeded. For example, if we see the football receiver hesitate or alter his pattern to avoid the safety, or if we see that the forward is afraid to go into the corners to get the puck, we assume that these players have been intimidated.

Regardless of whether one is attacked or is the attacker, another possible consequence of the altercation is an elevated arousal level. Anger or other emotions are often associated with involvement in an aggressive incident. Coupled closely with these emotions is an alteration in the individual's arousal level. The impact this altered state of arousal will have on the performance of the athlete was more fully discussed in the chapter on anxiety and arousal. In support of this suggestion, NHL referee Brad Watson was quoted as saying, "I find that a fight is, more times than not, a way to fire a team up" (Tuchman, 2000, ¶7).

Finally, penalization is the most common consequence that can occur to the aggressor and his or her team. In most sports, penalization is designed to discourage aggressive behaviour by reducing the individual's or team's chances of success.

Reflections 7.9
What are the various ways to reduce intimidation in sport?

Photo © Joe McBride/CORBIS.

Fan Violence

What happens to the observer of aggression in sport? Research suggests that fans like violence in their sports (Bryant, Comisky, & Zillman, 1981; Bryant, Brown, Comisky, & Zillman, 1982). One sports journalist stated, "The two loudest cheers you ever hear in a hockey game are when the home team scores a goal and when there is a fight" (Tuchman, 2000, ¶17).

Some people go to sport events not only to watch the aggressive behaviours of athletes but also even to instigate aggressive altercations themselves. Gord Russell of the University of Lethbridge (1995) and Russell and Arms (1995) found that individuals who are most likely to take part in aggressive behaviours in the stands at ice hockey games are young males who travel in groups, have a recent history of fighting, like to watch fights, attend hockey games in hopes of seeing fights, react impulsively, and score high on the trait of aggressiveness. These researchers have suggested that the individuals who tend to instigate aggression among fans have a false belief about the willingness of other fans to join in these acts of aggression. They refer to this perception as the **false consensus effect**.

In order to see how willing spectators actually are to become involved, the researchers asked fans at ice hockey games what they would do if a fight were to break out nearby in the stands. Of their respondents, 61% said they would watch, 26% said they would try to stop the fight, 7% said they would applaud or join in, and the remaining 6% said they would leave the area. The small percentage of people who indicated they would become involved gives support to the notion of the false consensus effect.

In addition to aggressive incidents that occur among the observers of athletic contests, there are many reports of altercations occurring between fans and athletes. Incidents of verbal abuse or the throwing of objects at athletes, coaches, or officials would be considered acts of hostile aggression if the intent of the fan is to physically or psychologically injure those individuals. Even if the intent is to gain an advantage for the fan's team by distracting the opposition, this could be considered an act of instrumental aggression (Tenenbaum, Stewart, Singer, & Duda, 1996).

We may believe that the majority of the aggressive acts that occur between fans and athletes happen at the professional level; however, a particularly disturbing incident occurred on January 16, 2005, between the father of a 9-year-old ice hockey player in Toronto and the child's coach. The team's policy was that if a player missed a practice, he would sit out for a couple of shifts during the next game. While the child was sitting on the bench, his father, who disagreed with the rule, reached over the glass partition, grabbed the coach by the neck, and choked the coach until he became unconscious.

Reflections 7.10

Tie Domi, Toronto Maple Leafs enforcer, stated, "When fans try to get involved in our work they gotta be ready to pay the price" ("Fans vs athletes," 2004, ¶5). What do you think should happen to fans who physically or psychologically abuse athletes?

Photo courtesy of AP Photo/Miles Kennedy.

Reduction of Aggression in Sport

Before we can even attempt to reduce aggressive behaviours in sport, we have to understand why they occur. By reading this chapter up to this point, you should have a clear understanding of some of the theories of why people behave aggressively and some of the personal, situational, and group factors that may influence a person's intent to physically or psychologically harm another living being. Based upon what we have discussed so far and suggestions presented elsewhere in the literature (e.g., Tenenbaum et al. 1996; Widmeyer, 2002), we are suggesting five broad methods that may be useful in helping individuals participating in, or even observing, sports to curb their aggressive behaviours. These methods are not necessarily directed specifically at the athletes themselves. Interventions targeted toward other individuals involved in the sporting system (e.g., coaches, parents, officials, and the media) may also prove to be beneficial in accomplishing successful behavioural change.

Punishment and Encouragement

Social learning theory suggests that people learn that aggression pays. Therefore, teaching individuals that aggression does not pay would be paramount for behavioural change. In order to make this shift, the individuals who strongly influence the athletes' learning process (i.e., coaches and parents) need to ensure that the penalty or punishment an athlete receives for an act of aggression is more meaningful to them than any reinforcement they may receive. To this end, coaches must emphasize the value of fair play and encourage and reward such behaviours as great moves, strong effort, unselfish play, teamwork, and courage. Parents also need to reinforce these assertive behaviours. Outside the field of play, parents should also focus on developing their child's ability to utilize a task goal orientation instead of an ego goal orientation. Finally, parents and coaches need to provide young athletes with positive role models, ones who demonstrate non-aggressive, yet effective, assertive behaviours.

In an attempt to ensure that positive behaviours are modelled by parents, the minister responsible for amateur sport in British Columbia was considering having parents of all young athletes in the province sign a contract ensuring that they (a) encourage their child to play by the rules and to resolve conflicts without resorting to hostility or violence, (b) never ridicule or yell at their child for making a mistake or losing a competition, and (c) never question the official's judgment or honesty in public ("Contracts for parents?", 2000, ¶1). A similar contract was used with athletes participating in the 2002 Arctic Winter Games. The rules for these Games included good sportsmanship, no violence, no racial slurs, no gender bashing, no drugs, and no alcohol ("Games code," 2002, ¶1).

Educational Interventions

One way we can help those involved in sport understand that aggression does not pay is through educational interventions. Some associations in Florida have built upon the contract suggested by British Columbia and required parents to take classes on how to behave at sporting events (Zarrella, 2000, ¶1). Similarly, in 2005, major league baseball collaborated with Northeastern University's Center for the Study of Sport in Society to offer this professional league's first violence-prevention training partnership. These workshops teach athletes, parents, coaches, officials, media personnel, and authority figures the meaning of aggression, why it occurs, the cost of aggressive acts, and how to control aggression.

Another aspect of educational programs should be the teaching of psychological skills. Such programs should not just focus on technical skills but also on teaching athletes to expect frustration, annoyance, and attack. Inherent in any sporting situation is an opponent's attempt to stop the athlete's ultimate goal of winning. The athlete has to be able to deal with these situations in an effective, yet non-aggressive, manner. The chapters on stress and coping (Chapter 6) and psychological interventions (Chapter 8) review the different types of psychological skills.

Another feature that any educational program should focus on is the consequences of anabolic steroid use. Athletes, parents, and coaches need to become more familiar with the extremely negative impacts that the use of these drugs has on the future health of the user.

Behavioural Modification Practices

In the International Society of Sport Psychology's (ISSP) position on aggression and violence in sport, Tenenbaum et al. (1996) state, "the tightening of rules, imposing of harsher penalties and changing of reinforcement patterns are only part of the answer to inhibiting aggression in sport. Ultimately, the athlete must assume responsibility for his/her behaviour" (p. 234). Part of assisting the athlete to assume this responsibility could involve the athlete's participation in programs designed to help reduce the desire to behave aggressively. As part of daily training, athletes should work on self-awareness and develop their strategies and coping skills.

When committing an instrumentally aggressive behaviour, a player has more control over his or her behaviour because the act is deliberate and is a means to an end; the player chooses to use aggression in those situations. Pure hostile aggression, however, may be slightly more difficult to curtail because this type of aggression typically occurs in a reactive manner, in a heightened state of arousal, and independent of meaningful cognitive processes. The aggressor needs to develop coping strategies to modify these behaviours (see Chapter 6). Brunelle, Janelle, and Tennant (1999) examined a promising method of dealing with anger and its subsequent behaviours in soccer. They found that a role-playing intervention, in which athletes simulated and practised strategies for dealing with angry feelings, was helpful in controlling these feelings and the typically aggressive behaviours that resulted from them.

Tenenbaum et al. (1996) also recognized that "like players, officials are placed under great stress during games" (p. 233). Consequently, they suggest that officials take measures to improve their psychological skills, for example, their ability to concentrate, to control unnecessary arousal, and to cope with pressure. Ultimately, the development of these skills will enable officials to become more competent and consistent in enforcing the rules of the sport. According to Tenenbaum et al., the subsequent decline in the incidence of errors will help to decrease athletes', coaches', and fans' levels of frustration, while also promoting fair play and minimizing aggressive behaviour.

Changes to the Sporting Environment

Even though we did not mention the use of alcohol previously, it is readily accepted knowledge that the ingestion of alcohol lowers an individual's inhibitions and consequently that individual is more prone to act aggressively. Therefore, the use of alcoholic beverages at sporting events should be banned, or at the very least limited and controlled. Cox (2002) suggests, "athletic events should be promoted and encouraged as family affairs" (p. 316). Sporting events should be an enjoyable experience, where parents and their children can learn about fair play.

Aggressive Behaviour in the Media

Previously we acknowledged the fact that fans like aggression in the sports they observe. Bryant and Zillman (1983) suggest that the media exploits this desire by (a) sensationalizing and replaying acts of aggression repeatedly, (b) focusing on and glorifying aggression in feature stories, and (c) promoting previous aggressive behaviours between competitors to encourage future attendance. Instead of making aggressive behaviours the highlights, the media should promote a campaign to decrease aggressive behaviours in sport, which would be more beneficial. Assertive (not aggressive) plays and players should be glorified and held up as role models in order to promote these acceptable behaviours.

Chapter Summary

The information we discussed in this chapter deals solely with the reasons that an individual may behave in an aggressive manner; ultimately, behaviour is a personal responsibility. In order for us to truly understand and attempt to control aggressive behaviour in sport, we must include other scientific disciplines (e.g., sociology, anthropology, etc.) in this quest. However, from a psychological viewpoint we know the following points regarding aggressive behaviour in sport.

Aggressive behaviour is *not* something we want to encourage or reinforce in athletes because the definition of aggression includes the intent to physically or psychologically harm another. We want to teach and encourage athletes to play assertively (i.e., with legitimate force and energy).

Aggression is sometimes in the eye of the beholder. Measuring aggressive behaviour is a complex and difficult task. Most of the time the aggressor's intent to harm the victim is inferred from the behaviour and the context surrounding the action. Because an observer is usually making this decision, aspects of the observer also come into play. One of the only ways to be certain of whether an act is aggressive is to ask the individual about her or his intent.

Many factors influence aggressive behaviour. Although many theories have helped us understand why people behave aggressively, the theory that provides the most promise for helping us control this behaviour in sport suggests that people behave aggressively because they have learned that aggression pays. Even though the social learning theory gives us a foundation from which to work, we need to be aware of many other personal, situational, and group factors that influence aggressive behaviour.

Reducing aggressive behaviour in sport involves everyone. Controlling aggression is not just an individual athlete's task. Many other actions or interventions could be implemented by, or even targeted at, other sports participants. Coaches, parents, officials, and the media are key stakeholders in the process of behaviour change.

Review Questions

1. Discuss the differences among aggression, assertion, and violence.
2. Lacrosse Canada has decided to examine the amount of aggression in its major leagues. How will you help them discover the extent to which aggressive behaviour occurs in their competitions?
3. Rugby Canada hires you as the consulting sport psychologist to provide seminars to their players, coaches, and officials regarding the underlying reasons that people behave aggressively. What will you tell them in your talk?
4. After a bench-clearing brawl in which four members of the Toronto Blue Jays were injured, the administration of the Jays approaches you to help curb the aggressive

behaviour of their players. What types of policies would you suggest to decrease this type of behaviour?

5.   As the educational sport psychologist for your university hockey team, you notice that one of the players frequently takes a slashing penalty after she loses the puck to an opposing player. How will you help her (a) understand why she behaves this way and (b) change her behaviour?

Suggested Reading

Stephens, D. E. (1998). Aggression. In J. L. Duda (Ed.), *Advances in sport and exercise psychology measurement* (pp. 277–292). Morgantown, WV: Fitness Information Technology.

Widmeyer, W. N. (2002). Reducing aggression in sport. In J. M. Silva III & D. E. Stevens (Eds.), *Psychological foundations of sport* (pp. 380–395). Boston: Allyn & Bacon.

Widmeyer, W. N., Bray, S. R., Dorsch, K. D., & McGuire, E. J. (2002). Explanations for the occurrence of aggression: Theories and research. In J. M. Silva III & D. E. Stevens (Eds.), *Psychological foundations of sport* (pp. 352–379). Boston: Allyn & Bacon.

References

Bandura, A. (1973). *Aggression: A social learning analysis.* Englewood Cliffs, NJ: Prentice Hall.

Berkowitz, L. (1989). Frustration-aggression hypothesis: Examination and reformulation. *Psychological Bulletin, 106,* 59–73.

Berkowitz, L. (1990). On the formation and regulation of anger and aggression: A cognitive-neoassociationistic analysis. *American Psychologist, 45,* 494–503.

Bloom, G. A., & Vanier, J. L. (2004). Coaches' perceptions of aggression in elite women's ice hockey. In D. J. Pearsall & A. B. Ashare (Eds.), *Safety in ice hockey* (Vol. 4, pp. 12–25). Philadelphia: American Society for Testing and Materials.

Bredemeier, B. J. (1994). Children's moral reasoning and their assertive, aggressive, and submissive tendencies in sport and daily life. *Journal of Sport & Exercise Psychology, 16,* 1–14.

Bredemeier, B. J., & Shields, D. L. (1984). The utility of moral stage analysis in the investigation of athletic aggression. *Sociology of Sport Journal, 1,* 138–149.

Brice, J. G. (1990). *Frustration in ice hockey: Extent, antecedents and consequences.* Unpublished master's thesis, University of Waterloo, Waterloo, Ontario.

Brunelle, J. P., Janelle, C. M., & Tennant, L. K. (1999). Controlling competitive anger among male soccer players. *Journal of Applied Sport Psychology, 11,* 283–297.

Bryant, J., Brown, D., Comisky, P. W., & Zillman, D. (1982). Sports and spectators: Commentary and appreciation. *Journal of Communications, 32,* 109–119.

Bryant, J., Comisky, P. W., & Zillman, D. (1981). The appeal of rough-and-tumble play in televised football. *Communication Quarterly, 29,* 256–262.

Bryant, J., & Zillman, D. (1983). Sports violence and the media. In J. Goldstein (Ed.), *Sport violence* (pp. 195–211). New York: Springer-Verlag.

Bushman, B. J. (2002). Does venting anger feed or extinguish the flame? Catharsis, rumination, distraction, anger, and aggressive responding. *Personality and Social Psychology Bulletin, 28,* 724–731.

Carron, A. V. (1988). *Group dynamics in sport.* London, ON: Spodym.

Carron, A. V., & Hausenblas, H. A. (1998). *Group dynamics in sport* (2nd ed.). Morgantown, WV: Fitness Information Technology.

Colburn, K. (1986). Deviance and legitimacy in ice-hockey: A microstructural theory of violence. *The Sociological Quarterly, 27,* 63–74.

Contracts for parents? (2000, October 3). CBC. Retrieved on January 8, 2005, from http://vancouver.cbc.ca/regional/servelet/PrintStory?filename=bc_ parentscontracts001003

Cox, R. H. (2002). *Sport psychology: Concepts and applications* (5th ed.). New York: McGraw-Hill.

Cullen, J. B., & Cullen, F. T. (1975). The structural and contextual conditions of group norm violation: Some implications from the game of ice hockey. *International Review of Sport Sociology, 10,* 69–78.

Dollard, J. C., Doob, L., Miller, N., Mowrer, O. H., & Sears, R. R. (1939). *Frustration and aggression.* New Haven, CT: Yale University Press.

Dorsch, K. D. (1992). *The extent and antecedents of aggression in peewee hockey.* Unpublished manuscript, University of Waterloo, Waterloo, Ontario.

Dorsch, K. D. (1997). *Examining aggressive behaviour from a group perspective.* Unpublished doctoral dissertation, University of Waterloo, Waterloo, Ontario.

Dorsch, K. D., McAuliffe, J., & Paskevich, D. M. (2000, April). Perceived stress, burnout, coping styles, and intentions to terminate among Canadian squash officials. *The Squash Official* [online newsletter], 6–7. Retrieved from http://www.squash.ca/e/officiating/tso/april2005/index.htm

Dorsch, K. D., Riemer, H. A., Kolmel, W., Hoeber, L., Howald, S., Park, I., et al. (2004, October). *Perceptions of aggressive behaviour in Atom ice hockey.* Paper presented at the meeting of the Canadian Society for Psychomotor Learning and Sport Psychology, Saskatoon, SK.

Dorsch, K. D., & Widmeyer, W. N. (1993). The extent and antecedents of aggression in PeeWee ice hockey. *Journal of Sport & Exercise Psychology, 15*(Suppl.), S24.

Dorsch, K. D., & Widmeyer, W. N. (1996). The influence of contextual information on observer's perceptions of actor's intentions to harm others. *Aggressive Behavior, 22,* 183–193.

Dorsch, K. D., Widmeyer, W. N., Paskevich, D. M., & Brawley, L. R. (1996). Exploring relationships among collective efficacy, norms for aggression, cohesion, and aggressive behaviour in Junior hockey. *Journal of Applied Sport Psychology, 8,* S55.

Duda, J. L., Olsen, L., & Templin, T. (1991). The relationship of task and ego orientation to sportsmanship attitudes and the perceived legitimacy of aggressive acts. *Research Quarterly for Exercise and Sport, 62,* 79–87.

Dunn, J. G. H., & Dunn, J. C. (1999). Goal orientation, perceptions of aggression, and sportspersonship in elite male youth ice hockey players. *The Sport Psychologist, 13,* 183–200.

Fans vs athletes: 10 ugly incidents. (2004, November 24). *CBC Sports Online.* Retrieved January 8, 2005, from http://www.cbc.ca/sports/columns/top10/fan_violence.html

Folkesson, P., Nyberg, C., Archer, T., & Norlander, T. (2002). Soccer referees' experience of threat and aggression: Effects of age, experience, and life orientation on outcome of coping strategy. *Aggressive Behavior, 28,* 317–327.

Freud, S. (1925). *Collected papers.* London: Hogarth Press.

Games code of conduct introduced. (2002, February 5). *CBC News.* Retrieved January 8, 2005, from http://north.cbc.ca/regional/servlet/View? filename=fe5conduct

Harrell, W. A. (1980). Aggression by high school basketball players: An observational study of the effects of opponents' aggression and frustration inducing factors. *International Journal of Sport Psychology, 11,* 290–298.

Hastorf, A. H., & Cantril, H. (1954). They saw a game: A case study. *Journal of Abnormal and Social Psychology, 49,* 129–134.

Katorji, J. K., & Cahoon, M. A. (1992). *The relationship between aggression and injury in junior B hockey.* Unpublished manuscript, University of Waterloo, Waterloo, Ontario.

Kirker, B., Tenenbaum, G., & Mattson, J. (2000). An investigation of the dynamics of aggression: Direct observations in ice hockey and basketball. *Research Quarterly for Exercise and Sport, 71*, 373–386.

Lefebvre, L. M., & Passer, M. W. (1974). The effects of game location and importance on aggression in team sport. *International Journal of Sport Psychology, 5*, 102–110.

Leith, L. M. (1977). *An experimental analysis of the effect of direct and vicarious participation in physical activity on subject aggressiveness.* Unpublished doctoral dissertation, University of Alberta, Edmonton.

Lemieux, P., McKelvie, S. J., & Stout, D. (2002, December). Self-reported hostile aggression in contact athletes, no contact athletes and non-athletes. *Athletic Insight: The online journal of sport psychology, 4.* Retrieved December 29, 2004, from http://www.athleticinsight.com/Vol4Iss3/SelfReportedAggression.htm

Luxbacher, J. (1986). Violence in sport: An examination of the theories of aggression, and how the coach can influence the degree of violence in sport. *Coaching Review, 9*, 14–17.

Martin, L. A. (1976). Effects of competition upon the aggressive responses of college basketball players and wrestlers. *Research Quarterly, 47*, 388–393.

McGregor, J. (2002). Girl charged in hockey scuffle. *The Toronto Star.* Retrieved April 3, 2002, from http://www.thestar.com

McGuire, E. J. (1990). *Antecedents of aggressive behaviour in professional ice hockey.* Unpublished doctoral dissertation, University of Waterloo, Waterloo, Ontario.

McGuire, E. J., Courneya, K. S., Widmeyer, W. N., & Carron, A. V. (1992). Aggression as a potential mediator of the home advantage in professional ice hockey. *Journal of Sport & Exercise Psychology, 14*, 148–158.

Meant no harm. (2000, September 28). *CNN/Sports Illustrated.* Retrieved January 3, 2005, from http://sportsillustrated.cnn.com/hockey/nhl/news/2000/09/27/mcsorley_ap/

Mummendey, A., Bornewasser, M., Löschper, G., & Linneweber, V. (1982). Defining interactions as aggressive in specific social contexts. *Aggressive Behavior, 8*, 224–228.

Mummendey, A., Linneweber, V., & Löschper, G. (1984a). Aggression: From act to interaction. In A. Mummendey (Ed.), *Social psychology of aggression: From individual behaviour to social interaction.* Berlin, Germany: Springer-Verlag.

Mummendey, A., Linneweber, V., & Löschper, G. (1984b). Actor or victim of aggression: Divergent perspectives—divergent evaluations. *European Journal of Social Psychology, 14*, 297–311.

Parrott, A., Choi, P., & Davies, M. (1994). Anabolic steroid use by amateur athletes: Effects upon psychological mood states. *Journal of Sports Medicine and Physical Fitness, 34*, 292–298.

Rainey, D. W. (1994). Assaults on umpires: A statewide survey. *Journal of Sport Behavior, 17*, 148–155.

Rehm, J., Steinleitner, M., & Lilli, W. (1987). Wearing uniforms and aggression: A field experiment. *European Journal of Social Psychology, 17*, 357–360.

Riefman, A. S., Larrick, R. P., & Fein, S. (1991). Temper and temperature on the diamond: The heat-aggression relationship in major league baseball. *Personality and Social Psychology Bulletin, 17*, 580–585.

Russell, G. W. (1993). *The social psychology of sport.* New York: Springer-Verlag.

Russell, G. W. (1995). Personalities in the crowd: Those who would escalate a sports riot. *Aggressive Behavior, 21*, 91–100.

Russell, G. W., & Arms, R. L. (1995). False consensus effect, physical aggression, anger, and a willingness to escalate a disturbance. *Aggressive Behavior, 21*, 381–386.

Sanszole, M. (1995). *The extent, antecedents and response to sport frustration by high school students.* Unpublished manuscript, University of Waterloo, Waterloo, Ontario.

Shapcott, K. M., Bloom, G. A., & Loughead, T. M. (2005). *Understanding aggression in women's ice hockey: An application of the theory of planned behavior.* Manuscript submitted for publication.

Sheldon, J. P., & Aimar, C. M. (2001). The role aggression plays in successful and unsuccessful ice hockey behaviors. *Research Quarterly for Exercise and Sport, 72,* 304–309.

Sherif, M., & Sherif, C. (1953). *Groups in harmony and tension: An integration of studies in inter-group behavior.* New York: Harper & Row.

Shields, D. L., Bredemeier, B. J., Gardner, D. E., & Bostrom, A. (1995). Leadership, cohesion, and team norms regarding cheating and aggression. *Sociology of Sport Journal, 12,* 324–336.

Silva, J. M. (1980). Understanding aggressive behavior and its effects upon athletic performance. In W. F. Straub (Ed.), *Sport psychology: An analysis of athlete behavior.* Ithaca, NY: Mouvement.

Silva, J. M. (1983). The perceived legitimacy of rule violating behavior in sport. *Journal of Sport Psychology, 5,* 438–448.

Smith, M. D. (1974). Significant others' influence on the assaultive behavior of young hockey players. *International Review of Sport Sociology, 3,* 45–56.

Smith, M. D. (1979). Social determinants of violence in hockey. *Canadian Journal of Applied Sport Sciences, 4,* 76–82.

Smith, M. D. (1983). *Violence and sport.* Toronto: Butterworth.

Stephens, D. E. (1998). Aggression. In J. L. Duda (Ed.), *Advances in sport and exercise psychology measurement* (pp. 277–292). Morgantown, WV: Fitness Information Technology.

Stephens, D. E. (2000). Predictors of likelihood to aggress in youth soccer: An examination of coed and all-girls teams. *Journal of Sport Behavior, 23,* 311–325.

Storr, A. (1968). *Human aggression.* London: Penguin.

Tenenbaum, G., Stewart, E., Singer, R. N., & Duda, J. (1996). Aggression and violence in sport: An ISSP position stand. *International Journal of Sport Psychology, 27,* 229–236.

Terry, P. C., & Jackson, J. J. (1985). The determinants and control of violence in sport. *Quest, 37,* 27–37.

Tuchman, G. (2000, September 26). Hockey player goes on trial for on-ice assault. *CNN.com.* Retrieved January 3, 2005, from http://archives.cnn.com/2000/ LAW/criminal/09/25/mcsorley. trial.02/

Vanier, J. L., Bloom, G. A., & Loughead, T. M. (2004). Athlete perceptions of aggression in elite women's ice hockey. Manuscript submitted for publication.

Wankel, L. M. (1973). An examination of illegal aggression in intercollegiate hockey. *Proceedings: Fourth Canadian psycho-motor learning and sport psychology symposium* (pp. 531–544). Waterloo, ON: University of Waterloo.

Wann, D. L. (1997, September). *The relationship between players' names on uniforms and athletic aggression.* Paper presented at the meeting of the Association for the Advancement of Applied Sport Psychology, San Diego, CA.

Widmeyer, W. N. (1997). *Aggressive penalties in university football.* Unpublished manuscript, University of Waterloo, Waterloo, Ontario.

Widmeyer, W. N. (2002). Reducing aggression in sport. In J. M. Silva III & D. E. Stevens (Eds.), *Psychological foundations of sport* (pp. 380–395). Boston: Allyn & Bacon.

Widmeyer, W. N., & Birch, J. S. (1984). Aggression in professional ice hockey: A strategy for success or reaction to failure? *Canadian Journal of Applied Sport Sciences, 4,* 91–94.

Widmeyer, W. N., Bray, S. R., Dorsch, K. D., & McGuire, E. J. (2002). Explanations for the occurrence of aggression: Theories and research. In J. M. Silva III & D. E. Stevens (Eds.), *Psychological foundations of sport* (pp. 352–379). Boston: Allyn & Bacon.

Widmeyer, W. N., Dorsch, K. D., Bray, S. R., & McGuire, E. J. (2002). The nature, prevalence, and consequences of aggression in sport. In J. M. Silva III & D. E. Stevens (Eds.), *Psychological foundations of sport* (pp. 328–351). Boston: Allyn & Bacon.

Widmeyer, W. N., Dorsch, K. D., & Sanszole, M. (1995, June). *Gender differences in the extent, antecedents of, and responses to frustration in sport.* Paper presented at the meeting of the North American Society for Psychology of Sport and Physical Activity, Monterey, CA.

Widmeyer, W. N., & McGuire, E. J. (1997). Frequency of competition and aggression in professional ice hockey. *International Journal of Sport Psychology, 26,* 57–60.

Yates, W. R., Perry, P. J., & Murray, S. (1992). Aggression and hostility in anabolic steroid users. *Biological Psychiatry, 31,* 1232–1234.

Zarrella, J. (2000, July 10). Florida youth league requires parents to learn sportsmanship. *CNN.com.* Retrieved January 3, 2005, from http://archives.cnn.com/2000/HEALTH/07/10/kids.sports. parents/index.html

Zillman, D., Johnson, R. C., & Day, K. D. (1974). Provoked and unprovoked aggressiveness in athletes. *Journal of Research in Personality, 8,* 139–152.

Krista Munroe-Chandler
Craig Hall

CHAPTER 8

Sport Psychology Interventions

Chapter Objectives

After reading this chapter, you should be able to do the following:

1. Define and describe each of the five psychological skills most often used in a psychological skills training program.

2. Explain why these psychological skills work.

3. Describe the measurement and implementation of the skills.

4. Describe the components of a psychological skills training program.

Stephanie is a 13-year-old novice-level figure skater representing a Toronto club. She consistently executes a double Axel and has been working for the past season on her triple jumps. She and her coach, Dave, have decided that for her to become a top performer she needs to work not only on her physical skills but also on her mental skills. Stephanie does not have a specific problem (e.g., extreme nervousness before competition); however, both she and Dave recognize the importance of enhancing mental skills. To help her improve her mental skills, they have asked for the help of an applied sport psychology consultant. The consultant meets with them, and together they develop a psychological skills training program.

After meeting with Stephanie and Dave, the applied sport psychology consultant first conducted performance profiling. Based on the results, the consultant determined that Stephanie needed to get psyched up for practices because she tended to be sluggish when she first stepped on the ice. She also needed to improve her focus during practice since she was spending too much time talking with friends and watching other skaters, rather than focusing on what she needed to do. Finally, she needed to enhance her confidence at competitions.

To accomplish these objectives, Stephanie began to do exercises and listen to upbeat music just before a practice. She developed and followed a practice plan that outlined in detail what she had to accomplish during a practice. In addition, she started to regularly do imagery and developed and used a set of confidence-building self-statements at competitions. This initial intervention proved very effective, and Stephanie continues to work with the applied sport psychology consultant on improving the mental side of her skating.

Athletes approach applied sport psychology consultants for two general reasons: (a) to seek help with specific problems, such as performance anxiety and lack of self-confidence and (b) to work to improve the mental side of sport, such as imagery and attention control. In the above scenario, Stephanie has decided to work with a sport psychology consultant for the second reason. Rather than dealing with a specific problem, the consultant is faced with generating a psychological skills training program for Stephanie. The challenge for the consultant will be to determine what techniques should be incorporated into the psychological skills training program (or intervention) and what emphasis should be placed on each. In this chapter we will address these and other issues.

Some Common Myths about Sport Psychology Interventions

MYTH: *Psychological skills training (PST) is a band-aid solution.*
Some athletes and coaches believe that the effective use of self-talk or imagery can be learned in one or two sessions to quickly fix a problem, such as lack of confidence. Just as physical skills take time and effort to develop, so too do psychological skills. There are no quick fixes to problems, and dedicating time to PST over an extended period will enhance athletes' performance and help them reach their full potential.

MYTH: *Only elite athletes can benefit from psychological skills training.*
Successful performance at any level of sport involves technical, tactical, physical, and mental components. Although elite athletes can benefit from highly developed psychological skills, even young athletes will experience the gains garnered from improved psychological skills. Therefore, PST can be implemented at any stage of an athlete's career, but ideally it should be initiated at the grassroots level in order to ensure the most effective development of the mental side of sport.

MYTH: *Athletes need a sport psychologist only when they are performing poorly.*
The third myth is that athletes need a sport psychologist only when they are performing poorly. Most successful athletes realize that achieving peak performance requires a detailed plan that includes an understanding of physiology and nutrition, implementation of cutting-edge technology, and employment of psychological skills training. It is harder to fix a problem once it has started than to keep a problem from occurring.

Introduction

For decades, sport psychology consultants have been studying and developing psychological skills interventions to help athletes enhance their performance and psychological well-being. A **psychological skills training** program, or intervention, entails the structured and consistent practice of psychological skills and generally has three distinct phases: education, acquisition, and practice. In the education phase, athletes recognize the importance of mental skills in sport and how the skills affect performance. There are various approaches to accomplishing this; however, one of the simplest ways is to ask athletes about the importance of mental skills in sport. Although most athletes realize the importance of the mental side of sport, very few actually spend time developing these skills in comparison with the time spent on physical skills.

Athletes often have some understanding of a psychological skill, but they do not fully comprehend its complexity and its optimal use. Therefore, in the acquisition phase, the focus is placed on helping athletes acquire the various psychological skills and learn how to most effectively employ them. In the practice phase, the goals are to have the athletes automate the various psychological skills through overlearning and to implement these skills in practice and competition.

The psychological skills that have been researched most extensively and incorporated into psychological skills training programs are the following: goal setting, imagery,

> Athletes approach an applied sport psychologist to seek help with specific problems and to work to improve the mental side of sport.
Photo courtesy of Joe Patronite/Getty Images.

self-talk, arousal regulation, and attention control. Each of these five skills will be discussed in turn. We will define each skill and discuss why it works, how it can be measured, and how it can be integrated into a psychological skills training program. Measurement tools are discussed in some detail since without proper assessment there cannot be a successful psychological skills training program.

Goal Setting

Goal setting is the most commonly used performance enhancement strategy in sport psychology. Leading sport psychology consultants working with Olympic athletes have reported that goal setting is the psychological intervention most often used (Gould, Tammen, Murphy, & May, 1989); however, most athletes rate their goals as being only moderately effective in enhancing sport performance (Burton, Naylor, & Holliday, 2001).

Types of Goals

A **goal** is a target or objective that people strive to attain. There are three types of goals that athletes can set. **Performance goals** focus on improving and attaining personal performance standards, such as learning an out-turn draw in curling or giving 100% effort at all times in a lacrosse match. **Process goals** focus on specific behaviours that an athlete must engage in throughout a performance, such as snapping the wrist when stroking a squash ball or pulling the arms in tight while executing a spin in figure skating. In contrast to the first two types of goals, **outcome goals** focus on social comparison and competitive results, such as winning a race or outscoring an opponent. Thus, outcome goals are dependent on the ability and performance of one's opponents. **Goal setting**, therefore, is the practice of establishing desirable objectives for one's actions. Research suggests incorporating all three types of goals when developing a goal-setting program (Filby, Maynard, & Graydon, 1999).

<
There are three types of goals athletes can set: *outcome*—to score a goal, *process*—to make an accurate pass to the winger, and *performance*—to give 100% effort.
Photo © Michael Kevin Daly/CORBIS.

Effectiveness of Goal Setting

Research suggests that goal setting works in various ways. According to Locke and Latham (1985), goals direct attention, mobilize effort, foster persistence, and promote the development of new learning strategies. In addition, goals may influence athletes' performance by enhancing their self-confidence and their sense of satisfaction (Moran, 2004). Research has consistently demonstrated the positive effects of goal setting. Burton et al. (2001) noted that 78% of sport and exercise studies have shown moderate-to-strong effects on behaviour. For example, Wanlin, Hrycaiko, Martin, and Mahon (1997) conducted a multiple baseline design in which youth speed skaters received training in goal setting. Over the course of the intervention, the skaters made improvements in their skating as a result of their goal setting.

Most athletes rate goals as being only moderately effective (Burton et al., 2001) even though goal setting is one of the most extensively employed interventions in sport psychology. This is likely due to the fact that athletes are not certain about how to effectively set goals, and as a result they do not think that goal setting works. Additionally, a number of barriers, such as lack of time and everyday distractions, hinder the practice of goal setting among athletes (Weinberg, 2002). Later in this chapter, we shall examine some ways of setting effective goals.

Assessing Goals

Performance profiling is a flexible assessment tool that allows for the identification of athletes' performance-related strengths and weaknesses. It is often used as a first step in developing an intervention program. In addition to its utility as a general assessment procedure, it can be used as an aid to goal setting (Butler & Hardy, 1992; Jones, 1993). There are five steps in performance profiling:

Step 1: Identify key performance characteristics of an elite athlete in your sport. Think of the best person in your sport and identify the characteristics of that athlete. These can include physical, technical, tactical, and mental characteristics.

Step 2: Identify the ideal rating for each of the athlete's characteristics. On a scale from 1 to 10, with 1 being *not at all important* and 10 being *extremely important*, indicate your ideal scores. This rating is also your target.

Step 3: Rate your current ability for each characteristic on a scale of 1 to 10, with 1 being *not at all like me* and 10 being *completely like me*. Be as honest as possible.

Step 4: Find your discrepancy score by subtracting your current rating from your ideal rating. The higher the discrepancy score, the weaker you perceive your ability for that characteristic.

Step 5: Prioritize your targets. After identifying your performance weaknesses (highest discrepancy scores), pick out the two or three that are most in need of correction.

Having identified performance characteristics most in need of urgent attention, you can now implement strategies (set goals) to improve these characteristics. Take the example of a field hockey player who, through performance profiling, has identified her penalty stroke as a weakness. Accordingly, she sets two goals: to improve her shot speed by 10% and improve the height of her shot by 30 cm over the course of four weeks. How to set effective goals, such as those established by the field hockey player, is discussed next.

Recommendations for Goal Setting

The acronym SMART has been recommended to help athletes remember five important guidelines for effective goal setting (Weinberg & Gould, 2003). Goals should be specific, measurable, adjustable, realistic, and timely (see Table 8.1).

Table 8.1   Field Hockey Goal-setting Example Using SMART Guidelines

GOAL: To increase the height of a shot by 30 cm over the course of four weeks

Specific	*Is the goal specific?* Yes ☐ No ☐ Set a goal that is specific rather than vague (e.g., to improve).	
Measurable	*Is the goal measurable?* Yes ☐ No ☐ Be sure you can measure your goal in order to assess progress.	
Adjustable	*Is the goal adjustable?* Yes ☐ No ☐ Don't be afraid to adjust your goal if necessary (i.e., having less playing time or having an injury).	
Realistic	*Is the goal realistic?* Yes ☐ No ☐ Set a goal that is moderately difficult. If a goal is too easy, it is of little value. If a goal is too difficult, it may lead to a decrease in confidence.	
Timely	*Is the goal timely?* Yes ☐ No ☐ Identify a point in time at which the goal is to be achieved, thereby increasing motivation.	

There are other important goal-setting guidelines that athletes should follow. First, athletes should set goals for both practice and competition. Often athletes focus only on competition goals; however, setting practice goals is important when one considers the time spent in practice compared with the time spent in competition. Second, it is important to write down your goals and make them public. In doing so, it is more likely that you will attempt to achieve your goals, given that people around you are aware of your objectives and can be helpful in motivating you to accomplish them. Third, goals should be stated positively, rather than negatively: "I want to run the best 100-metre time possible" rather than "I don't want to come in last in the 100-metre." Fourth, for teams to maximize potential, Dawson, Bray, and Widmeyer (2002) suggested four types of goals to be considered: (a) individual athlete's goals for self, (b) individual athlete's goal for the team, (c) the team's overall goal, and (d) the team's goal for individual members. Finally, the progress toward goal achievement should be reviewed on a regular basis. Conducting this regular review allows you to identify if your goals are appropriate (see Table 8.2).

An example of an intervention using SMART goals is the Wanlin et al. (1997) study previously mentioned (under "Effectiveness of Goal Setting"). All skaters in this study receiving the goal-setting package were first shown a videotape of the instructions to be followed throughout the duration of the study. Athletes were asked to develop a mission, set long-term goals, set subgoals and practice goals, and employ self-talk and visualization to help them achieve the goals. Moreover, athletes were asked to keep a logbook in which their daily practice goals were reported and measured. Athletes were told the goals must be flexible as well as challenging. The skaters made improvements in their skating performance over the course of the goal-setting intervention.

Table 8.2 Goal-setting Guidelines

- Set SMART goals.

- Set goals for practice and competition.

- Make your goals public.

- State goals positively rather than negatively.

- Consider the four types of team goals.

- Review your goals regularly.

Note: Adapted from "The PETTLER Approach to motor imagery: A functional equivalence model for sport psychologists," by P.S. Holmes and D. J. Collins, 2001, Journal of Applied Sport Psychology, 13, pp. 60–83. Copyright 2001 by Taylor and Francis, Philadelphia.

Reflections 8.1

Consider a goal that you have set (personal, athletic, or academic). Does it follow the SMART guidelines? If so, congratulations; if not, revise your goal so that it does follow the SMART guidelines. If you are having difficulties, use Table 8.1 as an example. Now set another goal using the SMART guidelines.

Common Goal-setting Problems

There are some common problems in implementing a goal-setting program. One of the most common mistakes made by athletes in implementing a program is setting too many goals. Athletes end up setting so many goals that they cannot properly monitor them, and they find the evaluation to be overwhelming and lose interest. Those who are just beginning a goal-setting program should work on achieving a small number of goals. Performance profiling will assist the athlete in determining those few goals in need of immediate attention.

Another common problem occurs when athletes do not willingly participate in the goal-setting program. Some individuals will not be excited about goal setting and may even have a negative attitude toward it. Forcing athletes to set goals is not very effective because individual commitment is required. One solution for recognizing individual differences is to expose all athletes to goal setting and work more with those who show the most interest.

Underestimating the time it takes to implement a goal-setting program is another common problem. Often a coach will implement a program with athletes early in the season. As the season progresses, however, less and less time is spent on goal setting, and toward the end of the season the goal-setting program is completely forgotten. Coaches and athletes need to recognize the time required to undertake a goal-setting program. It is better to devote 15 minutes a week throughout the season to goal setting than to attempt to devote 15 minutes a day and not be able to follow through on it.

Finally, failure to provide follow-up is one of the major problems with goal-setting programs. Evaluation of goals is imperative and the continued use of performance profiling throughout the season is one effective way to achieve this. Without follow-up and evaluation, goal setting is simply a waste of time and effort (see Table 8.3).

Table 8.3   Common Goal-setting Problems

- Setting too many goals

- Failing to recognize individual differences in interest in goal setting

- Underestimating the time required to set goals

- Failure to provide follow-up and evaluation

Conclusions about Goal Setting

It is almost impossible to conceive of a psychological skills training program that does not include goal setting. For athletes to enhance their performance, weaknesses must be identified and corrected. In overcoming weaknesses, it is almost inevitable that goals will be set. What becomes important is ensuring that athletes set SMART goals that are supported and evaluated. Although goal setting is a complex process that requires hard work and discipline, it can be extremely effective in helping athletes achieve excellence in sport (Burton et al., 2001). Thus, it is highly recommended that athletes of all competitive levels engage in goal setting.

Imagery

Canadian Olympic speed skater, Isabelle Charest stated,

A big part of my training has been visualization—I try to put myself in race situations. It starts when I lace up my skates and I go through every possible scenario in the race, the crowd, even the people watching at home. I see the race from various angles, starting first or second, leading and sometime coming from the back of the pack. (Kingsley, 1998)

Researchers and athletes alike have long been interested in imagery and its effect on sport performance. Some have gone so far as to hail it as the "central pillar of applied sport psychology" (Perry & Morris, 1995, p. 339). In addition, coaches view imagery as one of the most important psychological skills to teach their athletes (Rodgers, Hall, & Buckolz, 1991).

The Nature of Imagery

As the above quotation from Isabelle Charest suggests, imagery should involve as many perspectives as possible; however, referring to imagery as "visualization" is somewhat misleading. Visualization suggests that only one sense is being used, that of sight. It has been documented, however, that athletes try to incorporate as many senses as possible including, sight, auditory, olfactory, tactile, and kinesthetic. The latter sense is particularly important for athletes since it involves the feel or sensation of bodily movements. The more polysensory the image, the more real it becomes, and the more effective it will be on sport performance. Given the multidimensional nature of imagery, White and Hardy (1998) have defined imagery as:

An experience that mimics real experience. We can be aware of "seeing" an image, feeling movements as an image, or experiencing an image of smell, tastes, or sounds without actually experiencing the real thing. Sometimes people find that it helps to close their eyes. It differs from dreams in that we are awake and conscious when we form an image. (p. 389)

Analytic Model of Imagery

Most of the recent imagery research has stemmed from Paivio's (1985) analytic model, which suggests that imagery has cognitive and motivational functions that operate on either a specific or a general level. Thus, **cognitive general imagery** includes images of strategies, game plans, or routines—for example, imaging a floor routine in gymnastics; **cognitive specific imagery** includes images of specific sport skills—for example, imaging a free throw in basketball; **motivational general imagery** includes images relating to physiological arousal levels and emotions—for example, imaging feeling calm and relaxed in front of a crowd; and **motivational specific imagery** includes images related to an individual's goals—for example, imaging receiving a gold medal. More recently, Hall, Mack, Paivio, and Hausenblas (1998) divided the motivational general function into a **motivational general-arousal** function, encompassing imagery associated with arousal and stress, and a **motivational general-mastery** function, representing imagery associated with being mentally tough, in control, and self-confident (see Figure 8.1).

Based on the five functions, Martin, Moritz and Hall (1999) developed an applied model for depicting how imagery works in sport. Although the model shows that athletes use imagery in three different situations, they report using imagery most in competition and, more specifically, just prior to competition (Munroe, Giacobbi, Hall, & Weinberg, 2000). According to the model, the desired sport outcome should be matched to the correct function of imagery. For example, if an athlete wanted to reduce anxiety prior to a competition, the type of imagery used should be motivational general-arousal. Athletes have been found to use all five functions of imagery; however, they report using motivational general-mastery the most (Munroe, Hall, Simms, & Weinberg, 1998).

> When you use imagery, try to make it polysensory: see the ball, feel the ball, smell the fresh-cut grass, hear the crowd cheer, taste the sweat on your lips.

Photo © Thinkstock/Alamy.

Figure 8.1   The five functions of imagery

Level	Motivational Function	Cognitive Function
General	Mastery Arousal	Strategies
Specific	Goals	Skills

Note: Adapted from "Imagery Use by Athletes: Development of the Sport Imagery Questionnaire," by C. R. Hall, D. Mack, A. Paivio, and H. A. Hausenblas, 1998, International Journal of Sport Psychology, 29, pp. 73–89, Edizioni Luigi Pozzi; and from "Cognitive and Motivational Functions of Imagery in Human Performance," by A. Paivio, 1985, Canadian Journal of Applied Sport Sciences, 10, pp. 22S–28S. Canadian Association of Sports Sciences.

The model also illustrates that the effect of imagery function on outcome is moderated by imagery ability, which includes both visual and kinesthetic imagery. Although minimal research has been conducted on imagery use by injured athletes, Sordoni, Hall, and Forwell (2002) found that such athletes use imagery for three main reasons: cognitive, motivational, and healing imagery (see Figure 8.2).

There is considerable support for the main proposal of the model that the function of imagery should match the desired outcome. With respect to the cognitive functions of imagery, numerous studies conducted in a wide variety of contexts have shown that the use of cognitive specific imagery is conducive to enhancing the learning and performance of motor skills (see Driskell, Copper, & Moran, 1994 for a review). Case studies and anecdotal evidence suggest that cognitive general imagery can be beneficial when used for the learning and performance of play strategies. For example, the performance benefits of using cognitive general imagery have been reported for rehearsing football plays (Fenker & Lambiotte, 1987), wrestling strategies (Rushall, 1988), and entire canoe slalom races (MacIntyre & Moran, 1996).

Figure 8.2   Applied model of imagery use in sport.

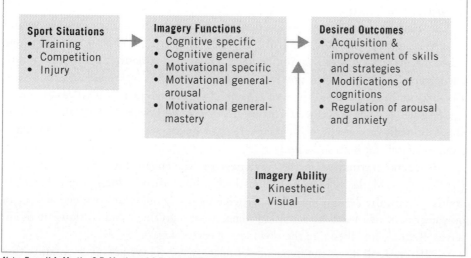

Note: From K.A. Martin, S.E. Mortiz and C.R. Hall, 1999, Imagery use in sport: a literature review and applied model, The Sport Psychologist 13(3): 248, figure 1. © 1999 by Human Kinetics Publishers, Inc. Adapted with permission from Human Kinetics (Champaign, IL).

With respect to motivational imagery, Munroe et al. (2000) reported that athletes use motivational specific imagery to develop goals, and Callow and Hardy (2001) argued that a benefit to using motivational specific imagery would be an increase in athletes' motivation to attain their goals. In another study, Callow, Hardy, and Hall (2001) investigated the effects of a motivational general-mastery intervention on the sport confidence of three elite badminton players. The researchers employed a single-subject multiple-baseline design. The two-week, six-session intervention was made up of motivational general-mastery imagery, consisting of images associated with control, confidence, and mental toughness in difficult situations. A significant increase in sport confidence was demonstrated for two of the players, and a stabilized confidence level was demonstrated for the third, thus indicating that a motivational general-mastery imagery intervention can improve sport confidence.

Lastly, research examining motivational general-arousal imagery has indicated that it can be used by athletes to regulate arousal and anxiety. More specifically, images of the emotions and arousal associated with competitive performance—for example, anger, anxiety, excitement, fear, pressure, psyched-up, etc.—are related to increased levels of state anxiety (Carter & Kelly, 1997; Hale & Whitehouse, 1998; Murphy & Woolfolk, 1987; Murphy, Woolfolk, & Budney, 1988; Vadocz, Hall, & Moritz, 1997). In contrast, images of performing in a relaxed and calm state are related to decreased levels of state anxiety (Murphy & Woolfolk, 1987; Murphy et al., 1988; Ryska, 1998).

Imagery Assessment Tools

Two types of imagery assessment tools have typically been used in sport psychology. One tool measures imagery ability, and the other assesses the frequency of imagery use. One of the most important factors influencing imagery effectiveness is imagery ability. Some athletes are better imagers than others even though most athletes report using imagery. In addition, Rodgers et al. (1991) in their intervention study with figure skaters found the imagery ability of the skaters improved with imagery practice. This suggests that imagery is not only an ability but also a skill that can be improved through regular practice.

Instruments have been developed to measure imagery ability. The Movement Imagery Questionnaire-Revised (MIQ-R; Hall & Martin, 1997) is an eight-item questionnaire that assesses an individual's visual and kinesthetic imagery ability. Participants are asked to first physically perform four different movements then visually or kinesthetically image the four movements. Each movement involves an arm, a leg, or a whole body movement. Participants then rate how well they felt they were able to visually or kinesthetically image the movement, and imagery scores are calculated separately for both subscales.

A second instrument is the Vividness of Movement Imagery Questionnaire (VMIQ; Isaac, Marks, & Russell, 1996), which assesses the vividness of visual imagery ability. Briefly, the 24-item scale has participants rating different imagined actions or movements in two ways, by watching someone else do them and by doing it themselves. Respondents then rate the vividness of each image.

Different tools assess the frequency of imagery use. There are questionnaires that provide information on imagery frequency (and other mental skills); examples are the Test of Psychological Skills (TOPS; Thomas, Murphy, & Hardy, 1999) and the Ottawa Mental Skills Assessment Tool (Durand-Bush, Salmela, & Green, 2001). These types of questionnaires provide considerable information about a number of psychological skills, but they do not provide detailed information about any one skill, such as imagery.

In comparison, other instruments have been designed to assess only imagery. The Sport Imagery Questionnaire (SIQ; Hall et al., 1998) is a 30-item self-report measure that asks athletes to rate how frequently they use the five functions of imagery as described in Figure 8.1 (see Table 8.4). A number of studies have employed the SIQ to examine and provide support for the applied model of imagery proposed by Martin et al. (1999).

Table 8.4   Sport Imagery Questionnaire Sample Items

Examples of Items in the SIQ

- I imagine my skills improving. (cognitive specific)

- I image alternative strategies in case my event/game plan fails. (cognitive general)

- I imagine winning a medal. (motivational specific)

- I imagine appearing self-confident in front of my opponents. (motivational general mastery)

- I get psyched up when imagining performing. (motivational general-arousal)

Recommendations for Using Imagery

Holmes and Collins (2001) have provided some guidelines in their PETTLEP model that are useful when conducting imagery interventions (see Table 8.5).

For imagery use to be effective, it must be incorporated into a daily routine. Bull, Albinson, and Shambrook (1996) suggest brief sessions (five minutes) once or twice a day for athletes who are beginning imagery. As athletes become more comfortable with and better at using imagery, they should systematically increase the amount of imagery employed. Cumming and Hall (2002) argue that imagery requires deliberate practice and just as for physical practice, more is better. Because imagery is a skill and improves with practice, athletes will become better imagers over the course of an imagery intervention. The better imagers they become, the more effective their imagery will be.

Here are other recommendations for using imagery:

- Images should be positive rather than negative (Hall, 2001).

- Athletes should be in a good mood when using imagery (Gregg, Hall, & Hanton, 2004).

- Athletes need to be encouraged to use imagery during those times when imagery use is typically less frequent, such as in the off-season and early competitive season (Munroe et al., 1998).

- Less skilled athletes need to be encouraged to use imagery (Hall, 2001).

- Athletes of all ages can benefit from imagery interventions (Munroe-Chandler, Hall, Fishburne, & Strachan, 2004).

Conclusions about Imagery

Imagery is an integral part of many psychological skills training programs because of its wide range applicability and the fact that imagery can be implemented virtually

Table 8.5   The PETTLEP Model of Imagery

A Guide for Using Imagery: The PETTLEP Model	
P = Physical	The physical nature of the imagery is dependent upon the task. You must determine whether relaxation or increased arousal is helpful prior to imaging.
E = Environment	The image should be as real or as close to the actual environment as possible. If you are unfamiliar with the competition venue, perhaps video footage or pictures will enhance your image.
T = Task	Depending on the task, your imagery perspective may vary. Skills that rely heavily on form have been found to benefit most from an external imagery perspective.
T = Timing	The temporal characteristics or timing of the image should be equal to that of your physical performance (e.g., if a skating routine takes three minutes to physically execute, so too should the imagery).
L = Learning	The content of the image should change based on the learning of the skill. For example, the content of your image when you are first learning a camel spin should be different from when you have mastered the skill.
E = Emotion	Images will be more effective if you attach meaning or emotion to them. If imaging winning a gold medal, feel the excitement and the joy that is a part of it.
P = Perspective	Consider both perspectives, internal and external, when imaging.

Note: Adapted from Holmes & Collins, 2001 / Holmes, Paul S., & Collins, David J. (2001)."The PETTLEP approach to motor imagery: A functional equivalence model for sport psychologists." Journal of Applied Sport Psychology, March 1, 2001, Vol.13:1, 60-83. Taylor & Francis, Philadelphia.

anywhere and anytime. Coaches, athletes, and sport psychology consultants have all recognized imagery as an effective intervention for influencing a number of factors as evidenced in Martin et al.'s (1999) applied model. Moreover, every athlete (novice to elite) can benefit from the use of imagery, providing the imagery is built into a daily routine and fits the needs of the athlete.

Self-talk

One of the skills most highly promoted by applied sport psychology consultants and frequently included in psychological skills intervention training programs is self-talk (e.g., Bull et al., 1996; Hanton & Jones, 1999). Although many different definitions have been forwarded, Hardy (2004) recently proposed a strong definition of self-talk, following his extensive research on athletes' self-talk at the University of Western Ontario. He argued that **self-talk** should be defined as "*overt* [out loud] or *covert* [in your head] sport related statements that are addressed to the self, multidimensional and somewhat dynamic in nature, include interpretive elements associated with the content of the self-statements, and seem to serve at least two functions for the athlete, instructional and motivational" (p. 145, italics added).

Functions of Self-talk

Self-talk serves two basic functions in sport: instructional and motivational. **Instructional self-talk** is used by athletes for skill development, skill execution, strategy development, and general performance improvement (Hardy, Gammage, & Hall, 2001). For example, Landin and Hebert (1999) investigated the effectiveness of instructional self-talk by having varsity tennis players use the cue words "split" and "turn" in order to improve their volleying technique at the net. These two cue words were constructed to represent the two phases of the volleying: splitting the legs shoulder width apart for a balanced position, and then turning the shoulders in order to reduce excessive raquet head movement. Improvements in the players' volleying performance were observed, indicating that sport performance can be improved by self-talk.

According to Hardy et al. (2001a), athletes employ **motivational self-talk** for three purposes: (a) for mastery, for example, building self-confidence, staying focused, being mentally ready, coping in difficult circumstances; (b) for arousal, for example, psyching up, relaxing; and (c) for drive, for example, increasing effort, increasing drive, reaching their potential. To date, there has been little research investigating motivational self-talk in sport. Nevertheless, one of the most consistent findings in sport psychology research is the direct relationship between positive thinking and successful performance. Undoubtedly, positive thinking entails considerable positive self-talk. Applied sport psychology books often stress that athletes need to change "I can't" to "I can" and "It's difficult for me" to "It's a challenge for me" if they want to be more successful (see Bull et al., 1996).

Assessment of Self-talk

Various approaches and measures have been employed by researchers to assess athletes' use of self-talk. The Self-Talk Grid (Hardy, Hall, & Alexander, 2001) measures two dimensions of self-talk: valence (positive vs. negative) and directional interpretation (motivating vs. de-motivating). Athletes simultaneously report on both dimensions by placing a check mark on a 9 × 9 grid: they indicate the valence of their self-talk, from *extremely positive* to *extremely negative*, as well as how they interpret their self-statements, from *extremely motivating* to *extremely de-motivating*. A weakness of the Self-Talk Grid is that it does not provide a detailed account of athletes' self-talk. As noted in Hardy's (2004) definition, self-talk is multidimensional, and the Self-Talk Grid assesses only two of the six dimensions of self-talk, valence and directional interpretation.

A more comprehensive questionnaire for assessing athletes' self-talk was recently developed by Hardy (2004). The Self-Talk Use Questionnaire (STUQ) is a 59-item self-report instrument that assesses the frequency of athletes' use of self-talk. The

---

Reflections 8.2
You have just been scored against and trail by one goal. What could you say to yourself in order to build confidence and stay positive?

STUQ has four sections: section 1 examines *when* athletes use self-talk; section 2, *what* athletes say to themselves; section 3, *why* athletes talk to themselves in both practice and competition; and section 4, *how* athletes use self-talk (see Table 8.6). The instrument appears to be both reliable and valid.

An alternative approach to using questionnaires, developed by Van Raalte, Brewer, Rivera, and Petitpas (1994), is a tennis-specific observational method called Self-Talk and Gestures Rating Scale (STAGRS). Independent judges rate athletes' usage of overt self-talk during a competitive tennis match. The STAGRS measures the use of positive, negative, and instructional self-talk (and gestures). Positive self-talk and gestures are the summed occurrences of complimenting opponents, fist pumps, and positive self-talk. Negative self-talk and gestures are the summed occurrences of ball abuse, frustration, hitting oneself, laughing in frustration, negative self-talk, opponent abuse, and racquet abuse. Finally, instructional self-talk are the summed occurrences of giving instructions to oneself (e.g., keep raquet head up) and practice motions without the ball. There are some limitations with the STAGRS. It assesses self-talk only in tennis, and it measures only overt self-talk; however, most of athletes' self-talk is covert.

Recommendations for Using Self-talk

Hardy (2004) identified six self-talk dimensions that should be used as a guide when developing a self-talk intervention for athletes. The first dimension, valence, refers to self-talk being positive or negative. Most of the self-talk research has compared positive versus negative self-talk and has consistently shown that positive self-talk is better. For example, Dagrou, Gauvin, and Halliwell (1992) found that a positive self-talk group significantly outperformed a negative self-talk and control group on a dart-throwing task. It is recommended that interventions focus on the use of positive self-talk.

The second dimension is concerned with how athletes' self-statements are verbalized, whether overtly or covertly. To date, there has been no direct comparison between the effectiveness of overt and covert self-talk in the sport domain. Nevertheless, it is known that both coping statements and goals are more effective if they are publicly

Table 8.6   Example Items of the Self-talk Use Questionnaire

Section on the STUQ	Example of an Item
When	How often do you use self-talk in relation to your sport before a practice?
What	In your opinion, generally what percentage of your self-talk is positive in nature? ____% generally what percentage of your self-talk is neutral in nature? ____% generally what percentage of your self-talk is negative in nature? ____% **(Percentages given should total 100%)**
Why	How often do you say things to yourself in practice to refine an already learned skill?
How	How often do you combine self-talk with mental imagery when using self-talk to help learn/fine tune a skill?

<
The Self-Talk Use Questionnaire
(STUQ) assesses the frequency of
athletes' use of self-talk: when, what,
why, and how.
Photo © Philippe Caron/Sygma/CORBIS.

known. It is recommended, therefore, that some of the self-talk in an intervention be overt.

The third dimension involves the self-determination of the statements used by athletes. Statements can be conceptualized as assigned or freely chosen. Research, such as the tennis study conducted by Landin and Hebert (1999), demonstrates that assigned self-talk can be very effective. However, Hardy (2004) has argued that self-talk freely chosen by the athlete might have a greater motivational influence. Given that there is no research comparing the effectiveness of assigned versus freely chosen self-talk in sport, it is recommended that the coach, the sport psychology practitioner, and the athlete collaborate in the development of the athlete's self-talk statements.

The fourth and fifth dimensions of self-talk are closely related and entail the motivational interpretation of self-talk. The fourth dimension, directional interpretation, is concerned with whether athletes view their self-talk as motivating or de-motivating. The fifth dimension is intensity and is concerned with the extent to which athletes interpret their self-talk to be motivating—*not at all* or *very much so*. Different from the directional interpretation dimension, intensity is achieved regardless of whether athletes view that self-talk as motivating or de-motivating. For interventions, we recommend that athletes use self-talk they perceive as very motivating.

The final dimension of self-talk is frequency (i.e., how often athletes employ self-talk). Research has found that successful athletes use more self-talk than unsuccessful athletes. For example, Mahoney and Avener (1977) found that male gymnasts who qualified for the U.S. Olympic team reported a greater use of self-talk in competition and practice than those gymnasts who did not qualify for the Olympics. Based on such findings, it is recommended that athletes be encouraged to use self-talk frequently (see Table 8.7).

Landin (1994) provided some additional guidelines for the use of verbal cues in sport. Verbal cues should be brief, phonetically simple, logically associated with the particular elements of the respective task, and be compatible with the rhythm and timing of the task.

Table 8.7   The Six Dimensions of Self-talk

1. Valence—Positive or Negative

2. Verbalization—Overt or Covert

3. Self-Determination—Assigned or Freely Chosen

4. Directional Interpretation—Motivating or De-motivating

5. Directional Intensity—Not At All or Very Much So

6. Frequency—Often or Never

Conclusions about Self-talk

It is important that athletes practise positive self-talk. We encourage athletes to analyze the content of their self-talk and be on the lookout for negatively framed statements. When negative statements enter your mind, they should be immediately replaced with positive ones. Furthermore, athletes need to ensure their self-talk incorporates both instructional and motivational statements. Athletes who invest in improving their self-talk will find their efforts well rewarded.

Arousal Regulation

The relationship between arousal and anxiety is complex (see Chapter 5). Given that athletes may require different levels of arousal for peak performance, it is important that athletes learn to identity which mental and emotional states are necessary for success. The following two quotations from Canadian athletes represent the diversity in arousal levels needed for peak performance. Tania Vincent, national level speed skater, said, "I need to be nervous before a race because it gives me that extra boost. I transfer my nervousness to adrenaline and it helps me keep going" (Wilson, 1998, ¶6). Recall Steve Podborski's quote from Chapter 5:

I discovered that after a certain point of nervousness, I would start to deteriorate pretty rapidly. There was a real drop off point in my ability to perform if I got too nervous . . . so it was just being able to find that little narrow comfort zone. (Orlick & Partington, 1986, p. 69)

Once athletes can identify their optimal level of arousal, they can learn to voluntarily program these responses. Because the theories and research pertaining to the arousal-performance relationship are covered elsewhere, this section will focus on techniques to reduce and increase levels of arousal.

Arousal was discussed in more detail in Chapter 5. For the purposes of our discussion, we will adopt the definition as proposed by Zaichkowsky and Baltzell (2001). **Arousal** is a multidimensional construct containing physiological, cognitive appraisal, and affective components. Coaches and athletes would concur that performance fluctuations in sport are many times the result of being overaroused or underaroused. Given the strong relationship between arousal and performance, it is not surprising that athletes use techniques to regulate their arousal levels.

Techniques to Reduce or Increase Arousal

TECHNIQUES TO REDUCE AROUSAL   Many performance problems arise because of overarousal. In order to avoid any detrimental effects on performance, learning to relax is vital. Below we discuss various techniques that have been shown to effectively reduce arousal level.

Breathing   If done properly, breathing is a simple technique used to relax. Diaphragmatic breathing, as opposed to quick shallow breathing, increases the amount of oxygen being delivered through the body and facilitates the removal of waste. When athletes feel overaroused prior to a competition, their breathing rate usually increases and breathing becomes very shallow. By learning to breathe better, athletes can achieve deep relaxation or momentary relaxation.

Breathing Exercise: Take a deep breath (dig down into the belly) and imagine your lungs are divided into three levels. Begin by filling the lower level of the lungs with air. You will notice the diaphragm moving down slightly and forcing the abdomen out. Next, fill the middle level of the lungs by expanding the chest cavity and raising the ribcage. Finally, fill the upper level of the lungs. Notice a slight rise in the chest and shoulders. Hold the breath for several seconds; then exhale slowly. Repeat this exercise until you feel comfortable with this breathing technique. To help enhance this technique, you may want to consider rhythmic breathing, in which you inhale for a count of four and exhale for a count of eight (a 1:2 ratio). This helps to slow the breathing and allows you to focus on the exhalation (Williams & Harris, 1998).

Progressive Relaxation   Jacobson (1938) first introduced this technique as a means to relax. Progressive relaxation was based on the notion that tension and relaxation are mutually exclusive. This means one cannot be relaxed and tense at the same time. Although the initial training program devised by Jacobson was lengthy and required a substantial amount of training, abbreviated exercises that are just as effective have evolved (Carlson & Hoyle, 1993). Once the technique has been mastered, athletes can achieve a relaxed state in a matter of minutes, thereby making it useful just prior to competition or during breaks in competition.

Progressive relaxation involves systematically tensing and relaxing specific muscles in a pre-determined order: left arm, right arm, left leg, right leg, abdomen, back, chest, shoulders, neck, and face muscles. The tensing (or contraction phase) teaches awareness and sensitivity while the letting go (or relaxing phase) teaches awareness of the absence of tension. Bernstein and Carlson (1993) propose that once the athlete can achieve the abbreviated version (normally takes several weeks of practice), an even shorter version can be attained. This includes tensing the entire body, holding for 5–10 seconds, and then releasing the tension to achieve a relaxed state.

Progressive Relaxation Exercise: In the following abbreviated version of progressive relaxation, tense each group of muscles and hold for 5–10 seconds, and then relax for 30–40 seconds.

a.   Make tight fists with both hands, tighten the biceps and the forearms, hold the tension, and then relax.

b.   Tighten the muscles of both thighs; at the same time you curl your toes and tighten the calves. Hold. Relax.

c.   Take a deep breath, hold it, and raise the shoulders while making the stomach hard and tightening the buttocks. Hold. Relax.

d.   Tense all the facial muscles while employing the tension procedure for the neck. Hold. Relax.

Meditation   **Meditation** allows for deep relaxation of the mind, which in turn, relaxes the body. Meditation has been found to facilitate athletic performance (Schaffer, 1992); however, these positive effects seem most prominent in activities involving gross motor movements, such as running. Meditation involves the uncritical focus of attention on a single thought, sound, or object (usually called the mental device). Although meditation is normally associated with eastern and western religious practice, Herbert Benson (1975) devised the relaxation response, which is a generalized version of meditation and one that is employed by athletes as a means to relax.

Meditation Exercise: Before you begin, find a quiet place where you can get comfortable and where distractions are minimal. Choose a mental device (mantra), such as the word "calm" or "warm." Adopt a passive attitude in which thoughts and images enter the mind but are not attended to. Close your eyes, and relax all your muscles, beginning at your feet and progressing up to your face. Focus on your breathing. With each exhalation, repeat your mantra. Breathe easily and naturally. Continue this for 10–20 minutes. Once finished, remain seated with your eyes closed. After a few minutes you may open your eyes. Practise the technique once or twice daily. Remember to remain passive by just letting the relaxation happen.

Autogenic Training   **Autogenic training** focuses on feelings associated with limbs and muscles of the body. More specifically, the training consists of three components: (a) warmth and heaviness of the limbs, (b) visualizing relaxing scenes at the same time as imagining the first component, and (c) specific relaxing themes in self-statements. Spigolon and Annalisa (1985) provide some anecdotal evidence that autogenic training works to improve athletic performance. Just as progressive relaxation takes time and training to master, so does autogenic training. Several months of regular training are needed to become skilled at this technique.

Autogenic Training Exercise: Autogenic training consists of six sequential stages. As described in progressive relaxation, allow the feelings to happen without interference. Allow yourself to learn each stage before progressing to the next. Repeat the suggestions in each stage six times followed by the word "quiet" once (see Table 8.8). Once the athlete has learned all the stages, the entire sequence can be practised.

TECHNIQUES TO INCREASE AROUSAL   Although the techniques mentioned thus far have dealt with relaxation, there are times when athletes need to psych themselves up and become energized. While relaxation training is used to lower arousal to optimal levels, **psyching up strategies** are used to increase arousal levels. When underaroused, athletes cannot perform effectively. Their reactions will be slowed down and their coordinations reduced. Many attempts by athletes to energize themselves or their teams have been done at the wrong time, thereby causing overarousal (Cox, 2002). Athletes and coaches must first identify the signs and symptoms of low energy, and then decide which of the following techniques is best suited to their needs. Below we discuss various techniques that have been shown to effectively increase arousal level.

Pep Talks   The pep talk is one of the most widely used and recognized energizing strategies. It is important, however, that the pep talk be meaningful and be applied at the correct time. If your player or team is already energized prior to a competition, you may want to think twice before giving the "win one for the gipper" speech.

Bulletin Boards   Catchy phrases or quotes displayed in a location that is visually prominent (e.g., locker room door, above athlete's stall) are an easy way to increase arousal (activation). Athletes seeing these on a daily basis will remember them and use them as reinforcement when needed.

Pre-competitive Workouts   A pre-competitive workout can enhance activation. It is not uncommon for athletes to feel fatigued on the day of competition. Therefore, a light workout several hours prior to competition can combat this fatigue.

Verbal Cues   Using energizing words such as "explode," "quick," or "go" can help a player or team to quickly become activated. There are situations where athletes do not have enough time to generate energy with a pre-competitive workout. In instances such as these, energizing words can be employed.

Breathing   Although breathing is a technique that can be used to relax, it can also be used as an energizer. By increasing the rhythm of breathing and imagining activation and energy with each inhalation, an athlete can increase arousal.

Table 8.8   Autogenic Training Stages, Sensations, and Suggestions

Stage	Sensation	Suggestion
Stage 1	Heaviness in the extremities	"My right (left) arm is heavy."
Stage 2	Warmth in the extremities	"My right (left) arm is very warm."
Stage 3	Regulation of cardiac activity	"My heartbeat is regular and strong."
Stage 4	Regulation of breathing	"My breathing rate is slow, calm, and relaxed: it breathes me."
Stage 5	Abdominal warmth	"My solar plexus is warm." (place hand on upper abdominal area while saying this phrase)
Stage 6	Cooling of the forehead	"My forehead is cool."

Imagery   Energizing images work in much the same way as energizing verbal cues. Be sure to formulate an image that is personally energizing. For instance, 2004 Olympic gymnastics floor champion Kyle Shewfelt stated, "The night before, I was trying to sleep, but I was going through my routine in my head. I wasn't too nervous, but I was trying to make it perfect.... [on competition day] I think I went through it about 5000 more times" ("Senior men," 2004, ¶3). As a result, he was full of energy when arriving at the competition venue.

Music   Many athletes use music to get psyched up. For many, music is part of their pre-competitive routine to help them achieve their optimal arousal level. Recently the NBA decided that athletes could no longer wear headphones and listen to music in the warm-up. Vince Carter, formerly of the NBA Toronto Raptors, noted that his pre-competitive routine would suffer as a result of this decision ("Carter told," 2004).

Measurement of Arousal Levels

Arousal can be measured in a number of ways, including physiological recordings, self-reports, and behavioural observations. A recent trend has been the construction of multidimensional self-report instruments, such as the Competitive State Anxiety Inventory-2 (CSAI-2; Martens, Burton, Vealey, Bump, & Smith, 1990). The measurement of arousal has been covered in Chapter 5.

Conclusions about Arousal Levels

Athletes' ability to effectively regulate arousal is one of the most important techniques in ensuring athletic success. Athletes need to know how and when to relax or become energized in both training and competition. Using the techniques and exercises outlined above will aid athletes in achieving optimal arousal levels.

Reflections 8.3

In previous chapters, we discussed the concepts of stress, anxiety, and coping, whereas this chapter has focused on specific psychological strategies. How would you develop a coping skills program for an athlete who reports experiencing debilitating high levels of cognitive anxiety during critical parts of a competition? Think carefully about what information you would need and the potential psychological or mental skills a trained and competent helper could teach the athlete.

Attention Control

Attention is fundamental to skilled motor performance (Abernethy, 2001). Players often attribute performing poorly to a loss of concentration or becoming distracted. Even a very temporary loss of focus can mar performance and spell the difference between winning and losing. For example, missing a short easy putt in golf as a result of simply not exerting enough concentration has cost numerous professionals tournament wins. Given the importance of attention to successful sport performance, it comes as little surprise that many psychological skills training programs include attention control training (e.g., Bull et al., 1996).

Recent research views **attention** as a multidimensional construct having at least two components (Abernethy, 2001). First, it is considered to be a limited resource. This refers to the known limitations people have in performing two or more tasks at

Research has shown that dual-task performance (e.g., dribbling a basketball while looking to make a pass) gets better with training.
Photo courtesy of Getty Images/ Digital Vision.

the same time. A basketball player, as an example, must dribble the ball and at the same time monitor the position of teammates and opponents. The second component of attention concerns the selective processing of specific information while ignoring other information. Alternatively, it can be considered as focusing on relevant cues while disregarding irrelevant ones. A goalie in hockey must determine from where a shot is being taken while disregarding the jostling players in front of the net.

Research has shown that performing multiple tasks, such as dribbling a basketball while looking to make a pass, gets better with training (Abernethy, 2001). In addition, performers become better with practice at selecting pertinent information or cues (e.g., the goalie determining from where the shot is taken) and are less likely to be distracted by irrelevant ones.

Assessing Attention as a Limited Resource

Probably the most common approach to measuring attention as a limited resource in experimental psychology has been the use of dual-task procedures. These procedures determine the attention demands and characteristics of two different tasks that are performed simultaneously. The **primary task** is the task for which attention demand is assessed. The **secondary task** provides the principal performance measure from which the implications concerning primary task demand are obtained. The following is an example of a dual task. A soccer player is required to dribble a ball down a field; this is the primary task. While dribbling, the player is required to change direction when a coach blows the whistle, and this reaction-time task (e.g., go right on the whistle blow) would be the secondary task. This signal could be given by the coach at various phases of the dribbling task, such as at the start, when a defender is encountered, or when the player is dribbling with no defenders nearby. Tasks similar to this one have shown that all phases of performing a skill do not require the same amount of attention. This dual-task procedure, unfortunately, has been rarely used to measure attention in sport because of the difficulty in determining an appropriate secondary task, as well as in achieving baseline measures of performance for both the primary and secondary tasks.

An alternative method of assessing attention demands has been to use physiological measures of information processing load. Researchers have used such measures as pupil diameter, cardiac acceleration or deceleration, cardiac variability, and EEG event-related potentials as indicators of information processing load. For example, researchers have proposed that when a task is performed that requires an external attentional focus, heart rate slows down immediately before the task is executed. This proposal has received some support. Boutcher (2002) found evidence of cardiac deceleration among elite rifle shooters just before they pull the trigger, which suggests they seem to be able to switch on their attention on demand. The limitations of using these physiological measures are that they can be quite costly and are only indirect measures of attention demands (i.e., they may not always be good measures of attentional resource limitations).

Assessing Selective Attention

There are multiple means to assess attention (see Table 8.9). One approach to assessing the selection of relevant information is the use of visual occlusion techniques. **Temporal occlusion** examines the amount of time people take to select the information they need in order to respond. Researchers show people a videotape of a skill. At various points during the action, the videotape is stopped and the observers are required to make a response. For example, Abernethy and Russell (1987) had badminton players watch video sequences of a player making different shots. When the video was stopped, the observers made predictions about the landing positions of the shuttle. To examine when, in the course of the observed action, accurate decisions were made, the video was stopped at different times prior to, during, and after the shuttle contact. Thus, the researchers could determine when during the action the observers could select the necessary information for making a correct decision.

Table 8.9   Summary of Selective Attention Assessment Tools

Assessing Selective Attention
Visual Occlusion Techniques: Temporal and Event
Eye Movement Recordings
Self-Report Measures
Test of Attentional and Interpersonal Style (TAIS)
Thought Occurrence Questionnaire for Sport (TOQS)

Event occlusion examines which characteristics of the performance people use to make a correct response. In this case, parts of the video are masked so the observers cannot see selected parts of the action. The logic of this approach is that if people make poorer decisions when they cannot see a specific cue (e.g., the hitting arm of a badminton player making a shot), then that cue is important for successful performance.

Another approach to investigating the selection of relevant information is the use of eye movement recordings. Sophisticated equipment tracks the movement of the eyes and records where they are looking at a particular time. The assumption is that what a person is looking at should provide insight into what information in the environment a person is attending to. The question is, can we relate eye movements to visual attention? The answer seems to be yes but with considerable caution. Although it is not possible to make an eye movement without a corresponding shift in attention, attention can be moved around the visual field without making eye movements. Therefore, visual fixation (periods when the eye remains relatively stationary) and attention are not one and the same. This means that eye movement recordings may underestimate what people are visually attending to.

A third approach to assessing selective attention is the use of self-report measures. These measures typically address how well people are able to focus their attention. Attentional focus is sometimes considered in terms of width (i.e., a broad or narrow focus) and direction (i.e., an external or internal focus). Taking a doubles tennis player as an example, the player would need a narrow external focus when volleying a ball at the net, but a broad internal focus when analyzing how to move at the net (e.g., to poach or not on a partner's upcoming serve). One of the most common measures of attentional focus is the Test of Attentional and Interpersonal Style (TAIS; Nideffer, 1976), and a number of sport-specific versions of this instrument have also been developed (e.g., baseball version (B-TAIS), Albrecht & Feltz, 1987). Research has indicated, however, that the TAIS has some inadequacies and should be employed with caution (Ford & Summers, 1992).

Although researchers have questioned the use of the TAIS, there is a promising new instrument for the assessment of concentration skills. The Thought Occurrence Questionnaire for Sport (TOQS; Hatzigeorgiadis & Biddle, 2000) is a 17-item test that measures the degree to which athletes experience cognitive interference from distracting thoughts during competition. The three subscales measure (a) task-related worries, such as "During the competition, I had thoughts that other competitors are better than I am"; (b) task-irrelevant thoughts, such as "During the competition, I had thoughts about what I'm going to do when I go home"; and (c) thoughts of escape, such as "During the competition, I had thoughts that I cannot stand it anymore."

Using Attention-control Strategies

There are different techniques for controlling attention (see Table 8.10 on next page). The most commonly used technique for learning to control attention is **attention simulation training**, in which athletes replicate the kinds of attention-demanding situations they find themselves in during competition. Players should practise simultaneously working on two tasks that typically must be performed together to produce optimal performance. Players should also practise focusing on relevant cues and disregarding irrelevant one. The practise, however, is only likely to be effective if it is sport specific. In other words, the training situations must allow the performer to practise the specific attention-sharing and cue-selection strategies required in the sport skill. A defenceman

Table 8.10   Summary of Attention-control Strategies

- Simulation Training

- Performance Routines

- Attentional Cues

- Imagery

in hockey should practise carrying the puck while looking to pass to one of the forwards, and a goalie should practise stopping shots with other players in front of the net.

Other attention-control strategies include performance routines, attentional cues, and imagery (Bull et al., 1996). **Performance routines** are a set sequence of thoughts and actions that are done before the performance of key skills. For example, professional golfer Mike Weir has a famous "waggle," which is part of a distinct pre-shot routine. What began as a physical move to counteract his hockey actions, the waggle has become part of his pre-shot routine (Wilson, 2003). It is now identical from one swing to the next. In order for performance routines to be effective in competition, they must be carefully planned and then extensively practised in training.

There are two types of routines used by athletes. Pre-event routines are the fixed thoughts and actions athletes undertake in the time leading up to competition (e.g., night before or morning of competition); pre-performance routines are the fixed thoughts and actions athletes undertake immediately before executing a skill (e.g., bouncing the ball three times before taking a foul shot). These routines work because they encourage athletes to focus on task-relevant information. They also remind athletes to remain in the present rather than dwell on past events of possible future outcomes. Finally, performance routines prevent the athlete from attending too much to skill technique instead of letting skills happen automatically.

Attentional cues are words and actions that direct the athlete's attention. These cues help athletes to focus their concentration on the task at hand and to refocus their concentration if lost. Three types of concentration cues are verbal, visual, and physical. A verbal cue is typically a single word, which is repeated at the appropriate moment. Some examples of verbal cues are *smooth, high, speed, ready*, and *power*. A visual cue entails focusing keenly on something in the athlete's surroundings. For example, looking at the strings of a squash racquet, staring at the logo on the shaft of a field hockey stick, and fixating on the button in curling are all visual cues an athlete may use. A physical cue involves doing an action, such as taking a deep breath, banging the stick on the ice, and slapping the thigh. Some athletes use a single cue while others prefer to use a combination. Just like performance routines, attentional cues need to be practised regularly and employed consistently before implementing them in competition.

Imagery, as a means of controlling attention, can be used in two ways. It can be used to prepare for various scenarios that ensure athletes will not be distracted by unexpected events. For example, a skater could imagine how to react if the music stops during the middle of her program. Moreover, imagery can be used as a means of parking errors in order to prevent dwelling on mistakes. For example, a volleyball player may image placing errors in the garbage can at the side of the court, or a soccer player may image placing errors in the tree at the end of the pitch. Just as with the other techniques discussed above, parking errors requires considerable practice. In doing so, the athlete creates a link between parking the image and focusing attention on relevant performance cues.

Conclusions about Attention Control

It is difficult to conceive of anything more important in sport than paying attention to the task at hand. Attention-control strategies are often perceived as inherent in elite athletes; however, the old adage "practice makes perfect" is apt when it comes to developing effective strategies. An athlete's control over attentional focus is learned through practice just like any other difficult physical skill. Using the techniques discussed above, athletes can improve their attention control and perform successfully during the critical moments in their sport.

Chapter Summary

A variety of psychological intervention strategies to enhance sport performance have been discussed in this chapter. These strategies involve the following five key psychological skills. Athletes should set SMART goals that are supported and evaluated. Imagery should be part of every psychological skills training program because of its wide application and the fact that it can be implemented virtually anywhere and anytime. Athletes should analyze the content of their self-talk and modify negatively framed statements. Athletes need to know how and when to relax or become energized during both training and competition. Athletes should improve their attention control so they can perform successfully during the critical moments in their sport.

The benefits of these strategies have been supported by research as well as by the anecdotal reports from athletes, coaches, and applied sport psychologists. It is important to remember that these psychological strategies can be learned, practised, and applied in a variety of settings, such as during training, competition, and injury rehabilitation. These strategies will be beneficial, however, only if athletes are committed to putting the time and effort into mastering them. Consider the results for Stephanie, the figure skater, in the opening vignette.

Review Questions

1. What are the five psychological skills discussed in this chapter?
2. Why are the five psychological skills effective?
3. Describe one way to measure each of these five psychological skills.
4. Describe the SMART guidelines for goal setting.
5. What are the guidelines for using imagery?
6. What are the six self-talk dimensions?
7. What are the techniques that effectively reduce arousal level?
8. What are the techniques that effectively increase arousal level?
9. Describe each of the four attentional control strategies and provide an example of each.

Suggested Reading

Abernethy, B. (2001). Attention. In R. N. Singer, H. A. Hausenblas, & C. M. Janelle (Eds.), *Handbook of sport psychology* (2nd ed., pp. 53–85). New York: Wiley.

Burton, D. (1989). Winning isn't everything: Examining the impact of performance goals on collegiate swimmers' cognitions and performance. *The Sport Psychologist, 3,* 105–132.

Butler, R. J., & Hardy, L. (1992). The performance profile: Theory and application. *The Sport Psychologist, 6,* 253–264.

Hall, C. R. (2001). Imagery in sport and exercise. In R. N. Singer, H. A. Hausenblas, & C. M. Janelle (Eds.), *Handbook of sport psychology* (2nd ed., pp. 529–549). New York: Wiley.

Williams, H. M., & Harris, D. V. (2001). Relaxation and energizing techniques for regulation of arousal. In J. M. Williams (Ed.), *Applied sport psychology: Personal growth to peak performance* (4th ed., pp. 229–246).

References

Abernethy, B. (2001). Attention. In R. N. Singer, H. A., Hausenblas, & C. M. Janelle (Eds.), *Handbook of sport psychology* (2nd ed., pp. 53–85). New York: Wiley.

Abernethy, B., & Russell, D. G. (1987). The relationship between expertise and visual search strategy in a racquet sport. *Human Movement Science, 6,* 283–319.

Albrecht, R. R., & Feltz, D. L. (1987). Generality and specificity of attention related to competitive anxiety and sport performance. *Journal of Sport Psychology, 9,* 231–248.

Benson, H. (1975). *The relaxation response.* New York: William Morrow.

Bernstein, D. A., & Carlson, C. R. (1993). Progressive relaxation: Abbreviated methods. In P. M. Lehrer & R. L. Woolfolk (Eds.), *Principles and practices of stress management* (2nd ed., pp. 58–87). New York: Guilford Press.

Boutcher, S. H. (2002). Attentional processes and sport performance. In T. Horn (Ed.), *Advances in sport psychology* (2nd ed., pp. 441–457). Morgantown, WV: Fitness Information Technology.

Bull, S. J., Albinson, J. G., & Shambrook, J. (1996). *The mental game plan: Getting psyched for sport.* Brighton, UK: Sports Dynamic.

Burton, D., Naylor, S., & Holliday, B. (2001). Goal setting in sport: Investigating the goal effectiveness paradigm. In R. N. Singer, H. A. Hausenblas, & C. M. Janelle (Eds.), *Handbook of sport psychology,* (2nd ed., pp. 497–528). New York: Wiley.

Butler, R. J., & Hardy, L. (1992). The performance profile: Theory and application. *The Sport Psychologist, 6,* 253–264.

Callow, N., & Hardy, L. (2001). Types of imagery associated with sport confidence in netball players of varying skill levels. *Journal of Applied Sport Psychology, 13,* 1–17.

Callow, N., Hardy, L., & Hall, C. (2001). The effect of a motivational general-mastery imagery intervention on the sport confidence of high-level badminton players. *Research Quarterly for Exercise and Sport, 72,* 389–400.

Carlson, C. R., & Hoyle, R. H. (1993). Efficacy of abbreviated progressive muscle relaxation training: A quantitative review of behavioral medicine research. *Journal of Consulting and Clinical Psychology, 61,* 1059–1067.

Carter, J. E., & Kelly, A. E. (1997). Using traditional and paradoxical imagery interventions with reactant intramural athletes. *The Sport Psychologist, 11,* 175–189.

Carter told to tune out. (2004, November 17). *The Windsor Star,* p. E2.

Cox, R. H. (2002). *Sport psychology: Concepts and applications* (5th ed.). New York: McGraw-Hill.

Cumming, J., & Hall, C. (2002) Deliberate imagery practice: The development of imagery skills in competitive athletes. *Journal of Sport Sciences, 20,* 137–145.

Dagrou, E., Gauvin, L., & Halliwell, W. (1992). Effets du langage positif, négatif, et neuter sur la performance motrice [Effects of positive, negative, and neutral self-talk on motor performance]. *Canadian Journal of Sports Sciences, 17,* 145–147.

Dawson, K. A., Bray, S. R., & Widmeyer, W. N. (2002). Goals setting by intercollegiate sport teams and athletes. *Avante, 8,* 14–23.

Driskell, J. E., Copper, C., & Moran, A. (1994). Does mental practice enhance performance? *Journal of Applied Psychology, 79,* 481–492.

Durand-Bush, N., Salmela, J. H., & Green, D. I. (2001). The Ottawa Mental Skills Assessment Tool (OMSAT-3). *The Sport Psychologist, 15*, 1–19.

Fenker, R. M., & Lambiotte, J. G. (1987). A performance enhancement program for a college football team: One incredible season. *The Sport Psychologist, 1*, 224–236.

Filby, W., Maynard, I., & Graydon, J. (1999). The effect of multiple-goal strategies on performance outcomes in training and competition. *Journal of Applied Sport Psychology, 11*, 230–246.

Ford, S. K., & Summers, J. J. (1992). The factorial validity of the TAIS attentional style subscales. *Journal of Sport & Exercise Psychology, 14*, 283–297.

Gould, D., Tammen, V., Murphy, S., & May, J. (1989). An examination of US Olympic sport psychology consultants and the services they provide. *The Sport Psychologist, 3*, 300–312.

Gregg, M., Hall, C., & Hanton, S. (2004). Perceived effectiveness of mental imagery. Manuscript submitted for publication.

Hale, B. D., & Whitehouse, A. (1998). The effects of imagery-manipulated appraisal on intensity and direction of competitive anxiety. *The Sport Psychologist, 12*, 40–51.

Hall, C. R. (2001). Imagery in sport and exercise. In R. N. Singer, H. A. Hausenblas, & C. M. Janelle (Eds.), *Handbook of sport psychology* (2nd ed., pp. 529–549). New York: Wiley.

Hall, C. R., Mack, D., Paivio, A., & Hausenblas, H. A. (1998). Imagery use by athletes: Development of the sport imagery questionnaire. *International Journal of Sport Psychology, 29*, 73–89.

Hall, C. R., & Martin, K. A. (1997). Measuring movement imagery abilities: A revision of the movement imagery questionnaire. *Journal of Mental Imagery, 21*, 143–154.

Hanton, S., & Jones, G. (1999). The effects of a multimodal intervention program on performers: II. Training the butterflies to fly in formation. *The Sport Psychologist, 13*, 22–41.

Hardy, J. (2004). *Describing athlete self-talk.* Unpublished doctoral dissertation, University of Western Ontario, London, Ontario.

Hardy, J., Gammage, K., & Hall, C. R. (2001a). A description of athlete self-talk. *The Sport Psychologist, 15*, 306–318.

Hardy, J., Hall, C. R., & Alexander, M. R. (2001b). Exploring self-talk and affective states in sport. *Journal of Sport Sciences, 19*, 469–475.

Hatzigeorgiadis, A., & Biddle, S. J. H. (2000). Assessing cognitive interference in sport: Development of the thought occurrence questionnaire for sport. *Anxiety, Stress and Coping, 13*, 65–86.

Holmes, P. S., & Collins, D. J. (2001). The PETTLEP approach to motor imagery: A functional equivalence model for sport psychologists. *Journal of Applied Sport Psychology, 13*, 60–83.

Isaac, A., Marks, D., & Russell, E. (1996). An instrument for assessing imagery or movement: The vividness of movement imagery questionnaire (VMIQ). *Journal of Mental Imagery, 10*, 23–30.

Jacobson, E. (1938). *Progressive relaxation.* Chicago, IL: University of Chicago Press.

Jones, G. (1993). The role of performance profiling in cognitive behavioral interventions in sport. *The Sport Psychologist, 7*, 160–172.

Kingsley, J. (1998, February 16). Canadians get back in the game. *The Canadian Press.* http://www.canoe.ca/SlamNaganoShortTrackSkatingArchive/feb16_can.html

Landin, D. (1994). The role of verbal cues in skill learning. *Quest, 46*, 299–313.

Landin, D., & Hebert, E. P. (1999). The influence of self-talk on the performance of skilled female tennis players. *Journal of Applied Sport Psychology, 11*, 263–282.

Locke, E. A., & Latham, G. P. (1985). The application of goal setting to sports. *Journal of Sport Psychology, 7*, 205–222.

MacIntyre, T., & Moran, A. (1996). Imagery use among canoeists: A worldwide survey of novice, intermediate, and elite slalomists. *Journal of Applied Sport Psychology, 8*, S132.

Mahoney, M. J., & Avener, M. (1977). Psychology of the elite athlete: An exploratory study. *Cognitive Therapy and Research, 6*, 225–342.

Martens, R., Burton, D., Vealey, R. S., Bump, L. A., & Smith, D. E. (1990). Development and validation of the competitive state anxiety inventory-2. In R. Martens, R. S. Vealey, & D. Burton (Eds.), *Competitive anxiety in sports* (pp. 117–190). Champaign, IL: Human Kinetics.

Martin, K. A., Moritz, S. E., & Hall, C. R. (1999). Imagery use in sport: A literature review and applied model. *The Sport Psychologist, 13,* 245–268.

Moran, A. P. (2004). *Sport and exercise psychology.* New York: Taylor & Francis Group.

Munroe, K. J., Giacobbi, P. R., Hall, C., & Weinberg, R. (2000). The four Ws of imagery use: Where, when, why, and what. *The Sport Psychologist, 14,* 119–137.

Munroe, K. J., Hall, C. R., Simms, S., & Weinberg, R. (1998). The influence of type of sport and time of season on athletes' use of imagery. *The Sport Psychologist, 12,* 440–449.

Munroe-Chandler, K. J., Hall, C. R., Fishburne, G., & Strachan, L. (2004, October). *Imagery use in youth sport from a developmental perspective: Current issues and future directions.* Symposium presented at the annual meeting of the Canadian Society for Psychomotor Learning and Sport Psychology, Saskatchewan, Canada.

Murphy, S. M., & Woolfolk, R. L. (1987). The effects of cognitive interventions on competitive anxiety and performance on a fine motor skill accuracy task. *International Journal of Sport Psychology, 18,* 152–166.

Murphy, S. M., Woolfolk, R. L., & Budney, A. J. (1988). The effects of emotive imagery on strength performance. *Journal of Sport & Exercise Psychology, 10,* 334–345.

Nideffer, R. M. (1976). The test of attentional and interpersonal style. *Journal of Personality and Social Psychology, 34,* 394–404.

Orlick, T., & Partington, J. (1986). *Psyched: Inner views of winning.* Gloucester, ON: Coaching Association of Canada.

Paivio, A. (1985). Cognitive and motivational functions of imagery in human performance. *Canadian Journal of Applied Sport Science, 10,* 22S–28S.

Perry, C., & Morris, T. (1995). Mental imagery in sport. In T. Morris & J. Summers (Eds.), *Sport psychology: Theory, applications and issues* (pp. 339–385). Brisbane, Australia: Wiley.

Rodgers, W. M., Hall, C. R., & Buckolz, E. (1991). The effect of an imagery training program on imagery ability, imagery use, and figure skating performance. *Journal of Applied Sport Psychology, 3,* 109–125.

Rushall, B. S. (1988). Covert modeling as a procedure for altering an elite athlete's psychological state. *The Sport Psychologist, 2,* 131–140.

Ryska, T. A. (1998). Cognitive-behavioral strategies and precompetitive anxiety among recreational athletes. *Psychological Record, 48,* 697–708.

Schaffer, W. (1992). *Stress management for wellness* (2nd ed.). New York: Harcourt Brace Jovanovich.

Senior men: Kyle Shewfelt. (n.d.). *Gymn.ca* Retrieved December 23, 2004, from http://gymn.ca/athletes/interviews/shewfelt_04.shtml

Sordoni, C., Hall, C., & Forwell, L. (2002). The use of imagery in athletic injury rehabilitation and its relationship to self-efficacy. *Physiotherapy Canada, 54,* 177–185.

Spigolon, L., & Annalisa, D. (1985). Autogenic training in frogmen. *International Journal of Sport Psychology, 16,* 312–320.

Thomas, P. R., Murphy, S. M., & Hardy, L. (1999). Test of performance strategies: Development and preliminary validation of a comprehensive measure of athletes' psychological skills. *Journal of Sport Sciences, 17,* 697–711.

Vadocz, E. A., Hall, C. R., & Moritz, S. E. (1997). The relationship between competitive anxiety and imagery use. *Journal of Applied Sport Psychology, 9,* 241–253.

Van Raalte, J. L., Brewer, B. W., Rivera, P. M., Petitpas, A. J. (1994). The relationship between observable self-talk and competitive junior tennis players' match performance. *Journal of Sport & Exercise Psychology, 16,* 400–415.

Wanlin, C. M., Hrycaiko, D. W., Martin, G. L., & Mahon, M. (1997). The effects of a goal-setting package on the performance of speed skaters. *Journal of Applied Sport Psychology, 9,* 212–228.

Weinberg, R. S. (2002). Goal setting in sport and exercise: Research to practice. In J. Van Raalte & B. Brewer (Eds.), *Exploring sport and exercise psychology* (2nd ed., pp. 25–48).

Weinberg, R. S., & Gould, D. (2003). *Foundations of sport and exercise psychology* (3rd ed.). Champaign, IL: Human Kinetics.

White, A., & Hardy, L. (1998). An in-depth analysis of the uses of imagery by high level slalom canoeists and artistic gymnasts. *The Sport Psychologist, 12,* 387–403.

Williams, J. M., & Harris, D. V. (1998). Relaxation and energizing techniques for regulation of arousal. In J. M. Williams (Ed.), *Personal growth to peak performance* (3rd ed., pp. 219–236). Mountain View, CA: Mayfield.

Wilson, L. (1998, January 31). Eyes on the prize. *The Calgary Sun.* http://www.canoe.ca/ SlamNagano ShortTrackSkatingArchive/jan31_nstss.html

Wilson, M. (2003). A master champion. Retrieved December 23, 2004, from http://www.thegolfer mag.com/the_golfer/archive/style03/story_style03_swingseq.htm

Zaichkowsky, L. D., & Baltzell, A. (2001). Arousal and performance. In R. N. Singer, H. A. Hausenblas, & C. M. Janelle (Eds.), *Handbook of sport psychology* (2nd ed., pp. 319–339). New York: Wiley.

Kevin S. Spink

CHAPTER 9

Group Cohesion

Chapter Objectives

After reading this chapter, you should be able to do the following:

1. Explain why the study of groups is important.
2. Provide a definition of *group dynamics*.
3. Provide a definition of *group cohesion*.
4. Explain how to measure group cohesion.
5. Describe the conceptual model of group cohesion.
6. Explain the important correlates of group cohesion.

＊ I would like to thank Joel Barnes, Mark Bruner, Darren Nickel, and Kathleen Wilson for their feedback on an earlier version of this chapter.

Brandon, Tyler, and Pam are discussing the fortunes of their recreational basketball team. Brandon thinks that they will win the city championship because they have so many talented players on the team. Accordingly he says, "Four of our five starters are good enough to play on the all-star team, and with that kind of talent you're bound to win lots of games. No other team in the league can match our firepower. We have the horses to go all the way."

Although Tyler and Pam agree that there is enough talent on the team to win games, they think that it takes more than just individual talent to win a championship. Tyler supports this by saying, "Remember last year. We had even more talent than this year, and we still couldn't win. Sure, we could beat the bottom teams easily with our talent, but we couldn't win any of the close games. In fact, by the end of the year, we weren't confident that we could win any of the close games. And remember what happened when we lost the 'Big Mo' in a tight game; we tanked it, pure and simple. It was pretty obvious to me that talent doesn't go very far if teamwork isn't there. Last year our best players were only interested in being the individual stars by scoring the most points. They were so driven to be the point leaders that they wouldn't even pass the ball to each other! No wonder we couldn't win the tough games."

Pam continues the point by stating, "And remember all the griping by the players coming off the bench. Those who didn't start the game were always complaining that they were good enough to be starting and wondering why others were playing ahead of them. And remember how the starters reacted when they got wind of this; they weren't very happy that they weren't being supported, not that the starters made any sacrifices themselves to make the others feel part of the team. The result, as you might remember, was that players stopped coming to practise, and those who came didn't work very hard. It's tough to win if you can't get a full team to practice and those who do show up don't work very hard."

To these comments Brandon responded, "Yeah, but you need talent to score points."

Who is right here? The two positions described above are captured in an axiom that is often stated by coaches and athletes alike: "A championship team will always beat a team of champions." This statement recognizes the basic fact that the contributions of individual team members are determined in part by the other members of the group. This fact results in a different group outcome than if the team members' contributions were simply added together. The result is a gestalt of sorts, the whole being not just the sum of its parts. The information in this chapter will focus on one property of a group that may contribute to the championship of a team—cohesion. The discussion above suggests that other factors may be associated with a champion team, including attendance, perceived effort, sacrifice, team confidence, and psychological momentum. These factors will be included in the discussion about group cohesion.

Some Common Myths about Group Cohesion

MYTH: *Cohesive teams are more successful.*
Although most coaches would agree that they would like to increase the cohesiveness of their teams in an effort to increase their teams' success, at the present time, the scientific results do not provide much support for this suggestion. In fact, the results from a review of sport teams found no difference between cohesion leading to performance success and performance success leading to cohesion (Carron, Colman, Wheeler, & Stevens, 2002).

MYTH: *Team harmony is required for cohesion to develop.*

For many coaches, team harmony is synonymous with team cohesion. Conversely, they see slim chances of cohesion developing within a team if there is any form of intrateam conflict. Although this has a nice intuitive feel, research suggests otherwise. As one example, a study by Sullivan and Feltz (2001) with ice hockey teams revealed that negative (destructive) intrateam conflict was associated with lower cohesion but that positive (constructive) intrateam conflict was associated with higher team cohesion.

MYTH: *There is no "I" in team.*

The standard locker-room fare of "There is no 'I' in team" makes good press, but it does not hold up well in the scientific literature. This statement implies that members of a group are generally less important than the group as a collective; however, there is little scientific evidence to support this contention. It is generally accepted by the scientific community that cohesion is a multidimensional construct that incorporates both group and individual components (Carron, Widmeyer, & Brawley, 1985). Individuals join and remain in groups for many reasons, and it has been acknowledged that the cognitions that individuals hold about the cohesiveness of their team reflect both the overall group as well as the manner in which the group satisfies individual needs (Carron, Brawley, & Widmeyer, 1998), suggesting that the needs and wants of the individual must be recognized when one examines group cohesion.

The task in this chapter is to give an explanation of the group cohesion construct. However, before group cohesion is presented, the importance of groups, in general and in sport, will be discussed.

Introduction

You do not have to think very long to recognize that a lot of our sport participation occurs in group settings. Sport groups come in the obvious guises of a hockey, football, basketball, volleyball, baseball, or soccer team. Although typically classified as individual sports, track and field, swimming, and wrestling involve participation in teams. The fact that we participate in a lot of sport groups parallels the fact that participation in group activities permeates most aspects of our non-sport lives as well, be it involvement in a drama club, debating group, band, choral group, or local Mensa group.

The reality is that we all belong to a number of different groups. Given that groups form a large part of our lives, it may not be surprising that a field of study has emerged that focuses on the behaviour of groups. The field is called group dynamics, and it is viewed as a major branch of social psychology. According to Cartwright and Zander (1968), **group dynamics** focuses on gaining knowledge about the nature of groups and their development and on understanding the interrelationships between groups and individuals, between groups, and between groups and larger institutions.

Implicit in the above description is the idea that a group is different from a mere collection of individuals. It has been known for many years that group composition, for instance, is an important variable in group settings. The term *assembly effect* refers to variations in group behaviour that are a function of the particular combinations of individuals in the group. Rosenberg, Erlick, and Berkowitz (1955) found that individuals contributed differently to a group's outcome, depending on the particular other individuals with whom they were grouped.

Although this difference (between a group and a collection of individuals) is recognized in the academic community, its significance is not lost on the sporting community. Michael Jordan, retired basketball player, acknowledged this difference when he said, "Me, I'd rather have five guys with less talent who are willing to come together as a team than five guys who consider themselves stars and aren't willing to sacrifice" (Jordan, 1994, p. 24). Similarly, former football coach Knute Rockne wrote, "The secret of winning football games is working more as a team, less as individuals. I play not my eleven best, but my best eleven" (Lynberg, 1993, p. 31).

As the preceding quotes illustrate, attempting to understand group behaviour in the sport setting may be a worthwhile pursuit resulting in a number of important practical consequences. In examining group behaviour, there are a number of variables that could be investigated, including group size, group composition, social power, and leadership behaviours. However, the one property that has been identified as fundamental to understanding groups is cohesion. In fact, cohesion has been described as the most important small group variable (Lott & Lott, 1965). This suggestion makes sense when one considers that most researchers who use the term cohesion agree that the term refers to the degree to which members are motivated to stay in the group (Shaw, 1976).

The recognition that cohesion is the glue that keeps the group together may be enough justification to examine the construct; however, there are other important reasons. One of the most important reasons is that the study of cohesion has revealed that enhanced levels of cohesion are associated with key outcomes for both the individual and the team in the sport setting. Consider the recognition of the importance of cohesion for team outcomes by one of the best individual basketball players of all time, Michael Jordan:

Naturally, there are going to be ups and downs, particularly if you are trying to achieve at a high level. But when we stepped between the lines, we knew what we were capable of doing. When a pressure situation presented itself, we were plugged into one another as a cohesive unit. That's why we were able to beat more talented teams. (1994, p. 23)

The Nature of Group Cohesion

There is some general understanding that cohesion is the glue that holds members in a group. However, in terms of specific scientific definitions, many have been expressed. Over the years, cohesion has been defined in various ways, including attraction to the group, level of motivation evidenced by group members, and coordination of group members (Shaw, 1976). One of the seminal definitions of cohesion stated that it is "the resultant of all forces acting on members to remain in the group" (Festinger, 1950, p. 274). In outlining his ideas, Festinger suggested that there are many reasons why individuals would want to remain in a group, including attractions to other members of the group, the specific activities of the group, and the prestige of the group. Although this important definition highlighted the multidimensional nature of cohesion, numerous studies that followed assumed that cohesion was unidimensional, with interpersonal attraction being the most common definition used in the early days of cohesion research (Lott & Lott, 1965). With so many definitions, it may not surprise many that after reviewing 50 years of empirical research on cohesion, Mudrack (1989) concluded that the construct of cohesion was difficult to define precisely or consistently.

Although Mudrack (1989) noted the confusion in defining cohesion, he did identify one definition as being important. It was one forwarded by Canadian sport psychology researcher Bert Carron, who defined cohesion as a "dynamic process which is reflected in the tendency for a group to stick together and remain united in the pursuit

> **Reflections 9.1**
> Examine the definition of cohesion outlined by Carron et al. (1998). Does their defi-
> nition differ from what you think cohesion is?

of its goals and objectives" (Carron, 1982, p. 124). Since this definition was formulated, Carron and two of his Canadian colleagues, Larry Brawley and Neil Widmeyer,
have refined and revised the definition of cohesion to state that it is, "the dynamic
process which is reflected in the tendency for a group to stick together and remain
united in the pursuit of its instrumental objectives and/or for the satisfaction of member affective needs" (Carron et al., 1998, p. 213). This is currently the most accepted
definition of group cohesion in sport.

Carron and Hausenblas (1998) noted that this definition captures the four key
characteristics of cohesion; it is dynamic, multidimensional, instrumental, and affective. One of the important characteristics of cohesion is that it is dynamic, not static.
This characteristic acknowledges that reasons for cohesion can change over time. For
instance, team members may be drawn to a team in its early stages because it is very
task oriented but stay with the group because they have all become good friends.

This definition also reflects the fact that the factors that hold the group together can
be varied and numerous, thus highlighting its multidimensional nature. Further, these
factors can also vary between groups. For instance, there could be two highly cohesive
intramural hockey teams that are being held together for very different reasons. On the
first team, the members remain in the group because the team is highly united around
winning the intramural championship (i.e., task reasons). On the other hand, the members of the second team stay together, not because they will win games, let alone the
championship, but because they are very socially compatible (i.e., social reasons).

Another important characteristic captured in the definition is the instrumental
nature of cohesion. This characteristic reflects the most basic of facts; namely, all
groups form for a reason. Whether it be a professional football team staying together to
pursue the Grey Cup or the "beer" league hockey team staying together to maintain
lifelong friendships, all groups form for a purpose. As such, it is important to keep in
mind this instrumental basis of cohesion when trying to define the construct.

Finally, affective relationships are important in understanding cohesion. Outside
of the instrumental reasons for members remaining in a group, sometimes groups stay
together because there are strong emotional ties among the individuals in the group.
For instance, a curling team may stay together because members make each other laugh
and feel comfortable. Likewise, members of a football team may form a tighter bond
because they have all gone through a gruelling initiation process in which those who
could not take it quit, and those who made it through developed a greater respect for
one another. A good example of this was portrayed in the movie *Remember the Titans*,
in which a new coach unites a racially diverse football team to make them very cohesive by exposing them to a series of very demanding tasks (e.g., early morning runs).

Measuring Group Cohesion

Numerous general measures have been used to assess cohesion in the sport setting.
These measures have included assumed similarity (Fiedler, 1954), esteem for teammates

(Myers, 1962), interpersonal relationships (McGrath, 1962), social and leadership choices (Lenk, 1969), and attraction to the group (Klein & Christiansen, 1969). In addition to these all-purpose measures, there have been sport-specific questionnaires developed to assess cohesion, including the Sport Cohesiveness Questionnaire (Martens, Landers, & Loy, 1972) and the Group Environment Questionnaire (GEQ, available from www.fitinfotech.com/geq/geqadmin.tpl) developed by the Canadian trio of Carron, Widmeyer, and Brawley (1985). The GEQ has been, by far, the most extensively used of the sport-specific cohesion instruments developed to date. Although there could be a number of reasons for the extensive use and longevity of the GEQ in the sport setting, its major strength likely stems from the fact that it is based on an accepted definition of cohesion (Carron, 1982) as well as on an accepted conceptual framework of cohesion by Carron et al (1985). Prior to the development of the GEQ, the theoretical basis for cohesion was not well developed, so to address this shortcoming, Carron et al. developed the conceptual model that served as the basis for operationalizing the GEQ.

Conceptual Model of Group Cohesion

The conceptual model of cohesion developed by Carron et al. (1985) portrays cohesion as a multidimensional construct that includes individual and group aspects. The individual aspect refers to the beliefs each member holds about personal benefits of group membership; the group aspect refers to beliefs each member holds about the group as a collective. These two aspects each divide into task and social cohesion. Task cohesion refers to the orientation toward achieving the group's objectives; social cohesion refers to the orientation toward developing and maintaining social relationships within the group. This results in four factors of cohesion in sport groups: individual attractions to the group-task, individual attractions to the group-social, group integration-task, and group integration-social (see Figure 9.1). These four related facets act together to create an integrated perception of cohesion. Although developed for the sport setting, this conceptualization of cohesion has broad acceptance in settings outside of sport (Cota, Evans, Dion, Kilik, & Longman, 1995).

Figure 9.1   Conceptual model of group cohesion

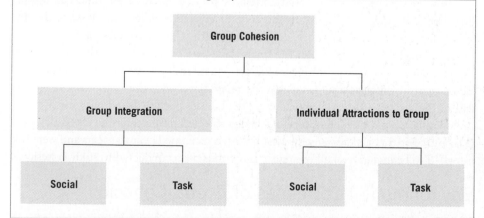

Note: From A.V. Carron, W.N. Widmeyer and L.R. Brawley, 1985, The development of an instrument to assess cohesion in sport teams: the Group Environment Questionnaire, Journal of Sport Psychology 7(3): 248, figure 2. © 1985 by Human Kinetics Publishers, Inc. Reprinted with permission from Human Kinetics (Champaign, IL).

It is from this two-dimensional (group-individual, task-social) conceptual model formulated by Carron et al. (1985) that the GEQ was developed to assess cohesion in the sport setting. The GEQ instrument contains 18 questions that are divided into four subscales, which reflect the four factors identified in the conceptual model.

The GEQ has been used extensively in the sport setting and has generally received good psychometric support across a wide range of teams and situations (cf. Carron et al., 1998). In addition, it has been modified for use in an exercise setting (Carron & Spink, 1992; Carron, Widmeyer, & Brawley, 1988, Study 1). Using the conceptual model of cohesion (Figure 9.1), Estabrooks and Carron (2000) further developed a measure called the Physical Activity Group Environment Questionnaire to assess cohesion in the exercise setting. There is preliminary evidence for the utility of the questionnaire as a test of cohesion in exercise groups (Estabrooks & Carron, 2000; Watson, Martin Ginis, & Spink, 2004).

Correlates of Group Cohesion

Now that you have some sense of what cohesion is and how to go about measuring it, let us turn our attention to factors that have been associated with cohesion. A framework outlined by Carron and Hausenblas (1998) illustrates the factors that correlate with group cohesion (see Figure 9.2). The use of the term *correlate* is intentional, given that most research in group cohesion is of a correlational nature, rather than of a cause-effect nature (see Chapter 2). In fact, it is likely that many of the relationships between these correlates and cohesion are bi-directional. For instance, it is just as likely that cohesion will influence satisfaction as it is that satisfaction will influence cohesion (Spink, Nickel, Wilson, & Odnokon, 2005). Similarly, it is equally likely that cohesion will influence intention to return as intention to return will influence cohesion (Spink, 1995).

In Figure 9.2, four categories of correlates are illustrated: environmental, leadership, personal, and team factors. In this chapter, selected studies will illustrate the different factors in each category. In keeping with the intentions of Carron and Hausenblas (1998) for the use of the framework, two caveats are worth noting. First, the four categories outlined in Figure 9.2 are not intended to be independent; that is, factors within different categories may be related. Second, the placement of factors within the categories was not intended to be absolute but was based on what was perceived to be a good fit. The factors and studies selected to illustrate the categories were chosen to give the reader a sense of what has been examined over the years and were not intended to be inclusive of all the research that has been conducted to study cohesion.

Environmental Correlates of Group Cohesion

GROUP SIZE Researchers and theoreticians alike have had a longstanding interest in the association between group size and cohesion. For the most part, an inverse relationship has emerged between cohesion and group size, generally, and within sport,

Figure 9.2 A general framework for examining the correlates of cohesion in sport and exercise groups

Note: From Group Dynamics in Sport, *2nd ed., (p. 244), by A. V. Carron and H. A. Hausenblas, 1998, Morgantown, WV: Fitness Information Technology. Reprinted with permission.*

specifically. In terms of examining groups generally, the results of a meta-analysis across a wide range of groups led Mullen and Copper (1994) to conclude that the smaller the group, the greater the level of cohesion. (A **meta-analysis** is a literature review wherein a number of studies in an area that meet criteria specified by the researcher are quantified to allow the use of statistical techniques as a means of analysis [Glass, 1976]). In sport, a similar relationship has been documented. For instance, Widmeyer, Brawley, and Carron (1990) examined the relationship between team size and cohesiveness using basketball teams playing 3-on-3 and found that as group size increased, task cohesion decreased. This inverse relationship between cohesion and group size has also been found in the exercise setting (Carron & Spink, 1995, Studies 1 & 2).

Reflections 9.3
Why do you think cohesion goes down as the size of the group increases? Do you think anything could be done to change this?

SPECIFIC ACTIVITY SETTING   Another environmental factor that has been associated with cohesion is the specific setting, or context, in which the activity occurs. As noted previously, cohesion is perceived to be multidimensional, and as such, it might be expected that the factors that hold the group together can be varied and numerous. Given that individuals likely come to different situations with different expectations, one might wonder whether a specific setting (context) would affect the perceptions of cohesiveness that develop. Research in the sport setting suggests that this may be the case. For example, Granito and Rainey (1988) found that a specific setting appeared to affect perceptions of cohesion: high-school football players endorsed task cohesion significantly more than university football players.

The effects of context on cohesion also appear to play out in the exercise setting. In two of our studies in the exercise setting, we found that the type of exercise context (i.e., university vs. club) tended to moderate the relationship between cohesion and adherence to an exercise program (Carron & Spink, 1995, Studies 1 & 2). Specifically, in the university context, those attending regularly held significantly greater perceptions of task cohesion than did eventual dropouts. On the other hand, in the club context, regular attendees held greater perceptions of social cohesion than did eventual dropouts. The finding that task-cohesion factors were more salient to adherence in the university context while social-cohesion factors were more related to adherence in the club context lends credibility to the suggestion that the specific context within the general setting may affect the type of cohesion that emerges.

Reflections 9.4

What might be different between the club and university exercise settings that would explain why social-cohesion factors were more salient in the former and task-cohesion factors were more important in the latter?

Photo courtesy of PhotoDisc/Getty Images.

Leadership Correlates of Group Cohesion

In sport, it might be expected that the development of cohesiveness would be associated with the behaviour of the coach. Research in the sport setting has provided abundant empirical support for the proposed association between coaching factors and cohesion across many different sports, including basketball teams (Pease & Kozub, 1994), football teams (Westre & Weiss, 1991), softball-baseball teams (Gardner, Shields, Bredemeier, & Bostrom, 1996), and ringette teams (Spink, 1998). In addition to researchers acknowledging the importance of the cohesion-leadership relationship, coaches also have recognized the importance of cohesion and their role in developing it. For instance, in one study using Canadian intercollegiate coaches, the role of the coach in developing cohesion was specifically addressed. The findings revealed that it was quite clear that coaches recognized the relationship between cohesion and performance and their important role in developing cohesion (Bloom, Stevens, & Wickmire, 2003).

LEADER'S BEHAVIOUR   In the leadership literature, examining the relationship between specific leader behaviour patterns and such criteria as member satisfaction and performance has been very important in determining leadership effectiveness. A similar tactic has been taken when examining the association between leadership and cohesion. Leadership behaviours have been assessed primarily through the Leadership Scale for Sports (LSS) developed by Chelladurai and Saleh (1980). The LSS contains five leadership subscales, with three of them reflecting behaviours (training and instruction, social support, and positive feedback) and the remaining two subscales reflecting decision style (autocratic style and democratic style). The behaviour subscales will be discussed in this section and the decision style subscales will be included in the next section.

According to Chelladurai and Saleh (1980), **training and instruction** was captured in behaviours by the coach that were geared to improving the team members' performance by emphasizing and facilitating hard training; providing instruction in skills, techniques, and tactics; clarifying the relationship among team members; and structuring and coordinating the activities of the team members. **Social support**, on the other hand, involved leader behaviours that were characterized by a concern for the welfare of the individual athletes, the fostering of a positive group atmosphere, and warm relationships with team members. Finally, behaviours by the coach that reinforced an athlete by recognizing and rewarding strong performance were categorized as **positive feedback**.

In several sport studies, it has been demonstrated that coaches who were perceived to engage in training and instruction, social support, and positive feedback behaviours had teams that were both more socially cohesive (Gardner et al., 1996; Spink, 1998) and task cohesive (Jowett & Chaundy, 2004; Westre & Weiss, 1991).

LEADER'S DECISION STYLE   Another leader variable that has received attention in the cohesion literature is the leader's decision style. **Decision style** refers to the degree to which a leader allows participation by subordinates in decision making. Much of the research examining leaders' decision style in the sport setting has used the LSS. As noted above, the LSS includes two decision-style subscales (Chelladurai & Saleh, 1980). One is the **autocratic style**, which signifies behaviour by the leader that involves independent decision making and stresses personal authority on the part of the leader. This translates into the leader making decisions alone. The other is the **democratic style**, which signifies behaviour by the leader that allows greater participation by the athletes in decisions relating to team goals, practice methods, and game tactics and strategies. In this approach, the final decision is made jointly, with the leader having no more or no less input into the final decision than any of the team members.

There appears to be some consensus in the cohesion literature that the more democratic the leader style, the greater the tendency for cohesion to develop. This relationship has been found across several sports (Brawley, Carron, & Widmeyer, 1993; Gardner et al., 1996; Jowett & Chaundy, 2004; Westre & Weiss, 1991).

Based on the studies outlined above, it appears that the cohesion of a team is associated with specific coaching behaviours and styles. Cohesion within a team tends to be associated with coaches who allow athletes input into team decisions, exhibit positive feedback, and provide solid instruction and training.

Reflections 9.5
It has been found consistently that higher levels of cohesion within a team tend to be associated with a more democratic style of leadership. Why do you think a democratic style is associated more with enhanced cohesion than is an autocratic style of leadership?

TEAM-BUILDING ACTIVITIES   In the research reported in the leadership section, the focus was on studies that have examined simple associations between cohesion and leadership variables. In this section, we will focus on some of our own work, as well as that of others, in which attempts were made to use the leader to create cohesion through the implementation of team-building protocols. Before the presentation of research in team building, a few terms require clarification. First, what is meant by *team building*? Although it has been defined in numerous ways, the definition by Newman (1984) forms the basis of our programs. According to Newman, **team building** refers to programs that are geared toward promoting an increased sense of team unity and cohesiveness, which then enables the team to function together more smoothly and effectively.

It is important to note that in our programs, the intervention that we created was filtered through the coach or exercise leader (Carron, Spink, & Prapavessis, 1997). This is an indirect form of team building because the intervention was done through a third party; it contrasts with more direct forms of team building in which the intervention is presented directly to the team members. In direct approaches, the intervention specialist works directly with the team members to provide them with greater insight and greater independence. It is assumed that, through the contact and education, team members will become more intrinsically motivated to team-build as a result of their enhanced competence and self-determination (Carron et al., 1998). One example of a direct team-building approach is outlined by Yukelson (1997) in his description of the program run in the athletics department at Penn State University. Stevens and Bloom (2003) also described a team-building intervention that combined both a direct and an indirect approach by involving both softball coaches and their athletes. Although examples of direct (and combined) interventions are interesting and can be effective forms of team building, they will not be included here, as the focus in this section of the chapter is on the relationship between leadership and cohesion. Thus, only those studies in which the coach or exercise leader (i.e., indirect team building) is the sole delivery agent of the intervention will be presented.

In our research in both sport and exercise settings, we created and implemented a four-stage **team-building (TB) model** (introduction, conceptual, practical, and interventions) using the coach or exercise leader as the agent of delivery (Carron & Spink, 1993, 1995; Prapavessis, Carron, & Spink, 1996; Spink & Carron, 1993; Watson et al., 2004). The first three stages of the TB model occur in a workshop conducted by the TB specialist with coaches or exercise leaders. The final stage involves the coaches or leaders going back to their team or group and implementing the TB strategies that were formulated during the workshop.

In the first stage of the team-building model, coaches or leaders are presented with a brief overview of the benefits of cohesion to their specific setting. For instance, if we were talking about team building to coaches, we would discuss the relationship between perceptions of cohesiveness and improved team outcomes as identified in the literature (Carron et al., 2002). On the other hand, if we were talking to exercise leaders, we would tailor the benefits to the type of exercise setting. For instance, if the leaders ran exercise classes for older adults (seniors) we would mention the positive relationships that have been established between elderly exercisers who perceive their group as more cohesive and better exercise class attendance (Estabrooks & Carron, 1999; Watson et al., 2004).

The second stage provides a frame of reference for the participants. This is accomplished by introducing a conceptual model. In the conceptual models that we have used in the sport and exercise settings, cohesion within the group is viewed as an output (or product) of conditions that arise from three different categories of group characteristics. Two categories are inputs: the environment of the group and the structure of the group; and one category is a throughput: group processes. Furthermore, within each of the three categories, specific factors are identified that have previously emerged as being associated with enhanced group cohesiveness. The conceptual model that we used in our TB programs in the exercise setting is presented in Figure 9.3.

As noted in Figure 9.3, distinctiveness has been identified in the group environment category as one factor to be manipulated to enhance cohesion in the exercise setting. When this was presented to the exercise leaders, they were told that when something in the group's environment is somehow made distinctive, members develop a stronger sense of "we," more readily distinguish themselves from non-members of the group, and ultimately develop stronger perceptions of cohesiveness (Carron & Spink, 1993). This procedure of presenting the leader with a research-based rationale justifying the inclusion of each factor was repeated for all factors outlined in Figure 9.3.

Figure 9.3   Conceptual framework used as a basis for the implementation of a team-building program in exercise classes

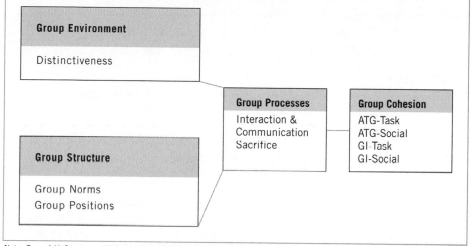

Note: From A.V. Carron and K.S. Spink, 1993, Team building in an exercise setting, The Sport Psychologist *7(1): 11, figure 1.* © 1993 by Human Kinetics Publishers, Inc. Reprinted with permission from Human Kinetics (Champaign, IL).

Although we used a similar conceptual model in our work in the sport setting, the specific factors that were highlighted were different from those in the exercise setting, which is consistent with Brawley and Paskevich's (1997) suggestion that TB factors may differ across situations because the importance of fundamental group processes change across groups. As one example, under the group environment category in the sport setting (see Table 9.1), togetherness and distinctiveness are both factors to be manipulated, whereas it was only distinctiveness in the exercise setting.

The practical stage is the final part of the workshop. The main purpose of this stage is to have the coaches and exercise leaders become active agents in developing practical strategies that they will use in their own group settings (Carron & Spink, 1993). This was done by having them use the conceptual framework to brainstorm as many specific techniques, procedures, or protocols as possible to be used for team building in their own groups. In the case of exercise groups, the leaders were asked to use distinctiveness, norms, positions, sacrifice, and communication/interaction as frames of reference for generating their techniques. Some representative examples of the specific strategies suggested by the leaders to enhance group cohesiveness in exercise

Table 9.1   Principles Underlying the Team-building Program in a Sport Setting

Categories	Principle
Team structure	
Role Clarity and Acceptance	When group members clearly understand their role in the group, cohesiveness is enhanced. When group members are satisfied and accept their roles in the group, cohesiveness is enhanced.
Leadership	Task and social cohesiveness in the group are influenced by the behaviour of the team leaders. A participative style of coaching leadership contributes to enhanced cohesiveness.
Conformity to standards	Conformity to group social and task norms contribute to enhanced cohesiveness. Group norms are highly resistant to change.
Team environment	
Togetherness	When group members are repetitively put in close physical proximity, feelings of cohesiveness increase.
Distinctiveness	The presence of group distinctiveness contributes to group cohesiveness.
Team processes	
Sacrifices	When high-status members make sacrifices for the group, cohesiveness is enhanced.
Goals and objectives	Group goals are more strongly associated with team success than are individual goals. Member participation in goal setting contributes to enhanced cohesiveness.
Cooperation	Cooperative behaviour is superior to individualistic behaviour for individual and group performance. Cooperative behaviour is superior to competitive behaviour for individuals and group performance. Cooperative behaviour contributes to enhanced cohesiveness.

Note: From "Team Building in Sport," by H. Prapavessis, A. V. Carron, and K. S. Spink, 1996, International Journal of Sport Psychology, 27, p. 275. Edizioni Luigi Pozzi.

classes are presented in Table 9.2. From the lists of practical suggestions generated, each coach or leader was free to take the suggestions that each felt would work best.

In the intervention stage, the coaches and exercise leaders take the team-building protocols that they have developed at the workshop and introduce them into their groups. The duration of the TB interventions vary across situations (Carron & Spink, 1993). Examples from our own research in both the exercise and the sport settings will now be presented to illustrate how the specific interventions are undertaken.

Our initial foray into team building was conducted in the exercise setting. The purpose was simple—to determine if cohesion in exercise classes could be enhanced through a psychological intervention program focusing on team-building concepts and delivered by the exercise leaders. The results revealed that the TB intervention significantly enhanced the class members' cohesion (Carron & Spink, 1993). In other tests of our team-building model, we found that a TB program was effective in negating any reduction in cohesion that resulted from increasing the size of the group (Carron &

Table 9.2   Examples of Specific Strategies Suggested by Instructors to Enhance Group Cohesiveness in Exercise Classes

Category Strategies Used	Examples of Intervention
Group Environment	
Distinctiveness	Have a group name Make up a group t-shirt Hand out neon head bands and/or shoelaces
Group Structure	
Individual positions	Have signs to label parts of the group Use specific positions for low, medium & high impact exercisers Let them pick their own spot & encourage them to remain in it throughout the year
Group norms	Encourage members to become fitness friends Establish a goal to lose weight together Promote a smart work ethic as a group characteristic
Group Processes	
Sacrifices	Ask 2 or 3 people for a goal for the day Ask regulars to help new people—fitness friends Ask people who aren't concerned with weight loss to make a sacrifice for the group on some days (more aerobics) and people who are concerned with weight loss to make a sacrifice on other days (more mat work)
Interaction and communication	Use partner work and have them introduce themselves to the person on the right and left Work in groups of 5 and take turns showing a move Use more partner activities

Note: From A.V. Carron and K.S. Spink, 1993, Team building in an exercise setting, The Sport Psychologist *7(1): 13, table 1. © 1993 by Human Kinetics Publishers, Inc. Reprinted with permission from Human Kinetics (Champaign, IL).*

Spink, 1995, Study 4). We also were able to increase cohesion though team building in exercise classes for the elderly (Watson et al., 2004).

We also extended our TB research into the sporting realm (Prapavessis et al., 1996) by implementing a team building intervention with soccer teams in Australia. Unfortunately, the results revealed that the TB intervention was not successful in enhancing levels of cohesion. One reason that we put forward to explain this result was the idea that sport teams are more complex than exercise groups, and, as such, the TB intervention may require a different focus (Prapavessis et al., 1996). The fact that team building may be more difficult to implement in the sport setting is echoed in the results of a study examining expert Canadian ice hockey and basketball coaches. This study found that cohesion was perceived to be a complex construct that unfolded over the course of the season (Schinke, Draper, & Salmela, 1997).

Given this complexity, the resulting message might be that one should not hastily discard this type of TB intervention in the sport setting. Based on the results that we have obtained thus far, it might be prudent to state that at this time the opportunities to increase cohesion through team building might be greater in the exercise setting than in the sport setting.

Personal Correlates of Group Cohesion

In this third category of correlates, we will present selected personal correlates that have been associated with cohesion. By personal correlates, we are referring to those factors that are characteristic of the team members.

Reflections 9.6
Cohesion has been associated with a number of personal correlates, such as higher perceived effort. Why do you think someone would work harder as a result of being in a more cohesive group?

INDIVIDUAL ADHERENCE   In our research in exercise settings, as well as that of others, one relationship that has been extensively examined is the one between perceptions of group cohesiveness and individual adherence. In a series of studies, a greater sense of group cohesiveness was associated with improved adherence behaviour across a number of exercise settings (Fraser & Spink, 2002; Spink & Carron, 1992, 1993; Watson et al., 2004).

In our earliest study, young adult exercisers who were less often late and absent for exercise class reported higher levels of cohesion (Spink & Carron, 1992). Another study, in a health-related exercise setting, examined the relationship between cohesion and attendance for individuals who were exercising in response to the instructions of a health-care practitioner (Fraser & Spink, 2002). This study is an example of a *compliance* situation (i.e., individuals are exercising because they are following the instructions of or using prescriptions assigned by a health-care provider). Similar to results in other exercise settings, it was found that those who attended classes very often endorsed task cohesion more so than those who attended classes less often.

Our research in the area of team building has also shown adherence effects. For example, with younger adults we found significantly fewer dropouts and late arrivals among the participants who were in the classes exposed to the TB intervention (Spink & Carron, 1993) as well as better class attendance in older adults who were presented with a team-building protocol (Watson et al., 2004).

To summarize, our work in the exercise setting, as well as that of others, has revealed that cohesion is related to a wide range of adherence measures, including lateness, attendance, and dropout behaviour. Also, relationships between cohesion and adherence have been found in young and older adults as well as when the individual is exercising freely versus being told to exercise by a health-care provider. Finally, research has demonstrated that cohesion can be enhanced in exercise classes through TB interventions delivered by the exercise leader.

It may not be too surprising to learn that cohesion has also been associated with adherence in the sport setting. In an examination of elite athletes from a number of sports, Carron et al. reported that individuals who maintained their involvement with their team scored higher on both task and social dimensions of cohesion than those individuals who dropped out (1988, Study 1). An examination of individuals participating in summer recreation sport leagues showed that those individuals who were never late or absent scored higher on social cohesion than those individuals who were frequently absent or late (Carron et al., 1988, Study 2).

INTENTION TO RETURN   In all of the previously mentioned studies examining dropout behaviour (Carron et al., 1988, Study 1; Spink & Carron, 1993, 1994), each used a short-term measure of adherence—withdrawal from the current group. Our intent in another set of studies was to determine whether perceptions of cohesion would be related to a longer term measure of adherence (i.e., intention to participate in the future). In two studies (Spink, 1995, 1998), both recreational and elite ringette players indicated that they would return to play with their team the next season if they perceived that their team was high in social cohesiveness, regardless of where their team ended up in the final league standings. We (Spink & Odnokon, 2001b) extended this result to ice hockey, where we found that players who reported higher perceptions of social cohesion at the end of the season indicated a greater intention to return for the next season, regardless of team success. Taken together, the results of these three studies suggest that previous research indicating a relationship between cohesion and in-group adherence may be extended to the longer term measure of intention to participate further with the team, in both male and female team sport settings.

Reflections 9.7
Study results have revealed that it is social cohesion that tends to be associated with wanting to return to the team for another season. Why do you think it is social rather than task cohesion that is associated with intending to return?

Photo courtesy of PhotoDisk/Getty Images.

INDIVIDUAL EFFORT   It has been suggested that individual adherence can manifest itself in other behaviours, such as apathy and reduced work output, which could be construed as a form of effort (Steers & Rhodes, 1978). In one study, Prapavessis and Carron (1997a) examined the relationship between cohesion and work output (i.e., effort) using participants from a variety of sports. They found that work output (measured by percentage of maximum oxygen consumption) was greater for athletes who held higher perceptions of the task cohesiveness of their team. In another study, Spink and Odnokon (2001a) found that ice hockey players who perceived their team to be high in task cohesion were the players who reported working the hardest over the season. Bray and Whaley (2001) obtained a similar finding when they examined players on basketball teams. These three studies provide evidence that perceptions of a team's cohesiveness are associated with an individual's actual or perceived level of effort in a team-sport setting.

SOCIAL LOAFING   An interesting twist on the cohesion-effort relationship is found in the social loafing literature. **Social loafing** is defined as the reduction in individual effort when individuals work collectively compared with when they work alone (Latane, Williams, & Harkins, 1979). A meta-analysis by Karau and Williams (1993) revealed that individuals tend to loaf when in groups and that the effect occurs consistently across many populations and with many different tasks. Although social loafing appears to be a pervasive force when individuals work in groups, increases in group cohesion appear to reduce or eliminate social loafing. In a study examining swimmers competing in a group setting (i.e., relay teams) versus swimming alone, it was found that perceptions of team cohesiveness influenced the amount of loafing that occurred (McKnight, Williams, & Widmeyer, 1991).

The first finding of interest was that when the swimmers' times in the relay (i.e., group setting) were not announced, they tended to swim slower than when they swam alone (i.e., they socially loafed). This finding is consistent with those of other researchers who have found that when times are not individually identified (i.e., announced) in a relay-race, swimmers tend to exert less effort (Williams, Nida, Baca, & Latane, 1989).

The second finding was that swimmers whose individual times were not publicly identified swam slower only in the relay versus alone condition when they perceived their team to be low in task cohesion. When they perceived their swim team to be high in task cohesion, they did not swim slower, regardless of whether their individual times were announced or not. In effect, social loafing did not occur when the team was perceived to be high in cohesiveness.

INDIVIDUAL SACRIFICE   Another interesting personal variable that has been related to cohesion is the sacrifice that individuals are willing to make for the group. From an intuitive perspective, it might be expected that individuals would want to remain in a group where team members were making sacrifices for the group. Holt and Sparkes (2001) examined the factors that members of a collegiate soccer team identified as contributing to team cohesion over the course of an eight-month season. One key theme that they identified as contributing to team cohesion was personal sacrifice by team members.

Prapavessis and Carron (1997b) provided more support for the relationship between cohesion and sacrifice in their investigation of high-level cricket teams in New Zealand. They had team members describe the extent to which they and their teammates regularly made individual sacrifices for their teams, and then the researchers related this to members' perceptions of team cohesiveness. Sacrifices were assessed along two dimensions. The first dimension reflected the distinction between internal sacrifices (e.g., playing another position) and external sacrifices (e.g., lowering work commitments to allow for more team practices). The second dimension captured the distinction between an individual social sacrifice (e.g., I give up my social life for the team) and teammate social sacrifice (e.g., My teammates give up their social lives).

Reflections 9.8

Do you think sacrifices made by high-profile players, like Jarome Iginla, would have a greater impact on developing cohesion than those made by lesser known players? Why or why not?

Photo courtesy of CP Photo/Jeff McIntosh.

The results supported the conclusion that reports of individual sacrifice and team-mates' sacrifice contributed to team task and social cohesion. In terms of specific findings, internal sacrifices made by individuals and teammates had the most powerful effect on cohesion.

SELF-HANDICAPPING   In terms of personal factors, it has also been found that what the individual brings to the group can affect cohesiveness. One such factor is the tendency to self-handicap. If you have ever remarked to a teammate before a big game that you may not play well because you were up all night with a cold, you may have been using a self-handicapping strategy. According to Jones and Berglas (1978), **self-handicapping** involves using strategies that protect one's self-esteem by providing excuses for forthcoming events. This is done by providing explanations wherein potential failure can be attributed to external factors (i.e., I was up all night), rather than to internal factors (i.e., I'm not prepared).

The relationship between team cohesiveness and self-handicapping has been examined in the sport setting (Carron, Prapavessis, & Grove, 1994; Hausenblas & Carron, 1996). In one study examining male athletes from a number of different sports, a negative relationship was found between the self-handicapping trait and perceptions of task cohesion (Carron et al., 1994). One possibility to explain this relationship might be that the high self-handicapper's perception of low task-cohesion might be ego-protective. If the team fails, the athlete can fall back on the thought, "I'm OK, but I'm not so sure about the team." The athlete externalizes the failure by blaming the team.

The purpose of another sport study conducted by Canadian researchers was to examine whether cohesion would moderate the use of self-handicapping strategies prior to competition (Hausenblas & Carron, 1996). Studying elite male and female athletes from a number of sports, Hausenblas and Carron found that athletes who scored high on self-handicapping and who perceived their team as more cohesive had a greater tendency to make excuses (i.e., self-handicap) before competition. On the other hand, when cohesion was perceived as low on their team, no relationship was found between the self-handicapping trait and the tendency to make excuses. In the case of the high self-handicapper, the tendency to make more excuses may simply reflect the fact that members on more cohesive teams feel a greater responsibility to the group and the use of prior claims of hindrances acts like an ego-protective mechanism in case the team fails.

Team Correlates of Group Cohesion

In the final category of correlates, selected team correlates that have been associated with perceptions of cohesion will be presented. With team correlates, the focus is on those factors that are associated with the team as a unit. Without doubt, the team factor that has been most associated with cohesion over the years is team outcome (team success). The assumption is that when team cohesion is strong, the group is motivated to perform well and is better able to coordinate activities that will lead to a positive team outcome (Cartwright, 1968).

TEAM SUCCESS   Given the insight provided by researchers (Cartwright, 1968) and the claims by coaches and athletes (see earlier quotes by Knute Rockne and Michael Jordan) about the proposed association between team cohesion and team success, it may come as a surprise that the research findings in this area have been mixed. There are studies showing that greater levels of team cohesion lead to success in intercollegiate ice hockey (Ball & Carron, 1976), studies showing lesser levels of team cohesion leading to success in international rowing teams (Lenk, 1969), and studies showing no relationship between cohesion and team success in intramural basketball teams (Melnick & Chemers, 1974).

Based on the results of a meta-analysis, Mullen and Copper (1994) concluded that a small but significant positive relationship exists between cohesion and performance across many groups and tasks. Three other specific suggestions from their analysis were the following. First, the cohesion-performance relationship was strongest when cohesion was measured as task commitment (similar to task cohesion) rather than as social cohesion. Second, the cohesion-performance relationship was stronger in real groups than in artificial groups. Third, within real groups, the link was strongest in sports teams.

Canadian researchers Carron et al. (2002) conducted a more focused meta-analysis wherein they examined the cohesion-performance relationship using only studies conducted with sport teams. Based on their analysis of 46 sport studies, they concluded that there was a moderate-to-large relationship between cohesion and performance. This is consistent with Mullen and Copper's (1994) suggestion that the cohesion-performance relationship is strongest in real groups, especially sport teams. In a third meta-analysis, Beal, Cohen, Burke, and McLendon (2003) also found that task and social cohesion related to performance across multiple group settings. They also reported that the relationship between cohesion and performance was stronger when performance was defined as **behaviour** (i.e., actions relevant to achieving the outcome) as opposed to **outcome** (i.e., results of behaviours).

Despite the mixed results from past research, the results from these three meta-analyses provide some strong evidence that cohesion and performance are related. Although this relationship appears to be established, one question concerning the direction still remains: which is stronger, cohesion leading to performance or performance leading to cohesion?

Reflections 9.9
Which do you think contributed more to Team Canada's success at the 2002 Olympics: the golden Loonie or cohesion?

This is an important question because it captures the essence of that age-old belief of coaches and athletes alike—having more cohesiveness will lead to more wins. Unfortunately, at the present time, the research does not support this belief. From the results of Mullen and Copper's (1994) meta-analysis, it was concluded that there was more support for success leading to cohesion than for cohesion leading to more success. The results from the Carron et al. (2002) meta-analysis using only sport teams found no difference between the cohesion-leading-to-success and the success-leading-to-cohesion relationships. Despite the lack of support for cohesion leading to more success, the fact still remains that there is some evidence that task and social cohesion are associated with better performance.

COLLECTIVE EFFICACY FOR COHESION   Performance (team success) is the team correlate that has received the most attention in the research literature; however, there are other proposed correlates of team cohesion. One such correlate is **collective efficacy**. The term was coined by Bandura (1977) to capture the idea that groups often have collective expectations for success. There has been speculation that different properties of a group, such as cohesion, have great potential to contribute to a team's sense of efficacy (Spink, 1990a), and this has been borne out in the sport literature. In one of my studies examining the relationship between cohesion and collective efficacy in volleyball teams, teams high in collective efficacy rated task and social cohesion higher than teams lower in collective efficacy (Spink, 1990b). Of interest, this relationship was found only for elite teams, not for recreational teams. In another study, which also examined volleyball teams in Canada, task cohesion measures differentiated between athletes who were low or high in their perception of their team's overall collective efficacy (Paskevich, Brawley, Dorsch, & Widmeyer, 1999).

Support for the relationship between cohesion and collective efficacy was also found by Kozub and McDonnell (2001) in a study involving rugby teams. They found that cohesion measures were highly associated with collective efficacy measures, with task cohesion having the strongest relationship with cohesion, thus supporting the results from the other sport studies mentioned previously (Paskevich et al., 1999; Spink, 1990b).

PSYCHOLOGICAL MOMENTUM   Psychological momentum is another team factor that appears to be related to team cohesion. **Psychological momentum** refers to a perception on the part of team members that the team is progressing toward its goal. This definition was adapted from one posited for individual behaviour by Vallerand, Colavecchio, and Pelletier (1988). The idea that cohesion and psychological momentum might be linked is not new. In one of the first works to discuss the effect of psychological momentum in sports events, Adler (1981) suggested that perceptions of psychological momentum and cohesion are linked. He went further by suggesting that coaches in team sports should attempt to develop a perception of cohesion in order to create a team climate favourable to momentum.

In the one test of this possible relationship, we examined the relationship between perceptions of task cohesion and psychological momentum in high-school volleyball teams (Eisler & Spink, 1998). Our results revealed that members of highly cohesive teams rated their team as possessing more psychological momentum than did the members of teams perceived as less cohesive. This finding supports Adler's (1981) contention that the development of cohesion creates a climate favourable to the perception of psychological momentum.

ATHLETE'S STARTING STATUS   Another team factor linked to cohesion is the impact of an athlete's starting status. In one of the first studies to examine this relationship, Granito and Rainey (1988) found that players at both the high school and the

---

Reflections 9.10

Spink (1992) found that it was only on less successful teams that starters and non-starters differed in their perceptions of team cohesion. Do you think this finding has any implications for the examination of the cohesion-success relationship?

Photo © George Blonsky/Alamy.

college levels who were selected to start games scored higher on measures of task cohesion than players who were not selected to start. I attempted to replicate and extend this study by examining the perceived cohesion levels of starters and non-starters on less successful and more successful volleyball teams (Spink, 1992). Results revealed that starters perceived more task cohesion on their team than did non-starters, which supports the Granito and Rainey (1988) result. However, this occurred only on teams that were less successful. On teams that were more successful, there were no differences in the levels of perceived cohesion between the starters and non-starters. From the results of this study, it appears that team success might serve to ameliorate the possible negative impact of not starting and help to maintain task cohesion.

Group Cohesion as a Mediator

Mediators are mechanisms that account for the effect of one variable on another variable. There has been a call by theoreticians for more research examining group-level mediators, such as cohesion, to help understand important relationships (Baron & Kenny, 1986). Since that call, examples have appeared in the literature that illustrate that cohesion does, in fact, act as a mediator in a number of important relationships.

In one study in the sport setting, I examined whether social cohesion would mediate the relationship between leadership behaviour and intention to return to sport (Spink, 1998). Using female ringette players, it was found that specific forms of leadership behaviour (i.e., training and instruction) predicted who intended to return to the sport the next season, but its effect was minimized when social cohesion was added to the prediction. The fact that the relationship between leadership and intention to return disappeared when social cohesion was entered suggests that social cohesion was the mechanism through which leadership behaviour was affecting intention to return (see Figure 9.4).

Two studies by Canadian researchers in the exercise setting provide further support for cohesion as an important mediator. The first study revealed that task cohesion mediated the relationship between an exercise leader's behaviours (i.e., availability, motivation, and enthusiasm) and both attendance and perceived exertion in older adult exercisers (Loughead, Colman, & Carron, 2001). This suggests that exercise leaders need to engage in availability, motivation, and enthusiasm to increase the group's task cohesion, which, in turn, will improve the attendance and perceived exertion of older exercisers.

Figure 9.4 Proposed mediation model

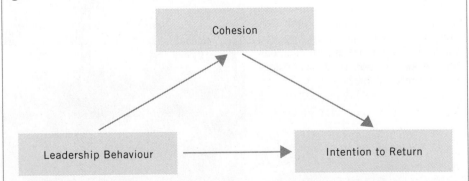

The second study examined whether task cohesion would mediate the relationship between leader behaviours and satisfaction of participants in recreational exercise programs (Loughead & Carron, 2004). Mediation was tested in several different relationships between leader behaviour and participant satisfaction, and in each case task cohesion was found to mediate the relationship between the specified leader behaviour and measures of participant satisfaction. The results from these three studies suggest that cohesion can be an important mechanism in mediating important relationships in the sport and exercise settings.

Reflections 9.11

Cohesion has been identified as a possible mediator in the relationship between leadership and both adherence and satisfaction measures. Can you identify any other relationships in which you think cohesion might act as a mediator?

Chapter Summary

It should be clear that team cohesion is a very important construct associated with many factors that are of consequence to the group and the individual. Also, the importance of understanding cohesion goes well beyond examining its relationship to team performance. There is still much more to understand about cohesion as it relates to sport and physical activity, so more research is needed. Despite the need for more research, several points about group cohesion have strong support within the research community. Cohesion has moved from being viewed as a unidimensional construct to being viewed as a multidimensional construct that incorporates at least two dimensions: the individual-group orientation and a task-social distinction. To assess cohesion in the sport setting, the Group Environment Questionnaire is the instrument of choice. The research literature is replete with examples demonstrating that cohesion is related to a number of important environmental, leadership, personal, and team factors. There is also evidence that team-building strategies implemented by exercise leaders can enhance cohesion, especially in the exercise setting.

Although it is typically believed by coaches and athletes that cohesion will increase team success, this is not fully supported in the research literature; however, the fact remains that there is some evidence that task and social cohesion contribute to better performance. There is also emerging evidence that cohesion can be used to account for other important relationships. For instance, some research has demonstrated that cohesion is one mechanism to explain why various leadership behaviours may be related to a number of important outcomes, including attendance, intention to return, perceived exertion, and satisfaction.

Review Questions

1. Why is it important to study groups?
2. What is the definition of *group dynamics*?
3. What are the main differences between the two definitions of cohesion involving Bert Carron?
4. Identify the four key characteristics of cohesion.
5. Identify and briefly describe the sport-specific questionnaires that have been used to assess cohesion.

6. Briefly outline the conceptual model of group cohesion.
7. What is the main difference between direct and indirect team-building procedures?
8. Outline the four stages in the team-building model.
9. Identify and briefly explain the relationship between cohesion and the six personal correlates.
10. Identify and describe two relationships in which cohesion has been examined as a mediator.

Suggested Reading

Carron, A. V., & Hausenblas, H. A. (1998). *Group dynamics in sport* (2nd ed.). Morgantown, WV: Fitness Information Technology.

Carron, A. V., Spink, K. S., & Prapavessis, H. (1997). Team building and cohesiveness in the sport and exercise setting: Use of indirect interventions. *Journal of Applied Sport Psychology, 9*, 61–72.

Mudrack, P. E. (1989). Defining group cohesiveness. A legacy of confusion? *Small Group Behavior, 20*, 37–49.

References

Adler, P. (1981). *Momentum: A theory of social action.* Beverly Hills, CA: Sage.

Ball, J. R., & Carron, A. V. (1976). The influence of team cohesion and participation motivation upon performance success in intercollegiate ice hockey. *Canadian Journal of Applied Sport Sciences, 1*, 271–275.

Bandura, A. (1977). Self-efficacy: Toward a unifying theory of behavioural change. *Psychological Review, 84*, 191–215.

Baron, R. M., & Kenny, D. A. (1986). The moderator-mediator variable distinction in social psychological research: Conceptual, strategic, and statistical considerations. *Journal of Personality & Social Psychology, 51*, 1173–1182.

Beal, D. J., Cohen, R., Burke, M. J., & McLendon, C. L. (2003). Cohesion and performance in groups: A meta-analytic clarification of construct relations. *Journal of Applied Psychology, 88*, 989–1004.

Bloom, G. A., Stevens, D. E., & Wickmire, T. L. (2003). Expert coaches' perceptions of team building. *Journal of Applied Sport Psychology, 15*, 129–143.

Brawley, L. R., Carron, A. V., & Widmeyer, W. N. (1993). The influence of the group and its cohesiveness on perceptions of group-related variables. *Journal of Sport & Exercise Psychology, 15*, 245–260.

Brawley, L. R., & Paskevich, D. M. (1997). Conducting team building research in the context of sport and exercise. *Journal of Applied Sport Psychology, 9*, 11–40.

Bray, C. D., & Whaley, D. E. (2001). Team cohesion, effort, and objective individual performance of high school basketball players. *The Sport Psychologist, 15*, 260–275.

Carron, A. V. (1982). Cohesiveness in sport groups: Interpretations and considerations. *Journal of Sport Psychology, 4*, 123–138.

Carron, A. V., Brawley, L. R., & Widmeyer, W. N. (1998). The measurement of cohesiveness in sport groups. In J. L. Duda (Ed.), *Advancements in sport and exercise psychology measurement* (pp. 213–226). Morgantown, WV: Fitness Information Technology.

Carron, A. V., Colman, M. M., Wheeler, J., & Stevens, D. (2002). Cohesion and performance in sport: A meta-analysis. *Journal of Sport & Exercise Psychology, 24*, 168–188.

Carron, A. V., & Hausenblas, H. A. (1998). *Group dynamics in sport* (2nd ed.). Morgantown, WV: Fitness Information Technology.

Carron, A. V., Prapavessis, H., & Grove, J. R. (1994). Group effects and self-handicapping. *Journal of Sport & Exercise Psychology, 16*, 246–258.

Carron, A. V., & Spink, K. S. (1992). Internal consistency of the Group Environment Questionnaire modified for an exercise setting. *Perceptual and Motor Skills, 74*, 1075–1078.

Carron, A. V., & Spink, K. S. (1993). Team building in an exercise setting. *The Sport Psychologist, 7*, 8–18.

Carron, A. V., & Spink, K. S. (1995). The group size-cohesion relationship in exercise groups. *Small Group Research, 26*, 86–105.

Carron, A. V., Spink, K. S., & Prapavessis, H. (1997). Team building and cohesiveness in the sport and exercise setting: Use of indirect interventions. *Journal of Applied Sport Psychology, 9*, 61–72.

Carron, A. V., Widmeyer, W. N., & Brawley, L. R. (1985). The development of an instrument to assess cohesion in sport teams: The Group Environment Questionnaire. *Journal of Sport Psychology, 7,* 244–266.

Carron, A. V., Widmeyer, W. N., & Brawley, L. R. (1988). Group cohesion and individual adherence to physical activity. *Journal of Sport & Exercise Psychology, 10,* 119–126.

Cartwright, D. (1968). The nature of group cohesiveness. In D. Cartwright & A. Zander (Eds.), *Group dynamics: Research and theory* (pp. 91–109). New York: Harper & Row.

Cartwright, D., & Zander, A. (1968). *Group dynamics: Research and theory.* New York: Harper & Row.

Chelladurai, P., & Saleh, S. D. (1980). Dimensions of leadership behaviour in sport: Development of a leadership scale. *Journal of Sport Psychology, 2,* 34–45.

Cota, A. A., Evans, C. R., Dion, K. L., Kilik, L., & Longman, R. S. (1995). The structure of group cohesion. *Personality and Social Psychological Bulletin, 21,* 572–580.

Eisler, L., & Spink, K. S. (1998). Effects of scoring configuration and task cohesion on the perception of psychological momentum. *Journal of Sport & Exercise Psychology, 20,* 311–320.

Estabrooks, P. A., & Carron, A. V. (1999). Group cohesion in older adult exercisers: Prediction and intervention effects. *Journal of Behavioral Medicine, 22,* 575–588.

Estabrooks, P. A., & Carron, A. V. (2000). The Physical Activity Group Environment Questionnaire: An instrument for the assessment of cohesion in exercise classes. *Group Dynamics, 4,* 230–243.

Festinger, L. (1950). Informal social communication. *Psychological Review, 57,* 271–282.

Fiedler, F. E. (1954). Assumed similarity measures as predictors of team effectiveness. *Journal of Abnormal and Social Psychology, 49,* 381–388.

Fraser, S., & Spink, K. S. (2002). Examining social support and group cohesion in the compliance behaviour of females in a health-related exercise setting. *Journal of Behavioral Medicine, 25,* 233–249.

Gardner, D. E., Shields, D. L., Bredemeier, B. J., & Bostrom, A. (1996). The relationship between perceived coaching behaviours and team cohesion among baseball and softball players. *The Sport Psychologist, 10,* 367–381.

Glass, G. V. (1976). Primary, secondary, and meta-analysis. *Educational Researcher, 5,* 3–8.

Granito, V. J., & Rainey, D. W. (1988). Differences in cohesion between high school and college football teams and starters and nonstarters. *Perceptual and Motor Skills, 66,* 471–477.

Hausenblas, H. A., & Carron, A. V. (1996). Group cohesion and self-handicapping in female and male athletes. *Journal of Sport & Exercise Psychology, 18,* 132–143.

Holt, N. L., & Sparkes, A. C. (2001). An ethnographic study of cohesiveness in a college soccer team over a season. *The Sport Psychologist, 15,* 237–259.

Jones, E. E., & Berglas, S. (1978). Control of attributions about the self through self-handicapping strategies: The appeal of alcohol and the role of underachievement. *Personality and Social Psychology Bulletin, 4,* 200–206.

Jordan, M. (1994). *I can't accept not trying.* San Francisco: Harper.

Jowett, S., & Chaundy, V. (2004). An investigation into the impact of coach leadership and coach-athlete relationships on group cohesion. *Groups Dynamics, 8,* 302–311.

Karau, S. J., & Williams, K. D. (1993). Social loafing: A meta-analytic review and theoretical integration. *Journal of Personality and Social Psychology, 65,* 681–706.

Klein, M., & Christiansen, G. (1969). Group composition, group structure and group effectiveness of basketball teams. In J. W. Loy & G. S. Kenyon (Eds.), *Sport, culture and society* (pp. 397–408). New York: Macmillan.

Kozub, S. A., & McDonnell, J. F. (2001). Exploring the relationship between cohesion and collective efficacy in rugby teams. *Journal of Sport Behavior, 23,* 120–129.

Latane, B., Williams, K., & Harkins, S. (1979). Many hands make light the work: The causes and consequences of social loafing. *Journal of Personality and Social Psychology, 37,* 822–832.

Lenk, H. (1969). Top performance despite internal conflict: An antithesis to a functional proposition. In J. W. Loy & G. S. Kenyon (Eds.), *Sport, culture and society* (pp. 393–397). New York: Macmillan.

Lott, A. J., & Lott, B. E. (1965). Group cohesiveness as interpersonal attraction: A review of relationships with antecedent and consequent variables. *Psychological Bulletin, 64,* 259–309.

Loughead, T. M., & Carron, A. V. (2004). The mediating role of cohesion in the leader behavior-satisfaction relationship. *Psychology of Sport and Exercise, 5,* 355–371.

Loughead, T. M., Colman, M. M., & Carron, A. V. (2001). Investigating the mediational relationship of leadership, class cohesion and adherence in an exercise setting. *Small Group Research, 32,* 558–575.

Lynberg, M. (1993). *Winning!* New York: Doubleday.

Martens, R., Landers, D. M., & Loy, J. W. (1972). *Sport cohesiveness questionnaire.* Washington, DC: AAHPERD Publications.

McGrath, J. E. (1962). The influence of positive interpersonal relations on adjustment and effectiveness in rifle teams. *Journal of Abnormal and Social Psychology, 65,* 365–375.

McKnight, P., Williams, J. M., & Widmeyer, W. N., (1991, October). *The effects of cohesion and identifiability on reducing the likelihood of social loafing.* Paper presented at the annual conference of the Association for the Advancement of Applied Sport Psychology, Savannah, GA.

Melnick, M. J., & Chemers, M. (1974). Effects of group social structure on the success of basketball teams. *Research Quarterly, 45,* 1–8.

Mudrack, P. E. (1989). Defining group cohesiveness. A legacy of confusion? *Small Group Behavior, 20,* 37–49.

Mullen, B., & Copper, C. (1994). The relation between group cohesiveness and performance: An integration. *Psychological Bulletin, 115,* 210–227.

Myers, A. (1962). Team competition, success and adjustment of team members. *Journal of Abnormal and Social Psychology, 65,* 325–332.

Newman, B. (1984). Expediency as benefactor: How team building saves times and gets the job done. *Training and Development Journal, 38,* 26–30.

Paskevich, D. M., Brawley, L. R., Dorsch, L. R., & Widmeyer, W. N. (1999). Relationships between collective efficacy and team measurement factors. *Group Dynamics, 3,* 210–222.

Pease, D. G., & Kozub, S. A. (1994). Perceived coaching behaviours and team cohesion in high school girls basketball team. *Journal of Sport & Exercise Psychology, 16,* S93.

Prapavessis, H., & Carron, A. V. (1997a). Cohesion and work output. *Small Group Research, 28,* 294–301.

Prapavessis, H., & Carron, A. V. (1997b). Sacrifice, cohesion, and conformity to norms in sport teams. *Group Dynamics, 1,* 231–240.

Prapavessis, H., Carron, A. V., & Spink, K. S. (1996). Team building in sport. *International Journal of Sport Psychology, 27,* 269–285.

Rosenberg, S., Erlick, D., & Berkowitz, L. (1955). Some effects of varying combinations of group members on group performance measures and leadership behaviors. *Journal of Abnormal and Social Psychology, 51,* 195–203.

Schinke, R. J., Draper, S. P., & Salmela, J. H. (1997). A conceptualization of team building in high performance sport as a season-long process. *Avante, 3,* 57–72.

Shaw, M. E. (1976). *Group dynamics: The psychology of small group behaviour.* New York: McGraw-Hill.

Spink, K. S. (1990a). Collective efficacy in the sport setting. *International Journal of Sport Psychology, 21,* 380–393.

Spink, K. S. (1990b) Group cohesion and collective efficacy in volleyball teams. *Journal of Sport & Exercise Psychology, 12,* 301–311.

Spink, K. S. (1992). Group cohesion and starting status in successful and less successful elite volleyball teams. *Journal of Sports Sciences, 10,* 379–388.

Spink, K. S. (1995). Cohesion and intention to participate of female sport team athletes. *Journal of Sport & Exercise Psychology, 17,* 416–427.

Spink, K. S. (1998). Mediational effects of social cohesion on the leadership-intention to return relationship in sport. *Group Dynamics, 2,* 92–100.

Spink, K. S., & Carron, A. V. (1992). Group cohesion and adherence in exercise classes. *Journal of Sport & Exercise Psychology, 14,* 78–86.

Spink, K. S., & Carron, A. V. (1993). The effects of team building on the adherence patterns of female exercise participants. *Journal of Sport & Exercise Psychology, 15,* 39–49.

Spink, K. S., & Carron, A. V. (1994). Group cohesion effects in exercise classes. *Small Group Research, 25,* 26–42.

Spink, K. S., Nickel, D., Wilson, K., & Odnokon, P. (2005). Examining the relationship between task cohesion and team task satisfaction in elite ice hockey players: A multilevel approach. *Small Group Research, 36,* 539–554.

Spink, K. S., & Odnokon, P. (2001a). Effects of team cohesion on male athletes' perceived effort. *Journal of Sport & Exercise Psychology, 23,* S32.

Spink, K. S., & Odnokon, P. (2001b). Examining the effect of team cohesion on male ice hockey players' intention to return. *Journal of Sport & Exercise Psychology, 23,* S33.

Steers, R., & Rhodes, S. (1978). Major influences of employee attendance: A process model. *Journal of Applied Psychology, 63,* 391–407.

Stevens, D. E., & Bloom, G. A. (2003). The effect of team building on cohesion. *Avante, 9,* 43–54.

Sullivan, P., & Feltz, D. (2001). The relationship between intrateam conflict and cohesion within hockey teams. *Small Group Research, 32,* 342–355.

Vallerand, R. J., Colavecchio, P. G., & Pelletier, L. G. (1988). Psychological momentum and performance inferences: A preliminary test of the antecedents-consequences psychological momentum model. *Journal of Sport & Exercise Psychology, 10,* 92–108.

Watson, J. D., Martin Ginis, K. A., & Spink, K. S. (2004). Team building in an exercise class for the elderly. *Activities, Adapation, & Aging, 28,* 35–47.

Westre, K. R., & Weiss, M. R. (1991). The relationship between perceived coaching behaviors and group cohesion in high school football teams. *The Sport Psychologist, 5,* 41–54.

Widmeyer, W. N., Brawley, L. R., & Carron, A. V. (1990). The effects of group size in sport. *Journal of Sport & Exercise Psychology, 12,* 177–190.

Williams, K. D., Nida, S. A., Baca, L. D., & Latane, B. (1989). Social loafing and swimming: Effects of identifiability on individual and relay performance of intercollegiate swimmers. *Basic and Applied Social Psychology, 10,* 73–81.

Yukelson, D. (1997). Principles of effective team building interventions in sport: A direct services approach at Penn State University. *Journal of Applied Sport Psychology, 9,* 73–96.

Gordon A. Bloom

CHAPTER 10

Coaching Psychology

Chapter Objectives

After reading this chapter, you should be able to do the following:

1. Describe the coach education structure and process in Canada.
2. Identify the steps to become an elite coach.
3. Describe the common characteristics and coaching principles of youth-sport coaches.
4. Describe the components of Chelladurai's sport leadership model and its relationship to coaching.
5. Define the different components of the coaching model.
6. Describe the coaching model and its relationship to effective coaching.
7. Explain the holistic (athlete-centred) approach adopted by many (non-professional) Canadian coaches.
8. Explain the model of coaching efficacy.

Coach C, an aspiring third-year coach of an elite women's basketball team, could not sleep for the past week. She was thinking about her team competing in the upcoming playoffs without her top player and league MVP. With this player, Coach C's team had been ranked as high as first in the province and fifth in the country. They were on a roll, and the playoffs were just around the corner. Coach C wanted to win to establish her reputation as an up-and-coming elite coach.

The loss of this key player was not due to injury, attitude, or academics; rather, it was due to an ethical dilemma that would create the defining moment of this young coach's career. If this athlete played one more game during the season, then she would forfeit a year of eligibility at an NCAA Division 1 university in the United States, for which she was being heavily recruited. Playing at an American Division 1 university would allow this athlete to realize her dream of competing against the best women basketball players in the world and possibly playing professional basketball for the Canadian national team upon her graduation.

The day before the playoffs began, Coach C received a text message from her athlete indicating her desire to continue playing this year. Would Coach C lessen her chance of coaching a national championship team by not encouraging her star athlete to play in this game? The answer is yes; Coach C convinced her league MVP not to play in the game, and the team subsequently lost a close game in the first round of the playoffs. Coach C knew her star athlete's heart was with the team but that deep down she was uncertain and nervous about the consequences of playing and forfeiting a year of NCAA playing eligibility. Coach C believed the value of a sound education for a student was far more important than adding a notch to her coaching resumé.

This scenario indicates how a coach's decision and behaviour affects many people in different ways. Thus, it is not surprising that research on expert performers in domains ranging from the arts and sciences to sport have found that the quality of teaching or coaching is an important factor contributing to an individual's rise to prominence (Bloom, 1985; Csikszentmihalyi, Rathunde, & Whalen, 1993; Salmela & Moraes, 2003). This may also explain the large amount of time, effort, and energy that some parents of gifted children spend searching for the right coach or teacher to help their child realize his or her potential.

Given this information, why then is so little respect afforded to many of Canada's greatest coaches by both the media and the general population? Possibly with the exception of professional or national team coaches in ice hockey—where the exploits of Toe Blake, Scotty Bowman, Danielle Sauvageau, and Pat Quinn are lauded—many of our elite-level Canadian coaches have received little acclaim or public adoration. For example, how many people in Canada are aware of the accomplishments of former Olympic basketball coaches Kathy Shields or Jack Donohue, or of current national team coaches Michel Larouche in diving, Paralympic coach Peter Eriksson in athletics, or Allison McNeill in basketball?

The relative anonymity of these great coaches leads to many interesting questions: Do people value and understand the importance of a good coach? As well, is there a recipe for coaching development and knowledge acquisition? By the time you have finished reading this chapter, you should not have any lingering doubts about the value and benefit of a proven coach. As well, you should understand how an individual becomes a coach, and moreover, what knowledge is used by coaches to develop healthy and well-balanced athletes.

Some Common Myths about Coaching Psychology

MYTH: *Outstanding athletes have an advantage in becoming excellent coaches.*

Although many people believe that elite athletes can more easily become elite coaches than less skilled athletes, the scientific (and non-scientific) results suggest otherwise. Although most expert coaches played at a high level in their sport, few were exceptional performers (Schinke, Bloom, & Salmela, 1995; Miller, 1996). Moreover, there are very few Hall of Fame athletes who reach the same level of success as coaches.

MYTH: *Aspiring coaches must emulate the most successful coaches in their sport, regardless of their own personality, beliefs, or philosophy.*

Studies have found that individuals should create their own coaching style based on their traits, beliefs, and philosophy, rather than emulate someone who has achieved success in their sport.

MYTH: *All elite-level coaches are focused solely on winning at the expense of athlete growth and development.*

Research on elite Canadian coaches at the university and Olympic levels have found these coaches to be just as concerned about the personal growth and development of their athletes as they are with their athletic growth and development (Côté, Salmela, Trudel, Baria, & Russell, 1995; Vallée, & Bloom, 2005). Similar findings have also emerged with some elite American coaches at similar levels of competition (Walton, 1992; Wooden, 1988).

MYTH: *Coaching confidence is determined solely by one's innate personality.*

Coaching confidence is similar to athlete confidence; it can be improved over time with positive performances, coach education seminars, community support, and perceived team ability.

Introduction

Explaining coaching psychology is a complex task. Before I begin, it is useful to have a brief historical overview of coaching science research. Gilbert and Trudel (2004) recently compiled and analyzed a database of 611 studies on coaching science published in English-language journals between 1970 and 2001 (the entire document can be accessed at www.aahperd.org/research/template.cfm?template=grantees.html). This project reviewed published research relevant to coaching science and involved an exhaustive search using computerized databases and encyclopedias. The results provided a foundation to help coach educators integrate coaching research into the development of coach training programs. Among their findings are the following points:

■ Coaching science research has increased significantly since 1970, now averaging approximately 30 published articles per year.

■ There is a relatively small core of authors who have developed a significant line of research in coaching science.

■ Research has branched from solely examining coaching behaviours to looking at coaching behaviours in combination with coaching cognition.

■ There is no single resource that lists and evaluates the assessment tools created to study coaching practices.

■ Coach gender issues are one of the most frequently studied topics in this field; as well, coaching effectiveness (knowledge) and career issues (e.g., burnout) are starting to receive increased attention.

- Coaching science research has seen a continuous increase of qualitative research studies, especially those incorporating an interview technique.
- There is a virtual absence of studies of coaches that include athletes, parents, and sport administrators.
- Most coaching scientific studies have focused on both team sport and school-based coaches; however, this excludes the youth and professional levels.
- Ninety percent of the studies have not used any criteria of coaching effectiveness.

Coach Education

The value and impact of coaching has grown tremendously since the word *coach* first came into existence following the 1860 American Civil War (Coakley, 1990). Yet, the path for becoming a coach is not clearly laid out. In Canada, coach education and development is governed by the Coaching Association of Canada (CAC, www.coach.ca). Created in 1970 following a task force recommendation on sport in our country, the CAC has a goal to promote quality coaching for the benefit of all Canadian athletes. This is accomplished by providing the foundation of skills, knowledge, and attitudes needed to ensure effective coaching leadership for Canadian athletes. In fact, government leaders in our country have recommended that all individuals obtain a Level 1 certification in their sport from the **National Coaching Certification Program (NCCP)** to ensure that each youth has a positive sport experience (Coaching Association of Canada, 2005).

The NCCP (www.coach.ca/e/nccp) is a knowledge- and course-based program run by the CAC with five levels of certification. Each sport determines its own content. Levels 1 to 3 are designed for coaches of community, school, and club sport programs and include theory, technical, and tactical components. The time commitment increases as one moves higher in coaching education levels: Level 1 is a one-weekend course whereas Level 2 is a two-weekend course. Levels 4 and 5 represent the top level of coaching and are designed for coaches of elite national and international-calibre athletes. These levels require more time commitment and cover a broader array of topics, including planning, sport psychology, biomechanics, and leadership (Coaching Association of Canada, 2005).

Presently, 65 sports are affiliated with the NCCP, and nearly 900 000 individuals have acquired various levels of the certification program. Approximately 700 of these coaches have received Level 4, and fewer than 100 have received Level 5 certification. Most sources have cited Canada's NCCP as the first widely adopted national coach education program. The NCCP is undergoing changes to meet emerging challenges, with the new NCCP model divided into three streams: community sport, competition, and instruction (see www.coach.ca/eng/certification/nccp_for_coaches/nccp_model.cfm).

Additional coach education and development information in Canada can be acquired through either the educational system or the National Coaching Institutes. Through the former, some universities in Canada offer specialized training in coach education. Perhaps the most well-known is the Master of Education in Coaching Studies program at the University of Victoria (www.educ.uvic.ca/phed/med_coaching.html). Canada presently has eight National Coaching Institutes (www.coach.ca/eng/institutes/index.cfm) across the country whose mission is to enhance the training environment for high-performance athletes and coaches through a variety of services. For coaches, the institutes are involved in the training and development of Level 4 and Level 5 coaches in the NCCP.

Similar in many ways to Canada, both Australia and the United Kingdom have coach education systems that are fewer than 30 years old and were developed in part with government participation and assistance. Created around the same time as Canada's, Australia's program (www.ausport.gov.au/coach) ensures that their 84 000 accredited coaches have received training in coaching principles (fundamentals of coaching and athletic performance), sport-specific skills, techniques and strategies, and coaching practice (application of coaching principles). The National Coaching Accreditation Scheme (NCAS) in Australia has guided the training and development of sport coaches from grassroots to all levels.

The United Kingdom's coach education program began in 1983 with their National Coaching Foundation, which then changed its name to sports coach UK (www.sportscoachuk.org). Its mandate is to guide the education and development of coaches at every level and to promote and establish coaching as a profession. Among its initiatives is a study that found approximately 6.25 million people in the United Kingdom were being coached by 1.2 million people involved in some capacity of coaching (www.sportscoachuk.org/research/researchreports.htm). Further to this, the report revealed that 38% of coaches had a coaching qualification, 19% were paid for their work, and just 5% worked full-time.

A different approach to coach training and education has taken place in the United States. Unlike the three countries already mentioned, the United States does not have one government-based national coaching organization for training its many volunteer and professional coaches, and coach education programs are rarely mandatory. Instead, several coaching development programs were created around the same time as the NCCP and NCAS. For example, the American Coaching Effectiveness Program was founded in 1976 (Douge & Hastie, 1993). It evolved into the American Sport Education Program (ASEP) and is arguably the most widely used program in the United States (Trudel & Gilbert, in press). According to Martens (2004), it is presently used by 250 organizations, ranging from the grassroots to Olympic levels. One of its newest initiatives is offering sport-specific coaching courses online (Martens, 2004). Positive Coaching Alliance (PCA) is another American organization that is responsible for educating coaches (www.positivecoach.org). Founded in 1998 at Stanford University, PCA provides research-based training workshops and practical tools for coaches.

Given the differences in coach education programs, it is not surprising that the knowledge acquisition of elite-level American coaches is different from that for coaches from the other three countries. For example, a group of American researchers found that observing other coaches and gaining coaching experience were the most important factors in their knowledge acquisition (Gould, Giannini, Krane, & Hodge, 1990). Further to this, these same coaches felt there was a need for a more structured coaching education program. To date, this recommendation does not appear to have been met in the United States.

The government-funded and supported coaching education programs in Canada, Australia, and the United Kingdom demonstrate that coaching is becoming recognized as an important field that can assist the growth and development of today's amateur and professional athletes. Coach education has grown tremendously in the last 35 years since certified programs were introduced. Presently, coach education is aided by the International Council for Coach Education (ICCE, www.icce.ws) whose mission is to improve the quality and exposure of coaching at all levels around the world. Based at the Wingate Institute for Physical Education and Sport in Israel, the ICCE has a

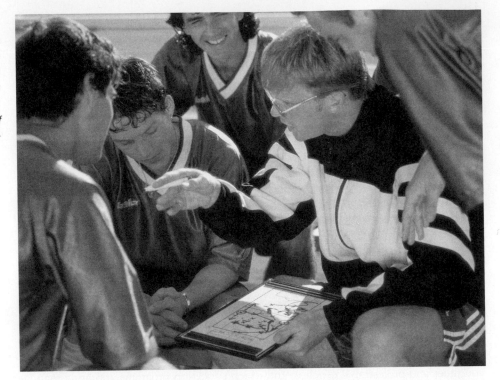

> Coaching education programs offered by National Coaching Institutes and higher education institutions can facilitate the effectiveness of coaches.
>
> *Photo courtesy of Superstock/Maxx Images.*

membership that includes contacts in 21 countries, according to the most recent statistics (Trudel & Gilbert, in press). Despite all of this, one could argue that the lack of consensus for coach education programs worldwide demonstrates there is still work to be done.

Reflections 10.1

Canada, the United Kingdom, and Australia have well-developed coach education programs that were partly developed with government participation and assistance. What do you think are the advantages of structured coaching education programs? Can you think of any possible drawbacks?

Coach Development

Despite the efforts of the ICCE and various coach education programs, there is a lack of scientific research on ways of becoming a successful (Canadian) coach. A small group of researchers have identified common developmental characteristics that shed light on what it takes to become a top-level coach in this country (Bloom, Salmela, & Schinke, 1995; Miller, 1996; Miller, Bloom, & Salmela, 1996; Schinke, Bloom, & Salmela, 1995). These studies looked at the career paths of elite team-sport coaches. As athletes, all of these elite Canadian coaches reported living active and successful sporting lives that began with a love of sports that was often fuelled by the encouragement of family members and accessibility to physical resources. They played and excelled in a number of sports as youths; perhaps more importantly, they were wholeheartedly committed to the pursuit of excellence in their sporting endeavours. Furthermore, they all had many leadership positions throughout their athletic careers (Miller et al., 1996). One could argue that their coaching potentials were recognized by many of their own coaches who often granted them leadership positions and shared coaching-related strategies and information with them.

All of these coaches played at a fairly high level in their sport, and they could be classified as above-average players on their university teams or as average or below-average players on their national teams, if they made it to that level (Schinke et al., 1995). Few, if any, reached star status either at the professional or Olympic level. In fact, this finding mirrors the top professional coaches in the four major North American team sports. For example, it is difficult to name more than a handful of athletes who had both athletic Hall of Fame status *and* coaching careers.

Most elite coaches were initiated into their profession either during their athletic careers or immediately after they finished competing (Miller, 1996; Schinke et al., 1995). With some, this was an extension of their leadership role as team captain, in which they regularly mentored younger, less experienced teammates. As well, many of these individuals volunteered in their community, either at camps during the off-season or at youth-sport practices during their seasons; these experiences often put them in direct contact with young athletes. Thus, for many, getting involved with sports at the grassroots level upon their retirement was a natural progression.

Up to this point in the chapter, the information on coach development has been organized and structured through coach education training programs or personal contacts in the community. One area that is very different, but that may be the most important factor in coaches' growth and development, is **mentoring**. There are many professions in which mentoring is a common and expected process. For example, pilots, doctors, and police officers spend years refining their skills with the assistance of experienced and well-respected colleagues who ensure they are allowed to grow and develop in an environment designed to minimize errors and build knowledge and confidence.

Although levels 4 and 5 of the NCCP ensure that coaches receive advice and training from a respected mentor, a question still remains: how much of an impact does good mentoring have on the growth and development of aspiring coaches? The answer to this question may never be known; however, an examination of the pedigree of some of sport's greatest coaches clearly shows the importance of solid mentoring. Former NHL coach Scotty Bowman learned from the greatest predecessor of his time, Toe Blake. Interestingly, many of Bowman's protégés have assumed top leadership roles in hockey: from Jacques Lemaire to Bob Gainey to Ken Dryden. Likewise, Bill Walsh, the successful coach of the San Francisco 49er's dynasty of the 1980s, apprenticed from a master coach, Paul Brown. Walsh then mentored a number of successful NFL head coaches including Mike Holmgren, Dennis Green, and George Seifert.

No discussion about coach and athlete mentoring in Canada would be complete without mentioning Kathy Shields—a former member of our Olympic basketball team, as well as former assistant coach and head coach for our national basketball team. She finished her coaching duties as head coach at the University of Victoria in 2005, where she compiled an astounding .865 winning percentage over her 25-year coaching career. Certified as a master coach in 1986 by the CAC, Shields has influenced nearly all of Canada's elite coaches and athletes in women's basketball for the last 25 years. No fewer than five former players and assistant coaches currently serve as head coaches for university teams.

Kathy Shields has influenced many of Canada's athletes and coaches in basketball for more than 25 years.

Photograph courtesy of University of Victoria Vikes.

An empirical examination of mentoring by researchers Bloom, Durand-Bush, Schinke, and Salmela (1998) found that all of the 21 expert coaches in their sample were mentored both as athletes and as developing coaches by well-respected individuals. The knowledge they acquired from their mentors helped mould their coaching ideas and philosophies. Interestingly, these coaches noted that it was important for them *not* to imitate everything about their mentors; rather, their own beliefs and personalities affected their coaching style. The importance of mentoring has also been highlighted by researchers in both the United States (Gould et al., 1990) and the United Kingdom (Jones, Armour, & Potrac, 2003).

Reflections 10.2
The chapter on motivation (Chapter 4) discussed several factors related to developing confidence in sport. How do you think mentoring fits into enhancing coaching confidence for less experienced coaches?

Youth-sport Coaching

Up to this point in the discussion, most information has been slanted toward coaches of elite sport. The context of youth sport has many interesting nuances that distinguish it from other levels of coaching. More specifically, the role of the coach in youth sport may have more important global implications than it does for elite-level coaches. For example, the medical and economic impact of physical inactivity accounts for $2.1 billion in Canadian health-care costs (Boudreault, 2003/04; Katzmarzyk, Glendhill, & Shephard, 2000). Only two in every five Canadian children are defined as being active enough for optimal growth and development (Cragg, Cameron, Craig, & Russell, 1999). One way to increase physical activity is to focus on factors that increase motives for youth-sport participation, specifically the nature of the environment surrounding the learning and implementation of physical skills (see Chapter 11 for more details). The person who is responsible for creating this positive youth-sport environment is the coach.

Characteristics of Youth Coaches

Trudel and Gilbert (in press) have reached a number of conclusions about the characteristics of youth-sport coaches. Their findings include the following points:

- Most are male.
- Most are in their mid-30s.
- As few as 10% of these coaches continue coaching for 10 years or more.
- Almost all of these coaches competed in sport, and most were above-average athletes.
- Most of these coaches acquired athletic experience for five years or more in the sport they now coach.
- Love of the sport, a desire to help young people develop skills, and a desire to serve as a leader and supervisor for young people were main reasons for coaching.
- Most coaches had a child on the team they coached.
- Just over half of the coaches were university educated.

Ideal Behaviours of Youth Coaches

Ideal behaviours for youth-sport coaches have been studied extensively by Smith and Smoll (2002a, 2002b). These researchers believed in the importance of training youth-sport coaches to ensure young athletes had fun, enjoyed being a part of a team, learned skills, and developed and increased their self-esteem. Their research over the past 30 years can be divided into two phases. The first phase involved the development of the mediational model of leadership and the coaching behaviour assessment system (CBAS) to categorize coaching behaviours (Smith, Smoll, & Hunt, 1977). Findings from their research using the CBAS demonstrated that coaching behaviours influenced children's self-perceptions, anxiety, and adherence levels. In addition, Smith, Smoll, and colleagues noted that coaching behaviours could be modified through structured coach training and education programs.

These findings influenced the second phase of their research, which involved the implementation of an intervention program, coach effectiveness training (CET), and the subsequent testing of the program in the youth-sport setting. Applied research using the CET has demonstrated that children playing for trained coaches, as opposed to untrained volunteers, had significant increases in self-esteem, had decreases in anxiety levels, enjoyed their sporting experience more, and evaluated their coach and teammates more favourably, regardless of the win-loss record (Smith & Smoll, 2002a). Results also indicated that children who played for trained coaches were also more likely to return the following season (Smith & Smoll, 2002a). Table 10.1 summarizes the researchers' key recommended coaching behaviours.

Lasting approximately three hours, a CET workshop follows five coaching principles (Smith & Smoll, 2002a; Smoll & Smith, 2002). The first principle is to create a healthy climate that is enjoyable and is focused on mastering skills instead of trying to beat an opponent. As well, coaches must understand that their success or failure is not

Table 10.1   Effective Practices for Coaching Youth Sport

■ Reinforce effort as much as results.

■ Give encouragement after a mistake but in positive and encouraging ways.

■ Establish clear expectations; involve athletes in behavioural guidelines and work to build team unity in achieving them.

■ Set a good example of behaviour, encourage athletes to be supportive of each other, and reinforce them when they do so.

■ Always give instructions positively and do so in a clear, concise manner.

■ Foster two-way communication, and respond to the needs of individual players appropriately.

Note: From Way to Go Coach! A Scientifically-proven Approach to Youth Sports Coaching Effectiveness *(2nd ed., pp. 31–48), by R. E. Smith and F. L. Smoll, 2002, Portola Valley, CA: Waroe.*

dependent on the outcome of the game or a win-loss record, but rather on their ability to get their athletes to give maximum effort. The second principle is to utilize a positive approach to coaching that involves positive reinforcement, encouragement, and appropriate instruction. Punitive behaviours are highly discouraged. The third principle is to establish norms that emphasize athletes' obligations to help and support one another, thereby increasing cohesion and personal commitment to the team. Coaches must also model and support these behaviours. The fourth principle is to include athletes in decision-making roles regarding team rules and compliance. The fifth principle is to engage in self-monitoring and assessment in order to focus on positive coaching behaviours.

> Coaches can be trained so that their behaviours improve the psychosocial development of their athletes.

Photo courtesy of Jonathan Dankner.

Many of today's successful high-profile coaches have gone through some common developmental patterns that began during their athletic careers and continued as they moved through the coaching ranks. While they were athletes, most of these experts had leadership roles that exposed them to different strategic information that may have helped their evolution to coaching. As well, most acquired information through the NCCP and supplemented this information with a developmental pattern that included exposure to positive role models (mentors). Their initiation into coaching, combined with the encouragement of their own coaches and their burning desire for sport, helped them excel as elite coaches. Although research on youth-sport coaching is comparatively lacking, some common characteristics and ideal coaching principles have been forwarded by experts in this field.

Coaching Knowledge

This section will focus on the knowledge of coaches, including their goals, roles, and responsibilities, as well as the extent to which they can affect the learning and performance of their athletes. In order to present this information, three bodies of literature in coaching psychology will be explained: (a) Chelladurai's sport leadership model, (b) Feltz and colleagues' coaching efficacy model, and (c) Côté, Salmela, Trudel, et al.'s coaching model.

Sport Leadership

Leadership has been defined as "a process whereby an individual influences a group of individuals to achieve a common goal" (Northouse, 2001, p. 3). Given its apparent practical appeal, it is not surprising that leadership has been one of the most studied areas in industrial and organizational psychology (Northouse, 2001). Leadership has been defined, constructed, and researched from numerous theoretical frameworks, such as trait theories or behavioural approaches (Klenke, 1993). In spite of the rich background of research on leadership, this concept is one of the least understood phenomena because almost every finding about leadership (e.g., personality characteristics, gender differences) can be contradicted by other results (Klenke, 1993). In sport, the importance of effective leadership has been cited by athletes and coaches as a vital component to achievement (Chelladurai & Riemer, 1998; Dupuis, Bloom, & Loughead, in press; Gould, Hodge, Peterson, & Petlichkoff, 1987) and athlete satisfaction (Riemer & Chelladurai, 1995). At the present time, most sport leadership research has focused on coaching effectiveness by identifying personality traits, behavioural attributes, and situational determinants.

Several models of sport leadership have been advanced, the most noteworthy being Chelladurai's (1978, 1993) **multidimensional model of leadership (MML)**, a linear model comprising antecedents, leader behaviours, and consequences (see Figure 10.1). Created specifically for sport situations, Chelladurai's MML conceptualizes leadership as an interactional process, and thus it allows researchers to evaluate leadership effectiveness through team member satisfaction and performance of athletes (consequences). These consequences are directly affected by the degree of congruence among the three states of leader behaviours, called required, preferred, and actual. **Required leader behaviours** are those that are expected of a coach. For example, coaches are not allowed to make physical contact with their athletes. **Preferred leader behaviours** are how a coach acts and are generally based on the athletes' preferences.

Figure 10.1   Diagram of multidimensional model of leadership

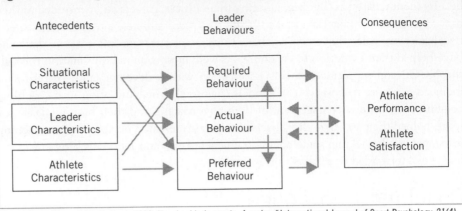

Note: Adapted from P. Chelladurai, 1990, "Leadership in sports: A review," International Journal of Sport Psychology 21(4): 328-354. By permission of P. Chelladurai.

For example, most professional coaches do not socialize with their players after games. Finally, **actual leader behaviours** are the behaviours that a coach exhibits, regardless of team standards. These leader behaviours are influenced by antecedent factors, which can be classified into situational (e.g., team goals, norms), leader (e.g., leader's experience or personality), and team-member characteristics (e.g., gender, ability).

Chelladurai's model benefited coaching research because it attributed coaches' success to more than great leadership skills. It stressed that success was a function of coaches' capacity to display actual leadership behaviours that responded to a combination of demands from the environment, the players, and the coaches themselves. Furthermore, successful coaches were able to adjust to these demands by incorporating the required and preferred behaviours into their actual behaviours. The majority of research using the MML has primarily focused on the leadership behaviours of adult coaches of elite sports.

> ## Reflections 10.3
> Who was your favourite coach that you played for? What were his/her actual leader behaviours? Did all players prefer these behaviours? Does the multidimensional model of leadership help explain your own experiences with this coach?

In order to examine the hypothesized relationships in the MML, Chelladurai and Saleh (1980) developed the **Leadership Scale for Sports (LSS)**, a 40-item inventory that measures five dimensions of leader behaviour. Specifically, the five dimensions include training and instruction, democratic behaviour, autocratic behaviour, social support, and positive feedback (see Table 10.2). Athletes completing the LSS provide information about preferred and actual coaching behaviours; coaches completing the LSS provide information about required coaching behaviours with respect to their own perceptions of how they coach. The LSS provides information in three areas: the athlete's preferences for specific coaching behaviours, the athletes' perceptions of their coaches' leadership behaviours, and the coaches' perceptions of their own behaviours. Zhang, Jensen, and Mann (1997) created a Revised LSS that supported the original five leadership behaviour dimensions and added a sixth dimension, situational consideration behaviour. This dimension considers situation factors, such as setting up individual goals or assigning an athlete to the right game position.

Table 10.2   The Leadership Scale for Sports

1. *Training and Instruction* (instructional behaviours): Coaching behaviour aimed at improving the performance of the athletes by providing a technically sound, rigorous, and coordinated training program.

2. *Democratic Behaviour* (decision-making style): Coaching behaviour that gives athletes a greater participation in the decisions pertaining to the team (in practices and games).

3. *Autocratic Behaviour* (decision-making style): Coaching behaviour that involves independence, authority, and sole responsibility of the leader over the decisions for the team. This precludes athlete input.

4. *Social Support* (motivational tendencies): Coaching behaviours that include a concern for the well-being of the athletes. It involves effort by the coach to instill a very strong team atmosphere that would lead to better relationships between team members.

5. *Positive Feedback* (motivational tendencies): Coaching behaviours that are used to reinforce the athletes by rewarding and praising them for good performances.

Research utilizing the MML has been extensive and has primarily been descriptive in nature. However, research examining the congruence between aspects of the model with respect to athlete performance and satisfaction can best be summarized by the following quote:

. . . athletes are satisfied with leadership to the extent that the coach emphasizes (a) training and instruction that enhances the ability and co-ordinated effort by members, which in turn contributes to task accomplishment, and (b) positive feedback that recognizes good performance. (Chelladurai, 1993, p. 654)

Coaching Efficacy

Sport psychology practitioners now generally believe that confidence levels can be changed and improved over time. Thus, the experts would argue that star athletes, like Wayne Gretzky, Steve Nash, and Chantal Petitclerc, were not born with exceptionally higher levels of confidence than their competitors. The same analogy can be made with elite coaches. In fact, the topic of confidence has recently been applied to the coaching psychology literature, under the title of *coaching efficacy*. This term is defined as "the extent to which coaches believe they have the capacity to affect the learning and performance of their athletes" (Feltz, Chase, Moritz, & Sullivan, 1999, p. 765). The authors have identified four key dimensions at the core of their model: game strategy, motivation, technique, and character building.

- *Game Strategy*: This refers to the degree to which coaches believe they can effectively coach (i.e., devise strategies) during competitions.
- *Motivation*: This refers to the degree to which coaches believe they can effectively affect their athletes' psychological attributes.
- *Technique*: This refers to the degree to which coaches believe they can teach the effective skills and techniques of their sport and recognize talent.
- *Character Building*: This refers to the degree to which coaches believe they can instill a sense of respect or fair play in their athletes.

Those coaches who scored high on each of these four areas were said to have teams that performed better with higher winning percentages, were more committed to their profession, used more praise and encouragement, and had more satisfied athletes who had higher levels of confidence. Furthermore, a coach's level of efficacy was affected by four sources: previous experiences and preparation, previous level of success, perceived skill of the athletes, and the level of community support (see Figure 10.2). The most important of these sources was prior success; coaches who had experienced success as either coaches or athletes felt more confident, especially in devising strategy and motivating athletes.

Figure 10.2   Model of coaching efficacy

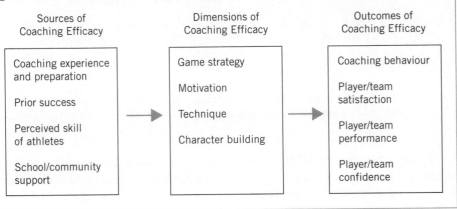

Sources of Coaching Efficacy	Dimensions of Coaching Efficacy	Outcomes of Coaching Efficacy
Coaching experience and preparation Prior success Perceived skill of athletes School/community support	Game strategy Motivation Technique Character building	Coaching behaviour Player/team satisfaction Player/team performance Player/team confidence

Note: From The Psychological Effect of Canada's National Coaching Education Program (Final Grant Report), *by P. J. Sullivan and D. L. Feltz, 2002, Ottawa: Social Sciences and Humanities Research Council of Canada. Reprinted with permission.*

Coaching Model

Côté, Salmela, Trudel, et al. (1995) created a coaching model (CM) that allows for connections to be established between the accumulated knowledge of how and why coaches perform as they do (Côté, 1998; see Figure 10.3). The CM infers that coaches begin their job by developing a mental model of the potential of their athletes or teams. This mental model is influenced by three peripheral components: coach's personal characteristics, athlete characteristics, and contextual factors. Coaches integrate these three peripheral components into their operational strategies to determine which of the three primary components—organization, training, and competition—must be used to maximize the development of the athlete and the team. The primary components of the CM are what distinguish it from other more specific models of coaching, including the MML. Moreover, the CM proposes that success includes more than a specific set of personality traits, organizational behaviours, or interpersonal skills of the coach. Overall, coaching success appears to be related to various interpersonal, cognitive, and operational aspects of leadership.

Research for the coaching model was carried out on expert individual-sport coaches (i.e., gymnastics coaches, Côté, Salmela, Trudel, et al., 1995). The components of the CM were supported in a single-case study of an elite university team-sport coach (i.e., hockey coach, Gilbert & Trudel, 2000). Finally, Moraes (1998) used the coaching model as a framework to study expert coaches of combat (martial art) sports. Given this information, it is not surprising that the CM has served as a theoretical framework for much research on expert Canadian coaching.

Figure 10.3 The coaching model (CM)

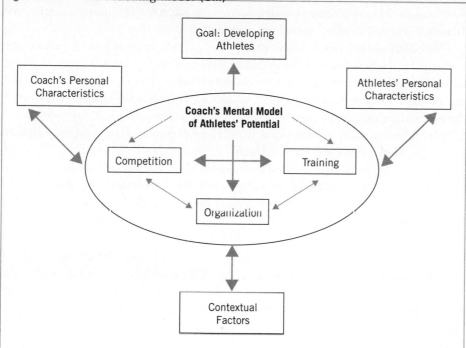

Note: From J. Côté, J.H. Salmela, P. Trudel, A. Baria and S.J. Russell, 1995, The coaching model: a grounded assessment of expert gymnastics coaches' knowledge, Journal of Sport & Exercise Psychology 17(1): 10, figure 1. © 1995 by Human Kinetics Publishers, Inc. Reprinted with permission from Human Kinetics (Champaign, IL).

OVERALL GOAL OF COACHING Too often, we read the horror stories of coaches who put winning above all else. For example, the coach of a novice hockey team who has a power play unit for the most skilled players or the youth softball coach who always bats the same two players at the bottom of the batting order. Although this winning-first philosophy may ultimately produce more victories, it certainly does not build the confidence and self-esteem levels of all the young players. In Canada, a body of research on successful university and Olympic coaches reveals that their main goal of coaching has a very positive, athlete-centred approach (e.g., Côté, Salmela, Trudel, et al., 1995; Gilbert & Trudel, 2000; Miller, Salmela, & Kerr, 2002; Vallée & Bloom, 2005). More specifically, although winning was important to these coaches, they were at least equally concerned with developing their athletes' personal and academic skills.

It is difficult to determine if this holistic approach to athlete development is specific to Canadian amateur sport, from which athletes rarely enter the professional setting (except perhaps for ice hockey). Two coaching books would suggest otherwise (Walton, 1992; Wooden, 1988). Gary Walton recounted the careers of six great coaches (five Americans) in a variety of sports: John Wooden, James "Doc" Counsilman, Woody Hayes, Vince Lombardi, Brutus Hamilton, and Percy Cerutty. Walton poignantly noted that although this group compiled extraordinary win-loss records and contributions to technical advances in their sports, they were more concerned about their contributions as educators and role models. In the same vein, John Wooden (1988) wrote, "I often told my players that, next to my own flesh and blood, they were the closest to me. They were my children. I got wrapped up in them, their lives, and their problems" (p. 62). Wooden's philosophy is even more impressive, considering the on-court success of his UCLA basketball teams: they set all-time records with 4 perfect 30-0 seasons, 88 consecutive victories, 38 straight NCAA tournament victories, and 10 national championships, including 7 in a row.

Wooden's secret to success undoubtedly lies in his *Pyramid of Success* (www.coach wooden.com), which explains the necessary steps to achieve success in basketball and in life. Wooden once explained that no building is better than its structural foundation and no man is better than his mental foundation. Two cornerstones at the bottom of the pyramid are industriousness and enthusiasm, which stress the value of each player's consistent hard work in games and practices. These two mental components are linked with team work principles, such as loyalty, friendship, and co-operation. Wooden's pyramid also highlights the value of establishing clear and realistic goals. As well, it shows that poise and confidence will be achieved only after hours of conditioning and drills in practice and a commitment to proper behaviour off the court. At the top of the pyramid is success, which is defined as knowing you did your best to become the best that you are capable of becoming. In other words, each block constitutes specific principles that must be in place in order to move up the pyramid. For example, a player cannot demonstrate poise and confidence at a high level until he or she masters the fundamental skills of the game, is morally and mentally stable, and achieves a high level of physical conditioning. In other words, the combination of sound preparation on the court and sound behaviour off the court directly influences a team's or athlete's level of self-confidence.

Pat Summitt, head coach of the University of Tennessee Lady Vols, is perhaps the most widely recognized women's head coach in North America. Besides being a co-captain of the 1976 silver-winning U.S. women's Olympic basketball team, Coach Summitt has won more national basketball championships than any other coach, man or woman, since John Wooden. Interestingly, she has attributed her coaching success to a change of coaching philosophy that involved adopting a more athlete-centred approach, about 10 years into her coaching career. She recounts:

Then, in 1987, we won our first title. And four more in the next ten years. What changed? For one thing, me. Over the years, I matured and learned from my experiences. I was forced out from behind my desk to deal with drugs, alcohol, injury, broken hearts, and emotional breakdowns of every other description. I was confronted by unwanted pregnancies, drinking problems, a player in a near-fatal car wreck, and countless instances of love gone wrong . . . I was learning that a coach is far more than a strategist or a disciplinarian. You are a peculiar form of crisis counselor and interim substitute parent. (Summitt & Jenkins, 1998, pp. 67–68)

Perhaps it can be concluded that all non-professional coaches in Canada should adopt an athlete-centred approach that includes their athletes' social, academic, and athletic pursuits. As well, an examination of both Pat Summitt's and John Wooden's philosophies clearly indicates that it is also possible for an elite amateur coach in the United States to follow a similar approach, even though media coverage and pressure to win are often greater than they are in Canada.

PRIMARY COMPONENTS OF THE COACH MODEL Organization   Côté, Salmela, Trudel, et al. (1995) stipulated that organization involves "applying one's knowledge towards establishing optimal conditions for training and competition by structuring and coordinating the tasks involved in reaching the goal" (p. 9). Desjardins (1996) alluded to the multitude of organizational tasks of team-sport coaches. These included the following seven tasks: creating a vision, establishing a seasonal plan, selecting a team, setting goals, developing team cohesion, working with support staff, and attending to administrative matters. By contrast, Côté and Salmela (1996) identified the following five organizational tasks for their group of expert gymnastics coaches: working with parents, working with assistants, helping gymnasts with personal concerns, planning training, and monitoring gymnasts' weight and aesthetics.

Whether in individual or team sports, organizational tasks are present before, during, and after the season and represent the foundation of the coaches' knowledge base. Moreover, a coach's ability to organize the season and to deal with organizational issues reveals much about his or her coaching and management skills. If a coach is organized, there will be a solid foundation from which to build a championship team. This should lead to more effective training sessions that in turn might improve the team's success at competitions (Bloom, 2002).

One of the fundamental elements of organization is creating and selling a coaching vision. Desjardins (1996) found that expert coaches began coaching their teams with a vision of where they could go and how they could get there. This vision involved both the long-term goal of program growth and development and the short-term goal of what the coach believed each athlete or the entire team could achieve in any given season. Desjardins stated that once the vision was established, the expert coaches transformed this vision into a **mission statement**, a tangible written statement that gave the team direction for the upcoming year. The mission statement then influenced the seasonal plan, daily practices, training regimens, team selection, and goal setting. Desjardins also mentioned that expert coaches drew up a complete plan for the upcoming season, taking into consideration the mental, physical, tactical, and technical aspects of training. In other words, a mission statement was not merely a target to aim for; it was the team's absolute reason for being.

<

Establishing optimal conditions for training and competition will help teams attain performance and personal goals

Photo courtesy of Stockbyte.

Further evidence about the need for a solid mission statement can be found in a Canadian study on expert basketball and volleyball university coaches (Vallée & Bloom, 2005). Interestingly, the participants in this study all took over losing programs, and in a short time, they turned the teams into perennial contenders with excellent reputations on and off the court. Although these authors also found that the primary goal of these coaches was the holistic development of their athletes, they found it was important for the coaches to possess strong organizational and interpersonal skills, including a vision for the team (highlighting personal growth and development). Early on in their appointments, coaches worked at changing past philosophies, setting higher standards and goals, and leading the team in a new direction. Coaches also emphasized the importance of athletes buying into the vision for the team to achieve success.

In sum, whether it is a high-school, university, or professional coach taking over a new team, it is important for the coach to create and articulate a clear vision. Besides the research presented in this section, comments from coaches like Phil Jackson (Chicago Bulls), Bill Belichik (New England Patriots), or Brent Sutter (Canadian National Junior Hockey Team) upon taking over their new coaching positions often alluded to a clearly thought out game plan. What is most impressive about these three coaches is that they were able to fulfill their visions in a short period.

> ## Reflections 10.4
> You are asked to develop a vision for a high-school basketball team. What would it be? What factors would you need to consider in developing this vision?

Training   Training encompasses the knowledge coaches utilize to maximize their athletes' ability to acquire and perform various skills during practice. Training has been found to include coaches' application of technical training, physical training, mental training, tactical training, and intervention style (Bloom, 2002; Côté, Salmela, Trudel et al., 1995; Durand-Bush, 1996).

Tharp and Gallimore (1976) performed a classic study on the technical skills of expert coaches by observing and analyzing coaching great John Wooden during basketball practice sessions over the course of one season. Results revealed that the majority of Wooden's cues were technical. He was focusing on the basic fundamentals of playing basketball, which in a recent reanalysis accounted for his apparent lack of positive praise (Gallimore & Tharp, 2004). This seemingly successful approach led to a new way of seeing coaching success. According to Tharp and Gallimore, Wooden was successful because of the quality of his teaching, interventions, and instructions. Additionally, research revealed that technical instructions were the most common form of instruction, and coaches stressed the importance of sound technical training to ensure their athletes were prepared for games and practices (Côté, Salmela, & Russell, 1995; Durand-Bush, 1996; Lacy & Darst, 1985).

Physical training focuses on the athletes' physical strength, endurance, and conditioning. With regard to physical training, expert coaches have commented on the uniqueness of each athlete and how they often created individualized training programs to meet their athletes' needs (Durand-Bush, 1996). Many of these coaches have utilized strength and conditioning specialists to work with their teams.

Over the years, there have been mixed messages, both anecdotally and empirically, about the use and importance of mental training by high-level coaches. Some elite coaches have given mental training less attention than physical and technical training (Durand-Bush, 1996). In contrast, some expert coaches have perceived mental training as an equally important component of training (Côté, Salmela, Trudel, et al., 1995; Wrisberg, 1990). These coaches felt it was beneficial to use a sport psychologist to work with their team on the more specific aspects of mental training, such as motivation, visualization, and controlling anxiety. As well, there are instances of Olympic and professional teams hiring sport psychologists. Thus, it appears that expert coaches are beginning to realize that in order to get the best out of their athletes, they must incorporate mental training, and perhaps the best way to do so is by utilizing the assistance of a sport psychologist.

Research has revealed that many expert coaches spend a large portion of practice time on tactical training—offensive and defensive strategies—as well as on creatively inventing drills to improve tactical difficulties (Bloom, Crumpton, & Anderson, 1999; Durand-Bush, 1996). According to Durand-Bush, elite coaches are knowledgeable about their sport and are able to adjust each practice to fit the current needs of their athletes.

Research has revealed that an authoritative intervention style was not present among top-level Canadian gymnastics coaches (Côté, Salmela, & Russell, 1995). However, two European studies present very different perspectives from that of Canadian coaches. For example, d'Arrippe-Longueville, Fournier, and Dubois (1998) reported that French judo coaches were not only authoritarian with their large number of World and Olympic champions, but they also used sarcasm and divisive training strategies to increase rivalry, and created hostility among players; however, this was associated with great international success. In another European study, Chantal, Guay, Dobreva-Martinova, and Vallerand (1996) found that elite Bulgarian athletes, while being self-determined, were not motivated by needs of inner fulfillment and ownership, but rather from external rewards and medals. Elsewhere, in Brazil, especially in soccer, the primary goal is winning; for coaches the consequence for losing is immediate dismissal (Salmela & Moraes, 2003). Thus, while more research is needed to reach any global conclusions, it appears that Canadian Olympic and university coaches use a different coaching style to some of their European and Brazilian counterparts. As well, there are likely differences based on the sport itself.

Competition   This primary component relates to coaching knowledge applied and tasks performed throughout the day of competition. Researchers have reported that elite coaches developed pre-match routines for both themselves and their athletes, mastered the contingencies they could control during a match (e.g., time-outs, rapport with officials), and dealt with emotions following the match to better deal with their athletes' performances (Bloom, 1996; Bloom, Durand-Bush, & Salmela, 1997; Côté, Salmela, Trudel et al., 1995). This section on competition will focus on team-sport coaches because of their active role on game day, compared with a more passive approach for individual and combat sport (martial art) coaches.

Pre-competition tasks involve coaches' activities leading up to their arrival on site. Research has indicated that these expert coaches are very meticulous in their plans for both themselves and their athletes on game day. With respect to themselves, coaches need time alone to mentally prepare and rehearse for their game. Often this occurred by taking a game-day jog. With respect to their athletes, coaches wanted them to have set routines so they were not wasting energy thinking about what to eat or how to get to the competition site. As well, coaches preferred that their athletes spend time together as a way of improving team cohesion.

An interesting finding from the research on expert Canadian coaches focused on the **pre-game pep talk** (Bloom, 1996; Bloom, Durand-Bush, & Salmela, 1997). Likely because of Hollywood's preoccupation with sensationalizing the pre-game talk (e.g., Knute Rockne's "win one for the Gipper" speech), many outsiders expect coaches to fire up the team prior to every competition. Nothing could be further from the truth, according to the expert Canadian coaches. These coaches preferred a calm, even-tempered pre-game pep talk. The coaches' final words were process-centred and reviewed three or four of the most important points stressed in the previous week's preparation.

Bloom's (1996) research revealed a number of important factors for expert team-sport coaches once competition began. Their coaching required attention to detail, an even-tempered demeanour, and an ability to out-think the opposing coach. This was accomplished in many ways: through strategically using time-outs and substitutions, relaying two or three important points of information during intermissions, developing productive relationships with officials, and providing athletes with appropriate playing time. The coaches' understanding of sport went beyond the basic textbook strategies. Some have compared expert team-sport coaches with grand chess masters because both have to think many steps ahead of the opposition. For example, while watching the game, these coaches put their players in the right position to maximize their strengths and minimize their opponents' strengths, and they regularly monitored their own behaviours, all with the goal of helping their team achieve success.

Post-competition activities of expert team-sport coaches dealt with four areas: how the coaches handled the outcome, how they coped with their own emotions, what they did and said in the locker room, and what was their post-game evaluation (Bloom et al., 1997). The content and focus of the post-competition meeting depended on both the outcome and the coaches' perceptions of whether the team played well or poorly. Most coaches gave their teams a few pointers, saving the in-depth analysis for the next practice or team meeting. Winning was the easiest outcome to handle. When the team played well and won, coaches emphasized effort and performance, not just outcome. When the team played poorly but won, coaches stressed areas needing improvement and acknowledged those individuals who gave a solid effort. The coaches did not want to spoil the thrill of victory, no matter how poorly they thought the team had played.

Losses were more demanding on the coaches. Most importantly, they had to decide if their players performed up to their capabilities. For example, when the team played well but lost, the expert team-sport coaches said it was important to remain encouraging, focusing on the positive aspects of their performance. However, when the team played poorly and lost, most of these coaches felt it was best to say little to their players because the emotional climate for themselves and their athletes was very high, and they worried about saying something they would later regret.

After any competition, the expert team-sport coaches also had to deal with their own emotions before entering the locker room. Many chose to take some time for themselves in order to "wind down." Most coaches said very little because they realized that both they and their athletes were still very emotional. They were especially aware that they should not single out any individual player. One reason for not analyzing the game in the locker room was that the coaches wanted to complete a thorough post-game evaluation, something that took place within 24 hours of the match. They wanted to consult a number of resources, such as videos, statistics, and assistant coaches, before finalizing their post-game evaluation. Regardless of the outcome, the coaches used every game as a learning experience to help prepare for future contests.

PERIPHERAL COMPONENTS OF THE COACHING MODEL   Coach's Personal Characteristics   Côté, Salmela, Trudel, et al. (1995) defined the coach's personal characteristics as "any variables that are part of the coach's philosophy, perceptions, beliefs, or personal life that could influence the organization, training, or competition components" (p. 11). A study specifically examining the characteristics of expert Canadian coaches was completed by Bloom and Salmela (2000). Their results included coaching preferences, goals, and beliefs. Among the results, it was found that expert coaches have an ongoing quest for personal growth and knowledge acquisition, display a strong work ethic, communicate effectively, empathize with players, and are good teachers. Many of these coaches noted that they work in a very competitive field and that the best way to succeed was by working harder than their colleagues. This involved spending long hours in their offices, which led to less time with their family and close friends. In fact, it also might explain why many expert Canadian coaches have been divorced (Salmela, 1996).

Bloom and Salmela (2000) also noted that a coach's personal characteristics greatly affected his or her ability to coach. They found that coaches who chose to regularly attend clinics or symposia, who shared information with other coaches, and who were willing to self-evaluate, likely devoted more time and energy to all other aspects of their profession. Thus, it could be hypothesized that their hard work and attention to detail resulted in more creative practices and perhaps better success at competition.

Interestingly, the expert coaches' personal characteristics mirrored those of high school teachers who help cultivate their students' talents (Csikszentmihalyi, Rathunde, & Whalen, 1993). Specifically, teachers who created the most ideal learning environments for their students shared three common characteristics. First, the teachers thoroughly enjoyed what they were doing and encouraged their students to excel beyond their current level of performance. Second, teachers created optimal learning conditions so that students were not bored or excessively frustrated, enabling them to maximize their level of concentration, self-esteem, potency, and involvement. Finally, the teachers showed reassuring kindness and genuine concern for the students' overall development, both inside and outside of school.

Reflections 10.5
What is your typical coaching style and philosophy?

Athletes' Personal Characteristics   Côté, Salmela, Trudel, et al. (1995) defined the athletes' personal characteristics as any variables relating to the athlete's stage of learning, personal abilities, and other personal characteristics that could affect the three primary components of the model. More specifically, it involved the coach's adjusting to the makeup of each athlete, whether this involved the athlete's personality, strengths, or weaknesses. The goal was to maximize their athletes' potential and output. Given the differences between coaching an individual athlete and a group of athletes, one would expect a number of differences to arise between coaches of individual sports and of team sports. Whereas individual-sport coaches can divert all of

their attention to one athlete all of the time, and thus create more personal decisions around a single athlete, team-sport coaches must be aware of how their interactions relate to the overall organization and effectiveness of the team.

Perhaps a good example of a coach being able to adapt to his athlete's idiosyncrasies was the legendary Phil Jackson; the athlete was Dennis "The Worm" Rodman. On the court, Rodman was a major rebounding presence throughout his career although he was suspended for assaulting referees, opponents, and even a photographer. However, his off-court behaviours were far more outlandish and possibly detrimental to the team. Some of Rodman's acts included posing nude, cross-dressing, dying his hair, and acquiring numerous body piercing and tattoos. Coach Phil Jackson obviously did not treat Rodman the same way he did his other notable stars, Michael Jordan and Scottie Pippen. Undoubtedly, his ability to adapt to Rodman, yet still put the team ahead of all else, may partially be attributed to the success of the Chicago Bulls during their NBA championship run in the 1990s.

Contextual Factors   Côté, Salmela, Trudel, et al. (1995) defined contextual factors as "unstable factors, aside from the athletes and the coach, such as working conditions, that need to be considered when intervening in the organization, training, and competition components" (p. 12). These could also be defined as situation-specific variables. Within the CM, the coaching context has been shown to be a determining factor that shapes all perceptions and behaviours. Available resources, pressures, and general lifestyles determine and affect coaches' views of their world. For example, a high-school team can gain a significant advantage over other schools if it receives more funding for equipment and training facilities than other schools.

Within team sports, Salmela (1996) listed a number of different contextual variables that could affect an elite Canadian coach's win-loss record and, hence, job security. These variables included the availability of athletic scholarships or funding (especially compared with the United States), the relationship between the coach and management, and the coaching salary. Some of these factors emerged in a recent study of the job satisfaction of elite male coaches at Canadian universities (Davies, Bloom, & Salmela, 2005). These coaches, who had all achieved a fair amount of success, noted that such factors as their relationship with their athletic director, recruiting challenges, lack of publicity, and low salary caused them some job dissatisfaction. However, these factors were more than compensated for by their passion for coaching and helping their athletes grow and mature both on- and off-court. As well, these coaches learned how to lead a balanced lifestyle that prioritized their family commitments.

Chapter Summary

Coaching science is one of the newest areas of sport psychology research. As such, there is a need for more empirical research at all levels of coaching, from the grassroots to the highest levels. The chapter presented information pertaining to the knowledge and leadership skills of coaches, as well as how to become a coach. A section specific to youth-sport coaching highlighted the characteristics and ideal behaviours of these coaches.

Canada has been a world leader in coach education and development through the NCCP's knowledge- and course-based program. The program teaches coaches theoretical, technical, and tactical elements of their sport. Nearly one million Canadians have passed through the certification program.

The chapter also summarizes research from a small group of Canadian researchers who reported various pathways to coaching taken by elite coaches. These pathways included (a) positive athletic experiences that fuelled a desire to be a coach, (b) leadership roles on teams (as captain), and (c) sharing of knowledge and strategies with coaches who recognized their cognitive and leadership abilities. For young coaches, this chapter points out the importance of mentoring and working with top professionals in their sport.

A larger section was devoted to expert coaches. One of the most important findings to emerge from research is that coaching is an *art* that requires years of hard work and practice; it also requires an ability to integrate and translate knowledge effectively to the specific sport environment. Moreover, many of Canada's top Olympic and university coaches were shown to possess an athlete-centred approach to coaching that indicated the primary goal of an elite Canadian coach was to develop the athlete, both as a person outside sport and as a participant inside sport.

Review Questions

1. Summarize the role of the NCCP in Canada.
2. How is mentoring important in the career progression of an elite coach?
3. An effective practice for coaching youth sport is to give encouragement after a mistake in a positive way. Provide a real-life game example to illustrate this recommendation.

4. List some effective practices for coaching youth sport.
5. Explain how coaching leadership is an interactional process.
6. What is meant by an athlete-centred approach to coaching?
7. What are the four key dimensions of coaching efficacy?
8. What can a coach do to improve the mental component of athlete development?

Suggested Reading

Lyle, J. (2002). *Sports coaching concepts: A framework for coaches' behaviour.* London: Routledge.

Smith, R. E., & Smoll, F. L. (2002). *Way to go coach!: A scientifically-proven approach to youth sports coaching effectiveness* (2nd ed.). Portola Valley, CA: Waroe.

Trudel, P., & Gilbert, W. D. (in press). Coaching and coach education. In D. Kirk, M. O'Sullivan, & D. McDonald (Eds.), *Handbook of physical education.* London: Sage.

References

Bloom, B. S. (1985). *Developing talent in young people.* New York: Ballantine.

Bloom, G. A. (1996). Competition: Preparing for and operating in competition. In J. H. Salmela (Ed.), *Great job coach! Getting the edge from proven winners* (pp. 138–179). Ottawa: Potentium.

Bloom, G. A. (2002). Coaching demands and responsibilities of expert coaches. In J. M. Silva III & D. E. Stevens (Eds.), *Psychological foundations of sport* (pp. 438–465). Boston: Allyn & Bacon.

Bloom, G. A., Crumpton, R., & Anderson, J. E. (1999). A systematic observation study of the teaching behaviors of an expert basketball coach. *The Sport Psychologist, 13,* 157–170.

Bloom, G. A., Durand-Bush, N., & Salmela, J. H. (1997). Pre- and postcompetition routines of expert coaches of team sports. *The Sport Psychologist, 11,* 127–141.

Bloom, G. A., Durand-Bush, N., Schinke, R. J., & Salmela, J. H. (1998). The importance of mentoring in the development of coaches and athletes. *International Journal of Sport Psychology, 29,* 267–281.

Bloom, G. A., & Salmela, J. H. (2000). Personal characteristics of expert team sport coaches. *Journal of Sport Pedagogy, 6,* 56–76.

Bloom, G. A., Salmela, J. H., & Schinke, R. J. (1995). Expert coaches' views on the training of developing coaches. In R. Vanfraechem-Raway & Y. Vanden Auweele (Eds.), *Proceedings of the ninth European congress on sport psychology* (pp. 401–408). Brussels, Belgium: Free University of Brussels.

Boudreault, J. P. (2003/04). Les couts de la sante ou les couts de l'activite physique. *Magazine Boutique Courir, 47.*

Chantal, Y., Guay, F., Dobreva-Martinova, T., & Vallerand, R. J. (1996). Motivation and elite performance: An exploratory investigation with Bulgarian athletes. *International Journal of Sport Psychology, 27,* 173–182.

Chelladurai, P. (1978). *A contingency model of leadership in athletics.* Unpublished doctoral dissertation, University of Waterloo, Waterloo, Ontario.

Chelladurai, P. (1993). Leadership. In R. N. Singer, M. Murphey, & L. K. Tennant (Eds.), *Handbook of research on sport psychology* (pp. 647–671). New York: Macmillan.

Chelladurai, P., & Riemer, H. A. (1998). Measurement of leadership in sport. In J. L. Duda (Ed.), *Advances in sport and exercise psychology measurement* (pp. 227–253). Morgantown, WV: Fitness Information Technology.

Chelladurai, P., & Saleh, S. D. (1980). Dimensions of leader behavior in sports: Development of a leadership scale. *Journal of Sport Psychology, 2*, 34–45.

Coaching Association of Canada (2005). *Results of the NCCP evaluation project: A blueprint for change.* Ottawa: Author.

Coakley, J. J. (1990). *Sport in society: Issues and controversies.* Toronto: Times Mirror/Mosby.

Côté, J. (1998). Coaching research and intervention: An introduction to the special issue. *Avante, 4,* 1–15.

Côté, J., & Salmela, J. H. (1996). The organizational tasks of high-performance gymnastic coaches. *The Sport Psychologist, 10,* 247–260.

Côté, J., Salmela, J. H., & Russell, S. J (1995). The knowledge of high-performance gymnastic coaches: Competition and training considerations. *The Sport Psychologist, 9,* 76–95.

Côté, J., Salmela, J. H., Trudel, P., Baria, A., & Russell, S. J. (1995). The coaching model: A grounded assessment of expert gymnastic coaches' knowledge. *Journal of Sport & Exercise Psychology, 17,* 1–17.

Cragg, S., Cameron, C., Craig, C. L., & Russell, S. J. (1999). *Canada's children and youth: A physical activity profile.* Ottawa: Canada Fitness and Lifestyle Research Institute.

Csikszentmihalyi, M., Rathunde, K., & Whalen, S. (1993). *Talented teenagers: The roots of success and failure.* New York: Cambridge.

d'Arripe-Longueville, F., Fournier, J. F., & Dubois, A. (1998). The perceived effectiveness of interactions between expert French judo coaches and their athletes. *The Sport Psychologist, 12,* 317–332.

Davies, M. J., Bloom, G. A., & Salmela, J. H. (2005). Job satisfaction of accomplished male university basketball coaches: The Canadian context. *International Journal of Sport Psychology, 36,* 173–192.

Desjardins, G. Jr. (1996). The mission. In J. H. Salmela (Ed.), *Great job coach! Getting the edge from proven winners* (pp. 1–35). Ottawa, ON: Potentium.

Douge, B., & Hastie, P. (1993). Coach effectiveness. *Sport Science Review, 2,* 14–29.

Dupuis, M., Bloom, G. A., & Loughead, T. M. (in press). Team captains' perceptions of athlete leadership. *Journal of Sport Behavior.*

Durand-Bush, N. (1996). Training: Blood, sweat, and tears. In J. H. Salmela (Ed.), *Great job coach! Getting the edge from proven winners* (pp. 103–139). Ottawa: Potentium.

Feltz, D. L., Chase, M. A., Moritz, S. E., Sullivan, P. J. (1999). A conceptual model of coaching efficacy: Preliminary investigation and instrument development. *Journal of Educational Psychology, 91,* 765–776.

Gallimore, R., & Tharp, R. (2004). What a coach can teach a teacher, 1975–2004: Reflections and reanalysis of John Wooden's teaching practices. *The Sport Psychologist, 18,* 119–137.

Gilbert, W., & Trudel, P. (2004). Analysis of coaching science research published from 1970–2001. *Research Quarterly for Exercise and Sport, 75,* 388–399.

Gilbert, W. D., & Trudel, P. (2000). Validation of the coaching model (CM) in a team sport context. *International Sports Journal, 4,* 120–128.

Gould, D., Giannini, J., Krane, V., & Hodge, K. (1990). Educational needs of elite U.S. national team, Pan American, and Olympic coaches. *Journal of Teaching in Physical Education, 9,* 332–344.

Gould, D., Hodge, K., Peterson, K., & Petlichkoff, L. (1987). Psychological foundations of coaching: Similarities and differences among intercollegiate wrestling coaches. *The Sport Psychologist, 1,* 293–308.

Jones, R. L., Armour, K. M., & Potrac, P. (2003). Constructing expert knowledge: A case study of a top-level professional soccer coach. *Sport, Education and Society, 8,* 213–229.

Katzmarzyk, P.T., Glendhill, N., Shephard, R. (2000). The economic burden of physical inactivity. *Canadian Medical Association Journal, 163,* 1435–1440.

Klenke, K. (1993). Meta-analytic studies of leadership: Added insights or added paradoxes? *Current Psychology: Developmental, Learning, Personality, Social, 12,* 326–343.

Lacy, A. C., & Darst, P. W. (1985). Systematic observation of behaviours of winning highschool head football coaches. *Journal of Teaching in Physical Education, 4,* 256–270.

Martens, R. (2004). *Successful coaching* (3rd ed.). Champaign, IL: Human Kinetics.

Miller, P. S. (1996). In the beginning. In J. H. Salmela (Ed.), *Great job coach! Getting the edge from proven winners* (pp. 69–100). Ottawa: Potentium.

Miller, P. S., Bloom, G. A., & Salmela, J. H. (1996). The roots of success: From athletic leaders to expert coaches. *Coaches Report, 2,* 18–20.

Miller, P. S., Salmela, J. H., & Kerr, G. (2002). Coaches perceived role in mentoring athletes. *International Journal of Sport Psychology, 33,* 410–430.

Moraes, L. C. C. D. A. (1998). *Influence in the development of beliefs of Canadian expert judo coaches and their impact on action.* Unpublished doctoral dissertation, University of Ottawa, Ontario.

Northouse, P. G. (2001). *Leadership: Theory and practice* (2nd ed.). Thousand Oaks, CA: Sage.

Riemer, H. A., & Chelladurai, P. (1995). Leadership and satisfaction in athletics. *Journal of Sport & Exercise Psychology, 17,* 276–293.

Salmela, J. H. (Ed.). (1996). *Great job coach! Getting the edge from proven winners.* Ottawa: Potentium.

Salmela, J. H., & Moraes, L. C. (2003). Development of expertise: The role of coaching, families and cultural contexts. In J. L. Starkes & K. A. Ericsson (Eds.), *Expert performance in sports: Advances in research on sport expertise* (pp. 275–296). Champaign, IL: Human Kinetics.

Schinke, R. J., Bloom, G. A., & Salmela, J. H. (1995). The career stages of elite Canadian basketball coaches. *Avante, 1,* 48–62.

Smith, R. E., & Smoll, F. L. (2002a). Youth sport as a behavioral setting for psychosocial interventions. In J. L. Van Raalte & B. W. Brewers (Eds.), *Exploring sport and exercise psychology* (pp. 341–371). Washington, DC: American Psychological Association.

Smith, R. E., & Smoll, F. L. (2002b). *Way to go coach!: A scientifically-proven approach to youth sports coaching effectiveness* (2nd ed.). Portola Valley, CA: Waroe.

Smith, R. E., Smoll, F. L., & Hunt, E. (1977). A system for the behavioral assessment of athletic coaches. *Research Quarterly, 48,* 401–407.

Smoll, F. L., & Smith, R. E. (2002). *Children and youth in sport* (2nd ed.). Dubuque, IA: Kendall/Hunt.

Sullivan, P.J, & Feltz, D.L. (2002). *The psychological effect of Canada's national coaching education program* (Final Grant Report). Ottawa: Social Sciences and Humanities Research Council of Canada.

Summitt, P., & Jenkins, S. (1998). *Raise the roof.* New York: Broadway.

Tharp, R. G., & Gallimore, R. (1976). What a coach can teach a teacher. *Psychology Today, 9,* 75–78.

Trudel, P., & Gilbert, W. D. (in press). Coaching and coach education. In D. Kirk, M. O'Sullivan, & D. McDonald (Eds.), *Handbook of physical education.* London: Sage.

Vallée, C. N., & Bloom, G. A. (2005). Building a successful university sport program: Key and common elements of expert coaches. *Journal of Applied Sport Psychology, 17,* 179–196.

Walton, G. M. (1992). *Beyond winning: The timeless wisdom of great philosopher coaches.* Champaign, IL: Human Kinetics.

Wooden, J. (1988). *They call me coach.* Chicago, IL: Contemporary Books.

Wrisberg, C. A. (1990). An interview with Pat Head Summitt. *The Sport Psychologist, 4,* 181–191.

Zhang, J., Jensen, B. E., & Mann, B. L. (1997). Modification and revision of the Leadership Scale for Sport. *Journal of Sport Behavior, 20,* 105–122.

Jean Côté
Jessica Fraser-Thomas

CHAPTER 11

Youth Involvement in Sport

Chapter Objectives

After reading this chapter, you should be able to do the following:

1. Define the objectives of youth sport.
2. Describe the positive and negative outcomes that can result from youth-sport participation.
3. Understand the principles of positive youth development as applied to youth sport.
4. Discuss youth-sport programs and the types of activities likely to lead to positive sport experiences.
5. Discuss how coaches and parents can influence positive youth-sport participation.
6. Understand the major theoretical frameworks of youth-sport motivation and development.

* Support for the writing of this chapter was given by doctoral and standard research grants from the Social Sciences and Humanities Research Council of Canada (SSHRC Grants # 752-2003-1319 and # 410-05-1949). The authors are grateful to Kristin Côté, Dany MacDonald, and Leisha Strachan for their helpful comments in the preparation of this chapter.

From ages 7 to 12, Sebastian and Olivia were neighbours and played on the same local hockey team. In the summer, they played soccer and tennis. They also liked swimming and playing pickup basketball and street hockey in their free time. Their soccer coach, Nick, was a physical education teacher and had many years of experience coaching youth sport. As a coach, Nick taught sport skills sequentially and logically, providing informative, positive, and constructive feedback to his players. Nick believed that sports offered children opportunities to learn important life skills, such as co-operation, responsibility, empathy, respect, and self-control. Accordingly, he used time during practices and games to deliberately teach and discuss these life skills with his players. Nick's teams were never the best in the league; however, Nick's goal was to make sure that all his players loved the game and felt good about their sport participation. At age 30, Sebastian and Olivia attribute many of their current successes to the values they learned through their youth-sport participation. Sebastian is now an award-winning teacher and a recreational tennis player. Olivia obtained a graduate degree in kinesiology, played university hockey, and is now a member of the women's national hockey team.

Two other children, Madelyn and Rachel, had very different experiences from each other in youth sports. They played hockey year round from ages 5 to 12. They were highly involved as early as age 5 in extra hockey training, such as power skating lessons and hockey schools. At age 13, Madelyn dropped out of hockey and did not get involved in any other sports. Now, at age 30, she has a successful career but is not regularly involved in any type of physical activity. She does not have particularly positive memories of her youth-sport experiences. Rachel, on the other hand, also 30, is now playing on a line with Olivia on the women's national hockey team. Rachel's life has always revolved around hockey, and she has not yet had a chance to think about what she will do when she retires from hockey.

The final example is Michael; he never had the opportunity to participate in youth sport or other extracurricular activities, such as music or art. He spent much of his youth in unstructured leisure activities, such as watching television or hanging out with friends. At age 30, he has a sedentary lifestyle, is overweight, and is struggling to find a meaningful career.

The above scenarios describe a number of different youth-sport experiences and outcomes. Sebastian and Olivia were fortunate to experience various sports during their childhood. They had coaches who taught them skills while being caring and understanding. For Sebastian, his youth-sport experiences did not lead to elite performance; however, his positive sport experiences helped him to understand the value of regular physical activity and health and gave him assets that helped his personal and professional development. Madelyn and Rachel were intensely involved in one sport from ages 5 to 12 and accordingly developed high-level skills. Rachel persisted with her training and eventually was selected for the national team; on the other hand, Madelyn showed signs of burnout and completely dropped out of hockey and other sports at age 13. Madelyn's intense training at a young age reduced her enjoyment of hockey and eventually led her to an inactive lifestyle. Unfortunately, Michael did not have opportunities to get involved in sports or other extracurricular activities. Spending less time in constructive leisure activities, such as sports, may have limited the number of developmental assets that Michael acquired as a child, which in turn may have led him to a more apathetic lifestyle.

The above scenarios illustrate explicit experiences and outcomes of youth sports that are not always evident. Nevertheless, the scenarios provide examples that raise a number of questions about youth-sport participation. What is the goal of youth sport? What are the best contexts and training patterns for youth-sport participation? How should contexts and training patterns change according to children's age and development? In this chapter we will provide answers to these and other questions related to youth-sport participation.

Some Common Myths about Youth Involvement in Sport

MYTH: *Involvement in youth sport builds character.*

Character building through sport is not automatic. Sport programs have to be specifically designed to foster positive development in youth. Positive outcomes depend on children's personal experiences, which are heavily influenced by the sport program activities and the coaches and parents who coordinate these activities.

MYTH: *Involvement in sport leads to negative outcomes, such as violence and aggression.*

Studies indicate some associations between sport and negative outcomes; however, well-designed programs aimed at promoting positive youth development, coupled with appropriate adult support, are less likely to lead to negative outcomes.

MYTH: *To become elite athletes, children must specialize in their sport by age six or seven.*

There is evidence that early specialization and sport-specific training are effective in producing elite performers; however, evidence also exists that suggests early involvement in a variety of sporting activities can also lead to elite performance in most sports. Current research suggests that there are many physical, psychological, and social benefits to early diversification while there are many costs associated with early specialization. For this reason, it appears that in most sports, early diversification is a healthier path to elite performance.

MYTH: *Parents should limit their involvement in their children's sport.*

Parents are an important source of various forms of support for their children. In addition, parents can influence their children's involvement through their behaviours and expectations. Sport programs must make a greater effort to proactively involve parents in their children's sport development. Parents should be informed about how their sport-related behaviours and beliefs influence their children's behaviours and beliefs.

MYTH: *Youth-sport coaches should be specialists in the sport that they are coaching.*

Past research indicates that coaches play a key role in children's competence beliefs, sport enjoyment, motivation for sport participation, and reasons for sport withdrawal. These responsibilities are as important as teaching sport skills. Thus, coaches play a critical role in children's sport involvement, and they must be trained to understand children's physical, cognitive, social, and psychological development.

Introduction

Almost 2.2 million Canadian children ages 5 to 14 (54%) participate in some kind of organized sport (Corbeil, 2000). The significance of sport involvement for youth is considerable, given that most children typically begin their involvement in organized sport when they are in their formative years (De Knop, Engström, & Skirstad, 1996; Smith & Smoll, 1990). The significance of sport as an integral avenue for youth development has been formally recognized as an important global issue. In 1999, the United Nations Educational, Scientific, and Cultural Organization (UNESCO) organized the third International Conference for Ministers and Senior Officials Responsible for Sport and Physical Education (MINEPS III). At the conference, a declaration was made to start a global movement toward youth sport and physical education participation. This declaration supports the significance of sport in the life of youth by acknowledging that sport is an essential and integral part of education and of individual and social development (United Nations Educational, Scientific, and Cultural Organization, 1999). Following this, the European Union proclaimed 2004 as the European Year of Education Through Sport. Furthermore, on November 3, 2003, the United Nations General Assembly adopted a resolution proclaiming 2005 as the International Year for Sport and Physical Education, as a means to promote education, health, development, and peace.

These organizations' recognition of the health and developmental benefits of youth sport comes at a critical time, as cultures around the world are experiencing the institutionalization of youth sports (De Knop et al., 1996). Socio-economic status and environmental factors are becoming greater barriers to youth-sport opportunities, given that programs are becoming increasingly expensive, competitive, and elitist. In this chapter, we highlight how sport must continue to be embraced and promoted as an activity that provides children with a chance to experience enjoyment and acquire positive outcomes, such as enhanced physical and mental health, challenge, social interaction, skill enhancement, and physical development.

Objectives of Youth Sports

Youth sport has the potential to accomplish three important objectives in children's development. First, sport programs provide youth with opportunities to be physically active, which can lead to improved *physical health*. Second, youth-sport programs have long been considered important to youth's *psychosocial development*, providing opportunities to learn important life skills, such as co-operation, discipline, leadership, and self-control. Third, youth-sport programs are critical for the learning of *motor skills*; these motor skills serve as a foundation for future national sport stars and recreational adult-sport participants.

These three objectives may appear to conflict; however, it is important that youth-sport programs focus on all three objectives, rather than focus on one or two at the cost of the other(s). For example, a youth-sport program that focuses solely on the learning of sport skills at the cost of children's physical health and psychosocial development would be inefficient. Similarly, a sole focus on children's physical health at the cost of developing fundamental sport skills and children's psychosocial assets would limit the potential influence of sport on children's overall development. Instead, youth-sport programs that focus on fun, skill development, and maximum participation encourage people to stay involved and achieve success at all developmental stages of life and at all levels of sport. To promote a culture of sport participation and performance, the roles of physical education, school sports, recreational sports, and performance sports should all be linked because the independent development of these programs is expensive and ineffective. Thus, by focusing on the common building blocks that all young people need, we can reduce costs and increase the benefits associated with sport participation.

Clearly, youth-sport programs have the potential to contribute to positive youth outcomes, but these positive outcomes do not occur automatically through youth-sport involvement. In the next section we will briefly review the positive and negative

physical, psychological, emotional, and social outcomes that have been associated with youth-sport participation. The rest of this chapter will focus on developmental activities and contexts of sport programs that are likely to lead to improved health, psychosocial development, and the learning of motor skills among youth.

Outcomes Associated with Youth-sport Participation

For the most part, we hear of the positive outcomes associated with youth-sport involvement: health benefits, increased self-esteem, friendships, discipline, teamwork, and competence. However, more and more frequently, we are hearing of less positive youth-sport experiences: insensitive coaches, pressure from parents, peer victimization, aggression, and decreased self-esteem. Although no studies have empirically shown a cause-effect relationship between youth-sport participation and developmental outcomes (due to methodological and ethical difficulties), Table 11.1 outlines the positive and negative outcomes associated with youth sport, based on research in the areas of physical health, psychological development, and social development (see Fraser-Thomas, Côté, & Deakin, 2005, for a review).

As Table 11.1 shows, sport involvement can contribute to physical health and positive psychological and social development; however, there is also evidence of less desirable relationships between sport participation and youth development. A key to understanding whether youth-sport programs foster positive outcomes is to first identify the processes that occur within them. Youth-sport programs provide a platform for positive youth development, and if structured appropriately, they can have direct effects on youth's present and future development and productivity. There is a growing body of literature in developmental psychology recognizing the importance of sports as pro-social activities that can contribute to youth's positive life trajectories and more civil societies (Eccles & Barber, 1999; Larson, 2000). Before discussing sport-specific contexts that are likely to lead to positive outcomes in youth, we will discuss major principles of positive youth development that could potentially be helpful in promoting the health, psychosocial development, and learning of motor skills in youth.

Table 11.1   Positive and Negative Outcomes of Youth Sport

	Positive Outcomes	Negative Outcomes
Physical Health	• Cardiovascular fitness • Weight control • Muscular strength/endurance • Adult physical activity • Decreased risk of adult heart disease • Decreased risk of diabetes • Decreased risk of osteoporosis • Decreased risk of cancer	• Overuse injuries • Eating disorders
Psychological Development	• Fun and enjoyable experiences • Challenging experiences • Increased self-esteem • Decreased stress • Increased life satisfaction • Increased happiness	• Decreased self-perceptions • Decreased confidence/self-esteem • Isolation from teammates • Excessive pressure • Burnout
Social Development	• Positive inter-group and • Peer relationships • Citizenship • Social status and success • Social mobility • Leadership skills • Increased academic performance • Enhanced adult career achievement • Decreased school dropout • Decreased delinquent behaviour	• Aggression • Assault • Poor sportsmanship • Decreased moral reasoning

Reflections 11.2

Many sport programs aim to promote positive youth development (see websites below). Examine the websites of these organizations and programs. What are the goals and values of these organizations? What kinds of environments do these programs aim to create?

www.ottawalions.com (Ottawa Lions Track and Field Club)
www.ymca.ca/eng_homepage.htm (YMCA Canada)
www.bwha.ca/ (Barrie Women's Hockey Association)
www.hcusoccer.ca/ (Halifax United Soccer Club)
www.stampedecitygym.com (Stampede City Gymnastics Club)
www.calkingston.on.ca (Church Athletic League of Kingston)
www.truesportpur.ca (True Sport Pur)

Principles of Positive Youth Development

Developmental Assets

Benson (1997) has outlined 40 **developmental assets,** commonly termed the "building blocks" for human development (see Table 11.2). The development of these assets in youth embodies a broad vision of communities and youth interacting in positive and effective manners. The assets fall into two broad categories: external and internal assets. Within each of these two broad categories, four types of assets exist. **External assets** comprise support, empowerment, boundaries and expectations, and constructive

Table 11.2 Forty Developmental Assets

External Assets (1–20)	Support (1–6)	1. Family support
		2. Positive family communication
		3. Other adult relationships
		4. Caring neighbourhood
		5. Caring school climate
		6. Parent involvement in schooling
	Empowerment (7–10)	7. Community values youth
		8. Youth as resources
		9. Service to others
		10. Safety
	Boundaries & Expectations (11–16)	11. Family boundaries
		12. School boundaries
		13. Neighbourhood boundaries
		14. Adult role models
		15. Positive peer influence
		16. High expectations
	Constructive Use of Time (17–20)	17. Creative activities
		18. Youth programs
		19. Religious community
		20. Time at home
Internal Assets (21-40)	Commitment to Learning (21–25)	21. Achievement motivation
		22. School engagement
		23. Homework
		24. Bonding to school
		25. Reading for pleasure
	Positive Values (26–31)	26. Caring
		27. Equality and social justice
		28. Integrity
		29. Honesty
		30. Responsibility
		31. Restraint
	Social Competencies (32–36)	32. Planning and decision making
		33. Interpersonal competence
		34. Cultural competence
		35. Resistance skills
		36. Peaceful conflict resolution
	Positive Identity (37–40)	37. Personal power
		38. Self-esteem
		39. Sense of purpose
		40. Positive view of personal future

Note: Adapted from All Kids Are Our Kids: What Communities Must Do to Raise Caring and Responsible Children and Adolescents, *by P. L. Benson, 1997, San Francisco: Jossey-Bass. Adapted with permission.*

use of time. **Internal assets** comprise commitment to learning, positive values, social competencies, and positive identity. Benson and others (Benson, 1997; Scales & Leffert, 1999) found that the more developmental assets an adolescent possesses, the greater his or her likelihood of developing in a positive and healthy manner. Specifically, the more assets an adolescent possesses, the more likely that she or he will "thrive" (show leadership, volunteer, get good grades, etc.) and the less likely that she or he will use alcohol or be depressed, suicidal, or violent.

Programs fostering Benson's 40 developmental assets have been found to lead to positive youth development. Sport programs cannot be expected to foster all 40 assets; however, we believe that sport programs have the potential to contribute to many of them. For example, involvement in sport programs can foster external assets in the areas of constructive use of time, emotional support from family, empowerment, positive social relationships, and high expectations. Past research also indicates that youth-sport programs have the potential to foster numerous internal assets, such as achievement motivation, school engagement, caring, responsibility, social competencies, conflict resolution skills, and a sense of positive identity (Benson, 1997; Scales & Leffert, 1999).

Desirable Youth-sport Program Settings

The National Research Council and Institute of Medicine (NRCIM, 2002) outlined eight features of settings that are most likely to foster positive assets in youth. All these features should be considered by policy makers, sport organizations, parents, and coaches when they are designing and implementing youth-sport programs. These eight features are shown in Table 11.3.

First, the NRCIM suggests that physical and psychological safety and security are essential to any setting aimed at promoting positive youth development. Although a child's physical safety is often a concern in sport settings, children's psychological and emotional sense of security must not be overlooked. If programs are implemented inappropriately, sport environments can often be intimidating or even frightening to youth. Second, settings must provide clear and consistent (age-appropriate) structure and appropriate adult supervision. All too often in youth-sport settings, coaches are

Table 11.3   Features of Positive Development Settings

1. Physical and psychological safety

2. Appropriate structure

3. Supportive relationships

4. Opportunities to belong

5. Positive social norms

6. Support for efficacy and mattering

7. Opportunities for skill building

8. Integration of family, school, and community efforts

Note: Adapted from Community Programs to Promote Youth Development, by the National Research Council and Institute of Medicine, 2002, Washington, DC: National Academy Press.

volunteers with insufficient knowledge of youths' developmental capabilities. The third and fourth setting features are supportive adult relationships (with parents and coaches) and opportunities to belong. Again, these relationships and opportunities must be worked toward, rather than assumed to occur.

The fifth setting feature, positive social norms, is usually assumed to be facilitated by youth-sport programs; however, much research continues to indicate that many programs promote exaggerated masculinity, aggression, and competitiveness (Eder & Parker, 1987). For the sixth feature, the NRCIM suggests that settings support youths' efficacy and sense of mattering. More specifically, youth-sport programs must be child-centred, and promote empowerment, autonomy, and opportunities to experience challenge. The seventh setting feature concerns skill-building opportunities, which are often provided in sport but occur only through developmentally appropriate program designs and coaching. Finally, programs that integrate family, school, and community create optimal environments for positive youth development because this integration creates opportunities for meaningful communication between different settings in youths' lives.

Fostering Initiative through Constructive Activities

Sport researchers have also taken an interest in the type of activities that lead to positive youth development. Children's activities have been classified into two categories: relaxed leisure activities and constructive leisure activities. **Relaxed leisure activities** (e.g., watching television, hanging out) are activities that are enjoyable but not demanding in terms of effort. **Constructive leisure activities** (e.g., sport, music, art) can also be enjoyable but require sustained effort toward the achievement of a clear goal. Larson (2000) argues that constructive leisure activities, rather than relaxed leisure activities, foster initiative development in children. He suggests that **initiative** is a core quality of positive physical, psychological, and social development in children, and that activities promoting initiative development must have three essential elements. First, they must be intrinsically motivating. Second, they must involve concerted attention toward specific goals. Third, they must occur over an extended period of time (i.e., regular involvement). Larson argues that constructive leisure activities provide these three elements and thus foster initiative.

When reviewing how youths spend their time around the world, Larson and Verma (1999) found sport participation to be the most popular constructive leisure activity for youth in North America and Europe. In addition, Larson and Kleiber (1993) reported that youths devote more attention to sports and games than to other daily life activities, such as schoolwork or watching television. These findings suggest that for many youths, sport may be more important than any other daily activity in contributing to positive development and the growth of critical adult skills, such as initiative and the capacity for autonomous action. Unfortunately, however, not all sport programs create enjoyable (intrinsically motivating) and challenging (effortful) environments that are able to sustain youth's engagement over time.

Five C's of Positive Youth Development

A final framework of positive youth development is reflected in Lerner, Fisher, and Weinberg's (2000) five desired outcomes of youth development or five C's of positive youth development: competence, character, connection, confidence, and caring (or compassion). Lerner et al.'s Model of National Youth Policy suggests that policies must be developed to allow families and programs to foster and promote positive development. If this occurs, youths will demonstrate the five C's of positive youth development. Collectively, these processes will lead to a sixth C of positive youth development: contribution. As healthy youths become adults, they will choose to contribute, or give back, to society. In doing so, they will be promoting the positive development of the next generation of youths.

Reflections 11.3

Take a moment and look at major periods in your development in sport. Think of your participation in sport from early childhood until now. Assess the different sport programs you were involved in, in terms of how they promoted the 40 developmental assets, integrated the 8 features of positive development settings, fostered initiative development, and fostered the 5 C's of positive youth development.

Photo courtesy of Stockbyte.

Considerations for Youth-sport Programs

The recent work of researchers in positive youth development constitutes a solid foundation on which youth-sport programs can be based. Developmental assets, setting features, and the five C's of positive youth development should be considered when sport programs are being constructed, in order to support the development of youths' health, psychosocial attributes, and motor skills. Although it can be assumed that most youth-sport programs intend to foster positive youth development, the research behind Table 11.1 indicates that many programs may be failing. This raises the challenging question: how do sport organizations, coaches, and parents ensure the concerted benefits of improved health, psychosocial development, and the learning of sport skills through sport participation? To do this most effectively, it is important first to examine the primary factors contributing to positive and negative experiences in youth sports, as identified in the literature: program activities and adult influences.

Youth-sport Program Activities

When coaches develop activities for youth practices and when sport organizations design youth-sport programs, they must consider the three objectives of youth sport. In particular, coaches and programmers must consider the differing implications of deliberate play, deliberate practice, and early specialization.

DELIBERATE PLAY, DELIBERATE PRACTICE, AND EARLY SPECIALIZATION
A common trend among adults involved in regular sport and physical activity is that they were involved in a broad range of organized sports and deliberate play activities during their youth. Côté and colleagues (Côté & Hay, 2002; Côté, Baker, & Abernethy, 2003) define **deliberate play** activities in sport as those designed to

maximize inherent enjoyment. These activities are regulated by flexible rules adapted from standardized sport rules and are set up and monitored by the children or by an involved adult. Children typically modify rules to find a point where their game most resembles the actual sport but still allows for play at their level. For example, children may change soccer and basketball rules to suit their environment and their needs (e.g., playing in the street, on a playing field, or in someone's backyard). When involved in deliberate play activities, children are less concerned with the outcome of their behaviour than with the behaviour per se. On the other hand, Ericsson, Krampe, and Tesch-Römer (1993) suggest that the most effective learning occurs through involvement in highly structured activities defined as **deliberate practice**. Deliberate practice activities require effort, generate no immediate rewards, and are motivated by the goal of improving performance rather than the goal of enjoyment. **Early specialization** is often characterized by high amounts of deliberate practice and low amounts of deliberate play. Early specialization is defined as limiting participation to one sport that is practised on a year-round basis.

The two concepts of deliberate play and deliberate practice could be placed at opposite ends of a continuum. Behaviours could be located along the continuum, from those that are primarily motivated by a process-experimentation perspective (deliberate play) to those that are motivated by a goal-directed perspective (deliberate practice). When individuals are involved in deliberate play, they experiment with new or different combinations of behaviours, but not necessarily in the most effective way to improve performance.

In contrast, when individuals are involved in deliberate practice, they exhibit behaviour focused on improving performance by the most effective means available. For example, the backhand skill in tennis could be learned and improved over time by playing matches or by creating fun practice situations. However, players could more

>

Early specialization is one of the most controversial areas in youth sport. Many parents believe that early specialization will enhance their child's prospects for later elite performance.
Photograph courtesy of Peter Crocker.

effectively improve their backhand performance by practising drills that might be considered less enjoyable. Although the drills used in deliberate practice might not be the most enjoyable, they might be the most relevant to improving performance. When one is considering the optimal amount of deliberate play, deliberate practice, and involvement in other sports that children should have in their early years, one has to consider the three objectives of youth sport: health, psychosocial development, and the learning of motor skills.

Reflections 11.4

How do the three objectives of youth sport influence the optimal amount of deliberate practice and deliberate play?

EARLY SPECIALIZATION AND DELIBERATE PRACTICE CONSIDERATIONS   From a health perspective, an overemphasis on deliberate practice at a young age and early specialization can lead to overtraining, muscle overuse, injury, and athletes' failure to develop transferable skills (Hollander, Meyers, & LeUnes, 1995). Early specialization often has harmful effects on emotional and psychological development. For example, early specialization can lead to decreased enjoyment and burnout in youth sports (Boyd & Yin, 1996; Seppa, 1996). Specialization can also lead to disappointment and discouragement in youth, as they may experience a sense of failure if they are unable to meet their goals after investing so heavily (Hill, 1988). Early specialization is also a concern for youth's social development because it can lead to missed social opportunities experienced through early diversification (Wright & Côté, 2003).

From a skill acquisition perspective, there is evidence that early specialization and an increased focus on deliberate practice activities during the early years can be effective in producing elite performers (Law, Côté, & Ericsson, in press); however, as outlined above, there are many costs associated with this pattern of activities. It appears that deliberate play and involvement in various sporting activities may serve as a more cost effective way for youth to explore their physical capacities in various contexts and to develop their sport skills. Analyses of elite athletes' early involvement in sports show that deliberate play activities and early diversification in sport activities are important during the first few years of sport participation. For example, Soberlak and Côté (2003) showed that elite ice hockey players spent slightly more time in deliberate play activities than deliberate practice activities before age 20. Although much research suggests that involvement in deliberate practice is a consistent factor that differentiates elite from non-elite athletes (e.g., Helsen, Starkes, & Hodges, 1998), the difference of time invested in deliberate practice activities generally occurs during the adolescent and adult years. Baker and Côté (2006) suggest that reducing the acquisition of sport skills to a single dimension (i.e., deliberate practice) fails to acknowledge important developmental, motivational, and psychosocial aspects of human abilities. However, the peak age in some sports, such as female gymnastics and figure skating, tends to be quite young. Athletes in these sports are sometimes required to specialize early in order to reach the highest levels. In these sports, extreme caution should be used. Training programs must always consider children's physical, psychological, social, and cognitive development.

Overall, early specialization and too much emphasis on deliberate practice activities during the early years of sport involvement may lead to health problems or withdrawal. Instead, an emphasis on various sport activities and deliberate play activities during childhood is likely to have immediate developmental and long-term health benefits. Some of the benefits and costs of early specialization are outlined in Table 11.4.

Many youth-sport programs are inherently designed to eventually expect specialization as athletes age and mature. Although this is a path that many young athletes choose to follow, it is not a route for all youth. Given that a lot of research attributes adolescent sport withdrawal to required time commitment and competitive focus (Linder, Johns, & Butcher, 1991), sport programmers should aim to offer both specialization (deliberate practice) and recreational (deliberate play) programs so that all adolescents can continue to enjoy and participate in sport.

Table 11.4   Benefits and Costs of Early Specialization in Sport

Dimensions of Children's Sport Involvement	Benefits	Costs
Physical	Learn sport-specific skills	Increased injuries and reduced health
Psychosocial	Self-confidence in one sport	Lack of diverse experiences Reduced enjoyment Parental expectations/pressure Coaching expectations/pressure Dropout Burnout

---

Reflections 11.5

Look back on your involvement in sport and recall all the activities that constituted your sporting experiences. Use the following categories to organize the different sporting activities you participated in during your development: deliberate practice, deliberate play, and competition. Did the number of activities and the nature of your sporting activities change during your development? If yes, how?

Role of Coaches

Coaches are a major adult influence in children's sport participation. They influence children's competence beliefs, sport enjoyment, and motivation for sport participation (Black & Weiss, 1992; Sinclair & Vealey, 1989). However, youth coaches who place primary emphasis on winning sometimes exploit their athletes rather than consider their psychological and social best interests (Gilbert, Gilbert, & Trudel, 2001a, 2001b). As Peterson (2004) points out, youth development programs, such as sport, have the potential to "build a better kid," but the personal characteristics of group leaders are critical to the success of all youth development programs. Côté (2002) suggests that studies examining coaches' influences on youth can be categorized into three main areas: psychological growth, social skills, and motor development.

COACHES' ROLES IN CHILDREN'S PSYCHOLOGICAL GROWTH The most influential studies examining coaches' influences on children's psychological growth were conducted by Ronald Smith and Frank Smoll and their colleagues at the University of Washington (see Smoll & Smith, 2002, for a review of their work). Their research took place in two phases and was centred on the development and assessment of a program called coach effectiveness training (CET), which was aimed at improving coaches' ability to interact effectively with their young athletes. Results from different studies generally showed that trained coaches were more supportive, provided more reinforcement and encouragement, and were less punitive than non-trained coaches. Additionally, participants who played for trained coaches exhibited a significant increase in self-esteem and a decrease in anxiety throughout the season, compared with participants from a control group. More recent studies have demonstrated that the CET program can also help to create more positive and cohesive team atmospheres in youth sport and reduce attrition rates among young athletes (Barnett, Smoll, & Smith, 1992; Smith & Smoll, 1997).

The coach-athlete relationship can also influence youth athletes' affective outcomes, such as sport enjoyment and perceived competence (for a review see Brustad, Babkes, & Smith, 2001). Numerous studies have shown that coaches have a significant influence on children's psychological development, affecting such characteristics as self-esteem, satisfaction, enjoyment, and stress. Coach behaviours most likely to positively influence children's psychological growth are appropriate reinforcement and praise, encouragement after mistakes, and skill instruction.

COACHES' ROLES IN DEVELOPING CHILDREN'S SOCIAL SKILLS Youth-sport coaches are in a prime position to increase children's pro-social behaviours, such as co-operation and responsibility, and decrease children's antisocial behaviours, such as cheating and aggression (Arnold, 2001). Hellison (2003) provides a framework for teaching personal and social responsibility through physical activity, and this framework can guide positive youth-development coaching. He highlights the roles of integration, transfer, empowerment, and coach-athlete relationships in leading youth from irresponsibility to respect, participation, self-direction, and caring. He also provides preliminary teaching strategies, including counselling time, awareness talks, group meetings, and reflection time.

Unfortunately, studies observing coaches in real-life situations indicate that most coaches do not explicitly teach players appropriate social behaviours. Despite valuing social skills, coaches often behave in manners that conflict with children's development of appropriate social behaviours. For example, several authors have reported that youth-sport coaches' behaviours during games are directed primarily toward winning, rather than toward players' actions and the development of players' social skills (Gilbert, Trudel, & Haughian, 1999; Wilcox & Trudel, 1998). Furthermore, youth-sport coaches sometimes set poor examples of fair play (Côté, Trudel, Bernard, Boileau,

& Marcotte, 1993). In their study of Canadian youth-sport coaches during ice hockey games, Côté et al. showed that when coaches were losing, they became hostile and shouted their grievances at referees significantly more than when they were winning.

In the realm of youth sport, coaches play a crucial role in enabling young athletes to become self-controlled constructive members of a team and, ultimately productive members of society. Unfortunately, for many young athletes, sport settings stimulate a change in social values and moral reasoning patterns. For example, children tend to believe violent acts are acceptable and would be supported by coaches and parents in game situations (Bredemeier & Shields, 1996). Youth-sport coaches should not "use language or techniques that might encourage participants to separate their sport experiences from 'real life'"(Bredemeier & Shields, 1996, p. 396). Youth sports should be seen as a medium through which social values can be learned and transferred to real-life situations.

COACHES' ROLES IN DEVELOPING CHILDREN'S MOTOR SKILLS   A goal for youth-sport coaches is to provide a context where all children have opportunities to learn physical skills. Key variables that affect children's learning of physical skills are on-task practice time and the coaches' instructional behaviours. Vickers (1994) presents five steps that are universal to teaching motor skills: (a) assess entry skill, (b) provide instruction, (c) facilitate practice, (d) provide feedback, and (e) evaluate learning. To teach skills effectively, one of these five steps in isolation is not sufficient. Rather, these five steps together compose a teaching process necessary for learning to occur; however, it is beyond the scope of this chapter to outline the appropriate specific pedagogical strategies to teach motor skills. We suggest that the promotion of quality instruction by coaches and participation in various sport contexts maximize children's learning of fundamental motor skills. In sum, coaches play critical roles in youth-sport participants' learning of motor skills. Further, the environment in which this learning occurs has important implications for later sport investment or recreational participation.

Reflections 11.6
Consider your own experiences as a coach or athlete. What behaviours do you demonstrate most frequently as a coach? How would you evaluate your coaches' behaviours during your youth?

Photograph courtesy of Jean Côté.

Role of Parents

Hellstedt (1987) suggests that parents' involvement in their children's sport participation can be conceptualized on a continuum from under-involved, to moderately involved, to over-involved. **Under-involved parents** show "a relative lack of emotional, financial, or functional investment" (p. 153). **Moderately involved parents** are characterized by "firm parental direction, but enough flexibility so that the young athlete is allowed significant involvement in decision-making" (p. 153). Finally, **over-involved parents** "have an excessive amount of involvement in the athletic success of their children" (p. 154). Frequent behaviours of over-involved parents include yelling during competitions, disagreeing with coaches about their child's playing time, consistently asking their child to try harder, and coaching their child when unsolicited to do so. Hellstedt suggests that a moderate level of parental involvement promotes the best interests of the child, even if this means that parents must sometimes sacrifice personal interests.

Although a typology of parental involvement in sport, such as the one presented by Hellstedt, is useful, it provides little insight into the specific types of parental behaviours that have the most favourable socialization effects on children in sport. Woolger and Power (1993) identified three dimensions of parent behaviour associated with children's sport socialization, motivation, and behaviour: parental support, modelling, and expectations.

PARENTAL SUPPORT Parents' psychosocial support is an essential element in the development of children's self-esteem, competence, and achievement. Côté and Hay (2002) suggest four categories of psychological needs for young athletes: emotional support, informational support, tangible support, and companionship. **Emotional support** is provided through parents' comforting gestures during times of stress and anxiety. When parents give their child positive feedback on his or her ability or express belief in their child's capabilities, the child believes that he or she is cared for. These supportive efforts and gestures can enhance a child's sense of competence and level of self-esteem (Cutrona & Russell, 1990). Children need to believe that what they do with their time, energy, and talent in sport is meaningful to themselves and others. **Informational support** refers to parents' provision of advice or guidance in problematic situations. For example, parents can provide general information on how to choose a suitable sport program or provide specific instructions to a child on how to learn a certain technique.

Tangible support refers to concrete assistance given to children in stressful situations; parents provide necessary resources to help their children cope with events. Examples of tangible support include providing the financial assistance or the time commitment necessary for lessons, equipment, and travel associated with sport participation. Overall, tangible support is required for participation in most sport programs, and the lack of it can certainly become a constraint to a child's sport participation. **Companionship** or "network support" reflects casual relationships that enable an individual to engage in various forms of social and recreational activities (Cutrona & Russell, 1990). Parents can be involved in various kinds of companionship related to their child's participation in sport. For instance, parents can attend sporting events with their child, collect sports cards for their child, or get involved in deliberate play with their child (Côté, 1999; Côté, Fraser-Thomas, Robertson-Wilson, & Soberlak, 2004).

PARENTAL MODELLING Research on the role of parental modelling in sport contexts has been mixed. For example, one study found that maternal modelling was positively associated with boys' and girls' enthusiasm for their sport, but paternal modelling was negatively associated with boys' enthusiasm for their sport (Power & Woolger, 1994). This and other studies suggest that sport-loving families are not a prerequisite for children's motivation in sport. Nevertheless, parents of committed individuals tend to espouse values related to the importance of achievement, hard work, success, being active, and being persistent (Howe, 1990; Csikszentmihalyi, Rathunde, & Whalen, 1993). Therefore, home environments that offer opportunities for children to witness physically active lifestyles and the successful outcomes of sustained efforts foster positive motivational climates for sport participation.

PARENTAL EXPECTATIONS   Parents' expectations can have a powerful effect on children's emotions and motivation in sport. There is a positive relationship between parental expectations and children's success and enjoyment in sport (Fredericks & Eccles, 2004). On the other hand, parental expectations can also become a source of pressure and stress that interferes with children's participation in sport. Power and Woolger (1994) found an inverted U-shaped relationship between parental expectations and children's enthusiasm for swimming. High and low parental expectations were associated with less enthusiasm from children while an intermediate level of expectation was associated with children's highest level of enthusiasm for swimming. Clearly, parents with inflated expectations can become a source of stress and anxiety for their children. Eccles and Harold (1991) proposed that parental expectations influence children's decisions to engage in particular activities, their intensity of effort expended in these activities, and their actual performance levels. Therefore, parents should be sensitive to the positive and negative impacts their expectations can have on their children's involvement in sport.

In sum, how children feel about themselves is largely related to how they are seen and treated by others, particularly their parents. Parents need to be constantly aware of their child's desire, motivation, and attitude toward sport so that they can modify and adjust their own behaviours.

Reflections 11.7
In 2005 in Toronto, the father of a nine-year-old boy reached over the plexiglass at a hockey arena and choked the team's coach. Before other parents could intervene, the coach collapsed to the ground. People involved with the team said the dispute arose when the coach, following team rules, benched the boy for missing a practice earlier in the week. The father was released on $2000 bail and faced charges for choking. He was ordered to take anger management courses and was banned from Toronto hockey arenas. Imagine that you were interviewed by the media as an expert on youth sport, parents, and coaches. Provide your personal analysis of the situation.

Models of Sport Motivation

In response to questions about why they play sports, children commonly cite reasons related to enjoyment (e.g., having fun), physical competence (e.g., learning skills), or social influence (e.g., being with friends). For a review, see Weiss and Williams, 2004. However, it is difficult to comprehend what constitutes enjoyment, competence, and positive social influence from a child's perspective. The mediational model of global self-worth (Harter, 1987), the achievement goal theory (Nicholls, 1989), and the self-determination theory (Deci & Ryan, 1985; Ryan & Deci, 2000) are prominent theories of motivation that have undergone substantial investigation to explain why children participate in sport. These theories were described in great detail in the motivation chapter; however, we will provide a short description of each in this chapter, to help explain children's motivation for sport.

Mediational Model of Global Self-Worth

The mediational model of global self-worth (Harter, 1987) suggests that children's competence-importance beliefs and their social support predict their sense of a global self-worth and their consequent motivation. For example, if children value sport as an important area for being successful, but are not very competent in sport, then their global self-worth and motivation to participate in sport will be reduced. On the other hand, if children value sport as an important area for being successful and are competent in sport, then their global self-worth and motivation will be enhanced. The social support construct of the model postulates that children's self-worth and subsequent motivation for sport are influenced by the children's perceptions of what significant others, such as coaches or parents, think of them. Children will have a high self-opinion if they perceive that coaches or parents have a high regard for them in sport. On the other hand, children will have a low self-opinion if they perceive that coaches or parents have a low regard for them in sport, and motivation will be affected.

Achievement Goal Theory

Achievement goal theory (Nicholls, 1989) suggests that children are not able to fully differentiate between ability and luck or between ability and effort until early adolescence. At approximately age 12, children gain a more mature conception of ability and become more capable of displaying task- or ego-involvement tendencies when participating in sports. When children are task-involved in sports, they focus on their own effort and improvement. Ego-involved children are more concerned with comparing themselves to others or winning. As outlined in Chapter 4, there are multiple benefits to task-involvement in sport. During childhood these benefits include increased enjoyment, effort, and motivation. Potential risks associated with ego-involvement in sport during childhood include increased anxiety and decreased motivation.

Self-Determination Theory

Self-determination theory (Deci & Ryan, 1985; Ryan & Deci, 2000) supports the notion that enjoyable experiences in sport over time will positively affect individuals' overall participation motivation. Ryan and Deci (2000) suggested that building a solid foundation of intrinsic motivation through involvement in activities that promote enjoyment (i.e., deliberate play) is paramount in the development of highly motivated, self-determined individuals. Thus, children's involvement in numerous enjoyable activities can provide them with opportunities to become more self-determined and committed in their future participation in sport.

Weiss and Williams (2004) reviewed some of the motivational theories outlined above and derived four practical guidelines for sustaining children's engagement in sport. First, they suggest that self-perceptions, such as perceived competence and global self-worth, are important determinants of motivated behaviour in youth sport. Therefore, parents and coaches should ensure through proper feedback and encouragement that youth maintain positive competence perceptions. Second, Weiss and Williams emphasize that affect, or emotion, is a critical influence on child motivation because it is the final influence. They suggest that positive emotions, such as enjoyment, excitement, and pleasure, increase future motivation participation whereas negative emotions, such as anxiety, sadness, and disappointment, decrease motivation. To promote positive emotion in sport, coaches should pay special attention to learning environments that encourage enthusiasm and playfulness, focusing on the positive behaviours of athletes and encouraging athletes' improvement (Bengoechea, Strean, & Williams, 2004; Strean, 1995). Third, Weiss and Williams recommend that coaches and parents implement a task-oriented climate, which focuses on self-improvement, instead of an ego-oriented climate, which focuses on comparison with others. This can be done by encouraging effort and improvement and being careful not to reward excessive competition, physical aggression, and cheating. Finally, Weiss and Williams highlight social support from coaches, parents, teachers, and peers as essential for continued engagement in youth sport. Through their behaviours and attitudes, significant adults and peers have an important influence on children's enjoyment, physical competence, self-worth, and, ultimately, their overall motivation to stay in sport.

Reflections 11.8

Weiss and Williams proposed four guidelines for motivating children and youth to stay involved in sport. How are these guidelines consistent with the three primary objectives of youth sport discussed at the beginning of the chapter? Do you think that these guidelines are reinforced in youth sport?

Photo courtesy of PhotoDisk/Getty Images.

Models of Sport Development

In the previous section, we outlined models that facilitated an understanding of children's motivation for sport participation. This section outlines three models that help to explain children's development in sport: the sport commitment model, the model of sport withdrawal, and the developmental model of sport participation.

Sport Commitment Model

Scanlan, Simons, Carpenter, Schmidt, and Keeler (1993) have conceptualized youth's motives for sport participation or dropout in their sport commitment model. The model was originally developed and empirically tested through questionnaires, administered to nearly 200 Little Leaguers. The original model consisted of five constructs that have the potential to increase or decrease sport commitment. The first construct, which positively affects sport commitment, is sport enjoyment, or the pleasure resulting from sport participation. The second construct, which negatively affects sport involvement, is involvement alternatives, which is defined as the opportunity to engage in other activities instead of participating in the sport. The third construct, which positively affects sport involvement, is personal investment, defined as personal resources invested in the sport, such as time, effort, and money. The fourth construct, social constraints, is described as positively affecting sport commitment and addresses the social pressure and obligations an athlete feels to participate. Involvement opportunities, such as the chance to improve skills, be with friends, or stay fit, is described as positively influencing sport commitment. Carpenter (1995) later added the construct of social support, which refers to perceived help and encouragement received from significant others, as a positive influence (see Figure 11.1).

These constructs may be better understood through the following two scenarios:

As a child, Sally is given the opportunity to participate in soccer. She enjoys it, and continues to enroll year after year (sport enjoyment [+]). Over time, her skills improve, she meets great friends, and she becomes a very good athlete (involvement opportunities [+]). She invests a great deal of time, and her parents invest a great deal of money, in soccer (personal investment [+]). All of these factors contribute to Sally's continued commitment to soccer.

Wendy was also introduced to soccer at a young age. Although she initially enjoyed the friendships and games, each year she felt that things became a little more serious. When she was 12, she started skipping practices and hanging out at her friend's house after school (involvement alternatives [–]). Her commitment to soccer decreased, and she eventually withdrew.

Figure 11.1   Sport commitment model

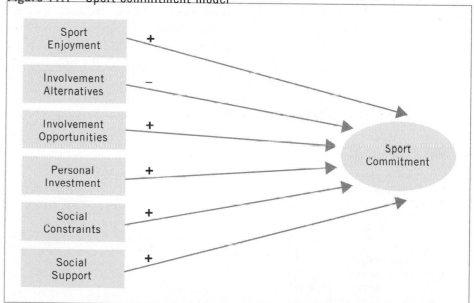

Note: From T.K. Scanlan, J.P. Simons, P.J. Carpenter, G.W. Schmidt and B. Keller, 1993, An introduction to the sport commitment model, Journal of Sport and Exercise Psychology 15(1): 5, figure 1. © 1993 by Human Kinetics Publishers, Inc. Adapted with permission from Human Kinetics (Champaign, IL).

Based on a study with junior tennis players, Weiss, Kimmel, and Smith (2001) recently modified the sport commitment model (see Figure 11.2). The new model suggests that sport enjoyment plays a more prominent role in sport commitment. Furthermore, based on past research, the new model includes an additional construct (perceived competence) and eliminates one construct (involvement opportunities). Weiss et al.'s model suggests that sport enjoyment is the central construct that predicts sport commitment, and that sport enjoyment serves as a filter through which other factors positively or negatively influence commitment.

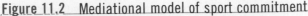

Figure 11.2 Mediational model of sport commitment

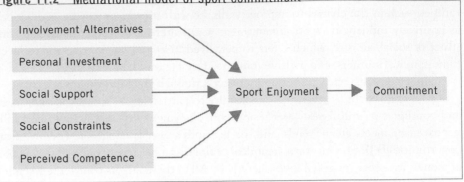

Note: From M.R. Weiss, L.A. Kimmel and A.L. Smith, 2001, Determinants of sport commitment among junior tennis players: enjoyment as a mediating variable, Pediatric Exercise Science 13(2): 134, figure 1b. © 2001 by Human Kinetics Publishers, Inc. Adapted with permission from Human Kinetics (Champaign, IL).

Sport Withdrawal Model

Linder et al. (1991) developed a model of voluntary youth-sport withdrawal, with the intention of providing a more extensive framework to understand youth-sport dropout. After an extensive review of the literature, they suggested that the dropout studies provided only intuitive, superficial, and subjective reasons for dropout. Accordingly, their model outlines three broad categories of factors that influence youths' withdrawal from sport: sport-related factors, milieu-related factors, and development-related factors (see Figure 11.3). The model suggests numerous sport-related factors that can influence participation and withdrawal: an individual's motivation for a sport, the time investment

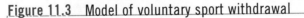

Figure 11.3 Model of voluntary sport withdrawal

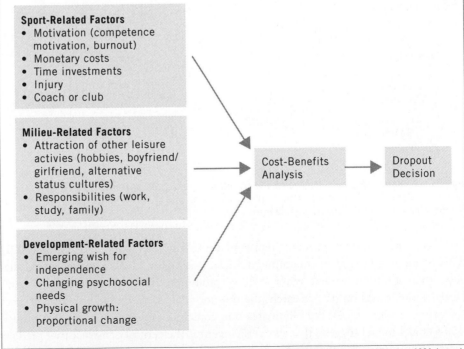

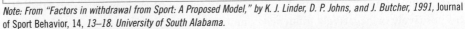

Note: From "Factors in withdrawal from Sport: A Proposed Model," by K. J. Linder, D. P. Johns, and J. Butcher, 1991, Journal of Sport Behavior, 14, 13–18. University of South Alabama.

required by a sport, coach and club characteristics, athletes' injuries, and monetary costs. The model also suggests milieu-related factors that may influence withdrawal: an individual's attraction to other things (e.g., hobbies, socializing), and personal responsibilities (e.g., jobs, school, family). Development-related factors that contribute to sport withdrawal include the following: psychosocial changes (e.g., increasing peer influence) and physical changes (e.g., proportional growth). This model proposed that youth athletes intuitively do cost-benefit analyses of all sport, milieu, and development factors related to their sport involvement. If benefits outweigh costs, youths will continue to participate in their sport, but if costs outweigh benefits, youths will withdraw from their sport.

This model holds that in order to fully understand youth-sport participation and withdrawal patterns, it is important to recognize different types of dropout athletes, and to understand how sport, milieu, and developmental factors influence each dropout type. Linder et al. (1991) categorize dropouts into three types: samplers, participants, and transfers. Samplers are defined as athletes who briefly engage in a sport for the purpose of trying it out. Sport participants are committed to one or more sports over several years and are further categorized by their levels of involvement (low, high, or elite). Finally, transfers are individuals who leave a sport because it no longer fulfills their needs; however, they become involved in other sports.

The Developmental Model of Sport Participation

The developmental model of sport participation (DMSP) by Côté (1999) and Côté & Hay (2002) emerged from extensive retrospective interviews with athletes in a variety of sports—hockey, baseball, gymnastics, rowing, tennis, triathlon (see Figure 11.4). The DMSP proposes three possible sport participation trajectories: recreational participation through sampling, elite performance through sampling, and elite performance through early specialization. Two of these trajectories, recreational participation and elite performance through sampling, have the same foundation from ages 6 to 12. After the sampling years, sport participants can choose to either stay involved in sport at a recreational level (recreational years, age 13+) or embark on a path that focuses primarily on performance (specializing years, ages 13–15; investment years, age 16+). These two trajectories have different outcomes in terms of performance but similar psychosocial and physical health benefits. A third possible trajectory consists of elite performance through early specialization (right side of Figure 11.4). Although this trajectory leads to elite performance, it can also result in reduced physical health (i.e., overuse injuries) and enjoyment.

TRAJECTORY 1: RECREATIONAL PARTICIPATION THROUGH SAMPLING   During the sampling years (ages 6–12), athletes participate in a variety of sports with the focus being primarily on deliberate play activities. These years are considered essential building blocks for recreational sport participation. The recreational years (age 13+) are usually seen as an extension of the sampling years, with the primary goals being enjoyment and health. Activities can involve deliberate play and deliberate practice, and sport programs are flexible enough to adapt to individual interests and ages. During the sampling and recreational years, coaches are primarily kind, supportive, and encouraging. Parents' roles include introducing their children to sports, enrolling their children in diverse activities, and providing their children with necessary resources and equipment.

Figure 11.4   Developmental model of sport participation

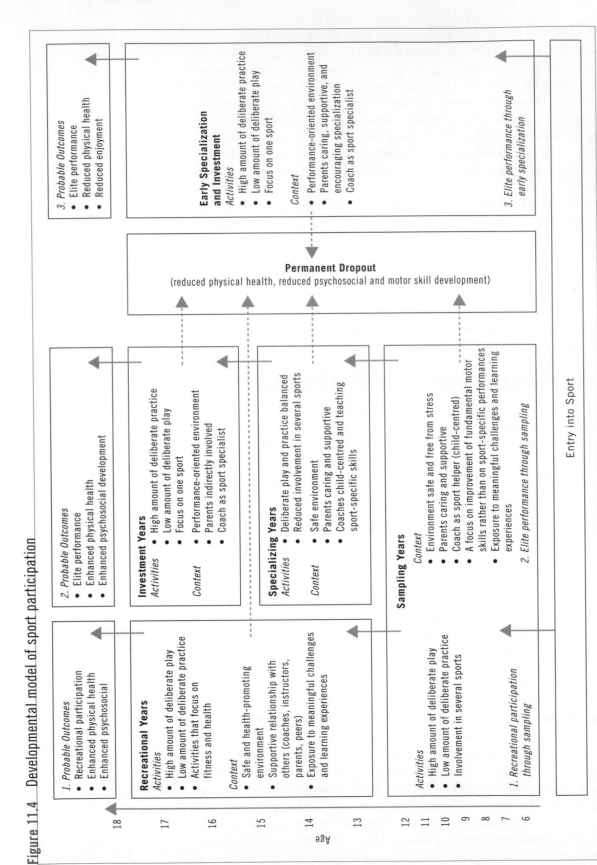

Note: Adapted from "The Influence of the Family Development of Talent in Sport," by J. Côté, 1999, The Sport Psychologist, 13, pp. 395–417; and from "Children's Involvement in Sport: A Developmental Perspective," by J. Côté and J. Hay, 2002, in J. M. Silva III and D. E. Stevens (Eds.), Psychological Foundations of Sport (pp. 484–502). Boston: Allyn & Bacon.

TRAJECTORY 2: ELITE PERFORMANCE THROUGH SAMPLING   For youth interested in a more performance-oriented path, a second trajectory of the DMSP suggests that specialization begins around age 13, after the sampling years (see Case Study 11.1). The specializing years (ages 13–15) are seen as a transitional stage to the investment years (age 16+). During the specializing years, youth engage in fewer activities, which are a mix of deliberate play and deliberate practice activities; during the investment years, youth commit to only one activity and engage primarily in deliberate practice. During both the specializing and the investment years, a more reciprocal coach-athlete respect develops, with coaches' styles becoming more skill oriented and technical. Parents become less involved but provide more financial and emotional support by helping their children through challenges and obstacles. Essentially, parents progress from a leadership role during the sampling years to a following and supporting role during the specializing and investment years (Côté 1999).

TRAJECTORY 3: ELITE PERFORMANCE THROUGH EARLY SPECIALIZATION   In sports where peak performance is achieved before puberty (e.g., women's gymnastics, figure skating), early specialization is often necessary to reach elite performance. Elite performers in these early-specialization sports usually skip the sampling years and, consequently, do not always experience the most positive psychosocial development. In addition, early specializers often experience overuse injuries, as outlined earlier in this chapter. The early specialization path is characterized by high amounts of deliberate practice and low amounts of deliberate play in a context that focuses on performance.

OTHER TRAJECTORIES   Opportunities for horizontal movement across stages, (e.g., going from investment to recreational) should be provided for participants, so individuals can change their level of participation at any age if they so desire. Unfortunately, in many sports it is difficult for a 16-year-old adolescent to invest in a sport if he or she has not been specializing in that sport since approximately age 13; however, in some sports, such as triathlon, investment in adulthood is possible (Baker, Côté, & Deakin, 2005).

Finally, at any stage of development, youth may also choose to disengage from sport and physical activity altogether. If this is the case, their youth-sport programs clearly failed to achieve the first objective of youth-sport programming: the long-term physical health of participants. Unfortunately, many youth-sport programs are failing to reach this objective, as evidenced by current adolescent and adult inactivity rates.

Case Study 11.1: Simon Whitfield, Canadian Triathlete

Simon Whitfield, a native of Kingston, Ontario, was almost unknown to Canadians on September 16, 2000, when he came from behind to win Canada's first gold medal of the 2000 Olympics in Sydney, Australia. Consequently, many immediately took an interest in his path to athletic stardom.

Simon participated in many sports from a very young age. As he suggests, he began playing soccer as soon as he could crawl. His parents played a huge role in his early childhood involvement by enrolling and supporting him in a variety of activities. His older sister was also an avid athlete. As she progressed in her sports, and eventually specialized in rowing, Simon looked up to her as a role model and appreciated her support.

Simon was 11 years old when he was first exposed to triathlons, competing in the local Sharbot Lake Kids of Steel triathlon. He raced on a clunky mountain bike in a pair of boxer shorts, and recalls the fun he had hanging out on the beach and enjoying a post-race barbecue.

It was not until age 15 that Simon decided to specialize in triathlons. His training increased in volume, intensity, and focus. Eventually, he relocated to the

Pacific National Training Centre in British Columbia and spent a year training in Australia. He worked closely with a variety of coaches, focusing especially on his weakness, the swimming component of the triathlon.

During the weeks and months following Simon's Olympic victory, Canadians sang his praises and were proud to call him their own. His model citizenship was apparent, as he travelled the country visiting schools, reaching out to children, and inspiring adults. A natural public speaker, Simon shared his positive sport experiences and served as a spokesperson for active, healthy living and fun-focused children's sports programs. Since Simon's victory, participation in Kids of Steel and adult triathlons has grown exponentially. He continues to share his contagious passion for sport, claiming that fun is the foundation to any successful youth-sport program.

Consider Simon's story in light of the chapter's content. Comment on Simon's sport development path using the models outlined in the final section of the chapter. Also, using the principles of positive youth development as a guide, comment on Simon's psychosocial development.

Chapter Summary

In this chapter, we outlined three objectives of youth-sport programs: physical health, psychosocial development, and the learning of motor skills. We reviewed the literature highlighting the positive (e.g., fitness) and negative (e.g., overuse injuries) outcomes of youth sports and suggested how to foster positive youth-sport experiences. Youth-sport programs should be conducted in desirable settings, and they should aim to foster developmental assets, initiative, health, performance, and the five C's of positive youth development (confidence, competence, character, connection, caring/compassion). To reach these objectives, youth-sport programs should promote participation in diverse activities and focus on deliberate play activities at a young age, rather than requiring children to specialize early and focus on deliberate practice activities. Coaches and parents, through their supportive behaviours and attitudes, have important roles in influencing children's psychological growth, social skills, and motor development.

In the last section of the chapter, we outlined models that help to explain children's motivation and development in sport. Motivation models suggest that children's motivation is linked to their competence beliefs, sport enjoyment, and the social support they receive. The models reinforce the important roles of parents and coaches in building children's competence beliefs, creating task-oriented climates, and facilitating environments that lead to positive emotions. The three sport development models presented highlight various factors that lead to prolonged participation, expertise, and dropout. These models show that youth's health, psychosocial development, and motor skill development must be considered by youth-sport programmers as a whole, instead of as separate entities. Youth should be encouraged to participate in diverse sports and extracurricular activities that focus on fun, play, excitement, recreation, personal involvement, games, friendships, variety, and choice. Activities and contexts that promote regular participation, enjoyment, and skill acquisition are the building blocks of all effective youth-sport programs.

We began this chapter by introducing you to Sebastian, Olivia, Madelyn, Rachel, and Michael, five young adults who had very different sport experiences during their youth, which in turn led them to very different paths as young adults. As you read through the chapter, you were introduced to some of the specific factors that led these individuals to have more or less positive youth-sport experiences. We hope that you will continue to consider these factors as you progress as professionals, coaches, administrators, programmers, and policy makers, in sport, physical activity, health, and other settings.

Review Questions

1. What are the three objectives of youth sport?
2. List positive and negative outcomes of youth-sport participation in the areas of health, psychological development, and social development.
3. Differentiate between relaxed leisure activities and constructive leisure activities. Provide examples.
4. Using developmental assets and setting features as frameworks, highlight some of the strengths and weaknesses of the youth-sport programs you were involved in.
5. What are the five C's of positive youth development?
6. Outline the two characteristics of youth-sport activities associated with positive youth-sport experiences.
7. What are the three dimensions of parent behaviour that can be associated with children's sport socialization, motivation, and behaviour? Briefly describe how each dimension influences children's sport experiences.
8. Coaches influence children's psychological growth, social skills, and motor development. Briefly describe findings of past studies on coaching in one of these three areas.
9. Name the three models of sport motivation and the three models of sport development outlined in this chapter. Compare and contrast key features of the models.

Suggested Reading

Smoll, F. L., & Smith, R. E. (2002). *Children and youth in sport: A biopsychosocial perspective* (2nd ed.). Dubuque, IA: Kendal Hunt.

Weiss, M. R. (Ed.). (2004). *Developmental sport and exercise psychology: A lifespan perspective*. Morgantown, WV: Fitness Information Technology.

References

Arnold, P. J. (2001). Sport, moral development, and the role of teacher: Implications for research and moral education. *Quest, 53*, 135–150.

Baker, J., & Côté, J. (2006). Shifting training requirements during athlete development: The relationship among deliberate practice, deliberate play and other sport involvement in the acquisition of sport expertise. In D. Hackfort & G. Tenenbaum (Eds.), *Essential processes for attaining peak performance*. (pp. 92–109) Aachen, Germany: Meyer and Meyer.

Baker, J., Côté, J., & Deakin, J. (2005). Expertise in ultra-endurance triathletes: Early sport involvement, training structure, and the theory of deliberate practice. *Journal of Applied Sport Psychology, 17*, 64–78.

Barnett, N. P., Smoll, F. L., & Smith, R. E. (1992). Effects of enhancing coach-athlete relationships on youth sport attrition. *The Sport Psychologist, 6*, 111–127.

Bengoechea, E. G., Strean, W. B., & Williams, D. J. (2004). Understanding and promoting fun in youth sport: Coaches' perspective. *Physical Education and Sport Pedagogy, 9*, 197–214.

Benson, P. L. (1997). *All kids are our kids: What communities must do to raise caring and responsible children and adolescents*. San Francisco: Jossey-Bass.

Black, S. J., & Weiss, M. R. (1992). The relationship among perceived coaching behaviors, perception of ability, and motivation in competitive age group swimmers. *Journal of Sport & Exercise Psychology, 14*, 309–325.

Boyd, M. P., & Yin, Z. (1996). Cognitive-affective sources of sport enjoyment in adolescent sport participants. *Adolescence, 31*, 383–395.

Bredemeier, B. J. L., & Shields, D. L. L. (1996). Moral development and children's sport. In F. L. Smoll & R. E. Smith (Eds.), *Children and youth sport: A biopsychosocial perspective* (pp. 381–404). Chicago: Brown & Benchmark.

Brustad, R. J., Babkes, M. L., & Smith, A. L. (2001). Youth in sport: Psychological considerations. In R. N. Singer, H. A. Hausenblas, & C. M. Janelle (Eds.), *Handbook of sport psychology* (2nd ed., pp. 604–635). New York: Wiley.

Carpenter, P. J (1995). Modification and extension of the sport commitment model. *Journal of Sport & Exercise Psychology, 17*, S37.

Corbeil, J. P. (2000). Sport participation in Canada. *Canadian Social Trends, 3*, 212–217.

Côté, J. (1999). The influence of the family in the development of talent in sport. *The Sport Psychologist, 13*, 395–417.

Côté, J. (2002). Coach and peer influence on children's development through sport. In J. M. Silva III & D. E. Stevens (Eds.), *Psychological foundations of sport* (pp. 520–540). Boston: Allyn & Bacon.

Côté, J., Baker, J., & Abernethy, B. (2003). From play to practice: A developmental framework for the acquisition of expertise in team sport. In J. Starkes & K. A. Ericsson (Eds.), *Recent advances in research on sport expertise* (pp. 89–114). Champaign, IL: Human Kinetics.

Côté, J., Fraser-Thomas, J., Robertson-Wilson, J., & Soberlak, P. (2004). L'utilisation d'entretiens pour quantifier l'implication des parents dans le développement de compétence sportives chez les athlètes [The use of interviews to quantify the influence of parental involvement in athletes' development of expertise]. *Revue Internationale des Sciences du sport et de l'Education Physique, 25*, 39–52.

Côté, J., & Hay, J. (2002). Children's involvement in sport: A developmental perspective. In J. M. Silva III & D. E. Stevens (Eds.), *Psychological foundations of sport* (pp. 484–502). Boston: Allyn & Bacon.

Côté, J., Trudel, P., Bernard, D., Boileau, R., & Marcotte, G. (1993). Observation of coach behaviors during different game score differentials. In C. R. Castaldi, P. J. Bishop, & E. F. Hoerner (Eds.), *Safety in ice hockey: second volume ASTM STP 1212* (pp. 78–87). Philadelphia: American Society for Testing and Materials.

Csikszentmihalyi, M., Rathunde, K., & Whalen, S. (1993). *Talented teenagers: The roots of success and failure*. Cambridge: Cambridge University Press.

Cutrona, C. E., & Russell, D. W. (1990). Type of social support and specific stress: Toward a theory of optimal matching. In B. R. Sarason, I. G. Sarason & G. R. Pierce (Eds.), *Social support: An interactional view* (pp. 319–366). New York: Wiley.

Deci, E. L., & Ryan, R. M. (1985). *Intrinsic motivation and self-determination in human behavior*. New York: Plenum.

De Knop, P., Engström, L-M., & Skirstad, B. (1996). Worldwide trends in youth sport. In P. De Knop, L-M. Engström, B. Skirstad, & M. Weiss (Eds.), *Worldwide trends in youth sport* (pp. 276–281). Champaign, IL: Human Kinetics.

Eccles, J. S., & Barber, B. L. (1999). Student council, volunteering, basketball, or marching band: What kind of extracurricular involvement matters? *Journal of Adolescent Research, 14*, 10–43.

Eccles, J. S., & Harold, R. D. (1991). Gender differences in sport involvement: Applying the Eccles expectancy-value model. *Journal of Applied Sport Psychology, 3*, 7–35.

Eder, D., & Parker, S. (1987). The cultural production and reproduction of gender: The effect of extracurricular activities on peer-group culture. *Sociology of Education, 60*, 200–213.

Ericsson, K. A., Krampe, R. T., & Tesch-Römer, C. (1993). The role of deliberate practice in the acquisition of expert performance. *Psychological Review, 100*, 363–406.

Fraser-Thomas, J. L., Côté, J., & Deakin, J. (2005). Youth sport programs: An avenue to foster positive youth development. *Physical Education and Sport Pedagogy, 10*, 49–70.

Fredericks, J. A., & Eccles, J. S. (2004). Parental influences on youth involvement in sports. In M. R. Weiss (Ed.), *Developmental sport and exercise psychology: A lifespan perspective* (pp. 145–164). Morgantown, WV: Fitness Information Technology.

Gilbert, W. D., Gilbert, J. N., & Trudel, P. (2001a). Coaching strategies for youth sports. Part 1: Athlete behavior and athlete performance. *Journal of Physical Education, Recreation and Dance, 72*, 29–33.

Gilbert, W. D., Gilbert, J. N., & Trudel, P. (2001b). Coaching strategies for youth sports. Part 2: Personal characteristics, parental influence, and team organization. *Journal of Physical Education, Recreation and Dance, 72*, 41–46.

Gilbert, W. D., Trudel, P., & Haughian, L. P. (1999). Interactive decision making factors considered by coaches of youth ice hockey during games. *Journal of Teaching in Physical Education, 18,* 290–311.

Harter, S. (1987). The determinants and mediational role of global self-worth in children. In N. Eisenberg (Ed.), *Contemporary topics in developmental psychology* (pp. 219–242). New York: Wiley.

Hellison, D. (2003). *Teaching responsibility through physical activity* (2nd ed.). Champaign, IL: Human Kinetics.

Hellstedt, J. C. (1987). The coach/parent/athlete relationship. *The Sport Psychologist, 1,* 151–160.

Helsen, W. F., Starkes, J. L., & Hodges, N. J. (1998). Team sports and the theory of deliberate practice. *Journal of Sport & Exercise Psychology, 20,* 12–34.

Hill, G. (1988). Celebrate diversity (not specialization) in school sports. *Executive Educator, 10,* 24.

Hollander, D. B., Meyers, M. C., & LeUnes, A. (1995). Psychological factors associated with overtraining: Implications for youth sport coaches. *Journal of Sport Behavior, 18,* 3–18.

Howe, M. J. A. (1990). *The origins of exceptional abilities.* Cambridge, England: Basil Blackwell.

Larson, R. W. (2000). Toward a psychology of positive youth development. *American Psychologist, 55,* 170–183.

Larson, R. W., & Kleiber, D. A. (1993). Structured leisure as a context for the development of attention during adolescence. *Society and Leisure, 16,* 77–98.

Larson, R. W., & Verma, S. (1999). How children and adolescents spend time across the world: Work, play, and developmental opportunities. *Psychological Bulletin, 125,* 701–736.

Law, M., Côté, J., & Ericsson, K. A. (in press). Characteristics of expert development in rhythmic gymnastics: A retrospective study. *International Journal of Sport and Exercise Psychology.*

Lerner, R. M., Fisher, C. B., & Weinberg, R. A. (2000). Toward a science for and of the people: Promoting civil society through the application of developmental science. *Child Development, 71,* 11–20.

Linder, K. J., Johns, D. P., & Butcher, J. (1991). Factors in withdrawal from sport: A proposed model. *Journal of Sport Behavior, 14,* 13–18.

Nicholls, J. G (1989). *The competitive ethos and democratic education.* Cambridge, MA: Harvard University Press.

NRCIM (National Research Council and Institute of Medicine) (2002). *Community programs to promote youth development.* Washington, DC: National Academy Press.

Peterson, C. (2004). Positive social science. *The Annals of the American Academy of Political and Social Science, 591,* 186–201.

Power, T. G., & Woolger, C. (1994). Parenting practices and age-group swimming: A correlational study. *Research Quarterly for Exercise and Sport, 65,* 59–66.

Ryan, R. M., & Deci, E. L. (2000). Self-determination theory and the facilitation of intrinsic motivation, social development, and well-being. *American Psychologist, 55,* 68–78.

Scales, P., & Leffert, N. (1999). *Developmental assets: A synthesis of the scientific research on adolescent development.* Minneapolis, MN: Search Institute.

Scanlan, T. K., Simons, J. P., Carpenter, P. J., Schmidt, G. W., & Keeler, B. (1993). An introduction to the sport commitment model. *Journal of Sport & Exercise Psychology, 15,* 1–15.

Seppa, N. (1996). Keeping young athletic fires burning. *APA Monitor.* Retrieved August 10, 1999, from http://web.isp.cz/jcrane/IB/Athletic_burnout.pdf

Sinclair, D. A., & Vealey, R. S. (1989). Effects of coaches' expectations and feedback on self-perceptions of athletes. *Journal of Sport Behavior, 11,* 77–91.

Smith, R. E., & Smoll, F. L. (1990). Self esteem and children's reactions to youth sport coaching behaviors: A field study of self-enhancement processes. *Developmental Psychology, 26,* 987–993.

Smith, R. E., & Smoll, F. L. (1997). Coach-mediated team building in youth sports. *Journal of Applied Sport Psychology, 9,* 114–132.

Smoll, F. L., & Smith, R. E. (2002). Coaching behavior research and intervention in youth sports. In F. L. Smoll & R. E. Smith (Eds.), *Children and youth in sport: A biopsychosocial perspective* (2nd ed., pp. 211–233). Dubuque, IA: Kendal Hunt.

Soberlak, P., & Côté, J. (2003). Developmental activities of elite ice hockey players. *Journal of Applied Sport Psychology, 15,* 41–49.

Strean, W. B. (1995). Youth sport contexts: coaches' perceptions and implications for intervention. *Journal of Applied Sport Psychology, 7,* 23–37.

United Nations Educational, Scientific, and Cultural Organization. (1999). *Draft recommendations.* Third International Conference of Ministers and Senior Officials Responsible for Physical Education and Sport (MINEPS III). Punta del Este, Uruguay: Author.

Vickers, J. N. (1994). Psychological research in sport pedagogy: Exploring the reversal effect. *Sport Science Review, 3,* 28–40

Weiss, M. R., Kimmel, L. A., & Smith, A. L. (2001). Determinants of sport commitment among junior tennis players: Enjoyment as a mediating variable. *Pediatric Exercise Science, 13,* 131–144.

Weiss, M. R., & Williams, L. (2004). The *why* of youth sport involvement: A developmental perspective on motivational processes. In M. R. Weiss (Ed.), *Developmental sport and exercise psychology: A lifespan perspective* (pp. 223–268). Morgantown, WV: Fitness Information Technology.

Wilcox, S., & Trudel, P. (1998). Constructing the coaching principles and beliefs of a youth ice hockey coach. *Avante, 4,* 39–66.

Woolger, C., & Power, T. G. (1993). Parent and sport socialization: Views from the achievement literature. *Journal of Sport Behavior, 16,* 171–189.

Wright, A. D., & Côté, J. (2003). A retrospective analysis of leadership development through sport. *The Sport Psychologist, 17,* 268–291.

Joseph Baker

CHAPTER 12

Aging and Physical Activity Involvement

Chapter Objectives

After reading this chapter, you should be able to do the following:

1. Present a profile of physical activity and sport involvement in older persons.

2. Understand the consequences of low levels of physical activity in this group.

3. Discuss and differentiate between models of skill maintenance.

4. Discuss the factors influencing sport and physical activity involvement in this group.

5. Consider the impact of societal perceptions of aging on physical and cognitive performance.

6. Identify strategies for increasing sport and physical activity involvement in older populations.

7. Discuss whether the Master athlete is an effective model of successful aging.

* Acknowledgments: Support for this chapter was provided by a standard research grant from the Social Sciences and Humanities Research Council of Canada (SSHRC # 410-04-1207). The author would also like to thank Sean Horton and Ann-Marie Kungl for their helpful comments.

Pawel grew up in rural Alberta and spent a great deal of his youth and adolescence working on his family's farm. As an adult, Pawel left the rural life and moved into a small city to start a family of his own. Recently, Pawel decided to make a change in his life after his doctor informed him that he was at an increased risk of having a heart attack, because of his high cholesterol, and that adding some physical activity to his daily routine would be a good idea. However, after decades of inactivity, Pawel finds it difficult to make changes to his routine. He tries joining a local fitness club but finds that he has little in common with the club's other members. He inquires about the aerobic and stretching programs available at the club, but the club's personal trainer informs him that their programs are likely too advanced for someone of his age and fitness level.

Pawel finally has some success when he begins a walking routine with his friend Nyla. This activity is well-suited to their neighbourhood since it has wide sidewalks and minimal traffic. However, after a few weeks, Nyla moves to live with her daughter's family, and Pawel quickly becomes discouraged walking by himself. At his checkup one year later, Pawel still hasn't made any consistent changes to his physical activity habits and remains at increased risk of having a heart attack.

In the above scenario, Pawel has difficulty making the necessary changes in his life to add a greater amount of physical activity. Unfortunately, this situation is commonplace among older adults (seniors) in Canadian society. In this chapter, we look at the factors influencing physical activity involvement in aging populations to determine the most effective courses of action for optimal health and performance in this group.

Some Common Myths about Aging and Physical Activity Involvement

MYTH: *Getting older involves the inevitable loss of the ability to function in society.*
Although a certain degree of ability loss appears to be inevitable with age, most of this loss is due to decreased participation in cognitively and physically stimulating activities. With continued involvement in challenging activities, older adults can maintain (and even increase) physical and cognitive abilities.

MYTH: *Stereotypes about "old people" are generally accurate.*
The stereotype commonly endorsed in North America is that older adults have diminished capacities, almost as though they are reverting to child-like levels of development. As mentioned in the first myth, this is not the case. In fact, the majority of stereotypes about older adults promoted in our society have no basis in empirical research.

MYTH: *Participating in competitive sports is too strenuous for older persons.*
The field of competitive sports for aging populations is rapidly growing. Masters-level competition is now possible in a wide range of organized sports throughout the world, and competitors regularly participate against regional, national, and international competitors.

Introduction

In 2007, the first wave of the Canadian baby boomer generation will reach 60 years of age. Persons over 85 years are the fastest growing segment of the population, and by 2026 the number of Canadian adults over the age of 65 is expected to double. Clearly, this is a section of the population that is of considerable importance in Canadian society. In the past 160 years, our average life expectancy has increased at a rate of about 3 months per year. In fact, the relationship between increasing life expectancy and the passage of time is so consistent that some researchers have considered it to be "the most remarkable regularity of mass endeavor ever observed" (Oeppen & Vaupel, 2002, pp. 1029). Although this is an exciting finding, since it suggests that we have a longer life to look forward to, an increased lifespan does not necessarily mean a better **quality of life**. In fact, many Canadians run the risk of spending a significant portion of their senior years in states of **morbidity** (being unhealthful) or in complete dependence. A significant factor contributing to this decreased quality of life is physical inactivity.

Data from the Canadian Community Health Survey (CCHS; Statistics Canada, 2005) for 2000–2001 support a robust and rather unsettling trend in physical activity research—physical activity levels decrease as we get older. These data indicate that among older adults 68% of women and 53% of men can be classified as inactive or sedentary. Furthermore, only 13% of women and 22% of men meet their recommended daily physical activity requirements. Although there is encouraging news indicating that this trend is improving, the fact remains that the majority of older men and women are not active enough for optimal health.

The most common physical activities for adults over 65 are outlined in Table 12.1. Walking, gardening, and exercising at home have the greatest rates of participation in older adult groups. These forms of physical activity are excellent avenues for staying active. However, because they are low in aerobic intensity, older adults need to be mindful of performing enough activity to meet their physical activity requirements. (The Canadian Fitness and Lifestyle Research Institute monitors physical activity involvement across Canada in various age groups [www.cflri.ca].)

Table 12.1 Most Popular Physical Activities among Canadian Adults over 65 and the Percent of the Population Participating in the Activity

Activity	%
Walking	66
Gardening	40
Home Exercise	23
Swimming	9
Social Dancing	9
Bicycling	7
Golf	6
Bowling	4
Fishing	4
Exercise Classes	3
Weight Training	1

Note: Adapted from Canadian Community Health Survey, 2000/01, 2005, Statistics Canada. Retrieved January 9, 2006, from http://www.statcan.ca/english/freepub/82-221-XIE/00502/tables/html/2165.htm.

Data indicate that involvement in aerobic exercise is not enough. To reduce the loss of muscle mass (**sarcopenia**) that typically occurs with age, older adults must also regularly participate in exercise that taxes their muscle strength (e.g., weight training). *Canada's Physical Activity Guide to Healthy Living for Older Adults* recommends up to 60 minutes of moderate to vigorous physical activity on most days, including a variety of endurance, flexibility, strength, and balance activities (Health Canada, 1999). There is overwhelming support that habitual involvement in these forms of physical activity is related to increased physical and mental health, as well as increased functional autonomy in aging populations (see Table 12.2). Physical activity guidelines for older adults (as well as for other age groups) are available on the Health Canada website (www.hc-sc.gc.ca).

Table 12.2   Benefits of Exercise in Older Adults

Increase in cardiovascular function
Decrease in cardiovascular-disease risk factors
Increased muscle mass and strength
Improved bone health and decreased risk of osteoporosis
Improved balance and postural stability
Improved flexibility
Improved psychological health

Note: Adapted from "Exercise and Physical Activity in Older Adults (Position Stand)," by ACSM, 1998, Medicine and Science in Sports and Exercise, 30, *pp. 992–1008.*

>
Weight training is essential
to prevent sarcopenia.
Photo courtesy of PhotoDisc/Getty Images.

Cognitive and Physical Decline with Advancing Age

Examinations of cognitive and physical performance across time indicate that these capacities decline as we get older. Some researchers indicate that 0.5% per year is a general rate of decline for *all* skills and capacities after we have reached peak performance (see Bortz & Bortz, 1996). Although there is consistent evidence indicating that physical and cognitive abilities decline as we age, there is conflicting evidence as to whether this is actually due to age. In a review article, Maharam, Bauman, Kalman, Skolnik, and Perle (1999) suggested that many of the physical and cognitive declines associated with aging were in fact the result of a "long-standing sedentary lifestyle or disuse" (p. 274). As mentioned earlier, involvement in physical activities also declines as we age. Current thinking is that these two factors—declining involvement and declining ability—are inextricably linked.

Studies of cognitive and motor skills suggest that performance can be maintained at high levels in spite of advancing age, provided there is continued involvement in the activity. For instance, studies of chess players (Charness, 1981), pianists (Krampe & Ericsson, 1996), and typists (Salthouse, 1984) have shown that high levels of performance could be maintained as the performers got older. The maintenance of skilled performance over time has been explained primarily using one of two models, the compensation model (e.g., Salthouse, 1984) or the selective maintenance model (Krampe & Ericsson, 1996).

The Compensation Model of Skill Maintenance

The basis of **compensation theory** is that although individual components of a skill may decline with age, it is possible for overall performance to remain the same because of an increased reliance on other aspects of performance (see Figure 12.1). Put more simply, the theory suggests that skilled performers strategically compensate for a decline in one skill area by developing or improving in another. Two excellent examples of this research come from studies examining chess players and typists. Charness (1981) found that skilled, older chess players could perform at the same level as younger skilled players despite age-related deficiencies in memory ability. Charness explained these results by suggesting that older players compensate for their declining memory by using more efficient information processing; they perform a more systematic search of the problem space and make a better global evaluation of chess positions.

Figure 12.1 The compensation model of aging: Although components of performance may decline (A), increases in a compensatory skill (B) allow for stability of performance over time (C)

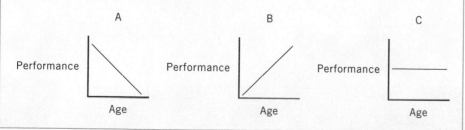

In addition, studies have found little decline in expert typing skill with advancing age (Bosman, 1993; Salthouse, 1984); the evidence indicates that expert typists compensate for age-related declines by scanning further ahead in the text, which allows them to begin keystroke preparation earlier. As a result of this advanced planning, aging typists can offset a deficiency in one area by improving performance in another.

The Selective Maintenance Model of Skill Maintenance

Ericsson and Krampe (Ericsson, 2000; Krampe & Ericsson, 1996) advocate that expert performance in skilled domains is maintained in very specific capacities. In their **selective maintenance model**, this is possible through appropriate attention to deliberate practice (see Chapter 11 for more on deliberate practice). Through extensive focus on appropriate training, experts are able to develop domain-specific mechanisms that allow them to circumvent general age-related limitations, and these mechanisms are more resistant to degradation over time, as long as training persists. For example, expert hockey players develop the ability to read offensive patterns of play and predict their opponents' actions (see Starkes, Helsen, & Jack, 2001, for a review of domain-specific characteristics).

To test this hypothesis, Krampe and Ericsson (1996) compared older and younger pianists on a range of performance-related measures. In addition, they compared performers at the expert and amateur levels (i.e., older expert, older amateur, younger expert, and younger amateur). They found that older performers, both amateur and expert, showed the same pattern of age-related decline on general measures of performance, such as reaction time; however, domain-specific measures of performance, such as finger-tapping speed and quality of performance, were maintained to a greater extent in older experts. In most cases differences in domain-specific measures of performance between younger and older experts were explained by differences in the amount of training and practice rather than age. Based on these results, the authors concluded that persistent regular involvement in a domain over time would allow aging performers to maintain their skills.

> Recent research indicates that golf skill is resistant to degradation over time.

Photo courtesy of AP/Orlin Wagner.

Reflections 12.2

Gordie Howe, one of the most successful hockey players in history, was able to continue playing in the National Hockey League (NHL) until he was 51 years of age. Compare explanations of this occurrence according to the compensation model and the selective maintenance model. Put yourself in the role of a researcher examining this issue. What evidence would you need to support each of the models?

Maintenance of Athletic Performance

Researchers have also examined the decline of athletic skill with age. In general, cognitive and motor skills appear to be more resistant to age-related decline than physiological factors, such as aerobic capacity. For example, data from running, rowing and swimming events indicate a decline in performance in the range of 0.35° to 0.5°% per year from peak performance (Bortz & Bortz, 1996; Starkes, Weir, & Young, 2003). However, examinations of cognitive-motor skills reveal that these skills are more resistant to the aging process. In a recent examination of performance in PGA golfers, Baker, Horton, Pearce, and Deakin (2005) found that although performance among elite golfers consistently declined with age, this rate of decline was less than half the rate of decline in physiological factors. Figure 12.2 shows their data on the decline in scoring average over time; the scoring average is the number of strokes required to play the entire course. Until age 50, players competed primarily on the PGA tour. After 50, players are eligible to play on the slightly easier Champions Tour, which accounts for the considerable decrease in scoring average from 49 to 51 years of age.

Figure 12.2   Performance decline data from Baker et al.'s (2005) study of elite PGA golfers

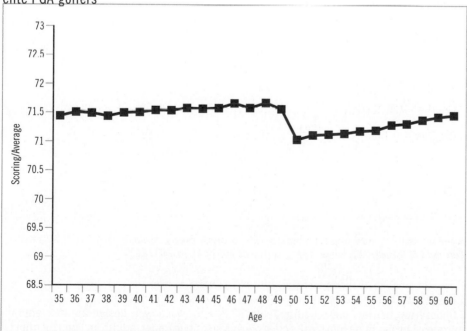

Note: Adapted from "A Longitudinal Examination of Performance Decline in Champion Golfers," by J. Baker, S. Horton, W. Pearce, and J. Deakin, 2005. Manuscript submitted for publication.

They also found that the rate of decline accelerated as the golfers got older (after 50 years of age), which matches previous examinations of athletic performance over time (e.g., Sterken, 2003; Stones & Kozma, 1981, 1984). This may not have been entirely due to age, however. Examinations of the training profiles of **Master athletes** (e.g., Starkes, Weir, Singh, Hodges, & Kerr, 1999) report significant differences in training volume and content compared with younger athletes, which may account for much of the decline. The age at which one qualifies for master-level competition various significantly across sports, but generally these athletes are 30 years or older. Just as more effective training leads to performance improvements (e.g., Ericsson, Krampe, & Tesch-Römer, 1993), decreased training intensity or duration leads to diminished performance. Collectively, these research studies indicate that, with proper attention to physical activity, the aging process can be much more positive than previously assumed. The logical question, therefore, is "why are more older adults not physically active?"

Barriers to Exercise for Older Adults

The idea that physical activity is useful for preventing premature morbidity and **mortality** is not new, and most of us are aware that involvement in physical activity leads to health benefits and a higher quality of life. However, for older persons, physical and psychological barriers can impede the adoption of a physically active lifestyle. In a recent study, Cohen-Mansfield, Marx, and Guralnik (2003) found that the most common barrier to physical activity involvement in older adults was an existing health problem or pain. In fact, nearly 60% of inactive older adults in their study reported this as a barrier to their physical activity and sport involvement. Other factors are listed in Table 12.3. As you can see, there is a combination of general and senior-specific barriers. Effective intervention programs to promote physical activity involvement in older populations should consider the diverse nature of these barriers.

Table 12.3   Barriers to Exercise in Seniors

Barrier	% Reporting This Barrier
Health Problems/Pain	53%
Lazy/Not Motivated	29%
Too Busy/No Time	25%
Fatigue	12%
Bad Weather	11%
Don't Like Exercise	8%

Note: From "Motivators and Barriers to Exercise in an Older Community-dwelling Population," by J. Cohen-Mansfield, M. S. Marx, and J. M. Guralnik, 2003, Journal of Aging and Physical Activity, *11, pp. 242–253.*

Reflections **12.3**
Choose two barriers presented in Table 12.3. How would you design an intervention strategy to facilitate physical activity involvement in older adults in light of these barriers?

<
Social support is an important
component to older adults' exercise
programs.
Photo courtesy of Kevin Dodge/Masterfile.

Determinants of Physical Activity and Sport Involvement in Older Adults

The factors influencing (younger) adults' participation in physical activity and sport (e.g., Trost, Owen, Bauman, Sallis, & Brown, 2002) fall into five categories, which are equally suited to describing the factors influencing participation in older adults

Demographic and Biological Factors

Among Canadian adults, age and gender are the most consistent predictors of physical activity involvement, with rates of participation declining as age increases and males being consistently more active than females (Stephens & Craig, 1990). As a matter of fact, gender is a fundamentally important variable in understanding exercise behaviour among older adults. In addition, other demographic factors also play significant roles. For instance, **socio-economic status** (SES) and educational level are two factors that are commonly linked with lifelong physical activity involvement (Dishman, 1990; Rudman, 1986). Older adults with a higher SES and a higher level of education are more likely to be involved in physical activity than those with lower SES and lower educational status. Research has also linked marital status and occupation with physical activity as an older adult (e.g., Dergance et al., 2003; O'Brien Cousins, 1998) although more research is necessary to determine precisely how these factors affect participation levels.

Behavioural Attributes

Patterns of behaviour throughout the lifespan have been good predictors of physical activity involvement. For instance, alcohol consumption is negatively related to physical activity involvement in older adults; that is, more activity means less alcohol use

(Smith & Storandt, 1997). Interestingly, some variables that would intuitively seem likely to be strongly related to adult physical activity level are not; one example is the amount of physical activity performed as a child or adolescent. Researchers involved in tracking studies have found that childhood and adolescent physical activity habits are only weakly correlated with physical activity as an adult (Seefeldt, Malina, & Clark, 2002; Trudeau, Laurencelle, & Shephard, 2004). There is also research that suggests that the strength of the relationship between childhood/adolescent physical activity and adult physical activity levels decreases as individuals age (Malina, 2001). For example, childhood physical activity may be a good predictor of involvement for a young adult, but it is not as effective at predicting physical activity for an older adult.

Social and Cultural Factors

Although individual barriers are often the focus of research and interventions, social and cultural barriers also play an important role. For instance, studies have reported that adequate levels of social support are critical to physical activity involvement (Chogahara, O'Brien Cousins, & Wankel, 1998). Researchers have found a variety of sources of support that can affect physical activity involvement. For instance, endorsement of physical activity by their spouse (Perusse, LeBlanc, & Bouchard, 1988), by members of their immediate family (Spreitzer & Snyder, 1983), by peers (O'Brien Cousins, 1998), or by physicians (Wechsler, Levine, Idelson, Rohman, & Taylor, 1983) can positively affect the likelihood that older adults will initiate and maintain physical activity involvement.

The dynamic interaction among members of an exercise group can also influence physical activity involvement. A study by Estabrooks and Carron (2000) used a team-building task to foster group cohesion. Their results showed that groups with greater cohesion had better rates of attendance and better adherence than control groups. Often, the dynamics of the group are influenced by the behaviour of the group's leader. Research examining the role of an exercise leader or class instructor has found that these individuals can have considerable influence on the quality of their participants' experience (McAuley & Jacobson, 1991).

Some expectations about behaviour are rooted in cultural beliefs, and these expectations can significantly impede an older individual's involvement in physical activity and exercise. A group that is particularly disadvantaged by cultural barriers is aging women. As mentioned earlier, women have typically been less physically active than men throughout the lifespan, and this certainly does not change as women age. Characterizations of female older adults as fragile or delicate reinforce the notion that physical activity for them is risky, and often these perceptions are reinforced by health care practitioners (Vertinsky, 1995).

Physical Environment Factors

Factors related to the physical activity environment can also impede physical activity involvement in older adults. An investigation by O'Neill and Reid (1991) examined barriers to physical activity in Canadian older adults and reported that between 5% and 15% felt that environmental factors negatively affected their participation. More specifically, the respondents indicated that difficulties getting to the facility, excessive costs of programs, unappealing activities, and inconvenient activity times were significant barriers to involvement. These factors may be less powerful predictors of physical activity participation than others (e.g., gender and age), and they are relatively easy to remedy. Simple changes to the way in which a program is administered can correct many environmental factors impeding physical activity involvement in older adults.

Psychological, Cognitive, and Emotional Factors

This final category of determinants is perhaps most applicable and salient to our discussion of the psychology of the older athlete. Several variables have been identified as important correlates of physical activity in adults: for example, locus of control, expected benefits, knowledge of health and exercise, perceived health or fitness, personality variables, body image, and perceived value of exercise outcomes (Trost et al., 2002). Despite the fact that more research is necessary to determine their relevance in predicting physical activity in older adults, several factors have been identified as central to understanding such activity. The two most common are enjoyment and perceived health and fitness.

ENJOYMENT   Researchers examining the factors that determine involvement in physical activity at any age have found that enjoyment is usually the best predictor (e.g., Lewis, Marcus, Pate, & Dunn, 2002; Salmon, Owen, Crawford, Bauman, & Sallis, 2003). Evidence indicates that this variable is an important predictor of physical activity involvement in older adults (Dergance et al., 2003; McAuley, Jerome, Elavsky, Marquez, & Ramsey, 2003).

PERCEIVED HEALTH AND FITNESS   A powerful barrier to physical activity involvement in older persons is a low perception of their current level of health and fitness. Many older adults believe that they are unable to participate in any type of exercise because of functional limitations (Cohen-Mansfield et al., 2003). Although in many cases these limitations are perceived rather than actual, they still limit older adults' inclination toward physical activities.

It is important to note that there is considerable interaction among the categories of barriers outlined above. For instance, demographic barriers, such as SES, affect physical environment barriers (e.g., proximity to exercise facilities) as well as psychological and emotional barriers (e.g., enjoyment and perceived health). These relationships reinforce the view that involvement in physical activity across the lifespan is an enormously complex issue and that successful physical activity programs and interventions should recognize this complexity.

Self-efficacy and Older Adults

A criticism of the majority of research available on older adults' motives for participating in sport and physical activity is that the research has been descriptive and atheoretical (Biddle & Nigg, 2000; Standage & Duda, 2004); this means it is not driven by a theory or hypothesis. Although descriptive studies are enormously important in initial stages of behavioural research, they are limited in that they do little to explain the motivational processes underlying behaviour.

One theory of motivation that has been considered in aging populations is Bandura's theory of **self-efficacy** (Bandura, 1986, 1997). As outlined in Chapter 4, self-efficacy refers to feelings of self-confidence in a given situation and has been found to be a central factor in explaining individuals' enthusiasm for different activities. Although a significant body of research has been amassed on the power of self-efficacy in predicting physical activity behaviour in youth (e.g., Bungum, Dowda, Weston, Trost, & Pate, 2000; Ryan & Dzewaltowski, 2002), recent research has confirmed its utility in older adults as well (e.g., McAuley et al., 2003).

Bandura's theory is based on the notion that individuals with high feelings of self-efficacy about physical activity are more likely to initiate and continue participation. Researchers examining this assumption in older adults have confirmed the importance of self-efficacy in predicting program initiation (McAuley, 1993), program attendance (Estabrooks & Carron, 2000), and adherence (McAuley, Lox, & Duncan, 1993). What is perhaps more interesting is that when older individuals participate in physical activity, their feelings of self-efficacy go up (Li et al., 2001; McAuley et al., 1993; McAuley et al., 1999); however, these levels decline when regular participation stops (McAuley et al., 1999). This finding suggests that feelings of self-efficacy and participation have a reciprocal relationship—feelings of self-efficacy promote participation which promotes increases in self-efficacy.

A positive finding from this research is that feelings of self-efficacy are readily modifiable. This has important implications for program design and interventions intended to promote physical activity in older populations. By focusing on increasing feelings of self-efficacy regarding physical activity, program administrators can support older individuals' exercise involvement in a powerful way.

Reflections 12.4

Although other theories of motivation have not been examined in aging populations, such theories may still explain the factors that influence older persons' participation in sport and physical activity. Recall one of the other theories discussed in Chapter 4, and consider how it might apply to motivation in older adults.

Negative Stereotypes: A Unique Barrier for Older Adults

The majority of the factors outlined in the sections above are significant barriers to physical activity for adults in general. In addition to these factors, older adults must contend with a barrier that is exclusive to their group—ageism. Studies have shown that attitudes toward aging in North America, held by the young and old alike, are predominantly negative (Levy & Langer, 1994). Such widespread agreement about a group can lead to the development of **stereotypes**, which in turn can lead to expectations about performance (Wheeler & Petty, 2001). These negative expectations can have considerable effect on the behaviour of members of the stereotyped group.

Sandra O'Brien Cousins' work at the University of Alberta has provided much insight into how societal beliefs about aging influence physical activity behaviour in older adults. Using qualitative interviews, she revealed that often "seniors say the darndest things" about physical activity and exercise (O'Brien Cousins, 2000, 2003). For example, she found that when confronted with the question "why are some older people less active?" many older adults responded with the equivalent of "why bother?" despite awareness of the benefits of physical activity. Dr. O'Brien Cousins suggested that this may be due to perceptions about the risks associated with physical activity in older adults. Older adults often reported that they are physically unable to participate in physical activity because "their heart couldn't take it." Although chronic periods of sedentary behaviour increase risk of various medical conditions, many older adults perceive exercise as high-risk behaviour. Contradictory messages may come from several sources, including significant others and society in general (Chogahara et al., 1998).

Becca Levy, a psychologist from Yale University has done extensive work on the ways in which stereotypes of aging can influence older adults' performance on cognitive and physical tasks. Her experimental research has examined how being exposed to a negative or positive stereotype about aging can influence performance in older adults. Levy used **implicit priming** to activate either a positive or a negative stereotype about aging in older adults. She found that priming older adults with a positive stereotype improved performance on cognitive measures, such as memory, as well as on physical measures, such as walking speed and handwriting (Hausdorff, Levy, & Wei, 1999; Levy, 2000). Her research also indicated that priming older adults with negative stereotypes of aging had marginal effects on performance. Arguably, this is due to the fact that negative stereotypes of aging are continually reinforced in our society. Older adults are continually exposed to negative stereotypes about aging (and therefore, about themselves) through media and social interactions and, as a result, live in an environment that perpetually emphasizes a negative view of aging.

Although the most obvious effects of negative stereotypes in studies to date have been immediate (e.g., decreased performance), some researchers have speculated that the most damaging effects may be long-term, such as feelings of dissatisfaction and ultimately disengagement (see Major, Spencer, Schmader, Wolfe, & Crocker, 1998). Steele (1997) postulated that under chronic situations of stereotype exposure, individuals become pressured to disidentify with the domain to preserve feelings of self-worth. **Disidentification** involves reconceptualizing your self-image to remove the value associated with a domain, thereby reducing the impact of negative performance. Although useful for maintaining self-image, disidentification can undermine the motivation required for long-term involvement in an activity.

As detailed in Chapter 4, sustained motivation is dependent on feelings of achievement and accomplishment. Older adults who believe that physical and cognitive decline is an inevitable part of growing older may disengage from activities that challenge these abilities in order to preserve their self-image. As discussed earlier, this can have important ramifications because the lack of physical and cognitive activity is believed to be the principal cause of the functional decline in aging populations (Maharam et al., 1999). Stereotypes have tremendous influence on behaviour. Older adults may be limiting their involvement in physical activity because of internalizing negative stereotypes about their group. Indeed, examinations of older adults' beliefs about physical activity confirm that negative stereotypes about the aging process have a significant effect on involvement (O'Brien Cousins, 2000).

Furthermore, the belief that old age is inevitably associated with the gradual loss of physical and cognitive functionality may promote a disengagement from other positive health behaviours. Levy and Myers (2004) used survey data from the Ohio Longitudinal Study of Aging and Retirement to examine this hypothesis. They examined how older adults felt about their own aging and whether those beliefs affected their health behaviours over a 20-year period. Health behaviours included wearing a seatbelt, eating a balanced diet, having regular physical examinations, and participation in some form of exercise. Their results revealed that older adults who had more positive self-perceptions of aging at baseline were more likely to practise preventive health behaviours, reinforcing the notion that older people's self-perceptions of aging is an important variable in their approach to preventive health behaviours.

Although these results point to a strong influence for age-related beliefs in determining physical activity involvement, the situation is certainly not as simplistic as current results would suggest. Research on the effects of exercise and physical activity involvement suggests that physical activity involvement can have significant positive effects on measures of emotional and psychological health (see Biddle & Mutrie, 2001, for a review). Thus, there may be a dynamic, reciprocal relationship between physical activity and age beliefs, such that positive age beliefs promote physical activity and physical activity promotes positive age beliefs.

Reflections 12.5

When you think of a 70-year-old, what words or images come to mind? Are they predominantly negative or positive? Consider ways in which your day-to-day experiences may reinforce negative stereotypes of aging.

Rewriting the record books:
Ed Whitlock, marathon runner

In 1896, the Olympic marathon was won in 2 hours and 56 minutes. In 2003, Ed Whitlock, a Canadian marathoner, ran just three minutes slower than this in the Toronto marathon. What is remarkable about this feat is that Whitlock was 72 years old when he achieved this performance and became the first person over 70 to break 3 hours for the marathon distance (2 hours 59 minutes). Throughout his running career, Whitlock has established numerous age-group records, and he continues to train and compete at the highest levels of competition, regularly representing Canada at international events. As remarkable as Whitlock is, he is not as rare as you might expect. With each passing year, aging athletes are rewriting the sports record books as they demolish previous standards of performance. This aging vanguard forces us to re-evaluate our perspective of what it means to grow older.

The Master Athlete: A Model of Successful Aging

The increasing popularity of Master-level competition is evident in such events as the World Masters Games and the Senior Olympic Games in the United States. These highly competitive events continue to grow with each passing year, providing older athletes with the opportunity to participate in sport at a highly competitive level against the best athletes in the world at their age. Canada has played an important role in the development of Masters sport. The first World Masters Games were held in Toronto in 1985, and in 2005 the sixth World Masters Games were held in Edmonton. Recent games have seen more than 20 000 athletes compete in 27 sports, which makes the games the largest multi-sport events in the world. (The World Masters Games are governed by the International Masters Games Association [www.imga-masters.com]).

Because of their ability to maintain high levels of physical and cognitive competency, Master athletes represent a unique population that defy the stereotypical views of aging we hold in North American. For instance, Master athletes consistently report high levels of physical and mental health (Shephard, Kavanagh, Mertens, Qureshi, & Clark, 1995).

A criticism of examining the performance of Master athletes and applying this information to models of general aging is that the Master data represent individuals who are at the highest level of performance in a given domain, and they may not accurately reflect the age-related decline of the average individual. Although this is a valid criticism, this population is still extremely valuable for age-related research, primarily because they reflect a group of individuals who have maintained involvement in physical activity and exercise for extended periods of time. They also serve as important role models (e.g., as stereotype busters). Data from Master athletes can be used to represent the performance levels possible for adults who perform high amounts of physical activity throughout their lifespan. In general, research on Master athletes indicates that maintaining a high level of involvement in physical activity as we age allows us to maintain high levels of ability. As a result, Master athletes appear to represent an ideal model of successful aging.

Although Master-level competition has been around for quite some time, we actually know very little about those who compete at this level, compared with performers at younger levels of competition. However, some general conclusions can be made from research conducted to date.

Participant Motives in Master Sport

An exploratory investigation of participant motives of Master track athletes found that the top-ranked motives were "to be physically fit" and "to meet new friends," while the lowest-ranked motives were "to get out of the house" and "to get rid of energy" (Fung, Ha, Louie, & Poon, 1992). These findings were echoed in a study of marathon runners by Ogles and Masters (2000), who found the primary motives for older runners were to improve general health, to deal with weight concerns, to give meaning to their lives, and to affiliate with other runners. In addition, the researchers found that the motives for participating in younger and older runners were appreciably different. While older runners were motivated by physical and social benefits of participation, younger athletes were more motivated by personal goal achievement (e.g., running a personal best, improving overall running speed).

Master-level Competitors vs. Non-competitor Older Athletes

Master runners have higher self-esteem, lower consumption of alcohol, better sleep patterns, and fewer physical problems than their non-active contemporaries (Morgan & Costill, 1996). In addition, Master athletes view their participation as an effective way to deal with stress and improve mood (Smith & Storandt, 1997).

Early Sport Involvement

An investigation of competitors, non-competitors (i.e., physically active but not competitive older athletes), and non-exercisers found that there was no difference among the groups with regard to activity levels during childhood and adolescence (Smith & Storandt, 1997). However, a critical time for Master athlete competition seems to be the third decade of life, when many adults are focusing on establishing families and careers. Master athletes were more likely to maintain involvement in sport and physical activity during this period while non-competitors and non-exercisers were less likely to.

Mood and Personality

In Chapter 3, authors Sedgwick and Crocker reviewed research using the Profile of Mood States (POMS) to describe the personalities of elite athletes. Similar investigations have been undertaken with Master athletes. Ungerleider, Golding, and Porter (1989) found that, similar to other athletes examined, Master track-and-field athletes demonstrated an iceberg profile: lower scores on tension, depression, fatigue, and confusion and higher scores on vigour than normative samples. In addition, the Master athletes' profile was also lower in depression and anger than reported by other athletes. A single study examining measures of personality (Smith & Storandt, 1997) found little difference between Master-level competitors and non-competitors. However, as outlined in Chapter 3, research using the POMS has been somewhat equivocal in distinguishing between athletes at different levels of ability.

Use of Psychological Skills

Ungerleider, Golding, Porter, and Foster (1989) have examined the use of different psychological skills by Masters track-and-field athletes. Their data indicated that 70% of their sample used imagery in training and competition. Furthermore, 35% used physical relaxation methods, 14% meditated, and 5% practised yoga. Prior research has supported the use of **associative strategies** by successful runners; however, there are conflicting data on this question with regard to Master runners. Ungerleider et al. reported that 76% of their sample used associative strategies, while Okwumabua, Meyers, and Santille (1987) found that the majority of their Master runners reported **dissociative strategies** during training and competition. Further research is clearly necessary to reconcile these inconsistent findings.

General Recommendations for Working with Master Athletes

Although many of the sport psychology concepts covered in this text are equally applicable to Master-level performers (e.g., goal setting and imagery), some concepts require an approach specifically designed with older athletes in mind. First, the specific needs of this population should be recognized. The psychological needs of Master athletes are unique; therefore, training programs and interventions must be designed with these needs in mind. Second, the athlete's experience and knowledge should be acknowledged. In the majority of cases, Master athletes will have an enormous depth of experience in their sport, in many cases superior to the knowledge of the sport psychologist working with them. Rather than attempting to learn as much or more than the athlete they are working with, sport psychologists should consider ways in which they can access the athlete's knowledge. This will reduce the amount of background reading needed and improve the rapport between the sport psychologist and the Master athletes. Third, one's attitudes toward older adults should be assessed for stereotypes. North American society reinforces a predominantly negative perspective about the aging process, and as a result, this attitude may be entrenched in your own outlook about aging. Changing your outlook to something more positive (and more accurate) is, unfortunately, not done overnight. Being aware of any preconceived beliefs you have will assist you in dealing with older athletes.

Chapter Summary

The focus of this chapter has been on physical activity and sport involvement in older persons. Unfortunately, there is a continuing trend among Canadians toward a decreasing level of physical activity as we age. There is, however, growing support for the notion that much of the cognitive and physical decline seen in aging populations is a result of disuse, rather than aging per se. The variables influencing involvement in physical activity in older adults include demographic and biological factors, behavioural attributes, social and cultural factors, physical environment factors, and psychological, cognitive, and emotional factors. In addition, negative cultural stereotypes about aging are unique barriers for older adults in our society.

One group of older adults seems to defy the typical profile of aging—Master athletes. This group has been able to maintain high levels of ability in the face of advancing age. Researchers examining these athletes have indicated that they are unique, different from sedentary older adults and younger athletes in several areas (e.g., mood, motives, use of psychological skills). Further research is clearly required to further describe the factors influencing sport involvement and competitive performance in this group.

Review Questions

1. Compare and contrast the compensation model and the selective maintenance model of skill maintenance.
2. Describe four characteristics of Master-level performers.
3. Briefly explain the influence negative cultural stereotypes of aging may have on older adults.
4. Define sarcopenia and explain why older adults should be aware of this condition.
5. Describe the typical profile of physical activity involvement in older adults.
6. Provide a list of barriers to physical activity involvement in older adults and provide a possible strategy to address this barrier.

Suggested Reading

O'Brien Cousins, S. (1998). *Exercise, aging, and health: Overcoming barriers to an active old age.* Philadelphia: Taylor and Francis.

O'Brien Cousins, S., & Horne, T. (1999). *Active living among older adults: Health benefits and outcomes.* Philadelphia: Taylor and Francis.

References

American College of Sports Medicine (ACSM). (1998). Exercise and physical activity in older adults (Position Stand). *Medicine and Science in Sports and Exercise, 30,* 992–1008.

Baker, J., Horton, S., Pearce, W., & Deakin, J. (2005). *A longitudinal examination of performance decline in champion golfers.* Manuscript submitted for publication.

Bandura, A. (1986). *Social foundations of thought and action: A social cognitive theory.* Englewood Cliffs, NJ: Prentice Hall.

Bandura, A. (1997). *Self-efficacy: The exercise of control.* New York: Freeman.

Biddle, S., & Mutrie, N. (2001). *Psychology of physical activity: Determinants, well being, and interventions.* Oxford, UK: Routledge.

Biddle, S. J. H., & Nigg, C. R. (2000). Theories of exercise behavior. *International Journal of Sports Psychology, 31,* 290–304.

Bortz, W. M., & Bortz, W. M. (1996). How fast do we age? Exercise performance over time as a biomarker. *Journal of Gerontology: Medical Sciences, 51,* 223–225.

Bosman, E. A. (1993). Age-related differences in the motoric aspects of transcription typing skill. *Psychology and Aging, 8,* 87–102.

Bungum, T., Dowda, M., Weston, A., Trost, S. G., & Pate, R. R. (2000). Correlates of physical activity in male and female youth. *Pediatric Exercise Science, 12,* 71–79.

Charness, N. (1981). Search in chess: Age and skill differences. *Journal of Experimental Psychology: Human Perception and Performance, 7,* 467–476.

Chogahara, M., O'Brien Cousins, S., & Wankel, L. M. (1998). Positive and negative social influences on the physical activity of older adults. *Journal of Aging and Physical Activity, 6,* 1–17.

Cohen-Mansfield, J., Marx, M. S., & Guralnik, J. M. (2003). Motivators and barriers to exercise in an older community-dwelling population. *Journal of Aging and Physical Activity, 11,* 242–253.

Dergance, J. M., Calmbach, W. L., Dhanda, R., Miles, T. P., Hazuda, H. P., & Mouton, C. P. (2003). Barriers to and benefits of leisure time physical activity in the elderly: Differences across cultures. *Journal of the American Geriatrics Society, 51,* 863–868.

Dishman, R. K. (1990). Determinants of participation in physical activity. In C. Bouchard, R. J. Shephard, T. Stephens, J. R. Sutton, & B. D. McPherson (Eds.), *Exercise, fitness and health: Consensus of current knowledge* (pp. 75–101). Champaign, IL: Human Kinetics.

Ericsson, K. A. (2000). How experts attain and maintain superior performance: Implications for the enhancement of skilled performance in older individuals. *Journal of Aging and Physical Activity, 8,* 346–352.

Ericsson, K. A., Krampe, R. T., & Tesch-Römer, C. (1993). The role of deliberate practice in the acquisition of expert performance. *Psychological Review, 100,* 363–406.

Estabrooks, P. A., & Carron, A. V. (2000). Predicting scheduling self-efficacy in older adult exercisers: The role of task cohesion. *Journal of Aging and Physical Activity, 8,* 41–50.

Fung, L., Ha, A., Louie, L., & Poon, F. (1992). Sport participation motives among veteran track and field athletes. *Journal of the International Council for Health Physical Education and Recreation, 29,* 24–28.

Hausdorff, J. M., Levy, B. R., & Wei, J. Y. (1999). The power of ageism on physical function of older persons: Reversibility of age-related gait changes. *Journal of the American Geriatric Society, 47,* 1346–1349.

Health Canada. (1999). *Canada's physical activity guide to healthy living for older adults.* Ottawa: Canada Communications Group.

Krampe, R. T., & Ericsson, K. A. (1996). Maintaining excellence: Deliberate practice and elite performance in young and older pianists. *Journal of Experimental Psychology: General, 125,* 331–359.

Levy, B. R. (2000). Handwriting as a reflection of aging self-stereotypes. *Journal of Geriatric Psychiatry: A Multidisciplinary Journal of Mental Health, 33,* 81–94.

Levy, B. R., & Langer, E. J. (1994). Aging free from negative stereotypes: Successful memory in China and among the American deaf. *Journal of Personality and Social Psychology, 66,* 989–997.

Levy, B. R., & Myers, L. M. (2004). Preventive health behaviors influenced by positive self-perceptions of aging. *Preventive Medicine, 39,* 625–629.

Lewis, B. A., Marcus, B. H., Pate, R. R., & Dunn, A. L. (2002). Psychosocial mediators of physical activity behavior among adults and children. *American Journal of Preventive Medicine, 23,* 26–35.

Li, F., Harmer, P., McAuley, E., Fisher, K. J., Duncan, T. E., & Duncan, S. C. (2001). Tai Chi, self-efficacy and physical function in the elderly. *Prevention Science, 2,* 229–239.

Maharam, L. G., Bauman, P. A., Kalman, D., Skolnik, H., & Perle, S. M. (1999). Masters athletes: Factors affecting performance. *Sports Medicine, 28,* 273–285.

Major, B., Spencer, S., Schmader, T., Wolfe, C., Crocker, J. (1998). Coping with negative stereotypes about intellectual performance: The role of psychological disengagement. *Personality and Social Psychology Bulletin, 24,* 34–50.

Malina, R. M. (2001). Adherence to physical activity from childhood to adulthood: A perspective from tracking studies. *Quest, 53,* 346–355.

McAuley, E. (1993). Self-efficacy and the maintenance of exercise participation in older adults. *Journal of Behavioral Medicine, 16,* 103–113.

McAuley, E., & Jacobson, L. (1991). Self-efficacy and exercise participation in sedentary adult females. *American Journal of Health Promotion, 5*, 185–191.

McAuley, E., Jerome, G. J., Elavsky, S., Marquez, D. X., & Ramsey, S. N. (2003). Predicting long-term maintenance of physical activity in older adults. *Preventive Medicine, 37*, 110–118.

McAuley, E., Katula, J., Mihalko, S. L., Blissmer, B., Duncan, T., Pena, M., et al. (1999). Mode of physical activity and self-efficacy in older adults: A latent growth curve analysis. *Journal of Gerontology: Psychological Sciences, 54B*, 283–292.

McAuley, E., Lox, C. L., & Duncan, T. (1993). Long-term maintenance of exercise, self-efficacy, and physiological change in older adults. *Journal of Gerontology, 48*, 218–223.

Morgan, W. P., & Costill, D. L. (1996). Selected psychological characteristics and health behaviors of aging marathon runners: A longitudinal study. *International Journal of Sports Medicine, 17*, 305–312.

O'Brien Cousins, S. (1998) *Exercise, aging and health: Overcoming barriers to an active old age.* Philadelphia: Taylor and Francis.

O'Brien Cousins, S. (2000). My heart couldn't take it: Older women's beliefs about exercise benefits and risks. *Journal of Gerontology: Psychological Sciences, 55*, 283–294.

O'Brien Cousins, S. (2003). Seniors say the "darndest" things about exercise: Quotable quotes that stimulate applied gerontology. *The Journal of Applied Gerontology, 22*, 359–378.

Oeppen, J., & Vaupel, J. W. (2002). Broken limits to life expectancy. *Science, 296*, 1029–1031.

Ogles, B. M., & Masters, K. S. (2000). Older vs. younger adult male marathon runners: Participant motives and training habits. *Journal of Sport Behavior, 23*, 130–143.

Okwumabua, T. M., Meyers, A. W., & Santille, L. (1987). A demographic and cognitive profile of master runners. *Journal of Sport Behavior, 11*, 212–220.

O'Neill, K., & Reid, G. (1991). Perceived barriers to physical activity by older adults. *Canadian Journal of Public Health, 82*, 392–396.

Perusse, L., LeBlanc, C., & Bouchard, C. (1988) Familial resemblance in lifestyle components: Results from the Canada Fitness Survey. *Canadian Journal of Public Health, 79*, 201–205.

Rudman, W. J. (1986). Life course socioeconomic transitions and sport involvement: A theory of restricted opportunity. In B. D. McPherson (Ed.), *Sport and Aging* (pp. 25–35). Champaign, IL: Human Kinetics.

Ryan, G. J., & Dzewalkowski, D. A. (2002). Comparing the relationships between different types of self-efficacy and physical activity in youth. *Health Education and Behavior, 29*, 491–504.

Salmon, J., Owen, N., Crawford, D., Bauman, A., & Sallis, J. F. (2003). Physical activity and sedentary behavior: A population-based study of barriers, enjoyment, and preference. *Health Psychology, 22*, 178–188.

Salthouse, T. A. (1984). Effects of age and skill in typing. *Journal of Experimental Psychology: General, 113*, 345–371.

Seefeldt, V., Malina, R. M., & Clark, M. A. (2002). Factors affecting levels of physical activity in adults. *Sports Medicine, 32*, 143–168.

Shephard, R. J., Kavanagh, T., Mertens, D. J., Qureshi, S., & Clark, M. (1995). Personal health benefits of Masters athletics competition. *British Journal of Sports Medicine, 19*, 35–40.

Smith, C. L., & Storandt, M. (1997). Physical activity participation in older adults: A comparison of competitors, noncompetitors, and nonexercisers. *Journal of Aging and Physical Activity, 5*, 98–110.

Spreitzer, E., & Snyder, E. E. (1983). Correlates of participation in adult recreational sports. *Journal of Leisure Research, 15*, 27–38.

Standage, M., & Duda, J. L. (2004). Motivational processes among older adults in sport and exercise settings. In M. R. Weiss (Ed.), *Developmental sport and exercise psychology: A lifespan perspective* (pp. 357–381). Morgantown, WV: Fitness Information Technology.

Starkes, J. L., Helsen, W., & Jack, R. (2001). Expert performance in sport and dance. In R. Singer, H. Hausenblas, & C. Janelle (Eds.), *Handbook of research in sport psychology* (2nd ed., pp. 174–201). New York: Macmillan.

Starkes, J. L., Weir, P. L., Singh, P., Hodges, N. J., & Kerr, T. (1999). Aging and the retention of sport expertise. *International Journal of Sport Psychology, 30*, 283–301.

Starkes, J. L., Weir, P. L., & Young, B. W. (2003). What does it take for older athletes to continue to excel? In J. L. Starkes & K. A. Ericsson (Eds.), *Expert performance in sports: Advances in research on sport expertise* (pp. 251–272). Champaign, IL: Human Kinetics.

Statistics Canada (2005). *Canadian Community Health Survey, 2000/01.* Retrieved January 9, 2006, from http://www.statcan.ca/english/freepub/82-221-XIE/00502/tables/html/2165.htm

Steele, C. M. (1997). A threat in the air: How stereotypes shape intellectual identity and performance. *American Psychologist, 52,* 613–629.

Stephens, T., & Craig, C. L. (1990). *The well-being of Canadians: Highlights of the 1988 Campbell's survey.* Ottawa: Canadian Fitness and Lifestyle Research Institute.

Sterken, E. (2003). From the cradle to the grave: How fast can we run? *Journal of Sports Sciences, 21,* 479–491.

Stones, M. J., & Kozma, A. (1981). Adult trends in athletic performance. *Experimental Aging Research, 17,* 269–280.

Stones, M. J., & Kozma, A. (1984). Longitudinal trends in track and field performances. *Experimental Aging Research, 10,* 107–110.

Trost, S. G., Owen, N., Bauman, A. E., Sallis, J. F., & Brown, W. (2002). Correlates of adults' participation in physical activity: Review and update. *Medicine and Science in Sports and Exercise, 34,* 1996–2001.

Trudeau, F., Laurencelle, L., Shephard, R. J. (2004). Tracking of physical activity from childhood to adulthood. *Medicine and Science in Sports and Exercise, 36,* 1937–1943.

Ungerleider, S., Golding, J. M., & Porter, K. (1989). Mood profiles of masters track and field athletes. *Perceptual and Motor Skills, 68,* 607–617.

Ungerleider, S., Golding, J. M., Porter, K., & Foster, J. (1989). An exploratory examination of cognitive strategies used by Masters track and field athletes. *The Sport Psychologist, 3,* 245–253.

Vertinsky, P. (1995). Stereotypes of aging women and exercise: A historical perspective. *Journal of Aging and Physical Activity, 3,* 223–237.

Wechsler, H., Levine, S., Idelson, R. K., Rohman, M., & Taylor, J. O. (1983). The physician's role in health promotion: A survey of primary care physicians. *New England Journal of Medicine, 308,* 97–100.

Wheeler, S. C., & Petty, R. E. (2001). The effects of stereotype activation on behavior: A review of possible mechanisms. *Psychological Bulletin, 127,* 797–826.

Diane E. Stevens
Kimberley L. Gammage
Lindsay Waddell

Female Athletes and Gender Issues

Chapter Objectives

After reading this chapter, you should be able to do the following:

1. Define *sex* and *gender* and explain how both concepts have been studied in sport.
2. Differentiate among various theoretical approaches to gender research.
3. Explain gender differences in cognitions and their relative influences.
4. Explain gender differences in social experiences and their relative influences.

Are women catching up? With the increased prevalence of women's sport participation, the belief that female athletes are catching up with their male counterparts has gained strength. This belief got a big boost when it was demonstrated that female runners were improving their performances at a faster rate than men (Whipp & Ward, 1992). For example, it was reported that the world-record pace for men, at distances ranging from 200 m to 10 000 m, was decreasing by about 5.7 to 7.6 metres per minute every 10 years. Women were getting faster at more than double that rate, from 14 to 18 metres per minute each decade. Public sentiment echoed scientific findings when a poll reported that 66% of respondents believed that "top female athletes will beat top males at the highest competitive levels" (Tharp, 1996).

A different perspective was advanced by Seiler and Sailer (1997), who acknowledged that although women's performances have been moving closer to those of men, the improvement for women has plateaued. In other words, as men continue to improve, the performances of females are now beginning to fall further behind, instead of catching up. The growth in the gender gap was attributed to women's performance in the mid-'90s, which was slower than in the previous decade. The relative slow-down in female performances documented by Seiler and Sailer served as a shock to sport scientists, coaches, and the public.

Are the differences between men's and women's performance times really becoming wider? To address this question, the differences between male and female athletes need to be understood. From a training perspective, both males and females respond in similar ways, for example, in maximum oxygen consumption and in decreased body fat percentage. Attention to physiological factors that may account for gender differences is beyond the scope of this chapter; instead, we will examine many of the most relevant psychosocial factors.

Some Common Myths about Female Athletes and Gender Issues

MYTH: *Women's participation in sport is associated with health risks.*

The belief that sport participation is harmful to women's health is one of the oldest myths used to deter women from sport participation. Fear of uterine displacement and damage to other reproductive organs were common reasons cited to prevent women from becoming physically active. Medical experts also proposed vitalist theories of energy, which reasoned (albeit incorrectly) that because the energy of each individual was limited and non-renewable, women were morally obligated to avoid intellectual and athletic pursuits in the interest of maintaining their health for childrearing and domestic chores. Today, there is no evidence that sport participation causes physical harm to women. The Women's Sport Foundation commissioned a report that outlined the numerous physical, psychological, social, and academic benefits associated with sport and physical activity (Sabo, Miller, Melnick, & Heywood, 2004). These benefits generally held across age and race.

MYTH: *Sport masculinizes the female athlete.*

The concern that sport masculinizes women has to do with both the appearance and the sexuality of the female athlete. Because sport has traditionally been a male preserve, female participants who acquire the skills necessary to become physically proficient have been assumed to become more masculine in the process. Since this masculinity has increasingly become associated with lesbianism (Cahn, 1994), many female athletes have been suspected of homosexuality. Nevertheless, it is easy to challenge both myths. As women (e.g., Catriona LeMay Doan, Therese Brisson, Perdita Felicien) rewrite definitions of appropriate behaviour and appearance, and thereby challenge the exclusive identification of muscles with masculinity, these myths seem empty.

MYTH: *Women are not interested in sport.*
A corollary of this view is the belief that female athletes will never attract as wide an audience as male athletes because their performance is inherently inferior. Such arguments assume that women's lack of interest precedes, and therefore justifies, lack of opportunity to perform. However, as Greendorfer (1992) argued, female participation and interest in sport may be a consequence of social learning, which directs women away from sport instead of predisposing them toward sport. Thus, because women have often been denied opportunities to participate, they have also been unable to demonstrate their interest in doing so. At the same time, there have been limited opportunities to view female performance and cultivate an appreciation for the unique talents and skills of female athletes.

MYTH: *Female athletes have to be coached differently from men.*
Anson Dorrance, the head women's soccer coach at the University of North Carolina (UNC) at Chapel Hill, is arguably the most successful coach in women's sport. Statistically, his teams have won 18 of the 23 national championships decided in the history of collegiate women's soccer. With a winning percentage of .946 (559-25-15), his coaching record is unsurpassed. Also a former coach of the men's soccer team at UNC, Dorrance (1996, 2002) believes that men and women need to be coached differently; he stressed the differences in leadership style and the importance of building cohesion with male and females athletes. There is very little empirical research on coaching the female athlete. Research conducted in the late 70s (Chelladurai & Saleh, 1979; Neil & Kirby, 1979) showed that gender partially influenced preferences for coach behaviour. However, as more and more women break through the physical, social, and psychological barriers imposed on their sport participation, the differences may be minimized. In fact, more recent research has demonstrated no differences in the coaching preferences between male and female athletes (Sherman, Fuller, & Speed, 2000). Furthermore, using meta-analytic techniques, Carron, Colman, Wheeler, and Stevens (2002) demonstrated that gender did not moderate the cohesion-performance relationship.

Introduction

Within sport, stereotypes and attitudes regarding appropriate male and female behaviour have served not only to prevent participation altogether (mainly of females) but also to direct athletes toward certain activities and away from others. With regard to the female athlete, negative attitudes surrounding participation have been especially resistant to change.

A Brief History of Female Athletes in Canada

Just as femininity has an established history of keeping women out of sport, masculinity has an equally well-developed legacy of encouraging men to participate. Since the middle nineteenth century, many have viewed sport as the primary way to "turn boys into men" (Whitson, 1990). Coined "muscular Christianity," a popular belief within the male boarding schools of England was that muscularity was synonymous with morality. The judgment and courage displayed on the fields were thought to transfer to other arenas of life. Canadians enthusiastically adopted the belief that sport could develop masculinity.

As the economic structure of Canada changed from an agrarian base to an industrial one, the legacy of property ownership passing from father to son became a dying tradition. Along with the fact that females dominated school-teaching and childrearing activities, the economic changes led to fears of "social feminization" and resulted in what Messner (1994) described as a masculinity crisis. The crisis manifested itself in an increased interest in sports, especially those that emphasized physical strength and toughness.

With the onset of World War I (1914–1918), women found employment in the factories and businesses. Many subsequently began participating in sport for recreation, and a grassroots movement was started that led to the establishment of women's athletic clubs. Alexandrine Gibb founded the first all-women's multi-sport club in Canada, the Toronto Ladies Athletic Club. In 1915, the most successful team in the history of basketball was founded by Percy Page in Edmonton; it was called the Edmonton Commercial Graduate Basketball team, or the Edmonton Grads. Until folding in 1940, the team's record was an impressive 502-20, with a consecutive winning streak of 147 games. In 1924, Cecil Eustace Smith became the first Canadian female to represent her country at the first official Olympic Winter Games. Four years later, six female track-and-field athletes competed for Canada in the Olympic Summer Games. Dubbed the "matchless six" (Jane Bell, Ethel Catherwood, Myrtle Cook, Fanny "Bobbie" Rosenfeld, Ethel Smith, and Jean Thompson), these athletes brought home four medals. Although female participation continued to increase through the 1930s, growing resistance to women's sport developed. Many feared that sport competition fostered "manly behaviours."

A second masculinity crisis occurred in the post–World War II era, as the economic structure of the country shifted once again (Messner, 1994). The economy was no longer dependent on physical labour to the extent it had once been. Bureaucracy, accessibility to women, and consumerism characterized the new service economy. The marriage of the media and sport played an important role in maintaining traditional beliefs about the superiority of male physicality and promoted the idea that women embrace femininity in all areas of life. Sports that emphasized aesthetic qualities (e.g., figure skating and synchronized swimming) enjoyed increased popularity for women whereas most female team sports lost their public appeal.

In 1961, the federal government enacted the Fitness and Amateur Sport Act (Bill C-131), which ensured that sport and fitness opportunities were available to all Canadians. At the grassroots level, team sports thrived; however, media focus on female sports continually emphasized sport replete with beauty and grace. Further government support has served to enhance the status of female athletes through the establishment of the Canadian Association for the Advancement of Women in Sport and Physical Activity and the Women in Coaching Program.

Not only is the female athlete more recognized and accepted in today's athletic world, but women have also broken down barriers in sports traditionally considered "men's only." Janet Guthrie became the first woman to race in the Indianapolis 500 in 1977, and in 1992, Manon Rheaume became the first female to play in the National Hockey League. In 1997, the National Basketball Association hired two female referees to officiate in the league. Finally, in 1998 and 2004 women's ice hockey and wrestling, respectively, became Olympic sports, which further challenged the dichotomy between masculine and feminine sports. More information on the history of women in sport can be found at the website of the Canadian Association for the Advancement of Women in Sport (www.caaws.ca).

> ## Reflections 13.1
> In 1984, twelve-year-old Justine Blainey was denied the right to play Pee Wee hockey on a boy's hockey team. Although the ensuing court decision was counter to the Canadian Charter of Rights and Freedoms, the decision to deny female participation on male teams was upheld. Although times have changed (e.g., Haley Wickenheiser played for a men's team in Finland, and Annika Sorenstam played a PGA event), controversy still exists as to whether females should be allowed to play against men. One side of the argument supports the females' right to play, while the other side suggests it would diminish the quality of the women's game. What do you think? And why?

Sex vs. Gender

The terms *sex* and *gender* are traditionally interchangeable. However, a more precise definition of the terms has been advanced, with **sex** referring to the biological distinctions between males and females and **gender** referring to those aspects of maleness and femaleness that are psychosocially determined (Hall, 1990). The sex differences (biological) approach assumes that not only will there be group differences between men and women on key traits (e.g., strength, confidence, body composition) but also that there will be non-overlapping distributions of scores for males and females. Some physical indices do demonstrate non-overlapping distributions (e.g., pregnancy), but for the majority of traits or characteristics, the distribution of scores for the genders overlap. For example, it is obvious that distributions of height for men and women overlap, that not *all* men are taller than *all* women. Males and females may differ in their average scores, but across any characteristic or level of ability, there are always representatives of both genders. As a result, researchers have offered arguments against studying gender differences at all, with some challenging the accuracy of the information produced and others focusing on the social consequences associated with an uncritical examination of the findings (Baumeister, 1988; Favreau, 1997).

In sport, the sex differences approach translated into the belief that women were not capable of performing physically at a high competitive level because of their supposedly inferior genetic makeup. The often quipped "she throws like a girl" implied that a girl's baseball throwing style was natural and inevitable and could not be altered by practice or coaching. Even though the biological approach to studying women in sport has since been criticized as narrow-focused and short-sighted, there are some apparent physical and hormonal differences between men and women (e.g., height, testosterone and estrogen levels).

Considering only the psychosocial approaches also has powerful implications. For example, the belief that men are "strong" and women are "weak" has powerful consequences for the way both sexes view and shape their bodies according to varied standards of beauty and health (Lowe, 1983). Distinguishing between sex and gender is useful as it suggests that many differences between males and females are not automatically the result of biology. Therefore, we often do not know whether a particular difference is the result of biological, psychological, or sociological influences. The following quotation highlights this point:

If a society puts half its children in dresses and skirts but warns them not to move in ways that reveal their underpants, while putting the other half in jeans and overalls and encouraging them to climbs trees and play ball and other outdoor games; if later, during adolescence, the half that has work trousers is exhorted to "eat like a growing boy", while the half in skirts is warned to "watch its weight and not get fat"; if the half in jeans trots around in sneakers or boots, while the half in skirts totters about on spiked heels, then these two groups of people will be biologically as well as socially different. Their muscles will be different, as will their reflexes, posture, arms, legs, and feet, hand-eye coordination, spatial perception, and so on . . . there is no way to sort out the biological and social components that produce these differences, therefore no way to sort nature from nurture. (Hubbard, 1990, pp. 115–116)

In fact, what seems apparent is that many differences result from an interaction of these forces (Hyde, 1994; Unger & Crawford, 1993) and emphasizing one approach (sex/biological vs. gender/psychosocial) over the other is dangerous. With the notion of biological differences alone accounting for variation in performance and behaviour discredited, researchers have turned toward examining psychosocial factors that may be responsible for creating the differences.

Reflections 13.2

Consider the role of the following factors in female athlete performance: better access to facilities and coaches, improved nutrition and health of females, relative increase in female participation, increased professionalism, more role models, increased acceptance of female athletes. Consider how the above factors may reduce the performance gender gap further! Do you care to examine performance differences yourself? Results of swim meets can be found at www.swimming.ca. Are female athletes catching up?

Theoretical Approaches to Understanding Gender

Theoretical approaches to studying gender differences have driven beliefs and influenced the questions asked, the issues investigated, and the conclusions drawn. Each theory considered below attempts to explain the acquisition of traits, behaviours, and roles that are generally associated with gender, a process referred to as **gender typing**. Lips (2005) suggested that two general types of theories have emerged—those that focus on *why* differences occur, and those that focus on *how* differences develop. Although some of these theories were previously introduced in the chapter on personality (Chapter 3), their application to gender will be highlighted.

Reasons for Gender Differences

Freud's psychoanalytic theory was one of the first and most influential theories of personality that assigned a central role to sexuality. According to Freud, identity formation for females begins when they realize that they are lacking one important anatomical feature—a penis. Females then develop a sense of inferiority to males that manifests itself through contempt for other women, an obsession with sexual attractiveness, a tendency to feel jealous, and a weaker superego. Horney (1939) extended this argument to suggest that it is not the anatomical feature that women envy but the power and authority it signifies. Building from perceived parental preferences for sons over daughters, females become more vulnerable and are more likely to develop a sense of inferiority.

Cultural theories of personality examine if the differences in social structure, practices, and ideological beliefs shape the development of gender roles. In most societies, men hold the majority of positions associated with power and status. According to this approach, males develop a more dominant style, which is supported and reinforced because of the more powerful roles they occupy. As such, society shapes gender roles in support of men's superior size and strength, women's reproductive capability, and the social and economic needs of the culture (Eagly & Wood, 1999).

Development of Gender Differences

Originally proposed by Mischel (1966), social learning theory holds that the social environment shapes gender development. Based on the principles of social learning, gender identity and gender roles are acquired through modelling, imitation, and behaviour (Bandura, 1977). Through being rewarded for appropriate gender-role behaviour, children learn what is acceptable. Bandura (1986) re-conceptualized social learning theory as social cognitive theory to account for the roles of active participation and cognition in identity development. Bussey and Bandura (1999) suggest that although children may initially learn gender roles through external rewards and punishments, they begin to self-regulate through an internal system of rewards and punishments. As they continue to develop, the influence of the social structure outside the family also becomes an important source of knowledge. Learning theories focus on how situations and contexts influence behaviour; therefore, their application to sport cannot be denied.

Cognitive development theory (Kohlberg, 1966) contends that gender identity is formed through a process of active learning whereby children purposefully search for patterns that govern gender-appropriate social functioning. Children then follow these "rules" in an attempt to adapt to social demands. A child's understanding of gender is tied to intellectual development, and an important marker occurs between the ages of 3 and 5. At this time, the child first realizes that gender is unchangeable, a process known as gender constancy. At this stage, children begin to value gender-appropriate behaviours, and engaging in these activities becomes an important, self-defining feature that is more self-reinforcing than engaging in those activities that are not gender-appropriate. Throughout this process, children seek their social world for information about which behaviours are gender-appropriate and which are not. Does this sound like social learning theory? Kohlberg contends they are quite different. According to social learning theory, rewards for gender-appropriate behaviour lead to the development of gender-appropriate behaviours and attitudes. Cognitive development theory argues that rewards for gender-consistent behaviour serve as a source of information for what is gender-appropriate; children engage in these behaviours because acting in a gender-consistent manner is, in itself, inherently rewarding.

Incorporating elements of social learning and cognitive development theories, gender schema theory (Bem, 1981) furthers our understanding of gender development and differentiation. Like social learning theory, it assumes that gender schema development stems from learning social norms and practices. Consistent with cognitive development theory, it contends that children develop an interrelated set of ideas about gender that guide their social perceptions and behaviours. However, gender schema theory differs notably from the above in that it postulates that the use of gender as an organizing principle is not inevitable. Femininity and masculinity are associated with **schemas** that represent a set of interrelated ideas that guide and organize the way an individual makes sense of a situation. People hold a variety of schemas, each developed around areas of functioning that are important to them (e.g., sport, gender, age). A person with a strong gender schema for femininity or for masculinity will process information and behave in a manner consistent with that concept of gender, as opposed to other relevant information, such as age or nationality.

Gender-role orientation reflects cultural definitions of masculinity (e.g., independence and assertiveness) and femininity (e.g., nurturance and understanding). According to this approach, masculine and feminine attributes are not mutually exclusive; people who score high on both orientations are labelled **androgynous** while those who score high on one orientation are labelled **sex-typed** (Bem, 1974). Research emanating from this approach challenged the traditional assumption that sex-typed individuals were the more psychologically healthy. Those classified as androgynous were considered to be most well-adjusted.

No one theory is adequate to explain all perspectives. All are useful, however, because they force researchers to examine similarities and differences between males and females. The remainder of this chapter will address the following question: To what extent are male and female athletes different from or similar to each other across psychosocial variables? Are they really world's apart? Which approach do the chapter authors endorse? Neither! Should the focus be exclusively on the similarities, what would be lost is the way in which males and females experience sport and physical activity differently. To focus on differences may only serve to promote the belief of female inferiority or male supremacy.

Gender Stereotypes vs. Sex Stereotypes

A popular stereotype forwarded to explain gender differences has been that males and females *think about* and *approach* situations differently. **Sex stereotypes** are socially shared beliefs that certain individual qualities are based on the biological classification of male or female whereas **gender stereotypes** are the behaviours considered appropriate for each gender. In other words, many of our stereotypes are based on the language of opposites: women are sensitive and creative, and men are aggressive and analytical. Stereotypes not only serve a descriptive function (what we are like) but are prescriptive as well (how we should act). How a person thinks has implications for achievement, and sport is one setting for achievement. Any differential treatment afforded to males and females in achievement situations may result in different levels of self-confidence, expectations for success, and motives.

Stereotypes do not occur in isolation; consequently, the influence of others cannot be ignored. The social environment, therefore, also plays a role in encouraging or discouraging sport achievement. Information conveyed by parents, teachers, coaches, teammates, and the media undoubtedly influences behaviour. As such, the gender salience of any situation ranges from negligible to central. Gender is most salient in contexts that are gender-typed. Thus, if sport in general (or a particular sport) is defined as "masculine" or "feminine," then social environmental beliefs about gender will influence participants. Consider how the sport of figure skating affects male skaters. Their participation in a "feminine" sport is likely to influence behaviours (to continue or discontinue participation), attitudes, friendship patterns, and self-awareness.

Because stereotypes are linked with the social environment, Deaux and Lewis (1984) suggested that gender stereotypes have multiple components (see Figure 13.1). They reflect personality traits but also include stereotypes about cognition, physical appearance, and role behaviours. Each component has a masculine and feminine version, and they are often considered independent; however, information about one influences assumptions about others. Consider the following example. A female athlete is described as *petite*. If asked, you would likely conclude that she competes in a sport in which aestheticism is integral to success, that her personality is gentle and emotional, and that she is heterosexual. However, this is not always the case. She could participate in a sport more traditionally defined as masculine (e.g., wrestling) and have a competitive and fiery nature.

Figure 13.1   The interrelationships among the components of gender stereotypes

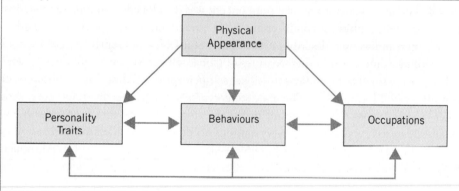

Note: Adapted from "Putting Gender into Context: An Interactive Model of Gender-related Behavior," by K. Deaux and B. Major, 1987, *Psychological Review, 94, pp. 369–389*. Adapted with permission.

Reflections 13.3
Consider your stereotypical beliefs. Walking down a darkened street alone at night you hear footsteps behind you. How would you react? Consider the ways you would describe a figure skater. Would your description differ if you knew the gender of the athlete?

Cognitions in Female and Male Athletes

Do male and female athletes differ in how they think, and if they do, what is the magnitude of these differences? This question will be addressed by considering a few of the most prominent constructs in sport psychology: self-perceptions, physique-related concerns, anxiety, stress, confidence, and motivation.

Self-perceptions

A developmental task faced by everyone is the construction of an **identity**, which can be defined as the integration of all self-perceptions (Brettschneider & Heim, 1997). A person's identity is formed as she or he becomes aware of, accepts, and labels different characteristics she or he possesses and organizes them in a meaningful way (Levine,

2003; Lips & Freedman, 1992). Inextricably linked to identity are self-concept and self-esteem. **Self-concept** is descriptive and refers to how individuals think about themselves; it is developed from environmental and experiential interpretations (Shavelson, Hubner, & Stanton, 1976). **Self-esteem** is an evaluation (either positive or negative) of what you think about yourself. It is the evaluative component of your self-concept or your sense of self-worth (Rosenberg, 1985).

For studying self-concept, Shavelson et al. (1976) proposed a model that reflects its multidimensional and hierarchical structure (see Figure 13.2). At the apex of the system is a stable global self-concept, which develops from academic and non-academic domains. Even more specific components that reflect specialized competencies within each domain influence these domain-specific self-perceptions. The physical self occupies an important position in the self-system because the body, through its appearance, attributes, and abilities provides a unique interface for the individual with the world (Fox, 1990). Fox and Corbin (1989) adopted this model to study the physical self. The more general physical self-concept was developed from four subdomains: sport competence, physical conditioning, body attractiveness, and physical strength.

Do men and women describe and evaluate themselves differently? There are consistent gender differences across measures of global self-esteem and self-concept, with men reporting small but significantly higher self-perceptions (Kling, Hyde, Showers, & Buswell, 1999; Marsh, 1989). There are stereotypical domain-specific differences, with males scoring higher on measures of math, emotional stability, and problem-solving. Females tend to report higher self-perceptions on dimensions reflecting verbal ability and social relationships (e.g., Marsh, 1989; Wilgenbusch & Merrell, 1999). Allthough these gender differences are consistent, they are relatively small. In domain-specific

Figure 13.2   The hierarchical nature of self-concept

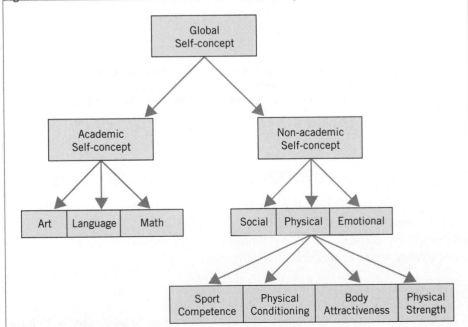

Note: Adapted from "Advances in the Measurement of the Physical Self," by K. R. Fox, 1998. In J. L. Duda (Ed.), Advances in Sport and Exercise Psychology Measurement (pp. 295–310). Morgantown, W V: Fitness Information Technology. Adapted with permission.

measures of self-concept, gender accounted for only 7%–8% of the variance, while in global measures of self-concept, gender accounted for about 1% (Marsh, 1989).

The largest gender differences are found across assessments of physical self-concept (Marsh, 1989; Shapka & Keating, 2005), and developmental trends suggest that physical self-concept decreases during adolescence, more notably for girls than for boys (Klomsten, Skaalvik, & Espnes, 2004). Crocker, Eklund, and Kowalski (2000) found that in children and adolescents aged 10–14 years, males scored higher on measures of sport competence and strength. Similarly, Hayes, Crocker, and Kowalski (1999) found that college men scored higher on the body attractiveness, sport competence, and physical conditioning subdomains than women. These findings hold for elite athletes as well although the magnitude of the difference is smaller than that found in other populations (Marsh, 1998; Marsh, Hey, Roche, & Perry, 1997). The cause of higher self-perceptions among elite athletes is unknown; perhaps the success experienced by top performers may serve an important ego-enhancing strategy.

Reflections 13.4

Consider your physical self-concept/self-esteem, and the components that make up physical self-concept. How would you describe yourself in each of these areas? How important is your physical self-concept (relative to other aspects of the self) to your overall self-esteem? Are you more efficacious or confident in the aspects of self that you ascribe the most importance to?

Physique-related Concerns

Physique-related concerns have received increased professional and public interest over the past two decades. Researchers have gained interest in the biological, socio-cultural, and psychological factors that contribute to the etiology of physique-related concerns. Popular magazines have contributed to the heightened attention afforded the physique; for example, a 2000 *People* magazine cover story was "The Search for the Perfect Body" (Dam, 2000). In some cases, the search for the perfect body may go to the extreme and result in serious physical, psychological, and social consequences. Physique-related concerns most often linked to sport include eating disorders and muscle dysmorphia.

EATING DISORDERS   Athletes are identified as an "at-risk" group for eating disorders (Kjelsas & Augestad, 2004). The pressure to compete and perform may lead to increased pressure for female athletes to be slim and for males to build muscle mass. Therefore, to achieve these ideals, an athlete may resort to disturbed eating behaviours, most notably anorexia and bulimia. A resistance to maintaining or gaining weight and an intense fear of gaining weight, even though underweight, characterizes **anorexia**. **Bulimia** is characterized by recurrent episodes of binge eating, accompanied by inappropriate compensatory behaviour to prevent weight gain (e.g., self-induced vomiting, excessive exercise).

Separate meta-analyses reported greater symptoms associated with eating disordered behaviour in athletes compared with other groups (Hausenblas & Carron, 1999; Smolak, Murnen, & Ruble, 2000); however, the difference was small. More specifically, Hausenblas and Carron found female athletes reported higher scores on measures of bulimic and anorexic behaviours but not on measures of drive for thinness (generally thought to be a defining feature of eating disorders). Hausenblas and Carron further report that those participating in aesthetic sports reported greater anorectic symptomology than those who competed in sports for which the physique was less salient (e.g., volleyball, distance running).

Consistent with differences in the general population, female athletes reported more eating disorder symptoms than males athletes. Of interest, however, was the fact that the magnitude of the difference between male athletes and their controls was greater than for corresponding females. In other words, although male athletes report a lower incidence of eating disordered behaviour than female athletes, the magnitude of the difference between male athletes and male non-athletes was greater than that observed for female athletes and non-athletes.

There are several explanations of why athletes are at greater risk. A trait approach holds that athletes may possess certain psychological traits that predispose them to eating disordered behaviour (Davis, 1992). Their characteristics thought to be beneficial for success in sport—such as perfectionism, high achievement orientation, high levels of control, and neuroticism—are similar to those found in clinical eating-disorder populations (Davis, Fox, Cowles, Hastings, & Schwass, 1990). Alternatively, the nature of the sport may lead athletes to engage in unhealthy behaviours (Sykora, Grilo, Wilfley, & Brownell, 1993). The emphasis placed on physique-type, leanness, and performance intensifies existing societal pressures to maintain or achieve the ideal physique. This belief may explain why athletes in lean or aesthetic sports report more eating disordered behaviours.

MUSCLE DYSMORPHIA   Men are becoming obsessed with their body image in higher numbers than ever before and in ways different from those seen in women (Olivardia, 2001). Researchers propose that muscular mesomorphic bodies characterize attractiveness for men: well-developed shoulders, arms, and chest combined with slim waist, hips, and buttocks. As the female ideal is becoming increasingly unrealistic for many to attain, so is the ideal for males, some of whom fear that they are too small, weak, or skinny. The prevalence rates of dieting to increase weight and/or muscle size in adolescent and young adult males has been found to range from 21.2% to 47% (Cafri et al., 2005). **Muscle dysmorphia** involves a disturbance in body image wherein individuals believe they are smaller or weaker than they really are despite typically having a very well-defined physique and low body fat.

There is an uncertainty surrounding the prevalence of muscle dysmorphia. However, research suggests about 10% of males perceive themselves to be less muscular than they were in reality (Pope & Katz, 1994). Feelings of inadequacy associated with muscle dysmorphia are very intrusive and consuming. For example, weightlifters typically report spending about 40 minutes a day thinking about being too small, not being big enough, or getting bigger. Those with muscle dysmorphia report being preoccupied with such thoughts approximately five hours per day (Olivardia, Pope, & Hudson, 2000). People also tend to believe that this is a disorder that is most commonly found in weightlifters and is not a problem with the general population. However, only a small percentage of reported cases of muscle dysmorphia occur in body builders (Pope, Gruber, Choi, Olivardia, & Phillips, 1997; Olivardia et al., 2000).

It is likely that those with muscle dysmorphia may experience higher levels of the drive for muscularity. The **drive for muscularity** has been defined as the desire to achieve an idealized, muscular body type (McCreary & Sasse, 2000). Morrison and colleagues have demonstrated that the drive is related to individual perceptions (body dissatisfaction, vanity, social comparison, appearance self-esteem) and to the increased media exposure of the muscular ideal (Morrison, Morrison, Hopkins, & Rowan, 2004). Furthermore, perceived social and physical benefits for muscularity (such as strength) were linked to the desire to be more muscular.

Anxiety

Much research in sport psychology has focused on the construct of anxiety: how it manifests, its antecedents, and its consequences (for more detail refer to Chapter 5). An examination of gender differences in anxiety reveals equivocal results. Some researchers suggest that women experience higher levels of competitive state anxiety compared with men (Krane & Williams, 1994; Martens, Vealey, & Burton, 1990) while others report no differences (Perry & Williams, 1998). These studies all considered anxiety at a single point in time. However, does anxiety change during the precompetitive period? Results have shown that men's cognitive anxiety remained relatively stable; however, women showed increased cognitive anxiety 2 hours prior and then again at 30 minutes prior to competition (Jones, Swain, & Cale, 1991; see Figure 13.3). The athletes' interpretation of the symptoms experienced with anxiety is an important consideration in understanding anxiety's influence on performance. Perry and Williams (1998) reported that men interpreted cognitive and somatic anxiety as more facilitative than did women, although the magnitude of the differences was small.

Figure 13.3   Gender differences in temporal patterning of anxiety prior to competition

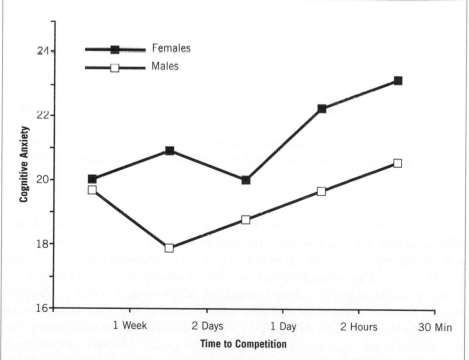

Note: From G. Jones, A. Swain and A. Cale, 1991, Gender differences in pre-competition temporal patterning and antecedents of anxiety and self-confidence, Journal of Sport and Exercise Psychology 13(1): 7, figure 2. © 1991 by Human Kinetics Publishers, Inc. Adapted with permission from Human Kinetics (Champaign, IL).

The above differences support the necessity of examining environmental conditions that manifest themselves as anxiety-provoking. For women, cognitive anxiety was predicted by perceived readiness to compete and by the importance they placed on themselves to do well in competition (Jones & Cale, 1989). Conversely, thinking they would win, the rating of the opposition, and the importance of the match contributed to cognitive anxiety in males. Thus, cognitive anxiety may result from different concerns for men and women. There were no gender differences in the antecedents to somatic anxiety.

Reflections 13.5

Do you experience anxiety prior to or while competing in sport? Consider the anxiety in terms of its type (somatic or cognitive), intensity, and direction. Does your experience of anxiety change in the days and hours preceding competition? What factors lead to the experience of anxiety for you personally?

Stress

Stressors are events or conditions that are appraised as threatening by an individual and thus are the source of upset, worry, and discomfort (for more detail, see Chapter 6). All athletes experience stress, physically and psychologically. According to Lazarus (1999), stress involves a primary evaluation of the impact of a situation on one's well-being, a secondary appraisal of one's personal resources to deal with that evaluation, and an assessment of one's coping potential. As the experience of stress depends on an individual's interpretation, the same stressor may be a source of stress for one athlete, but not for another.

There is some evidence that male and female athletes report different athletic environments as sources of stress. Goyen and Anshel (1998) found that being hassled or booed by spectators, being criticized by teammates, and being yelled at or pressured by the coach was less stressful for men than for women. They concluded that social evaluation stressors were more intense for women than for men. In addition, Hammermeister and Burton (2004) found that gender differences existed in the secondary appraisal of personal resources to deal with the stress. Specifically, female athletes perceived that they had less control over environmental threats than males did. This difference occurred despite the fact that men and women perceived the same amount of threat.

Confidence

Confidence is the belief an individual has in his or her ability to be successful (Vealey, 1986), and it is often cited as one of the most important variables in predicting sport performance and differentiating more-successful from less-successful athletes. Lirgg (1991) conducted a meta-analysis in an attempt to examine gender differences in confidence more systematically. Results revealed that men were more confident about performing physical activity tasks than were women, although the size of the differences varied greatly among studies. Further, the analysis showed that the more traditionally masculine the task (e.g., football), the greater the gender difference in confidence. There were no gender differences in confidence for competitive tasks.

Thus, it appears that it may be the nature of the task being performed that contributes to gender differences in confidence and not competition per se. Labelling a

There are gender differences in confidence for tasks that are considered "masculine," for which females report lower confidence levels.
Photo courtesy of Lee Strickland/ Getty Images.

task as "feminine" or "masculine" raised the expectations of what group is more likely to experience success. Early research reported that males do better on "masculine" tasks and females on "feminine" tasks (Deaux & Farris, 1977; Lenney, 1977). This is a consistent finding across several domains, including academics (e.g., math and science) and sport. However, researchers in sport psychology have noted that when tasks are perceived as appropriate for females and clear feedback is offered, gender differences in confidence disappear (Petruzzello & Corbin, 1988; Solmon, Lee, Belcher, Harrison, & Wells, 2003). Coaches, teammates, and parents can facilitate enhanced confidence through offering clear and appropriate feedback to female athletes.

Comparable with that found with anxiety, gender differences in the temporal patterning of confidence have also been reported (Jones et al., 1991). Male athletes' confidence remained relatively stable until 2 hours prior to the event and then decreased with a second reduction 30 minutes prior to competition (see Figure 13.4). Females also showed a decline in confidence, but the decrease started earlier than in men. Antecedent conditions for confidence were also different, with "thinking about winning" positively predicting confidence in males and "perceived readiness" and "the importance of performing well" being the most important predictors for females.

Motivation

There are numerous theoretical frameworks to explain motivation in sport and physical activity (see Chapter 4). Generally, men and women differ in the strength of their motives, most notably with respect to the reasons for participation and attribution style.

From youth-sport participants to college students, males tend to rate competition and winning as more important motives for participation than do females; by contrast, women athletes endorse participation for fun and social motives more frequently (Flood & Hellstedt, 1991; Gill, Gross, & Huddleston, 1983). Furthermore, Fortier,

Figure 13.4   Gender differences in temporal patterning of confidence prior to competition

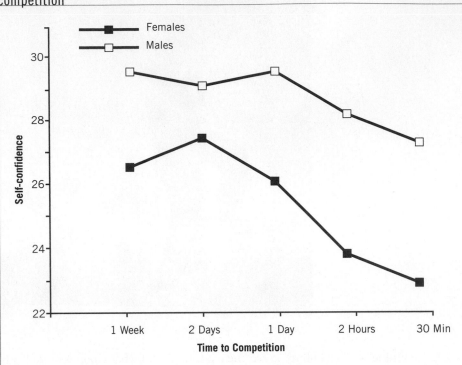

Note: From G. Jones, A. Swain and A. Cale, 1991, Gender differences in pre-competition temporal patterning and antecedents of anxiety and self-confidence, Journal of Sport and Exercise Psychology *13(1): 8, figure 3. © 1991 by Human Kinetics Publishers, Inc. Adapted with permission from Human Kinetics (Champaign, IL).*

Vallerand, Brière, and Provencher (1995) examined differences in intrinsic and extrinsic motivation in male and female athletes. They found that females scored higher in intrinsic motivation (had a more self-determined motivational profile) while males scored higher on extrinsic motivation and amotivation.

> ## Reflections 13.6
> Identify the reasons that you engage (or engaged) in sport. Relative to each other, how important were such motives as competition, success, and affiliation? Were your reasons consistent with those advanced for your gender?

Motivation has also been studied from the standpoint of attribution style. **Attribution** refers to how people explain their successes and failures (see Chapter 4). In general, male athletes' attributions have been found to be *self-enhancing* (i.e., make themselves look and feel better and more competent); their own success is attributed to stable, internal factors, such as ability, while failure is often attributed to unstable, external factors, such as luck. By contrast, female athletes sometimes use what is referred to as a *self-defeating* pattern of attributions (i.e., make themselves look less positive or competent); success is attributed to luck, or to help from others, while failure results from their lack of ability (e.g., Riordan, Thomas, & James, 1985; White, 1999). Coaches and parents can help female athletes develop a more internal attribution style through discussing effort, challenge, and strategy. If taught that a disappointing

Females and males participate in sport for different reasons. Females are more likely to be motivated by social and intrinsic reasons; males, by competition.

© Tom Carter/Photo Edit

performance is not due to lack of ability or luck but perhaps to inadequate effort, then female athletes may be better able to handle challenging situations.

In contrast to sport, what effect does gender have on motives underpinning exercise participation? The Canadian Fitness and Lifestyle Research Institute (2001) reported that 57% of Canadian adults were not active enough to achieve optimal health benefits. Therefore, it is important to understand what motivates people to engage in exercise so that these motivating factors can be addressed to facilitate participation.

Garcia, Broda, Frenn, and Coviak (1995) found that girls engaged in much less leisure-time physical activity and needed more support from their families for sustained involvement than did boys. Moreover, this trend extends into adulthood, with men on average engaging in more leisure-time physical activity than women (Bruce & Katzmarzyk, 2002). Body-related concerns specific to weight control and appearance are more significant motives for exercise participation in women, especially younger women (Koivula, 1999). However, Davis, Fox, Brewer, and Ratusny (1995) found that when age was taken into consideration, the situation could be quite different, with men in their middle years reporting exercising for weight control more so than similar-aged women do. Another form of motivation that is relatively controlling may influence female exercisers. Wilson, Rodgers, Fraser, and Murray (2004) reported that introjected regulation predicted exercise behaviours for female participants only. For those motivated by introjected regulation, avoiding guilt or anxiety or to gain ego enhancement, such as pride, may drive exercise behaviours.

Gender differences in motivation are more likely to be observed in public than in private settings (Maccoby, 1990), and the exercise setting may be one such environment. An explanation for this finding may reflect self-presentational motives. **Self-presentation** involves the selective presentation and omission of aspects of the self to create desired impressions and avoid undesired impressions with specific people in a social encounter (Leary, 1992). If individuals feel they cannot create a certain image or are subject to negative evaluation, then they may change or discontinue exercise. Although few studies have examined gender differences in self-presentational motives in exercise settings, research has shown that females higher in self-presentational concerns are more likely to exercise alone or prefer same-sex exercise environments (Kruisselbrink, Dodge, Swanburg, & MacLeod, 2004).

Role of the Social Environment

Although gender differences in cognitions are often small or inconsistent, what seems to be stable is the societal belief that males and females do differ. Deaux (1984) emphasized that how people *think* males and females differ is more important than how they *actually* differ. In other words, gender is mediated by specific social contexts (Deaux & LaFrance, 1998; Deaux & Major, 1987). This results in a gender belief system that reflects characteristics and cognitions of the individual and others, but the salience of these influences and situational cues varies tremendously.

The salience of gender cues may help to explain why people sometimes behave in a manner congruent with their gender and at other times in an incongruent manner. Therefore, gendered behaviour is context dependent and flexible, which helps to explain why despite consistent pressures to be different, at times males and females behave similarly. For example, males are more likely to aggress against other males than against females (Maccoby, 1998), and females are more likely to use relational aggression (hurt or damage another person through threatening relationships) than are males (Crick, Casas, & Mosher, 1997). In these examples, social norms and expectations may be influencing aggressive behaviour: to aggress against a female is inappropriate for a male, and females may be more likely to use relational aggression, as it is a more socially acceptable form for them. Conversely, female athletes have reported greater perceptions of perceived legitimacy of aggressive acts in sport than non-athletes (Silva, 1983). In this example, the influence of the social context cannot be ignored as the immediate social situation (i.e., sport) promotes behaviour that is incongruent with social norms of femininity. The influences of two important environmental variables are considered below. Then, the possible impact of the social environment on aggression in sport is considered.

Gender Socialization

Parents serve as the first source of gendered learning. Lytton and Romney (1991) demonstrated that on most dimensions of socialization (e.g., warmth, intimacy) differences in the ways parents treat their sons and daughters were small and insignificant. However, considerable evidence shows that parents display different behaviours in areas related to gender expectations. There are examples in children's play environments, even in infancy. Parents were more likely to furnish children's rooms with sex-appropriate toys, particularly for boys, who were more likely to have sports equipment and instrumental toys (i.e., tools, vehicles), which are more complex and require more motor activity (Pomerleau, Bolduc, Malcuit, & Cossette, 1990; Wood, Desmarais, & Gugula, 2002). Parents were more flexible about the toys they chose when they played with their daughters.

We cannot ignore the implications for sport. There is little question that parents transmit their beliefs about appropriate behaviour in sport settings through processes of reinforcement, modelling, stereotyping appropriate behaviour, and labelling. In

< Parents communicate information (albeit sometimes unconsciously) about behaviours that they consider gender-appropriate.

Index Stock/Maxx Images

sport, parental expectations influence physical activity participation, the intensity of effort expended, and the child's performance level (Bois, Sarrazin, Brustad, Trouilloud, & Cury, 2005; Carriere, 2003; Eccles & Harold, 1991). Research has indicated that actual levels of participation in physical activity are related to parents' expectations and beliefs regarding physical competence (Fredricks & Eccles, 2005). The home environment, toy selection, styles of play, and parents' own physical activity levels all convey important information. These and other factors may translate into the degree to which sport is important in a child's life and the type of sports considered gender-appropriate. Furthermore, Giuliano, Popp, and Knight (2000) found that playing with "masculine" instead of "feminine" toys, playing with predominantly male or mix-gendered groups, and being considered a tomboy distinguished between women who became intercollegiate athletes and those who did not.

Reflections 13.7

Consider how your parents influenced your sport participation through the toys and games they provided and how they interacted with you in play. Did female family members (e.g., mother, grandmother) differ in their interaction styles compared with male family members (father, grandfather)? How do you think your family would have reacted had you chosen to participate in a "gender inappropriate" sport? Would they have reacted as the families did in the movies *Billy Elliot* (male dancer) or *Million Dollar Baby* (female boxer)?

Media Portrayal of Athletes

Canadian children and adolescents spend approximately 14 hours a week watching television, with numbers increasing to 22 hours for adults (www.statscan.ca). Combine these totals with time spent listening to the radio, reading newspapers and magazines, and playing video games! There can be little doubt that the media are important sources of information that people derive about their social world in general and about sport. Female athletes occupy a place within sport culture that was unthinkable 20 or 30 years ago, but does this mean that the world is ready for an all-women's sports network? In September 2001, CTV Specialty Television Inc. launched WTSN, the world's first 24-hour, national network devoted exclusively to women's sport programming. Despite paying big dollars for programming, the network did not get the audience it expected. The channel's business plan projected 714,000 subscribers in the first year of operation, but only 438,000 had signed up after two years. Subscribership ranked lowest among the sports digital cable channels, as did its advertising revenue (Houston, 2003).

Research has demonstrated that the media promotes gender-stereotyped messages (Davis, 1990; Lausen & Dozier, 2002), and one area in which sport gender differences are particularly evident is in the media's portrayal of male and female athletes. Consistently, athletes are presented differently based on their sex, and these differences occur in both newspaper and television coverage and at almost all competitive levels and types of sport (Koivula, 1999; Wann, Schrader, Allison, & McGeorge, 1998). At the most basic level, female sports receive quantitatively less coverage than male sports across all media (Higgs, Weiller, & Martin, 2003; Salwen & Wood, 1994). Even in sports in which women make up the majority of competitors, or in sports considered to be feminine (e.g., gymnastics), this pattern emerges. Not only is the quantity of the coverage different, but the quality is as well. In all types of sports (i.e., masculine, feminine, or gender-neutral), women's sports are more likely to (a) be marked, or labelled, specifically as women's sport, (b) be broadcast with poorer technical quality, (c) be televised in shorter segments, and (d) be more heavily edited (Higgs & Weiller, 1994; Koivula, 1999).

The descriptions of the female athletes also differ from those of the male athletes. Women are often portrayed as women first and athletes second, and they are more likely to be referred to by their first names than are male athletes (Koivula, 1999). This difference may serve to make the female athletes seem less mature, and may reinforce the idea that female athletes should not be taken seriously. Male athletes are often described as strong, aggressive, or powerful while female athletes are described as emotional, feminine, attractive, or graceful (Weiller & Higgs, 1999).

Television viewers notice the different portrayals of females and males (Lavine, Sweeney, & Wagner, 1999). The messages conveyed have a direct effect on attitudes (Cobb, Stevens-Long, Goldstein, 1982). Whether it is deliberate or not, the media reinforces the traditional gender stereotypes that exist in society, which results in a hierarchy of quality in sport (i.e., male athletes are superior to female athletes) and a reinforcement of gender differences (Knight & Giuliano, 2002; Koivula, 1999). In effect, media helps to reinforce gender schemas! When people contradict the stereotypes, or schemas, that we hold about certain groups, we perceive them more negatively (e.g., Knight, Giuliano, & Sanchez-Ross, 2001).

Reflections 13.8

Select any media outlet. It could be Sportscentre on TSN, the sports section of your newspaper, or a magazine, such as *Sports Illustrated*. Pay attention to how often women's sport or female athletes receive coverage. How much coverage do they receive? How are female athletes described? How are female athletes portrayed? Do the media portrayals reinforce existing gender stereotypes?

Sporting Environment and Aggression

The roles of parents and the media cannot be denied, but what about the influence of the sporting environment itself? Are cognitions or behaviours altered when athletes enter a competitive situation? One dimension that has received research attention is aggression. Many of the approaches to studying gender identified earlier in the chapter (e.g., cultural and social learning theories) predict that males would exhibit more aggression than do females.

Maccoby (1998) suggested that male aggression is not a personality trait but is more likely a product of particular situations. In other words, certain situations allow for and encourage more aggressive behaviours among males than among females. Gender differences in aggression in laboratory and real-world environments support the idea. In laboratory settings, Knight, Fabes, and Higgins (1996) reported moderate gender differences in aggressive behaviours whereas weak gender differences were reported when aggression was studied in real-world settings (Archer, 2004). Consistent with gender stereotypes, the magnitude of the difference was greater when aggression was conceptualized as physical than when it was conceptualized as verbal.

Few studies of aggression in sport have examined female intent to aggress or gender differences in perceptions of aggressive behaviours. Widmeyer, Dorsch, and Sanzole (1995) surveyed female intercollegiate athletes to determine the extent to which they wanted to physically injure or psychologically harm their opponents. Between 44% and 66% wanted to psychologically intimidate an opponent at least once per game, and 11% to 13% wanted to physically injure an opponent at least once per game. These frequencies are considerably less than for males at 83% to 89% and 23% to 50%, respectively, in similar male sports. Team norms specific to aggression appear to be significant predictors for aggressive tendencies in female athletes. Perceptions of teammates' aggressive behaviours in similar situations and perceived desires of coaches contributed to aggressive behaviours (Stephens, 2000, 2001).

Explaining the Differences and Similarities

There is support for the idea that gender differences exist in the way male and female athletes think and in their social environments (see Table 13.1). However, across many constructs the magnitudes of the differences are quite small, and there are some similarities. A central question then becomes, how can we explain the similarities and differences observed? The theoretical approaches to understanding gender reported earlier in this chapter offer a starting point. Psychoanalytic theories promoted individual personality differences resulting from parent-child relationships. Cultural theories focused on the role of status and social practices in maintaining gender differences. Social learning/social cognitive theories emphasize that children will act in ways that will facilitate reinforcement (from themselves or others). Cognitive development theory stresses children's active attempts to learn social rules that result in competence in social settings. Finally, Deaux and Major's (1987) gender belief system integrates many of these theoretical orientations to suggest that gendered behaviour results from an interaction of forces that include people's perceptions of themselves and of others within a social context. What may be the best approach to consider? Perhaps it is one that recognizes that gender differences reflect interactions among social experiences, predispositions, and circumstances.

Table 13.1   Overview of Differences and Similarities between Female and Male Athletes

Area of Cognition	Research Findings
Global Self-esteem	Small differences favouring males
Physical Self-concept	Large male-female differences, with males describing themselves more favourably across most dimensions of physical self-concept
Physique-related Concerns	Females athletes more likely to report symptoms of disturbed eating
	Magnitude of the difference between athletes and non-athletes greater for males than for females
	More muscle dysmorphia reported by males
Anxiety	Inconclusive results on intensity of anxiety experienced
	For females symptoms more debilitative,
	For females earlier increase in symptoms in the pre-competitive period
Stress	No differences in intensity
	Stress experienced from different sources
Confidence	Greater confidence reported by males when performing physical tasks, most notably sex-typed tasks
	No gender differences in competitive settings
Motivation	Gender differences in reasons for participating in sport and physical activities
	Gender differences in attribution style
Social Factors	**Research Findings**
Socialization	Gender expectations conveyed by parents through the home environment, style of play, and toys
Media Coverage	Media portrayal of female athletes and sports of lesser quantity and quality than that for males
Sporting Environment	Small gender differences in aggression
	Nature of the aggressive act differs between males and females
	Greater desire for and greater perceived legitimacy of aggressive acts for males than for females

Earlier we discussed how stereotypes translate into gender-appropriate behaviour. For example, it is commonly believed that boys are better at physical skills and athletics and that girls are stronger in social and relationship behaviours. Reported differences in physical self-concept are consistent with this stereotype. Given that global self-esteem and self-concept develop from many domains, some believed to be stereotypical of males and others of females, the small differences reported are not surprising.

Differential beliefs in the appropriateness of competitive sport participation for males and females may result in differences in the quality and quantity of parental encouragement, training, and reinforcement for sport participation. All of these factors may contribute to what Steele (1997) identified as **stereotype threat**, a tendency for individuals to perform poorly if they fear they will likely be judged negatively for performing what is considered to be gender-inappropriate behaviour. Gender differences in confidence on tasks considered "masculine" or differences identified in athletes' desire to aggress (either physically or psychologically) against an opponent may offer support to the existence of this threat.

Reflections 13.9

Research suggests differences between males and females in cognitions and behaviours, including the physical self, anxiety, confidence, motivation, and socialization. Can you link these cognitions and behaviours to gender and sex stereotypes?

Chapter Summary

Much of this chapter was devoted to developing an appreciation for the psychosocial variables that contribute to sport performance. Although differences exist across some constructs, the differences are not as large as what stereotypes may have us believe. Furthermore, as former female athletes retire and move into other sporting roles (e.g., coaching and administration), they will influence sport participation by females and will continue to encourage and inspire Canadians to celebrate the achievement of female athletes. There will be challenges to traditional definitions of femininity as more and more females compete in sport. This may result in changed expectations for sport achievement and, in the end, bring about more similarities than differences between male and female athletes.

A question was posed in the chapter-opening vignette: are women catching up? So, will women ever catch up? Only time will tell. A bigger question may be "do they need to?" Those interested in studying gender in sport should be aware of the following key points. There are many myths associated with women's sport participation. However, these myths have been refuted, and women are enjoying many health, social, and physical benefits associated with sport participation. Another point is that sex differences are separate from gender differences. There are numerous approaches to understanding gender. All contribute to explaining the similarities and differences across gender, but no one perspective is fully equipped to explain all aspects of gender. Greater attention should be directed to complementary factors that explain achievement in sport. These factors include biological, psychological, and sociological influences.

There are differences in athletes' cognitions related to sport performance. Most notably, females tend to report lower levels of physical self-concept and demonstrate different motivational qualities regulating participation in physical activity and sport. There are physique-related differences, with females reporting higher levels of eating disorders compared with males (although the difference between athletic males and their controls was greater than that for females athletes and theirs); males reported greater muscle dysmorphia. However, there are also similarities in cognitions related to sport performance. Similarities have been reported for intensity of anxiety experiences, confidence in doing gender-neutral tasks, or when informative feedback is provided.

There are differences caused by the social environment. Parents and the media are influential sources of gendered messages. These messages influence expectations, attitudes, and gender-learned behaviours. We cannot ignore the influence of personality, social experiences, and circumstances when considering gender in sport. Current definitions of masculinity and femininity and appropriate gendered behaviour need not be binding. As sport evolves and challenges traditional definitions, qualities stereotypically ascribed to each gender may be more interchangeable than ever imagined.

Review Questions

1. Differentiate between the terms *sex* and *gender* as they relate to sport participation.
2. Numerous theories applicable to the study of gender were identified. Take any construct of interest (e.g., confidence, muscle dysmorphia, socialization). How might these theories explain the different experiences reported for males and females?
3. What is the difference between how male and female athletes think? Answer this question with specific reference to the physical self, anxiety, stress, and motivation.
4. Deaux and colleagues argued that to fully understand gendered behaviour, consideration of individual/other characteristics and the social environment must be made. According to this framework, how may confidence be influenced for male and female athletes?
5. It was suggested that the gender salience of any situation influences behaviour. In a gender-salient situation, is an individual more or less likely to conform to gender-appropriate behaviours?

Suggested Reading

Gill, D. (2002). Gender and sport behavior. In T. S. Horn (Ed.), *Advances in sport psychology* (2nd ed., pp. 355–375). Champaign, IL: Human Kinetics.

Hall, A. M. (1996). *Feminism and sporting bodies: Essays on theory and practice.* Champaign, IL: Human Kinetics.

Messner, M. A. (2002). *Taking the field: Women, men and sports.* Minneapolis: University of Minnesota Press.

Theberge, N. (2000). Gender and sport. In J. Coakley & E. Dunning (Eds.), *Handbook of sport studies* (pp. 322–333). London: Sage.

References

Archer, J. (2004). Sex differences in aggression in real world settings: A meta-analytic review. *Review of General Psychology, 8,* 291–322.

Bandura, A. (1977). *Social learning theory.* Englewood Cliffs, NJ: Prentice Hall.

Bandura, A. (1986). *Social foundations of thought and action: A social cognitive theory.* Englewood Cliffs, NJ: Prentice Hall.

Baumeister, R. (1988). Should we stop studying sex differences altogether? *American Psychologist, 43,* 1092–1095.

Bem, S. L. (1974). The measurement of psychological androgyny. *Journal of Consulting and Clinical Psychology, 42,* 155–162.

Bem, S. L. (1981). Gender schema theory: A cognitive account of sex typing. *Psychological Review, 88,* 354–364.

Bois, J. E., Sarrazin, P. G., Brustad, R. J., Trouilloud, D. O., & Cury, F. (2005). Elementary schoolchildren's perceived competence and physical activity involvement: The influence of parents' role modeling behaviors and perceptions of their child's competence. *Psychology of Sport and Exercise, 6,* 381–397.

Brettschneider, W. D., & Heim, R. (1997). Identity, sport, and youth development. In K. R. Fox (Ed.), *The physical self: From motivation to well-being* (pp. 205–228). Champaign, IL: Human Kinetics.

Bruce, M. J., & Katzmarzyk, P. T. (2002). Canadian population trends in leisure-time physical activity levels, 1981–1998. *Canadian Journal of Applied Physiology, 27,* 681–690.

Bussey, K., & Bandura, A. (1999). Social cognitive theory of gender development and differentiation. *Psychological Review, 106,* 676–713.

Cafri, G., Thompson, K. J., Ricciardelli, L., McCabe, M., Smolak, L., & Yesalis, C. (2005). Pursuit of the muscular ideal: Physical and psychological consequences and putative risk factors. *Clinical Psychology Review, 25,* 215–239.

Cahn, S. K. (1994). *Coming on strong: Gender and sexuality in twentieth-century women's sport.* London: Harvard University Press.

Canadian Fitness and Lifestyle Research Institute (2001). *2000 Physical Activity Monitor.* Retrieved November 16, 2002, from http://www.cflri.ca/cflri/pa/surveys/2000survey/2000survey.html

Carriere, G. (2003). Parent and child factors associated with youth obesity. *Supplement to Health Reports, 14,* Ottawa: Statistics Canada.

Carron, A. V., Colman, M., Wheeler, J., & Stevens, D. (2002). Cohesion and performance in sport: A meta-analysis. *Journal of Sport & Exercise Psychology, 24,* 168–188.

Chelladurai, P., & Saleh, S. D. (1979). Person-task congruence in sports. *Canadian Journal of Applied Sport Sciences, 4,* 172–177.

Cobb, N. J., Stevens-Long, J., & Goldstein, S. (1982). The influence of televised models on toy preference in children. *Sex Roles, 8,* 1075–1080.

Crick, N. R., Casas, J. F., & Mosher, M. (1997). Relational and overt aggression in preschool. *Developmental Psychology, 33,* 579–588.

Crocker, P. R., Eklund, R. C., & Kowalski, K. C. (2000). Children's physical activity and physical self-perceptions. *Journal of Sports Sciences, 18,* 383–394.

Dam, J. K. L. (2000). Searching for the perfect body: How do I look? *People Magazine, 54,* 114–122.

Davis, C. (1992). Body image, dieting behaviours, and personality factors: A study of high-performance female athletes. *International Journal of Sport Psychology, 23,* 179–192.

Davis, C., Fox, J., Brewer, H., & Ratusny, D. (1995). Motivations to exercise as a function of personality characteristics, age, and gender. *Personality and Individual Differences, 19,* 165–174.

Davis, C., Fox, J., Cowles, M. P., Hastings, P., & Schwass, K. (1990). The functional role of exercise in the development of weight and diet concerns in women. *Journal of Psychosomatic Research, 34,* 563–574.

Davis, D. M. (1990). Portrayals of women in prime-time network television: Some demographic characteristics. *Sex Roles, 23,* 325–333.

Deaux, K. (1984). From individual differences to social categories: Analysis of a decade's research on gender. *American Psychologist, 39,* 105–116.

Deaux, K., & Farris, M. (1977). Attributing causes for one's own performance: The effects of sex, norms and outcomes. *Journal of Research in Personality, 11,* 59–72.

Deaux, K., & Lewis, L. L. (1984). Structure of gender stereotypes: Interrelationships among components and gender label. *Journal of Personality and Social Psychology, 46,* 991–1004.

Deaux, K., & LaFrance, M. (1998). Gender. In D. T. Gilbert, S. T. Fiske, & G. Lindzey (Eds.), *The handbook of social psychology* (Vol. 1, pp. 788–827). Boston: McGraw-Hill.

Deaux, K., & Major, B. (1987). Putting gender into context: An interactive model of gender-related behavior. *Psychological Review, 94,* 369–389.

Dorrance, A. (with Averbuch, G.). (2002). The vision of a champion: Advice and inspiration from the world's most successful women's soccer coach. Chelsea, MI: Sleeping Bear Press.

Dorrance, A. (with Nash, T.). (1996). *Training soccer champions.* Apex, NC: JYC Sports.

Eagly, A. H., & Wood, W. (1999). The origins of sex differences in human behavior: Evolved dispositions versus social roles. *American Psychologist, 54,* 408–423.

Eccles, J. S., & Harold, R. D. (1991). Gender differences in sport involvement: Applying the Eccles' expectancy-value model. *Journal of Applied Sport Psychology, 3,* 7–35.

Favreau, O. E. (1997). Sex and gender comparisons: Does null hypothesis testing create a false dichotomy? *Feminism and Psychology, 7,* 63–81.

Flood, S. E., & Hellstedt, J. C. (1991). Gender differences in motivation for intercollegiate athletic participation. *Journal of Sport Behavior, 14,* 159–167.

Fortier, M. S., Vallerand, R. J., Brière, N. M., & Provencher, P. J. (1995). Competitive and recreational sport structures and gender: A test of their relationship with sport motivation. *International Journal of Sport Psychology, 26,* 24–39.

Fox, K. R. (1990). *The physical self-perception profile manual* (PRN Monograph). De Kalb, IL: Northern Illinois University Office for Health Promotion.

Fox, K. R., & Corbin, C. (1989). Physical self-perceptions profile: Development and preliminary validation. *Journal of Sport & Exercise Psychology, 1,* 408–430.

Fredricks, J. A., & Eccles, J. S. (2005). Family socialization, gender and sport motivation and involvement. *Journal of Sport & Exercise Psychology, 27,* 3–31.

Garcia, A. W., Broda, M. A. N., Frenn, M., & Coviak, C. (1995). Gender and developmental differences in exercise beliefs among youth and prediction of their exercise behaviour. *The Journal of School Health, 65,* 213–220.

Gill, D. L., Gross, J. B., & Huddleston, S. (1983). Participation motivation in youth sports. *International Journal of Sport Psychology, 14,* 1–14.

Giuliano, T. A., Popp, K. E., & Knight, J. L. (2000). Footballs versus Barbies: Childhood play activities as predictors of sport participation by women. *Sex Roles, 42,* 159–181.

Goyen, M. J., & Anshel, M. H. (1998). Sources of acute competitive stress and use of coping strategies as a function of age and gender. *Journal of Applied Developmental Psychology, 19,* 469–486.

Greendorfer, S. L. (1992). Sport socialization. In T. S. Horn (Ed.), *Advances in Sport Psychology* (pp. 201–218). Champaign IL: Human Kinetics.

Hall, M. A. (1990). How should we theorize gender in the context of sport? In M. A. Messner & D. F. Sabo (Eds.), *Sport, men, and the gender order: Critical feminist perspectives* (pp. 223–239). Campaign IL: Human Kinetics.

Hammermeister, J., & Burton, D. (2004). Gender differences in coping with endurance sport stress: Are men from Mars and women from Venus? *Journal of Sport Behavior, 27,* 148–164.

Hausenblas, H. A., & Carron, A. V. (1999). Eating disorder indices and athletes: An integration. *Journal of Sport & Exercise Psychology, 21,* 230–258.

Hayes, S. D., Crocker, P. R., & Kowalski, K. C. (1999). Gender differences in physical self-perceptions, global self-esteem, and physical activity: Evaluation of the physical self-perceptions profile model. *Journal of Sport Behavior, 22,* 1–14.

Higgs, C. T., & Weiller, K. H. (1994). Gender bias and the 1992 Summer Olympic Games: An analysis of television coverage. *Journal of Sport and Social Issues, 3,* 234–246.

Higgs, C. T., Weiller, K. H., & Martin, S. B. (2003). Gender bias in the 1996 Olympic Games. *Journal of Sport and Social Issues, 27,* 52–64.

Horney, K. (1939). *The neurotic personality of our time.* New York: Norton.

Houston, W. (2003, September). CTV's women's sports network was doomed from beginning. *The Globe & Mail.* Retrieved from http://209.47.161.50/articles/GlobeandMail/globe030903.htm

Hubbard, R. (1990). *The politics of women's biology.* New Brunswick, NJ: Rutgers University Press.

Hyde, J. S. (1994). Should psychologists study gender differences? Yes, with some guidelines. *Feminism & Psychology, 4,* 507–512.

Jones, G., & Cale, A. (1989). Precompetition temporal patterning of anxiety and self-confidence in males and females. *Journal of Sport Behaviour, 12,* 183–195.

Jones, G., Swain, A., & Cale, A. (1991). Gender differences in precompetition temporal patterning and antecedents of anxiety and self-confidence. *Journal of Sport & Exercise Psychology, 13,* 1–15.

Kjelsas, E., & Augestad, L. B. (2004). Gender, eating behaviour, and personality characteristics in physically active students. *Scandinavian Journal of Medicine & Science in Sports, 14,* 258–268.

Kling, K. C., Hyde, J. S., Showers, C. J., & Buswell, B. N. (1999). Gender differences in self-esteem: A meta-analysis. *Psychological Bulletin, 125,* 470–500.

Klomsten, A. T., Skaalvik, E. M., & Espnes, G. A. (2004). Physical self-concept and sports: Do gender differences still exist? *Sex Roles, 50,* 119–127.

Knight, G. P., Fabes, R. A., & Higgins, D. A. (1996). Concerns about drawing causal inferences from meta-analyses: An example in the study of gender differences in aggression. *Psychological Bulletin, 119,* 410–421.

Knight, J. L, & Giuliano, T. A. (2002). He's a Laker; she's a looker: The consequences of gender-stereotyped portrayals of male and female athletes by the print media. *Sex Roles, 45,* 217–229.

Knight, J. L., Giuliano, T. A., & Sanchez-Ross, M. G., (2001). Famous or infamous? The influence of celebrity status and race on perceptions of responsibility for rape. *Basic and Applied Social Psychology, 23,* 183–190.

Kohlberg, L. A. (1966). A cognitive-developmental analysis of children's sex-role concepts and attitudes. In E. E. Maccoby (Ed.), *The development of sex differences* (pp. 82–172). Stanford, CA: Stanford University Press.

Koivula, N. (1999). Sport participation: Differences in motivation and actual participation due to gender typing. *Journal of Sport Behavior, 22,* 360–381.

Krane, V., & Williams, J. M. (1994). Cognitive anxiety, somatic anxiety, and confidence in track and field athletes: The impact of gender, competitive level, and task characteristics. *International Journal of Sport Psychology, 25,* 203–221.

Kruisselbrink, L. D., Dodge, A. M., Swanburg, S. L., & MacLeod, A. L. (2004). Influence of same-sex and mixed-sex exercise settings on the social physique anxiety and exercise intentions of males and females. *Journal of Sport & Exercise Psychology, 26,* 616–623.

Lausen, M. M., & Dozier, D. M. (2002). You look mahvelous: An examination of gender and appearance comments in the 1999–2000 prime-time season. *Sex Roles, 46,* 429–437.

Lavine, H., Sweeney, D., & Wagner, S. H. (1999). Depicting women as sex objects in television advertising: Effects on body dissatisfaction. *Personality and Social Psychology Bulletin, 25,* 1049–1058.

Lazarus, R. (1999). *Stress and emotion: A new synthesis.* New York: Springer.

Leary, M. R. (1992). Self-presentational processes in exercise and sport. *Journal of Sport & Exercise Psychology, 14,* 339–351.

Lenney, E. (1977). Women's self-confidence in achievement settings. *Psychological Bulletin, 84,* 1–13.

Levine, C. (2003). Introduction: Structure, development, and identity formation. *Identity: An International Journal of Theory and Research, 3,* 191–195.

Lips, H. M. (2005). *Sex and gender: An introduction* (5th ed.). New York: McGraw-Hill.

Lips, H. M., & Freedman, S. A. (1992). Heterosexual feminist identities: Private boundaries and shifting centres. *Feminism & Psychology, 2,* 441–444.

Lirgg, C. D., (1991). Gender differences in self-confidence in physical activity: A meta-analysis of recent studies. *Journal of Sport & Exercise Psychology, 13,* 294–310.

Lowe, M. (1983). The dialectic of biology and culture. In M. Lowe & R. Hubbard (Eds.), *Women's nature. Rationalizations of inequality* (pp. 39–62). New York: Pergamon Press.

Lytton, H., & Romney, D. M. (1991). Parents' differential socialization of boys and girls: A meta-analysis. *Psychological Bulletin, 109,* 267–296.

Maccoby, E. E. (1990). Gender and relationships: A developmental account. *American Psychologist, 45,* 513–520.

Maccoby, E. E. (1998). *The two sexes: Growing up apart, coming together.* Cambridge, MA: Harvard University Press.

Marsh, H. W. (1989). Age and sex effects in multiple dimensions of self-concept. Preadolescence to adulthood. *Journal of Educational Psychology, 81,* 417–430.

Marsh, H. W. (1998). Age and gender effects in physical self-concepts for adolescent elite athletes and non-athletes: A multi-cohort-multi-occasion design. *Journal of Sport & Exercise Psychology, 20,* 237–259.

Marsh, H. W., Hey, J., Roche, L. A., & Perry, C. (1997). Structure of physical self-concept: Elite athletes and physical education students. *Journal of Educational Psychology, 89,* 369–380.

Martens, R., Vealey, R. S., & Burton, D. (1990). *Competitive anxiety in sport.* Champaign, IL: Human Kinetics.

McCreary, D., & Sasse, D. (2000) An exploration of the drive for muscularity in adolescent boys and girls. *Journal of American College Health, 48,* 297.

Messner, M. A. (1994). *Sex, violence, and power in sports: Rethinking masculinity.* Freedom, CA: The Crossing Press.

Mischel, W. (1966). A social learning view of sex differences in behavior. In E. E. Maccoby (Ed.), *The development of sex differences* (pp. 56–81). Stanford, CA: Stanford University Press.

Morrison, T. G., Morrison, M. A., Hopkins, C., & Rowan, E. T. (2004). Muscle mania: Development of a new scale examining the drive for muscularity in Canadian males. *Psychology of Men & Masculinity, 5,* 30–39.

Neil, G. I., & Kirby, S. L. (1979). Coaching styles and preferred coaching behaviors among rowers and paddlers. *Journal of Sport Behavior, 8,* 3–17.

Olivardia, R. (2001). Mirror, mirror on the wall, who's the largest of them all? The features and phenomenology of muscle dysmorphia. *Harvard Review of Psychiatry, 9,* 254–259.

Olivardia, R., Pope, H. G., & Hudson, J. I. (2000). Muscle dysmorphia in male weightlifters: A case-control study. *American Journal of Psychiatry, 157,* 1291–1296.

Perry, J. D, & Williams, J. M. (1998). Relationship of intensity and direction of competitive trait anxiety to skill level and gender in tennis. *The Sport Psychologist, 12,* 169–179.

Petruzzello, S. J., & Corbin, C. B. (1988). The effects of performance feedback on female self-confidence. *Journal of Sport & Exercise Psychology, 10,* 174–183.

Pomerleau, A., Bolduc, D., Malcuit, G., & Cossette, L. (1990). Pink or blue: Environmental gender stereotypes in the first two years of life. *Sex Roles, 22,* 359–367.

Pope, H. G., Gruber A. J., Choi, P., Olivardia, R., & Phillips, K. A. (1997). Muscle dysmorphia. An underrecognized form of body dysmorphic disorder. *Psychosomatics. 38,* 548–557.

Pope, H. G., & Katz, D. L. (1994). Psychiatric and medical effects of anabolic-androgenic steroids. A controlled study of 160 athletes. *Archives of General Psychiatry 51,* 375–382.

Riordan, C. A., Thomas, J. S., & James, M. K. (1985). Attributions in a one-on-one sports competition: Evidence for self-serving biases and gender differences. *Journal of Sport Behavior, 8,* 42–53.

Rosenberg, M. (1985). Self-concept and psychological well-being in adolescence. In R. L. Leahy (Ed.), *The development of the self* (pp. 205–246.). Orlando, FL: The Academic Press.

Sabo, D., Miller, K. E., Melnick, M. J., & Heywood, L. (2004). *Her life depends on it: Sport, physical activity and the health and well-being of American girls.* East Meadow, NY: Women's Sports Foundation.

Salwen, M. B., & Wood, N. (1994). Depictions of female athletes on Sports Illustrated covers, 1957-89. *Journal of Sport Behavior, 17,* 98–107.

Seiler, S., & Sailer, S. (1997) The gender gap: Elite women are running further behind. *Sportscience News.* Retrieved from http://www.sportsci.org/news/news9705/gengap.html

Shapka, J. D., & Keating, D. P. (2005). Structure and change in self-concept during adolescence. *Canadian Journal of Behavioural Science, 37,* 83–96.

Shavelson, R. J., Hubner, J. J., & Stanton, G. C. (1976). Validation of construct interpretations. *Review of Educational Research, 46,* 407–441.

Silva, J. M. (1983). The perceived legitimacy of rule violating behavior in sport. *Journal of Sport Psychology, 5,* 438–448.

Smolak, L., Murnen, S. K., & Ruble, A. E. (2000). Female athletes and eating problems: A meta-analysis. *International Journal of Eating Disorders, 27,* 371–380.

Solmon, M. A., Lee, A. M., Belcher, D., Harrison, L., & Wells, L. (2003). Beliefs about gender appropriateness, ability, and competence in physical activity. *Journal of Teaching Physical Education, 22,* 261–279.

Steele, C. M. (1997). A threat in the air: How stereotypes shape intellectual identity and performance. *American Psychologist, 52,* 613–629.

Stephens, D. E. (2000). Predictors of likelihood to aggress in youth soccer: An examination of co-ed and all-girls teams. *Journal of Sport Behavior, 23,* 311–325.

Stephens, D. E. (2001). Predictors of aggressive tendencies in girls' basketball: An examination of beginning and advanced participants in a summer skills camp. *Research Quarterly for Exercise & Sport, 72,* 257–266.

Sykora, C., Grilo, C. M, Wilfley, D. E., & Brownell, K. D. (1993). Eating, weight, and dieting disturbances in male and female lightweight and heavyweight rowers. *International Journal of Eating Disorders, 14,* 203–212.

Tharp, M. (1996, July 22). Ready, set, go: Why we love our games. *US News & World Report.* pp. 33–34.

Unger, R., & Crawford, M. (1993). Commentary: Sex and gender: The troubled relationship between terms and concepts. *Psychological Science, 4,* 122–124.

Vealey, R. S. (1986). Conceptualization of sport-confidence and competitive orientation: Preliminary investigation and instrument development. *Journal of Sport Psychology, 8,* 221–246.

Wann, D. L., Schrader, M. P., Allison, J. A., & McGeorge, K. K. (1998). The inequitable newspaper coverage of men's and women's athletics at small, medium, and large universities. *Journal of Sport and Social Issues, 22,* 79–87.

Weiller, K. H., & Higgs, C. T. (1999). Television coverage of professional golf: a focus on gender. *Women in Sport and Physical Activity Journal, 8*, 83–100.

Whipp, B. J., & Ward, S. A. (1992). Will women soon outrun men? *Nature, 355*, 25.

White, S. A. (1999). The effect of gender and age on causal attributions in softball players. *International Journal of Sport Psychology, 24*, 49–58.

Whitson, D. (1990). Sport in the social construction of masculinity. In D. Sabo & M. Messner (Eds.), *Sport, men and the gender order*. Champaign, IL: Human Kinetics.

Widmeyer, W. N., Dorsch, K. D., & Sanzole, M. (1995). *Gender differences in the extent, antecedents of, and responses to frustration in sport*. Paper presented at the annual meeting of the North American Society for Psychology of Sport and Physical Activity, Monterey CA.

Wilgenbusch, T., & Merrell, K. W. (1999). Gender differences in self-concept among children and adolescents: A meta-analysis of multidimensional studies. *School Psychology Quarterly, 14*, 101–120.

Wilson, P. M., Rodgers, W. M., Fraser, S. N., & Murray, T. C. (2004). The relationship between exercise regulations and motivational consequences. *Research Quarterly for Exercise & Sport, 75*, 81–91.

Wood, E., Desmarais, S., & Gugula, S. (2002). The impact of parenting experience on gender stereotyped toy play of children. *Sex Roles, 47*, 39–49.

Glossary

Chapter 2: Research Perspectives in Sport Psychology

Alternative hypothesis: A researcher's educated guess about what he or she expects to find in the study.

Alternative hypothesis: A researcher's educated guess about what he or she expects to find in the study.

Anonymity: The inability to identify a participant involved in a research project.

Applied research: Focuses on generating solutions to immediate problems, irrespective of mechanistic minutia.

Authorities: Experts whose opinions are considered the final world in knowledge acquisition.

Basic interpretive qualitative studies: Studies that look at perspectives and perceptions through interviews, observation and document analysis.

Basic research: Category of research that tests the fundamental mechanisms producing conditions or events, without undue concern for practical utility.

Beneficence: The degree to which the proposed research should be the ones who will derive the benefits from the results.

Case study: Intensive description and analyses of a single person, program, event and so on.

Causal agent: Agent that, when manipulated, will bring about the desired changes in the dependent variable of interest.

Confidentiality: Retention of participant data in confidence whereby participants are not identifiable to others.

Convenience sampling: A non-probability based approach to sampling that has the researcher collect data from accessible samples.

Dependent variable: Variable not under the control of the researcher and expected to change as a result of manipulating the independent variable.

Descriptive research: Method of research used to generate in-depth portrayals of a phenomenon of interest, usually answering questions of how much, when and where.

Error of measurement: Anything that can inadvertently cause an error in a score on the variable of interest.

Ethnography: The study of the culture operating within or around a group or team.

Extraneous variable: Any variable other than the independent variable that could influence the dependent variable in a research study; also called a confounding variable.

Grounded theory: A theory derived from participants' data.

Hypothesis: An educated guess regarding the outcome of a research study.

Idiographic: A concept that is used to describe research concerning a special or unique case that does not apply to most people on the majority of occasions.

Independent variable: The manipulated variable or cause, under the researcher's control, that explains the study outcomes.

Informed consent: An ethical process indicating that the research participants have been informed of what their participation will entail and how the data provided will be treated during the research project.

Internal validity threat: Another plausible explanation for the study findings.

Internal validity: The extent to which the results of a study can be attributed to a treatment of intervention rather than to a design flaw.

Interval: A level of measurement that consists of an ordered set of categories or assignment of numbers to variables so that the distances between the numbers are equal; equal differences in magnitude reflected by equal distances between the numbers.

Intuition: The development of an implicit understanding of the phenomena of interest in the absence of formal training.

Justice: The notion that participants in a study should be the ones who will derive the benefits from the results.

Levels of measurement: Different ways of assigning numbers to variables.

Logic: Knowledge generated through the application of formal rules of reasoning to a problem.

Measurement: The process of assigning numbers to variables according to specific rules.

Narrative analysis: An approach to qualitative inquiry that collects data to present a story told in the first person.

Nominal: The most rudimentary level of measurement in which numbers have no quantitative values and are assigned to represent sets of categories with different names.

Nomothetic: A research method that concerns attempts to isolate rules or observations that pertain to most cases on most occasions or in most contexts; relates to or involves the search for abstract universal principles.

Non-experimental design: Studies that establish patterns of relationships between the variable(s) of interest in absence of group assignment or variable manipulation.

Non-probability based sampling: The target population isn't defined before collecting data.

Null hypothesis: Indicates that there is no relationship between the variables or no difference between groups in a study.

Observed score: Actual numerical value derived from a test that is composed of an individual's true score plus some error of measurement.

Ordinal: A level of measurement that reflects the assignment and categorization of numbers that are ranked in terms of magnitude.

Phenomenology: A philosophical tradition that concerns the structure or essence of an experience for a group or an individual.

Population: The entire group under study.

Predictive research: Method of research used to establish directional relationships between phenomena of interest.

Probability-based sampling: Every element of a population has an equal chance of being selected.

Psychometrics: Concerned with the measurement of psychological variables.

Purposive sampling: A non–probability-based approach that has the researcher collecting data from samples that have the defining set of unique characteristics of interest to the researcher.

Qualitative inquiry: An approach to knowledge acquisition that is used to understand the phenomenon of interest from the participant's point of view.

Quantitative inquiry: An approach to knowledge acquisition that focuses on quantifying or counting the amount of a particular variable or set of variables.

Quasi-experimental design: Studies in which participants are not randomly assigned to different conditions.

Ratio: A level of measurement wherein numbers are assigned in such a way that a true zero exists, representing a complete absence of the variable under study.

Reliability: The consistency or stability of scores derived from a test or measurement procedure applied on one or multiple occasions.

Research design: A plan to follow when executing a study.

Research Ethics Board (REB): An administrative body that ensures research in conducted in a manner that protects the integrity and safety of participants and researchers.

Respecting participants: Concerns the anonymity and confidentiality of participant data.

Sample: A selection of observations for study in the research project.

Sampling: The process of selecting observations for the purposes of study.

Science: A dynamic yet imperfect process of knowledge accumulation through the process of research.

Scientific method: A series of steps that are organized sequentially to generate knowledge.

Study population: All of the accessible elements of a population.

Substantive theory: A theory that deals with a particular real-life situation.

Theoretical population: All of the possible elements of a population.

Theory: An interconnected set of concepts that explain how and why phenomena work together.

Tradition: Knowledge that is historically rooted, with no emphasis on current information.

True experimental design: A study that randomly assigns participants to different conditions and manipulates the independent variable(s).

True score: A person's score on the variable of interest.

Validity: The extent to which test scores serve their intended function.

Variable: Any attribute or characteristic that can change or vary.

Chapter 3: Personality in Sport

Competitiveness: A disposition for motivation toward achievement.

Credulous side: A group of individuals who believed that personality was an important factor in sport and that personality traits could predict success.

Disposition: A broad, natural or acquired habit or characteristic tendency in a person. (In sport research, the term disposition is often applied to constructs that are relatively stable, such as competitiveness, optimism, and motivational orientation.)

Dynamic interaction: Involves the reciprocal effects between a person and a situation.

Ego: The reality principle (of Freud) which mediates the individual's relationship with the environment.

Ethical principles: Guidelines that shape professional judgment and behaviour.

Healthy or adaptive perfectionism: A subtype of perfectionism that is characterized by realistic goal setting, judging success through personal improvement and effort (task orientation), self-discipline, and achievement striving.

Id: The instinctual and driving force of personality.

Maladaptive perfectionism: A subtype of perfectionism that is characterized by excessive, unrealistic standards of performance; high doubt; high self-criticism; fear of failure; and high distress.

Mechanistic interaction: The structure of the interaction between a person and a situation versus the process.

Mental toughness: A combination of personal characteristics and psychological skills that allow individuals to cope with stress and anxiety while remaining focused on competition demands.

Objective test: Highly standardized instrument that does not require the tester to integrate the meaning of the participant's responses.

Perfectionism: A relatively stable multidimensional personality construct that involves setting unrealistic high standards, inappropriate levels of expectations, and high self-criticism.

Personality: A relatively stable construct of the distinct characteristics that make an individual unique, including patterns of behaviour, thoughts, and feelings.

Projective test: A subjective instrument with open-ended questions.

Psychodynamic approach: A personality approach suggesting that all behaviour is interconnected and driven by unconscious forces.

Psychological core: The most basic foundation of an individual's personality, containing the values, motives, attitudes, memories, and expectations that make each person unique. (It is the hardest element of personality to change.)

Risk taking: Narrowing of the margin of safety, both physically and psychologically.

Role-related behaviour: The immediate situation and expectations of how an individual should behave. (It is the easiest component of personality to change.)

Self-actualization: An individual's attempt to be the best he or she can be or a desire to fulfill one's potential.

Skeptical side: A group of individuals who argued there was no consistent scientific evidence that personality could provide a meaningful prediction of success.

States: Momentary feelings and thoughts that change depending on the situation and time.

Stimulus seeking: A trait defined as the seeking of varied, novel, complex, and intense sensations and experiences, and the willingness to take multiple risks for the sake of such experiences.

Superego: The voice of the conscience and morality.

Trait: A relatively stable characteristic or quality that may represent a portion of one's personality; a quality used to explain an individual's behaviour across time and situation.

Trait anxiety: A general disposition to respond to a variety of situations with feelings of concern or worry along with heightened physiological arousal.

Typical responses: The way in which an individual would react to various contexts/situations and temporal factors.

Chapter 4: Motivation in Sport

Achievement goal theory: A motivational theory that focuses on differences in how individuals evaluate competence and define success and failure.

Amotivation: The absence of motivation, perceiving that there is no connection between one's actions and outcomes.

Attribution theory: A motivational theory that focuses on how individuals explain success and failure.

Autonomy: The feeling that one has choice and is in control of one's own behaviour.

Competence: The perception that one has the ability to handle challenges and achieve desired outcomes.

Controllability: Whether or not manipulating factors are within one's power.

Controlling factor: The aspect of a reward that affects how much an individual feels her or his behaviour is internally determined.

Differentiated concept of ability: An individual's ability to, or choice to, differentiate between ability and effort.

Direction of effort: Those situations that an athlete seeks out, approaches, or is attracted to.

Effectance motivation: An intrinsic need to deal effectively with the environment.

Ego goal orientation: A tendency to focus on outcome and being better than others, also called outcome orientation.

Ego involvement: Judging success by and focusing on comparing oneself favourably with or outperforming others.

Enactive mastery experience: Previous performances that could influence one's belief in his/her capability to repeat such actions in a similar setting.

External regulation: Involved in actions performed to fulfill an external demand, achieve a reward, or avoid punishment.

Extrinsic motivation: Motivation for behaviours to attain rewards or outcomes that lie outside of the sport activity itself.

Identified regulation: Involved in engaging in the behaviour because it is linked to personal importance and value.

Informational factor: Aspect of a reward that affects how competent one feels.

Integrated regulation: Involved in engaging in a behaviour because it is in line with one's view of the self.

Intensity of effort: The amount of effort one is willing to put forth in a particular situation or event.

Interaction-centred view: The view that motivation is determined by the interaction of personal characteristics with the situation, rather than from each factor alone.

Intrinsic motivation: Motivation to perform a behaviour because it is inherently satisfying interesting, or enjoyable.

Intrinsic motivation to accomplish: Motivation to participate for the satisfaction of striving to improve one's personal best performances and achieve new personal objectives.

Intrinsic motivation to experience stimulation: Motivation to engage in an activity to experience sensations such as sensory pleasure, aesthetic experience, fun, excitement, etc.

Intrinsic motivation to know: Motivation to perform a behaviour for the sake of learning, exploring, or understanding something new.

Introjected regulation: Involved in performing a behaviour to avoid negative emotions such as guilt or to enhance positive emotions such as pride.

Involvement alternatives: Alternative activities that are more, or less, desirable in relation to participating in a current sport program.

Involvement opportunities: Opportunities that arise through playing in the sport.

Locus of causality: Whether the cause of the attributed quality is internal or external to the athlete.

Motivation: The hypothetical construct of the internal and/or external forces that produce the initiation, direction, and persistence of behaviour.

Motivational climate: Athletes' perceptions of achievement goals promoted by coaches and significant others such as parents.

Outcome expectations: Expected consequences associated with specific behaviour.

Persistence: Maintaining intensity of effort over a continuous period.

Personal investment: Personal resources devoted to the sport.

Physiological and affective states: Physical and emotional cues associated with performance.

Relatedness: The perception of being connected with others and involved in the social context.

Self-efficacy: Beliefs in one's capabilities to organize and execute the courses of actions required to produce desired attainments.

Self-serving bias: The tendency to attribute outcomes to more internal causes when one is successful, and to more external causes when one is unsuccessful.

Situation-centred view: The view that environmental features determine motivation levels.

Social constraints: Social expectations or norms that make a person feel obligated to remain in the sport.

Social support: Perceived help and encouragement received from significant others while participating in the sport.

Sport commitment: The psychological state representing the desire or resolve to continue sport participation.

Sport enjoyment: The positive feelings related to the sport experience.

Stability: The extent to which the attributed quality is relatively enduring or stable over time.

Task goal orientation: a tendency to engage in mastery and skill improvement behaviour, also called mastery orientation.

Task involvement: Judging success by and focusing on learning, mastery, and improvement.

Trait-centred view: The view that sources of motivation are personal dispositions or individual characteristics, also called the participant-centred view.

Undifferentiated concept of ability: An inability or a choice not to differentiate between ability and effort.

Verbal persuasion: Self-talk and encouragement from coaches and significant others.

Vicarious experiences: Comparing oneself with others who have similar skills and attributes.

Chapter 5: Arousal, Anxiety, and Sport Performance

Anxiety: A negative emotional state caused by worries and apprehension.

Arousal: Physiological and psychological activation which varies in intensity on a continuum ranging from deep sleep to peak activation or frenzy.

Attentional focus and selectivity hypothesis: An elevation in state anxiety reduces the ability to attend to and process information.

Cognitive anxiety: The mental component of competitive trait anxiety.

Competitive trait anxiety: The specific trait anxiety associated with sport competition. (See *trait anxiety*.)

Cusp catastrophe theory: The theory that attempts to describe the combined influences of the multiple components of anxiety (cognitive state anxiety and physiological arousal) on athletic performance.

Directional interpretation of competitive anxiety: How cognitive and physiological anxiety symptoms are perceived on a debilitative-facilitative continuum.

Home-team advantage hypothesis: Athletes should perform better and be more successful in front of a supportive home-team crowd than before a less supportive and antagonist opposition crowd.

Hyperdistraction: The state in which athletes' attentional focus shifts rapidly between different sources of stimuli.

Self-handicapping behaviours: Displaying diminishing efforts during training, exaggerating the pain associated with an injury, or complaining illegitimately about the unfairness of the referee.

Social physique anxiety: The anxiety resulting from perceived evaluation of one's physique in social settings.

Somatic anxiety: The physiological and affective elements of anxiety.

State anxiety: The type of anxiety associated with worries and apprehension that change from moment to moment.

Trait anxiety: The stable part of an individual's personality predisposing the individual to perceive situations as physically or psychologically threatening.

Chapter 6: Stress and Coping in Sport

Acute stress: The stress occurring over a short period of time with a sudden onset.

Avoidance coping: The attempt to get out of a stressful situation.

Bad news coping: Rigid, disorganized, and derogatory responses to unmanageable levels of stress.

Challenge: The stress resulting from the interpretation of potential benefits from succeeding in a situation that presents difficult demands.

Chronic stress: The stress that presents over a long period of time.

Cognitive appraisal: Someone's interpretation of a situation.

Competitive stressors: Those stressors experienced prior to, during, or immediately following competition, such as injury, poor officiating, and expectations from others.

Coping: Cognitive and behavioural efforts to manage specific external or internal demands that are appraised as taxing or exceeding the resources of the person.

Coping style: Consistent ways of managing stress over different situations.

Distress: Bad stress, which debilitates performance and well-being.

Emotion-focused coping: Attempting to change the way a situation is attended to or interpreted.

Eustress: Good stress, which facilitates performance and well-being.

Expected stressor: A stressor that an athlete plans or prepares for.

Gender socialization hypothesis: Males and females learn to use different coping strategies to manage the same kinds of situations.

Goodness of fit model of coping: The effectiveness of coping depends on two fits: (1) The match between what is actually going on and how someone views it and (2) the match between the perceived controllability of a situation and the actual control someone has.

Good news coping: Ways of coping that are organized, flexible, and constructive.

Harm/loss: A type of stress arising from an appraisal of a situation in which psychological damage has already been done and the loss is irrevocable.

Macro-level: Looking at the goals or functions of coping strategies that are used to deal with stress.

Management skills: Routine behaviours that help prevent stress from happening.

Micro-analytic: Looking at specific coping strategies to deal with stress or families of such coping strategies.

Non-competitive stressors: Stressors that are related to sport but not directly part of an actual competition performance, such as having to deal with the media, travel, rehabilitation, and team meetings.

Outcome of coping: Result of coping efforts.

Personal resources: Inner resources (such as psychological skills) that an individual is able to use when attempting to manage stressful situations.

Primary appraisal: An evaluation of what is at stake for an athlete in a situation.

Problem-focused coping: Efforts that help athletes to change the actual situation in some way.

Role constraint theory: Differences in stress between men and women are primarily the result of the different roles they play in society, rather than of any inherent gender differences.

Secondary appraisal: An evaluation of what can be done in the situation, which will depend on an athlete's available resources, level of perceived control, and expectations regarding what is likely to occur in the future.

Stress: An experience that is produced through a person-situation relationship that is perceived as taxing or exceeding the athlete's resources.

Stressors: The external events, forces, or situations that have the potential to be interpreted as stressful.

Threat: The anticipation of harm that might occur or is likely to occur.

Unexpected stressors: Stressors that are not anticipated.

Chapter 7: Aggression in Sport

Aggression: Any overt verbal or physical act that is intended to either psychologically or physically injure another living organism.

Assertive behaviour: Actions that are forceful, vigorous, legitimate, but the individual performing this behaviour does not intend to harm another living being.

Catharsis: To purge/cleanse the self of aggressive feelings; typically, venting of aggressive tendencies through socially acceptable means.

Cognitive neoassociation theory: Paying attention to and focusing on angry feelings primes more angry feelings, thereby increasing the possibility of further aggression.

Collective efficacy for aggression: A team's perception of their ability to use aggressive behaviour as a tactic or strategy.

Deindividuation: The process occurring when an individual feels less identifiable by others.

External perspective: Measures of aggression that focus on behaviours in the sport that are generally thought to be performed with the intent to harm.

False consensus effect: When individuals instigating aggression among fans have a false belief about the willingness of other fans to join them in acts of aggression.

Group norms: Standards for the behaviour that is expected of members of the group.

Instrumental aggression: Aggressive acts when the aggressor's ultimate goal is not the injury of the person, but some other tangible reward like praise or victory.

Internal perspective: Measures of aggression in which individuals are asked to describe their desire to behave aggressively or their perceptions of what is an aggressive behaviour.

Reactive or hostile aggression: Aggressive acts undertaken for the purpose of harming or injuring the victim.

Revised frustration-aggression theory: Aggression can have causes other than frustration and frustration can lead to behaviours other than aggression.

Self-presentation: The way individuals present themselves (i.e., behave, dress) in social situations.

Violent behaviours: Extreme acts of physical aggression which bear no direct relationship to the competitive goals of sport; incidents of uncontrolled aggression outside the rules of sport.

Chapter 8: Sport Psychology Interventions

Arousal: A multidimensional construct containing physiological, cognitive appraisal, and affective components.

Attention: A multidimensional construct having at least two components (limited resources and selectivity).

Attentional cues: Words and actions that direct the athlete's attention.

Attention simulation training: Training in which athletes replicate the kinds of attention demanding situations they find themselves in during competition.

Autogenic training: Training that focuses on feelings associated with limbs and muscles of the body.

Cognitive general imagery: Images of strategies, game plans, or routines.

Cognitive specific imagery: Images of specific sport skills.

Event occlusion: The process of examining which characteristics of the performance people use to make a correct response.

Goal: A target or objective that people strive to attain.

Goal setting: The practice of establishing desirable objectives for one's actions.

Instructional self-talk: The overt or covert speech that individuals use for skill development, skill execution, strategy development, and general performance improvement.

Meditation: A relaxation technique that allows for deep relaxation of the mind, which in turn, relaxes the body.

Motivation specific imagery: Images related to an individual's goals.

Motivational general imagery: Images relating to physiological arousal levels and emotions.

Motivational general-arousal: Imagery associated with arousal and stress.

Motivational general-mastery: Imagery associated with the notion of being mentally tough, in control, and self-confident.

Motivational self-talk: The overt or covert speech that individuals use for mastery, arousal control, and drive.

Outcome goals: Goals that focus on social comparison and competitive results.

Performance goals: Goals that focus on improvement and attainment of personal performance standards.

Performance profiling: A flexible assessment tool that allows for the identification of athletes' performance related strengths and weaknesses.

Performance routines: A set sequence of thoughts and actions before the performance of key skills.

Primary task: Typically the task of main interest; the task for which an assessment of attention demand is sought.

Process goals: Goals that focus on specific behaviours in which athletes must engage throughout a performance.

Psyching up strategies: Strategies used to increase arousal levels.

Psychological skill training: A program or intervention that entails a structured and consistent practice of psychological skills and generally has three distinct phases (education, acquisition, and practice).

Secondary task: The task that provides the principal performance measure from which the implications concerning primary task demand are obtained.

Self-talk: Overt or covert sport-related statements that are addressed to the self, are multidimensional, somewhat dynamic in nature, and seem to serve at least two functions for the athlete, instructional and motivational.

Temporal occlusion: The process of examining the amount of time people take to select the information they need in order to respond.

Chapter 9: Cohesion

Autocratic style: A decision style that involves independent decision making and stresses personal authority on the part of the leader.

Behaviour: Actions relevant to achieving the outcome.

Collective efficacy: A group's shared perception of the group's capabilities to succeed at a given task.

Decision style: The degree to which a leader allows participation by subordinates in decision making.

Democratic style: A decision style that allows participation by team members in joint decision making with the leader.

Group dynamics: The study of the nature of groups and their development, and the interrelationships of groups with individuals, other groups, and larger institutions.

Mediators: Mechanisms that account for the effect of one variable on another variable.

Meta-analysis: A technique of literature review wherein a number of studies in an area that meet criteria specified by the researcher are quantified to allow the use of statistical techniques as a means of analysis.

Outcome: Results of behaviours.

Positive feedback: Behaviours by a coach that reinforce an athlete by recognizing and rewarding strong performance.

Psychological momentum: A perception on the part of team members that the team is progressing toward its goal.

Self-handicapping: Using strategies that protect one's self-esteem by providing excuses for forthcoming events.

Social loafing: The reduction in individual effort when individuals work collectively compared to when they work alone.

Social support: Leader behaviours that are characterized by a concern for the welfare of the individual athletes, the fostering of a positive group atmosphere, and warm relationships with team members.

Team building: Programs promoting an increased sense of unity and cohesiveness within a team.

Training and instruction: Behaviours by the coach that are geared to improving team members' performance.

Chapter 10: Coaching Psychology

Actual leader behaviours: Behaviours that a coach exhibits, regardless of team standards.

Coach effectiveness training (CET): A program to improve coaching behaviours through structured coach training and education programs.

Leadership scale for sports: A 40-item inventory that measures five dimensions of leader behaviour.

Mentoring: The assistance of more experienced and well-respected colleagues who ensure growth and development in an environment that is designed to minimize errors and build knowledge and confidence.

Mission statement: A written statement that gives a team direction for the upcoming year.

Multidimensional model of leadership: A linear model comprising antecedents, leader behaviours, and consequences.

National Coaching Certification Program: (NCCP) A knowledge- and course-based program run by the Coaching Association of Canada (CAC).

Organization: The establishing of optional conditions for training and competition in order to reach a goal.

Preferred leader behaviours: Ways in which coaches act that are generally based on the athletes' preferences.

Pre-game pep talk: Words used to fire up a team prior to competition.

Required leader behaviours: Behaviours that are expected of a coach.

Chapter 11: Youth Involvement in Sport

Companionship: Casual relationships that enable an individual to engage in various forms of social and recreational activities.

Constructive leisure activities: Activities that require sustained effort towards the achievement of a clear goal (e.g., sport, music, art).

Deliberate play: Sport activities designed to maximize inherent enjoyment.

Deliberate practice: Sport activities that are highly structured, require effort, generate no immediate rewards, and are motivated by the goal of improving performance rather than its inherent enjoyment.

Developmental assets: Social and psychological "building blocks" for human development.

Early specialization: Limiting participation to one sport that is practiced on a year-round basis.

Emotional support: Comforting gestures from others during times of stress and anxiety.

External assets: Developmental assets in the areas of support, empowerment, boundaries and expectations, and constructive use of time.

Informational support: Provision of advice or guidance to an athlete by others in problematic situations.

Initiative: A core quality of positive physical, psychological, and social development in children.

Internal assets: Developmental assets in the areas of commitment to learning, positive values, social competencies, and positive identity.

Moderately involved parents: Parents characterized by firm parental direction, but enough flexibility so that the young athlete is allowed significant involvement in decision making.

Over-involved parents: Parents who have an excessive amount of involvement in the athletic success of their children.

Relaxed leisure activities: Activities that are enjoyable but not demanding in terms of effort (e.g. watching television, hanging out).

Tangible support: Concrete assistance given by others in stressful situations.

Under-involved parents: Parents who show a relative lack of emotional, financial, or functional investment in their children's sport participation.

Chapter 12: Aging and Physical Activity Involvement

Associative strategies: An approach in which cognition is focused on performance-relevant thoughts.

Compensation theory: A theory of aging based on the notion that age-related losses in one area can be offset by improvements in another area.

Disidentification: Reconceptualizing your self-image to remove the value associated with a domain, thereby reducing the impact of negative performance.

Dissociative strategies: An approach in which cognition is focused on thoughts that are irrelevant to performance (e.g., distracting).

Implicit priming: A technique used to activate or reinforce a belief without conscious awareness (i.e., subliminal).

Master athletes: Athletes who are 30 years or older competing at the masters level of competition.

Morbidity: The quality or state of being morbid or unhealthful.

Mortality: Frequency of number of deaths in proportion to a population; death.

Quality of life: A multidimensional construct referring to an overall sense of well-being with a strong relation to a person's health perceptions and ability to function; includes aspects of physical and mental health and functioning, and social support.

Sarcopenia: A deficiency in the amount of skeletal muscle tissue.

Selective maintenance model: A model of aging emphasizing the role of high quality training and practice in acquiring and maintaining the domain-specific characteristics required for high levels of skill.

Self-efficacy: A person's belief about his or her capacity to produce a designated level of performance.

Socio-economic status: The relative position of a family on a societal hierarchy based on access to, or control over, wealth, prestige, and power.

Stereotype: A popularly held belief (which does not take into account individual differences) about a type of person or a group of people.

Chapter 13: Female Athletes and Gender Issues

Androgynous: The label given to those who score high on both masculine and feminine attributes.

Anorexia: A resistance to maintaining or gaining weight and an intense fear of gaining weight, even though underweight.

Attributions: The explanations people give for their successes and failures.

Bulimia: Recurrent episodes of binge eating, accompanied by inappropriate compensatory behaviour to prevent weight gain.

Confidence: The belief an individual has in his or her ability to be successful.

Drive for muscularity: The desire to achieve an idealized, muscular body type.

Gender constancy: An understanding that one's gender is unchangeable.

Gender stereotypes: The behaviours that are considered appropriate for each gender.

Gender typing: The acquisition of traits, behaviours, and roles that are generally associated with one's gender.

Gender: Psychologically and socially determined aspects of maleness and femaleness.

Identity: The integration of all self-perceptions.

Muscle dysmorphia: A disturbance in body image whereby individuals see themselves as smaller or weaker than they really are.

Schema: A set of inter-related ideas that guide and organize the way an individual makes sense of a situation.

Self-concept: The concept that an individual has about herself or himself.

Self-esteem: The evaluative component of self-concept.

Self-presentation: The selective presentation and omission of aspects of the self to create desired impressions and avoid undesired impressions with specific people in a social encounter.

Sex stereotypes: Socially shared beliefs that certain qualities can be assigned to individuals based on their biological classification as male or female.

Sex: Biological distinctions between males and females.

Sex-typed: The label given to those who score high on either masculine or feminine attributes.

Stereotype threat: a tendency for individuals to perform poorly if they fear they will likely be judged negatively for performing what is considered to be gender-inappropriate behaviour.

Index